Work, Happiness, and Unhappiness

Work, Happiness, and Unhappiness

Peter Warr
Institute of Work Psychology, University of Sheffield

LEA

LAWRENCE ERLBAUM ASSOCIATES, PUBLISHERS

2007   Mahwah, New Jersey   London

Lawrence Erlbaum Associates, Inc., Publishers
10 Industrial Avenue
Mahwah, New Jersey 07430
www.erlbaum.com

Cover design by Tomai Maridou

Library of Congress Cataloging-in-Publication Data

Warr, Peter B. (Peter Bryan)
  Work, happiness, and unhappiness / Peter Warr.
    p. cm.
  Includes bibliographical references and index.
  ISNB 978-0-8058-5710-8 — 0-8058-5710-9 (cloth)
  ISBN 978-0-8058-5711-5 — 0-8058-5711-7 (pbk.)
  ISBN 978-1-4106-1595-4 — 1-4106-1595-2 (e-book)
  1. Work—Psychological aspects. I. Title.
  BF481.W273 2007
  158.7—dc22

                                                              2006017872

                                                                    CIP

Books published by Lawrence Erlbaum Associates are printed on acid-free paper, and their bindings are chosen for strength and durability.

Printed in the United States of America
10 9 8 7 6 5 4 3 2 1

Felix qui potuit rerum cognoscere causas
(Virgil: *Georgics*, ii, 490)

Translated as: Happy is the person who understands the
causes of things
(Motto of the University of Sheffield)

Contents

Preface

In 1975 Penguin Books published **Work and Well-Being,** written by Toby Wall and myself. That examined how and why people feel good or bad about their life, with a particular emphasis on the settings of paid employment. It examined both traditional and novel themes that were important 30 years ago, and consolidated my interest in the issues that have been brought together in the present volume.

Paid work is a primary arena of human activity, in which many practical and moral questions demand attention. It has become the object of scientific study by energetic and creative psychologists in many parts of the world, and we now have available a substantial research base about happiness and unhappiness in work settings. Building on that knowledge, the book sets out a broad framework with wide applicability. The primary question asks "Why are some people at work happier or unhappier than others?", but the answers and occupational examples can also be applied in other settings. The environmental and personal sources of happiness are similar in whatever role is examined.

The book has four main sections, although those are not numbered as such. First (in chaps. 1 and 2) we look at the nature and measurement of happiness. That construct has of course been pondered and written about for centuries, and the emphasis here is on recent explorations by research psychologists. I have long been troubled by the limitations of many psychologists' focus on the narrow variable of job satisfaction or the inflated construct of work stress. We need to examine within a single framework a comprehensive range of experiences and to recognize that happiness has several different aspects.

With that in mind, chapters 1 and 2 present an account in terms of "happiness as well-being" and "happiness as self-validation." The first of those has been studied much more frequently than the second, and the book draws attention to three axes for its measurement and three levels of scope. For example, we need to distinguish between more energized and more tranquil forms of well-being, and between broad happiness in general and more narrow happiness about a particular feature in, say, your job.

The book's two main sections cover separately what can be identified as "environment-centered" and "person-centered" approaches to the study of happiness. In the first case (chaps. 4 to 8), the goal is to identify the principal aspects of an environment that influence people. A framework is presented for understanding similarities and differences between employment-related roles and the effects of those roles. The model has three main themes.

First, the environments of paid work, unemployment, and retirement can helpfully be described and investigated in terms of the same features. The beneficial or harmful consequences of particular environments may be attributed to the nature of those features as experienced in whatever role, and sources of happiness or unhappiness in any setting can be interpreted in the same terms. Using this specification, jobs can be profiled to show the elements that affect particular groups of individuals. In those terms, some jobs may be seen to have a content that is less psychologically desirable than, for example, some forms of unemployment.

The second theme develops an analogy with vitamins and physical health. Increases in an environmental feature are unlikely to have the same magnitude of increased impact as that feature's level becomes ever greater. Instead, a leveling off at moderate levels is proposed, such that (like vitamins) a deficiency is harmful but benefits do not continue to accrue at very high levels. Furthermore, as with several vitamins, it is possible in some cases to "have too much of a good thing."

Third, the book is written in the belief that much research into environmental characteristics has been excessively narrow. Traditional perspectives have focused on a limited set of undoubtedly important features (demands and control, for instance), to the exclusion of others that can substantially affect happiness or unhappiness. With that in mind, a broad framework is presented, extending across 12 characteristics that require attention. Job content may be studied either in those 12 terms or through more specific subcategories; for example, chapter 8 derives an expanded set of 26 influential features from the basic 12.

However, discussions with people about their jobs soon make it clear that there is no standard pattern of environmental impact. Apart from similar reactions at extreme levels of input, people differ widely in their experience in response to the same conditions. We therefore need person-centered approaches to complement the environment-centered emphasis of, for instance, the "vitamin" model described here. Chapters 9 to 13 develop approaches of that person-centered kind, comprising the book's third section.

Those chapters explore the mental processes that take place in people's assessment of their happiness or unhappiness, reviewing judgments made in the face of environmental features of the kinds introduced in the earlier chapters. Here we need to consider how people make mental comparisons with other individuals, other situations, and other times, as well as their assessments of personal salience and novelty. Variations between people in their application of those judgments ensure that happiness responses to a particular environment can be far from uniform.

Other person-centered issues are considered through an investigation of cultural and demographic differences. For instance, in what respects are men and women similar or different in their happiness? Personality patterns are also reviewed. It is clear that certain continuing traits are linked to people's happiness, and that both traits and associated happiness arise in part from a person's genetic makeup.

Separate consideration of environment-centered and person-centered themes leads naturally to what has been labeled "person–environment fit." It is shown in several chapters that happiness or unhappiness in response to an environmental input depends crucially on the personal salience of that input—how much the feature matters to a particular person. Linked to that, broad happiness differences in terms of personality, gender and other attributes can be partly accounted for through variations in personal salience. One general perspective on salience is through the operation of "values," which provide the basis for prioritizing some features over others. The exploration of work values thus becomes of central importance at the present stage of understanding in this area.

The final chapter contains the book's fourth section, asking about the consequences of being happy or unhappy. Research into that issue is still limited. Although significant cross-sectional correlations with behavior are available, the underlying direction of causality is not always clear. Nevertheless, evidence is strong for the influence of happiness on several outcomes. Attention is directed here to job performance, certain mental and social processes, absence from work, and staff turnover.

The book has evolved over several years, and I am indebted to many people. Most generally, I thank the researchers in many countries who have laid the foundations for my own work. More locally, I am very grateful to colleagues in the Institute of Work Psychology at the University of Sheffield for their valued suggestions and helpful advice. Most particularly among those colleagues, my thanks go to Toby Wall for his continuing assistance in working through unresolved issues and clarifying conceptual ambiguities.

—Peter Warr

1

The Principal Concepts

This chapter introduces the two central concepts of the book. "Work" is commonly discussed in terms of paid employment, and that will be the main focus of the chapters which follow. "Happiness" has received centuries of attention from philosophers, poets, and other commentators. It is here viewed in terms that are primarily psychological, identifying three principal dimensions of people's experience that need to be examined in organizations and in life as a whole. The framework developed in this first chapter is used throughout the book.

The book's primary question is: Why are some people at work happier or unhappier than others? Among possible answers is one in terms of job titles. We might observe that people in jobs with a certain title tend to be more happy or less happy than others. Examining overall job satisfaction, Rose (2003) reported some British findings of that kind. The most satisfied individuals in national surveys worked, for instance, as gardeners, hairdressers, or care assistants. On the other hand, job dissatisfaction was greatest among, for example, bus drivers, postal workers, and assembly-line workers. In another British survey, chefs and members of the clergy emerged as among the most happy, with architects and secretaries scoring particularly poorly (City and Guilds Institute, 2005). Across seven national studies in the United States, most satisfied with their job were managers and administrators, and least satisfied were machine operators and laborers (Weaver, 1980).

However, findings from this kind of investigation depend in part on which measure of happiness is applied; as is elaborated later, satisfaction is only one of several indicators of happiness. Furthermore, the content of different people's job can vary markedly within the same title; a single average score for a job title as a whole can conceal wide diversity between job holders in their activities and experiences. Linked to that, results can depend on how broadly or narrowly a job category is defined. And in practical terms, the number of individuals in a research subsample with the same job title has sometimes been very small, perhaps less than 20, so that average scores as published can be unreliable estimates of general values.

However, the major limitation of statements about happiness linked to job titles is that they are unable to provide much by way of explanation. Even if we found reliable large-sample differences in average happiness between the holders of jobs with different titles, we would lack an understanding of their cause. What is it about jobs with a particular title that affects the happiness of those who work in them? To answer the book's question more informatively, we need to identify the factors that are important for any job title. By specifying key features of a work role that are linked in general to happiness or unhappiness (such as the nature of task demands, social contact, and so on), we can better understand any one job in relation to others. Happiness is expected to be greater if those desirable features are present, whatever job title is being considered.

A second answer to the book's question (beyond an account in terms of job title) is thus along these lines: People at work are happier if their jobs contain features that are generally desirable. However, this can only be partly accurate. Individuals are not all happy or unhappy to the same degree, even if their jobs have the same characteristics. There is something about people themselves that influences their happiness, not necessarily connected with their current environment. We need also to look at aspects of job holders as well as at the content of their jobs.

Therefore, a more comprehensive answer might be: People at work are happier if their jobs contain features that are generally desirable and if their own characteristics and mental processes encourage the presence of happiness. An answer of that kind is developed in this book.

In addition to paid work itself, other employment-related roles are here placed within a common framework. The environmental and personal factors that bear on job holders' happiness or unhappiness are also present to varying degrees in retirement and unemployment, and investigations into those two roles are also examined. Furthermore, the identified factors are important beyond a formal employment relationship, so that much of the book's content is applicable to activities across a life space as a whole.

WORK AND ITS IMPLICATIONS

The term *work* is used in many different ways. The printout of its entry in the *Oxford English Dictionary* runs to nearly 50 pages. Meanings set out there include "what a person has to do; occupation, employment, business, task, function," "action involving effort or exertion directed to a definite end, especially as a means of gaining one's livelihood; labor, toil," and "a particular act or piece of labor; a task, job."

The concept is of course wider than merely paid employment, also taking in many other activities. Examples include housework, voluntary work, schoolwork, repair and decorating ("do-it-yourself") work, and a large number of activities not explicitly identified through their titles as work. In its essence, work is an activity with a purpose beyond enjoyment of the activity itself. It can be arduous and/or tedious, involving effort and persistence beyond the point at which it is pleasurable. The term connotes difficulty and a need to labor or exert oneself against the environment; the objective is to achieve something that is physically and/or psychologically difficult. Linked to that, there is often a suggestion that work is obligatory, being required in some way; it is seen as an unavoidable aspect of living. Barringer's (2005) summary is that work is "quintessentially performative; an expressive act of doing or making; the purposeful exercise of body or mind; the overcoming of obstacles with a particular end in sight" (p. 26). In broad terms, it is also a precondition of existence, being essential for continued living.

Work is often seen as an undesirable burden. In the Bible's Book of Genesis, it was presented as the "wages of sin," such that it was only through labor ("in the sweat of thy face") "shalt thou eat bread" (Genesis 3:19). In medieval times, work almost always involved hard physical labor, with obvious potential for exhaustion and bodily damage. Adam Smith (1723–1790) observed that repetitive work leads to people becoming "as stupid and ignorant as it is possible for a human being to become." By Victorian times, mechanization had taken over some of the load, but also added to pressures through the industrialization and intensification of production and the increased competition brought about by improved transportation.

In the 1960s and 1970s workforces were said to be substantially "alienated" from their jobs, and debilitating occupational stress has since then allegedly become widespread in certain countries. Some painful themes were described by Terkel (1972): "This book, being about work, is by its very nature about violence—to the spirit as well as to the body. It is about ulcers as well as accidents, about shouting matches as well as fistfights, about nervous breakdowns as well as kicking the dog around. It is, above all (or beneath all), about daily humiliations. To survive the day is triumph enough for the walking wounded among the great many of us" (p. xi). In a historical review, Thomas (1999) emphasized "the inescapable fact that, through the centuries, the lot of most of the human race has been hard toil for small reward" (p. xviii).

Yet work has long been recognized as desirable as well as a struggle. Denis Diderot (1713–1784) incorporated this ambivalence in his definition: "the daily occupation to which man is condemned by his need, and to which at the same time he owes his health, his subsistence, his peace of mind, his good sense and perhaps his virtue." George Berkeley (1658–1753) concluded that "there can be no such thing as a happy life without labor"; and for Thomas Hobbes (1588–1679) "work is good; it is truly a motive for life." Sigmund Freud (1856–1939) saw work as one of two important foundations of psychological health (the other being love); and for Noel Coward (1899–1973) "work is much more fun than fun." Thomas (1999) noted that work "absorbs our energies and preoccupies our thoughts. It involves us in close relations with other people and gives us our sense of identity. It provides us with the means of subsistence, and it makes possible all the pleasures and achievements of civilization" (p. v).

Linked to those and other positive views, individuals who are unemployed ("out of work") overwhelmingly want to gain a job. Surveys have repeatedly indicated that most people would continue in a job even if they won a large sum of money, and that employed people generally report feeling positively about their work. For example, between 70% and 90% of workers in a wide range of countries say that they are satisfied with their job (Sousa-Poza & Sousa-Poza, 2000; Weaver, 1980). (Precise conclusions depend on where the threshold is set for "satisfaction.") Examining workers' experiences through reports obtained on several occasions in the course of a day, Miner, Glomb, and Hulin (2005) found that positive job events occurred about four times as frequently as negative ones. Terkel (1972) continued the account excerpted earlier to recognize the favorable as well as the negative features of work: "It is about a search, too, for daily meaning as well as daily bread, for recognition as well as cash, for astonishment rather than torpor; in short for a sort of life rather than a Monday through Friday sort of dying. Perhaps immortality, too, is part of the quest. To be remembered was the wish, spoken and unspoken, of the heroes and heroines of this book" (p. xi).

The fact that work has both negative and positive aspects has been central to discussion over the centuries. Martin Luther's (1483–1546) religious perspective included the view that people should diligently pursue the "calling" into which they had been born: "The human being is created to work as the bird is created to fly." Luther believed that God valued good work of any kind, including that which is hard and punishing: "Your work is a very sacred matter. God delights in it, and through it wants to bestow His blessing on you." John Calvin (1509–1564) emphasized that everyone, including the rich, must work, because that is the will of God and work is the way through which He is to be glorified. Calvin argued that potential gains should not be desired in terms of personal wealth; instead, hard work should be valued for its own sake, it was a duty, and it provided its own reward.

These ideas fed into the development of Protestantism, with its "emphasis on the moral duty of untiring activity, on work as an end in itself, on the evils of luxury and extravagance, on the necessity for foresight and thrift, and on the beneficial effects of moderation, self-discipline, and rational calculation" (Applebaum, 1992, p. 331). However, the unpleasantness of much work could not be ignored, and negative as well as positive emphases were retained in Victorian commentators' accounts of what were sometimes described as "instrumental" versus "expressive" features. In the former case, struggle through labor was recognized as necessary in order to meet the needs of individuals and society. However, in "expressive" terms, work could bring out the goodness in a person. Thomas Carlyle (1795–1881) wrote, "There is a perennial nobleness, and even sacredness, in work," such that "a man perfects himself by working." For John Ruskin (1819–1900), work was the process through which human identity is formed. Embedded within these forms of Protestantism "was the notion that work tests, and displays, the moral fibre of the individual, by which he can earn a place for himself, not only on earth but also thereafter" (Barringer, 2005, p. 29).

Work, unpleasant or pleasant, is undoubtedly of great importance to us, with or without any religious connotations. As with other important aspects of life, it has been the target of humor as well as of serious observation. Oscar Wilde (1854–1900) described it as "the curse of the drinking classes," inverting a traditional view of alcohol as the curse of the working classes, and the opinion of Alfred Polgar (1873–1955) was that "work is what you do so that some time you won't have to do it any more." Referring particularly to paid work in large organizations, Northcote Parkinson (1909–1993) proposed "Parkinson's Law," that "work expands so as to fill the time available for its completion," and Laurence Peter (1919–1990) offered the "Peter Principle," that "work is accomplished by those employees who have not yet reached their level of incompetence."

The majority of adults spend much of their life in paid employment ("at work" or "working"), and that expenditure of time and effort is essential to earn money for oneself and one's family. The personal value of work comes partly from the demands and opportunities inherent in a work role, exposing a person to goals, challenges, situations, and people not otherwise present in his or her life, but its importance derives also from consequences and indirect effects. For example, money from a job can purchase pleasures and access to other pleasures that themselves have no direct link to their origins in a person's employment. Jobs also place people in different locations in society, exposing them to particular values, norms, and pressures. For example, the leisure activities and social networks of many professional employees are quite unlike those of many manual workers. Similarly, long-term unemployed people live their lives and interact with society in ways that contrast sharply with the activities and experiences of people in stable employment.

Jobs are thus a primary reflection, and also cause and effect, of a person's place in society. They strongly influence the nature and quality of other environments to which a person is exposed, and factors operative in those correlated nonjob environments have effects far from their partial source in paid employment.

Paid employment is often identified as either full-time or part-time, in the first case taking an average of between 35 and 45 hours per week. Traveling to and from a place of full-time employment typically adds several hours per week, with jobs in large cities often requiring considerably more travel time (e.g., Williams, 2004). Part-time jobs of course vary in their duration, but 30 or 35 hours per week is often taken as their upper limit for statistical and survey purposes.

Recent years have seen changes in the content of jobs. For instance, expansion has occurred in technical, professional, and managerial work. That shift is particularly marked in larger organizations, and is commonly attributed to greater use of technology, more complex working processes, more international competition and transfer of knowledge, and an increased emphasis on customer requirements. At the same time, there has been a general trend away from agriculture and production industries into service work. Developed countries have lost many jobs in farming, textiles, iron and steel, mining, and the wood industry. The principal growth sectors in those countries have been health and social work, business services, hotels and restaurants, education, and recreational services. Most developed countries now have approximately three-quarters of their jobs in service sectors.

PERSPECTIVES ON HAPPINESS

The words *happiness* and *unhappiness* are avoided by most academic psychologists in their professional life. Instead, they have often used terms that are less widely familiar, such as *affect* or *well-being*. In addition, much of psychologists' thinking and empirical research exhibits a general bias in favor of negative states, such as anxiety, depression, or strain. Myers and Diener (1995) and Schaufeli and Bakker (2004) recorded negative and positive emphases in recent research studies in the ratio of 17 to 1 and 15 to 1, respectively. Examining reported correlates of job satisfaction, Thoresen, Kaplan, Barsky, Warren, and de Chermont (2003) found that previous investigators had examined negative job attributes more then twice as often as positive attributes.

The use of happiness as an organizing construct, rather than affect, well-being, or similar notions, has four principal advantages. First, people are fascinated by the presence or absence of happiness, recognizing a strong personal relevance and wishing better to understand the experience. Kim-Prieto, Diener, Tamir, Scollon, and Diener (2005) reported from a survey of college students in 47 countries that happiness was overwhelmingly rated as the most important of all personal values, above wealth, health, love, and similar others. Citizens' "inalienable right" to "the pursuit of happiness" has been affirmed in political documents in the United States since the Declaration of Independence in 1776. This enduring personal and political interest means that research into people in organizations and other settings is likely to have greater impact on the wider population if it is framed in terms of happiness or unhappiness, rather than through the more technical concepts that are usual in the academic world.

Second, apparently diverse variables can be brought together within a single framework. Happiness and unhappiness include many subordinate constructs, whose interrelationships can be more clearly identified and analyzed as members of a single conceptual structure. Third, philosophical examination of happiness has pointed to themes that so far have remained largely outside psychologists' research and conceptualization. Those need to be incorporated in a more comprehensive account than is traditional, in order better to understand a construct that has so far been examined in too narrow a manner.

A fourth reason for using the term *happiness* in scientific research derives from its connotative rather than denotative meaning. The latter (a question of literal, representational, or dictionary meaning) is considered shortly. The connotative meaning of a term concerns its implied associations based on personal and sociocultural interpretations. These color a literal (denotative) meaning with emotional and value-laden possibilities.

Most terms employed by psychologists in this area have connotative meanings that tend to be either negative or passive. Thus, *strain* is a concept with clearly unpleasant connotations, and *well-being* tends to imply in many cases a sense of positivity that is desirable but inert. On the other hand, the connotative meaning of *happiness* emphasizes associations that are more active and energy-related. Not only are such implied themes essential to the concept, but they can also be important in scientific understanding of the experience and its consequences.

The term's denotative meaning derives in part from the Middle English *hap*, meaning "chance" or "luck," as also in *happenstance, perhaps, hapless*, and *mishap*. (A character in Shakespeare's *Comedy of Errors* [c1592] believes that his life would have been better "had not our hap been bad," and elsewhere Shakespeare used "haply" to mean "by chance" and "good hap" as "good luck.") Current usage has moved away from that emphasis on fortunate events outside the self. Although the word's present meaning can include an element of chance, it rarely concerns something that is exclusively a matter of happenstance. Indeed, Western thinking is now likely to emphasize a person's own activities that may create happiness; in very broad terms, happiness may be described as a positive state that people seek. For that denotation, the *Oxford English Dictionary* suggests "the state of pleasurable content of mind, which results from success or the attainment of what is considered good."

Two Aspects of Happiness

Philosophical examinations of the concept have drawn attention to several uncertainties and ambiguities (e.g., den Uyl & Machan, 1983).

A commonly made philosophical distinction has been between accounts that are either subjective (experienced by a person himself or herself) or somehow independent of that person. Subjective forms of high or low happiness include the experience of pleasure or pain, and some theories (often labeled as "hedonism") assert that happiness should be viewed entirely in those terms; being happy would then be described as a preponderance of positive feelings over negative ones.

Related terms within hedonic perspectives include delight, elation, exhilaration, joy, contentment, comfort, satisfaction, serenity, and bliss. Pleasurable experiences of that type involve positive feelings of some kind, and are here termed "happiness as well-being." Subjective well-being was considered by Diener, Suh, Lucas, and Smith (1999) to be "a broad category of phenomena that includes people's emotional responses, domain satisfactions, and global judgments of life satisfaction" (p. 277). The term "refers to people's evaluations of their lives" (Diener & Lucas, 1999, p. 213). It was described by Røysamb, Tambs, Reichborn-Kjennerud, Neale, and Harris (2003) as "a general tendency to hold a positive life view" (p. 1143). For Keyes (2002), "Subjective well-being is individuals' perceptions and evaluations of their own lives in terms of their affective states and their psychological and social functioning" (p. 208). Differences between more activated and less activated forms of well-being are considered in chapter 2.

However, philosophers' consideration of happiness has suggested that happiness can be more than evaluations in terms of pleasure (e.g., Arneson, 1999). Some accounts argue that certain features independent of a person should be treated as constituents of happiness irrespective of a person's feelings. For example, Parfit (1984) identified themes that could be viewed as ("objective") elements of a particular person's happiness whether or not he or she felt them to be positive. Parfit noted (without selecting from among them) that less subjective elements of happiness "might include moral goodness, rational activity, the development of one's abilities, having children and being a good parent, knowledge, and the awareness of true beauty" (p. 499). In those terms, a person can be said to be happy, even if he or she does not experience positive feelings at the time. Although happiness is often a question of hedonic experience, "objective" philosophical accounts suggest that it can also occur without personal enjoyment.

This second form of happiness is thus conceptually distinct from pleasure. It often relates to standards that can exist independently of a person, addressing the notion that some actions or personal states are more fitting or appropriate than others (Veenhoven, 1984). This idea has been explored by many writers, using different labels and with different aims, but it remains difficult to characterize in a precise manner. Constituent themes include a sense that one is using well one's attributes, is fulfilling oneself, is exploiting one's potential, is truly alive, is fully functioning, is enacting central human functions, is self-affirming, or that one somehow means something. Other themes are a sense of wholeness, self-realization, being authentic (as one "should be"), experiencing one's true nature, being true to oneself, or acting in some respect that is harmonious or morally desirable. Self-transcendence, going beyond one's everyday self, has also been cited. This second notion is here labeled "happiness as self-validation."

Ideas about this form of happiness have roots in the writing of early Greek philosophers. Much-discussed in that and later literature is "eudaimonia," in particular as articulated by Aristotle (384–322 BC). Although often translated as "happiness," Aristotle's account of eudaimonia was not a primarily hedonistic one, and an alternative translation is "human flourishing" (Cooper, 1975). His concern was for the attainment of one's true self, a fulfilled life, the proper functioning of a human being (e.g., Hughes, 2001). He viewed happiness (with an emphasis on long-term state, rather than short-term feelings) as based on virtuous behavior in seeking the greatest fulfilment in living of which a person is capable. In Aristotle's framework, virtue particularly arose through contemplation about relationships with other members of society. Eudaimonia thus derived from thoughts or actions that are appropriate, worthwhile, or fitting in relation to one's community. It was viewed in terms of personal attainments in respect of valued standards or obligations, not merely as experienced pleasure.

A happy person in Aristotle's model was one who has achieved what is worth desiring (or is fit to be desired), rather than one who has merely gained what it is that he or she desired (Telfer, 1980). Eudaimonia was thought to come from the gratification of only some desires, those that are appropriate or fitting, not from the gratification of any desire. In that framework, happiness as well-being may sometimes be a consequence of eudaimonia, but the two are conceptually distinct.

A similar theme occurs in Buddhist perspectives. Those associate true or genuine happiness with a sense of personal meaning and inner peace. That form of happiness is considered to derive from the cultivation of appropriate attitudes and from individual and interpersonal activities based on central human values (e.g., Dalai Lama & Cutler,

2003). By training oneself to emphasize tolerance, compassion, and harmony with one's context, a person may experience positive states of inner peace that are independent of pleasure in a hedonic sense. Buddhism argues that pleasure resulting from the achievement of goals cannot deliver true happiness. It describes how an "enlightened" person emphasizes the current potentialities of any situation, the interfusion of all things, and the uniqueness of the moment. Experiences in those respects may yield true contentment, whereas that positive state is not considered attainable through goal-related pleasure (Gaskins, 1999).

Happiness as self-validation thus invokes some standards of appropriateness or rightness. In some cases, a standard of worth is defined in terms external to the individual, perhaps based on a developed religious or ethical doctrine, being "objective" in the sense introduced above. Other standards arise from a person's own view of what is fitting for him or her, for example, in terms of a personal ideology, core values, or a vague awareness of "being how I should be." External and internal standards overlap with each other in several ways. For example, standards of worth that were initially independent of the person may become internalized, also providing benchmarks of a personally valued kind.

Associated with the conceptual separation between well-being and self-validation, happiness of the second kind may or may not be accompanied by experienced pleasure. In some cases, the two might be in opposition to each other. For example, altruistic behavior may be experienced as unpleasant, requiring unselfish activities that are unwanted but also contribute to a sense of personal validation through consistency with valued standards. Behaving in a way deemed to be fitting or morally desirable, a person may forego pleasures that would otherwise be attainable or perhaps enter situations that are threatening to the self; high self-validation is then accompanied by lower pleasure or even pain. In other cases, a person may be unsure about one or the other element. "I don't know whether I'm happy or not, but I've made the best of what I've got" or "I'm not really enjoying myself, but I wanted to make a contribution."

Both forms of happiness may be considered as short-term or long-term states. For example, subjective well-being may be examined in a single, short episode, perhaps as an immediate reaction to an input from the environment. Alternatively, one might ask about the nature of a happy life or about happiness across some other extended period of time.

The importance of self-validation as an aspect of happiness is particularly clear in long-term perspectives. Much philosophical discussion concerns an entire life, rather than examining current happiness in a short episode (which has tended to be psychologists' interest). For example, long-term retrospective appraisals (e.g., "has my life been a happy one?") do of course invoke happiness as well-being (avoidance of pain and a generally pleasurable existence), but issues of self-fulfilment are often also included. That is also seen in long-term anticipation of the future. For instance, in wishing a newborn child "a happy life," the hope is usually more than merely for pleasure and the absence of pain, although those are of course important (McFall, 1982).

Happiness as self-validation thus requires an evaluative conception of human life—the assertion that certain activities or experiences are in some way more appropriate than others. "These normative notions are not easily understood or operationalized" (Tiberius, 2004, p. 303), both for conceptual reasons and because of the difficulty of empirically tapping into complex mental processes. Psychologists' approaches to measurement are illustrated in chapter 2. Note that those have rarely used the term *self-validation*. That is adopted here as a broad descriptor to encompass many specific accounts of overlapping constructs; those have themselves been labeled in many different ways.

Multiple Experiences of Happiness

Happiness may thus be viewed as an overarching concept with two principal aspects, well-being and self-validation. However, almost all research by psychologists inside or outside organizations has examined only the first of those, with very little attention to what is here termed self-validation. In part, this arises from the elusiveness of the second form of happiness and the difficulty of its definition and operationalization; verbal specifications tend to be abstract, and measures have usually been indirect and not always convincing.

In addition, there may be a hierarchical or sequential element in the two experiences, such that self-validation matters less to people lower down the experiential hierarchy or earlier in the sequence. Unless a person has achieved a certain level of well-being, avoiding substantial unhappiness of the first kind, self-validation may be of little personal concern (e.g., McGregor & Little, 1998). Many people are persistently occupied in seeking an acceptable level of pleasure or escaping from displeasure, and the first form of happiness may take priority for them.

For harassed people in difficult situations, the notion of happiness as self-validation may seem irrelevant.

The possibility of a hierarchy within happiness was central to Maslow's (e.g., 1968) account. He identified five classes of basic need, labeled as physiological, safety, social, esteem, and self-actualization. Earlier needs in that list were viewed as prepotent, being personally most significant until they became satisfied to some acceptable degree; only then did the higher ones (including aspects of what is here termed self-validation) come into play. The higher order needs were taken to be particularly important, but only after the others had been satisfied; before that, they were thought to be of limited impact. Such a possibility appears immediately plausible, although empirical research has been unable to confirm detailed predictions.

As noted earlier, a particular level of hedonic happiness can occur in conjunction with either high or low self-validation—or without a sense of self-validation at all. Similarly, high self-validation may or may not be accompanied by pleasure. Overall, however, self-validation seems more likely to be accompanied or followed by high (rather than low) well-being. That is because self-validating activity can itself give rise to well-being (you feel pleased because you have met a standard of worth), and/or because experiences of self-validation and well-being can both arise from the same activity.

A moderate positive association is thus expected in general between the two forms of happiness, with relatively stronger or weaker links occurring in particular situations. That association has been recorded by several investigators, although the measurement of self-validation has sometimes been uncertain. Measures of the two kinds of happiness (differeing between the studies) examined by Sheldon, and Kasser (1995), Rothbard (2001), and Keyes, Schmotkin, and Ryff (2002) were intercorrelated on average by factors of +0.25, +0.33, and +0.34, respectively. Examining the statistical structure of self-report questionnaires in community samples, Compton, Smith, Cornish, and Qualls (1996) and Keyes et al. (2002) both found that indicators illustrating the two forms of happiness emerged as separate but partially overlapping factors. Quinn (2005) recorded experiences of "flow" in particular work situations (a specific form of self-validation; see chap. 2). Flow and enjoyment of a situation (here an example of happiness as well-being) were overall positively intercorrelated to a moderate degree.

Those findings illustrate that a person can have different experiences of happiness at about the same time. At any moment, a process of selective mental attention leads to concentration on a particular theme, both in response to conscious direction and in reaction to environmental and other internal stimuli. Subsequent switches of attention lead to possibly different experiences, without necessarily negating the previous ones. For example, short-term happiness in a particular setting may contrast with a person's more extended level or experience in a different setting, but that short-term state does not itself deny the reality of other states. This phenomenological diversity is difficult to capture in empirical research. Although people have available for attention a wide variety of happiness-related experiences, only one can be conscious at any moment.

The important point at this stage is that any measure that is taken of happiness does not exclude the potential presence of different experiences; it is inevitably selective. Variability between several forms of happiness is of course constrained by their conceptual interdependence and their common sources in the environment and the person, but some differences in causes and consequences are to be expected. Research thus has to select certain processes for emphasis, recognizing that others have been excluded from consideration. A particular index provides only partial information about a person's happiness.

CONTENT AND STRUCTURE OF THE BOOK

Chapter 2 examines in more detail the nature and measurement of well-being and self-validation. As illustrated earlier, happiness varies in its scope, and degrees of abstractness are here treated at three levels, identified as "context-free," "domain-specific," and "facet-specific." In the first case, we are concerned with an overall evaluation of life as a whole; domain-specific happiness involves experiences related to one part of a life space, such as paid employment or the family; and facet-specific happiness is restricted to one aspect of a particular domain, such as income received (in the job domain) or relations with children (in the domain of family life).

Happiness as well-being has both affective and cognitive elements. Chapter 2 describes how those have different priority in different kinds of experience. With an affective emphasis we are particularly concerned with feelings and emotions, whereas more cognitive forms of happiness involve reflective judgments of, for instance, satisfaction. In both cases, subjective well-being is here viewed in terms of two principal dimensions—degree of psychological arousal or activation, and degree of pleasure. For example, high pleasure can be reflected either in excited and energized well-being (with higher activation) or in terms of calm contentment or tranquility (with lower activation). Presenting pleasure and activation as orthogonal to each other, three axes of measurement are proposed in chapter 2, ranging from displeasure to pleasure, from anxiety to comfort, and from depression to enthusiasm. Subsequent chapters are organized around those three axes of subjective well-being.

Psychologists' measurement of that form of happiness is also covered in chapter 2, covering, for instance, life satisfaction, anxiety, depression, job satisfaction, job-related tension, burnout, and specific satisfactions with particular features of the environment. The measurement of self-validation is similarly reviewed in that chapter, examining a range of inventories about involvement in activities that are felt to be worthwhile, fitting, or that somehow meet standards beyond pleasure alone. Overlaps of happiness with related concepts, for example, emotion, strain, and mental health, are also examined.

In considering why some people are happier than others, the book is structured around perspectives that are either "environment-centered" or "person-centered." In the first case, studies of unhappiness or happiness have concentrated on possible influences from the settings in which a person is located, whereas person-centered perspectives have emphasized between-individual differences in demographic characteristics, personality, behavior, or ways of thinking.

An overall framework of environment-centered explanation is developed in chapters 4 to 8. Principal aspects of any environment are identified, and their relationships with different forms of happiness are reviewed. Addressing employment-related roles beyond merely a job, central themes are also considered (in chap. 3) in settings of unemployment or retirement from paid work. How does happiness or unhappiness vary between those settings, and what factors might influence their level in each?

The book argues against the idea that environmental features are related to happiness in a linear manner, such that a certain increment in an environmental characteristic is accompanied by a fixed increment in happiness at any level of that characteristic. Instead, the environment–happiness association is viewed as analogous to the relationship between vitamin intake and aspects of physical health. Vitamins are important for physical health up to but not beyond a certain level, after which there is no benefit from additional quantities. Furthermore, certain vitamins become harmful in very large quantities, so that in those cases the association between increased vitamin intake and physical health becomes negative after a broad range of moderate amounts.

This analogy is presented in chapter 4, where a "vitamin" model envisages two classes of environmental input to happiness. In both cases, associations with happiness are treated as nonlinear, with their impact stabilizing across moderate levels. However, differences between the two kinds of input are proposed for very high amounts. In one case, a constant effect on happiness is expected across high input levels, and for other features a decrement in happiness is proposed at very high levels.

The identified "vitamins" are important in environments of any kind, for example unemployment and retirement as well as a paid job. Chapter 5 reviews the operation in job settings of six of the key features in jobs, those with an expected "constant effect" across high levels. Those are labeled as availability of money, physical security, valued social position, supportive supervision, career outlook, and equity. The six remaining characteristics in the vitamin framework are examined in chapters 6 and 7: opportunity for personal control, opportunity for skill use, externally generated goals, variety, environmental clarity, and contact with others. In those "additional decrement" cases, very high levels of input are viewed as psychologically harmful, and the nonlinear expectation is for an inverted U pattern.

Environment-centered issues of a more general kind are examined in chapter 8. For example, possible combinations of different job features are reviewed, and methodological issues of measurement and causal interpretation are explored. Previous perspectives and empirical findings are then brought together to suggest a multiattribute account of environmental characteristics that range across bad and good jobs of all kinds. Including subcategories of those environmental characteristics (e.g., opportunity for new learning, or conflict between work and home), a rating procedure for profiling any job in terms of 26 happiness-related features is outlined. In that way, profiles may be constructed for the psychologically important features of current jobs or of anticipated jobs.

Chapters 3 to 8 together illustrate the substantial impact that environmental features have on unhappiness or happiness. However, their effects are not always uniform, and patterns vary between individuals. Themes of a person-centered kind are considered in chapters 9 to 13. First are processes of judgment that can intervene between an environmental input and the experience of happiness. Ten kinds of mental process that can vary between individuals and between situations are introduced. Those involve mental comparisons with other people, with other situations and with other times, and also comparisons with an individual's own reference points such as personal salience, self-efficacy, and novelty or familiarity. Research into those judgments is reviewed in chapter 9. That chapter also examines studies of self-help exercises, which guide people to apply judgments of the kind outlined in seeking to enhance or maintain their level of happiness.

Chapter 10 explores differences between sets of people. For example, patterns of unhappiness or happiness in men and women and among younger and older workers are examined, as are similarities and differences between full-timers and part-timers and between more permanent and temporary staff. Other person-centered themes are explored in chapter 11, which reviews research findings about personality and happiness. The presentation is primarily organized in terms of the Big Five factors of neuroticism, extraversion, openness to experience, agreeableness, and conscientiousness, but also covers, for instance, positive affectivity, negative affectivity, hardiness, core self-evaluations, and perfectionism.

In examining possible personality influences, chapter 11 draws attention to the overlap between several concepts that are widely applied in considering differences between people. It is shown that personality attributes are similar to values, interests, motives, and wants, in having a common focus on self-relevant evaluations. High or low scorers on inventories of each of those (however they are labeled) differ in the importance that they attach to particular targets. Chapter 12 explores how indicators of personal salience can moderate the association between environmental characteristics and happiness. Research from several areas is brought together to show that environmental features have a greater impact on unhappiness or happiness when they are of greater salience to an individual. Those themes are set within traditional perspectives on "person–environment fit" in chapter 13. Twelve types of occupational value are introduced there, which parallel the 12 environmental "vitamins" examined in earlier chapters. Those occupational values reflect differences in judgmental salience, as reviewed in previous chapters, and are proposed to moderate the impact of job characteristics on happiness, both at the individual level and between groups.

Chapter 14 reviews research into the consequences of unhappiness or happiness for people's behavior. Earlier chapters primarily concern the nature and the causes of those experiences, and this final chapter instead examines their possible effects. Evidence is brought together about job performance, cognitive processes of perception, remember-ing and creativity, energy and persistence, interpersonal relationships, absence from work, and staff turnover. Particular attention is paid to possible directions of causality: from happiness to behavior, from behavior to happiness, in both directions, or due to the impact of additional variables. Significant associations are reviewed between the level of employees' well-being and, for instance, their job perfor-mance. Although a behavioral impact from happiness or unhappiness can be inferred, other causal influences are also considered.

These topics and research themes are of central importance to many areas of industrial-organizational, work, or occupational psy-chology. However, the book's concepts and theoretical frameworks are more widely applicable, in nonoccupational settings as well as in employment-related roles. Linked to that broad applicability, research findings from clinical and social psychology, and less often from socio-logy or economics, are incorporated throughout.

2

Well-Being and Self-Validation

How can we specify and measure the forms of happiness introduced in chapter 1? Research has primarily examined happiness as well-being, and procedures are more established in that respect than for self-validation. In addition, the fact that happiness and unhappiness are strongly dependent on affective experiences suggests overlap with other feeling-based constructs, such as emotion, mood, or strain. Some similarities and differences will be considered later in this chapter.

HAPPINESS AS WELL-BEING

Since the early days of psychology as a scientific discipline, the feeling of pleasure or displeasure has been identified as a fundamental dimension of conscious experience, often described in academic research as "psychological well-being" or "subjective well-being." However, labeling variations have been common in this area. For instance, Ryff and her colleagues (e.g., Keyes et al., 2002; Ryff, 1989; Ryff & Keyes, 1995; Schmutte & Ryff, 1997) used the term "subjective well-being" to refer to hedonic aspects of happiness (as here), but treated "psychological well-being" as a different concept, emphasizing instead what is here termed happiness as self-validation; their conceptualization is considered later. In contrast, "subjective" well-being and "psychological" well-being are treated as equivalent in the present framework. For Cropanzano and Wright (1999, p. 253), Easterlin (2001, p. 465), Lyubomirsky (2001, p. 239), Seligman (2002, p. 261), and others, "well-being" was interchangeable with "happiness" as a whole, but in the present book well-being is examined as only one of two main components of the broader concept. Similarly, life satisfaction was said to "denote" overall happiness in Veenhoven's (1984) framework, but that is only one component of well-being (itself one component of happiness) in the present book. It is clearly important to check each author's definition of terms.

Two principal kinds of pleasurable feelings are suggested by dictionary definitions, which often refer to what Freedman (1978, pp. 30–31) described as "happiness as peace of mind and contentment" and "happiness as fun, excitement." That general distinction was reflected in Hartman's (1934) definition of happiness as a "state of well-being characterized by dominantly agreeable emotions ranging in value from mere contentment to positive felicity" (p. 202). In empirical research, this spread of feelings has sometimes been examined in terms of mental activation, in addition to the positive or negative direction of an experience. The framework set out in Figure 2.1 has been supported in many investigations (e.g., Cropanzano, Weiss, Hale, & Reb, 2003; Feldman Barrett & Russell, 1998; Reisenzein, 1994; Remington, Fabrigar, & Visser, 2000; Russell, 1980, 2003; Seo, Feldman Barrett, & Bartunek, 2004; van Katwyk, Fox, Spector, & Kelloway, 2000; Yik, Russell, & Feldman Barrett, 1999) that have pointed to the importance of two independent dimensions, labeled in Figure 2.1 as "pleasure" and "arousal."

We may describe a person's subjective well-being in terms of its location relative to those two dimensions (representing the content of feelings) and its distance from the midpoint of the figure (such that a more distant location indicates a greater intensity). A particular degree of displeasure or pleasure (the horizontal dimension) may be accompanied by low or high levels of mental arousal (the vertical dimension, sometimes described as ranging from "deactivation" to "activation"), and a particular quantity of mental arousal may be either pleasurable or unpleasurable to varying degrees. Experiences that can be viewed in terms of the two dimensions are illustrated around the outside of Figure 2.1. Those descriptors have slightly different meanings in different contexts, but broadly summarize possible combinations of pleasure and arousal. In general, subjective well-being is based more on a level of pleasure than on arousal (Feldman, 1995).

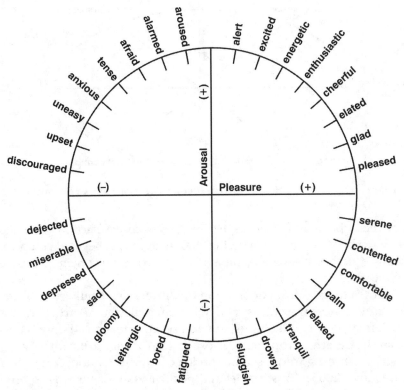

Figure 2.1.   A two-dimensional view of subjective well-being.

Axes of Subjective Well-Being

Within that framework, Figure 2.2 suggests three principal axes for the empirical measurement of this first form of happiness. In view of the central importance of displeasure or pleasure, the first axis is in terms of the horizontal dimension alone. The other two axes take account of mental arousal as well as pleasure, by running diagonally between opposite quadrants through the midpoint of the figure.

The two poles of the first (horizontal) axis reflect overall negative or positive experiences, from feeling bad to feeling good, without reference to a person's degree of psychological arousal. The second axis runs diagonally from anxiety to comfort. Feelings of anxiety combine low pleasure with high mental arousal, whereas comfort is illustrated as low-arousal pleasure. Employees in the lower right ("comfortable") quadrant have

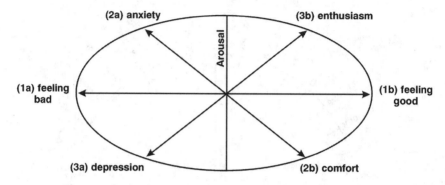

Figure 2.2.   Three axes for the measurement of subjective well-being.

sometimes been described as having "resigned satisfaction" (Büssing, 1992; Grebner, Semmer, & Elfering, 2005); although they find acceptable their job or other situation, they have limited commitment, energy or aspirations.

Third is the axis from depression to enthusiasm. Feelings of depression and sadness (low pleasure and low mental arousal) are in the bottom left quadrant, and enthusiasm and positive feelings (being actively pleased) are at the top right. Those latter feelings are central to the model of "thriving" proposed by Spreitzer, Sutcliffe, Dutton, Sonenshein, and Grant (2005). This defines the positive state of thriving in terms of the joint experience of learning and vitality. "Vitality refers to the positive feelings of having energy available, reflecting feelings of aliveness" (p. 538). The notion of thriving is broader in some respects than subjective well-being, but is overlapping both in its nature and in some of its causes and consequences.

Note that although the dimensions of pleasure and arousal can be treated as orthogonal to each other, the three axes of well-being are expected to be intercorrelated through strong loadings on the core experience of pleasure. Self-reports on those measurement axes are indeed empirically associated with each other. For example, Warr (1990a) recorded a correlation of +0.66 between axes 2 and 3; similar values in other studies are cited throughout the book. The overarching involvement of pleasure suggested to Tellegen, Watson, and Clark (1999) that a hierarchical account might be appropriate. They envisaged activation-loaded states (on axes 2 and 3 of Fig. 2.2) to be accompanied by an overall, higher-level emphasis on feeling bad or feeling good (axis 1).

Despite the overlap between axes of subjective well-being, different associations exist with certain other variables. For example, a person's organizational level is linked in opposite ways with job-related anxiety and job-related depression. People in higher-level jobs report significantly *less* job-related depression than those in lower-level jobs, but also significantly *more* job-related anxiety (Mullarkey, Wall, Warr, Clegg, & Stride, 1999; Totterdell, Wall, Holman, Diamond, & Epitropaki, 2004; Warr, 1990a). This differential pattern of subjective well-being (both better and worse at higher organizational levels) may be interpreted in terms of the dimension of mental arousal; people in higher level positions experience greater arousal, on both the diagonal axes in Figure 2.2. Differences also exist in relation to certain job characteristics. For example, high job demands are more closely linked to unhappiness in terms of axis 2 (raised anxiety) than in terms of axis 3 (from depression to enthusiasm). Systematic differences also occur between people. For instance, women on average have significantly lower well-being than men on axes 2 and 3, but have similar average scores on the first axis. These and similar patterns are detailed throughout the book.

Environmental Threat or Deficit

Although they are moderately intercorrelated, well-being axes 2 and 3 are likely to have different priorities with respect to either escape from danger or avoidance of deprivation. Low well-being in terms of anxiety (on axis 2) may arise more from a need to escape from or avoid threats and potential harm, whereas feelings of depression to enthusiasm (axis 3) might be more linked to a desire to move toward something that is wanted but currently lacking. This separation between the mental processes associated with either anxiety or depression has been explored by clinical psychologists more than by occupational researchers. It is extended here to examine different hedonic patterns associated with either low or high levels of specified job characteristics.

Feelings of anxiety and depression are highly intercorrelated in samples of both clinical patients and nonpatients (around +0.68 in research by Clark & Watson, 1991), but research has indicated that accompanying thought processes are partly distinct from each other. Anxiety-related thoughts primarily concern personal problems and threats, with perceptions of danger leading to aroused feelings of tension and fear and to increased autonomic activation. On the other hand, the thoughts of depressed individuals revolve more around loss and deprivation, triggering deactivated feelings of sadness, gloom, hopelessness, and physical weariness (Burns & Eidelson, 1998; Feldman, 1993).

Although many symptoms of anxiety and depression are not specific to only one of those conditions (reflecting the high empirical correlation between them), experienced anxiety is thus targeted mainly on thoughts of harm and danger, whereas depression is linked to cognitions of loss, deficit, and the absence of desired features (Clark, Beck, & Brown, 1989). In addition, anxiety is accompanied by raised psychological and psychosomatic arousal, toward the top of the vertical dimension in Figures 2.1 and 2.2, whereas depression involves low-arousal listlessness, at the bottom of those figures. The present concern is primarily with individuals who are not clinical patients, and those partly distinct reactions can also be envisaged in respect of job and other environmental characteristics. Consistent with observed links between perceived threat from the environment and feelings of anxiety (above), it may be that variation in the level of threat in the high range of a job feature (e.g., too many demands) is generally accompanied more by anxiety (i.e., low scores on well-being axis 2) than with depression (low well-being on axis 3). On the other hand, the absence of a desirable environmental feature (e.g., lack of an opportunity to use your skills) could be more linked to a low score on well-being axis 3 (from depression to enthusiasm) than on axis 2.

This possibility is supported by research in clinical populations in respect of "stressful life events." For example, Finlay-Jones and Brown (1981) studied the recent life events reported by three groups of psychiatric patients—those diagnosed as suffering from depression, from anxiety, or from mixed depression and anxiety. In addition to the presence of several nondifferentiating events, severe loss in the previous 3 months (of people, resources, or envisaged possibilities) was particularly related to a diagnosis of depression, whereas a person's perception of danger to the self was associated with the development of anxiety. Conversely, there was no association between perceived danger and the onset of depression, or between experienced loss and the development of anxiety. Similar findings with larger samples have been reported by Kendler, Hettema, Butera, Gardner, and Prescott (2003) and others, although several authors emphasize also the presence of inputs to negative affect that are nonspecific in those content terms. Those two different processes in job settings, either from the threat of harm or from the absence of what is desired, will be explored throughout chapters 5 to 7.

The presentation so far has mainly considered the absence or presence of an environmental feature. In addition, a person's feelings are likely to be influenced by his or her movement relative to that feature

(Carver & Scheier, 1990, 1998; see also chap. 9). Consistent with the preceding argument, the two axes of well-being may be linked in different ways to movement toward or away from a target. Progress in getting closer to an absent desired feature is likely to be reflected primarily in increased well-being on axis 3 (a reduction in depression, moving toward activated positive feelings). On the other hand, success or failure in moving away from or reducing a harmful threat to the person is expected to show up mainly on axis 2 (from anxiety to comfort). "In this view, approach processes yield affective qualities of sadness or depression when progress is very poor; they yield such qualities as eagerness, happiness, or elation when progress is very high [i.e., along the present axis 3]. Avoidance processes yield anxiety or fear when progress is very poor; they yield relief, calmness, or contentment when progress is very high [here, along axis 2]" (Carver, 2003, p. 245, bracketed material added).

Unhappiness based on the presence of (or slow progress from) a negative, threatening feature may thus take the form of anxiety more than depression. On the other hand, unhappiness due to the absence of (or only slow progress toward) something desirable may be more a question of depression than anxiety. This possibility has rarely been considered in employment-related research, but it is examined throughout the book with respect to the well-being axes summarized in Figure 2.2.

Three Levels of Scope

In addition to the dimensions of pleasure and arousal, subjective well-being also requires specification in terms of level or scope, the breadth of a life-space area to which feelings are directed. In general, a person who is happy in terms of subjective well-being is one who feels good about his or her life. However, his or her feelings might either have a broad focus or be more narrowly directed at a particular domain or part of that domain. We need to distinguish between experiences that have a comprehensive reference and those that are more limited in their scope.

How many different levels of scope should be addressed? Any decision about that is in part arbitrary, but a three-level approach is attractive. The broadest form of subjective well-being is in terms of life in general, overall and without restriction to a particular setting. Let us call that "context-free" well-being. Second, a medium-range focus is in terms of "domain-specific" well-being, directed at one segment of a life space. Particular domains of well-being include one's job, family, health, leisure, or oneself (Diener et al., 1999; Headey, Holmström, & Wearing, 1984). Well-being that is job-related is the domain-specific form, which is of particular interest in this book. However, domain-specific well-being that is concerned with the self or with one's health will also receive attention. Third, we might examine "facet-specific" well-being, targeted at one particular aspect of a domain. For example, satisfaction with one's pay relates to a single facet within the job domain.

As expected from their conceptual overlap, experiences at the three levels of abstractness (context-free, domain-specific, and facet-specific) are empirically interrelated. For example, Rice, Frone, and McFarlin (1992) reported correlations between (context-free) life satisfaction and (domain-specific) satisfactions with job, family, and leisure that averaged +0.46. The meta-analysis by Faragher, Cass, and Cooper (2005) yielded average uncorrected correlations between job satisfaction and context-free anxiety of –0.35 and with context-free depression of –0.37.

Nevertheless, subjective well-being at different levels of scope is influenced in part by different factors. For example, job-related well-being is more responsive to conditions and activities in the domain of employment than other domains, and context-free well-being is also significantly influenced by health, family, and community factors (e.g., Warr, 1987). Very narrow forms of (facet-specific) well-being are by definition targeted on a single feature (e.g., satisfaction with one's income), and are expected to be particularly closely correlated with characteristics of that feature. All levels also reflect people's dispositional characteristics, with happiness being somewhat stable across time and between situations (e.g., Dormann & Zapf, 2001; Heller, Judge, & Watson, 2002) and being significantly related to aspects of personality. Aspects of dispositional consistency are examined in chapters 9 to 13.

Links between well-being that is context-free and the domain-specific form targeted on paid employment have sometimes been examined respectively in terms of life satisfaction and job satisfaction. Some overlap between those two levels of abstractness is in part logically necessary, because feelings about a job are themselves one component of wider life satisfaction. The review by Tait, Padgett, and Baldwin (1989) revealed an average uncorrected intercorrelation across 57 data sets of +0.35. In later research, life satisfaction and job satisfaction have been found to be intercorrelated, for instance, at +0.49 (Rice et al., 1992), +0.42 (average of two occasions; Judge & Watanabe, 1993),

+0.29 (Adams, King, & King, 1996), +0.43 (Tepper, 2000), +0.46 (average of two occasions; Heller et al., 2002), and +0.30 (Rode, 2004). Heller et al. (2002) also measured this association across a period of six months (average $r = +0.44$) and with another person's assessment of a target individual's job satisfaction or life satisfaction (average $r = +0.33$ both concurrently and across time).

Reports of strain (rather than satisfaction) were studied by Gallie, White, Cheng, and Tomlinson (1998); the correlation between job-related and context-free strain was +0.38. For overall job satisfaction and context-free distress, Moyle (1995) reported a correlation of −0.48, and Payne, Wall, Borrill, and Carter (1999) obtained a value of −0.36. Many similar correlations between happiness at the domain-specific and happiness at the context-free levels have been published (e.g., Faragher et al., 2005). Warr (1990a) asked about context-free well-being after the exclusion of paid work ("in your life outside your job"), rather than about a life space including a job. He reported an average correlation of +0.46 between employees' nonjob well-being and their well-being in a job.

Across a period of more than 2 years, Headey et al. (1984) observed that changes in several domain-specific satisfactions (with friends, marriage, leisure, job, etc.) were significantly associated with changes in context-free well-being. Judge and Watanabe's (1993) results suggested a pattern of mutual influence: The two levels of happiness affected each other. However, the effect from life satisfaction to job satisfaction was greater than in the opposite direction. A person's overall well-being thus has a significant impact on his or her job-specific well-being, and job well-being also affects wider happiness. The latter process was illustrated by Judge and Ilies (2004) in terms of employees' mood at home in the evenings after work. Evening mood was found to be significantly predicted by mood during the day's job activities and by job satisfaction assessed during those activities.

The existence of different levels of abstractness illustrates again that, despite some consistency between levels, a person may in different ways be happy or unhappy to varying degrees at about the same time. For example, several dissimilar feelings about different aspects of one's job may coexist within a single overall well-being at the context-free level. Similarly, domain-specific well-being with respect to oneself or one's health may be high despite low satisfaction with one's job. Research to date has tended to examine merely one index on its own, without placing that in a framework of concurrent happiness at the same or different levels of abstractness. Multiple experiences may be evaluatively consistent with each other, but ambivalence can also occur, when a person is both happy and unhappy in different respects at about the same time.

Affective or Cognitive Emphases

Another difference between aspects of happiness as well-being has been studied through a varying emphasis on either affective or cognitive reactions. Subjective well-being necessarily involves affective (feeling) states, but in addition has sometimes been examined as a more cognitive outcome, deriving from reflective appraisal of oneself and one's position beyond merely the experience of negative or positive feelings. Cognitive elements are clearly present in typical measures of satisfaction. For example, Pavot and Diener (1993) referred to life satisfaction as "a judgmental process, in which individuals assess the quality of their lives" (p. 164). In those terms, a person "weighs the good against the bad, and arrives at a judgment of overall satisfaction" (Lucas, Diener, & Suh, 1996, p. 616). All experiences of happiness are likely to draw to some extent on recollections and interpretations of previous activities and feelings, but judgments of satisfaction (more reflective than direct measures of affect) are particularly likely to involve cognitive processes of that kind.

In research into well-being at the context-free level, the two kinds of indicator (of affect and satisfaction with one's life) have been found to be factorially separate from each other (e.g., Diener, 1994; Diener et al., 1999). Their discriminant validity at that context-free level has also been demonstrated by lower correlations between the two kinds of measure than within either affect or life satisfaction (Lucas et al., 1996). However, statistical separation between more affective and more cognitive well-being at the domain-specific level of abstractness (e.g., in relation to paid work) has rarely been investigated. In respect of satisfaction with one's job, some instruments emphasize reflective appraisals, whereas others more directly assess employees' feelings. The observed level of association between job affect and job satisfaction may be expected to depend on that relative emphasis in the particular measure of satisfaction that has been applied.

Niklas and Dormann (2005) obtained information on three occasions within 4 weeks about current job satisfaction recorded in either a more affective or a more reflective manner. The average correlation between those two kinds of satisfaction measure with different emphasis was +0.38. As expected, the affective measure (indicating

TABLE 2.1

Six Types of Happiness as Well-Being, Based on Breadth of Scope and
Relative Emphasis

	Broad Scope: Context-Free Well-Being		Moderate Scope: Domain-Specific Well-Being		Narrow Scope: Facet-Specific Well-Being	
	More Affective Emphasis	More Cognitive Emphasis	More Affective Emphasis	More Cognitive Emphasis	More Affective Emphasis	More Cognitive Emphasis
Example indicator	Global affect	Life satisfaction	Feelings about one's job	Job satisfaction	Feelings about work colleagues	Satisfaction with pay in one's job
Type of well-being	1	2	3	4	5	6

Note. Examples of indicators at the domain-specific and facet-specific levels here concern the domain of paid work. Similar instruments are available in other domains.

feelings in a situation) was much less stable between different occasions (average $r = +0.38$) than was the more cognitive assessment of satisfaction (mean $r = +0.89$).

An overview of subjective well-being in terms of levels of scope and the relative emphasis of assessment is presented in Table 2.1. In addition to the three suggested levels of abstractness introduced above (shown in the top row), each possibility is viewed as either more affective or more cognitive in emphasis, yielding six approaches to measurement. The suggested affective-cognitive separation is in practice not a dichotomy, since both processes are involved in any particular experience. In that way, although Lyubomirsky, King, and Diener (2005) emphasized affect in their definition of happiness as "the frequent experience of positive emotions over time" (p. 806, type 1 in Table 2.1), they considered life satisfaction (type 2) to be a "defensible proxy" (p. 822) for that affect-based construct.

Illustrative indicators are also included in Table 2.1, with alternatives labeled as well-being types 1 to 6. Consistent with the book's primary concern, the domain-specific and facet-specific illustrations concern job settings. Alternatively, with respect to, for instance, the domain of self, one might instead consider indicators of self-esteem, assessed primarily either in terms of negative or positive feelings about oneself (type 3) or in terms of more cognitive satisfaction with one's attributes (type 4).

MEASURING HAPPINESS AS WELL-BEING

Procedures for the measurement of this first, hedonic form of happiness typically involve self-reports, such that individuals describe a relevant mental state. Overall scale scores (averages or totals) thus usually summarize responses across themes identified by an investigator. In addition to self-reports, some research has obtained assessments of a person's well-being by a knowledgeable observer such as a spouse or friend, revealing moderate associations between responses made by oneself and the other rater. For example, self–other correlations of context-free well-being were typically in excess of +0.40 in studies by Lucas et al. (1996), and averaged +0.44 in research by Judge and Locke (1993). This section illustrates measurement approaches for each of the six types of subjective well-being summarized in Table 2.1.

Context-Free Well-Being

Global affect (an example of well-being type 1 in Table 2.1) is usually studied through scales whose items cover a range of positive and negative states. For example, the General Health Questionnaire (GHQ; Goldberg & Williams, 1988) asks people whether they have recently been feeling unhappy, nervous, hopeful, and so on. The scale is internally reliable (e.g., Mullarkey et al., 1999), and responses are meaningfully correlated with a range of other variables. (High scores in this case indicate unhappiness rather than happiness.) A 12-item context-free scale described by Warr, Butcher, Robertson, and Callinan (2006) covers feelings that are similar to those in the GHQ. However, response options there are in terms of "some of the time," "most of the time," and so on, rather than asking about current feelings in comparison with usual feelings (e.g., "much more than usual"), as is the case with the General Health Questionnaire.

Other investigators of type 1 well-being have obtained separate reports of positive and negative feelings, for example, in the factors of psychological well-being and psychological distress (i.e., positive and negative respectively) of the Mental Health Index of Veit and Ware (1983). In the Positive and Negative Affect Schedule (PANAS) created by Watson, Clark, and Tellegen (1988), positive items include alert, proud and inspired, and negative affect is covered by upset, hostile, jittery and similar terms (20 in total). Respondents in different studies may be requested to use differing time frames—the present moment, today, the past week, and so on. Other instruments of this kind, yielding separate positive and negative scores, include that by Kehr (2003). This indexed positive affect in terms of elation and activation, and negative affect as depression and energy deficit.

Note that the PANAS and similar scales tap only certain kinds of positive or negative affect–high-arousal feelings in the two upper segments of Figure 2.2 (e.g., Cropanzano et al., 2003; Feldman Barrett & Russell, 1998). This restricted coverage was later recognized by Tellegen et al. (1999). They indicated that, "to avoid terminological ambiguity, we have renamed the two factors Positive Activation and Negative Activation respectively, and use the abbreviations PA and NA in reference to these new labels" (p. 298). However, this renaming has been widely ignored by subsequent researchers.

More extended coverage along axes 2 and 3 is provided by Warr's (1990a) scales, whose content explicitly ranges from negative to positive. These scales cover dimensions from anxiety to comfort and from depression to enthusiasm. In their context-free application, they ask about the frequency with which people have in the past few weeks felt anxious, relaxed, and so on (for anxiety to comfort) and gloomy, enthusiastic, and so on (for depression to enthusiasm). Negative items are reverse scored, so that higher values always indicate greater happiness.

A general point should be made here about inappropriate conclusions that have sometimes been drawn from factor analyses of positively evaluated and negatively evaluated items. It has often been found that sets of items that cover both of the evaluative directions tend to yield evaluatively opposite statistical factors (e.g., Emmons & McCullough, 2003; Lucas et al., 1996; Veit & Ware, 1983). Items are likely to cluster in groups restricted to either positive or negative content, and on that basis it has sometimes been inferred that positive and negative affect should be treated as distinct from each other, for instance, through separate measures. However, this statistical bifurcation appears to be largely artifactual, caused by procedural factors and error patterns in the responses submitted to analysis, rather than representing the construct of subjective well-being itself.

Of particular importance is between-person variation in acquiescence response bias, shifting all assessments toward "agree" irrespective of their evaluative meaning. Statistically controlling for this bias has been shown to remove the directional separation and reveal bipolar axes of the kind shown in Figure 2.2. For example, Russell (1979) indexed individuals' agreement bias as the sum of all responses irrespective of item direction. Analyses that controlled for that tendency revealed an item structure of the expected form. Warr (1990a) summarized other earlier studies demonstrating that impact. Once the biasing effects of agreement response style had been offset by statistically controlling for the number of items checked or the positivity of responses, patterns of correlations were found in several studies to support a bipolar structure. That was also the case in research by Sevastos, Smith, and Cordery (1992).

With respect to the present framework, summarized in Figure 2.2 (p. 22), Warr (1990a) showed that well-being items extending all the way along either axis 2 or axis 3 emerged as separate factors after control for agreement acquiescence in that manner. The expected factorial distinction between anxiety–comfort and depression–enthusiasm was also obtained by carrying out separate analyses of items that were either all positive or all negative. In those evaluatively consistent conditions (restricted to entirely positive or negative material), acquiescence response bias cannot pull apart items that are differently evaluated, and the separate content-based factors of well-being were found to be clearly present.

Schmitt and Stults (1985) demonstrated the impact of a related artifactual process. Focusing on unintentional agreement with negative items, they showed that statistical separation between negative and positive items can arise from careless responding by even a small minority of individuals. Schmitt and Stults examined through simulated data sets the tendency to agree with some negative items when one in fact disagrees with them. When only 10% of respondents were careless in that fashion, a clearly definable negative factor was generated regardless of the substantive meaning of the items. That type of response error was identified as consistent with agreement acquiescence (described earlier), as a person accepts a statement that he or she in fact finds unacceptable.

Spector, van Katwyk, Brannick, and Chen (1997) also drew attention to the effect on observed factor structure of response unreliability, particularly to negative items (Schriesheim, Eisenback, & Hill, 1991). They too concluded that separate negative and positive factors were "artifacts of wording direction" (p. 660). Spector and colleagues examined the distribution of responses across a negative-to-positive response continuum. They showed that, rather than agreeing with one and disagreeing with the other, individuals may disagree with extreme items near to both poles of a continuum, because extreme responses in either direction tend to be contrary to their own more moderate position. "The result is that extreme items at opposite ends of a continuum have quite skewed distributions, with few people agreeing with them. ... This produces low correlations between extreme items with opposite wording direction and high correlations between items with the same wording direction" (pp. 673–674). Spector et al. (1997) confirmed that a two-factor, evaluatively separated structure emerged from that process by analyzing sets of simulated data that incorporated the response tendency. Similar arguments have been presented by van Schuur and Kiers (1994).

Bipolarity in positive and negative responses may be masked in other ways. For example, Green, Goldman, and Salovey (1993) considered several biases due to random and nonrandom response error, demonstrating in research with students that when those forms of error are taken into account, a largely bipolar structure is found. González-Romá, Schaufeli, Bakker, and Lloret (2006) drew attention to another source of statistical separation, showing that the presence of two distinct factors depends on an assumption of linearity in the relationships between item responses. They examined aspects of job-related burnout (discussed later) in three samples of employees, analyzing responses by nonparametric Mokken scaling as well as through conventional principal component procedures. In each sample the conventional approach gave rise to factors that were, as usual, evaluatively either positive or negative. However, the nonparametric analyses, which do not assume linearity of correlations, produced response dimensions extending from negative to positive, for example from feelings of exhaustion to vigor.

Subjective well-being can thus appropriately be viewed in terms of bipolar continua that extend between evaluatively opposite extremes (as can almost every other concept examined by psychologists), despite the fact that separate factors tend to be found in conventional statistical examination. The apparent separation of negative and positive content arises from one or more processes of agreement acquiescence, unreliable or unintended responding, consistent disagreement with both directions of extreme item, and an assumption of linearity in the relation between responses. The construct of well-being has both negative and positive elements, but those are opposite evaluations on a single continuum, not separate components.

The other category of context-free well-being shown in Table 2.1 (labeled as type 2) has a more reflective, cognitive emphasis than the affective aspects considered so far. For example, life satisfaction is often measured through the Satisfaction with Life Scale (Diener, Emmons, Larsen, & Griffin, 1985). This asks for broad-ranging assessments through five items like "In most ways my life is close to my ideal" and "If I could live my life over, I would change almost nothing." More complex mental processing is required in these cases than when indicating directly one's current feelings (for instance, in measures of type 1 in the table). The Satisfaction with Life Scale has been shown to be reliable internally and across time, and to be significantly responsive to changes in life circumstances (e.g., Pavot & Diener, 1993).

Domain-Specific Well-Being

Job-related affect (one form of domain-specific well-being, type 3 in Table 2.1) has sometimes been investigated in terms of job "burnout" (Maslach, 1982; Maslach, Schaufeli, & Leiter, 2001). The principal component of this has been defined as emotional exhaustion, which "refers to feelings of being emotionally overextended and depleted of one's emotional resources" (Maslach, 1998, p. 69). Conventional questionnaire items emphasize tension, strain, anxiety, and fatigue arising from one's work activities, primarily but not exclusively covering well-being axis 2 (from anxiety to comfort). Job-related emotional exhaustion measured in this way was found to be correlated with overall job satisfaction (described later) on average at –0.26 in the meta-analysis by Lee and Ashforth (1996).

Also within well-being type 3 of Table 2.1, the two diagonal axes of Figure 2.2 (from anxiety to comfort and from depression to enthusiasm) are covered by Warr's (1990a) scales (discussed earlier) when those are applied specifically to work ("Thinking of the past few weeks, how much of the time has your job made you feel...?"). The Job Affect Scale (Brief, Burke, George, Robinson, & Webster, 1988; Burke, Brief, George, Roberson, & Webster, 1989) also covers the four quadrants of Figures 2.1 and 2.2, with items about positive and negative feelings at work in the previous week. For example, employees describe how often they have felt excited, relaxed, sluggish, and nervous. As described in the previous section, although evaluatively distinct factors are often found, it is appropriate to view well-being themes in bipolar rather than separated terms. The statistical contrast between positive and negative items is an artifact arising from processes of response and data analysis.

Most frequently measured in the area of this book has been job satisfaction (Cook, Hepworth, Wall, & Warr, 1981). Both affective and cognitive themes were incorporated in Locke's (1969) definition of job satisfaction as a "pleasurable emotional state resulting from the appraisal of one's job" (p. 317). Feelings were more stressed by Cranny, Smith, and Stone (1992), whose account was in terms of "an affective (that is, emotional) reaction to one's job" (p. 1).

Measures in this area have either addressed overall satisfaction or been directed at satisfaction with individual facets of a job. Overall job satisfaction has sometimes been examined through a single question (e.g., "all things considered, how satisfied are you with your job in general"), but more often through multiple items. Those may request overall evaluations, as in the scale devised by Brayfield and Rothe (1951). This asks for disagree or agree responses to statements like "I feel fairly satisfied with my present job" and "I find real enjoyment in my work." Alternatively, separate items can cover specific job features. For example, the scale developed by Warr, Cook, and Wall (1979) asks about a person's degree of satisfaction with 15 work themes (physical conditions, your fellow workers, the freedom to use your own judgment, and so on), and an overall score is taken. Twenty job features of that kind are covered in the Minnesota Satisfaction Questionnaire (Weiss, Dawis, England, & Lofquist, 1967). Internal reliability of established scales of this kind is high; Bruk-Lee, Goh, Khoury, and Spector (2005) reported an average reliability coefficient from 13 scales of +0.87.

Job satisfaction is sometimes described in terms of a relative emphasis on "intrinsic" or "extrinsic" features. For example, the scale of Warr et al. (1979; described earlier) also yields scores of those two kinds, focusing either on satisfaction with job content (e.g., with amount of responsibility or personal freedom of action) or with features extrinsic to task activities such as one's rate of pay. Those two forms of job satisfaction are significantly intercorrelated, for example, at +0.72 in the source publication. The correlation between intrinsic and extrinsic satisfaction scores from the Minnesota Satisfaction Questionnaire was reported to average +0.60 by Weiss et al. (1967). (Consistent responding to intermingled intrinsic and extrinsic items in a single questionnaire does of course enhance this observed overlap.)

Those and similar instruments obtain evaluations of job features that require some reflective consideration about one's situation, falling within type 4 of Table 2.1 (with a more cognitive emphasis). A more affective measure of job satisfaction (type 3) was proposed by Kunin (1955). This presents outlines of faces that range in appearance from unhappiness to happiness, and respondents are asked to choose the one that best reflects their current feeling. The original instrument contained a set of 11 male faces, but later versions have varied both in faces' number (five or more) and gender (Dunham & Herman, 1975). More recently, asexual "smiley" faces have been used.

Other domain-specific aspects of happiness, at the same level of scope as job-related well-being, include self-related well-being. This has been indexed, for instance, through Rosenberg's (1965) scale of self-esteem, which includes items such as *I feel I'm as good a person as anybody*. Self-related well-being measured in that way is significantly associated with a person's happiness at the context-free level. For example, the average correlation with life satisfaction was +0.57 in research by Lucas et al. (1996); Watson, Suls, and Haig (2002) presented correlations averaging –0.70 with context-free depression and –0.43 with context-free anxiety; the mean correlation between self-esteem and context-free negative affect was –0.31 in research by Chen, Gully, and Eden (2004); in the studies reviewed by Lyubomirsky et al. (2005), the average correlation of self-esteem with a variety of indicators of context-free happiness was +0.60.

Correlations between self-esteem (here viewed primarily as well-being in the self domain) and subsequent life satisfaction and job satisfaction (2 months later) were +0.50 and +0.40, respectively, in separate studies by Judge, Bono, Erez, and Locke (2005). In a meta-analysis of cross-sectional research, an average uncorrected correlation of +0.35 with job satisfaction was reported by Faragher et al. (2005). Another established scale of self-esteem is by Coopersmith (1967). This overlaps strongly with Rosenberg's measure; for example, the intercorrelation was +0.78 in research by Watson et al. (2002).

Facet-Specific Well-Being

Facet-specific well-being (illustrated as types 5 and 6 in Table 2.1 on p. 29) has been measured in many ways, with separate scales that focus0 on particular targets. For example, the Job Descriptive Index (JDI; Kinicki, McKee-Ryan, Schriesheim, & Carson, 2002; Smith, Kendall, & Hulin, 1969) covers satisfaction with five aspects of a job (the work itself, pay, opportunities for promotion, supervision, and coworkers). Employees indicate whether or not, for instance, their supervisor is tactful, praises good work, and so on. Separate scores are computed for each facet.

Satisfaction with one of those factors, the work itself, is usually taken to represent "intrinsic" satisfaction (see earlier discussion). Scores of that kind are more closely associated with overall job satisfaction than are "extrinsic" facet satisfactions. For example, Ironson, Smith, Brannick, Gibson, and Paul (1989) reported a correlation of +0.78 between satisfaction with the work itself and overall job satisfaction; on the other hand, that intercorrelation for the other four JDI facet satisfactions averaged only +0.38. Based on that and other published investigations, Lapierre, Spector, and Leck (2005) computed average correlations between job-facet satisfactions and overall job satisfaction. Those average levels were +0.72 for satisfaction with the work itself, +0.43 for coworker satisfaction, +0.42 for satisfaction with promotion opportunities, +0.40 for supervisor satisfaction, and +0.27 for pay satisfaction.

In the study by Taber and Alliger (1995), the correlation between overall job satisfaction and work-itself satisfaction was +0.59. Those researchers also examined feelings about the specific tasks undertaken in each person's job. Average rated enjoyment of those tasks (averaging 13 in a job) was correlated at +0.41 with an employee's satisfaction with the work itself and at +0.30 with overall job satisfaction. Published correlations between job-facet satisfactions and employees' life satisfaction were reviewed by Kinicki et al. (2002). Although the average correlation of life satisfaction with work-itself satisfaction was +0.27, that value for satisfaction with coworkers or with supervision was only +0.15 in each case.

Facet-specific well-being has also been examined in other domains. For example, the domain-specific concept of self-related well-being (described earlier) has sometimes been broken down into separate facets, such as social self-esteem or academic self-esteem. At that level of scope, Pierce and Gardner (2004) have focused on "organization-based self-esteem," defined as "the degree to which an individual believes him/herself to be capable, significant, and worthy as an organizational member" (p. 593). They presented self-descriptive items to tap this facet-specific form of well-being.

In overview of this section about measurement, happiness as well-being has been studied at several levels of specificity and with an emphasis that is either more affective or more reflective. As illustrated in Table 2.1, it is convenient to think in terms of six overlapping forms of subjective well-being, and the measurement approaches outlined here cover all those possibilities. Although conventional statistical analyses have suggested that negative items might be treated as distinct from positive items, that apparent separation by evaluative content has been shown to arise artifactually from agreement biases and other sources of response error. It is preferable to treat subjective well-being as a bipolar construct extending from negative to positive, rather than in terms of two separately evaluated components.

Face validity and content validity of well-being scales are often very high, because items directly cover the topic of interest. Instruments' construct validity may be appraised in terms of factor structure and associations with relevant affective, behavioral, and environmental variables. Considerable information about validity in that sense is presented in later chapters and in the many publications that are cited. As for criterion-related validity, associations might be examined with happiness-relevant cognitions and behaviors. Much supporting research of that kind is reviewed later, although it is not always clear on conceptual grounds what should serve as criteria in the validation of happiness measures.

In practice, issues of validity have rarely been explicitly addressed in this domain. Given the clear face validity of most measures, their conceptual closeness to happiness as a criterion, and their meaningful associations with other variables, instruments have been widely accepted as appropriate. However, in view of the many different measures that have been produced and the variations in perspective illustrated in Table 2.1, it would now be appropriate to investigate more systematically networks of overlapping happiness concepts and their measures. In particular, issues of convergent and discriminant validity deserve attention; how similar or different are measures in the scores they yield and in their associations with other variables?

HAPPINESS AS SELF-VALIDATION

Next, let us look at psychologists' examination of the second form of happiness. This has been interpreted in diverse ways, but a core theme (as outlined in chap. 1) is that happiness should not only be viewed in terms of pleasure. It also involves worthwhile activities or a realization of the self, somehow meeting a standard of fittingness in relation to what one should be. This second form of happiness is here referred to as "self-validation," although (as indicated in chap. 1) many different terms have been used in the research literature.

Self-validation involves feeling positive for reasons that are in some sense appropriate relative to certain standards. Some standards may be entirely personal to oneself, and others reflect external definitions of morality or religion (e.g., McFall, 1982). Conceptions of what is fitting may thus originate in part from social definitions of what is considered meaningful to people in a given society, so that the nature of appropriateness (and hence of self-validation) is in part specified by other people. Although a central core of valued human attributes and experiences is also involved, some variations may thus be expected between different societies or time periods. For example, a general difference between Western and Eastern cultures may be linked to a more collective (and less individualistic) emphasis in the East. Self-validation through meeting group obligations may thus be a more significant form of happiness in some cultures than in others. This possibility is examined in chapter 10.

The second form of happiness has been examined by markedly fewer psychologists than have studied happiness as well-being. Researchers in this subfield have varied among themselves in the elements to be emphasized, and (as illustrated later) their measuring instruments reflect that divergence. Almost no research has examined self-validation in samples of job holders.

The construct here labeled as "self-validation" is central to Seligman's (2002) notion of "authentic happiness." He distinguished between a "pleasant life" and a "good life." A pleasant life reflects the first form of happiness introduced earlier—positive states through the avoidance of pain and the experience of pleasure. However, authentic happiness (described as a life that is "good") was considered to arise from the application of personal strengths and virtues. Seligman identified six principal virtues: wisdom and knowledge, courage, love and humanity, justice, temperance, and spirituality (later termed "transcendence"; Seligman, Steen, Park, & Peterson, 2005). These virtues embody standards independent of the person, inherent in the notion of self-validation.

Seligman explicitly disapproved of the narrowness of what he called "'happiology' or hedonics—the science of how we feel from moment to moment" (2002, p. 6). Furthermore, happiness "sometimes refers to feelings, but sometimes refers to activities in which nothing at all is felt" (Seligman, 2002, p. 261). That separation of happiness as well-being from other forms of happiness was further emphasized by Peterson, Park, and Seligman (2005). In a study of people's orientations (rather than their actual happiness), they suggested that being engaged in a valued activity (irrespective of current feelings of displeasure or pleasure) was itself one way of being happy.

That view has some similarity with the earlier arguments of Ferguson (1767/1966), who believed that happiness is not to be found in the satisfaction of desires but more in active engagement against adversity. "The mind, during the greater part of its existence, is employed in active exertions, not in merely attending to its own feelings of pleasure or pain" (p. 42). People seem most to be happy "when placed in the middle of difficulties, and obliged to employ the powers they possess" (p. 44). "The most animating occasions of human life are calls to danger and hardship, not invitations to safety and ease" (p. 45); happiness "is not the succession of mere animal pleasures...[and it is not] the state of repose" (p. 49). Instead,

Ferguson argued that happiness occurs within purposeful activity, whether that is experienced as pleasurable or painful.

Themes of that kind are present in the more recent concept of "thriving" in job settings, which has been emphasized by Spreitzer et al. (2005). This covers both a sense of vitality and the awareness of new learning and forward movement. The construct was presented as combining both hedonic and eudaimonic (see chap. 1) perspectives, emphasizing that individuals, in their role as employees as well as elsewhere, seek to realize their full potential as human beings. "Thriving focuses on the positive psychological experience of increased learning and vitality to develop oneself and grow at work" (p. 538).

McGregor and Little (1998) examined the second form of happiness in terms of personal "meaning." Deriving from personal standards, that notion was viewed as "the extent to which participants appraise their personal projects as consistent with their values, commitments, and other important aspects of self-identity" (p. 496). "Meaning refers to feelings of connectedness, purpose, and growth" (p. 508). That theme was developed by King, Hicks, Krull, and Del Gaiso (2006) in terms of people's experiences of meaning in life. "A life is meaningful when it is understood by the person living it to matter in some larger sense. Lives may be experienced as meaningful when they are felt to have significance beyond the trivial or momentary, to have purpose, or to have a coherence that transcends chaos" (p. 180).

Other psychologists have also focused on the characteristics of a person's goals. For example, Sheldon and Kasser (1995) considered patterns of congruence, viewed as the degree to which goals are linked to each other and determined by the person himself or herself. Such "self-concordance" of goals was described by Sheldon and Elliott (1999) as "their consistency with the person's developing interests and core values" (p. 482), arguing that their achievement does "not necessarily feel 'good' nor are they necessarily self-gratifying" (Sheldon & Elliott, 1999, p. 484). In longitudinal research with students, Sheldon and Houser-Marko (2001) found that the attainment of self-concordant goals of that kind was particularly beneficial for later personal adjustment and a sense of growth.

In these studies, standards of fittingness were self-set, in terms of people's own aims and values; what is here described as "self-validation" was treated as the attainment of personally meaningful goals. Note that this particular view is individualistic and achievement-oriented, as are many other Western models of self-realization (Waterman, 1984). Alternative accounts of happiness as self-validation can of course be more community-oriented, or linked to universal moral standards, or based on a belief in the value of contemplation or a willing acceptance of one's life condition. In that respect, Buddhism argues that hedonic happiness is ultimately unattainable, and that contentment should be sought through an openness to alternative perspectives and a recognition of the connectedness between all things.

From a Western perspective, self-determination was emphasized by Nix, Ryan, Manly, and Deci (1999). Undertaking salient, intrinsically motivated activities was said to yield "a special sense of being restorative or regenerative" (p. 267), together with a feeling of subjective vitality. The latter was construed by Ryan and Frederick (1997) as a positive feeling of aliveness, and was explicitly distinguished from hedonic happiness, although the two were viewed as sometimes inter-correlated. (See also the notion of "thriving," discussed earlier.) Waterman's (1993) perspective was in terms of "personal expressiveness," experienced when activities are characterized by intense involvement and a sense of special fit with what a person is meant to do. He argued that feelings of personal expressiveness were likely to derive from "self-realization through the fulfilment of personal potentials in the form of the development of one's skills and talents, the advancement of one's purposes in living, or both" (p. 679).

People's attainment of goals that are intrinsically important to them has sometimes been approached through themes of "psychological growth" or "self-actualization" (e.g., Herzberg, 1966; Maslow, 1943; Schultz, 1977). For example, Maslow distinguished between "becoming" and "being." We were assumed to be in the process of moving toward our full potential, toward the actualization of what we might be. The state of self-actualization was described as an episode "in which the powers of the person come together in a particularly efficient and intensely enjoyable ways, and in which he [sic] is more integrated and less split, more open for experience, more idiosyncratic, more perfectly expressive or spontaneous, or fully functioning, more creative, more humorous, more ego-transcending, more independent of his lower needs, etc. He becomes in these episodes more truly himself, more perfectly actualizing his potentialities, closer to the core of his Being, more fully human" (Maslow, 1968, p. 97). That broad conceptualization extends beyond what is meant here by happiness as self-validation, but it captures several central themes. Maslow's work was extremely popular in earlier decades, perhaps because many readers recognized the experiences he described, despite the fact that his accounts were diffuse and imprecise.

Herzberg's (1966) approach was similar, in terms of people's need "to realize the human potential for perfection" (p. 70). In particular, he emphasized the importance of attainments that are cognitive, arguing that people have strong needs to increase their knowledge, enhance understanding, and be creative. He pointed out that satisfaction of those needs is actively sought in jobs as well as elsewhere, but that attempts to overcome obstacles necessarily give rise from time to time to negative affect in the pursuit of personal growth.

Ryff (e.g., 1989) moved beyond happiness as pleasure to consider six additional dimensions of psychological functioning. Two of those are similar to themes considered earlier, identified as "personal growth" and "purpose in life." Personal growth was seen in terms of continued development, a sense that one's potential is being realized, and changes to oneself that reflect increasing self-knowledge. Purpose in life was taken to imply the presence of personal goals that contribute to a feeling that one's life is meaningful. In addition, Ryff explored four more dimensions: autonomy, environmental mastery, positive relations with others, and self-acceptance.

Self-reports on scales to assess these six themes are positively intercorrelated, and scores are located within a single higher-order factor. They are also significantly associated with parallel ratings of a target person made by knowledgeable other people, such as spouses (Schmutte & Ryff, 1997; mean $r = +0.43$), and with measures of happiness as subjective well-being (Keyes et al., 2002; Ryff, 1989; Ryff & Keyes, 1995).

The constructs of personal growth and purpose in life would generally be accepted as falling within happiness as self-validation as treated here. However, the conceptual location of the other four themes is less certain. For instance, Ryan and Deci (2001, p. 147) pointed out that autonomy, environmental mastery, and positive interpersonal relations might better be viewed as features that foster happiness, rather than being defining attributes of that concept itself.

A common theme in characterizing self-validation is some involvement in activities that are important to the person. As pointed out earlier, perceived importance arises from external value standards as well as from consistency with one's own values and motives. A short-term form of consistency with personal motives has been emphasized by Csikszentmihalyi (e.g., 1997). He showed that many motivated activities yield a sense of "flow," in conditions where goals are clear and difficult, a person's skills match the level of challenge, and he or she is motivated to achieve success.

Being "in flow" is described as "the subjective experience of engaging just-manageable challenges by tackling a series of goals, continuously processing feedback about progress, and adjusting actions based on this feedback. Under these conditions, experience seamlessly unfolds from moment to moment" (Nakamura & Csikszentmihalyi, 2002, p. 90). The process may include intense and focused concentration and absorption, automaticity of action, experiences of self-transcendence, unity, and fusion with the world, together with a sense that time has raced by. It is one of dynamic equilibrium, a balance between action capacities and perceived opportunities for action, and is intrinsically rewarding. Flow thus embodies aspects of self-fulfilment and self-transcendence, themes within the notion of self-validation as described here.

However, Quinn (2005) pointed out that there is no agreed definition of flow, and that it has been specified only loosely. He built on Csikszentmihalyi's account to define flow as "the experience of temporarily merging one's situation awareness with the automatic application of activity-relevant knowledge and skills" (p. 615), and treated other possible elements of the construct as either antecedents (e.g., goal clarity and high concentration) or outcomes (e.g., sense of control and loss of self-consciousness). "Situation awareness" in that definition involves the perception of current circumstances, response requirements, and likely future developments. Quinn (2005) thus suggested that flow occurs when "awareness and application occur simultaneously rather than sequentially" (p. 615) in situations where levels of environmental challenge and personal skill are appropriately balanced.

Particular flow experiences may be brief, but in the longer term Csikszentmihalyi (e.g., 1999) saw a "good life" as requiring extended involvement in appropriate activities. That involvement is often through episodes of flow during motivating and challenging tasks. The second form of happiness was thus viewed in his framework as less dependent on the actual content of an activity than on the presence of a combination of characteristics giving rise to flow.

However, the relationship between flow and subjective well-being (the first kind of happiness) is "not entirely self-evident" (Csikszentmihalyi, 1999, p. 825). During a flow experience, people do not necessarily feel pleasure, because they are too involved in the task to consider subjective states. Nevertheless, in retrospect they can often report having been in a specially positive mode. The frequency and intensity of such positive states are likely to influence more extended feelings of well-being, so that experiences of flow and subjective well-being can be interdependent over time, although they remain conceptually distinct.

That is also the case with forms of self-validation more generally; they are conceptually different from happiness as pleasure, but sometimes linked to it. This point is considered again later in the chapter.

Finally in this section we should consider together the sense of self-validation as construed here and the related concept of self-esteem. The latter was earlier conceptualized as a form of domain-specific (here self-related) subjective well-being (type 3 or 4 in Table 2.1). How does self-validation, identified as the second broad component of happiness, differ from self-esteem, a domain-specific instance of the first component?

Both involve positive perceptions of oneself, but a clear conceptual distinction should be stressed. Happiness as well-being (the first aspect) was illustrated earlier as a consequence of the satisfaction of desires in general, whereas happiness as self-validation was seen to depend on satisfaction of one particular kind—relative to some standards of fittingness or appropriateness. In other words, self-validation (the second component of happiness) does not derive from all experiences, but only from a subset of experiences, those that are linked to a standard of worth. On the other hand, self-esteem (a domain-specific instance of happiness as well-being) involves feelings about oneself relative to whatever activity is under consideration. Self-validation thus has a more restricted content than self-esteem, focusing only on standards of worth. Despite that limitation, the concept labeled here as self-validation is clearly very diffuse, and agreement about definition and operationalization is still lacking.

MEASURING HAPPINESS AS SELF-VALIDATION

Self-report scales in this area vary widely, and few investigators seek to place their constructs within a broader notion such as self-validation. Measures have here been brought together under that heading, but they were originally presented in more specific frameworks that differed between themselves. As mentioned earlier, the term *self-validation* does not usually occur in the papers cited, and has been applied in the present framework as an overarching label for interconnected themes.

For example, emphasizing personal meaning and intrinsic motivation, McGregor and Little (1998) measured students' sense of self-determination, with items about the presence of "very clear goals and aims in life" and a sense of "meaning, purpose, and mission in life." Those items were developed by King et al. (2006), and were applied both to extended experiences and to a short-term sense of purpose (e.g., *Today, I had a sense that I see a reason for me being here*). Subjective vitality was assessed by Ryan and Frederick (1997) through items describing feelings of being truly alive. Ryff's (1989) scale of Personal Growth asked about one's continued development, openness to new experiences, and similar themes. Her Purpose in Life scale covered, for instance, the existence of life goals, a sense of directedness, and beliefs that give life a purpose.

Waterman (1993) examined eudaimonic happiness with respect to five activities nominated by each person as important to him or her. For each activity, items for disagreement or agreement included *This activity gives me my greatest feeling of really being alive* and *When I engage in this activity, I feel that this is what I was meant to do*. By combining these ratings, an overall measure of self-validation was obtained. (That was labeled in the paper as "personal expressiveness," and was said to "signify self-realization"; p. 680.)

The attainment of personally meaningful or "self-concordant" goals has been emphasized by Sheldon and Kasser (1995), Sheldon and Elliot (1999), and others (see the previous section). Individuals were asked to record six short-term goals (or another specified number) and then to describe their reasons for pursuing each one, for instance, in terms of external demands or intrinsic interest. Self-concordance scores have been derived in terms of the total of intrinsically determined choices minus those based on external pressures or because of a sense of guilt or obligation.

As noted earlier in the chapter, self-concordance assessed in this way has a focus on goals that are personal to each individual. External standards are not the primary focus in such a framework, such that (for instance) pursuing a particular goal because of obligation or in order to avoid feeling guilty has been given a negative score, considered to be in opposition to self-concordance (see the previous paragraph). However, although it is generally difficult to identify the primary reason for actions that may be multiply determined (see chap. 6), it seems desirable to view an obligation to meet external moral standards (or guilt because of failure to pursue those) as linked to self-validation, rather than in opposition to it, as done in the research described earlier.

The more localized experience of flow in a particular activity was assessed through a 36-item scale by Jackson and Marsh (1996). Respondents rated a recent episode in terms of the presence of key attributes in Csikszentmihalyi's (e.g., 1999) model (loss of self-consciousness, transformation of time, etc.), and an overall flow score was taken. Quinn (2005) emphasized as the central element of experienced flow the merging of situation awareness and the application of expertise (described earlier), through items such as *I could sense why the decisions I made were correct.* The absorption scale of Rothbard (2001) emphasized how people can lose themselves in a role, one aspect of the broader notion of flow. Items include *When I am working, I often lose track of time.*

It is not clear how these different measures are interrelated within the same construct, here labeled as self-validation, and broad-based examination and empirical comparison of several such instruments are needed. Studies of the factor structure and relative validity of multiple indicators in this field would now be very valuable, especially in employment-related settings. As was indicated for subjective well-being, it is generally desirable to examine more systematically the validity of measures across different aspects of happiness.

It is also important to create self-report scales that more directly cover principal themes of self-validation. In parallel with questionnaires to directly record specific types of subjective well-being (see the earlier section), items need to describe different possible experiences of self-validation, obtaining self-reports about their occurrence at levels that are context-free, domain-specific (e.g., job-related), and possibly facet-specific.

In developing these scales, it would be helpful to examine separately different dimensions of self-validation experience. For example, as noted earlier, standards of worth may be more socially oriented or more individually oriented. Socially oriented self-validation is likely to involve unselfish or altruistic behaviors, whereas individually oriented happiness of that kind derives more from consistency with one's personal motives, illustrated earlier in terms of personal meaning or goal achievement. (However, an individual's goals can themselves be socially oriented.) Both emphases in self-validation need examination through targeted questions. Another feature that warrants separate measurement is the extent to which standards applied by a person are part of a formal system of religion or morality, rather than being criteria of worth that he or she has individually adopted.

THREE DIMENSIONS OF HAPPINESS: PLEASURE, AROUSAL, AND SELF-VALIDATION

The two-dimensional approach to happiness as well-being in Figure 2.1 can be extended to yield the more complete framework shown in

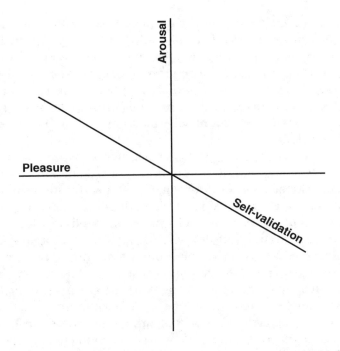

Figure 2.3.   A three-dimensional view of happiness, covering both well-being (through arousal and pleasure) and self-validation. (From left to right, self-validation extends from behind other two dimensions to a position in the front.)

Figure 2.3. Self-validation is presented there as a third dimension of experience, in addition to the well-being themes of pleasure and arousal. (That third dimension should be viewed as running from behind the other two at the left, through the midpoint, to a frontal position at the right.) Although pleasure and arousal are, as previously, laid out as orthogonal to each other, representing subjective well-being as reviewed earlier, self-validation is set at an angle of less than 90° to well-being, indicating the empirical correlation between those two aspects of happiness.

We can in this way consider any experience of happiness in terms of the three sub-concepts together. Happiness as subjective well-being (embracing the dimensions of pleasure and arousal in Fig. 2.1) may be captured through the intercorrelated measurement axes of feeling bad to feeling good, anxiety to comfort, and depression to enthusiasm (see

Fig. 2.2). However, any experience on those axes also has a loading on self-validation. In practice, that self-validation loading may be around zero, in cases when self-validation (the third dimension of happiness in Fig. 2.3) is not part of an experience. (Possible experiential hierarchies or sequences were discussed earlier.) On the other hand, some experiences on the axes of subjective well-being are also clearly positive or negative with respect to self-validation, with nonzero loadings on all dimensions.

In these terms, the experience of happiness involves an amount (including zero) of pleasure, arousal, and self-validation. Within the three-dimensional framework of Figure 2.3, greater intensity can be shown by increased distance from the midpoint. The scope and content of a particular experience of happiness depend on which aspects receive mental attention at the time, in response to intentional and other influences on cognitive selection. Attention may be directed at context-free happiness, at happiness that is specific to a particular domain (such as a job, family or oneself), or at facet-specific happiness, for example, in relation to one's pay or colleagues. The emphasis may be more affective or more cognitive, as illustrated in Table 2.1.

Some combinations of experience are phenomenologically more straightforward than others. For example, high levels of both self-validation and subjective well-being together can readily be envisaged, as can low levels of each. However, mixed compounds introduce the notion of ambivalence. High self-validation with low well-being, and low self-validation with high well-being, both imply two sets of awareness that cannot be amalgamated within a single summary description. A person is happy in one sense but unhappy in the other.

Given that mental life contains a large number of thoughts and feelings at about the same time, mental inconsistencies of that kind are common. In addition to possible contrasts between levels of the two forms of happiness (described earlier), people often experience contradictions within subjective well-being itself. For example, at the facet-specific level (types 5 and 6 in Table 2.1), responses can vary between different aspects of a job (wages and colleagues, for instance), linked to a divergent quality of these separate targets. In that way, one can feel ambivalent within the domain: Some aspects of your job make you happy and others make you unhappy. Between domains, one can, for instance, feel both low pleasure about one's job and high pleasure about one's family. In studies of subjective well-being at the context-free level, survey respondents often report that life is both quite satisfying and quite stressful (e.g., Headey & Wearing, 1992). Describing subjective well-being in terms only of a single statement may thus conceal differences between the valence of different aspects.

More generally, it is clear that happiness takes many different forms. In addition to a principal difference between subjective well-being and self-validation, variations occur in terms of scope and emphasis. The differentiations suggested in this chapter are used throughout the book: three levels of scope (context-free, domain-specific, and facet-specific), and well-being indicators that are more affective (emphasizing feelings) or more cognitive (e.g., reflective satisfaction). (Table 2.1 thus summarized six types of subjective well-being.) In addition, the varying involvement of psychological arousal in hedonic experience points to three axes for the measurement of well-being: from feeling bad to feeling good, from anxiety to comfort, and from depression to enthusiasm. As illustrated in Figure 2.2, these are moderately intercorrelated. Variations in temporal duration can also be important. Short-term feelings that are quickly replaced can have causes and consequences quite different from those that are extended and unchanging. We thus need to examine differences between forms of happiness as well as seeking general statements about happiness as a whole.

SOME CONCEPTS RELATED TO HAPPINESS

The book's focal concept is both similar to and different from others that are important in this field. In particular, happiness as well-being overlaps with several other notions through a common involvement of affect. This section briefly considers links with emotion, mood, attitude, quality of life, stress, and mental health.

Emotion and Mood

The first of those constructs, emotion, has several affect-based similarities with happiness. The term *affect* is traced by the *Oxford English Dictionary* back to the 1300s, and is defined as "the way in which one is affected or disposed." In psychological writings it is treated as an elementary feeling, described by Russell (2003) as "primitive, universal, and irreducible on the mental plane" (p. 148). Feelings are inherent in emotions as well as in subjective well-being. Miner, Glomb, and Hulin (2005) "use the term affect to generally describe the positive and negative quality of emotions and moods" (p. 171).

However, despite a common presence of affect, the concepts of emotion and well-being differ from each other in several ways. For example, emotions focus on a personally significant target (for instance, anger is directed at something or somebody), whereas well-being often lacks a specific referent. Both constructs can involve measurable physiological processes, but those are usually more pronounced for emotions than for well-being. Particular emotions usually have a brief time span, but well-being may be of long duration.

In addition, emotions are conventionally placed in discrete categories, such as fear, anger, surprise, or guilt. Most of those have a specific content that is conceptually distinct from the feelings that are central to subjective well-being, and the experiences in most emotions are clearly different from states of happiness or unhappiness. Nevertheless, two emotions among the several possible are usually identified as "joy" and "contentment" (e.g., Fredrickson, 2001). Those correspond to the two positive poles of well-being identified earlier in the chapter (e.g., Fig. 2.2; see p. 22). When joy and contentment are viewed as emotions, they are usually discussed in relation to a particular target, but that is not always the case for well-being itself.

A similar notion is that of mood. Moods are affective states that are usually considered to be less intense than emotions, more broad-ranging, and less likely to be targeted at a particular object; they tend to be somewhat more long-lasting than emotions (Barsade, 2002; George, 1996; Russell, 2003). George and Brief (1992) noted that "moods provide the affective coloring for day-to-day events" (p. 314). Sy, Côté, and Saavedra (2005) defined them as "generalized feeling states of relatively low intensity with no clear antecedent causes" (p. 295). Having a less obvious precursor, moods may have limited cognitive (rather than affective) content (Forgas & George, 2001).

Consistent with the central involvement of affect in both moods and subjective well-being, indicators of the two constructs tend to be inter-correlated. For example, Fisher (2000) examined the overlap between domain-specific well-being, in terms of overall job satisfaction, and average mood at work (ranging from unhappy to happy feelings) in the previous 2 weeks. Employees' average pleasantness of mood at work was found to be correlated at +0.30 with their subsequent job satisfaction. For averaged job satisfaction (both before and after the period of mood ratings) the correlation with average mood was +0.53. In a longitudinal examination, Judge and Ilies (2004) showed that employees' job satisfaction during the day was significantly associated with their mood in the evening. More generally, as indicated earlier in the chapter, the magnitude of association between measures of mood, satisfaction, and similar constructs varies according to the degree of content overlap between scales.

Attitude

Another concept linked to subjective well-being through the involvement of affect is that of attitude. Eagly and Chaiken (1993) defined an attitude as "a psychological tendency that is expressed by evaluating a particular entity with some degree of favor or disfavor" (p. 1). Evaluation is "the imputation of some degree of goodness or badness to an entity" (p. 4), in other words feeling good or bad about it. Petty, Wegener, and Fabrigar (1997) made the point like this: Attitudes are "summary evaluations of objects (oneself, other people, issues, etc.) along a dimension ranging from positive to negative" (p. 621). Subjective well-being has here been treated as bad or good feelings about one's life space, but another possibility is to describe those feelings in terms of an attitude to that life space.

However, attitudes also include themes that extend beyond the notion of well-being. An attitude is usually described as having three principal components, affective, cognitive, and behavioral, which are reflected in feelings, beliefs, and actions, respectively. For Kraus (1995), "Perhaps the most fundamental assumption underlying the attitude concept is the notion that attitudes, in some way, guide, influence, direct, shape or predict actual behavior" (p. 58). Tendencies to action are thus central to the construct, but those are less part of the notion of well-being. In that way, an attitude is characterized by a predisposition to respond in a consistently favorable or unfavorable manner to a particular target, but such an action-tendency (although it may be present) is not at the core of well-being. Other differences between subjective well-being and attitude include the fact that attitudes more explicitly involve a network of multiple beliefs and perceptions. Those cognitive extensions mean in part that attitudes can merge into broader ideologies that are far removed from the experience of subjective well-being.

Specific forms of well-being (narrower in scope than context-free experiences) are more similar to attitudes than is the context-free construct. Relevant domains have been introduced earlier in terms of a job, family, health, self, and so on; well-being in those individual domains has sometimes been viewed as an attitude. For instance, Fisher (2000) was explicit that "job satisfaction is an attitude" (p. 185), Miner (1992) saw "job satisfaction as generally equivalent to job attitudes" (p. 116), and Brief (1998) described it as "an attitude toward one's job" (p. 10). Studies of job-related (domain-specific) well-being and research into attitudes to one's job clearly have much in common.

Even more targeted states are investigated in research into well-being at the facet level. For example, within the domain of a job the facets of interest include pay, colleagues, and working conditions, and those have often been treated as the objects of specific attitudes. Facet-specific well-being, such as pay satisfaction, is conceptually similar to an attitude toward the facet in question, with similar implications for associations with other variables.

Perceived Quality of Life

Another member of this family of concepts is the "quality of life," with an illustrative domain-specific focus on the "quality of working life." This notion was particularly popular in the 1970s, measured either objectively in terms of actual living conditions (e.g., availability of housing) or through the perceptions of research participants. In practice, requested perceptions were similar to those examined in studies of subjective well-being. For example, Andrews and Withey (1974) studied perceived quality of life by asking people to consider their house, neighborhood, family life, and so on, in each case responding affectively through a scale from "terrible" to "delighted." Quality of life measured in this way can also be tapped through assessed satisfaction with particular domains. For example, the Comprehensive Quality of Life Scale (Cummins, McCabe, Romeo, & Gullone 1994) asks about people's satisfaction with their health, things they own, place in the community, and so on.

A partial summary of these similarities and differences is suggested in Table 2.2. First (in column 2) is each concept's primary emphasis on either affect, cognition, behavior, or bodily state. Each construct is heavily loaded with affect, being based on feelings, but they differ among themselves in their other emphases. In that way, affect, cognition, and behavior are all important in an attitude, but behavior is not central to specification of the other constructs. In addition, cognition is less involved in mood, in more affective forms of context-free well-being (types 1, 3, and 5 in Table 2.1), or in affective measures of life quality. Bodily state can be particularly significant in certain emotions.

In the third column, emotions are shown as being typically of brief duration and moods as being somewhat more extended (of "moderate" duration). Subjective well-being is described there as usually being of moderate duration, although in practice a research focus can range from short-term (e.g., "at this moment") through moderate durations (e.g., "in the past month") to extended periods (e.g., "in the past year"). That is also the case with attitudes and quality of life, although in general they can be thought of as relatively long-lasting. In terms of directedness (the right-hand column), emotions and attitudes are more

TABLE 2.2
Subjective Well-Being and Other Constructs

Construct	Primary Emphasis: Affect, Cognition, Behavior, or Bodily State	Typical Duration	Typical Directedness
More affective subjective well-being (types 1, 3, and 5 in Table 2.1)	Affect	Moderate	Less directed
More cognitive subjective well-being (types 2, 4, and 6 in Table 2.1)	Affect and cognition	Moderate	Less directed
Emotion	Affect and bodily state	Brief	Directed at a target
Mood	Affect	Moderate	Less directed
Attitude	Affect, cognition, and behavior	Long-lasting	Directed at a target
Quality of life	Either affect or affect and cognition (depending on the measure)	Long-lasting	Less directed

focused on a particular target than are the other constructs. Although not demonstrable through the structure of Table 2.2, greater directedness occurs in more specific (rather than more general) forms of well-being and life quality. For instance, job satisfaction (domain-specific) and pay satisfaction (facet-specific) are each more closely directed at a particular target than is life satisfaction (context-free).

Stress

The notion of stress has received considerable attention in recent decades, covering unhappiness beyond a threshold of severity. The term has been used in three different ways, referring (a) to a negative response to environmental inputs (for instance, as a person "experiences stress"), (b) to causal inputs themselves (e.g., describing "stress in my job"), or (c) to an overarching construct (as in discussing "the topic of stress"). It seems desirable to separate people's negative responses (the first of those) from the environmental causes of those responses (the second, sometimes specified as "stressors"), and the term *strain* is often used to describe reactions in this area (e.g., being "under strain"). Strain is typically studied as a form of low subjective well-being, perhaps with an emphasis on bodily or psychosomatic states, such as stomach complaints, cardiovascular disorders, physical tension, or sleeping problems.

From an early and targeted meaning in terms of the amount of pressure from an external load, the psychological notion of "stress" has since the 1970s become devalued, being applied in an overly inclusive manner. In addition to ambiguities about the referent of "stress" (discussed earlier), two problems may be noted. The term is often applied more broadly than is appropriate, and it is regularly extended to conditions that are not sufficiently serious to warrant the label.

In terms of breadth, Harkness et al. (2005) noted that "stress" has become a general label for a growing number of work-place concerns, such that it "appears to be everywhere and unavoidable, with reports of ever increasing stress levels, often described as reaching 'epidemic' proportions in the Western world" (p. 121). The professional literature and the mass media have included many different feelings, bodily conditions, and behaviors within a single umbrella construct. Recent publications have described as "work stress" all of the following: absenteeism, alcohol consumption, anger, anxiety, burnout, cardiovascular impairment, cigarette smoking, depression, distress, drug abuse, eating disorders, emotional exhaustion, fatigue, frustration, heart attack, hormonal changes, job dissatisfaction, lack of confidence, lethargy, low commitment, low morale, poor concentration, psycho-physiological symptoms of many kinds, raised blood pressure, and tension.

Those variables are clearly important, but many of them differ so greatly from others that joint treatment in the same broad category is inappropriate. Unless variables' content and correlates are substantially alike, it is an error to merge them together within a single composite. Describing all of the these as "work stress," implying common characteristics, causes, and consequences, is misleading and unhelpful. Instead of "this tendency to treat stressors as if they were all the same" (Lepine, Podsakoff, & Lepine, 2005, p. 770), we need to consider each one in terms of its own characteristics. As argued by Spector, Chen, and O'Connell (2000), we must move away from the widespread assumption that "job stressors in general lead to job strains in general" (p. 216). A more differentiated account is needed.

This book examines separately a number of job characteristics, which each create reactions of strain or more positive well-being in their own specific manner. A categorization of intermediate scope is in terms of "good stress" and "bad stress." It has long been recognized that some kinds of stressor might have positive outcomes, even if most instances within the category are negative. "Good stress" is sometimes viewed in terms of intensity level, such that "a bit of stress is good for you" whereas higher levels are harmful.

Instead of that categorization by intensity, Lepine et al. (2005) drew attention to a distinction between "challenge" stressors and "hindrance" stressors. The former involve environmental demands that bring about activation and goal achievement, whereas "hindrance" stressors were viewed as constraints and hassles. Podsakoff and colleagues showed in a meta-analysis of previous results that those two kinds of stressor can be distinguished empirically in relation to job performance. On average, "challenge" stressors were modestly positively associated with performance (uncorrected mean $r = +0.09$), whereas the correlation with "hindrance" stressors tended to be negative (average $r = -0.14$). Stress researchers have rarely made that conceptual distinction.

With respect to the second overextension, application of the term when intensity is low, "work stress" is now commonly used (especially in mass-media presentations) for relatively benign mental states, sometimes apparently in order to bolster their negative significance. The concept has in this way been inflated to include many conditions that do not reach its true threshold of seriousness. In a study of the discourse of female clerical workers, Harkness et al. (2005) concluded that "talking about stress has become so normal that effectiveness as a worker is judged by how stressed you appear to be" (p. 127).

The term "work stress" has thus been excessively applied, with respect to both breadth and depth. Barley and Knight (1992) argued that the notion has taken on its wide content by drawing in a range of earlier societal concerns. It thus operates as a symbol with expressive and political applications. They illustrated how the term has been used by the mass media, trade unions, professional organizations, and other bodies as a rhetorical device to build solidarity and further their own aims. For example, they suggested that the labor movement has emphasized stress claims in order to gain public support. Briner and Reynolds (1999) concluded that developments of those kinds mean that "stressors [now] essentially include almost anything that a person may not like ..., and strain includes almost any state that a person finds aversive or any behavior they, or others, may view as negative" (pp. 651–652).

A related concern about the recent emphasis on stress is that the focus becomes excessively negative, exaggerating threat and unpleasantness and discouraging a consideration of positive aspects of life. In practice, happiness is often possible only as a result of work directed toward difficult goals, and negative experiences during that process are essential as part of a happy life. Yet many researchers have treated even mild strain as an unacceptable experience. It has become customary to argue that the presence of strain requires changes to the situation or person, and that such changes call for the intervention of other people or professional institutions.

Objecting to the current overconcern with negative issues and excessive involvement of society in individuals' own personal problems, Wainwright and Calnan (2002) viewed the contemporary notion of stress as a historically unusual phenomenon that "brings into being a passive subject, a diminished self, and promotes a profoundly antihumanist lowering of expectations about human potential" (p. vii). From the perspective of this book, extending across several kinds of happiness, it is inappropriate to use the biased construct of "stress" as currently applied. Rather than diminishing our knowledge by an undue concentration on experiences that are unpleasant, we need also to examine positive life themes and to treat different experiences separately rather than subsuming all negative themes within a single category.

That view was developed by Bonanno (2004) in terms of processes of resilience. Examining individuals who had suffered trauma, bereavement, sexual abuse, and other negative events (with no direct occupational involvement), he noted that psychologists have consistently argued for clinical intervention, assuming that some form of assistance from others is widely desirable. Instead, he reviewed research indicating that for many people this well-meaning approach is of no benefit and may sometimes in fact be harmful. (However, he recognized the value of psychotherapeutic assistance in a minority of cases.)

Bonanno argued that an excessive emphasis on negative outcomes from aversive events has distorted and limited our theoretical understanding. "It is imperative that future investigations of loss and trauma include more detailed study of the full range of possible outcomes; simply put, dysfunction cannot be fully understood without a deeper understanding of health and resilience" (p. 26). We need "to take a fresh look at the various ways people adapt and even flourish in the face of what otherwise would seem to be potentially debilitating events" (p. 27).

A more positive approach to the study of happiness, in settings that inevitably include negative as well as positive features, is thus likely to investigate resilience, agency, tenacity, courage, and capacity to overcome adversity; or perhaps explore threatening events as a spur to creative activity or as a test of moral fiber (Pollock, 1988). Such outlooks emphasize that unhappiness and happiness are interdependent, they less restrict attention to potential harm or see a need for the involvement of society in personal lives, and they more often explore proactivity in functioning and experiences of both positive and negative kinds.

Mental Health

Processes of that kind are also included within the construct of mental health. That has been described in many ways by authors and practitioners of different orientations. A summary of previous views by Warr (1987, 2005) treats mental health not as a construct that is separate from and in opposition to "mental ill-health" (such that a person is designated as either "ill" or "well"), but in terms of a continuum from negative to positive states. Accounts of mental health may be viewed in terms of five principal themes: subjective well-being, competence, aspiration, autonomy, and integrated functioning. The first of those is also the first component of happiness described earlier. Happiness and mental health thus overlap in respect of subjective well-being, and that component can be described and examined through the same measurement axes in both areas of study.

However, some differences in emphasis occur between the nature of well-being in the two constructs. For example, psychosomatic symptoms (e.g., stomach or cardiac complaints, sleep problems, sweating, or bodily agitation) tend to have greater priority in discussions of low mental health than of unhappiness. In addition, different domain-specific and facet-specific emphases can be identified. For example, one domain-specific form of well-being has a focus on the self. Self-related well-being, feeling bad or good about yourself (e.g., in terms of self-esteem, self-acceptance, feelings of self-worth, or positive self-regard), falls within both concepts, but has been examined more within discussions of mental health than it has been treated as an aspect of happiness. Similarly, specific facets of particular domains fall more clearly in one construct rather than the other. For instance, facet-specific well-being within the job domain, illustrated as satisfaction with one's pay or one's supervisor, is more obviously a narrow aspect of people's happiness than of their mental health.

Other elements of mental health may be viewed as behavioral constructs that fall less clearly within the definition of happiness. These behavioral themes can be described as "competence," "aspiration," and "autonomy." In addition, consideration of mental health (e.g., by clinical psychologists) brings in theory-based constructs and perspectives that are not usually introduced into discussions of happiness. Those will be referred to here as "integrated functioning."

Competence.   Behaviors collectively referred to as "competence" have been emphasized by many writers on mental health (e.g., Bradburn, 1969; Jahoda, 1958). Terms have included effective coping, environmental mastery, effectance motivation, and so on. This feature covers a person's ability to handle life's problems and act on the environment with at least a moderate amount of success. It is sometimes viewed broadly in terms of positive functioning in life (e.g., Keyes, 2002). As in other cases, competence may be viewed as either context-free (concerning life in general) or with a domain-specific (e.g., job-related) focus. Competence that is specific to particular activities has been viewed as activity-related self-efficacy, linked to behaviors and processes of self-regulation (e.g., Bandura, 1997).

Low competence is not always a sign of low mental health; everyone is incompetent in some respects. The key factor is a link with low subjective well-being. Inability to cope with important environmental demands is often associated with negative feelings (e.g., Nezu, 1985), but that is not the case for all activities. For personally nonsalient activities, low competence does not normally reflect low mental health.

Aspiration.   The mentally healthy person has also been viewed as someone who establishes realistic goals and makes active efforts to attain them (e.g., Herzberg, 1966; Maslow, 1943; Schultz, 1977). Such people show an interest in the environment, they engage in motivated activity, and they seek to extend themselves in ways that are personally significant. On the other hand, low levels of aspiration are seen in apathy and acceptance of the status quo, no matter how unsatisfactory that is.

To characterize people in these terms in a context-free manner is difficult, because a person's aspirations can have many different targets. However, a broad-ranging scale of goal-directedness has been shown to be significantly related to employees' subjective well-being (Payne, Robbins, & Dougherty, 1991). In occupational settings, where the interest may be in purely job-related aspiration, it is sometimes appropriate to examine intrinsic job motivation. That concerns the degree to which a person desires challenging goals in his or her job, a feature that is central to aspiration in that domain.

Autonomy.   Another aspect of mental health, autonomy, has been emphasized more by Western than by Eastern writers. For example, in the United States, Angyal (1965) identified the tendency to strive for independence and self-regulation as a key aspect of mental health, and Loevinger (1980) included in her account of personal development a high-level "autonomous stage." Mentally healthy people are usually considered able to resist the influence of environmental features and to determine their own opinions and actions. A factor analysis of questionnaire items by Kafka and Kozma (2001) identified an autonomy factor along those lines.

However, too much as well as too little autonomy can be undesirable. We should thus think in terms of a continuum of personal autonomy, ranging from extreme dependence on other people all the way to extreme counterdependence, with both interdependence and independence located between the extremes. A balance between interdependence and independence reflects good mental health of this kind.

Integrated Functioning.   A final aspect of mental health, here identified as "integrated functioning," concerns the person as a whole and relationships between other components. People who are mentally healthy exhibit several forms of balance, harmony, and inner relatedness. Different writers have their own preferred theoretical perspective on integrated functioning. For example, some psychoanalytic approaches include concepts of ego, id, and superego; models of identity and the self may focus on coherence between goals and values or between cognitive and affective subsystems. One self-report questionnaire investigation revealed a factor of mental integration of that kind as well as separate factors of subjective well-being and personal growth (Compton et al., 1996). However, current perspectives on integrated functioning as an aspect of mental health (usually within clinical psychology) rarely consider paid employment.

The literatures covered in this section, on emotion, mood, attitude, quality of life, stress, and mental health, are thus all in part relevant to a book on happiness. All are later brought in where relevant, placing themes within the framework introduced here. As set out in Figure 2.3, the broad construct of happiness is characterized in terms of pleasure, psychological arousal, and self-validation, with the first two dimensions together comprising subjective well-being. And, as summarized in Figure 2.2, that first form of happiness will be examined in terms of three intercorrelated axes, from feeling bad to feeling good, from anxiety to comfort, and from depression to enthusiasm. The perspective embraces positive as well as negative forms of well-being, and seeks evidence about high as well as low self-validation.

3

Unemployment and Retirement: Role Preference and Other Influences

C hapters 1 and 2 have considered psychologists' ideas about the nature of happiness and their procedures to measure its two main components, labeled here as subjective well-being and self-validation. The book's primary question was identified as "Why are some people at work happier or unhappier than others?" and answers to that question have been seen to require an understanding not only of the environment but also of the person. We now move on to consider variables in those two domains.

Environmental and personal themes for later development are introduced in this chapter by examining other employment-related roles which provide a context for paid work—unemployment and retirement. Although an extended period in a job is usual for most adults in most countries, many people are instead unemployed, non-employed, or retired. "Unemployed" individuals are usually defined as those who lack a job and are seeking one or would like to have one, whereas the "nonemployed" include people who are without a job by their own choice. Retirement involves a withdrawal from the labor market, usually at the end of a working life.

Precise specification of those roles can sometimes be difficult in psychologically relevant terms. For instance, a person identified as unemployed may indeed be seeking a job but not really want one, because he or she is responding only to official requirements in order to claim welfare benefits. People who are defined as retired in the sense that they receive a state pension may also undertake paid work on an intermittent or part-time basis, so that their retirement does not mean complete absence of a job. For all groups, category membership can be for reasons that are to some degree more voluntary or more involuntary, so that personal motivation requires consideration in addition to environmental causation. For instance, some mothers choose to be nonemployed as they look after their children, but others may be reluctantly in the nonemployed category, because a chronic illness or lack of job opportunity prevents them from obtaining paid work.

In seeking psychological understanding of unemployment, nonemployment, or retirement, additional information beyond a person's formal status is thus needed. However, much research has merely examined groups defined by their formal position, such as "unemployed and seeking benefit" or "beyond state retirement age." This chapter reviews research findings, asking also about possible additional influences, such as personal preferences and the features of a typical life space in each role that might bear on happiness or unhappiness. Influential variables identified here are set within a framework of in-job processes in later chapters.

UNEMPLOYMENT AND UNHAPPINESS

Research into the psychological effects of unemployment began during the economic depression of the 1930s (e.g., Eisenberg & Lazarsfeld, 1938; Jahoda, Lazarsfeld, & Zeisel, 1971). Studies have typically examined happiness as well-being, the first aspect discussed in chapters 1 and 2, with particular emphasis on context-free types 1 and 2 in Table 2.1. Opportunities for self-validation (the second form of happiness) are likely also to be affected during unemployment, as external constraints and personal discouragement combine to restrict a person's activity and aspirations, but these have been less frequently considered.

Main Effects

Research has been either cross-sectional, at one point in time, or longitudinal, following people as they move between one employment-related category and another. Cross-sectional comparisons between people in jobs and those who are unemployed have consistently revealed more context-free distress and other forms of unhappiness in the latter group (e.g., Bradburn & Caplovitz, 1965; Warr, 1987). For example, several studies have obtained responses to the General Health Questionnaire (see chap. 2), which asks about felt strain, finding life a struggle, losing sleep through worry, thinking that life is not worth living, and feeling depressed, worthless, and hopeless. Distressed experiences of that kind are substantially more common among the unemployed than among people in jobs. Meta-analytic findings from 60 different comparisons between unemployed and employed individuals, using a variety of indicators, have revealed a consistent pattern of substantially lower subjective well-being among the unemployed (McKee-Ryan, Song, Wanberg, & Kinicki, 2005).

Unhappiness is also found to be greater among unemployed people after statistical controls for other possibly relevant attributes. For example, Grzywacz and Dooley (2003) reported significantly greater depression despite controls for age, sex, race and socioeconomic status. As in other cases, cross-sectional comparisons do not allow strong inferences about causality: If unemployed people are more distressed, did that difference arise from their unemployment or were they also more distressed before unemployment? Longitudinal research is desirable to demonstrate that unemployment itself is cause of the unhappiness.

Studies that follow individuals from a job to unemployment or in the reverse direction have regularly found transitional patterns that indicate causal effects. For example, Cobb and Kasl (1977) examined blue-collar workers before and after a factory closure, finding significant deterioration in several aspects of well-being; particular impact occurred for feelings of anxiety. Dooley, Catalano, and Wilson (1994) found that, controlling for prior levels of depression, a transition into unemployment led to a near doubling in depressive symptoms. Warr and Jackson (1985) obtained repeated information from unskilled and semiskilled men, showing, for example, that context-free unhappiness improved substantially for those who regained a job.

Earlier longitudinal investigations have been summarized by Warr (1987) and Warr, Jackson, and Banks (1988). Murphy and Athanasou (1999) reviewed later studies, confirming that transitions both into unemployment and into reemployment had substantial psychological effects, in opposite directions as expected. That pattern was also present in the larger set of investigations reviewed by McKee-Ryan et al. (2005). Lucas, Clark, Georgellis, and Diener (2004) found that although reemployment did indeed increase life satisfaction, that returned on average to a lower level than prior to unemployment.

Studies in this field have applied a wide range of instruments to assess happiness or unhappiness. Although the focus has usually been on subjective well-being that is context-free, some domain-specific indicators have also been found to change. For example, shifts in self-esteem (here viewed as self-related well-being) were recorded by Warr and Jackson (1983) and Waters and Moore (2002). Shamir (1986a) confirmed that self-reports of that kind changed significantly after shifts in employment status, but noted that more personality-like aspects of self-esteem were not greatly affected.

General reviews of this field have been provided by Winefield (1995), Hanisch (1999), McKee-Ryan and Kinicki (2002), and McKee-Ryan et al. (2005). It is clear that the families of unemployed individuals also experience unhappiness, with direct effects from a person's joblessness and subsequent negative consequences through a reduction in financial resources (e.g., Jackson & Walsh, 1987; Westman, Etzion, & Horovitz, 2004).

Moderator Variables

Given that unemployed people in general experience significantly more negative feelings than do those in jobs, we need to ask about possible sources of variation: which unemployed individuals are more affected or less affected than others? Research has suggested seven variables of importance, some within the person and some in the environment.

1. Employment Commitment. Between-person differences in role preference occur in many areas of investigation. Relevant to this section are differences between unemployed people in the strength of their desire to be in paid work. In part, the personal salience of employment reflects a person's need to earn money, but (as will be illustrated throughout the book) there are also nonfinancial reasons for wishing to be in a job. Aspects of employment commitment (sometimes termed "perceived work-role centrality") have been measured through multi-item scales tapping a person's desire for a job. Significant associations have repeatedly been found between employment commitment and indicators of unhappiness during unemployment.

For example, Stafford, Jackson, and Banks (1980) examined negative affect and employment commitment in young adults who were either in a job or seeking one. For employed people, the correlation between employment commitment and happiness was positive (more commitment was accompanied by more happiness), whereas for those currently unemployed the correlation was negative (more commitment to a job, less happiness). That difference between the two associations was statistically significant, as it was in the study of young adults described by Hannan, Oriain, and Whelan (1997). In research with unemployed men, Jackson and Warr (1984) observed a correlation between employment commitment and context-free well-being of −0.39. Across 19 unemployed samples, McKee-Ryan et al. (2005) found an average correlation with employment commitment of −0.26 for a variety of affective indicators of well-being. In the review of previous research by Paul and Moser (2006), average correlations with unemployed people's context-free distress, anxiety, and depression were +0.23, +0.21, and +0.21, respectively.

The importance of this form of role preference was illustrated in a study of married women by Ross, Mirowski, and Huber (1983). Levels of context-free depression were found to be in general unrelated to whether or not a woman had a job. Instead, a significant interaction was found with a person's preference for paid employment or housework. Among wives who preferred domestic activities, having a job was associated with greater depression; among those who preferred a job, employment was accompanied by lower depression. Other studies observing this moderating impact of role preference on women's happiness or unhappiness have been reviewed by Warr and Parry (1982) and Klumb and Lampert (2004). (See also chap. 10.)

Employment commitment has also been found to be important in transitions into or out of unemployment. In separate studies, Jackson, Stafford, Banks, and Warr (1983) and Shamir (1986b) found that individuals highly committed to a job, in comparison with low-commitment others, showed greater shifts in well-being on becoming either unemployed or reemployed, negative and positive, respectively. That differential pattern was replicated in research by Nordenmark (1999), who also observed that continuously unemployed people who lowered their employment commitment after a period of joblessness showed an improvement in subjective well-being.

The importance of this variable has been illustrated in several studies of employed samples. For example, Agho, Mueller, and Price (1993) reported a correlation of +0.35 between employment commitment and employees' overall job satisfaction (axis 1 in Fig. 2.2). Birdi, Warr, and Oswald (1995) examined data from several thousand employees from 10 countries, finding a significant correlation with job satisfaction of +0.14. In a national sample of British workers (Warr, 1992), employment commitment was associated with significantly higher well-being in terms of job-related anxiety-comfort and depression-enthusiasm (axes 2 and 3 in Fig. 2.2).

A significant statistical interaction was present in the meta-analysis by Paul and Moser (2006). In four separate reviews, of context-free distress, anxiety, depression, and positive forms of subjective well-being, employment commitment was positively related to raised well-being for employed people but negatively associated for those who are unemployed. In summary, employed individuals who more want to be in a job are happier than those for whom paid work is less valued, and unemployed people who more want to be in a job are less happy than others who are less committed to paid work. Links between this form of role preference and broader notions of personal salience are developed in later chapters.

2. Age.   A curvilinear age pattern has been found consistently in this area, with younger and older unemployed people exhibiting less distress than those between 20 and 59 years (e.g., Warr, 1987; Warr et al., 1988). That difference is also reflected in longitudinal changes. Following a sample across nine months of continuous unemployment, Warr and Jackson (1985) found that men aged between 20 and 59 showed significantly more psychological deterioration than did those who were younger and older. A parallel curvilinear association has also been found with employment commitment, which is also greater in the middle years (e.g., Warr, 1987; Warr et al., 1988).

Although differences in age involve some variations in individual psychological and physiological functioning, there are also systematic changes in role responsibilities that contribute to age-related differences in unemployed people's unhappiness. For example, teenagers have fewer financial pressures than older unemployed people, perhaps living in their parents' home. They may carry forward from school a network of friends and established patterns of leisure activities that can be sustained without paid work. Furthermore, the income differential between having a job and being unemployed is sometimes not very great for teenagers, especially those with few qualifications and little employment experience. At the other extreme of the age range, older unemployed people are likely to have fewer financial commitments and family responsibilities than those of medium age. They may be able to see themselves as out of the labor market and hence under less pressure to get a job, especially as they come close to the conventional retirement age. It is medium-age people who are most subject to personal, social, and financial demands, and those become particularly severe during unemployment.

This curvilinear pattern of unhappiness in relation to age is not restricted to the unemployed. Greater family and personal commitments in the middle years are also accompanied by less positive affect among employed people. In a study of job holders, Clark, Oswald, and Warr (1996) showed that lowest happiness (both context-free and job-related) occurred in the mid thirties. This context-free curvilinear trend has also been found in the British population as a whole (Warr, 1997; Clark, 2003). Further details are presented in chapter 10.

3. Financial Pressures. Linked to the previous features, the extent to which an unemployed person suffers financial problems has a substantial impact on his or her well-being (e.g., Winefield, 1995; Hanisch, 1999; McKee-Ryan & Kinicki, 2002; McKee-Ryan et al., 2005). For example, economic hardship was correlated at +0.45 (average from two occasions) with context-free anxiety in the study by Westman et al. (2004) and at +0.61 with general distress in research by Creed and Macintyre (2001).

Across 9 months of continuing unemployment, Warr and Jackson (1985) found that distress increased most for those lacking financial support. Price, Choi, and Vinokur (2002) described a chain of adversity during unemployment, central to which is the impact of financial pressures. In addition to their negative personal impact, these pressures reverberate widely through families, undermining interpersonal support and relationships between partners (e.g., Vinokur, Price, & Caplan, 1996). Financial difficulties tend to be particularly pressing in the middle years, when family and personal needs are often greatest (e.g., Warr et al., 1988).

4. Duration of Unemployment. Cross-sectional analyses have found on average a small negative correlation between the duration of unemployment and people's subjective well-being (McKee-Ryan et al., 2005). However, cross-sectional comparisons (at a single point in time) may be misleading in this respect, because the composition of a sample changes across a period as some individuals regain a job and others remain unemployed. Long-duration research participants have all failed to obtain paid work, whereas short-duration unemployed samples include both potential job gainers as well as those who will remain without a job.

Preferable are longitudinal analyses, examining the same individuals at different times. Analyses of that kind have revealed a nonlinear pattern of change. Warr and Jackson (1984) found significant increases in general distress during the first months out of work, but some stabilization occurred after about 6 months. In addition, a small but significant improvement in well-being was observed between 12 and 24 months (Warr & Jackson, 1985).

The adaptation that gives rise to stabilization or improvement may be of two kinds. "Constructive adaptation" involves positive steps to develop interests and activities outside the labor market, perhaps taking up hobbies, expanding social networks, or helping with voluntary work in the community. Those positive changes can sometimes be aided by mutual accommodation at the family level (e.g., Jackson & Walsh, 1987). Second is "resigned adaptation," involving reduced aspirations and lower emotional investment in the environment. People may withdraw from job seeking, depend on limited routines of behavior, and protect themselves from threatening events by avoiding new situations and potentially stressful or expensive activities. Although such resigned adaptation can be accompanied by a slight improvement in subjective well-being (linked to a reduction in employment commitment, 1 described earlier), happiness as self-validation is likely to remain at a low level.

5. State of Health.   Unhappiness during unemployment is also linked to a person's health or ill-health. This is most apparent if health is measured through self-report rather than through objective indicators. For instance, Price et al. (2002) assessed health with four questions such as, "In general, would you say your health is excellent, good, fair, or poor?" Across three measurement points, the average correlation of reported health with unemployed people's depression was −0.40. The correlation between self-described health and a broad measure of context-free well-being was +0.50 in research by Røysamb et al. (2003). This health–happiness overlap during unemployment has been confirmed in multiple regression analyses holding constant a range of other variables (e.g., Clark, 2003), and has been found to be stronger with more affective than cognitive forms of subjective well-being, type 1 rather than type 2 in Table 2.1 (Warr, Butcher, Robertson, & Callinan, 2004).

As summarized from nonoccupational research by Lyubomirsky et al. (2005), this pattern is found more widely than merely during unemployment. The significant association between wider well-being and people's reported health may be interpreted as arising in part from conceptual overlap. Hedonic forms of happiness involve feeling good about your life, either in context-free terms or focused on domains such as your job, your family, or your health. Self-reports about how bad or good is your health thus provide an index of one form of domain-specific (health-related) well-being.

The general consistency between overall and specific levels of happiness illustrated in chapter 2 implies a moderate association between context-free well-being and reported health as is indeed found. However, that association is expected to be reduced if indicators of health or ill-health are targeted reports about specific medical conditions or are otherwise independent of self-ratings, for instance through assessment by physicians, visits to the doctor, hospitalization, and so on. As predicted, the correlation between health and subjective well-being is consistently found to be smaller with independent measures of those kinds (e.g., Diener et al., 1999; Faragher et al., 2005; Okun, Stock, Haring, & Witter, 1984).

6. Local Unemployment Rate.   The personal impact of unemployment is likely to be in part a function of local social standards. In settings where lack of a job is rare, personal stigma, feelings of extraordinary failure, and an absence of informal support networks might yield even greater unhappiness than when unemployment is the typical condition. This pattern was shown in relation to neighborhood unemployment rates by Jackson and Warr (1987). British unemployed men in areas of chronically high unemployment were found to be significantly less unhappy than those in areas of moderate or lower unemployment. This difference persisted after controls for age, length of unemployment, employment commitment, and family composition.

Clark (2003) investigated possible social norms of three kinds: regional unemployment rate (as just described), spouse or partner's employment status, and the overall unemployment in a person's household. In all cases, the greater the unemployment in a person's lifespace, the less was his or her unhappiness. This comparative effect was particularly strong for men. "Loosely speaking, unemployment hurts less the more there is of it around" (Clark, 2003, p. 326).

McKee-Ryan et al. (2005) acknowledged this possible beneficial effect of high local unemployment, but drew attention to the fact that a high rate is likely to be problematic for unemployed people because it reduces the probability of regaining employment. Their meta-analysis of 30 studies failed to find a significant link between subjective well-being and local unemployment rate. However, they noted possible inaccuracies in their examination of this issue, because it had often been necessary for researchers to introduce proxy or estimated rates of local unemployment.

7. Social Relationships. There is considerable evidence from research in different areas that, irrespective of a person's employment-related role, happiness is linked to interactions with other people. With respect to unemployment, Warr et al. (1988) reported from several studies that context-free distress, depression, and anxiety in young jobless people were associated negatively with the amount of time spent with friends in the past month; also, more limited social support was consistently accompanied by greater unhappiness. Early research into social relationships in unemployment was reviewed by Ullah, Banks, and Warr (1985). Subsequent studies include that by Drew, Bromet, and Penkower (1992), who showed that involuntary job loss led to greater subsequent depression in women when support from a husband or partner was low. In a sample of both male and female unemployed individuals, Creed and Macintyre (2001) reported that amount of social contact was correlated at -0.34 with context-free distress. The meta-analysis by McKee-Ryan et al. (2005) revealed an average correlation between unemployed people's reported social support and their subjective well-being of $+0.21$.

In overview, it is clear that being unemployed causes considerable unhappiness. That is well substantiated in terms of low levels of happiness as well-being, but quantitative evidence is lacking with respect to self-validation, the second form of happiness described in chapters 1 and 2. However, the constraints of enforced joblessness and typical psychological responses to that condition suggest that this second aspect is likely also to be severely impaired; it clearly deserves greater research attention.

Low self-validation was identified (but not with that name) in a classic investigation in the Austrian community of Marienthal (Jahoda et al., 1971). In a foreword to the 1971 edition of that report, Lazarsfeld emphasized "the vicious circle between reduced opportunities and reduced level of aspiration," through which "prolonged unemployment leads to a state of apathy in which the victims do not utilize any longer even the few opportunities left to them" (p. vii). Marienthal was a particularly deprived environment, but similar processes are likely to occur in many other unemployment settings.

Nevertheless, not all unemployed people are equally unhappy. As illustrated above, an absence of financial pressure, good health, and positive social support can reduce distress, as does role preference in terms of a weaker desire to be in a job. A curvilinear association with age has been found, as has some adaptation after an extended period out of work. Local norms can also be important, with the negative impact of unemployment apparently reduced in settings where it is more common. Several of those factors are placed in general frameworks of environmental and personal influences in later chapters.

RETIREMENT AND HAPPINESS

Although unemployment and retirement are similar in that people in both roles lack a job, retirement is socially sanctioned and an expected part of later life. As with unemployment, research into happiness or unhappiness during retirement has focused on subjective well-being rather than self-validation.

Midanik, Soghikian, Ransom, and Tekawa (1995) pointed out that the literature in this area is "confusing and difficult to summarize" (p. S60). Findings vary in several respects among investigations. For instance, having a job after the formal age of retirement was accompanied by greater life satisfaction (compared to nonemployed people) in research by Aquino, Russell, Cutrona, and Altmeier (1996), Kim and Feldman (2000), and Palmore, Burchett, Fillenbaum, George, and Wallman (1985). Findings about depression by Reitzes, Mutran, and Fernandez (1996) also favored older people's nonemployment over employment. On the other hand, no difference was observed above 60 years by George, Okun, and Landerman (1985) or in studies of employed and nonemployed older people by Ross and Drentea (1998) and Warr, Butcher, Robertson, and Callinan (2004b). Both Herzog, House, and Morgan (1991) and Harlow and Cantor (1996) found that life satisfaction was unrelated to the amount of paid work undertaken by older adults.

Discrepancies between findings are likely to arise from variations in the nature of a sample studied and in the specific measures applied. For example, investigations have differed in the age range covered. Although respondents were above 60 or 65 years in many studies, the range examined was (for instance) between 58 and 64 and between 52 and 66 in the studies by Reitzes et al. (1996) and Robbins, Lee, and Wan (1994), respectively, and extended from 39 to 88 in research by Bossé, Aldwin, Levenson, and Ekerdt (1987). The definition of employment-related categories also varies between projects. For example, the "retired" category typically includes any person who chooses to describe himself or herself by that term, but some definitions are more restrictive. Thus, Herzog et al. (1991) excluded people who had retired for reasons of ill health. Conversely, some definitions are broader than others. For instance, "retirement" included part-time work in the study by Bossé et al. (1987), and "working" in research by Herzog at al. (1991) covered anyone who had worked for pay for any hours in the last 12 months, not necessarily at present.

Moderator Variables

It seems appropriate to conclude from the research just summarized that in overall terms there is no great difference in happiness between being retired or being employed at older ages. Short-term transitional disruption might be envisaged, but in general happiness appears to be similar across the roles. However, specific patterns are likely to vary between situations (as illustrated by the wide variation in research findings), and we need to consider possible moderating factors. Seven possible influences were identified in reviewing the impact of unemployment; these should also be considered in relation to retirement.

1. Employment Commitment.   As illustrated earlier in the chapter, people's role preferences have sometimes been examined in terms of their commitment to paid work. During unemployment, a negative association with happiness is found: people who more want a job when unemployed are even less happy than others. That negative pattern also occurs during retirement. Warr, Butcher, Robertson, and Callinan (2004b) found that for retired individuals aged between 50 and 74 the correlations of employment commitment with affective well-being and life satisfaction (types 1 and 2 in Table 2.1) were −0.25 and −0.30, respectively. (For those members of the sample who were in paid jobs, the correlations were positive rather than negative.) A single-item measure of work-role salience was significantly negatively associated with men's satisfaction with their retirement in the study by Quick and Moen (1998).

The importance of personal preference is also shown with respect to an individual's influence over the timing of his or her retirement. Swan, Dame, and Carmelli (1991) reported that individuals who had been required to retire, rather than choosing to do so, exhibited more depression and more negative feelings about being retired (the latter being a form of domain-specific well-being, type 3 in Table 2.1).

Similar findings were described by Palmore et al. (1985). In practice, many involuntary retirements occur because of ill-health, and greater health problems among involuntary retirees are likely also to contribute to their poorer subsequent well-being. In the study by Warr, Butcher, Robertson, and Callinan (2004b), individuals who had been forced to retire early through ill-health reported significantly lower subjective well-being and life satisfaction than did those who themselves chose to retire early.

2. Age. Although age patterns in happiness have been studied during the years of retirement, gerontological publications rarely identify participants' employment status. In many cases, it is safe to assume that members of a sample were all out of the labor market. Associations with age have varied from positive to negative between studies (e.g., Campbell, 1981; Diener & Suh, 1998; George et al., 1985; Horley & Lavery, 1995; Ryff, 1989), and a meta-analysis of results from samples with a mean age above 50 years yielded an average correlation of subjective well-being with age of –0.01 (Pinquart, 2001).

However, the observed association is in practice influenced by the range of years studied. For instance, Warr (1997) reported a cross-sectional increase in well-being between the mid-30s and the mid-60s, but a small decrease thereafter. In Horley and Lavery's (1995) study, well-being was higher up to 65–74 years but slightly lower at ages above 74. Mroczek and Kolarz (1998) summarized survey findings that the percentage of Americans reporting themselves "very happy" increased across age-groups up to about 70 and then declined slightly. Pinquart's (2001) meta-analysis confirmed the presence of this nonlinearity for both positive and negative affect, and Warr, Butcher, Robertson, and Callinan (2004b) observed its presence between 50 and 74 for context-free well-being. The latter investigation suggested that nonlinearity occurs more for affective forms of well-being than for reflective indicators of life satisfaction. However, a nonlinear pattern was demonstrated for life satisfaction in longitudinal research by Mroczek and Spiro (2005), with a decline after about 65 years. Additional studies of age patterns are reviewed in chapter 10.

Given that older people tend to suffer ill health, the illness or death of family and friends, and other deprivations, it is often assumed that age across adulthood is negatively associated with happiness. The fact that average subjective well-being is at least as high at older ages as among younger people (except perhaps among the very old) is likely to be due to processes of emotional regulation. Brandstädter and Rothermund (1994) illustrated this longitudinally in a sample aged initially between 30 and 59. They reasoned that "personal control and well-being in later life critically hinge on accommodative processes that keep goals and ambitions commensurate with personal resources and situational constraints" (p. 266). Over an 8-year period, it was found that the reduction of a person's control in a particular domain had a smaller negative effect on well-being if that domain had become downgraded in personal importance.

Carstensen (e.g., 1995) viewed processes of this kind in terms of emotional regulation linked to socioemotional selectivity, arguing that older people more than younger ones gear their activities to maximizing positive affect and minimizing negative affect; well-being is maintained through choices to enter some situations and avoid others, and those choices become more definite at older ages. Another process is likely to be through changes in comparison standards. At all ages, people compare their behavior and feelings with those perceived in other people, and it may be that a person judges his or her own attainments and experiences more positively in later years, as accumulating knowledge indicates that other people's levels are lower than he or she had previously assumed. Judgment processes bearing on experiences of happiness or unhappiness are explored more generally in chapter 9.

The importance of age in studies of retirement arises also from the existence of a national age for receipt of a state pension. It is relatively unusual to retire before a country's pension age or to be employed after it. In the United Kingdom, 70% of people aged within the 10 years before state pension age have a job, and only 10% are employed after that age (Office for National Statistics, 2005). In the United States, those figures are 62% and 13%, respectively (Toossi, 2004). Individuals only slightly above the pension threshold are of course more likely to be in paid work than those who are still older; for example, in the United States 20% versus 5% are employed in the ranges between 65 and 74 and from 75 upward (Toossi, 2004). Among the minority of people employed after the state pension age, most are in jobs that are part-time; for instance, the figure is 70% in the United Kingdom (Whiting, 2005).

The level of a person's happiness in early retirement or in late employment (before or after state pension age, respectively) is likely to depend on how much his or her role is personally desired. That preference for employment or retirement may be externally caused, for example, through a need for income (hence a person is under pressure to continue work) or because of ill health (hence forced early retirement). On the other hand, it may be more voluntary in the sense that a person is able actively to choose nonemployment or employment without particular concerns about income or health. For instance, older people who remain in good health can often themselves decide whether or not to continue working after retirement age, whereas those who are unhealthy frequently have no option but to retire. Both Bossé et al. (1987) and Warr, Butcher, Robertson, and Callinan (2004b) found that people employed after the standard retirement age exhibited particularly high context-free well-being compared to individuals who retired at the normal time.

However, in the study by Bossé and colleagues, early retirees had lower well-being than people who continued working until the normal age, whereas Warr and colleagues found that those who retired early were particularly happy. The inconsistency between findings is probably due to a difference in self-selection into early retirement. In the latter study, early retirees were relatively wealthy and chose to leave the labor market before the formal age of retirement, whereas in the project by Bossé and colleagues early retirement appeared to be largely enforced. As indicated earlier, variations in employment commitment are a central influence on happiness or unhappiness in employment-related roles.

3. Financial Pressures. As described for unemployed samples, happiness is to some extent based on a person's financial situation. A significant association between financial pressure and low well-being has long been reported for older people (e.g., Markides & Martin, 1979; Hanisch, 1994). The meta-analytic review by Pinquart and Sörensen (2000) of studies whose participants' mean age exceeded 55 revealed average correlations of income with affective well-being and life satisfaction of 0.21 and 0.18, respectively. In addition, a person's financial position affects whether he or she can select a retirement age (Beehr, Glazer, Nielson, & Farmer, 2000). Those who are more wealthy and have the ability to choose are in general likely to be early rather than late retirees (Swan et al., 1991; Warr, Butcher, Robertson, & Callinan, 2004b).

4. Duration of Retirement. Although duration of unemployment (as already described) can be important in relation to a person's increasing need to escape from that condition, retirement is seen to be a more permanent state of affairs. Associations between length of retirement and happiness have therefore received limited research attention.

It is to be expected that retired individuals will to some extent adapt to their new role, perhaps with an improvement and then a leveling off in subjective well-being (Gall, Evans, & Howard, 1997). Bossé et al. (1987) and Robbins et al. (1994) found that the association between time elapsed since retirement and subjective well-being was nonsignificant. More generally, transitions that are in the distant past are less likely to serve as causal factors, because more recent features have become important. As people continue in retirement, they become open to influence from a wide range of personal and environmental factors, and it is reasonable to focus on those other features rather than seeking explanations of happiness levels in terms of retirement duration.

5. State of Health. As indicated earlier, a person's health (especially as self-reported) is in general significantly associated with subjective well-being. Within that pattern, there is considerable evidence that differences in health can account for some of the variation in subjective well-being during retirement, both context-free and retirement-related (e.g., Feldman, 1994; Hanisch, 1994; Hardy & Quadagno, 1995; Quick & Moen, 1998; Warr, Butcher, Robertson, & Callinan, 2004b): Less healthy retired people are less happy. Associated with that, individuals with impaired health are more likely to retire early.

6. Local Retirement Rate. Although local prevalence rate can be associated with unhappiness during unemployment (see earlier discussion), this variable appears less important in retirement. It may be relevant in extreme cases (e.g., in a retirement community, with a rate of 100%, or when a retired person is isolated among young people), but variations in this respect have not been systematically investigated.

7. Social Relationships. As in other roles, it is clear that differences in happiness are associated with a retired person's links with other people. Positive relationships can assist in coping with day-to-day problems, and they can provide both emotional support and instrumental support. In a review of research with older adults, Pinquart and Sörensen (2000) found significant positive associations with both the quantity and quality of a person's interactions. Reported social support was correlated at +0.57 with older people's life satisfaction in the study by Aquino et al. (1996), and the correlation of social activities with life satisfaction was +0.26 in research by Warr, Butcher, and Robertson

(2004a). Social contact is clearly important to people in many roles, and it is explored in more detail in later chapters.

MULTIPLE ROLES ACROSS TIME

In overview, comparisons between people in different employment-related roles have shown that unemployment generally creates unhappiness, but that retired people's well-being is overall similar to that among individuals who continue working. In both cases, a primary influence is a person's preference for his or her role. For example, a stronger commitment to paid employment is significantly associated with lower subjective well-being in both unemployment and retirement; people who less want to be in their current role exhibit lower well-being.

Financial pressures, state of health, and social relationships have also been shown to influence unhappiness or happiness in both unemployment and retirement. People whose wealth or health is acceptable to them are likely to be more happy than are individuals lacking money or experiencing ill-health, and social support is important in all employment-related roles. A curvilinear association with role duration has been found during unemployment, with an initial decline in unhappiness and then some stabilization or slight improvement in well-being. However, linked to the fact that the retired role becomes established as a person's regular way of living, duration of retirement has rarely been investigated. It may be that the pattern observed in unemployment occurs in reverse during retirement, with a slight increase in well-being and then some decline at long durations. Such a decline should be viewed in terms of changes related to age, rather than caused merely through duration of retirement itself. The remaining feature examined earlier in this chapter, local prevalence rate, has been shown to be important in relation to unemployment, but has not been examined in retirement.

For individuals with less marketable skills or in labor markets subject to disruption through economic or technological change, unemployment can be a recurrent rather than a one-time experience. In examining the impact of enforced joblessness on people's happiness, it is thus necessary to think also in terms of cumulative processes across time. Repeated periods of unemployment can reduce a person's overall income, impair future employability, and lead him or her into jobs that are insecure, low-skilled and poorly paid. Analyses of work histories over a 5-year period by Gallie et al. (1998) showed that people who became unemployed were more likely than others to move into temporary or low-paying jobs, which provided little opportunity for self-development. Extended exposure to negative environmental features can create low levels of well-being irrespective of whether a person happens to be unemployed at the time of an investigation. Grzywacz and Dooley (2003) found greater context-free depression among individuals in jobs that were defined as economically or psychologically poor, over and above statistical controls for other personal characteristics. Perceived job insecurity can be associated with levels of unhappiness similar to those experienced in unemployment itself (de Witte, 1999).

Several researchers have examined happiness or unhappiness among employed people as a function of prior unemployment. Tausig and Fenwick (1999) described a longitudinal study of people in full-time jobs at the second of two measurement points. Life dissatisfaction at that time was strongly predicted by a period of unemployment between the two points. Dooley, Prause, and Ham-Rowbottom (2000) examined depression levels in people experiencing adverse employment changes that led to jobs that were involuntarily part-time or which paid only poverty-level wages. In a 2-year study, individuals who were adequately employed at first contact showed substantial increases in depression after those downward transitions (still within employment), almost as great as in people who instead became unemployed. Feldman, Leana, and Bolino (2002) studied reemployed managers who had been laid off from their jobs in the previous 12 months, finding a variety of negative impacts from current underemployment, defined in terms of substantially reduced income, job status, and skill utilization. Lucas et al. (2004) also observed that employed peoples' life satisfaction was lower if they had previously been unemployed. Furthermore, although gaining a job after unemployment was beneficial, it did not shift life satisfaction back to its previous level; on average, a continuing negative impact of earlier unemployment was present.

Overlaps are also possible between employment and retirement. A person may retire from a job, but then or later take up temporary or part-time work (e.g., Herz, 1995; Mutchler, Burr, Pienta, & Massagli, 1997; Myers, 1991). "Bridge" jobs of this kind are more common among men than women (e.g., Davis, 2003; Ruhm, 1990). They are often located in a different organization or involve self-employment, and are typically paid less than a person's preretirement position (e.g., Haider & Loughran, 2001). Kim and Feldman (2000) found that retired individuals with bridge employment exhibited greater life satisfaction and satisfaction with retirement than did their counterparts without such work.

Factors predicting whether or not a retired person will take up bridge employment in retirement are likely to be similar to those considered earlier in the chapter. For example, Mutchler et al. (1997) and Kim and Feldman (2000) found that a retired person's health was positively linked to taking up a bridge job, and a negative association with age was reported by Myers (1991) and Davis (2003). Bridge workers are likely to be healthier and younger than nonemployed retired people.

Two other factors examined earlier also predict whether or not a person will take up a job during retirement. First is financial pressure: Retirees in need of increased income may choose to obtain that through part-time or temporary employment (e.g., Mutchler et al. 1997; Myers, 1991). Second is employment commitment, with continuation in a job more likely if a retired person has a positive orientation to paid work. The latter variable appears not to have been studied directly in this area, but its importance has been shown through the proxy variable of education level: Bridge employment is more common among more educated people (Haider & Loughran, 2001; Myers, 1991; Whiting, 2005). This difference may be due partly to the greater availability of job opportunities for older professional and managerial ex-employees than for manual workers, and is linked to the fact that employment commitment is generally greater for individuals of higher socioeconomic status (Warr, 1982).

The importance for happiness of part-time or intermittent employment during retirement draws attention to the fact that other kinds of desired work (those without payment) are likely to be valuable in the same way. For example, Kim and Feldman (2000) observed that retired individuals who choose to engage more in volunteer or leisure activities have significantly higher life satisfaction than others. Research into activity and well-being at older ages, without the present concern for employment-related roles, has also found that participation in voluntary or charitable work is linked to greater well-being (Harlow & Cantor, 1996). Warr, Butcher, and Robertson (2004a) reported that this association is stronger for nonemployed than for employed people aged between 50 and 74.

The centrality of personal role preference in happiness or unhappiness raises the question: What might underlie such preferences for particular roles, and thus in part determine people's happiness? Role preferences are likely to reflect two sets of influence: personal values and motives, and also the opportunities and demands in a current life space. In terms of life-space characteristics, it would be useful to identify a set of features common to any role that can help to account for happiness or unhappiness in the same way in any role. Different settings of, for instance, employment, retirement or unemployment might then be characterized in standard terms. Identified desirable characteristics of an environment are also expected to be linked to personal preferences themselves: A setting that has many attractive features is preferred to one lacking them.

We thus need to examine principal roles in terms of characteristics that are important in any environment: What are the features of any setting that influence happiness or unhappiness? A person's happiness in any role might then be partly explained in terms of the level of those features available to him or her. Unemployment or retirement (for instance) are not causally important in their own right. It is the features that are experienced in those roles that cause unhappiness or happiness. Principal environmental features are reviewed in the next chapter.

4

The Vitamin Analogy

Research frameworks to learn about the causes of happiness or unhappiness are of three broad kinds, based primarily on the environment, the person, or combinations of those two. It is clear that an approach that joins environments and people (the third option) is needed for a complete understanding, but a first step is to characterize the features of each contributing domain and to identify their modes of operation. Much research in this field has therefore been either primarily environment-centered or primarily person-centered. An emphasis of one or the other kind does not necessarily deny the need for a joint account, but a more focused approach can be methodologically more appropriate at this stage of understanding. Environmental inputs to happiness are explored in this and the following four chapters, chapters 9 to 11 emphasize person-centered issues, and research into both influences simultaneously is examined in chapters 12 and 13.

NINE PRIMARY FEATURES OF ANY ENVIRONMENT

Two important aspects of any situation were examined in the previous chapter's discussion of unemployment and retirement, in terms of the availability of money and social relationships. An additional seven environmental features are included in the framework developed by

Warr (1987). This identified nine primary features of any environment that can account for psychological effects of employment, unemployment, and retirement in the same terms. These features are introduced next, with some illustrations from nonemployed roles. More detailed accounts in chapters 5 to 8 examine the environmental features in settings of paid work. Three specifically occupational features are there added to the nine in-general characteristics.

There is no single "correct" number of categories in a framework of this kind. Greater precision can be gained by listing a larger number of more specific features, but conceptual and presentational complexity can then be more than is desirable. The present grouping in terms of nine primary features has been selected as pragmatically appropriate, recognizing that specific subcategories need also to be examined in more detailed accounts. Several subcategories are considered later. For example, Table 8.1 in chapter 8 contains 26 job features within the primary categories.

The logical status of the framework should also be mentioned here. There is a need for empirical examination of detailed hypotheses about each of the primary features and elements of those, but their overall importance is not in question. They have been included on the basis of prior research that makes it clear that variations between low and high values of each feature are accompanied by differences in unhappiness or happiness. Research by many people has provided evidence of that kind (e.g., summarized by Warr, 1987, 1994a, 1999), and a large number of illustrations are provided later.

The principal environmental characteristics have been labeled as follows:

1. Opportunity for personal control.
2. Opportunity for skill use.
3. Externally generated goals.
4. Variety.
5. Environmental clarity.
6. Contact with others.
7. Availability of money.
8. Physical security.
9. Valued social position.

Such features can in principle be examined in two ways: either objectively, with verifiable external measurement, or subjectively, as perceived by the individuals under investigation. For research investigations, objective assessment of factual conditions may initially appear preferable to subjective reports, recording information about frequencies, times, activities, and so on. In practice, such measures may be unacceptably limited, covering only a few surface-level attributes. For example, opportunity for personal control and environmental clarity (numbers 1 and 5 in the preceding list) are difficult to index in objective terms. Furthermore, the personal impact of the environment depends in part on individuals' own appraisals, and a single, standard environmental value for all people in a role misses this important between-person variation in input to their happiness. These themes are expanded in chapter 8.

The limitations of objective measurement in the area of this book have led most researchers to specify the environment through descriptions by a person himself or herself. Central to those descriptions is the notion of a perceived opportunity, in terms of facilitation or encouragement from the environment. Perceived opportunities have in some circumstances been referred to as "affordances" (e.g., Gibson, 1979; von Hofsten, 1985). These are properties of the world that are personally significant to a perceiver or a group of perceivers; they indicate that an environment affords certain possibilities or permits certain actions that are important to the person. That potential is partly (but not completely) suggested by current usage in the design of computer graphics, where an affordance is viewed as a visual clue to the function of an object. Gibson (1979) considered affordances to be natural units of perception.

Environmental features that can influence happiness or unhappiness are introduced next in a summary manner. More detailed aspects of each (and additional characteristics in paid employment) are examined in subsequent chapters.

1. Opportunity for Personal Control. Happiness is strongly determined by the opportunities provided in an environment for a person to have some control over activities and events. Such opportunities allow personal influence over one's own actions as well as those of family or friends, and sometimes extend into major discretion over other people's lives. An absence of this opportunity creates unhappiness in jobs, unemployment, retirement, and outside the labor market.

At a general level, we may be concerned for the amount of freedom or democracy in a country; more narrowly, research in job situations has examined employee discretion over, for example, work pace or scheduling. Given that individuals desire personally relevant outcomes, the potential to achieve goals through self-determination is essential to happiness, perhaps even being "the essence of humanness" (Bandura, 2001, p. 1).

A person's sense of control in a particular setting is a function both of environmental features and of personal attributes. Different researchers have tended to emphasize one or the other of those influences, and the focus in this chapter and the next four is on the nature of environments. Opportunity for control as an aspect of the environment has a dual importance in the framework of this book. The feature is beneficial in its own right, and also because it can affect the operation of the other primary features. If a person has some influence over his or her environment, other features may perhaps be manipulated with consequential impacts on happiness.

2. Opportunity for Skill Use.   A related characteristic is the degree to which an environment inhibits or encourages the use and development of a person's skills. Skilled performance is valued not only because it contributes to the solution of problems and progress toward goal achievement but also because it is satisfying in its creative, challenging and/or familiar aspects.

Skilled behavior involves the effective handling of particular situations, and depends on prior acquisition of expertise through learning. It requires some degree of knowledge, which may be described as either "declarative" or "procedural." Declarative knowledge comprises factual information about what is the case, whereas procedural knowledge is made up of routines specifying how to do something. Those routines may be either physical or mental. Aspects of knowledge and skill are similar, but knowledge is more declarative and skill is more procedural.

Skill use thus involves the application of expertise. Experts have a superior and more organized knowledge base; they perceive and recall larger meaningful patterns in their domain, search for and locate information more effectively, are better at anticipating future developments and potential faults, make more sophisticated plans, and can more quickly process new information within their established knowledge structure (e.g., Sonnentag, 2000). Expertise facilitates goal achievement, creating benefits for an individual or group, and its application can be a satisfying activity in itself.

Environmental restrictions on the use of skill are of two kinds, concerning application or extension. First are those that prevent people from applying already-acquired expertise, constraining them to behaviors that are within a basic capability. Second are restrictions on new learning, requiring individuals to remain at low levels despite their potential for advancing into more complex activity through the expansion of their expertise. Conversely, environments can promote both the use and acquisition of skill through the creation of opportunities, challenges, and demands.

This second environmental characteristic is often associated with the previous one, in that skill use typically implies some control of the environment. However, a high opportunity for personal control (feature number 1) can itself be present in conjunction with a low level of skill use, when a person influences a situation in ways that are simple and require no expertise.

3. Externally Generated Goals. A third environmental feature influencing happiness or unhappiness is the presence of goals generated by a situation. Goals are also set by individuals themselves, deriving from personal needs, values and desires. The focus in this chapter is on influences from the environment, rather than personal inputs to happiness, which are reviewed in chapters 9 to 12. Overlaps between goals that are externally generated and internally generated are considered in chapter 6.

Externally generated goals arise partly from physical deficits (e.g., a drop in temperature), but also from obligations and targets deriving from formal and informal roles. These roles introduce requirements to behave in certain ways, to follow certain routines, to solve certain problems, and to be in specified locations at certain times. Role-generated requirements give rise to organized sequences of actions, drawing people toward objectives and often into interaction with others.

An environment that makes no demands on a person sets up no objectives and encourages no activity or achievement. On the other hand, a setting that gives rise to the establishment and pursuit of goals can yield activities whose consequences are immediately or consequentially beneficial. However, some situations generate goals that are too numerous or too difficult; it is possible to "have too much of a good thing." Possible nonlinear associations between environmental features and happiness are considered later in the chapter.

4. Variety. It sometimes happens that externally generated goals and associated actions are invariant and repetitive. Required activity of a repetitive kind is often felt to be less attractive than are more diverse requirements, which introduce novelty and break up uniformity of activity and/or location. Low environmental variety is often accompanied by reduced levels of the previous features: personal control, skill use and development, and challenging goals. Shifts in perceived value after repetition also arise in part from processes of adaptation, as a repeated stimulus comes to have a weaker impact over time. As illustrated in chapter 9, research has demonstrated that continued exposure to a situation tends to reduce its capacity to reward or punish.

5. Environmental Clarity. A fifth feature is the extent to which a person's environment is clear or opaque. Three aspects of this seem to be of particular significance. First is the degree to which other people and systems in the environment are predictable, so that a person can foresee likely developments and the consequences of his or her actions. Some clarity about the future is a minimum requirement for establishing personal control and developing skills; if perceptual relationships and action interdependencies do not continue much as expected, purposeful behavior is threatened. The inability to plan and take action because of future uncertainty can lead to a failure to cope, a sense of helplessness, and associated feelings of anxiety (e.g., Miller, 1981).

A second aspect of this environmental feature is the clarity of role requirements and normative expectations about behavior. Are required standards explicit in the environment (e.g., clearly communicated by a supervisor or coworkers), or must a person make assumptions about which particular activities or emphases might lead to positive or negative responses from others? Third is the availability of feedback about the consequences of one's actions; are the results of particular actions subsequently made clear or do they remain hidden? These three aspects of environmental clarity are considered in job settings in chapter 7.

6. Contact With Others. Environments also differ in the opportunity they provide for interaction with other people. This is important for several reasons. First, interpersonal contact can give rise to friendships and reduce feelings of loneliness. "Social drives" were central to early models of motivation (e.g., McDougall, 1932), and personal benefits of social relationships have been widely examined since then. Second, contact with other people may provide help and support of many kinds. Social support may be "emotional," helping with the management of feelings, or "instrumental," contributing to the resolution of problems. Another form is "motivational" support, when other people encourage continued problem-solving, for example, through reassurance that persistent efforts will be successful.

A third importance of interpersonal contact is in terms of social comparison, as proposed by Festinger (1954). He pointed out that people are motivated to compare their opinions and abilities with those of others, in order better to interpret and appraise themselves. Social encounters provide opportunities for comparisons between oneself and others, and Festinger suggested that such encounters are in part steered with this in mind. Comparative judgments in the experience of well-being are examined in chapter 9. Fourth, contact with others is important in learning about appropriate behaviors through norms and routines. Some behavioral conformity underlies any community, and also provides one input into a person's status within that community; moderate conformity is usually required for enhanced social standing. A fifth importance arises from the fact that many goals can be achieved only through the interdependent efforts of several people. Membership of formal or informal groups makes possible the establishment and attainment of goals that could not be realized by an individual alone. This environmental characteristic may thus combine with other features that are concerned with, for instance, goals, variety, control and skill use.

In identifying the importance of social contact for happiness or unhappiness, it is important to distinguish between indicators that are either quantitative or qualitative. In the first case, we might ask about the amount of contact that is available irrespective of its quality, for instance, through quantitative indices of social encounters, the proximity of other people, or the number of close-working colleagues. An environment that encourages social contact in quantitative terms is one that brings individuals into closer proximity with people or requires greater interdependence in activity, or both of those. Conversely, low quantitative contact is a question of isolated functioning, with little interaction with others.

Qualitative aspects of this feature may be viewed in terms of the personal value of these forms of contact. In addition to numerical indicators of social contact, environments may be described with respect to their provision of emotional, instrumental, or motivational support from others. Conversely, low levels of qualitative social features can be illustrated in aggression, hostility, and abusive relationships, beyond merely an absence of positive input.

7. Availability of Money.   Financial pressures during unemployment and retirement have already been considered, and the importance of money for happiness is clear. When personal and family requirements exceed a person's financial resources, activities and pleasures are curtailed, and small changes in either needs or resources can generate major problems. Poverty is in several ways self-perpetuating. For example, poor individuals are liable to pay more than others for equivalent goods or services. Heating costs may be greater because of an inability to finance insulation or energy-efficient equipment; bulk purchases of household items at reduced prices are impossible; a car is not available to travel to cheaper retail outlets. More generally, shortage of money means that payment of some bills is possible only if others are left unpaid, and debts may accumulate to a level that provokes substantial anxiety.

Poverty is also likely to affect other environmental features. For instance, it reduces the opportunity for personal control (feature 1) in activities that require money, and inhibits skill use (feature 2) in hobby or educational activities. Variety (4) becomes less achievable through lack of financial resources, and social contact (6) may be reduced through an inability to pay for travel or entertainment. Money thus has indirect as well as direct effects on happiness. It is important for what it makes possible with respect to other environmental features as well as for its own immediate benefits.

On the other hand, an extremely large amount of money might not be beneficial beyond lesser large amounts. Although lack of money creates unhappiness in several ways, continued increases in its availability may not be accompanied by ever-growing happiness; a possible nonlinear association is considered shortly.

8. Physical Security.   The eighth primary environmental feature is a physically secure setting. A person needs to be protected against physical threat, and to have adequate heating, space, and facilities for everyday activities. Settings vary in their structure, construction, content, and location, and thus in their potential to provide security of these kinds.

Different aspects of physical security are of principal importance in different roles. For retired individuals, low physical security can involve problems of inadequate domestic heating or needed adaptations to household equipment, whereas for many people at work physical security involves safety provisions in their job or ergonomic aspects of their computers or other equipment. Some of these are examined in the next chapter.

9. *Valued Social Position.* The ninth environmental characteristic affecting happiness or unhappiness is one's position in a social structure, in particular the potential afforded for esteem or recognition for one's social worth. In practice, a person is likely to be a member of several such structures (for instance, a family, a manufacturing company, and a local community), so that esteem may possibly derive from several external sources.

The value allotted to a position in a social structure derives mainly from the contribution it makes to other people and the structure itself. Ryff (1989) asked people, "What does personal fulfilment mean to you?" and found that "making a contribution" was among the primary elements. However, objective and subjectively perceived social position may differ from each other. Particular role activities may be considered important to different degrees by different people, and external indicators of social value do not always coincide with the value which a person accords to his or her own contributions. Perceived, rather than externally defined, esteem may therefore be of special importance in this area.

These nine aspects of any environment are here examined mainly in employment-related roles, but the framework may also be applied to other kinds of setting, for example, in families or social groups. As illustrated earlier, the features are psychologically important in two ways. Each one bears on happiness or unhappiness because of its own nature and implications, but in addition each can affect several other aspects of the environment. For example, the opportunity for personal control (feature 1) influences all other possibilities, and availability of money (7) also has a wide-ranging impact. Greater environmental variety (4) can expand the range of externally generated goals (3), and future ambiguity (an aspect of feature 5) or very high interdependence with others (an aspect of 6) tend to reduce the potential for control by oneself.

Although most research into environmental characteristics has targeted only one or a few features, a broad perspective on them all is clearly desirable for understanding the impact of different situations. One possibility is to describe a particular setting in terms of a profile of the characteristics, perhaps including more specific elements of each. This possibility is developed in chapter 8.

THE PRIMARY FEATURES IN EMPLOYMENT, UNEMPLOYMENT, AND RETIREMENT

The primary environmental characteristics are considered in detail in the next four chapters. The main focus is on settings of paid work:

How do job variations in those nine respects bear on employees' happiness or unhappiness? Chapter 3 was more concerned with other roles, those of unemployment and retirement, and some impacts of role membership on unhappiness or happiness were reviewed there. That discussion is extended here to consider all of the primary environmental features introduced earlier.

An important conceptual basis for research into the environment of unemployed people has been the "latent functions" model of Jahoda (e.g., 1981, 1982). She described the psychological value of paid work in terms of its manifest and latent functions, and argued that unemployment is harmful because it impairs functions of both of those kinds. Earning a living was viewed as the manifest function of a job, and in addition five latent functions were suggested: that "employment imposes a time structure on the working day," it "implies regularly shared experiences and contacts with people outside the nuclear family," it "links people to goals and purposes that transcend their own," it "defines aspects of personal status and identity," and "employment enforces activity" (Jahoda, 1981, p. 188).

The nine-component framework examined here builds on Jahoda's theorizing, in that her second and fourth latent functions appear as environmental features 6 and 9 (contact with others and valued social position). Her other three latent functions are here subsumed within feature 3, externally generated goals, and other environmental characteristics have been added. That extension is not inconsistent with Jahoda's observation that "the five broad categories do not cover all the available research on employment. There are other latent by-products" (1981, p. 189).

In general, the environment experienced by people who are unemployed provides only limited inputs in all nine respects (Warr, 1987). Opportunity for personal control (feature 1) is low, as unemployed individuals have a reduced chance to decide and act in chosen ways. Lack of success in job seeking, inability to influence employers, and increased dependence on welfare bureaucracies all contribute to a reduction in a person's ability to affect what happens to him or her. Reduced personal control also arises from other characteristics of an unemployed person's environment. For instance, shortage of money (feature 7) constrains self-initiated activities and goal-achievement in many ways. In addition, low opportunity for control has an impact on other features in a life space, as an unemployed person is less able to influence, for instance, environmental variety or valued social position. Low opportunity for control is thus harmful to an unemployed person both in its own right and also because it gives rise to power-lessness with respect to other primary features, which can themselves become damaging. Note, however, that control opportunity may also be restricted in paid employment, as a person's activities can be closely specified within his or her job role; see chapter 6.

The second environmental feature, opportunity for skill use, is also likely to be affected during unemployment. People are necessarily prevented from using job skills to meet personal challenges in their employment, and they usually have little opportunity to extend them-selves through the acquisition of new expertise. Third, externally gen-erated goals are necessarily reduced, as a person is less subject to job-related demands, and purposeful activity is less encouraged by the environment. Several investigators have confirmed that unemployed people can have difficulty filling their days, with long periods spent without activity, merely sitting around or watching television (e.g., Kilpatrick & Trew, 1985). Creed and Macintyre (2001) have summa-rized previous investigations showing that unemployed people's activ-ity level is linked to less unhappiness; in their own sample, the correlation with general distress was −0.33.

A reduction during unemployment in the fourth environmental characteristic, variety, is linked with fewer externally generated goals and arises in part from a loss of contrast between job and nonjob activities. Experience is also narrowed through the reduction in activ-ity that follows an unemployed person's drop in income.

Aspects of environmental clarity, the fifth feature, are also affected by unemployment. Three forms of low clarity were introduced earlier. First, an unemployed person's future becomes unpredictable in many ways, as outcomes of job seeking are uncertain, and potential conse-quences of personal development activities are unclear. Needed infor-mation is lacking for decisions, plans, and actions. Second, role requirements in society and in one's own family can be ambiguous in an unfamiliar situation. Third, feedback about one's behaviors and their outcomes is likely to be reduced as a person becomes separated from continuing institutional frameworks.

The sixth primary characteristic (contact with others) has been con-sidered earlier and in chapter 3. In many cases relationships with other people can be harmed during unemployment, for instance, as low income prohibits attendance at some social events, or disputes about limited financial resources threaten within-family harmony. Both quan-titative and qualitative aspects of this feature are likely to be impaired, as the number of contacts and also their supportive value are affected.

Reduced availability of money (7) has already been considered as a principal source of unhappiness. Many earlier studies of increased financial pressure during unemployment were described by Warr (1987), with clear negative impacts on family relationships as well as on personal well-being. This point has been developed in chapter 3. Low levels of the eighth primary characteristic (physical security) are usually associated during unemployment with low availability of money. Environments need to protect a person against physical threat, and provide adequate warmth and space for food preparation, relaxation and sleeping. The physical setting of some unemployed individuals can be problematic in some of those respects, in part because of a shortage of money for repairs or a move to somewhere else.

Finally, valued social position is clearly undermined by enforced joblessness. On becoming unemployed, a person loses a socially approved role and the positive self-evaluations that go with it. The new position is widely felt to be one of lower prestige, deviant, second-rate, stigmatized, or not providing full membership of society. Even when welfare benefits remove the worst financial hardship, there may be shame attached to receipt of public funds and a seeming failure to provide for one's family or contribute to society more widely. In studies by Haworth (1997) and Creed and Macintyre (2001), comparing different environmental features during unemployment, low perceived status was particularly strongly associated with context-free distress.

Between-Role Comparisons

Before moving on to examine the nature and consequences of paid work itself, we should ask about other employment-related roles. Three summary questions may be raised at this stage. First, what differences and similarities are present between the average environments of unemployment, retirement, and paid work? Second, are average differences in environmental features between the roles accompanied by average differences in role-incumbents' happiness or unhappiness? And, third, within each of the roles are differences in individual persons' happiness or unhappiness associated with differences in the degree to which those individuals are exposed to particular environmental features? Those questions have been touched upon in the earlier accounts, and were addressed directly in research by Warr, Butcher, Robertson, and Callinan (2004b).

Questionnaires were completed by 1,167 older British men and women, aged between 50 and 74. Participants were either employed, unemployed, or retired. As well as providing information about context-free affect and life satisfaction (well-being types 1 and 2 in Table 2.1 of chap. 2), each person completed multi-item scales to tap perceptions of each of the nine environmental features. (Contact with others, feature 6, was measured in both quantitative and qualitative terms.)

First, were there average between-role differences in the primary environmental characteristics? As expected from the considerations raised earlier, levels were found to differ significantly between the three respondent groups. The average perceived environment of unemployed people was substantially impoverished in every respect relative to that of both employed and retired people. In addition, employed individuals in comparison to those who were retired reported significantly lower opportunity for control and significantly more externally generated goals, a higher quantity of social contact, and a more valued social position.

Examining the second question raised earlier (are there between-role average differences in happiness or unhappiness?), unemployment was accompanied by significantly lower average well-being on both measures than in the other two roles. However, comparisons between employed and retired persons indicated that on average those two groups were equally happy in both respects, consistent with their broadly similar environments.

Third, how closely within each role were between-person differences in environmental features linked to individual differences in happiness? Correlations between the perceived environmental characteristics and context-free affect averaged +0.26, +0.36, and +0.28 for employed, unemployed, and retired individuals, respectively; for life satisfaction, those values were +0.37, +0.43, and +0.41, respectively. The nine characteristics were thus important for people in the three kinds of environment, slightly more so with respect to life satisfaction (average $r = +0.40$) than for the more affective indicator (average $r = +0.30$).

Multiple regression analyses were carried out in order to examine the impact on happiness of each environmental characteristic after statistical control for a person's employment role and for the other features. The pattern of associations set out in detail by Warr, Butcher, Robertson, and Callinan (2004b) is summarized in Table 4.1.

Consider first the results for context-free affect, in columns 2 and 3. The first two entries in column 2 show that, when examined as predictors on their own (in step 1), individuals' employment-related role

TABLE 4.1

Two Hierarchical Regression Analyses in a Study of Employment-Related Roles
(Employment, Unemployment, and Retirement): Associations of Individuals'
Role and Age With Their Context-Free Affect and Life Satisfaction, Without
Environmental Features (step 1) and With Environmental Features (step 2)

Predictor Environmental Variables	Associations With Context-Free Affect		Associations With Life Satisfaction	
	Step 1: Two Predictors on Their Own	Step 2: Also With Environmental Features	Step 1: Two Predictors on Their Own	Step 2: Also With Environmental Features
Employment-related roles	Significant	Not significant	Significant	Not significant
Age (50–74 years)	Significant positive	Not significant	Not significant	Not significant
1. Opportunity for personal control		Significant positive		Significant positive
2. Opportunity for skill use		Not significant		Not significant
3. Externally generated goals		Significant negative		Not significant
4. Variety		Significant positive		Significant positive
5. Environmental clarity		Significant positive		Significant positive
6a. Quantity of contact		Not significant		Not significant
6b. Quality of contact		Not significant		Significant positive
7. Availability of money		Not significant		Significant positive
8. Physical security		Significant positive		Significant positive
9. Valued social position		Not significant		Significant positive

(employment, unemployment or retirement) and age were both significantly associated with that form of happiness. This between-role
difference was outlined earlier. However, inclusion in the regression
equation of the environmental characteristics (step 2, in column 3)
removed those significant associations. In other words, perceived features of the environment, whether in employment, unemployment, or
retirement, statistically accounted for the previously observed effects
on happiness of employment-related role and age. As shown in column
3, several aspects of the environment were found to be important in this

process. For the affect measure, significant features in any employment-related role were opportunity for personal control, externally generated goals, variety, environmental clarity, and physical security. The same hierarchical analysis for life satisfaction, in columns 4 and 5 of Table 4.1, pointed to the impact on that form of happiness of four of those features and also quality of contact, availability of money, and valued social position.

Recall that these environmental features have been selected on the basis of previous research evidence that they are all important for happiness. The fact that they are found to be associated with subjective well-being in this sample is therefore not empirically surprising. The noteworthy point of Table 4.1 is that differences in well-being between and within employment-related roles are accounted for by these features. It is not being unemployed, or in any other role, that itself matters in the causation of happiness or unhappiness; it is the content of a particular role that counts. The same primary characteristics affect happiness in all cases. Irrespective of a person's role, differences in these primary features account substantially for variations in happiness.

Environment-centered approaches to happiness in work and other roles must therefore cover the principal characteristics introduced here. Chapters 5 to 8 explore in more detail their operation in settings of paid employment. First, however, we should examine the likely nature of environment-happiness associations. Are these linear or nonlinear?

VITAMINS AND ENVIRONMENTAL CHARACTERISTICS

One possibility is that happiness is influenced by the environment in a manner analogous to the effect of vitamins on physical condition. Vitamins are important for physical health up to but not beyond a certain level. At low levels of intake, vitamin deficiency gives rise to physiological impairment and ill-health (sometimes referred to in a medical context as "deficiency disease"), but after a moderate level has been reached ("the recommended daily allowance") there is no benefit from additional quantities. In a similar manner, it may be that an absence of the primary environmental characteristics leads to unhappiness, but that their presence beyond a certain level does not further increase happiness.

Certain vitamins become harmful in very large quantities. In those cases, the association between increased vitamin intake and physical

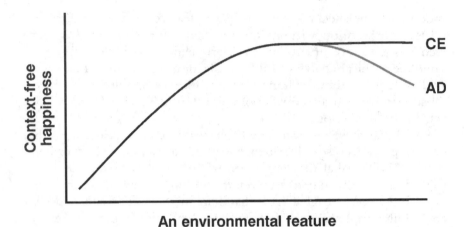

An environmental feature

Figure 4.1.   The vitamin analogy: "additional decrement" (AD) and "constant effect" (CE) relationships between environmental features and context-free happiness.

health becomes negative after a broad range of moderate amounts. This relationship may also occur for certain aspects of the environment, particularly with respect to context-free (rather than more restricted forms of) happiness. The possibility is summarized in Figure 4.1, where low ("deficiency") values of an environmental feature are depicted as particularly harmful and those in the middle range are shown as having a constant beneficial effect on happiness. A second, smaller decrement is proposed at particularly high ("toxic") values for certain environmental features (labeled "AD") but not for others ("CE").

Those two labels are also based on abbreviations in the vitamin analogy. There are no toxic consequences from very high intakes of certain vitamins: deficiency causes ill-health, but additional doses beyond a moderate amount have a constant effect. Vitamins C and E are of this kind (Barker & Bender, 1980, 1982; Hathcock et al., 2005). The abbreviation "CE" reflects this fact, and can also stand for "constant effect." On the other hand, vitamins A and D are toxic at very high levels (Barker & Bender, 1980, 1982), and "AD" in the figure may be read as an "additional decrement."

The "vitamin model" suggests that six of the primary environmental features considered so far may be viewed as analogues of vitamins A and D, and that three features instead parallel vitamins C and E. Suggested AD vitamins are numbers 1 to 6 in the previous account: opportunity for personal control, opportunity for skill use, externally generated goals, variety, environmental clarity, and contact with others. The three features thought to have a constant effect beyond moderate levels are numbers 7 to 9: availability of money, physical security, and valued social position.

Why should certain features of the environment, desirable at moderate levels, become harmful when extremely high? The "too much of a good thing" pattern seems likely for both intrinsic reasons and because of associated effects from other features. Very high levels of some environmental characteristics can become punishing in themselves, and they are likely also to be accompanied by extremely high levels of other features that yield an additional decrement.

The two features identified as "opportunities" (for control and for skill use; numbers 1 and 2) are expected to give rise to decrements at the right-hand side of Figure 4.1, because an "opportunity" becomes an "unavoidable requirement" at very high levels; behavior is then coerced rather than encouraged or facilitated. Environments that call for unremitting control (a very high level of feature 1) through difficult decision making and sustained personal responsibility, or that demand continuous use of extremely complex skills (2), can give rise to overload problems as very high demands exceed personal capabilities. In part, those come about through a correlated shift to a particularly high level of externally generated goals (feature 3). As those goals become extremely difficult and/or numerous, the load may become unmanageable, with an inability to cope with environmental requirements and an accumulation of harmful effects. In these settings, extremely high goal demands often include some that are incompatible with others, yielding additional pressures in the form of between-goal conflicts.

Extremely high variety (4) requires constant switching of attention and activity, with resulting low concentration and limited attainment of single goals; conflict between contradictory goals may be present; and extreme diversity may prohibit the development and use of skills. Feature 5 (environmental clarity) appears also to be of this "additional decrement" (AD) kind. At extremely high levels, there is no uncertainty about the future, events are entirely predictable and never novel, and a fixed set of role requirements permits no new experiences. Such settings prevent risk taking, contain little potential for skill development, and provide no opportunity to expand one's control over the environment.

A similar downturn of the happiness curve is expected at very high levels of contact with other people (feature 6). Very substantial social inputs can bring about reduced well-being through overcrowding and lack of privacy in high-density situations, or through a lack of personal control, frequent interruptions, and the prohibited initiation of valued activities because of other people's excessive demands. Behavioral procedures and physical structures to prevent excessive social contact have been created in cultures of all kinds (e.g., Altman & Chemers, 1980).

Several environmental features in the vitamin model are thus assumed to be of the "additional decrement" kind, with their positive association with happiness leveling off across the moderate to high range and becoming reversed at very high levels. Underlying processes are considered in greater detail later in the book. The proposed decline at very high levels is likely to be smaller than at very low levels, because deficiencies in a feature (at the left of Fig. 4.1) carry particularly negative implications for the person. The additional decrement (AD) assumption about happiness as a function of certain environmental features thus takes the form of an asymmetrical, flattened, inverse U-shaped association. That pattern is particularly likely for context-free (rather than domain-specific or facet-specific) happiness; the basis of that probable difference is reviewed shortly.

The other three features introduced earlier are proposed to yield a constant effect (CE) with respect to (especially context-free) happiness: availability of money, physical security, and valued social position (7, 8, and 9). Although extremely high levels of these can create unhappiness in particular cases, they do not appear likely to have that effect for people in general. The high-range negative impact proposed for "additional decrement" features was suggested to arise from two sources: each one's inherent harmful impact, and associated harm from other variables. Neither of those impacts is expected for high levels of "constant-effect" features. Instead, the assumption is that high to very high values of those environmental characteristics are on average accompanied by similar context-free happiness.

In all cases, a nonlinear association between the level of an environmental feature and people's happiness is thus proposed. Environmental increments of a certain size at lower values (to the left of Fig. 4.1) are suggested to give rise to greater increases in happiness than do increments of the same magnitude at moderate to high values. But why suggest a plateau in context-free happiness at middle environmental levels—a horizontal line in Figure 4.1—rather than nonlinearity in the form of either a smooth curve of steadily reducing steepness (for CE features) or an inverted U (for AD features)?

The justification for a plateau in this benign mid-range has two elements. First, differences between environmental stimuli of a given magnitude are likely to have a reduced personal importance away from the extremes of that characteristic. If a feature is broadly unproblematic (in the middle of the range), it is of little concern to someone whether its level becomes slightly higher or slightly lower; variations within the no-threat middle range are thus likely to be unrelated to happiness, which across this range is consistently high.

Second, happiness is always influenced by more than a single characteristic of the environment. In the middle range of an environmental feature, when variations in that feature do not shift it into a zone of potential danger, additional factors, perhaps more intense or otherwise more personally salient, can more strongly determine happiness. In that benign middle range, many other features can together be more troublesome or more attractive than is a mid-range feature on its own. These other inputs can combine in many different ways, with different impacts on happiness. They also vary in their direction and force between individuals, so that individuals' opposed directional effects may be canceled out in multiperson analyses. Variations in a single aspect of the environment within the middle range are thus less likely to be correlated with context-free happiness than when that feature poses a threat. In the latter case, when an environmental characteristic is personally problematic, for instance to the left of Figure 4.1, variations in level are expected to have a stronger impact, overriding other less threatening (mid-range) variables in the determination of happiness.

A stronger association between an environmental feature and happiness within the low range of that feature has been proposed in other research frameworks. For instance, Cummins (2000a) argued that subjective well-being is held at a stable level under personal homeostatic control at those levels of the environment that are nonthreatening. In threatening conditions (to the left of Fig. 4.1), a significant correlation with happiness is expected, but above some threshold value of an environmental feature people are likely to adjust their perceptions and feelings around their own personal "set point" or "equilibrium level" (Headey & Wearing, 1989, 1992). This homeostatic model considers that subjective well-being is maintained by each person in his or her narrowly defined range (which is thought to be largely determined by genetic factors), until environmental features move into a zone of potential danger. Cummins (2000a) illustrated that possibility by calculating environment–happiness correlations for samples either considered to be in difficult circumstances (e.g., suffering from spinal injury) or unselected in terms of their likely exposure to threat. Average correlations between environmental features and context-free subjective well-being were +0.26 and +0.12 for the two groups, assumed to be to the left or in the mid-range of Figure 4.1, respectively.

The limited importance of an environmental feature outside a zone of harm has been interpreted by Marmot (2004) in terms of changed standards of judgmental comparison. Examining associations between income and health, he argued that for those in or near to poverty (when feature 7 is well to the left of Fig. 4.1), the availability of money is judged in absolute terms; in that range, the important question is how much money one has. However, above a certain level of income, Marmot suggested that money availability is judged in relation to that of other people; comparisons are made in relative rather than absolute terms. Income and health are thus positively correlated with each other at low levels of income, but above a "threshold of absolute deprivation" (Marmot, 2004, p. 75) health is more determined by a variety of other factors, which individually can have either a positive or negative effect and collectively may become neutral in multiperson analyses.

More generally, the nonlinear pattern proposed here implies that the observed correlation between an environmental feature and an indicator of happiness will vary according to a sample's location on the environmental dimension. For example, if a study sample has generally moderate levels of a feature (falling in the assumed benign mid-range plateau), the correlation of that feature with happiness will be smaller than in a sample located in the lower range of the feature. This implication should be borne in mind when interpreting different studies' correlations; varying between-study environment-happiness correlations can arise from samples' different locations on the horizontal axis of Figure 4.1.

Nonlinearity and the Scope of Happiness

However, differences in the shape of relationships with a single environmental characteristic are expected between the three levels of scope identified in chapter 1: happiness that is context-free, domain-specific, or facet-specific. The extended plateau for "constant-effect" characteristics and the benign mid-range plateau for "additional decrement" features shown Figure 4.1 are most likely to be found for context-free indicators. As noted in chapter 2 and in the previous section, that global form of happiness is a function of inputs from multiple domains, and those varied inputs can combine in many different ways to influence overall well-being. A single environmental feature on its own is merely one of many possible influences on this broad form of happiness. Outside its range of deficiency values (away from the left of Fig. 4.1), one feature on its own is likely to be of limited concern, for reasons set out earlier. Also as discussed earlier, a negative impact is predicted for "additional decrement" (AD) characteristics when they reach a very high, threatening level. This asymmetric, flattened inverse U-shaped relationship is re-presented (as Fig. 4.2a) at the top of Figure 4.2.

Figure 4.2 summarizes expected patterns at each level of scope: context-free, domain-specific, and facet-specific. In each case, the vitamin model's overarching assumption of nonlinearity is shown, with a downturn in happiness at very high levels of "additional decrement" characteristics and stability for "constant effect" features. However, between-scope differences are envisaged in the width of the plateau occurring at moderate and high levels of an environmental feature. Those differences in plateau width are linked to variations in the strength of linear association between a particular environmental feature and the three levels of happiness. Consistent with a smallest departure from a linear pattern, a target facet is expected to be most strongly correlated with happiness that is specific to that facet (Fig. 4.2c). The least strong relationship is expected with respect to the feature's association with context-free happiness (Fig. 4.2a). Domain-specific happiness is likely to be correlated with a single environmental feature to an intermediate degree (Fig. 4.2b).

Happiness is always influenced by other variables in addition to the one under investigation. For facet-specific happiness, concerned with a single feature, conceptual interdependence is very high between the content of the feature and happiness focused on that feature. Thus, for instance, the nature of one's working conditions (an aspect of feature 8) has a strong impact on satisfaction with those conditions themselves, because that specific form of satisfaction is defined in terms of the feature itself; other environmental features, such as level of pay or family relationships, are of less direct consequence for that targeted evaluation. However, for medium-scope happiness (e.g., concerned with a job overall, being domain-specific), other variables in the same domain are additionally influential. And at the broadest level (context-free happiness), even more features are potentially relevant to the global judgment that is made, from other areas of a life space as well as from the job domain itself. As a result, a single facet of a job (e.g.,

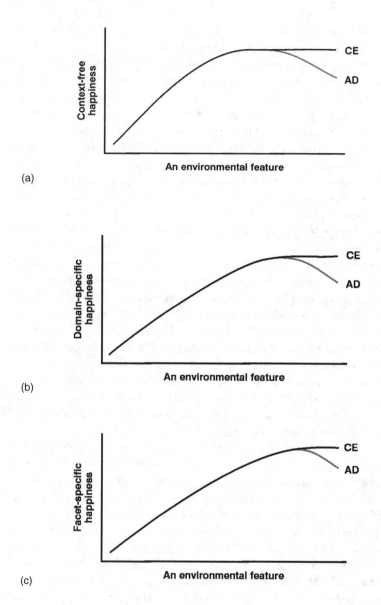

(a)

(b)

(c)

Figure 4.2. Expected relationships between environmental features and happiness at three levels of scope (CE is "constant effect"; AD is "additional decrement"). (a) For context-free happiness, a benign plateau beyond a zone of deficiency, with a smaller zone of threat at very high AD levels. (b) For domain-specific happiness, an asymmetric inverted U for AD features, and a benign plateau for CE features. (c) For facet-specific happiness, a linear association except at very high levels of environmental features.

working conditions) is alone likely to have least impact at that broad level (e.g., with respect to life satisfaction).

In general, mid-range stability of environmental features' impact on happiness is thus wider in proportion to the comprehensiveness of an indicator. A broad plateau is most likely for global, context-free happiness and least likely for narrow, facet-specific indicators, with an intermediate probability in relation to domain-specific measures. The smaller impact of ancillary influences on happiness as one moves from context-free to facet-specific outcomes is thus reflected across Figures 4.2a to 4.2c in a shortening of the assumed plateau at higher levels of an environmental feature.

Context-Free Illustrations of Nonlinearity

Most research into the association between environmental features and happiness has looked merely for linear relationships; as indicated earlier, all the primary characteristics identified here are known to be linked to subjective well-being in that manner. However, a limited amount of empirical evidence is available about nonlinearity. Studies of context-free happiness are illustrated in this section; chapters 5 to 8 examine in more detail research evidence in job situations.

A possible "additional decrement" at high levels of "vitamin" 1 was examined by Burger (1989), who reviewed a range of nonoccupational studies to identify circumstances in which a very high opportunity for personal control is undesirable. He presented laboratory findings showing that extremely large amounts of control give rise to negative affect because of excessive personal responsibility, anxiety about possibly poor decision-making and about others' perceptions of one's inadequacy, perceived high probability of overload from multiple inputs, and the unpredictability of multiple consequences in combination with each other. High personal control was seen to be particularly troublesome when all the available options are negative; extensive and continuing decision making with inevitably unpleasant outcomes has a particularly harmful impact on subjective well-being.

Later experimental studies of choice-making options by Iyengar and Lepper (2000) yielded similar findings about the undesirability of high levels of feature 1. An extensive array of options from which a decision has to be made was consistently found to create choice overload and subsequent dissatisfaction with outcomes. Iyengar and Lepper pointed out that these overload problems may be further exacerbated when faulty decisions have a major detrimental impact on oneself or others, or when needed information is not available for consideration.

Extremely high levels of personal control opportunity have also been examined by Schwartz (2000, 2004). He observed that a proliferation of options can reduce well-being for three main reasons. First, people become anxious about the need to obtain yet more information in order to make a sound choice; second, as options expand, standards for what is an acceptable result become raised, with accompanying increases in the perceived probability of failure; and third, individuals can come to believe that any suboptimal outcome is their personal fault, because the large number of alternatives available surely includes a better one. Developing those ideas, low levels of context-free satisfaction and a raised concern about faulty decision-making were observed in several experimental settings of multiple options by Schwartz et al. (2002). It is clear that very high levels of the first environmental characteristic in the present framework, opportunity for personal control, can operate in an "additional decrement" manner.

The third feature (externally generated goals) has also been discussed in terms that are consistent with the AD curve in Figures 4.1 and 4.2a, as both "underload" and "overload" are deemed to be harmful. Overload, a very high level of the feature, may be either quantitative, having too much to do, or qualitative, as a person is faced with demands perceived as excessively difficult. From low to moderate levels, increases in externally generated goals can be linked to increasing well-being through goal-achievement, but at very high levels (within the toxic range of "vitamins" of the AD kind) substantial loads are liable to produce a surfeit of demands and an inability to cope. Examples of nonlinearity in job settings are considered in chapter 6.

Availability of money (environmental characteristic 7) was introduced earlier as having a "constant effect" of the form shown in Figures 4.1 and 4.2a. Evidence in support of that possibility has been reported in both between-person and between-nation research. (In the latter case, average scores for each nation are analyzed, rather than examining individual people.) As indicated earlier, the overall pattern is one of positive association. At the individual (rather than national) level of analysis, Easterlin (2001) reported a correlation of +0.20 between income and context-free happiness. Across 11 previous studies, that average correlation was +0.19 in a review by Diener and Biswas-Diener (2002). The association appeared to be stronger for affective forms of happiness (type 1 in Table 2.1), in comparison with the more reflective life satisfaction (type 2), and was particularly great for facet-specific indicators of financial satisfaction (which overlap conceptually with income itself), as proposed in Figure 4.2c. In addition, at the national level of analysis Diener and Biswas-Diener (2002) reported a mean correlation from earlier studies of about +0.60; a nation's average subjective well-being is greater in countries with greater national income (additional details were provided by Diener, Diener, & Diener, 1995). In a later nation-level investigation, Steel and Ones (2002) reported a correlation between average income and average context-free happiness of +0.41 across 36 countries.

Hagerty and Veenhoven (2003) examined several data points from different times within each of 21 nations. Analyzing cross-sectional patterns at individual measurement points, they found that national happiness and national wealth had a mean intercorrelation of +0.27. Furthermore, lagged analyses within each nation across time showed that in many cases an increase in a country's average wealth was followed by an increase in its average happiness.

There is also evidence of nonlinearity of the "constant effect" kind. In nation-level analyses, Veenhoven (1991), Diener and Suh (1999), and Frey and Stutzer (2001) all described a positive association between average context-free well-being and national income at lower levels of income, but reported that the income-happiness association was substantially reduced across wealthier nations. However, that pattern was not replicated by Diener et al. (1995).

At the individual level of analysis, Diener and Biswas-Diener (2002) summarized stronger associations between people's income and their well-being in poorer countries than in rich ones; variation in income made a greater difference to people's context-free well-being in countries with lower average levels of income than in more wealthy ones. They also reported stronger associations within the same country among poorer than wealthier individuals. For instance, Diener, Sandvik, Seidlitz, and Diener (1993) found a nonlinear association between income and context-free subjective well-being in the United States; the income–happiness correlation was strong among poorer people, but for higher income individuals it was reduced. At higher levels of income (when basic needs are easily satisfied), it may be that individuals come to adapt to their raised financial input, with an associated leveling off in happiness with ever-increasing income (Diener et al., 1999). Processes of adaptation are considered in chapter 9.

The nonlinear pattern is expected within Cummins's (2000a, 2000b) homeostatic model (see earlier discussion). This predicts that "provided homeostasis is being maintained, there will be little or no relationship between objective variables such as money and subjective well-being. However, as soon as the person's resources become insufficient to maintain homeostasis, subjective well-being will move below its normal range under the control of the challenging agent" (Cummins, 2000b, p. 140). Drawing from previous publications, Cummins (2000b) compared samples with low income against those with average income, finding average correlations between income level and subjective well-being that matched this prediction: +0.26 and +0.14, respectively.

There is thus some published evidence for the "additional decrement" (AD) and "constant-effect" (CE) patterns of context-free happiness suggested in Figures 4.1 and 4.2. In addition, those patterns are strongly supported on conceptual grounds, as outlined earlier. However, investigations into possible nonlinearity have been infrequent, and relevant information is lacking about several of the primary environmental features. Research into nonlinearity has generally suffered from inadequately small samples and poor coverage of the extremes of a range. Large samples are needed to provide adequate statistical power, and an adequate test of a nonlinear pattern is not possible unless a study examines substantial numbers of people away from the middle range, those with extremely low or extremely high levels of an environmental characteristic (e.g., Muse, Harris, & Feild, 2003). Available evidence about happiness in relation to the characteristics of people's jobs is reviewed in chapters 5 to 8.

ENVIRONMENTAL FEATURES AND DIFFERENT FORMS OF HAPPINESS

The preceding discussion has examined happiness without consideration of the different measurement axes introduced in Figures 2.2 and 2.3. However, it may be that environmental features are associated in different ways with different aspects of subjective well-being or differentially with happiness as self-validation. Table 4.2 considers possible variations of that kind.

All environmental characteristics in the book's framework have been selected because of their association with happiness in general, so that significant correlations with feeling bad to feeling good, the first measurement axis for subjective well-being in Figure 2.2, are taken for granted. The primary differential question about subjective well-being is thus: Which of the two other measurement axes (diagonal in Fig. 2.2) is likely to be more strongly associated with each environmental feature? Given that different aspects of happiness tend to be interrelated, sharp differences in association not expected. Table 4.2 thus presents relative emphases, such that one association is proposed to be more likely than another.

Because the environmental features are assumed to be linked to happiness in nonlinear ways (either "additional decrement" or "constant effect"; AD or CE), we also need to consider patterns in different segments of the range of environmental scores. Separate columns in Table 4.2 thus cover expected correlations with happiness at low and very high environmental values.

This table embodies the assumption set out in chapter 2 that variations in low levels of an environmental feature are more associated with feelings of depression–enthusiasm than with anxiety–comfort. That emphasis on axis 3 (from depression to enthusiasm) rather than axis 2 (from anxiety to comfort) at low environmental levels is linked to the argument (e.g., Carver, 2003) that those different forms of well-being have divergent priorities in relation to either approach or avoidance goals. Depression (a low score on axis 3) is expected to be particularly associated with the absence or loss of something desired in the environment and a wish to move toward that missing feature (Finlay-Jones & Brown, 1981). Hence the suggested positive associations with depression–enthusiasm throughout column 4 of Table 4.2, referring to low environmental values. On the other hand, very high levels of an "additional decrement" (AD) feature are more likely to be viewed as threats from which a person wishes to escape; such threats provoke worry and tension, represented by low scores on the anxiety–comfort measurement axis (Clark et al., 1989). On that basis, negative associations of high AD features (numbers 1 to 6) are all predicted in column 3 to be primarily in relation to the anxiety–comfort axis of subjective well-being.

Table 4.2 also proposes some additions to those overall expectations. Low levels of four environmental characteristics are viewed (in column 2) also as a threat (and thus linked with anxiety–comfort), rather than only being an absence of something desirable. For example, low values of feature number 1 (opportunity for personal control) are expected to generate anxiety as people are unable to act on their negative environment to avoid danger and potentially harmful events. Other features of that kind, both posing a threat and representing an undesired absence at low levels, are suggested in Table 4.2 to be numbers 5, 7, and 8.

TABLE 4.2

Expected Principal Correlations Between the Primary Environmental Characteristics and Different Forms of Happiness (In Addition, Associations With Well-Being Axis 1 Are Present in Every Case)

| Environmental Features | Happiness as Well-Being: Diagonal Measurement Axes of Figure 2.2 | | | | Happiness as Self-Validation | |
| | (2a) Anxiety to (2b) Comfort | | (3a) Depression to (3b) Enthusiasm | | | |
	Low Environmental Values	Very High Environmental Values	Low Environmental Values	Very High Environmental Values	Low Environmental Values	Very High Environmental Values
1. Opportunity for personal control (AD)	Positive	Negative	Positive		Positive	Negative
2. Opportunity for skill use (AD)		Negative	Positive		Positive	Negative
3. Externally generated goals (AD)		Negative	Positive			
4. Variety (AD)		Negative	Positive			
5. Environmental clarity (AD)	Positive	Negative	Positive			
6. Contact with others (AD)		Negative	Positive			
7. Availability of money (CE)	Positive		Positive		Positive	
8. Physical security (CE)	Positive		Positive			
9. Valued social position (CE)			Positive		Positive	

For each of those characteristics, a deficiency is likely to be experienced as actively harmful rather than only suggesting a desirable goal (removal of the deficiency) to be aimed at. For instance, a low level of environmental clarity (5) can render a person's unpredictable situation less controllable and potentially dangerous; as suggested in Table 4.2, low control opportunity is itself likely to generate anxiety in many situations. Similarly, as discussed earlier, low availability of money (7) can reduce both personal control (1) and environmental clarity (5). In addition, low physical security (feature 8) can in some circumstances yield anxiety about one's own physical welfare. Substantial associations with anxiety–comfort at lower levels of features 1, 5, 7, and 8 are thus proposed.

These suggestions about varying environmental impact on different axes of well-being have not so far been examined empirically, because research has typically been based on only a single indicator, such as life satisfaction. There is a clear need at present to test these possibilities in studies that take a more differentiated view. Some multiple-outcome investigations have been reported into forms of job-related well-being, and those are reviewed in chapters 5 to 8.

The need for more differentiated research extends also to the second aspect of happiness—in terms of self-validation. As discussed in chapters 1 and 2, this involves experiences of self-worth in activities felt to be right, appropriate or in some sense proper for oneself, whether or not those are experienced as pleasurable. The right-hand columns of Table 4.2 suggest that self-validation is particularly linked to variations in two features that permit proactivity and personal initiative: opportunity for personal control and for skill use (features 1 and 2). At low levels of these features, there is an absence of choice, challenge, and potential for self-expression and personal growth. Low personal control or skill use is thus likely to be linked to unhappiness in terms of low self-validation. In addition, very high opportunities of those (AD) kinds are expected to impair self-validation, as a person is prevented by excessive demands from steering his or her own course to meet perceived standards of worth.

Availability of money (7) and valued social position (9) are also suggested to be correlated at low levels with experiences of self-validation. In poverty or near-poverty, a person's activities are directed at the reduction of current hassles and distress, so that little possibility exists for self-validation. However, availability of money is proposed to be a "constant effect" feature, so that no correlation with self-validation is expected at higher levels. The right-hand cell is thus blank for feature 7.

A similar pattern appears probable for valued social position ("vitamin" 9). Being located in a setting of very low social worth is likely to inhibit the development of self-validating activities and experiences, so that a positive correlation between increasingly valued social position and self-validation is expected in the lower range of that environmental feature. However, across positions with moderate and high social value (as in column 7), self-validation is likely to be determined more by other aspects of the environment and the person, so that no impact of variation in this feature (as a CE characteristic) is anticipated.

An indirect impact of environmental variation on self-validation may also be envisaged, arising from the sequential expectation introduced in chapter 1: Self-validation is expected to become important mainly when a person's well-being is at least at a moderate level. In settings of very low environmental quality, people are likely to be primarily concerned with their low subjective well-being and ways to increase that well-being. However, when principal environmental features reach a moderate level, that first form of happiness may be raised to a point beyond which a person becomes open to self-validating concerns.

This possibility may be illustrated through feature 7, the availability of money. Given that money is required to buy necessities which can avoid or reduce personal and family distress, some moderate income appears to be essential for even a modest level of well-being. Without money, self-validation in many societies may therefore be of limited concern. An instance from Buddhist thinking is the Dalai Lama's suggestion that "if someone is economically deprived, desperately poor, then the practice of human values [an aspect of self-validation in the present account] is difficult for them" (Dalai Lama & Cutler, 2003, p. 54, bracketed material added). But when money availability is at least moderate, people may turn to issues of self-validation.

These expectations about differential associations with different forms of happiness are examined in this book mainly within the domain of paid employment. The focus is on happiness or unhappiness in relation to the primary environmental features in job settings. Features of the "constant effect" kind are reviewed in chapter 5, with "additional decrement" variables considered in chapters 6 and 7. Some wide-ranging issues about the environment and happiness are addressed in chapter 8.

5

Constant Effects Beyond a Threshold

The preceding chapters have identified two principal aspects of happiness. The first is subjective well-being, which may be measured on three axes of experience: from feeling bad to feeling good, from anxiety to comfort, and from depression to enthusiasm (see Fig. 2.2 on p. 22). Assessments tend to be either more affective, particularly emphasizing current feelings, or more reflective, drawing on recollections and interpretations to generate reports of satisfaction or similar constructs. Experiences of happiness also differ in their scope, with context-free happiness concerning life in general and domain-specific happiness focused on a particular area, such as one's family, job, health or self. As described earlier, single domains can themselves be subdivided, so that attention might be directed at separate facets of, say, a job or one's family life. This chapter and the following three are concerned with the characteristics of jobs, and mainly emphasize job-related (domain-specific) happiness and forms of facet-specific happiness within the job domain.

A second form of happiness was earlier termed self-validation. This involves activities and experiences that may or may not be pleasurable, reflecting a sense that certain actions are personally fitting, appropriate, or worthy. This second form of happiness is difficult to specify, and there may be a hierarchical or sequential pattern such that self-validation matters less to people experiencing considerable unhappiness of the first kind; the presence or absence of self-validation may be of concern primarily to those who have already achieved a certain level of happiness as pleasure.

Psychologists' research in organizations has almost always examined subjective well-being, with little attention paid to happiness as self-validation. Well-being itself is influenced by features in a person's environment, by aspects of himself or herself, and by the interaction between self and environment. Within an environment-oriented perspective, nine important environmental characteristics were introduced in chapter 4. Those were all selected on the basis of research findings that each one is in general associated with greater happiness.

Environment–happiness associations were suggested to be nonlinear, with a pattern analogous to the effect of vitamins on physical health: Increases in an environmental feature are important when below a moderate level, but they are not increasingly valuable beyond that level (see Fig. 4.1). Some evidence about the features' nonlinear relationship with happiness that is context-free was reviewed in the previous chapter. That presentation ended with suggestions about possible differential relationships between the environmental features and different aspects of happiness (Table 4.2 on p. 108). For example, opportunity for personal control (feature 1) was expected to be related to both happiness as well-being and as self-validation, whereas physical security (8) was considered to be primarily associated only with happiness of the first kind.

THREE ADDITIONAL FEATURES IN JOB SETTINGS

This chapter turns to the settings of paid employment. It was pointed out in chapter 3 that all roles expose people in varying degrees to the same key features, so that variations in those characteristics can provide an overarching explanation of happiness levels in any role. (However, a person's own mental processes also contribute to happiness, so that an environmental account can only be partially adequate; see chaps. 9 to 13.) In examining research in job settings, the general treatment of environmental characteristics in previous chapters can be made more concrete through more localized (here, job-related) examples of each one.

Three questions are addressed about each characteristic. First, how is the general association between that environmental feature and people's happiness illustrated in specific aspects of a job? Because the characteristics have been selected because they are known to be important for happiness, positive associations are overall to be expected. However, research findings can depend on the form of the construct that is addressed and the specific measure that is applied. For instance, patterns can contrast markedly between different levels of scope (happiness that is context-free, domain-specific, or facet-specific). Second, what evidence is available about the nonlinear patterns of association suggested in the last chapter? For example, has research in job settings uncovered "constant-effect" relationships for some environmental features, and have other ("additional decrement") characteristics been shown to be harmful at very high as well as low levels? The chapter's third question asks whether the differential proposals of Table 4.2 are empirically supported in occupational research, with different job features being of different importance for different aspects of happiness.

The principal features have been investigated in job settings with a variety of labels. They are listed again here, in terms that have been used in job-related research. As originally proposed within a "vitamin" framework (Warr, 1987), and summarized in chapter 4, nine characteristics cover primary aspects of the environment in employment, unemployment, and retirement. However, three additional aspects also require consideration in occupational settings—the support provided by a supervisor, the career prospects offered, and the extent to which relationships with an organization are equitable. These job features, less appropriate in discussion of other roles, have been included as numbers 10 to 12 in this chapter. The job-related framework thus comprises 12 features, the first 9 of which (from chap. 4) are broadly applicable across roles in general.

The key characteristics in any job are as follows, with illustrative job-relevant labels presented after each one's formal title. As elsewhere in the book, "AD" indicates that an environmental feature is assumed to be associated with happiness in an "additional decrement" nonlinear manner; "CE" refers to an assumed "constant effect" above moderate levels. Those patterns have been introduced in chapter 4.

1. *Opportunity for personal control* (AD): employee discretion, decision latitude, autonomy, absence of close supervision, opportunity for self-determination or independence, freedom of choice, participation in decision-making, influence over the organization.
2. *Opportunity for skill use* (AD): (a) skill utilization, utilization of valued abilities, required skills, multiskilling, applying expertise; (b) opportunity for learning, self-development or skill acquisition, becoming an expert, developing new skills.

3. *Externally generated goals* (AD): job demands, task demands, quantitative or qualitative workload, attentional demand, work pressure, role responsibility, challenge, normative requirements, traction, conflicting demands, role conflict, work–family conflict.

4. *Variety* (AD): variation in job content and location, nonrepetitive work, avoidance of repetition, skill variety, task variety.

5. *Environmental clarity* (AD): (a) information about the future, absence of ambiguity about the future; (b) information about required behavior, low role ambiguity, role clarity, clarity of role requirements; (c) information about the consequences of behavior, task feedback.

6. *Contact with others* (AD): (a) quantity of interaction, frequency of social contact, social density, adequate privacy; (b) quality of interaction, good relationships with others, social support, good communications, freedom from abuse or bullying.

7. *Availability of money* (CE): income level, amount of pay, salary, financial resources.

8. *Physical security* (CE): absence of danger, good working conditions, ergonomically adequate equipment, a low-hazard environment, safe levels of temperature and noise.

9. *Valued social position* (CE): status in society, importance to the organization, task significance, valued role incumbency, meaningfulness of job, contribution to the community or wider society.

10. *Supportive supervision* (CE): leader consideration, boss support, supportive management, concern for employee welfare.

11. *Career outlook* (CE): (a) security of employment, job security, availability of extended tenure; (b) opportunity for promotion, advancement, or a shift to other roles.

12. *Equity* (CE): (a) fairness in one's employment relationship; distributive and procedural justice; equitable psychological contract; absence of unfair discrimination; (b) morality in an employer's relationship with society.

For all these aspects of a job environment, increases from low to moderate levels (analogous to the "deficiency range" of vitamins) are likely to be associated with greater happiness. (Alternatively stated, their absence is likely to promote unhappiness.) However, chapter 4 described how stronger associations with job characteristics are expected for well-being in the domain of work than for (broader) well-being that is context-free. As in other domain-specific cases, job-related happiness is influenced primarily by features of that same domain (i.e., in one's job), whereas context-free happiness can be affected also by a large number of elements in other domains of a life space. At the third level of scope, facet-specific happiness is the most narrowly defined indicator. Associations between (for instance) satisfaction with a facet and the content of that facet can be expected to be particularly strong, because the two are conceptually interdependent.

However, environment–happiness associations have been proposed to be nonlinear, with some leveling off at moderate and high levels. As set out in the three diagrams of Figure 4.2 in chapter 4, different patterns are predicted for forms of happiness that vary in scope. Nonlinear associations with an environmental feature are most probable for context-free happiness, and least probable for facet-specific indicators. Particularly in the case of happiness that is context-free, a constant effect beyond a moderate environmental level is envisaged for the characteristics identified as "CE" earlier. In other ("AD") cases, a high-level decrement is expected on average, when extremely high values (analogous to toxic, excessive amounts of certain vitamins) are linked to a decrease in happiness. (Differences around these average trends are considered later.)

Note that the "additional decrement" features (1 to 6) can be distinguished from those assumed to have a "constant effect" (7 to 12) in terms of their intrinsic or extrinsic focus. Research has sometimes examined "intrinsic" features within job tasks themselves (or "intrinsic satisfaction" with those features; see chap. 2), and the vitamin framework suggests that intrinsic characteristics have in common the possibility of "too much of a good thing" (referred to as an "additional decrement," numbers 1 to 6). On the other hand, more extrinsic features (concerned primarily with attributes external to job tasks) are likely to yield a "constant effect" across moderate and high levels (features 7 to 12).

This chapter examines happiness in relation to the six assumed "constant effect" characteristics in job settings: availability of money, physical security, valued social position, supportive supervision, career outlook, and equity. The other six environmental features (thought to involve an additional decrement at very high levels) are considered in chapters 6 and 7.

JOB FEATURE 7: AVAILABILITY OF MONEY

Availability of money has often been studied in terms of an employed person's wage or salary level. The amount of pay one receives is personally important not only for the purchases and the lifestyle that it makes possible, but also as an indicator of public recognition, equitable treatment, and a sign of one's achievements (e.g., Srivastava, Locke, & Bartol, 2001).

Research into money and happiness across several nations or within community samples has been illustrated in chapter 4. Many studies in employing organizations have examined merely one facet-specific form of happiness—satisfaction with pay received. Not surprisingly, income level has been found to be associated with that targeted and content-linked form of subjective well-being. Correlations with employees' pay satisfaction were +0.41 (averaged across three samples), +0.50, +0.30, and +0.19 (averaged across four samples) in research by Dyer and Theriault (1976), Rice, Phillips, and McFarlin (1990), Griffin (1997), and Sweeney and McFarlin (2005), respectively.

Other investigations have examined overall job satisfaction (i.e., at the domain-specific level), again finding significant (but lower) associations with income level. For example, the correlation was +0.25 in a study by Caplan, Cobb, French, Van Harrison, and Pinneau (1975) and +0.24 in research by Agho et al. (1993). In analyses of data from different British national samples, significant associations with overall job satisfaction were found by Clark (1996), Sloane and Williams (2000), and Rose (2003), but bivariate correlation values were not cited. Clark (1996) presented multivariate analyses showing that income received was substantially more associated with pay satisfaction than with overall job satisfaction, but that the association was statistically significant in both cases.

Findings about the psychological correlates of pay are of course open to influence from other aspects of a job. Given that subjective well-being is determined by many different features, it may be that additional job characteristics partly account for bivariate associations with income alone. Nevertheless, the correlation of income with job satisfaction remained significant in multivariate analyses by Dyer and Theriault (1976), Birdi et al. (1995), Clark (1996), Griffin (1997), Sloane and Williams (2000), Bender, Donohue, and Heywood (2005), Clark (2005b), and Sweeney and McFarlin (2005) after controlling for different sets of demographic and other factors.

What about a worker's income and his or her happiness of the context-free kind? As summarized in chapter 4, community samples (not restricted to people in jobs) yield an average correlation around +0.20 with context-free well-being. In two studies of blue-collar employees, low pay was significantly associated with more context-free anxiety

(Gardell, 1971) and with a low score on an interview measure of mental health (Kornhauser, 1965). Adelmann's (1987) national U.S. sample of full-time employees yielded a correlation of +0.15 with a broad measure of happiness. However, in a nationally representative sample of British employees, Clark et al. (1996) reported that generalized distress was unrelated to income level after controls for age, gender, education, and other variables.

It is possible that the association between income and happiness is stronger among poorer employees (e.g., in the blue-collar samples examined by Gardell and Kornhauser, described earlier) than among more wealthy ones, as found for the population as a whole (see chap. 4). For example, even within the blue-collar sample studied by Kornhauser (1965), separate analyses at different levels of skill indicated that income variation "has its greatest impact at the lower job levels" (p. 125). On that basis, we might expect that income level will be less important in samples of high earners. That reduction of association was illustrated in the study of medical practitioners by Simoens, Scott, and Sibbald (2002). They recorded nonsignificant correlations in that sample with job satisfaction and job-related strain, but values were not cited. Additional research into this nonlinear possibility among job holders would be valuable.

In assessing their pay satisfaction, people view their income relative to personal standards of comparison. Studies in this area are often based on a version of equity theory (Adams, 1963; Walster, Walster, & Berscheid, 1978), proposing that employees compare the ratio of their pay received relative to their inputs against those outcome–input ratios for other people. "Inputs" are usually defined in terms of skill, effort, qualifications, working conditions, hours of work, and so on. Persons who compare themselves unfavorably with others in these ratios tend to feel negatively about the level of their pay.

Possible social referents in these perceptual comparisons were examined by Goodman (1974), who showed that pay satisfaction could be affected by many different comparisons, with people both outside and inside one's organization. Studies by Dyer and Theriault (1976), Rice et al. (1990), and Sweeney and McFarlin (2004, 2005) included actual income level in their analyses of multiple judgmental comparisons, finding that comparative assessments against referent standards remained associated with pay satisfaction over and above a person's income itself. Research by Sweeney, McFarlin, and Inderrieden (1990) examined in multiple regression analyses a range of personal expectations as well as actual salary, needed salary, and the salary level considered to be appropriate. Even after those controls, social comparisons were significantly associated with pay satisfaction in four different samples.

Clark and Oswald (1996) examined possible comparisons with an external standard that was more objectively defined than are perceptions about other people. They constructed an econometrically determined "going rate" for each person, in terms of equivalent job type and demographic characteristics. Both overall job satisfaction and pay satisfaction were found to be linked to that standard, such that a received income below a person's econometric comparison rate was accompanied by lower satisfaction. This pattern occurred despite control for actual income level, and income level itself remained significant in the multivariate analyses.

The discussion of this environmental feature in job settings has so far mainly covered the first question raised earlier in the chapter. Significant associations between income received and several forms of subjective well-being have been consistently reported. Those are particularly high for the facet-specific index of satisfaction with pay, as would be expected from narrow and overlapping content. The medium-scope, domain-specific construct of overall job satisfaction is also correlated with pay level, but to a lesser extent than is pay satisfaction. Associations at both those levels remain significant despite statistical controls for other relevant variables. As for context-free happiness, several studies of community samples and of employees only have found significant associations with income level. Linked to decreases in conceptual overlap, income and subjective well-being are less intercorrelated as one moves from facet-specific to context-free happiness. Even in the latter case, a significant association is retained, but other factors are also implicated.

Turning to the chapter's second question, about a possible "constant-effect" pattern, although chapter 4 illustrated that associations between income and context-free well-being appear to be nonlinear in that way, systematic evidence in job settings is limited. Kornhauser's (1965) observation of a stronger association at lower levels of skill (see earlier discussion) is supportive, but that study covered only blue-collar workers. Nevertheless, it is reasonable to suppose that variations in the availability of money are more important in circumstances of financial difficulty than when one is wealthy. As suggested by Cummins's (2000a, 2000b) homeostatic theory, a person's happiness may be held within a fixed personal range as long as he or she remains outside a zone of threat and potential harm, in this case after income has become sufficient for day-to-day living.

The chapter's third question asks about the differential possibilities suggested in Table 4.2: Do associations with this environmental feature (7 in the table) vary in relation to different kinds of happiness? For the first axis of subjective well-being (from feeling bad to feeling good), a significant association is known to be present; that association (illustrated in terms of satisfaction in previous paragraphs) was one basis for selection of the "vitamins" in the present framework. In addition, availability of money was proposed in Table 4.2 to be important at low levels for both diagonal measurement axes of subjective well-being: from anxiety to comfort (axis 2) and from depression to enthusiasm (axis 3). Because organizational research into pay and happiness has almost always examined merely axis 1, little can be said about those other possibilities. However, the anxiety and mental health indicators examined by Gardell (1971) and Kornhauser (1965; described earlier) provide some support for Table 4.2's dual expectation at low levels of income. At high income levels, associations with both axes of well-being are expected to be nonsignificant, consistent with the predicted "constant effect" above an elevated threshold. (On that basis, columns 3 and 5 for feature 7 are left blank.) Some support for this possibility has been described earlier, but further investigation with samples of very high-income workers remains desirable.

Table 4.2 (p. 108) also suggested that very low levels of money availability are linked to an absence of self-validation. That second aspect of happiness has rarely been investigated in job settings, and no evidence about self-validation as a function of employees' income level appears to be available. However, Rainwater's (1974) theoretical argument is persuasive. He emphasized that in the absence of financial and related resources self-validating activities are not possible, noting that poor people lack such resources. "The basic obstacle to the [happiness] of people in poverty comes from the fact that families do not have available to them the resources in the form of goods and services that would allow them to carry out the validating activities [that are] required" (Rainwater, 1974, p. 21, bracketed material added).

When other environmental inputs are impoverished through an absence of money and perhaps accumulated debts, many possibilities for self-validating activity are removed. This theme has been presented more generally in chapters 1 and 2; self-validation is likely to be of limited concern to people living in extremely negative conditions of any kind. However, increasing levels of money availability at least open up the possibility of self-validating activities, and that is indicated by the positive association suggested in column 6 of Table 4.2.

JOB FEATURE 8: PHYSICAL SECURITY

A second "constant-effect" aspect of the environment introduced in chapter 4 concerns the physical conditions in which one lives. Physical security takes many different forms, with the primary elements depending on which group of people or which setting is under investigation. For example, during retirement a principal concern might be for the usability of domestic equipment or the adequacy of heating in a home. In job settings, key issues are the absence of danger and the presence of good working conditions, ergonomically adequate equipment, and safe levels of, for instance, temperature and noise.

These aspects of physical security are often omitted from research into employees' subjective well-being. Taber, Beehr, and Walsh (1985) pointed out that "this omission is consistent with the bias in modern theories to classify working conditions arbitrarily as 'extrinsic' to the job and then to ignore them.... Early studies in industrial psychology focused on the importance of working conditions, but they play almost no part in modern social science theories of work" (p. 42). Key features of physical security in job settings were identified by Carlopio (1996) in terms of environmental design (lighting, air quality, the nature of surfaces, etc.), equipment and tools, hazards and danger, and toilet, eating, and resting facilities. Poulton (1978) considered levels of illumination, noise, vibration, temperature, wind, and atmospheric pollution,

It is clear that the level of physical security in a job is significantly associated with employees' subjective well-being. For example, Campion and Thayer (1985) developed a broad scale of physical characteristics, recording noise, tool design, lifting and postural requirements, and vibration and safety levels. Jobs were rated by independent observers in those respects, and the correlation between overall observer ratings of negative physical features and employees' health complaints and physical discomfort was found to be +0.50. (See also Campion, 1988.) In a multination study by Huang and van de Vliert (2004), employees' own ratings of physical working conditions ("ventilation, temperature, space to work, etc.") were correlated at +0.28 with overall job satisfaction; this association remained significant despite controls for many other variables.

An investigation by Kirjonen and Hänninen (1986) recorded employees' working conditions in terms of physical, chemical, and ergonomic hazards. Across a 5-year period, they found that increases or decreases in those respects were accompanied by parallel changes in both job-related and context-free well-being. Those longitudinal associations were present despite statistical controls for changes in other job characteristics, relations with colleagues, and satisfaction with pay.

Warr (1992) and Birdi et al. (1995) also reported significant associations of poor working conditions with low subjective well-being, on axes 2 and 3 and on axis 1 respectively (see Fig. 2.2 in chap. 2); those were retained despite controls for other job and demographic variables. In the study by Wilson, DeJoy, Vandenberg, Richardson, and McGrath (2004), perceptions of hazardous physical work conditions were correlated at –0.38 and +0.41 with overall job satisfaction and negative job affect, respectively. In research by Zaccaro and Stone (1988), greater perceived danger in a job was significantly associated with lower overall job satisfaction (a domain-specific indicator) and satisfaction with work activities themselves (facet-specific). Those associations remained significant despite statistical controls for a large number of other job characteristics.

Job-related emotional exhaustion (mainly low levels of well-being axis 2; see chap. 2) was studied by Demerouti, Bakker, Nachreiner, and Schaufeli (2001). The correlation with perceived poor quality of the physical environment was +0.32. Context-free forms of subjective well-being have less often been examined in this area, but a significant association with context-free distress was found by Loscocco and Spitze (1990), both before and after statistical control for other variables. The correlation between hazardous work conditions and context-free depression was +0.22 in the study by Wilson et al. (2004).

Poor physical security of this kind is expected to reduce employees' well-being in three ways. First is a direct effect: Adverse physical conditions are likely themselves to give rise to negative feelings. Second, an indirect impact may occur through job-induced deterioration in physical health. Negative physical consequences of work (such as a chronic back complaint from heavy lifting or a damaged leg after an industrial accident) are likely to be harmful in psychological as well as bodily terms. Unhappiness can in these cases arise from chronic pain, restriction of mobility, sleeping or eating problems, and reduced ability to undertake rewarding work tasks.

A third influence of job feature 8 might occur through correlated levels of other features. For instance, low physical security indexed as dangerous working conditions can be associated with low perceived controllability; employees may see their hazardous job environment as one that they cannot adequately control (feature 1) or cannot sufficiently predict (5). Similarly, poor working conditions might be considered to illustrate a lack of support from supervision (10; Barling, Kelloway, & Iverson, 2003).

Specific aspects of physical security in jobs have been examined by researchers with particular interests. For example, Sundstrom, Burt, and Kamp (1980) studied architectural features including the noisiness of a work environment. Across three samples of employees, noisiness was correlated on average at −0.45 with satisfaction with one's work-space and at −0.21 with overall job satisfaction. The review by McCoy and Evans (2005) indicated that high levels of noise are particularly troublesome when they are extended or unpredictable and when employees have no control over them.

In many cases, environmental characteristics have been studied in relation to facet-specific satisfaction (linked to the feature in question) or in terms of actual or potential bodily harm. For example, ambient noise has been found to be annoying as a function of its frequency as well as intensity (e.g., Crocker, 1997). Indicators of atmospheric conditions, in terms of air temperature, humidity, air movement, and/or radiant temperature, are closely linked to bodily discomfort or comfort (e.g., Kantowitz & Sorkin, 1983). Inadequate equipment can both be intrinsically undesirable (creating facet-specific unhappiness) and also cause distress through consequential errors and interruptions to work flow (e.g., Bullinger, Kern, & Braun, 1997).

Many studies have explored cognitive and ergonomic aspects of computer equipment. There is considerable evidence that poorly designed hardware, software, and computer-based networking systems can reduce operator well-being. For example, the handbook edited by Helander, Landauer, and Prabhu (1997) identified a large number of computer-related features that can have impact on facet-specific well-being. The design of these features can give rise to specific work problems with respect to, for example, input devices, visual displays, interface design, schemes of notation, menu provision, task allocations between a user and the system, computer-mediated group interaction, and decision support systems.

It is not surprising that problems in all these (and similar) respects have an impact on subjective well-being that is targeted on the equipment in question (Smith, 1997). For example, Clegg, Carey, Dean, Hornby, and Bolden (1997) examined computer users' reactions in terms of system-related (i.e., facet-specific) anxiety, depression and satisfaction. However, research has almost never considered domain-specific (job-related) or context-free happiness as a function of computer equipment in a work environment.

The occurrence of accidents at work might be considered a proxy measure of low physical security. Barling et al. (2003) examined the reported occurrence in the past year of six forms of injury at work in relation to overall job satisfaction. A low but statistically significant correlation (–0.12) was found between satisfaction and employees' number of injuries of those kinds.

The chapter's three questions ask about specific associations between an environmental feature and employee happiness, possible nonlinear associations, here of the "constant effect" (CE) kind, and variations in an environmental feature's relationships with different forms of happiness. Examples of significant associations (the first question) have been presented already. Low levels of physical security are consistently correlated with reduced well-being of a facet-specific kind, targeted on the feature in question; both direct and consequential effects are envisaged. A finding that certain aspects of working conditions are undesirable in that narrow, conceptually linked sense is not surprising, although the prevalence of poor conditions of that kind in an organization certainly warrants investigation. However, as illustrated earlier, significant associations with broader, domain-specific well-being, such as overall job satisfaction, have also been established.

Links between physical working conditions and employees' well-being that is context-free have more rarely been investigated. Nevertheless, as cited earlier, correlations are significant with perceived hazard in one's job. On the other hand, many single features of the physical work environment or of employees' equipment are not expected individually to have an impact on happiness that extends beyond the job domain, because context-free happiness is also determined by a wide range of other factors and processes.

The second question asks about nonlinear associations. It was proposed in chapter 4 that physical security is a "constant-effect" (CE) feature, such that variations at high levels of security do not affect well-being; when feature 8 is outside a zone of threat (away from the left of Figs. 4.1 and 4.2), additional increases in its level are expected to have no further impact on well-being (which is high to the right of the figures). The traditional research focus has been primarily on low environmental levels, for which significant associations have been reported earlier, and evidence for the proposed CE pattern at higher levels is not yet available.

As described in chapter 4, such a pattern is especially likely for context-free indicators, because many additional features also contribute to happiness at the context-free level. These different inputs are

expected to influence context-free happiness both positively and negatively, over and above the impact of physical security alone. Although
variations in physical security are likely to influence unhappiness in
the zone of threat to the left of Figure 4.1, at moderate levels of that
feature the combined influence of other features is expected to be of
greater importance. (In all cases, this canceling-out of other influences
at moderate levels is expected to be particularly marked in multiperson analyses, as the diversity of other inputs will be greater across
a sample of people than for a single person alone.) On the other hand,
as illustrated in Figure 4.2c, facet-specific indicators (for instance, satisfaction with working conditions) might be expected to be more linearly associated with the nature of their target (the working conditions
themselves), because that measure of well-being is defined in the same
narrow content terms as the job feature itself.

The chapter's third question asks about the differential proposals in
Table 4.2; are those supported in job settings? In the present case, is
physical security associated to a similar degree with the second and
third axes of subjective well-being (from anxiety to comfort and from
depression to enthusiasm)? Studies of physical security in job settings
have usually been restricted to facet-specific satisfaction (linked to the
environmental feature in question), and do not adequately cover multiple aspects of happiness. Systematic examination of separate links
with different aspects of happiness is still needed.

JOB FEATURE 9: VALUED SOCIAL POSITION

The third "constant-effect" characteristic in the present framework
(identified in Table 4.2 as feature 9) concerns the significance that is
attached to a particular role. Jobs differ from each other in the value
that is attached to them within a particular society, and aspects of job
holders' happiness have been found to be associated with that attributed value.

For example, Bradburn (1969; but the author of the cited chapter
was identified inside the book as C. E. Knoll) distinguished between
jobs within either white-collar or blue-collar groups according to their
prestige rankings in an established sociological classification. Among
male principal wage earners, context-free well-being and positive
affect were found in each case to be greater in jobs with higher prestige. In a study of women as well as men, Xie and Johns (1995) found
that greater job prestige was significantly linked to lower job-related
emotional exhaustion.

Such a pattern may of course arise from the fact that prestige ratings are based also on other job characteristics in the present framework. It is not clear from bivariate associations with publicly attributed prestige what particular aspects of a job give rise to an observed pattern. Bradburn (1969) emphasized that variation in the esteem accorded to a position was an important contributor to differential happiness, but also drew attention to other correlated factors. For the white-collar sample, job autonomy and promotion prospects emerged as important to both occupational prestige and employee happiness, whereas in the blue-collar sample differences in income level were of greater relevance.

In addition to these examinations of publicly defined social position, esteem has also been measured through the perceptions of a job holder. For example, the "task significance" scale of the Job Diagnostic Survey (Hackman & Oldham, 1975, 1980) records employees' assessment of the importance of their job. Many studies (e.g., Hackman & Oldham, 1975; Wall, Clegg, & Jackson, 1978) have found significant correlations between perceived task significance and overall job satisfaction, and that association has been replicated longitudinally by Hackman, Pearce, and Wolfe (1978). In a review of results from 28 cross-sectional studies, Loher et al. (1985) found an average correlation with overall job satisfaction of +0.25; in a later study, that value was +0.37 (Agho et al., 1993).

For the five facet-level satisfactions measured by the Job Descriptive Index (see chap. 2), task significance is most correlated with (conceptually related) satisfaction with the work itself (an average r from previous research of +0.38; Kinicki et al., 2002). However, for facet satisfactions that have less conceptual overlap with the job feature, correlations are lower; for instance, that average value was +0.10 for satisfaction with promotion opportunities in the review by Kinicki and colleagues. Perceived task significance was unrelated to subjective well-being that was context-free in the study by Wall et al. (1978).

This characteristic of a job is, more than several others, open to subjective interpretation; the value accorded to a particular role can vary between occupants of that same role. Wrzesniewski, McCauley, Rozin, and Schwartz (1997) examined the extent to which employees viewed their work as either "a job" (undertaken because of necessity rather than for pleasure or personal fulfilment), "a career" (with a focus on advancement in the future), or "a calling" (involving activities that are fulfilling and socially useful). Of their sample, approximately one-third of employees viewed their work in each category, with greatest job satisfaction and life satisfaction among those who reported a calling. Even within a single job (administrative assistant), approximately constant proportions of job, career, or calling were observed. Thus, although a third of administrative assistants saw their work as a calling (with positive social value), another third saw it merely as a necessity. Those proportions will of course vary between positions and as a function of job content in the same position, but estimates of a job's social value are likely always to derive from both objective features and employees' own interpretation of those.

That theme was developed with respect to a career (rather than a single job) by Hall and Chandler (2005). They emphasized that subjective assessment of a career (rather than through objective indicators in terms of income, job category, etc.) are central to the investigation of its personal meaningfulness. In the case of careers viewed as a "calling" ("doing work out of a strong sense of inner direction," p. 160), periods of transition and challenge can involve anxiety and worry. However, in the longer term Hall and Chandler argued that successful careers of the "calling" kind are particularly likely to give rise to raised well-being at several levels of scope and also to outcomes that are here described as self-validation.

The importance of personal (and also work-group) interpretations of a job's value can be illustrated with respect to what Hughes (1951) termed "dirty work," examining jobs that are widely perceived as disgusting, degrading, or immoral. Examples include cleaners of public toilets and other soiled environments, workers in some form of sexual interaction, animal exterminators, people in extremely servile roles, garbage collectors, and others whose activities are physically, socially, or morally tainted.

Jobs characterized as "dirty" are likely to be treated with little public respect, but their holders do not necessarily view them in terms of similarly low occupational esteem. Given that a job feeds into one's self-identity, it can be important to find personal worth in what one is doing. Ashforth and Kreiner (1999) described cognitive and social processes undertaken "to transform the meaning of the stigmatized work by simultaneously negating or devaluing negative attributes and creating or revaluing positive ones" (p. 421). For example, a "dirty" worker may find particular social value in his or her activities, or alter perceptual standards so that job content is evaluated less negatively than it is by outsiders. Those processes are likely to be supported at the group level, through a local culture and common perspectives that appreciate job holders' activities and perhaps criticize outsiders for their lack of awareness.

As well as being based on objective differences, assessments of social position thus derive in part from personal and group processes of interpretation. Within those processes, employees may build on specific cues provided by other people. Wrzesniewski, Dutton, and Debebe (2003) illustrated how job holders are frequently exposed to information that conveys other people's appraisals of their worth and the perceived value of their job. Self-perceptions may be enhanced proactively by selecting for attention cues from other people that suggest a positive social value, or adjusting behavior to seek out interactions and activities that are likely to affirm that value.

Wrzesniewski et al. (2003) viewed this aspect of the attribution of value as an instance of employees' sense-making in their organizational environment. More generally, individuals are more likely to engage in sense-making activity when they meet some problems (Weick, 1995; Weick, Sutcliffe, & Obstfeld, 2005), and sense-making processes are thus expected particularly to occur in settings of low or ambiguous social value.

The chapter's second question asks about possible nonlinear associations between an environmental characteristic and level of happiness, in this case about a proposed "constant effect" of valued social position at moderate and high levels. It appears that studies have always examined linear patterns, so no empirical conclusions can yet be drawn. In conceptual terms, it remains unlikely that among jobs all of which are of high social value, small differences in that feature will be associated with variations in job holders' happiness, especially of a context-free kind.

The third question concerns the differential proposals in Table 4.2 (p. 108). As well as an expected association with axis 1 of subjective well-being (from feeling bad to feeling good), illustrated in findings summarized above, that table suggested that a principal correlate of valued social position is well-being axis 3, from depression to enthusiasm (see Fig. 2.2 in chap. 2). No research into that comparative possibility has been located.

Table 4.2 also viewed this environmental feature as tending to promote self-validation, an awareness that one is meeting some standards of appropriateness or rightness. Given that a role's socially attributed worth reflects in part its value in a community of people, an empirical association with this second aspect of happiness is to be expected. However, the possibility does not appear to have been examined by psychologists in organizational settings.

JOB FEATURE 10: SUPPORTIVE SUPERVISION

A fourth "constant-effect" feature concerns inputs from a worker's supervisor, long recognized as crucial to job satisfaction (e.g., Ronan, 1970). Research in this field has often been reported in terms of "leadership," focusing on a supervisor's or manager's impact on the behavior and attitudes of his or her subordinates. Between the 1950s and 1970s, aspects of leadership were often examined through items completed by subordinates to record their perceptions of behaviors conventionally labeled as "consideration." Questions asked about a boss's support and respect for staff, his or her concern for their welfare, and his or her tendency to express appreciation for work well done. Behaviors defined as "consideration" included a willingness to listen to and accept subordinates' suggestions, and the feature was thus linked to opportunity for personal control, "vitamin" 1 in the present framework.

As in other facet-specific cases, it is not surprising (because of targeted conceptual overlap) that a leader's considerate behavior has been found to be significantly associated with employees' positive feelings about that leader. A review by Judge, Piccolo, and Ilies (2004) found an average uncorrected correlation with the facet-specific indicator of satisfaction with one's supervisor across 49 samples of +0.68. Kinicki et al. (2002) reported from previous facet-level studies average uncorrected correlations with leader consideration of +0.68 (satisfaction with supervision), +0.26 (satisfaction with work), +0.24 (satisfaction with pay), +0.23 (satisfaction with promotion opportunities), and +0.22 (satisfaction with coworkers).

What about well-being at the domain-specific level? In the meta-analysis by Judge et al. (2004), the average correlation between leader consideration and overall job satisfaction across 76 samples was +0.40. Another meta-analysis by Podsakoff, MacKenzie, and Bommer (1996) examined overall job satisfaction as a function of employees' ratings of their leader's supportiveness. The average correlation (+0.52 across 15 studies) remained significant (+0.43) after statistical control for other leader behaviors. The association with job satisfaction also occurs in aggregate form at the level of entire organizations. For example, Patterson, Warr, and West (2004) examined employees' average overall job satisfaction in 42 manufacturing companies. Across those organizations (rather than at the level of individuals) a company's average job satisfaction was correlated at +0.46 with its employees' average perception of the amount of supervisory support available.

With respect to job-related emotional exhaustion (emphasizing well-being axis 2; see chap. 2), Seltzer and Numeroff (1988) reported a correlation of –0.55 with employees' descriptions of their boss's consideration, an association that remained significant after control for other variables. That form of low well-being was correlated –0.27 with perceived supervisor support in research by Wilk and Moynihan (2005), again remaining significant after control for other variables.

Use of scales tapping supervisory behaviors labeled as "consideration" became unfashionable in the 1980s, as ideas about "transformational" and "transactional" leadership instead attracted researchers' interest. Leader behaviors identified as transformational include inspirational or charismatic activities that inspire motivation and pride, forms of intellectual stimulation to encourage new ways of working, and individualized forms of consideration similar to those assessed in earlier scales with that name (e.g., Avolio, Bass, & Jung, 1999; Bass, 1985).

Research in this area has often focused on (facet-specific) satisfaction with one's supervisor, rather than examining broader aspects of an employee's well-being. Not surprisingly, the subordinates of more transformational leaders report greater satisfaction with those leaders than do employees whose supervisor lacks the characteristics illustrated above. For example, the correlation between transformational leadership and leader satisfaction in an American study was +0.81 (Bycio, Hackett, & Allen, 1995), and a Norwegian value was +0.76 (Hetland & Sandal, 2003). The latter investigation also obtained ratings of transformational behavior from a leader's own supervisor (as well as from his or her subordinates); the correlation of supervisors' ratings of a manager's transformational behavior with subordinates' satisfaction with that manager was +0.69. A meta-analysis by Judge and Piccolo (2004) indicated that average correlations with transformational leadership (corrected for unreliability in predictor and criterion) were +0.71 and +0.58 for satisfaction with one's supervisor and overall job satisfaction, respectively.

Other supervisor behaviors have been labeled as "transactional." Principal activities of that kind include the provision of rewards that are contingent on desired performance and taking corrective action in anticipation of likely problems. (Transactional and transformational behaviors are moderately intercorrelated, and a leader can exhibit both of them; the two should not be treated as mutually exclusive.) Transactional behaviors of those kinds are also associated with subordinates' satisfaction with their leader, averaging a correlation of +0.47 in the study by Bycio et al. (1995) and +0.39 in the project by Hetland and Sandal (2003).

What about particularly low levels of this environmental feature? Unpleasant behaviors by a supervisor can take many forms. Several of those were viewed by Ashforth (1994) within the construct of "petty tyranny," said to occur when a leader abuses his or her power. Factor analysis of subordinates' perceptions of their supervisor suggested six forms of behavior under that heading: favoritism in decision making, belittling subordinates, lack of consideration, forcing conflicts to a resolution, discouraging initiative, and punishment that is not contingent on actual performance. Those and similar behaviors were studied by Tepper (2000) under the label of "abusive supervision." Perceived abuse was found to be correlated with well-being measured 6 months later—negatively with overall job satisfaction (–0.35) and life satisfaction (–0.19), and positively with job-related emotional exhaustion (+0.36) and context-free anxiety and depression (+0.21 and +0.18).

Other studies have focused on leaders' "social-emotional" behavior more generally. For example, Landeweerd and Boumans (1994) found such behavior to be correlated at +0.57 with overall job satisfaction after statistical control of gender, job level, full- or part-time tenure, and length of service. Notions of social support (an aspect of feature 6) have sometimes been applied specifically to helpful behaviors exhibited by a supervisor. Scales to tap supervisory support (very like "consideration" as used earlier) were found by Rafferty, Friend, and Landsbergis (2001) and Bakker, Demerouti, and Euwema (2005) to be correlated at –0.40 and –0.22 with employees' job-related emotional exhaustion. For job-related strain, the correlation was –0.23 with rated supervisor support (labeled as "relational justice") in research by Elovainio, Kivimäki, and Helkama (2001). Huang and van de Vliert (2004) found that employees' reports of a boss's recognition for good work were correlated at +0.29 with overall job satisfaction, and that this association remained significant despite many statistical controls.

Context-free (rather than domain-specific or facet-specific) well-being has less often been examined as a function of supervisory behavior. However, global distress was found by Jones, Smith, and Johnston (2005) to be correlated at –0.23 with support received from managers. Gilbreath and Benson (2004) created an index covering a leader's consideration, communication and supportive activities. Subordinates' descriptions of a boss in those respects (scored so that high values were positive) were found to be correlated at –0.39 with a general measure of context-free distress. Furthermore, that association remained significant after statistical control for other variables also linked to this form of low well-being: support from colleagues, support from relatives and friends, reported health practices (exercise, eating, etc.), and recent stressful life and work events.

The chapter's second question asks about evidence for or against nonlinear relationships. As pointed out by Judge et al. (2004), a leveling off in well-being at higher levels of consideration is not excluded by the frequent reports of associations that are linear. A "constant-effect" pattern is expected within the vitamin framework. Extremely high levels of support from a supervisor are unlikely to actually reduce subordinate happiness in an "additional decrement" pattern. However, nonlinearity appears to be inevitable, because happiness cannot continue to increase at the same rate with more and more support at high levels. This possibility has rarely been considered.

One relevant study was by Fleishman and Harris (1962). Consistent with the expected nonlinear pattern (see Figs. 4.1 and 4.2), they reported diminishing returns to leaders' consideration with respect to subordinates' grievances and turnover. Those behaviors (analyzed in terms of a work group rather than a person) were found to be correlated with supervisors' consideration at low levels but not at medium to high levels of consideration. Rice, Gentile, and McFarlin (1991) examined the amount of employees' contact with their supervisor, a quantitative indicator rather than the more qualitative aspects of supportive supervision considered above. In a study of facet satisfactions, amount of contact was again found to be related to satisfaction with that contact in the nonlinear manner proposed here. Additional enquiries into nonlinearity with other indicators of both supervisor support and happiness are required.

Third, is there evidence that associations with degree of supportive supervision vary between different aspects of happiness? Although all the characteristics examined in this book were selected because they are known to be associated with the first axis of subjective well-being (from feeling bad to feeling good; see Fig. 2.2 in chap. 2), specific relations with axes 2 and 3 and with happiness as self-validation were suggested in Table 4.2. That included the nine environmental features of the initial vitamin model (Warr, 1987), applicable to settings of any kind. As described earlier in the chapter, three additional factors (supportive supervision, career outlook, and equity) also require consideration in occupational environments (but not, for instance, in retirement). The differential possibilities shown in Table 4.2 for all kinds of environment have been extended to embrace those additional job features in Table 5.1.

TABLE 5.1

Expected Principal Correlations Between the 12 Primary job Characteristics and Different Forms of Happiness (In Addition, Associations With Well-Being Axis 1 Are Present in Every Case)

| Environmental Features | Happiness as Well-Being: Diagonal Measurement Axes of Figure 2.2 | | | | Happiness as Self-Validation | |
| | (2a) Anxiety to (2b) Comfort | | (3a) Depression to (3b) Enthusiasm | | | |
	Low Environmental Values	Very High Environmental Values	Low Environmental Values	Very High Environmental Values	Low Environmental Values	Very High Environmental Values
1. Opportunity for personal control (AD)	Positive	Negative	Positive		Positive	Negative
2. Opportunity for skill use (AD)	Negative	Positive			Positive	Negative
3. Externally generated goals (AD)		Negative	Positive			
4. Variety (AD)		Negative	Positive			
5. Environmental clarity (AD)	Positive	Negative	Positive			
6. Contact with others (AD)		Negative	Positive			
7. Availability of money (CE)	Positive		Positive		Positive	
8. Physical security (CE)	Positive		Positive			
9. Valued social position (CE)			Positive		Positive	
10. Supportive supervision (CE)	Positive		Positive		Positive	
11. Career outlook (CE)	Positive		Positive			
12. Equity (CE)	Positive		Positive		Positive	

Supportive supervision is there presented as feature 10. As shown in columns 2 and 4, similarly significant positive associations are expected at low levels with both axes 2 and 3 of subjective well-being. Lack of supervisory support is likely to increase feelings of anxiety (generating low well-being on axis 2) for several reasons. For example, support from a boss that is extremely low may involve "petty tyranny" as illustrated earlier. Or an unsupportive boss may behave in ways that increase the ambiguity of a job setting (feature 5), also making it less controllable (1). Well-being axis 3 (depression to enthusiasm) is implicated in part because of the general assumption (in all entries in column 4) that low values (tending to an absence) of these desirable features can generate feelings of depression. Furthermore, greater supervisor support seems likely to encourage more enthusiastic and active forms of well-being (the positive pole of axis 3). However, evidence about these two possibilities is not available, because measurement attention has been concentrated on indicators of job satisfaction (on axis 1).

Happiness as self-validation is also proposed in Table 5.1 to be linked in the lower range to the level of supervisor support available to an employee. Many supervisors have the power to discourage or encourage subordinates' activities that are experienced as personally worthy or fulfilling. Such a process does of course vary between job settings; in some roles there is greater potential for self-validating activities than in others. Although an association of this kind appears to be likely in some circumstances, research evidence has not been located, either for its general prevalence or for possible contingency factors encouraging or discouraging its presence.

The differential suggestions on Table 5.1 will often be revised in this and later chapters. In order that they are readily available for consideration later, an abbreviated version is presented inside the book's front cover.

JOB FEATURE 11: CAREER OUTLOOK

Another assumed "constant-effect" characteristic in occupational environments (also shown in Table 5.1) was introduced earlier in terms of the opportunity for progress in one's career. A career is often seen as upward progression in an employment hierarchy, probably within a single area of work or even a single organization. However, careers also take other forms, including lateral movements, shifts to alternative roles, and educational activities of several kinds. Arnold (1997) suggested as a broad definition "the sequence of employment-related positions, roles, activities and experiences encountered by a person" (p. 16).

Recent changes in the labor markets of developed countries have been accompanied by greater between-role flexibility and the requirement for more individuals to acquire different skills throughout their paid employment (e.g., Hall & Chandler, 2005). Active management of one's career thus requires forward planning and appraisal of the prospects offered by one's current and other positions. In that context, the 11th job characteristic in Table 5.1 can be an important contributor to employee well-being.

Two aspects of career outlook require examination. First, jobs differ in the security that is offered. In some cases, a job is expected to be available for many years, whereas in other positions an employee is more likely to be declared redundant or otherwise forced to move on. A second aspect of career outlook is the potential for movement to other roles. For many people, this is viewed in terms of opportunities for promotion: Does the job provide me with experience and expertise that will be useful in moving to a higher status position, and/or will such a position be available to me in the future? However, consistent with a broad definition of career (as described earlier), prospects of this kind also include possible opportunities for transitions into other activities that do not necessarily involve upward movement in a hierarchical structure. The availability of sideways transitions is often important to prevent skills becoming obsolescent, opening up future possibilities as well as providing direct benefit in terms of increased skill development (feature 2), more challenging or less challenging goals (number 3), and increased variety (4).

The first aspect of career outlook, job security, has been examined in terms of the perceived likelihood of losing one's job (e.g., Ashford, Lee, & Bobko, 1989; Hellgren, Sverke, & Isaksson, 1999). The prospect of job loss, an anticipation of future harm, has been shown to be associated with impaired context-free as well as job-related well-being. De Witte (1999) summarized several investigations with those findings, and in a review by Sverke, Hellgren, & Näswall (2002) job insecurity was on average correlated at –0.32 with job satisfaction (across 50 samples) and –0.19 with context-free well-being (across 37 samples). Significant associations of those kinds are retained after statistical controls for other job factors and personal characteristics (e.g., Clark, 2005b; de Witte, 1999; Dooley, Rook, & Catalano, 1987; Lim, 1996; Näswall, Sverke, & Hellgren, 2005; Probst, 2005b; Probst & Lawler, 2006).

Note that job security might sometimes be viewed as an aspect of environmental clarity (feature 5 in the present framework). That notion includes the extent to which future events are predictable, but it is evaluatively more varied than is job security as discussed here. Job security involves the prediction merely of one kind of (desirable) outcome, whereas environmental clarity embraces predictability in all respects and with both positive and negative valence. Despite that conceptual separation, an empirical association between the two environmental features may be envisaged. For instance, in making broad assessments of future clarity, employees are likely to include the security of their job as one basis for an overall judgment.

Although this form of career outlook is clearly associated with employee well-being, only limited evidence is available about job security or insecurity with respect to the chapter's second and third questions.

Strazdins, D'Souza, Lim, Broom, and Rodgers (2004) observed similar associations of perceived job insecurity with both context-free anxiety and depression after controls for several job and demographic features. Additional context-free investigations remain desirable. Nevertheless, it seems likely on conceptual grounds that variations in job security will be equally linked to the well-being axes of anxiety-to-contentment and depression-to-enthusiasm (see Table 5.1). A "constant-effect" pattern is also proposed. There is likely to be a (high) level of positive expectation beyond which greater job security becomes of no additional value to a person.

Those patterns can also be envisaged for the second aspect of feature 11 introduced earlier—opportunity for promotion or for another desired transition. In a nationally representative sample of British employees, Clark (1996) reported a significant association of overall job satisfaction with the perceived presence of promotion prospects. A significant positive association of that kind after controls for many other variables was also found by Clark (2005b) in a multination investigation. A nonlinear pattern was reported by Rice et al. (1991) with respect to facet-specific satisfaction with promotion prospects. However, additional research into the wider happiness implications of this aspect of an occupational environment is still required.

JOB FEATURE 12: EQUITY

The final characteristic proposed to have a "constant-effect" in the present framework concerns two aspects of equity: the fairness of a person's relationship with his or her employer, and the fairness of one's organization's relationship with society more widely. Organizational equity of the second kind is sometimes linked to "corporate social responsibility." Equity of the first kind (within the organization itself) has been investigated under the heading of "organizational justice," with particular attention to either "distributive" or "procedural" issues. Distributive justice is concerned with the fairness or otherwise of allocations to different members of a social system, and procedural justice refers to the fairness of the processes that lead to those allocations (e.g., Cropanzano, Goldman, & Benson, 2005). Attention may be directed at unfair discrimination with respect to age, gender or race, for example in choices made between people in the operation of procedures for recruitment and selection, allocation to roles, promotion, training, or encouragement to retire from a job.

Notions of distributive justice derive in part from Homans's (1961) application of social exchange theory, with its emphasis on the value attached to reciprocity in social relationships. Adams (1963) developed this theme with particular respect to financial and material allocations to argue that people are less concerned with the absolute level of certain allocations than with whether they are perceived as fair. Fairness was operationalized through the ratio of one's contributions ("inputs") of effort, knowledge, commitment, and so on to one's outcomes (e.g., pay received, status, etc.), in relation to that input–outcome ratio of relevant other people. The validity of this general approach to distributive justice has been illustrated earlier with respect to employees' pay and subjective well-being.

Procedural justice is a matter of the consistent and fair application of the processes that lead to outcomes of the kind considered earlier. In addition, it has typically been viewed in terms of the opportunities provided for employees to express their opinions about relevant issues. For example, Leventhal's (1980) criteria for the fairness of procedures included consistency of application, freedom from bias, accurate information use, and accordance with perceived moral standards, but also some participation by individuals affected by the process.

Questionnaire items to assess those two aspects of organizational justice have been found to generate separate factors as expected (e.g., Colquitt, 2001). However, outcomes (relevant to distributive justice) and processes (in procedural justice) tend to be linked to each other both conceptually and in practice—for instance, because procedural evaluations are based in part on the outcomes of those procedures. An average correlation of +0.48 between the two aspects of justice was reported from 45 different employee samples by Colquitt, Conlon, Wesson, Porter, and Ng (2001). That value was +0.60 in a later study by Wilson et al. (2004). Other themes have been examined under the label of "interactional" justice, sometimes subdivided into interpersonal treatment (respect and consideration, for instance) and informational provision (adequate communication about relevant issues). However, those themes are not intrinsically part of the concept of equity, and have been placed elsewhere in the present framework, under job feature 6 or 10 (contact with others or supportive supervision).

Distributive and procedural justice are likely to be viewed as desirable in their own right, in that fairness and reciprocity are themselves morally loaded as well as providing personal benefits. In addition, justice helps to establish order in one's world. Low levels of justice carry with them the possibility of apparently arbitrary and unpredictable events, so that injustice can bring about a reduction in environmental clarity (feature 5). That arbitrariness is likely to impair individuals' ability to control their environment (feature 1), so that level of equity is expected to be correlated with both those environmental characteristics. Furthermore, a source of fairness or unfairness may be seen as either an organization itself or an individual representative of that organization, particularly one's supervisor (Cropanzano, Byrne, Bobocel, & Rupp, 2001). When equity or inequity is viewed primarily in terms of supervisory behavior, perceived justice is expected to be linked also with job feature 10, supportive supervision.

These considerations point to the fact that equity can affect happiness in several ways. First is a direct impact: Unjust outcomes or procedures are themselves experienced as negative. Second, equity is associated with other environmental features that are themselves influential. For example, ratings of equity within one's organization were on average correlated at -0.44 with the perceived presence of abusive supervision (an aspect of feature 10) in research by Tepper (2000). Both abusive supervision and inequity were found to significantly predict subjective well-being. Third, the feature may operate with respect to other influential job characteristics. For example, injustice may occur in the allocation to different employees of personal control (1), skill development (2), workload (3), pay (7), or promotion opportunities (11).

Researchers in the area of this book have taken for granted the personal undesirability of injustice, and specific associations with employee unhappiness appear not to have been reported. However, some research has obtained broad assessments of distributive or procedural justice in a person's organization as a whole, finding significant associations with subjective well-being. Colquitt et al. (2001) reported from previous studies average correlations with overall job satisfaction of $+0.46$ and $+0.51$, respectively. In later research by Wilson et al. (2004), those values were $+0.58$ and $+0.55$; in addition, distributive and procedural justice were in that study correlated at -0.21 and -0.19 with context-free depression. Both forms of justice were significantly predictive of job-related emotional exhaustion 6 months later in the study by Tepper (2000; $r = -0.39$ and -0.38 for distributive and procedural perceptions). With respect to life satisfaction at the later time, both correlations were $+0.28$.

Research focusing only on procedural justice includes a study by Lee and Allen (2002). They found that perceptions of that form of equity were correlated at $+0.38$ with activated forms of job-related positive affect (in the top-right section of Figs. 2.1 and 2.2) and at -0.49 with a broad measure of job-related negative affect. Elovainio et al. (2001) reported a correlation of -0.24 with job-related strain, and Kivimäki, Elovainio, Vahtera, Virtanen, and Stansfeld (2003) showed that procedural inequity significantly predicted later context-free distress, despite statistical controls for other job characteristics and several individual behaviors and attributes.

Taris, Kalimo, and Schaufeli (2002) reported that job-related emotional exhaustion (mainly tapping well-being axis 2; see chap. 2) was correlated at –0.22 with equity measured in terms of a comparison made between one's own investment-outcome ratio and that ratio estimated for similar others. Employees' investments were recorded in terms of reported skill and energy, and outcomes were assessed as income, job benefits, recognition, and personal satisfaction. Two aspects of equity theory were examined. First, the researchers asked whether comparison with similar other people (rather than merely one's own personal ratio) was important in that prediction, as argued by Adams and other equity theorists (see the earlier discussion). They found that the within-person ratio of inputs to outcomes was more closely associated with job-related emotional exhaustion ($r = -0.38$) than was that index in comparison with other people (–0.22, discussed earlier). It may thus be that employees' assessment of organizational justice does not depend strongly on comparative judgments about other people, being instead mainly a function of a person's own mental comparisons.

Second, Taris et al. (2002) examined the curvilinear assumption of equity theory. According to Adams (1963), receiving too much (in relative terms) of a positive feature, as well as receiving too little, should create a mental discrepancy that results in negative affect. Examination of three subgroups of employees (underbenefited, equally treated, and overbenefited) revealed a "constant-effect" pattern of the kind proposed in this book. Inequity was linked to reduced well-being (greater emotional exhaustion) in the underbenefited subgroup, but well-being was at a similarly higher level in the other two subgroups; there was no well-being decrement for employees reporting an excess of benefits. This nonlinear pattern occurred for both the within-person and between-person indicators described in the previous paragraph.

Siegrist's (e.g., 1998) model of effort–reward imbalance is also based on the importance of reciprocity in social exchange. However, this model views only negative imbalance (receiving too little) as harmful. Such a lack of reciprocity between inputs and outcomes is assumed to give rise to emotional distress that may lead to cardiovascular and other health disorders. In empirically examining the model, an employee's input to a job has conventionally been assessed narrowly, through a scale of invested "effort" in relation to demands, explicitly omitting other possible troublesome features (Siegrist et al., 2004). Such an index fails to consider many aspects of the environment that may be important in the assessment of equity or inequity.

Reciprocity is sometimes addressed through the notion of a "psychological contract." This has been defined as "an individual's beliefs, shaped by the organization, regarding terms of an exchange agreement between individuals and their organizations" (Rousseau, 1995, p. 9). For McLean-Parks, Kidder, and Gallagher (1998), a psychological contract is "the idiosyncratic set of reciprocal expectations held by employees concerning their obligations (i.e., what they will do for the employer) and their entitlements (i.e., what they expect to receive in return)" (p. 698).

As pointed out by Sutton and Griffin (2004), "psychological contracts have more often been theorized about rather than empirically investigated" (p. 497). It is not surprising that employees have been found to value an employer's upholding of their expectations of that kind. Conway and Briner (2002) recorded perceptions of the degree to which an organization was thought to have kept its promises to an individual. Across two different companies, the average correlation with overall job satisfaction was found to be +0.54. In research by Sutton and Griffin (2004), ratings of the extent to which an employer had broken obligations about job features and human relations practices were correlated at –0.57 with overall job satisfaction.

It is clear that perceived organizational injustice of the first kind introduced above is linked to employees' reduced subjective well-being, although detailed research into different aspects of happiness is still required. The chapter's second question asks about the predicted "constant effect" pattern, as illustrated in Figures 4.1 and 4.2. Nonlinearity appears necessary on logical grounds, in that happiness cannot continue to increase without limit as justice becomes even greater. Level of equity is thus likely to be personally important in the left-hand section of Figures 4.1 and 4.2, but to be less influential, in combination with other inputs to happiness, once a threshold of acceptability has been reached. Findings by Taris et al. (2002; described earlier) support this possibility, but more empirical investigations are needed.

The third question asks about differential relationships, as summarized in Table 5.1 (presented on p. 132 and in abbreviated form inside the book's front cover). In addition to an association with well-being axis 1 (from feeling bad to feeling good; see Fig. 2.2 in chap. 2), it is expected that low to moderate levels of within-organization equity will be associated with both anxiety to comfort (axis 2) and depression to enthusiasm (axis 3). Depression–enthusiasm is expected to be influenced in a lower range because that range covers the lack of something desirable; as summarized in chapter 2, depression arises particularly from an absence of something that is wanted. In addition, low levels of equity are predicted to generate anxiety, because (as illustrated earlier) organizational unfairness or a broken psychological contract can affect other job characteristics that are themselves linked to anxiety.

Given that research in this field has typically investigated only a single aspect of well-being, few comparative findings about multiple axes are available. However, Conway and Briner (2002) examined both diagonal axes of subjective well-being. They found that an employer's perceived adherence to an employee's psychological contract was correlated on average at +0.36 with job-related anxiety–comfort (axis 2) and +0.41 with job-related depression–enthusiasm (axis 3).

Table 5.1 also envisages an association at low to moderate levels between organizational equity and employees' happiness as self-validation (but not at higher levels of equity, within a "constant-effect" relationship). That expectation is based on the possible occurrence of inequity in respects that are of particular personal or moral importance. Given that an employee has remained in an inequitable job setting, he or she is subject to pressures that may violate significant standards, with an associated reduction in experienced self-validation. Greater inequity might in that way lead to a greater sense of moral failure and inauthenticity. Empirical investigations of this possibility would be valuable.

A second form of equity was introduced at the beginning of this section in terms of an organization's relationship with society. It is sometimes the case that a provider of employment is appraised through broad ethical principles, for example, with respect to an organization's treatment of its customers, its concern for global climate change, the management of its waste products, its exploitation of labor in developing countries, or harmful ecological consequences from its products or services. Those ethical aspects of an organization's functioning have rarely been examined by psychologists concerned with employees' happiness or unhappiness, but they undoubtedly are influential in some cases. This second aspect of equity is linked to some themes of feature 9 (valued social position). For example, a job whose activities tend to harm the local community (i.e., with a low score on this aspect of feature 12) is likely also to be viewed as having a low social value (9).

Ethical themes in organizational functioning deserve more research attention than they have received. For some employees or in some organizations, the possibility of unethical dealings with customers or community is of little relevance or concern. But in other cases, low levels of equity can be expected to create unhappiness. The feature is predicted to be of particular significance in the left-hand section of Figure 4.2, with a leveling off (a "constant effect") above moderate levels.

6

Control, Skill, and Goals

Chapters 6 and 7 examine the remaining environmental features of the vitamin model in job settings: opportunity for personal control, opportunity for skill use, externally generated goals, variety, environmental clarity, and contact with others. Those are all viewed as "additional decrement" features (as in Figs. 4.1 and 4.2), such that significant positive associations with happiness at lower levels of a feature are expected to be accompanied by negative associations at very high levels. In effect, for each of these characteristics a person can "have too much of a good thing."

As in the previous chapter, three questions are asked in each case. First, what evidence is available in particular studies about specific associations and possible mechanisms? Second, has the nonlinear proposal been supported empirically? And, third, is the environmental feature linked differentially to different forms of happiness in the ways proposed in Tables 4.2 and 5.1 (also inside the front cover)?

JOB FEATURE 1: OPPORTUNITY FOR PERSONAL CONTROL

Research in many areas of psychology has confirmed the wide-ranging importance of having some personal control over aspects of the environment. That is particularly apparent in negative situations, where, for example, increased control is associated with less unhappiness during illness (Thompson, 2002) and reduces the adverse impact of financial strain on well-being during unemployment (Price et al., 2002).

The benefits of control may be viewed in evolutionary as well as personal terms. An inability to control aversive situations reduces the probability of survival for oneself and one's offspring, as well as being experienced as unwanted and unpleasant. An individual's perception of control is, like several other features, a function of his or her dispositions and cognitive processes as well as of inputs received from the environment. The focus of this chapter is on environmental characteristics, and some within-person themes are considered in chapters 9 to 13.

Control and Happiness

Opportunity for personal control has often been studied in job settings, described as discretion, autonomy, absence of close supervision, self-determination, or participation in decision making. Ganster's (1989) broad definition was "the ability to exert some influence over one's environment so that the environment becomes more rewarding or less threatening" (p. 3). Using similar definitions, Wall and Lischeron (1977) and Greenberger, Strasser, Cummings, and Dunham (1989) showed that most employees in a range of samples desired more control over their job activities than they currently possessed.

Karasek's (1979) approach was in terms of "job decision latitude," defined as "the working individual's potential control over his tasks and his conduct during the working day" (pp. 289–290). Karasek reanalyzed data from male workers in two earlier national surveys, administered in the United States and in Sweden. Measures of job decision latitude varied between the surveys, and involved a combination of experts' assessments with perceptions by job incumbents. Karasek examined both job-related and context-free unhappiness, through employees' reports of job dissatisfaction and broad-ranging distress. He found that both types of well-being were significantly associated with job decision latitude, with greatest unhappiness among employees most lacking that feature.

Karasek's measure of decision latitude covered job characteristics beyond merely opportunity for personal control (e.g., including questions about skill requirements), and other investigators have applied more focused instruments to obtain descriptions from job holders. (See, e.g., the review by Terry and Jimmieson, 1999.) Hackman and Oldham (1975, 1976) examined autonomy, which they defined as "the degree to which the job provides substantial freedom, independence, and discretion to the individual in scheduling the work and in determining the procedures to be used in carrying it out" (1976, p. 258). Their Job Diagnostic Survey included items to measure that aspect of a job, covering personal decisions, the chance to use initiative, and the opportunity for independence in one's work.

Many projects have confirmed those authors' finding that autonomy at work is significantly associated with overall job satisfaction. For example, Loher, Noe, Moeller, and Fitzgerald (1985) carried out a meta-analysis of 28 studies, with a total sample size in excess of 15,000. They reported that the average uncorrected correlation between job autonomy and overall job satisfaction was +0.34. Spector's (1986) average correlation from 44 samples was +0.29, and Fried's (1991) mean value from 20 data sets was +0.50. Later studies of job satisfaction, using different measures of employee-reported control, include those by Greenberger et al. (1989; average $r = +0.33$), Warr (1990b; $r = +0.40$), Moyle (1995; $r = +0.39$), Wall, Jackson, Mullarkey, and Parker (1996; $r = +0.37$), de Jonge, Reuvers, Houtman, Bongers, and Kompier (2000; $r = +0.24$), Spector, Chen, and O'Connell (2000; $r = +0.55$), Jeurissen and Nyklíček (2001; $r = +0.28$), Bond and Bunce (2002; $r = +0.53$), Grebner, Semmer, Lo Faso, Gut, Kälin, and Elfering (2003; $r = +0.32$), Lewig and Dollard (2003; $r = +0.56$), Bordia, Hunt, Paulsen, Tourish, and DiFonzo (2004; $r = +0.30$), Janssen, Peeters, de Jonge, Houkes, and Tummers (2004; average $r = +0.28$), and Wilson et al. (2004; $r = +0.50$).

Opportunity for personal control is thus widely found to be associated with employees' job-related well-being on axis 1 of Figure 2.2. Workers deprived of an opportunity to influence their job activities exhibit greater unhappiness in their work. However, given that job control is itself linked with other variables (such as organizational level, educational qualifications, or certain other job features), it might be argued that these other variables are instead the influential ones. As another example, consider conflict between work and home (an aspect of job feature 3; discussed later). Control opportunity at work is significantly negatively associated with work–home conflict (Butler, Grzywacz, Bass, & Linney, 2005), and that conflict might instead have a major influence on unhappiness.

It is thus necessary also to examine the pattern after statistical control for other relevant features. That has been done in many analyses, and the central finding remains strong. Significant associations between opportunity for personal control and job-related well-being after statistical controls have been reported by, for instance, O'Brien (1982, 1983), Chay (1993), Landeweerd and Boumans (1994), de Jonge et al. (2000), Rafferty et al. (2001), Holman (2002), Janssen et al. (2004), Probst (2005b), and van Vegchel, de Jonge, and Landsbergis (2005). Other features can of course also have an impact on happiness or unhappiness, but the opportunity for personal control (here environmental feature 1) remains significant in itself.

That association is also present at the level of an organization. For example, Patterson et al. (2004) showed that companies in which the opportunity for personal control is perceived on average to be high tend to have employees whose job-related well-being is on average higher than others. Across 42 companies, the correlation between average perceived level of control opportunity and average overall job satisfaction was +0.36.

What about axes 2 and 3 of subjective well-being, from anxiety to comfort and from depression to enthusiasm, respectively? It appears that variations in job control opportunity (usually studied in the lower range) are more associated with job-related depression–enthusiasm (axis 3) than with the other diagonal axis in Figure 2.2 (from anxiety to comfort). For example, personal control opportunity was correlated at only −0.08 with job-related anxiety, but −0.17 with job-related depression, in research by Caplan et al. (1975). In a British national sample, Warr (1990b) found correlations with axis 2 (anxiety–comfort) and axis 3 (depression–enthusiasm; where high scores indicate better well-being) of +0.06 and +0.32, respectively. Those values averaged +0.10 (for anxiety–comfort) and +0.20 (for depression–enthusiasm) in Holman's (2002) investigation, and +0.08 and +0.23 in the report by Holman and Wall (2002). They were +0.09 and +0.21 in Parker's (2003) study, and +0.02 and +0.38 in research by Totterdell, Wood, and Wall (2006). (Note that this differentiation occurs despite the fact that well-being axes 2 and 3 are themselves intercorrelated; the average r value in those studies was +0.54.)

That pattern of difference between correlations also occurs in comparisons between job-related forms of axis 1 (e.g., satisfaction) and axis 2 (anxiety–comfort); associations between control opportunity and anxiety-related forms of well-being are lower than with measures of job satisfaction. For example, Jex and Spector (1996) found that the opportunity for personal control was correlated (on average across two samples) at +0.36 with overall job satisfaction, but only −0.15 with job-related anxiety; in research by Spector and O'Connell (1994), those values were +0.56 and −0.25, respectively. Consistent with this general pattern, de Jonge and Schaufeli (1998) observed within structural equation analyses that variations in job autonomy were more related to job-related axes 1 and 3 than with axis 2 (anxiety–comfort). The relationship with job-related strain (on axis 2) was almost zero in research by Gallie et al. (1998).

In the study by Janssen et al. (2004), opportunity for personal control was more associated with overall job satisfaction (axis 1) than with job-related emotional exhaustion (covering mainly the negative pole of axis 2; see chap. 2). Bakker et al. (2005) found that almost all job features they examined were more strongly linked to emotional exhaustion than was autonomy. Similarly, Peeters and Rutte (2005) reported that job-related emotional exhaustion was less correlated with control opportunity than with work demands (−0.31 and +0.57, respectively).

In addition to links with (domain-specific) job happiness, relevant forms of well-being at the facet level are also associated with this environmental characteristic (e.g., Sims, Szilagyi, & Keller, 1976). In a study by Mathieu, Hofmann, and Farr (1993), the opportunity for control in a job was correlated at +0.49 with satisfaction with growth opportunities and +0.31 with satisfaction with supervision. Spector's (1986) meta-analysis yielded an average correlation across 30 samples of +0.32 with satisfaction with work content; that value in a later study was +0.33 (Probst, 2005b). Associations with facet-level satisfactions depend (as in other cases) on the degree of conceptual overlap between control opportunity and the type of well-being under investigation; stronger correlations occur when the facet and response are more conceptually related. Thus Kinicki et al. (2002) reported average correlations from previous publications of +0.32 with satisfaction with the work itself, +0.25 for satisfaction with supervision, +0.19 for satisfaction with coworkers, +0.16 for pay satisfaction, and +0.13 for satisfaction with promotion opportunities.

Some research has examined separately intrinsic and extrinsic forms of job satisfaction. Payne et al. (1999) found that job control was correlated at +0.37 with intrinsic satisfaction (with features integral to the work content), whereas for extrinsic job satisfaction (with respect to contextual features like working conditions or promotion possibilities) the correlation was +0.19. In Holman's (2002) research, those values averaged +0.29 and +0.11, and for intrinsic satisfaction alone Morrison, Cordery, Girardi, and Payne (2005) reported correlations that averaged +0.27 in two studies. Quinn (2005) examined employees' enjoyment of specific work activities across a week. The availability of personal control over an activity was correlated at +0.57 with enjoyment of that activity.

Other research has looked at associations with control opportunity at the third level of scope, with respect to happiness that is context-free. As noted earlier, Karasek's (1979) examination of national samples in the United States and Sweden found a significant negative association between job discretion and job holders' general distress. That negative association was also observed for life dissatisfaction in the U.S. data and for the consumption of tranquilizers and sleeping pills in the Swedish data. Adelmann (1987) recorded a significant association with a global index of context-free happiness, both before and after statistical controls for employees' age, education, income, and other job features. In studies by Karasek, Triantis, and Chaudhry (1982) and de Jonge et al. (2000), decision authority was correlated respectively at –0.27 and –0.18 with context-free depression.

Chay (1993), Moyle (1995), de Witte (1999), Schat and Kelloway (2000), Beehr, Glaser, Canali, and Wallwey (2001), and Waldenström, Lundberg, Waldenström, and Härenstam (2005) reported correlations with job autonomy of –0.23, –0.26, –0.10, –0.33 (average value), –0.11 (average value), and –0.10, respectively, with generalized distress (score on the General Health Questionnaire [GHQ]; see chap. 2). That measure of context-free distress was examined by Wall, Kemp, Jackson, and Clegg (1986) in relation to autonomy at the level of a work-group. In a comparison between groups, significantly lower distress was found in conditions of greater work-group autonomy.

In research with self-employed workers, Parasuraman, Purohit, Godshalk, and Beutell (1996) recorded a correlation between perceived opportunity for job control and context-free strain of –0.20. The correlation was –0.18 in a study by Wilson et al. (2004) of employees' context-free depression. Kelloway and Barling (1991) examined the association of job autonomy with satisfaction with the work itself and also with general context-free distress. As is typically found, the job characteristic was more closely linked to job-related well-being than to the context-free indicator (+0.45 and –0.22, respectively). Furthermore, path analysis suggested that job-related affect mediated the association with context-free well-being; the context-free association from the job environment was indirect, through happiness or unhappiness that was job-related.

In summary, although this job feature is strongly correlated with job-related happiness, the association with context-free measures (although often significant) tends to be less strong. For example, with respect to axis 1 of Figure 2.2 in chapter 2, the average correlation between opportunity for personal control and job satisfaction is probably between +0.35 and +0.40 (see earlier). However, with context-free distress (measured through the GHQ, as mentioned earlier) that average value is less than –0.20. As considered in chapters 2 and 4, context-free happiness is influenced by a variety of environmental factors in many domains of life, whereas job-related well-being is more exclusively influenced by features in the job domain alone. Correlations with primary job features thus tend to be larger with respect to job-related well-being than with respect to context-free measures.

Research examined so far in this section has typically examined the opportunity for control as a single construct, using an overall measure of that job feature. In addition, some investigators have asked about its more specific forms. For example, Jackson, Wall, Martin, and Davids (1993) created separate indicators of timing control ("the individual's opportunity to determine the scheduling of his or her work behavior," p. 754) and method control ("choice in how to carry out given tasks," p. 754). Another, broader, distinction is between two principal aspects: personal control in relation to local job content (as examined so far) and a wider participation in the organization's decision making. Those may be referred to as "intrinsic" and "extrinsic" control, being focused respectively on a person's job tasks themselves and on broader issues within an organization (Warr, 1987).

The first of these, intrinsic control, has been shown to be important for several aspects of subjective well-being, but least so for the anxiety–comfort axis. In addition to those specific associations, a second-order mode of operation should be noted. With substantial personal control, an employee is able to determine the amount of control that he or she exerts at any point in time. The nature of one's work can thus to some extent be adjusted temporarily or more permanently, increasing or reducing the amount of influence that is exerted. This form of adjustment is not available to those whose control opportunities are restricted; such people must work at levels of control that are both low and unchanging. More generally, raised levels of intrinsic control permit manipulation of other job features, for instance, allowing people to adjust from time to time their level of skill use, goals or variety (features 2, 3, and 4 in the present framework).

Intrinsic control of this kind has sometimes been examined in terms of "job crafting" (Wrzesniewski & Dutton, 2001). Many employees are able to make some adjustments to the content of their work and their relationships with other people. Such job crafting is more possible when a role permits greater discretion (a higher level of feature 1), but it is also a function of the closeness of coupling with other roles; considerable between-employee task interdependence reduces the possibility of modifying one's own activities.

The second form of control, labeled earlier as "extrinsic," concerns influence on other aspects of the work environment, such as wages, hours, refreshment facilities, product designs, and broader company policy. Such influence may be exerted by an employee himself or herself, or be indirect through trade union or other representatives, perhaps involving worker–management negotiations or conflict. Both kinds of extrinsic control have been viewed as forms of employee participation in decision making.

Research into the well-being of employees as a function of their involvement in decision making of those extrinsic kinds has yielded inconsistent findings. In part, this variability comes from between-study differences in the measures applied. Some investigations have examined extrinsic control through employees' reports of achieved influence, parallel to the more proximal focus of many intrinsic control studies (described earlier). For example, Jackson (1983) asked about the amount of influence that individuals had exerted over 13 organizational issues. She found a correlation of +0.28 with overall job satisfaction, and +0.34 and +0.15 with intrinsic and extrinsic job satisfaction, respectively. In general, employees' reports about the level of extrinsic control achieved are significantly associated with overall job satisfaction. For example, Spector (1986) reported an average correlation of +0.35.

However, rather than recording the actual achievement of control (as described earlier), many studies have asked only about the occurrence of problem-solving meetings or some other procedure intended to increase employee participation. Such studies, identifying merely the existence of organizational systems rather than recording achieved influence, are less likely to find a positive association with employee well-being for a range of reasons (Ganster, 1989; Wall & Lischeron, 1977). For example, the meetings may be infrequent, badly run, or inconclusive; topics for discussion may be limited or perceived as irrelevant; an employee may not wish to attend, or indeed may not attend, the meetings; he or she may feel uneasy in discussions of wider company policy; employee opinions may not be acted on; and the meetings may draw attention to additional issues of contention that cannot in practice be resolved.

In settings where procedures for extrinsic control do actually increase employees' influence in decision making, some research has found that job satisfaction is relatively high (e.g., Gardell, 1982). Bond and Bunce (2001) described a quasi-experimental study in which one group of employees engaged in problem-solving discussions to increase their participation in decision making, whereas no such opportunity was provided to a second group. Meetings continued across 3 months, and some 9 months after their termination the experimental group showed a significant reduction in context-free distress relative to the control group. However, no difference was found with respect to overall job satisfaction.

Bond and Bunce speculated that the absence of impact on job satisfaction might have been because changes in that form of well-being were in fact temporary, having dissipated in the intervening 6 months, when no measurements were taken. Alternatively, participative discussions can sometimes impair rather than enhance job-related happiness, as suggestions about desired changes are rejected by management. Extrinsic control procedures can in that way lead to an increase in employee frustration and dissatisfaction, in relation to desires that have been raised by the participative procedures themselves. Findings about well-being as a function of this second form of control opportunity are thus still uncertain.

Nonlinearity and Control

The chapter's second question concerns the proposed nonlinear association between a job feature and employee happiness. In this case, is there evidence for a leveling off and an "additional decrement" for personal control opportunity in relation to context-free happiness as suggested in Figures 4.1 and 4.2a, with a mid-range plateau and a decline in happiness at very high levels of the feature? And is the association increasingly linear for domain-specific and then facet-specific indicators, as proposed in Figures 4.2b and 4.2c? Almost all published research has ignored nonlinear possibilities. However, patterns have sometimes been examined for intrinsic, but not extrinsic, forms of control.

Chapter 4 reviewed arguments and laboratory evidence for relative unhappiness when personal control is very high. For instance, Burger (1989) examined negative affect arising from excessive personal responsibility, in terms of anxiety about poor decision making, cognitive overload, and worry about the unpredictability of multiple outcomes; harmful outcomes from very high levels of personal control were found to be especially likely when decision options are negative. Have those laboratory findings been replicated in job settings?

There is considerable evidence, already described, that very low personal control in a job (analogous to the vitamin-deficiency range) is accompanied by greatest unhappiness, and that more control up to moderate levels is linked to greater subjective well-being. But does that positive relationship extend linearly to the highest levels of control occurring in a job, or (as proposed here) does control opportunity come to exhibit harmful effects above levels that are moderately high? As pointed out earlier, adequate tests of the additional decrement possibility require a substantial number of individuals scoring within the high range of an environmental feature. In practice, few employees with extremely high control are likely to be included in a typical research sample, so that measured opportunity for control often extends only up to moderate values.

Nevertheless, both a leveling off across moderately high control and a downturn at highest levels have been observed in occupational settings. Karasek (1979) found much the same context-free well-being scores across a range of moderate levels of job decision latitude. In addition, there was typically a reversal of association at very high levels of control, when well-being was lower than in jobs of moderate latitude. For example, the probability of severe depression in groups arrayed from very low to very high decision latitude was 0.37, 0.31, 0.18, and 0.22 in American data and 0.23, 0.13, 0.09, and 0.16 in Swedish results. (Different measures and scores were used in the two studies.) For severe life dissatisfaction, a similar pattern, but without a reversal at the highest level, was reported in the American data; from very low to very high job decision latitude, proportions were 0.18, 0.09, 0.03, and 0.04. For job dissatisfaction the pattern was also nonlinear without an "additional decrement" (0.40, 0.20, 0.16, and 0.14). (Those measures were not examined in Sweden.)

Another study testing for nonlinearity was by van Dijkhuizen (1980). Participation in job decisions was found to be significantly negatively associated with job dissatisfaction in the predicted asymmetric curvilinear manner. For employee groups ranging from low to high participation, mean job dissatisfaction scores were 2.90, 2.41, 1.87, 1.60, and 1.73, respectively.

Warr (1990b) examined the three measurement axes of job-related well-being (as in Fig. 2.2 in chap. 2). In a nationally representative British sample, opportunity for personal control was significantly nonlinearly correlated with job satisfaction, with a leveling off but no reversal at the highest level. Mean satisfaction scores were (from low to high control opportunity) 2.60, 3.06, 3.22, 3.47, 3.55, 3.61, and 3.69. However, the associations for job-related anxiety–comfort and depression–enthusiasm were merely linear. Nonlinearity was also present in relation to facet-specific satisfaction with decision-making opportunity in research by Rice et al. (1991). In a study of health care workers, de Jonge and Schaufeli (1998) examined the pattern with respect to overall job satisfaction, job-related anxiety, and emotional exhaustion; in no case was the hypothesized nonlinear pattern observed. (Note that there were few employees with very high personal control in this sample, so that the range of environmental scores was truncated. The authors also speculated that a generally high desire for autonomy in their sample may have encouraged positive reactions to control opportunities at all of the levels investigated.)

Fletcher and Jones (1993) observed significant nonlinearity in the relation of job discretion with job satisfaction and life satisfaction (well-being axis 1) for men but not for women; however, associations with context-free anxiety and depression (axes 2 and 3, respectively) were only linear. The authors pointed out that "job features may need to be much more extreme to produce curvilinear relationships with the context-free measures of strain used in the present study" (p. 328). Data from a sample of nurses also failed to reveal a nonlinear correlation with opportunity for personal job control (Jeurissen & Nyklíček, 2001), a finding that was viewed as probably due to range restriction in the environmental feature; "there were practically no very high scores" (p. 262). As pointed out by Cohen, Cohen, West, and Aiken (2003), tests of curvilinearity "are uninformative at extreme values if data at these extreme values are sparse" (p. 207).

Possible nonlinearity in the relationship between job autonomy and employee happiness was also examined by de Jonge et al. (2000). Combining within a single multiple-regression equation several quadratic functions, they failed to obtain evidence for a nonlinear pattern. Note that the inclusion of squared values for several job features simultaneously tests a different hypothesis from examination of a single quadratic possibility on its own (about job autonomy in this case). By including together several variables in squared form, one is asking whether (here) job autonomy has a unique nonlinear relationship with the happiness index after variance explained by the other quadratic terms has been taken out. That is not the same as asking the more direct question, whether a nonlinear pattern exists with respect to that one variable on its own, and the presence of several other quadratic predictors may modify the observed significance level of the target one. Furthermore, that level of statistical significance can vary between analyses of this kind, depending on which other (in this case, quadratic) terms have been included in an equation.

There is thus some doubt about the appropriate answer to the second question, of whether the predicted nonlinearity occurs with respect to opportunity for personal control. The absence of nonlinearity in some studies may be due to sampling limitations, with an organizational focus on low scores and few respondents with high levels of control, or to the use of combined analyses that extract other nonlinear variance before examining the pattern that is of immediate concern. In conceptual terms, it appears logically necessary that additional increases in control cannot continue to increase happiness at an unchanging rate across ever-increasing control. That conceptual limitation is supported by laboratory investigations (already described) and by some, but not all, studies in employment settings. In practice, of course, if a studied sample of employees has only low to moderate opportunities of this kind, the presence of a merely linear association with subjective well-being is consistent with both the "vitamin" assumption and the traditional perspective, because those two make the same prediction across the lower range of environmental values.

Control and Different Aspects of Happiness

The chapter's third question is about predicted differences in associations with different aspects of happiness. It was suggested in Tables 4.2 and 5.1 that at low levels of control opportunity this environmental feature was likely to be equally correlated with depression–enthusiasm and anxiety–comfort. The limited research into this question has concerned job-related rather than context-free well-being, and points clearly to a stronger association for depression–enthusiasm (measurement axis 3) than for anxiety–comfort (axis 2). Correlations cited earlier in the chapter averaged +0.27 and +0.07. That pattern is consistent with the general supposition in chapter 2 that deprivation or loss (here seen in a lack of control opportunity) more generate feelings of depression than of anxiety.

However, the smaller associations with job-related anxiety–comfort than with job-related depression–enthusiasm clash with the specific expectation in Tables 4.2 and 5.1, that low opportunity for control will provoke both anxiety as well as depression. It is possible that such a pattern is found with respect to a life space more generally and for anxiety that is context-free rather than job-specific. Within a job, a low opportunity for personal control is not usually linked to threat and danger, being more a routine lack of influence or an absence of something desirable, but in life more broadly a low level of personal control can be critically threatening to the self in substantial ways, as one is unable to escape from danger or handle obstacles to living.

A different contrast between axes 2 and 3 is expected at high levels of this and other "additional decrement" features. As discussed in chapter 2, anxiety arises primarily from settings of threat or excessive load, rather than from the absence of a desirable feature. Very high levels of personal control are thus more likely to increase anxiety (on axis 2) than affect a person's level of depression (axis 3). Comparative between-axis information at high levels of opportunity for personal control appears not to be available.

We also lack research findings about self-validation as a function of this environmental feature. Tables 4.2 and 5.1 proposed that this second form of happiness is linked to control opportunity at both low and high levels (positively and negatively respectively), because this environmental characteristic offers choice and sometimes the potential for personal growth. Waterman's (1993) research with undergraduate students applied a measure of personal expressiveness (introduced in chap. 2 as an instance of self-validation), finding that this was correlated on average at +0.23 with feelings of being in control of an activity. In the absence of direct evidence in employment settings, possible links with self-validation might be viewed indirectly, through employees' satisfaction with opportunities for personal growth in their job. Spector's (1986) meta-analysis across eight studies revealed an average correlation of growth satisfaction with the opportunity for personal control of +0.49. It remains very likely that this environmental feature is associated with happiness as self-validation, but support is so far clearly limited.

JOB FEATURE 2: OPPORTUNITY FOR SKILL USE

The second "additional decrement" feature to be considered in this chapter is the extent to which a job provides opportunities for the use and development of skills. Skills involve procedural knowledge in both physical and mental activities, and there is considerable evidence that employees who are restricted in their use of skill are less happy than others.

The personal value of skill use may be illustrated through studies described by Lewin, Dembo, Festinger, and Sears (1944). They examined success and expected success in moderately difficult laboratory situations of practical problem-solving or sensorimotor performance. A recurrent finding was that success at a task led to a raised aspiration level, where that was defined in terms of how high to set the goal on the next attempt. This fact may be interpreted in terms of a tendency for people to set higher and higher goals until success becomes uncertain. People like to undertake moderately difficult tasks, where they can apply their skills in the search for goal attainment.

Opportunity for learning was a key environmental feature in the model of thriving at work proposed by Spreitzer et al. (2005). This defined thriving as the joint experience of learning and vitality, which together permit and encourage a sense of forward movement and self-development. Both vitality and processes of learning were viewed as essential within thriving and its "desirable subjective experience" (p. 37). Without some opportunities for learning, thriving at work becomes impossible.

Skill Use and Happiness

Two aspects of this job variable are important to happiness: the potential to use skills already possessed, and the opportunity to acquire new skills. With respect to skill use, all adults have acquired over time a range of competencies and expertise, and they value situations which will channel those into rewarding activities. For instance, Kornhauser (1965) studied manual workers in a car-assembly factory, finding sharp differences in overall job dissatisfaction based on answers to "Does your job give you a chance to use your abilities?" Many workers in that setting, especially those on an assembly line, reported being required to carry out only simple tasks that made no use of their abilities. Job-related well-being was particularly low in that subsample. "Decidedly the strongest influence is exerted by workers' feelings that the job does or does not give them a chance to use their abilities" (p. 129).

Similar associations have been reported in many subsequent studies. For example, the mean correlation between perceived opportunity for skill use and job satisfaction across six investigations cited by Warr (1987, p. 93) was +0.40; in research by Neil and Snizek (1988), that value was +0.37, and the average correlation across two samples in Ganzach's (2003) research was +0.48. In O'Brien's (1982) comparison, the effect of this job feature was more substantial than that of any other job characteristic, and in multiple regressions by Allen and van der Velden (2001), self-rated skill underutilization was strongly correlated with low overall job satisfaction despite controls for a wide range of job and demographic characteristics. For intrinsic job satisfaction, Morrison et al. (2005) found an average bivariate correlation with skill use in two samples of +0.53, and for job-related emotional exhaustion Lee and Ashforth (1996) reported an average value of –0.20 across seven studies.

The negative impact of working at too low a level of skill comes partly from frustration of a desire to undertake challenging activity (as illustrated by Lewin et al., 1944, described earlier) and to experience positive feelings from the application of expertise and the achievement of goals. Considerable pleasure can be gained from the application of skills to meet acceptable challenges. Aspects of that process are examined as experienced "flow" later in the chapter. At this stage the general point is that the presence of this second "vitamin" can significantly enhance subjective well-being.

Variations in the opportunity for skill use can be accompanied by differences in other important environmental characteristics. Jobs that prevent skill use tend to be simple and repetitive, providing few externally generated goals and little task variety (features 3 and 4 in the present framework). Low skill use also implies little opportunity for personal control (feature 1); for example, the average correlation between those features was +0.50 in two studies by Morrison et al. (2005). Note, however, that raised control in a job can sometimes involve routine activities, without a need for high skill use.

This environmental characteristic also varies with occupational level, educational qualifications, and socioeconomic status, and it might be thought that differences in those respects are primarily responsible for the observed impact of skill use in a job. A broader influence of that kind does seem likely, but the strong association of skill use with subjective well-being is maintained after holding constant other features. For example, this has been found in multiple regression analyses that control for occupational level and other job characteristics (Allen & van der Velden, 2001; Huang & van de Vliert, 2004) and also in studies restricted to narrow occupational groupings (O'Brien, 1982). Kornhauser (1965) examined the issue among manual employees "within the same or similar types of work" (p. 98) in car factories in a single locality, finding that perceived opportunity for skill use was strongly negatively linked to job dissatisfaction even in that very homogeneous sample.

Turning to subjective well-being of broader scope, context-free indicators have also been found to be significantly correlated with opportunity for skill use in a job. For example, de Witte (1999) reported a correlation of –0.24 with generalized distress (General Health Questionnaire score; see chap. 2), finding that this association remained significant after statistical controls for other variables. Kornhauser's (1965) investigation involved interviews lasting several hours to identify employees' happiness in terms of life satisfaction, attitudes, activities, and neurotic symptoms. A significant difference in context-free happiness was found between employees with less and more opportunity for skill use in their job; that difference was also present in separate analyses of subsamples based on age and skill level. O'Brien (1980) obtained similar findings with another broad index at the context-free level.

Studies reviewed so far in this section have concerned the first of the feature's two aspects introduced earlier. In addition to the application of skills already possessed, the opportunity to acquire new skills is also important. Those two are in practice interrelated, as skill use in challenging situations often requires a person to extend his or her expertise to meet new or difficult demands. The acquisition of new skills is itself likely to be encouraged by other job features (e.g., in conditions of high goal-related challenge or job variety, features 3 or 4) and is central to some people's assessment of career outlook (11). Examining forms of career progression, Hall and Chandler (2005) emphasized interdependency between skills and goals ("vitamins" 2 and 3) through the notion of repeated "learning cycles" in new challenging situations. "Within each learning cycle we would expect to see yet smaller cycles of goal-setting, effort, psychological success, and identity change, as the person gains experience and achieves a high level of performance and mastery" (p. 158). Hacker's (1986) application of action theory in work settings emphasized that skill enhancement to meet job challenges is central to personal development.

In research reported by Wilson et al. (2004), employees' perceptions of the opportunities available for them to update current skills or to acquire new skills were more strongly associated with subjective well-being than almost any other job characteristic. Correlations with overall job satisfaction and negative job-related affect were +0.59 and –0.36 respectively, and for context-free depression that value was –0.25. This pattern is also present for organizations as a whole; higher average levels of skill development are linked to higher average job-related well-being. Across 42 companies, Patterson et al. (2004) found that average employee perceptions of a company's emphasis on staff development were correlated at +0.74 with average overall job satisfaction.

Nonlinearity and Skill Use

Is opportunity for skill use in a job related to employees' happiness in the nonlinear pattern identified here as one of additional decrement? A little information is available about the application of skills already possessed (the first aspect of this feature), but no evidence has been located about the nonlinearity with respect to new acquisition possibilities. Van Dijkhuizen (1980) presented mean scores of job dissatisfaction for subgroups defined by their perceived opportunity for skill use. For those arrayed from low to high skill use, job dissatisfaction means were 2.69, 2.07, 1.89, 1.65, and 1.71, respectively. That is as predicted, with an asymmetric U-shaped pattern. However, analyses of subjective well-being in terms of job-related anxiety and depression yielded inconsistent results. O'Brien (1982) indicated that "some evidence obtained from the present sample" (p. 234) suggested that excessively high opportunity for skill use was associated with reduced job satisfaction, but numerical values were not presented. There is thus some support for the expected nonlinearity, but additional investigations are clearly needed before a definite conclusion can be reached.

Skill Use and Different Aspects of Happiness

The chapter's third question concerns possibly different associations with different aspects of happiness. It was suggested in Tables 4.2 and 5.1 that, in addition to significant correlations with the first axis of subjective well-being, opportunity for skill use in the low range would be more associated with depression–enthusiasm (axis 3) than with anxiety–comfort (axis 2). There is little published information about this possibility, but limited empirical support comes from the project by Caplan et al. (1975). Skill underutilization was found to be correlated at only +0.09 with context-free anxiety (the negative pole of axis 2) but +0.17 with depression (a low score on axis 3). A parallel comparison is between axes 1 and 2. Research reviewed earlier in the section has shown that job-related emotional exhaustion (mainly covering negative forms of axis 2) is correlated at around –0.20 with the opportunity for skill use, whereas for job satisfaction (axis 1) that average value is much larger, being above +0.40.

Consistent with a shift from being a desirable input at low levels of the opportunity to being a coercive requirement at very high levels, the correlation is expected to turn negative and to be stronger for anxiety than for depression at extremely high levels of skill use. No evidence about that possibility has been found.

As summarized in Tables 4.2 and 5.1, opportunity for skill use is also likely to bear upon employees' happiness as self-validation. Skills enhance a person's potential contribution to others and can be at the core of activities which are personally meaningful. Their importance to self-validation is reflected in Kornhauser's (1965) conclusion that skill utilization was the most important aspect of job content studied. "One set of characteristics is outstandingly influential: the chance the work offers a man to use his abilities, to perform a worthwhile function, to fulfil his role as a competent human being, and to find interest in his work and a sense of accomplishment and self-respect" (p. 131).

Waterman (1993) argued that feelings of personal expressiveness (identified as "self-realization"; see chap. 2) "occur specifically in connection with activities affording opportunities for individuals to develop their best potentials, that is, further the development of their skills and talents, advance their purposes in living, or both" (p. 680). In two investigations with students, an average correlation of +0.45 was found between personal expressiveness and reported opportunities of that kind.

One particular aspect of self validation was described in chapter 2 as "flow" (e.g., Csikszentmihalyi, 1999; Quinn, 2005). This experience can occur when a person has skills that are in balance with a challenging level of task demands. In those moderately difficult situations, a person can become absorbed in task activities, applying his or her skills and adjusting activities in response to feedback received. Flow can be experienced only when a person is required to work at a high level of skill; jobs that do not call for skill utilization necessarily prohibit the experience of flow. This and other forms of self-validation now require examination in job settings.

JOB FEATURE 3: EXTERNALLY-GENERATED GOALS

A third "additional decrement" feature within the vitamin framework was identified in chapter 4 as externally generated goals. Environments vary in the demands they make on a person for mental or physical activity. At low levels of this situational characteristic a person is set few objectives and is under little external pressure for action. At intermediate levels, he or she is encouraged by the environment to work toward goals that are to varying degrees easy or difficult to reach. Very high levels of externally generated goals require people to work toward many and/or difficult objectives, often causing them to feel rushed, unable to maintain quality or quantity of output, and perhaps to fail to cope with the heavy demands upon them.

Goals may be defined as "internal representations of desired states" (Austin & Vancouver, 1996, p. 338). They vary between themselves in many different respects, but have in common an essential concern for the management of affect; for Judge et al. (2005), goals are "the central organizers of affect" (p. 265). Broadly speaking, they may be self-set or externally generated. The two sources of goals (oneself and the environment) are interdependent in several ways, and a mixture of sources is common. For example, activity that is internally generated often places a person in settings that themselves create new or additional demands. Similarly, external pressures can themselves link with personal motives to yield a combined influence. That combined process has sometimes been viewed as a blending of both "intrinsic" and "extrinsic" motivation.

Ryan and Deci (2001) emphasized that those two sources of goals are not mutually exclusive, and that extrinsically motivated activities (via externally generated goals) are internally regulated to varying degrees. They proposed a continuum of internalization of demands, from those that remain completely externally determined to forms of autonomous motivation. (See also Gagné & Deci, 2005.) On the one hand, activity that is entirely externally determined has no personal motivation, being mere compliance or undertaken solely for extrinsic reward or to avoid punishment. However, some external demands lead to actions that are also internally motivated through the involvement of personal values and objectives. Many situations thus give rise to a mixture of both external and internal regulation, and goals that are originally externally generated can contribute to happiness or unhappiness in both those ways.

The overlap between externally and internally generated goals has long been of interest to psychologists outside job settings. Flügel (1948) drew attention to processes whereby a person may have to commence an activity without a desire to do so (e.g., eat a meal when not hungry), but "very soon the food to which we were at first indifferent becomes attractive" and "we end by consuming a fair-sized meal with enjoyment" (p. 171). This self-sustaining process may be viewed in terms of the "functional autonomy of motives" (Allport, 1937), such that a line of activity, once started, may perpetuate itself without further input from the motives that originally prompted it.

It is clear that not all motivation is functionally autonomous in that sense, but self-sustaining processes based initially on external goals are likely to occur frequently in work situations. Baldamus (1961) analyzed activities in repetitive factory tasks, noting that even in those monotonous activities some satisfaction is often derived from the "traction" that is present. Traction "is a feeling of being pulled along by the inertia inherent in a particular activity. The experience is pleasant and may therefore function as a relief from tedium" (p. 59). Baldamus saw traction as similar to the rhythm, swing, or pull of work, such that "there is usually a distinctly pleasant sensation in being guided or pulled along by the process in completing a given work cycle" (p. 63). His focus was on short-cycle manual tasks, but positive affect may also derive from the traction in many other work activities. External demands can in that way give rise to activities that may yield some pleasure quite unconnected to the original source of those activities.

Goals and Happiness

Linked to the themes just discussed is the possibility that activity itself can be enjoyable, in addition to its potential value as a means to goal attainment. For example, Murray (1938) distinguished between sources of pleasure either in activity or in achievement. In language more fashionable several decades ago, he saw "activity pleasure" as accompanying the rise of "energy" and its discharge, whereas "achievement pleasure" was associated with "the conquest of oppositions to the will" (p. 91).

The personal value of pressures to action has since been stressed in research into the harmful psychological effects of unemployment. Being unemployed reduces the external requirements for activity, through both an absence of regular times for work-place attendance and the removal of task-related problem solving within a job. As noted in chapter 3, those reductions in externally generated goals can be a major contributor to impaired well-being for many unemployed people (Jahoda, 1982; Warr, 1987).

The temporary absence of external demands was central to some early psychoanalytic conceptions of a "Sunday neurosis." Ferenczi (1918/1926), writing at a time when Sunday was often the only day free of work, observed that removal of job obligations and disciplines was sometimes associated with neurotic and psychosomatic symptoms on that day. He viewed this in terms of an external and inner "liberation," which permitted repressed impulses and punishment fantasies to be mobilized against the self. That account was consistent with Freud's (1930) view of work as a person's strongest tie to reality, providing links and commitments that prevent a person from becoming overwhelmed by fantasy and emotion. Abraham (1918/1950) extended the notion of Sunday neuroses to holidays and vacation periods of all kinds. "A considerable number of persons are able to protect themselves against the outbreak of serious neurotic phenomena only through intense work. In this way the mental balance which has been maintained with difficulty through working is overturned for the duration of a Sunday, a holiday, or possibly even for a longer period" (pp. 313–314).

A general beneficial impact of demands from the environment can be seen more specifically in the association between goal achievement and subjective well-being. Several studies have shown that reduced distance from a goal (a "desired state"; see earlier discussion) is in general likely to be associated with better well-being. For example, progress in the achievement of goals is a significant predictor of change in university students' well-being (Brunstein, 1993; Koestner, Lekes, Powers, & Chicoine, 2002). The same pattern has been found in employment settings, where attainment of work goals contributes to people's overall job satisfaction (Maier & Brunstein, 2001; Roberson, 1990), to their end-of-shift job-related affect (Harris, Daniels, & Briner, 2003), and to improvements in their well-being in subsequent months (Kehr, 2003).

In a 3-year longitudinal study, Wiese and Freund (2005) showed that progress toward work goals was significantly related to improvements in context-free affect and in overall job satisfaction. However, that was only the case for more difficult goals; attainment of easy goals was unrelated to improvements in subjective well-being. It seems likely that the magnitude of impact of goal achievement on happiness is a function of the level of personal challenge that is provided. Judge et al. (2005) focused on congruence with an employee's own wants, viewing the attainment of personally congruent goals as a likely source of subjective well-being. In a study of students, reported attainment of six previously identified life goals was found to be correlated at +0.32 with life satisfaction. However, in a sample of employees that correlation with respect to the attainment of prior work goals and overall job satisfaction was only +0.16, perhaps because goals considered important several weeks ago were no longer of central concern at the time of later data collection. Happiness as a function of movement toward a goal is further considered in chapter 9.

A goal has by definition some personally attractive qualities, and achievement of a goal can thus directly yield happiness. However, this aspect of people's interaction with their environment illustrates that the pursuit of happiness can involve sustained and unpleasant effort to overcome obstacles and restrictions. As suggested by a longitudinal examination of goal attainment, "you can hope to make yourself happier, but it will take hard work to get there, and more hard work to stay there" (Sheldon & Houser-Marko, 2001, p. 161). Extended happiness, often built around the generation and attainment of a succession of goals, is a matter of negative as well as positive feelings at different times and in different respects.

Some researchers have argued (as illustrated in chap. 2) that goal attainment linked to extrinsic motivation is less productive of happiness than is the attainment of goals that are intrinsic. Despite that possible difference, interdependence between the two sources of motivation (examined earlier) ensures in practice that externally generated activity can become linked to more internal sources of positive experience. Furthermore, failure to meet external demands in a job can result in clearly negative outcomes, so that (despite an extrinsic source) the personal significance of demands imposed by a role can be substantial. Note also that progress toward the attainment of goals, whether externally or internally generated, usually involves enhanced (probably desirable) environmental variety (feature 4). Lack of progress implies an unchanging environment as well as indicating that a goal is as far away as previously.

Low Demands.   As with other primary job features, short periods of low environmental demand may be attractive, for example, providing relaxation or an opportunity to engage in different activity. However, extended situations of unchanging low demand in a job or elsewhere are likely to have a negative impact on a person's well-being. In addition to a linked reduction in goal achievement (discussed earlier), a lack of demands from the environment tends to be accompanied by low levels of other environmental features, such as opportunity for control (1), opportunity for skill use (2), and variety (4). Low levels of externally generated goals tend also to be accompanied by high environmental clarity (5), another "additional decrement" feature with a negative impact at high levels.

Low job demands were investigated in Britain by the Industrial Fatigue Research Board during the 1920s. (The organization's title was changed to "Industrial Health Research Board" in 1927 [Warr, 2006a].)

For example, with a focus on repetitive work in machine-feeding situations, Wyatt and Langden (1938) emphasized the importance of a moderate workload to maintain motivation and satisfaction. "Machine speeds which are much below the capacity of the workers are almost as undesirable as those which exceed this level" (p. 9). Underload in that research took the form of extremely simple actions that were frequently repeated in manual workers' response to machine requirements.

Many other situations with low externally generated goals require few actions of any kind, described by Johansson (1989) as "uneventful monotony." Those situations provide very little stimulation and elicit almost no action, but they can demand continuous attention in case action becomes needed. They may involve vigilance, inspection, monitoring, or merely waiting for long periods for some demands to present themselves.

More generally, low-demand jobs were shown by Caplan et al. (1975) to be associated with substantially greater job dissatisfaction than other jobs. Melamed, Ben-Avi, Luz, and Green (1995) examined reported underload in a sample of blue-collar employees, recording correlations with intrinsic job satisfaction of –0.21 and –0.42 for men and women, respectively. However, recent research has rarely focused on job demands that are low.

Task Identity. One specific aspect of goals within a job is the degree to which they give rise to a coherent structure of activities, sometimes referred to as "task identity." Hackman and Oldham (1975, 1980) defined that as "the degree to which the job requires completion of a 'whole' and identifiable piece of work; that is, doing a job from beginning to end with a visible outcome" (1975, p. 257). That and similar definitions (e.g., Sims et al., 1976) link task identity to the availability of feedback, which is considered in the next chapter, and in practice measures of the two constructs are positively intercorrelated.

It is consistently found that workers whose jobs have greater task identity exhibit higher overall and intrinsic job satisfaction (e.g., Hackman & Oldham, 1980). The meta-analysis by Loher et al. (1985) found from 28 studies an average uncorrected correlation with overall job satisfaction of +0.24. The average correlation with intrinsic job satisfaction in Fried's (1991) meta-analysis was +0.27. For (facet-level) satisfaction with growth opportunity and satisfaction with supervision, correlations with task identity were +0.43 and +0.25 in research by Mathieu et al. (1993). Across the five facet satisfactions covered by the Job Descriptive Index (see chap. 2), average correlations with task identity range (in parallel with degree of conceptual overlap) from +0.12 (for satisfaction with promotion opportunities) to +0.31 (for satisfaction with the work itself; Kinicki et al., 2002). The presence of a coherent internal structure in one's work is clearly linked to conceptually related forms of job-related happiness.

In overview, research of several kinds has shown that low levels of externally generated goals in a job, as well as goals that fail to create a coherent whole, are accompanied by low subjective well-being. The studies cited earlier have examined domain-specific (job-related) or facet-specific forms of well-being, but overlaps between goal demands and other key features of the environment (discussed previously) suggest that links might also be present in this low range with happiness that is context-free. Future studies of low demands need to extend across a wider range of happiness indicators.

High Demands.   What about the proposed decrease in happiness to the right-hand side of Figures 4.1 and 4.2, the "additional decrement" of the vitamin model? That possibility is reflected in common use of the term *overload* for that right-hand segment, whereas *underload* can describe the deficiency range examined above. Similarly, employees sometimes refer to an "optimum level of stress," indicating that they aspire to a moderate level of demand that will require some effort but that does not become excessive. There is considerable evidence (described later) for a negative association with well-being in conditions of high work demands, when employees are subject to pressures that are difficult to cope with. Overload can be "quantitative" when one has too much work to do in the time available, "qualitative" when required tasks are beyond one's abilities, or both quantitative and qualitative together.

Some projects have examined particular aspects of overload. For example, Jackson et al. (1993) created separate measurement instruments for problem-solving demand, monitoring demand and production responsibility. Load scores of a physical (rather than mental) kind were studied by MacDonald, Karasek, Punnett, and Scharf (2001). They developed assessment procedures for upper-extremity load (on employees' shoulders, neck, arms, etc.) and for demands made on their back and legs. Physical load of both kinds was greatest in repetitive jobs with a short cycle time and a machine-regulated pace. Other particular instances of overload include emotional dissonance, role conflict, and interference between work and family activities; those are considered shortly.

Common to many situations of overload is a high level of unwanted interruption. In a job that places heavy demands on an employee, goal achievement becomes increasingly difficult if activities are frequently interrupted by demands from other people or the work process itself. Externally imposed interruptions are often unpredictable in their timing and duration, and thus provide at irregular intervals obstacles to achieving one's goals as well as creating additional demands to be met within a period of task activity.

Kirmeyer (1988) recorded the nature and frequency of interruptions in particular work settings. She observed three ways in which additional demands of that kind were handled. Most straightforward was sequential processing, when an ongoing task was completed before an interrupting demand was dealt with. More problematic was "preemption," when an incoming demand brought to an end a current task, leaving it unfinished while the interruption was dealt with. Also difficult was "simultaneity," when both demands were handled together for a period before an interruption's goals became predominant. Those processes are likely to be found in jobs of many kinds, being important elements in the development of overload.

Leitner and Resch (2005) examined work interruptions in terms of the amount of consequential time devoted to extra tasks without improving performance. Office employees were observed for between 2 and 8 hours, recording "hindrances to task performance that have to be dealt with in addition to the regular task, without resources being made available by management for this purpose" (p. 20). The study found that the average amount of time devoted to coping with hindrances of that kind was nearly 6 hours in a week.

There is no doubt that greater job demands in the high range of this environmental feature are associated with greater unhappiness of several kinds. With respect to the first axis of job-related well-being, Warr (1987) cited previous investigations yielding an average correlation with job satisfaction of -0.31. Later studies with similar findings include those by de Jonge and Schaufeli (1998; average $r = -0 20$), Payne et al. (1999; $r = -0 20$), de Jonge et al. (2001; average $r = -0 35$), Janssen (2001; $r = -0 21$), Jeurissen and Nyklíček (2001; $r = -0.49$), Lewig and Dollard (2003; $r = -0 24$), Janssen et al. (2004; average $r = -0 30$), and Wilson et al. (2004; $r = -0 28$). With respect to a facet-specific indicator, satisfaction with workload, Caplan et al. (1975) recorded a correlation of -0.35. Significant associations of high demands with low job satisfaction have been retained after statistically controlling for other variables in analyses by, for instance, Karasek

(1979), O'Brien (1982), Landeweerd and Boumans (1994), de Jonge et al. (2001), Janssen (2001), and Janssen et al. (2004),

Nevertheless, several studies with diverse samples have observed correlations between job demands and overall job satisfaction that are around zero. These include Caplan et al. (1975; $r = +0.04$), Warr (1990b; $r = +0.10$), Chay (1993; $r = -0.05$), Spector and O'Connell (1994; $r = 0.00$), Moyle (1995; $r = +0.11$), Wall et al. (1996; $r = +0.02$), de Jonge et al. (2000; $r = -0.08$), Spector et al. (2000; $r = +0.01$), van Yperen and Janssen (2002; $r = -0.07$ with intrinsic job satisfaction), van Rijswijk, Bekker, Rutte, and Croon (2004; $r = -0.13$), Aryee, Srinivas, and Tan (2005; $r = -0.08$), and Morrison et al. (2005; $r = +0.07$ in Study 1).

The inverted U shape proposed across the range of the environmental feature in Figures 4.1 and 4.2 implies that the correlation between externally generated goals and happiness will vary according to the location of respondents along the horizontal axis. For example, employees in wide-ranging samples, as studied by Caplan et al. (1975) and Warr (1990b), may extend broadly across the range, with positive and negative associations expected at different levels of demand and thus an overall absence of intercorrelation. Similarly, when the demands on study participants fall mainly in the moderate range, correlations between demands and happiness are expected to be close to zero. And research that reveals strong negative associations is instead likely to involve a sample primarily in the "additional decrement" zone of high demands.

A high level of externally generated goals has also been found to be associated with low scores on axis 2 of job-related well-being. That measurement axis, from feelings of anxiety to comfort as shown in Figure 2.2, includes unhappiness in terms of tension and strain. Negative feelings of that kind are expected to flow from excessive demands, a hectic pace, and an awareness of potential coping collapse. The correlation with job-related anxiety reported by Spector et al. (2000) was +0.49, and Glazer and Beehr (2005) reported a consistent pattern in four different countries, with an average correlation with job anxiety of +0.48. Note that the job feature was there recorded overtly as "overload," with items explicitly covering "too much" work rather than being merely descriptive of job content. That was also the case in research by Geurts, Kompier, Roxburgh, and Houtman (2003), who found an average correlation of +0.52 across three samples with a scale primarily tapping job-related anxiety. Correlations between workload and job-related anxiety–comfort (axis 2, where a high score indicates greater well-being) were −0.21 (average; Martin & Wall,

1989, study 2), –0.26 (Warr, 1990b), –0.27 (average; Daniels & Guppy, 1997), –0.22 (average; Holman & Wall, 2002), –0.30 (average; Parker, 2003), and –0.20 (Totterdell et al., 2006).

On the other hand, associations of job demands with the third measurement axis, from depression to enthusiasm, are often nonsignificant. Correlations with job-related depression–enthusiasm in projects by Martin and Wall (1989), Warr (1990b), Holman and Wall (2002), Parker (2003), and Totterdell et al. (2006) were 0.00 (average), +0.05, –0.03 (average), –0.04 (average) and +0.04. A similar contrast is found between correlations with axis 2 (anxiety–comfort) and with axis 1 (e.g., job satisfaction). Those correlations with workload in two samples averaged –0.42 and –0.16, respectively, in research by Jex and Spector (1996), and were –0.29 and – 0.08, –0.55 and –0.07, and –0.48 and 0.00 in studies by Keenan and McBain (1979), Chen and Spector (1991), and Spector and O'Connell (1994). (In all of those cases, scales have been presented so that a higher score indicates raised well-being.)

As described in chapter 2, well-being has sometimes been investigated in terms of job-related "burnout." The principal feature of this has been viewed as job-related emotional exhaustion (Maslach, 1982; Maslach et al., 2001), in terms of negative reactions to a job particularly of tension, strain, and fatigue. Emotional exhaustion as conventionally measured thus primarily covers anxiety-related aspects of axis 2 in the present framework, but the construct is somewhat broader than specified by that axis.

Maslach (1998) saw the principal sources of emotional exhaustion as being "work overload and personal conflict" (p. 69). Studies of workload in relation to this form of job-related unhappiness yielded an average correlation of +0.52 in the meta-analysis by Lee and Ashforth (1996). Subsequent investigations obtained, for instance, correlations of +0.51 (average of two values; de Jonge et al., 2001), +0.52 (Rafferty et al., 2001), +0.54 (Zellars & Perrewé, 2001), +0.46 (Bakker, Demerouti, de Boer, & Schaufeli, 2003), +0.39 (Harvey, Kelloway, & Duncan-Leiper, 2003), +0.44 (Houkes, Janssen, de Jonge, & Bakker, 2003), +0.32 (Lewig & Dollard, 2003), +0.41 (average of three measurement occasions; Demerouti, Bakker, & Bulters, 2004), +0.51 (average of two samples; Janssen et al., 2004), +0.28 (Schaufeli & Bakker, 2004), +0.39 (Bakker et al., 2005), +0.57 (Peeters & Rutte, 2005), and +0.26 (average of two samples; van Vegchel et al., 2005). All those studies also found that workload remained significantly associated with job-related emotional exhaustion in analyses controlling for a range of other variables.

Unhappiness that is context-free has less often been studied as a function of high job demands. Work overload was found by Major, Klein, and Erhart (2002) and by Geurts et al. (2003) to be correlated at +0.23 and +0.18, respectively, with context-free depression (the negative pole of well-being axis 3). De Jonge et al. (2000) reported a significant bivariate correlation of that kind, which remained significant after controls for demographic features and other job characteristics. That was also found for generalized context-free distress (covering the negative pole of both axes 2 and 3) by Roxburgh (1996) and de Witte (1999). The correlation of high workload with a broad measure of negative affect was +0.34 in research by Parasuraman et al. (1996).

Other studies have found a significant association of high workload with context-free unhappiness assessed through the General Health Questionnaire (GHQ; see chap. 2). For instance, Parkes (1990), Chay (1993), Moyle (1995), Payne et al. (1999), Harvey et al. (2003), and Waldenström et al. (2005) reported correlations of +0.33, +0.31, +0.18, +0.33, +0.27, and +0.17, respectively; the correlations remained significant in multivariate analyses by several of those authors and by Gallie et al. (1998). On the other hand, the correlation between workload and GHQ score averaged only +0.09 across two indicators of load in the project by Wall and Martin (1989), and the job feature was correlated at only +0.02 and +0.05 with context-free depression in research by Beehr, Jex, Stacy, and Murray (2000) and Wilson et al. (2004). This varying pattern could arise from samples' different location on the horizontal axis of Figures 4.1 and 4.2, as suggested earlier.

Leitner and Resch (2005) examined context-free depression and life satisfaction as a function of the amount of time devoted to coping with job hindrances (as recorded by observers; see earlier in this section). Across two measurement occasions, the average correlations with those two forms of well-being were +0.19 and –0.30, respectively. Zohar (1999) also studied environmentally created hassles that interrupt task activities and increase the number of goals to be achieved. Frequently encountered hassles were found to include unexpected delays within one's work process, a lack of equipment or materials, temporary communication breakdowns, staff errors, administrative confusion, late changes to a program, and similar troubling events. Employees' negative mood in the evening after work was found to be correlated at +0.30 with supervisors' ratings of the severity of hassles they had faced during that day. However, self-reports of overall workload (rather than hassles themselves) were related only +0.15 with evening negative mood. In Sonnentag and Bayer's (2005) diary study, employees' positive context-free mood after return home was correlated –0.28 with their retrospective report of time pressure at work earlier in the day.

Geurts et al. (2003) viewed unhappiness and high workload in terms of employees' need to recover from high demands after leaving the job setting. Given that meeting high demands throughout a period of work depletes a person's resources, those need to be replenished by relaxation after work. (An "effort-recovery" model is outlined in chap. 8.) However, the recovery process can be impeded by hassles at home or in some other nonwork location. Geurts and colleagues recorded interference between employees' work and home (see later in the chapter) to explore whether an accumulation of such interference might account for some of the extended impact of workload itself. Results suggested that the relationship between workload and unhappiness was indeed mediated by work–home interference, partly so in the case of job-related anxiety and fully mediated for context-free depression.

Similar themes were examined by Sonnentag and Bayer (2005) in terms of the extent to which employees mentally "switch off" from their job in the evening. Consistent with findings about physiological unwinding, when more stressful work days can be followed by more extended physiological indications of strain (Meijman, Mulder, van Dormolen, & Cremer, 1992), they found that psychological detachment from a job was significantly impaired after days with higher quantitative workload ($r = -0.19$). High work demands thus tend to be accompanied by job thoughts and activities outside working hours that can themselves affect subjective well-being.

Job demands have sometimes been viewed in terms of the time a person spends at work, on the assumption that more working hours are likely to create unhappiness. That association is indeed sometimes found, for instance, in relation to lower job satisfaction among doctors by Simoens et al. (2002) and in male employees in a U.S. national sample by Bender et al. (2005). However, a nonsignificant pattern is also common. For example, the correlation of work hours with overall job satisfaction in between-person research by Birdi et al. (1995) was only +0.02, and in the within-person investigation by Sonnentag and Bayer (2005) the number of a person's job hours was correlated –0.05 with his or her positive mood on return home. The psychological meaning of this time variable on its own is thus not clear.

Findings will depend in part on the range of hours involved in a comparison (e.g., from low to medium values, or from high to very high) and crucially with respect to the other job features involved. Extension of time in a paid job involves the continuation of whatever features happen to be present in that job. Longer working hours might thus bring about, for instance, a continuation of overload or merely an extension of a moderate level of demands (feature 3), a longer period of either social isolation or excessive interpersonal contact (feature 6), or an increased or unchanging income (7). Similarly, conflict between work and home (an aspect of 3) may or may not be increased by longer hours, depending on a person's own situation. Reverse causal influences can also be important. For example, Tucker and Rutherford (2005) illustrated that a heavy workload (with associated low well-being) can lead an employee to choose to work overtime to help cope with current demands.

In addition, role preference was shown in earlier chapters to influence the impact of role membership (and is considered as a form of more general personal salience in chap. 9). Differences between employees in their wish to be at work for long periods are thus also important in this area; some people seek long hours, but others do not. Linked to that, some investigations into hours worked have included both full-time and part-time employees. Many part-timers (who by definition work fewer hours) have explicitly chosen that form of contract, and their number of hours worked cannot be appropriately combined with those of full-timers. Overall, the impact on employee happiness of variation in working hours depends on many different contingencies, and research needs to address those in a more differentiated manner than has been customary.

Emotional Dissonance.   A specific form of high work demand arises when job holders are required to act in ways that reflect "emotional dissonance," expressing organizationally desired emotions that they do not in fact experience, or concealing felt emotions that are organizationally inappropriate (e.g., Morris & Feldman, 1996). For example, a person may be expected to communicate positive feelings when unhappy or to remain neutral in the face of a customer's insulting behavior. Glomb, Kammeyer-Mueller, and Rotundo (2004) demonstrated from independent analysts' ratings that demands of this kind are particularly likely in service, health, or counseling work; telephone call centers have been much discussed in this respect (e.g., Grandey, Dickter, & Sin, 2004; Wilk & Moynihan, 2005).

Dissonance themes have sometimes been considered in terms of "emotional labor" and the "display rules" established by an organization.

For example, Gosserand and Diefendorff (2005) defined "emotional labor as the process of regulating one's emotional displays in response to display rules so that work goals can be achieved. The basic purpose of display rules is to dictate the emotions that employees express" (p. 1256). Two commonly discussed procedures for regulating one's emotional displays are "surface acting," which involves suppressing experienced emotions and displaying those that are organizationally desired, and "deep acting," when underlying feelings are modified in order to display those considered to be appropriate (e.g., Grandey, 2000). Surface acting is likely to occur in work situations more frequently than deep acting (Zapf & Holz, 2006).

Although emotional dissonance can occur in many kinds of social interaction (e.g., Côté, 2005), demands for high and continuing amounts of incongruent emotional expression may be thought likely to impair workers' subjective well-being. Zapf, Vogt, Seifert, Mertini, and Isic (1999) and Lewig and Dollard (2003) found significant negative associations of such dissonance with job satisfaction (r values of −0.30 [average from three samples] and −0.24, respectively) and positive correlations with job-related emotional exhaustion (an average of +0.41 and a single correlation of +0.43). The latter authors also carried out multivariate analyses, finding that associations with emotional dissonance remained significant despite statistical controls for the opportunity for personal control and other job features. They observed that emotional dissonance was itself independent of job demands as traditionally studied (see earlier discussion); the two forms of externally generated goals were intercorrelated only at +0.06. Zapf (2002) examined 12 previous studies of emotional dissonance, finding an average correlation with job-related emotional exhaustion of +0.32. In a later project, that correlation averaged +0.25 from two samples, remaining significant after controls for other variables (Zapf & Holz, 2006).

What about the second form of happiness introduced in chapter 1? Most research has examined aspects of subjective well-being, as illustrated earlier, but in addition happiness as self-validation involves a sense that one is living a life that is worth living, meeting some valued standards, or being authentically appropriate or fitting. As described in chapter 2, this dimension of happiness tends to be positively associated with subjective well-being, but the two can occur to different degrees; high self-validation may be accompanied by low or high well-being. Happiness as self-validation is likely to be affected by emotional dissonance in one's job if dissonant demands become intense. Being required to express many or strong emotions contrary to what is genuinely felt can lead a person to behave in ways that require inauthenticity and a sense of self-estrangement (Brotheridge & Lee, 2002).

It seems probable that some employees faced with goals that induce emotional dissonance treat such pretence as a form of role-playing without negative psychological consequence. However, for people in particularly demanding or extended situations these emotionally dissonant external goals can be expected to have a negative impact on both subjective well-being and self-validation.

Role Conflict. High goal demands have also been examined in terms of role conflict, when the requirements from different environmental sources are incompatible with each other. In those cases, it becomes difficult or impossible to meet one set of demands (from a supervisor, for instance) and also cope with other demands, such as completing a particular task, handling interruptions from a colleague, or responding to another, conflicting, request from a supervisor at a different time. Sometimes, externally generated goals are both numerous (as in the previous section) and in opposition to each other (as here), but role conflict can also occur in settings of low overall load.

Perceived role conflict of this kind has often been shown to be associated with impaired subjective well-being. For example, Fisher and Gitelson (1983) reviewed data from 59 employee samples, finding average correlations of role conflict with job dissatisfaction and job-related tension of +0.35 and +0.28. In a subsequent investigation, Netemeyer, Johnston, and Burton (1990) reported correlations of +0.55 and +0.44 for those indicators, respectively; in the study by Payne et al. (1999), the values were +0.42 and +0.40. Reviewing a selection of previous investigations, Podsakoff, MacKenzie, and Bommer (1996) found that perceived role conflict on average correlated at –0.36 with overall job satisfaction.

Published studies of job satisfaction at the facet-specific level were brought together by Kinicki et al. (2002). Across the five factors in the Job Descriptive Index (see chap. 2), average correlations with in-job role conflict ranged from –0.33 for satisfaction with work content to –0.22 for satisfaction with pay. For job-related emotional exhaustion (mainly axis 2 in the present framework; see chap. 2), Zellars and Perrewé (2001) found a correlation with role conflict of +0.52, which remained significant after control for other job and personal variables. Glazer and Beehr (2005) reported an average correlation with job-related anxiety (the negative pole of axis 2) of +0.40 across four countries.

Work–Home Conflict. Role conflict has also been considered in terms of the combined set of demands from both employment and domestic responsibilities. Greenhaus and Beutell (1986) defined work–family conflict as "a form of inter-role conflict in which the role pressures from the work and family domains are mutually incompatible in some respect" (p. 77). They drew attention to three forms of such conflict: time-based, when multiple roles compete for a person's limited time; strain-based, when negative affect in one role influences behavior and feelings in the other; and behavior-based, when behavior in one role (e.g., as a father at home) is incompatible with expectations in another role (e.g., as a manager in an employing organization).

A specific form of time-based conflict between job and family activities was recorded by Williams, Suls, Alliger, Learner, and Wan (1991) in terms of employed mothers' juggling of the two roles. They viewed role juggling in terms of interruptions to goal-oriented activity (see earlier description), and obtained several reports about the current presence or absence of juggling in the course of each of 8 days. Within-person comparisons between mood ratings at times of inter-role juggling and of no juggling revealed that current mood was significantly more negative when both work and family issues demanded a mother's attention.

Several studies have found that overall conflict between work and home (i.e., without separation into different directions of conflict) is negatively associated with job satisfaction (on the first axis of job-related well-being; e.g., Eby, Casper, Lockwood, Bordeaux, & Brinley, 2005). Published correlations with job holders' reports include −0.20 (Rice et al., 1992), −0.46 (Thomas & Ganster, 1995), −0.26 (average from two samples, Janssen et al., 2004), and −0.22 (average from two occasions, Kinnunen, Guerts, & Mauno, 2004). The average uncorrected correlation between work–family conflict and job satisfaction was −0.27 in the review of previous studies by Kossek and Ozeki (1998). For job-related emotional exhaustion (primarily reflecting low scores on well-being axis 2), the correlation was +0.55 in research by Bakker et al. (2005) and averaged +0.54 across three measurement occasions in the study by Demerouti et al. (2004). Several of those researchers applied statistical controls for a range of demographic and other variables, finding that correlations between work–family conflict and job-related well-being remained significant over and above links with other variables.

Significant associations are also present with context-free happiness or unhappiness (e.g., Bellavia & Frone, 2005). Reported bivariate correlations with overall indicators of work–family conflict include –0.20 (life satisfaction, Rice et al., 1992), +0.42 (depression, Thomas & Ganster, 1995), +0.27 (general negative affect, average value from two occasions, Kinnunen et al., 2004), and +0.31 (depression, Wiesner, Windle, & Freeman, 2005). The review of previous research by Kossek and Ozeki (1998) yielded an average correlation with life satisfaction of –0.26.

Findings described thus far have all concerned overall work–family-conflict. However, some studies have obtained employees' reports separately for the two directional possibilities: work-to-family conflict and family-to-work conflict. The latter two are themselves intercorrelated, for example, +0.59, +0.30, +0.33, +0.28, +0.44, +0.51, +0.50, and +0.36 (average of two studies), in research by Frone, Russell, and Cooper (1992), Adams et al. (1996), Frone, Russell, and Barnes (1996), Frone, Russell, and Cooper (1997), Tepper (2000), van Rijswijk et al. (2004), Wayne, Musisca, and Fleeson (2004), and Aryee et al. (2005), respectively. The meta-analysis by Mesmer-Magnus and Viswesvaran (2005) included some of those studies with additional investigations, yielding an average correlation between the two forms of conflict of +0.38; after correction for measurement error, that average value in the meta-analysis by Byron (2005) was +0.48. Frone et al. (1992) demonstrated in path analyses that the two directional processes appear to influence each other reciprocally.

In separate examinations of the two directions of conflict, Kossek and Ozeki (1998) reported that the negative correlations with job satisfaction in previous publications tended to be stronger with conflict from work to family (average $r = -0.23$) than with family-to-work conflict (average $r = -0.14$). That difference was also present in Kossek and Ozeki's review of correlations with employees' life satisfaction (mean values of –0.31 and –0.20, respectively).

In a meta-analysis restricted to conflict in the direction from work to family (i.e., excluding family to-work processes), the average uncorrected correlation with overall job satisfaction in previous research was found to be –0.23 (Allen, Herst, Bruck, & Sutton, 2000). The review by Mesmer-Magnus and Viswesvaran (2005) produced a lower correlation between work-to-family conflict and job satisfaction, averaging –0.12 without correction. Subsequent studies have obtained correlations of –0.26, –0.29, –0.36, and –0.33 (Aryee et al., 2005; Judge & Colquitt, 2004; van Rijswijk et al., 2004; Wayne et al., 2004). For job-related strain and job-related burnout (on well-being axis 2), average correlations with work-to-family conflict in the meta-analysis by Allen et al. (2000) were +0.41 and +0.40, respectively.

In the other direction, from family to work, the meta-analysis by Mesmer-Magnus and Viswesvaran (2005) yielded an uncorrected average correlation between job satisfaction and family-to-work conflict of −0.14. Later correlations between family-to-work conflict and job satisfaction were −0.31, −0.13, and −0.21 in studies by van Rijswijk et al. (2004), Wayne et al. (2004) and Aryee et al. (2005).

There appear to be few direct comparisons between job-related forms of well-being axes 2 and 3 (anxiety to comfort and depression to enthusiasm) as a function of work–family conflict. Within the book's general expectation about the consequences of either loss or threat (with primary impacts on axes 3 and 2 respectively; see chap. 2), stronger associations are predicted between work–family conflict (a threat) and job-related anxiety–comfort than with epression–enthusiasm. As described earlier, that is also expected for demands within a job itself (e.g., Table 5.1). Job-related emotional exhaustion (mainly tapping axis 2, from anxiety to comfort) was measured by Tepper (2000); correlations with work-to-family conflict and family-to-work conflict were +0.49 and +0.26, respectively. Comparable values for axis 3 appear not to be available.

Some research has examined a second form of domain-specific well-being, in terms of satisfaction with one's family. The meta-analysis of work-to-family studies reported by Allen et al. (2000) found an average uncorrected correlation between that form of conflict and marital satisfaction of −0.24. Wayne et al. (2004) found that both work-to-family conflict and family-to-work conflict were significantly associated with low family satisfaction (r = −0.21 and −0.23 respectively), and that those associations remained significant after controls for demographic and personality features. However, in other studies the links with marital satisfaction have been less strong. The average correlation (from two occasions of measurement) with overall work–family conflict in the study by Kinnunen et al. (2004) was −0.13. Well-being in the marital domain is likely to be influenced by many other aspects of a person's interactions and relationships, and findings presumably depend on which particular aspects of a person's marriage are assessed.

With respect to context-free indicators of happiness as a function of the two separate directions of conflict, life satisfaction was included in the meta-analyses by Allen et al. (2000) and Mesmer-Magnus and Viswesvaran (2005). Average uncorrected correlations with work-to-family conflict were −0.28 and −0.26, respectively. Family-to-work conflict was on average correlated (without correction) at −0.20 with life satisfaction in the second of those reviews. Allen et al. (2000) also examined employees' context-free strain and depression; wide-ranging measures of those were both associated at +0.34 on average (uncorrected) with work-to-family conflict. For a broad index of context-free negative affect, the correlation was greater with work-to-family conflict (+0.53) than with family-to-work conflict (+0.33) in research by Parasuraman et al. (1996); that difference was retained after control for several other variables.

Associations of the two kinds with context-free depression appear on average to be similar. Correlations with work-to-family conflict were found to be +0.26, +0.22 (mean from two studies), +0.18, and +0.28 (averaged across eight analyses) in research by Frone et al. (1992), Frone et al. (1996), Frone et al. (1997), and Hammer, Cullen, Neal, Sinclair, and Shafiro (2005). For family-to-work conflict, those values were +0.42, +0.33 (mean from two studies), +0.38, and +0.23 (mean value), respectively. Separate values for men and for women were reported by Grandey, Cordeiro, and Crouter (2005) and Hammer et al. (2005). For work-to-family conflict, average correlations in those studies with context-free depression were +0.25 for men and +0.26 for women; for family-to-work conflict, they were +0.21 and +0.25 respectively. Frone et al. (1997) examined depression across 4 years. Although both longitudinal bivariate associations with context-free depression were themselves significant, only family-to-work (and not work-to-family) conflict predicted later depression after control for demographic variables and the other form of conflict.

Correlations with job-related and context-free unhappiness have sometimes been found to be stronger for women than for men (Frone, 2000; Kossek & Ozeki, 1998). For example, Kinnunen et al. (2004) analyzed patterns across 12 months, finding that level of overall work–family conflict at the initial measurement significantly predicted later job satisfaction and context-free distress for women but not for men. Viewing this form of conflict in terms of the depletion of emotional resources, Rothbard (2001) found a work-to-family effect only for women. She speculated that the absence of association for men might be due to men's greater segmentation of the two roles.

In similar terms, Grandey et al. (2005) pointed out that women are more likely than men to see the family role as part of their social identity. They examined overall job satisfaction as a function of the two directions of conflict as well as of context-free affect and some job attributes. After controlling for the additional variables, work-to-family conflict was more strongly associated with job satisfaction for women than for men, but not to a statistically significant degree. In longitudinal analyses, work-to-family conflict predicted changes in job satisfaction after a year (more initial conflict was followed by a greater reduction in satisfaction) for women but not for men.

Nevertheless, not all research has found stronger associations between work–family conflict and low subjective well-being for women than for men (e.g., Frone et al., 1996). With respect to context-free depression, Grandey et al. (2005) and Hammer et al. (2005) reported very similar correlations for men and women; see the earlier summary. Patterns are likely to depend on additional variables that might differ between investigations, such as the level of personal salience attached to one or both roles (see chap. 9) and aspects of the environment that remain unmeasured. In the latter respect, work–family conflict tends to be greater when additional (job or other) demands also press upon an individual or couple (Bakker et al., 2005; Bellavia & Frone, 2005; Byron, 2005; Eby et al., 2005; Grzywacz & Marks, 2000). Across four samples, Geurts et al. (2003) reported an average correlation of +0.50 between workload in one's job and work–home conflict. That correlation remained significant after controls for gender, parental status, and working hours (Geurts, Taris, Kompier, Dikkers, van Hooff, & Kinnunen, 2005). In research by Parasuraman et al. (1996), Demerouti et al. (2004), Janssen et al. (2004), and Butler et al. (2005), correlations between job demands and work–home conflict were +0.61, +0.38 (average of two measurement points), +0.42 (average from two samples), and +0.48, respectively.

Number of hours worked has been found to be significantly related to work-to-family conflict, but conflict in the other direction (from family to work) appears to be unrelated to hours worked. That differentiated pattern was documented in the meta-analysis by Byron (2005). Also apparent from that review was the fact that employees whose job permits some flexibility of scheduling report significantly fewer conflicts of both kinds. Kossek and Ozeki (1998) observed that employees' work–family conflict is greatest when both partners are employed, especially affecting dissatisfaction that is job-related.

A three-component investigation was reported by Bruck, Allen, and Spector (2002). They asked about the three forms of work–family conflict introduced earlier in this discussion: time-based, strain-based, and behavior-based. Correlations between overall job satisfaction and work-to-family conflict were –0.21, –0.31, and –0.42, respectively. With respect to family-to-work conflict, correlations with job satisfaction were –0.12 (time-based), –0.13 (strain-based), and –0.43 (behavior-based). As in the less fine-grained research summarized earlier, time-based and strain-based conflicts from work to family were more related to low well-being than was a family's interference in work (average r-values above of −0.26 and −0.13). However, no difference in the magnitude of correlation was found for behavior-based conflict.

Most research into work–home conflict has been cross-sectional, limiting our knowledge about causal patterns. A longitudinal study across 3 months by Demerouti et al. (2004) pointed to reciprocal influences between job demands, work-to-home conflict, and job-related emotional exhaustion. For example, not only did conflict lead to emotional exhaustion, but exhaustion also created more conflict. A spiral of impact was assumed, such that environmental conditions harmed subjective well-being and available psychological resources; in turn, reduced resources were thought to generate more work–home conflict, as impaired individuals either failed to cope or used up excessive resources in their coping efforts.

Overlaps between work and home can be positive as well as negative. For example, qualitative research by Piotrkowski (1978) identified several forms of positive carryover from husbands' jobs to their home, as well as negative effects. In positive cases, a husband came home cheerful, and was described as both "emotionally available" and "interpersonally available" to other family members. He introduced personal energy into family activities, laughed and joked, initiated warm and interested interactions, and responded positively to other people. Greenhaus and Powell (2006) examined facilitation of that kind in two categories. "Instrumental" facilitation (which they termed "enrichment") was viewed as the direct transfer of skills, knowledge, perspectives, and other resources from one domain to the other; "emotional" facilitation was said to occur when positive affect in one role enhances a person's functioning in another.

In research by Wayne et al. (2004), perceived facilitation (and also conflict) was measured in both directions—from work to home and from home to work. Reports of conflict and facilitation between the roles were found to be unrelated to each other (average $r = +0.01$), rather than occurring as opposites. (In studies by Aryee et al. [2005], Butler et al. [2005], and Hammer et al. [2005], that correlation was −0.29, −0.16, and −0.10 [average of eight measurements].) Furthermore, Wayne and colleagues found that facilitation from work to home was significantly associated with job satisfaction ($r = +0.25$) but not with family satisfaction ($r = +0.06$), and that home-to-work facilitation was more related to family satisfaction ($r = +0.30$) than to job satisfaction ($r = +0.11$). That pattern was retained despite controls for demographic and personality variables.

Thus, when individuals saw facilitating benefits from one role (either work or home), they tended to report more well-being in that particular domain. (However, Aryee et al. [2005] obtained a more substantial correlation, +0.25, between family-to-work facilitation and overall job satisfaction.) Placing their results about facilitation in the context of their findings about conflict (described earlier), Wayne et al. (2004) emphasized that job satisfaction and family satisfaction were each a function of both kinds of directional influence, but that job satisfaction was more linked to a job's impact, whereas family satisfaction was more associated with influences from the home environment. Related research by Grzywacz and Marks (2000) showed that experienced levels of work-to-family or family-to-work conflict or facilitation were each primarily influenced by job factors or family factors respectively, that is, from within their originating domain.

Hammer at al. (2005) examined context-free depression as a function of both directions of role facilitation. They recorded larger negative associations between depression and facilitation from family to work (mean $r = -0.28$) than with facilitation from work to family (mean $r = -0.19$). A review of previous studies by Greenhaus and Powell (2006) indicated that differences in level have been widely observed: Family-to-work facilitation has been found to be substantially stronger than work-to-family facilitation.

Conflict between the two domains is placed in the present subsection of the book because it is a particular form of those conflicts that can arise from externally generated goals (environmental feature 3); those are the topic of the section as a whole. However, positive aspects of dual role occupancy, described here as "facilitation," bring in a range of other job variables, extending beyond merely the present section. The possible benefits of multiple role occupancy (here in both job and family activities) can in principle arise from most of the environmental sources in the book's framework. For example, having a job as well as being a family member generates additional variety (feature 4), increases income (7), and can provide a valued social position (9). Work–family facilitation is thus appropriately examined as a broader construct involving a multiplicity of environmental features, rather than being treated as the opposite process to conflict between the two roles; conflict (an aspect of feature 3) is necessarily more limited in its nature than is the multifeature construct of facilitation.

Nonlinearity and Goals

Studies reviewed so far in this section about externally generated goals have illustrated themes relevant to the chapter's first question: What evidence is available about specific associations with this job feature (number 3 in the vitamin framework) and about possible mechanisms of influence? The second question concerns nonlinearity: Is there evidence for the "additional decrement" pattern summarized in Figures 4.1 and 4.2?

As demonstrated earlier, associations between externally generated goals and employee well-being have been found to be positive and negative in separate studies of low and high demands, respectively. Research that examines a broad range of external demands in a single analysis is thus likely to reveal the proposed inverted U shape.

Early examples of that pattern were presented by Karasek (1979). In the American survey described earlier, he examined four levels of job demand. Results indicated that both job dissatisfaction and life dissatisfaction (job-related and context-free forms of the first measurement axis in Fig. 2.2) were curvilinearly related to magnitude of workload. The percentages of each subsample identified as dissatisfied with their job were 24, 17, 22, and 28 from very low to very high job demands. For dissatisfaction with life, the corresponding values were 9, 5, 6, and 11. However, for measures of context-free exhaustion and depression (well-being axes 2 and 3, respectively), greatest unhappiness was again found with highest job demands, but scores were similar to each other across medium to low demands.

In a national sample of British workers, Warr (1990b) examined nonlinearity in the demands-happiness association for the three principal measurement axes (as in Fig. 2.2): job satisfaction, job-related anxiety–comfort, and job-related depression–enthusiasm. In all cases, significant nonlinearity of the predicted kind was present. For subgroups ranged from low job demands to high demands, overall job satisfaction scores were 2.98, 3.31, 3.38, 3.49, 3.42, 3.39, and 3.35 respectively ($p < .001$). For job-related anxiety–comfort, the scores from low demand to high demand were 4.29, 4.47, 4.37, 4.23, 4.07, 3.96, and 3.78 ($p < .005$), and for job depression–enthusiasm they were 4.33, 4.60, 4.65, 4.59, 4.52, 4.55, and 4.54 ($p < .01$). (As elsewhere in the book, high scores on the two axes indicate raised well-being.) Job-related happiness thus increased cross-sectionally from the lowest levels of externally generated goals (analogous to the zone of vitamin deficiency), and decreased after a moderate level (having reached the toxic zone of excessive "vitamins").

Rice et al. (1991) examined one aspect of externally generated goals—the physical demands from a job. In relation to employees' satisfaction with that particular facet, significant nonlinearity was present. This included a leveling off at higher demands, but no details were presented. Janssen (2001) examined the possibility that the inverted-U pattern was more likely in certain organizational settings than in others. Focusing on possible moderation by the perceived fairness of one's effort-reward balance, he found substantial curvilinearity of the expected shape between job demands and work satisfaction for those employees reporting a fair balance of that kind.

De Jonge and Schaufeli (1998) observed this nonlinear pattern for job-related anxiety, but reported that associations of job demands with job satisfaction and job-related emotional exhaustion were merely linear. On the other hand, job-related emotional exhaustion was found in another sample to be related to job demands in the expected manner (de Jonge et al., 2000), although nonlinearity was absent in relation to context-free depression. Fletcher and Jones (1993) also failed to observe nonlinearity with context-free anxiety or depression, but the expected pattern was observed for male employees' job satisfaction.

Findings are thus inconsistent, possibly because of variations in samples' location on the environmental feature (see the earlier discussion), but there is accumulating evidence for the expected nonlinear pattern in relation to the first two axes of subjective well-being. In particular, the inverted U shape of Figures 4.1 and 4.2 is strongly supported with respect to experiences of anxiety–comfort. As shown in those correlations that are restricted to the high-demand range (summarized earlier), that is the measurement axis that is most associated with workload in that range.

Such a difference between axis 2 (anxiety–comfort) and axis 3 (depression–enthusiasm) may be interpreted in terms of contrasting emphases on approach or avoidance goals. Chapter 2 pointed out that variations in anxiety–comfort may be primarily dependent on the need to avoid a personal threat (such as excessive workload), whereas low scores on the well-being axis from depression to enthusiasm are likely to be more linked to approach activities as an individual moves toward something that is desirable (in this case, toward moderately challenging goals, from low to medium values in Figs. 4.1 and 4.2; Carver, 2003).

Goals and Different Aspects of Happiness

That avoid–approach difference bears on the chapter's third question: Is the environmental feature under consideration linked differentially to alternative forms of happiness in the ways suggested in Tables 4.2 and 5.1? (An abbreviated form of Table 5.1 is presented inside the front cover.) Externally generated goals were in those tables proposed to be particularly associated (negatively) with anxiety–comfort (well-being axis 2, rather than with axis 3) at high levels of goals (in the zone of threat), and to be more linked (positively) with depression–enthusiasm (axis 3) than with axis 2 at low levels (in the zone of deficiency). That divergent pattern at high levels of workload was demonstrated earlier in this section, with average correlations of –0.30 and 0.00 with job-related anxiety–comfort (axis 2) and depression–enthusiasm (axis 3), respectively. (Recall that in describing those axes, high scores indicate higher well-being.)

However, research in the left-hand segment of Figures 4.1 and 4.2 (examining underload) has been infrequent in recent decades, and information about the two diagonal measurement axes at low levels of the environmental feature is lacking. In addition, more information is needed about those well-being axes in their context-free forms. It is also desirable to examine more systematically well-being associations with the separate components described in this chapter. Although some comparative findings are available for externally generated goals as a whole (reviewed earlier), information about nonlinearity and differential associations with axes of well-being still has to be gathered with respect to task identity, emotional dissonance, role conflict, and work–family conflict. This environmental characteristic is undoubtedly linked to unhappiness or happiness in specifiable ways, but particular patterns still require more targeted investigation.

7

Variety, Clarity, and Social Contact

T his chapter continues the examination of primary job features that are thought to be associated with happiness in an "additional decrement" manner (see chap. 4 and Figs. 4.1 and 4.2). As in the last two chapters, three issues are addressed: specific associations and possible mechanisms, linearity or nonlinearity of associations, and possibly different relationships with different aspects of happiness. The features to be covered were identified earlier as variety, environmental clarity, and contact with others.

JOB FEATURE 4: VARIETY

This component of the vitamin model concerns variation in the conditions to which a person is exposed and in the activities he or she is required to perform. Low variety occurs as a relative constancy in the physical and/or social environment and in the tasks to be undertaken in a role. In job settings this may involve extended repetition of the same operations, possibly with short cycle times and/or a fixedness of location and environmental stimulation. People's dislike of an unchanging environmental input is reflected in several popular sayings: the recommendation that "a change is as good as a rest," the observation made in some routine settings that "the novelty has worn off," and the statement of personal disinclination that "I've been there, done that." In some cases, "I've heard it all before" can indicate a lack of interest in overly familiar themes.

Variety and Happiness

Low variety is likely to generate low subjective well-being for two sets of reasons. First, an absence of variation is often experienced as unpleasant in itself. People like some diversity in their experiences to balance the sense of comfort and ease of operation that can arise from routines and habits. In part, such a preference derives from processes of psychological adaptation to previous inputs. Continued exposure to an environmental feature tends across time to reduce its affective potential, so that a familiar input comes to generate feelings that are less extreme than previously. In response to a constant or repeated stimulus, feelings can thus become reduced or give way to indifference (Frederick & Loewenstein, 1999). (Chap. 9 provides a more substantial review of this process.) This adaptation to a low-variety situation can lead people to seek out novel activities, which themselves have a stronger initial reward potential.

Second, low variety tends to be correlated with other negative environmental characteristics, such as low opportunity for control and for skill use (features 1 and 2). Other undesirable aspects of the environment are thus also likely to contribute to unhappiness in settings of low variety.

Links between variety and other characteristics are also important with respect to the latters' duration. Exposure to negative stimuli can often be tolerated without psychological harm if those stimuli are relatively brief, whereas negative conditions that extend across longer periods of time are more likely to impair well-being. Longer inputs do of course illustrate low variety; the conditions do not change. Low variety in conjunction with other negative job characteristics (e.g., work overload or inadequate income) is thus a form of long-duration negative input, and is harmful because of the duration as well as the content of those characteristics.

Unhappiness associated with low variety in a job has often been demonstrated. Investigations in the 1920s by the Industrial Fatigue ("Health" from 1927) Research Board studied British workers in highly repetitive jobs such as packaging, wrapping, folding, weighing, and assembling (e.g., Wyatt & Ogden, 1924). The performance and attitudes of employees were recorded under normal conditions and also after changes had been made to increase variety. Employees responded favorably to that increase: "Operatives who have had experience of both uniform and varied conditions of work generally prefer the latter" (Wyatt, Fraser, & Stock, 1928). However, consistent with the present "additional decrement" proposal, very high levels of variety were found to be undesirable for disrupting employees' work rhythm.

Warr (1987) summarized early evidence for a significant association between low well-being and low variety in a job. For example, Kornhauser's (1965) examination of semiskilled car workers included comparisons between those who were in repetitive and nonrepetitive jobs. A substantial difference in overall job satisfaction between the two sets of job holders was accompanied by a similar divergence in context-free unhappiness; workers in jobs that were repetitive were considerably less happy in both job-related and context-free terms than their counterparts in nonrepetitive work. Independent associations with overall job satisfaction were demonstrated by O'Brien (1982), who showed that job variety remained a significant predictor of satisfaction despite statistical controls for opportunity for personal control, opportunity for skill use, and externally generated goals. In the review by Podsakoff et al. (1996), task routineness was on average (across 15 previous studies) correlated at −0.22 with overall job satisfaction. Mathieu et al. (1993) reported associations at the facet-specific level. For example, variety in a job was correlated at +0.59 with satisfaction with opportunity for personal growth, but only +0.12 with the conceptually less related satisfaction with pay.

A job analytic project by Melamed et al. (1995) revealed significant associations of independently assessed variety with intrinsic job satisfaction ($r = +0.26$ for men and $r = +0.38$ for women) and with context-free distress ($r = -0.14$ for men and $r = -0.30$ for women). Employees' own reports of variety were themselves correlated strongly with job satisfaction ($r = +0.52$ for men and $+0.58$ for women) and (less strongly, as usual) with (broader scope) context-free distress ($r = -0.21$ for men and -0.35 for women). Roxburgh's (1996) analyses included statistical controls for other job features and demographic characteristics; low variety in a job remained significantly correlated with a wide-ranging index of distress despite those controls.

Aspects of this job feature were covered in a scale of "skill variety" in the Job Diagnostic Survey of Hackman and Oldham (1975). This describes variation in the use of different skills, but the scale's construct validity is compromised by some coverage of "a number of complex or high-level skills" (i.e., addressing the level of skill as well as its variety). Skill variety measured in that way has repeatedly been found to be associated with job-related well-being. For example, the average correlation with intrinsic job satisfaction across 20 studies was +0.45 in the analysis by Fried (1991). O'Brien (1983) showed that this job feature remained significant despite statistical controls for other job characteristics.

With respect to the five facet satisfactions covered by the Job Descriptive Index (see chap. 2), a particularly high correlation with skill variety is found for satisfaction with the work itself (mean r = +0.44; Kinicki et al., 2002). Conceptually less relevant facet satisfactions are, as expected, less strongly associated with this job feature. For instance, satisfaction with promotion opportunities was on average correlated with skill variety at only +0.19 in the review by Kinicki and colleagues.

Employees may introduce variety into their work by personal adjustments to their activities. Several informal procedures of that kind were described by Roy (1960), for example, through the establishment of variations in personal task schedules. Those informal work plans "yielded a continuous sequence of short-range production goals with achievement rewards in the form of activity change" (p. 161). Self-set goals of those kinds can also be beneficial in permitting some personal control in establishing particular targets or their method of attainment (feature 1), in raising ambiguity from very low levels ("Will I or won't I hit my target?"; feature 5), in generating feedback about goal attainment (5), and in enhancing task identity for segments of the job (an aspect of 3). Broadbent (1981) and Fisher (1993) outlined a range of other activities to reduce the monotony of low-variety work, such as daydreaming, singing, working on a crossword puzzle (a non-work form of 3), or chatting with other people (6). It is clear that in many ways employees create additional structure or content for low-variety work, to hurry it along and to make more positive their affect.

Nonlinearity and Variety

What about very high levels of variety in a job or other environment? Linked to its classification as an assumed "additional decrement" feature, extremely high variety is expected to cause unhappiness. That is for two reasons. First, very high variety gives rise to harmful levels of some other environmental features. For example, the number of different external goals (feature 3) is likely to become excessive when tasks are extremely varied, and the traction or task identity (see chap. 6) of particular activities can become broken, as a person is unable smoothly to complete an entire operation. Similarly, it can be difficult or impossible to control all of a widely diverse set of activities (feature 1).

A second negative aspect of very high variety is more intrinsic to the environmental feature itself. Having a very wide range of tasks to undertake requires a person repeatedly to shift concentration and attention. Frequent shifts of that kind are problematic in several ways. For example, they demand additional expenditure of mental and physical energy, using resources on multiple activities imposed by the high level of variety and preventing the application of those resources elsewhere. Frequent shifts can also impair progress toward particular task goals, as unfolding sequences of behavior become disrupted by new requirements. In part, very high diversity in one's activities can be viewed as a series of repeated interruptions; negative outcomes of interruptions in general have been illustrated in the previous chapter.

Limited evidence for the harmful impact of very high variety has been noted earlier (e.g., Wyatt et al., 1928), but empirical study of this job feature has almost always been restricted to low values on the horizontal axis in Figures 4.1 and 4.2. It is thus not yet possible to document an additional decrement at very high levels of job variety. Given the lack of research in that segment of the proposed curve, it is not surprising that the entire curve has not been investigated in a single study. The chapter's second issue (about available evidence for non-linearity) thus remains unresolved with respect to job feature 4, although the logical bases for that expectation remain strong.

Variety and Different Aspects of Happiness

The chapter's third question asks about the different associations with happiness summarized in Tables 4.2 and 5.1. As with all the environmental features examined here, a significant association with the first axis of happiness (from feeling bad to feeling good) is well established. (That is one reason for inclusion of each feature in the framework.) With respect to the other two measurement axes, it was proposed in chapter 4 that environmental variety is likely to be more associated (positively) at low levels with depression–enthusiasm (axis 3), whereas at high levels the stronger (negative) association is expected with anxiety–comfort (axis 2). (Recall that those axes are described throughout the book with a higher score indicating greater well-being.) At low levels of variety, people experience a lack of stimulation and seek movement toward the goal of moderate environmental diversity. As argued in chapter 2, fulfilling an approach-oriented motive is expected to give rise to a reduction in depression and an increase in activated forms of happiness with greater proximity to the goal (Carver, 2003). Conversely, very high variety creates over-stimulation, and a desire to avoid a threatening situation. Following a shift away from potential harm (here in terms of excessive variety), the predominant affective experience is likely to be a reduction in anxiety.

Associated with a recent lack of research into variety in job settings, this differential possibility still requires systematic exploration. Investigations into job variety need to look more closely at different aspects of subjective well-being, paying attention separately to low and high levels of input and the several forms of unhappiness and happiness that may accompany them.

JOB FEATURE 5: ENVIRONMENTAL CLARITY

The fifth environmental feature in the present framework concerns the degree to which a person can successfully anticipate what is likely to happen in his or her life space. Some uncertainty is of course almost always present, but variations in the clarity of an environment have often been shown to be related to a person's subjective well-being.

Clarity and Happiness

Low environmental clarity is experienced as undesirable in itself, restricting an understanding of one's current or probable situation and generating tension as conceptual closure is prevented. Some knowledge of "what the future might bring" is widely felt to be needed. For example, in thinking and making plans about possible events, a lack of clear information can obstruct interpretation of a situation and give rise to doubts and confusion about interdependencies between aspects of the environment and about actions that might be taken. Experimental research by Iyengar and Lepper (2000) demonstrated that decision makers are particularly uncomfortable in conditions of uncertain information.

Low predictability reduces people's self-efficacy (their subjective competence in a situation), because they are less able to assess probabilities and risks. Associated with that, uncertainty is harmful for its impact on the opportunity for personal control (feature 1; e.g., the correlation between those two features in jobs was −0.43 in the study by Bordia et al., 2004). If people cannot predict future developments and the consequences of their actions with moderate confidence, they cannot act to influence their environment in a desired manner; low environmental clarity thus brings about powerlessness as well as unpredictability. (On the other hand, when clarity is moderately high, the opportunity for control may be either high or low, depending on other aspects of the situation.) In these ways, goal achievement is impaired in settings of low environmental clarity through both unpredictability and low potential for personal control.

In addition to that link with control opportunity, this primary job feature also bears on other components of the present model. Those were selected because of their relevance to happiness or unhappiness, and variations in clarity may be considered with respect to each other feature. One might thus investigate, for example, how predictable in a future period are the availability of money (feature 7) or externally generated goals (3), and also ask about the happiness-related consequences of each feature's clarity or unclarity. Environmental clarity is thus important in itself, for its effect on self-efficacy and associated goal achievement, and because it can operate through other environmental features that themselves generate happiness or unhappiness.

Three principal types of clarity were introduced in chapter 4. First is the degree to which a future is predictable, so that one is able to think and plan ahead and exercise some control over events. A second aspect is more specific: Are normative expectations in a role clear to a person, so that he or she can predict which behaviors will lead to positive or negative evaluation by others? Third, environmental clarity is partly reflected in the amount of feedback that is received about particular actions and their effectiveness.

Predictability.   In examining the first aspect, Caplan et al. (1975) developed a measure of "job future ambiguity," covering a worker's uncertainty about likely career developments and the future value of one's job skills. In a broad sample of male employees, perceived future ambiguity was associated at +0.39 with job dissatisfaction, +0.24 with job-related depression, and +0.12 with job-related anxiety. In van Dijkhuizen's (1980) sample, those correlations were +0.26, +0.26, and +0.17, respectively. Significant associations have also been reported in subsequent research.

For instance, Landeweerd and Boumans (1994) examined together several forms of reported job-related clarity, obtaining a correlation of +0.61 with overall job satisfaction, and Hellgren et al. (1999) found that future uncertainty was correlated at –0.52 with job satisfaction and –0.35 with a general index of context-free well-being. For job-related emotional exhaustion, the correlation with job future ambiguity was +0.33 and +0.43 in research by Zellars and Perrewé (2001) and Bordia et al. (2004), respectively. For overall job satisfaction, that correlation was –0.24 in the second of those studies, and the average correlation with context-free distress from two samples was –0.23 in research by Schat and Kelloway (2000).

Problems can arise when seeking to distinguish between future predictability (this aspect of feature 5) and the notion of job security, which has been placed here within feature 11, career outlook. Those two clearly overlap with each other, but they are different in themselves and in their links to other constructs. The present allocation to two different categories is based on the more comprehensive nature of predictability (concerning any kind of future development; 5) in comparison with a narrow focus on future role tenure (11). The predictability component of environmental clarity can concern many aspects of the future, whereas the 11th feature concerns only possible developments in one's career.

Role Ambiguity.   A second aspect of environmental clarity concerns the degree to which a setting provides clear information about what behaviors and levels of attainment are required. Following Kahn, Wolfe, Quinn, and Snoek (1964), low values of this feature have sometimes been examined as "role ambiguity." For example, the perceived role ambiguity scale developed by Rizzo, House, and Lirtzman (1970) contains items like "I know exactly what is expected of me." Greater ambiguity in those terms (i.e., low environmental clarity) has often been found to be associated with low subjective well-being. The meta-analysis by Jackson and Schuler (1985) recorded average correlations with employees' overall job satisfaction and job-related anxiety of –0.30 and +0.30 respectively. Subsequent investigations found, for instance, correlations of –0.36 and +0.28 (Netemeyer et al., 1990) and –0.38 and +0.30 (Spector et al., 2000) with those two aspects of job well-being.

Research with different measures of role ambiguity has obtained correlations with overall job satisfaction of –0.41 (Payne et al., 1999), –0.31 (Grebner et al., 2003), and –0.47 (Wilson et al., 2004). An average value from nine previous studies was –0.55 in the review by Podsakoff et al. (1996). Correlations with facet-level satisfactions have been found to range between averages of –0.35 (satisfaction with supervision) and –0.13 (satisfaction with pay; Kinicki et al., 2002). For job-related anxiety (the negative pole of well-being axis 2), Glazer and Beehr (2005) reported from four countries an average correlation with role ambiguity of +0.34.

Three facets of in-job ambiguity were identified by Breaugh and Colihan (1994). First is "performance criteria ambiguity" with respect to employees' uncertainty about standards of required performance; second, "work method ambiguity" concerns the procedures to be used in a job; third, "scheduling ambiguity" is uncertainty about how to schedule or sequence task activities. The three kinds of perceived ambiguity were found to be significantly associated with both intrinsic job satisfaction and satisfaction with one's supervisor, with highest correlations (averages across three studies of –0.34 and –0.62, respectively) for ambiguity about performance criteria.

Feedback. Feedback about one's performance (the third form of environmental clarity introduced earlier) is essential to establish and maintain personal control over the environment and for the development and use of skills. It would be impossible to interact successfully with the environment if information did not become available about the effectiveness or otherwise of one's actions. In addition, feedback can be important for the public recognition it accords to a person's good performance. This job feature thus has both instrumental and emotional value.

A person can learn about the consequences of his or her job actions through information from other people and/or from the manner in which task events subsequently unfold. In the meta-analysis by Jackson and Schuler (1985), perceived levels of both those forms of feedback were correlated with measures of more general role ambiguity, on average at –0.35 from other people and –0.22 from the task.

However, research in the area of this book has typically obtained merely an overall report of feedback received of all kinds. Feedback scores on the Job Diagnostic Survey (Hackman & Oldham, 1975) were correlated on average at +0.29 with overall job satisfaction in the review of previous research by Loher et al. (1985). Fried's (1991) meta-analysis of findings about two indicators of general job feedback yielded an average correlation with intrinsic satisfaction of +0.38, and the average correlation with overall job satisfaction (for a range of feedback indicators) was +0.42 in the review by Podsakoff et al. (1996). Across 42 manufacturing companies, average level of performance feedback rated by employees was found by Patterson et al. (2004) to be correlated at +0.57 with average overall job satisfaction in that company.

Illustrative facet-level correlations in the study by Mathieu et al. (1993) were +0.59 with satisfaction with supervision and +0.45 with satisfaction with the opportunity for personal growth. For the five facet-level satisfactions covered by the Job Descriptive Index (see chap. 2), the highest average correlation with perceived job feedback (+0.40) was reported by Kinicki et al. (2002) to occur for (the conceptually related) satisfaction with supervision. Job-related emotional exhaustion (mainly on well-being axis 2) was correlated at –0.20 and –0.25 with the availability of feedback in studies by Schaufeli and Bakker (2004) and Bakker et al. (2005), respectively. Examining employees' enjoyment of particular work activities in the course of a week, Quinn (2005) recorded a correlation between enjoyment and feedback clarity of +0.49. However, no evidence about links with context-free indicators of happiness has been located; the availability of feedback in job situations has apparently been examined only with respect to job well-being.

Nonlinearity and Clarity

Research into forms of environmental clarity has been overwhelmingly directed at low levels of its components: ambiguity, uncertainty, and lack of feedback. We thus have little information about situations of very high clarity. As noted in chapter 4, clarity to the right-hand side of Figures 4.1 and 4.2 removes surprise, risk, and variety of outcomes; role requirements are completely specified with no ambiguity; and extreme predictability removes personal control by imposing strong and certain information from the environment.

The possibility of an additional decrement at very high levels ("too much of a good thing"; the chapter's second question) may be examined through some findings by van Dijkhuizen (1980). A significant curvilinear trend was present for role ambiguity, with mean levels of job dissatisfaction for subgroups arrayed from low environmental clarity to high clarity of 2.40, 1.93, 1.76, and 1.87. However, the range of clarity scores was not great in that study. As noted previously, research must cover an extensive range of environmental levels to provide an adequate empirical test of nonlinear proposals.

Ilgen, Fisher, and Taylor (1979) raised the possibility of harm at very high levels in respect specifically of the feedback provided to employees. They "questioned the generally accepted notion that more feedback is always better" (p. 366), because "very frequent feedback may connote a loss of personal control to the recipient" (p. 367). That argument provides conceptual support for the "additional decrement" classification of environmental clarity in the vitamin model. However, more substantial empirical evidence is still required.

Clarity and Different Aspects of Happiness

The chapter's third question asks about the differential associations predicted in Tables 4.2 and 5.1 (also inside the front cover). It was there suggested that (as with other features) environmental clarity is likely to be particularly correlated with well-being axis 3 (depression to enthusiasm) in its lower range, because low clarity represents a deficit of desirable input and deficits in general give rise to depression rather than anxiety (see chap. 2). However, this aspect of a job was considered also to create threats and potential harm at lower values, as low clarity prohibits personal control and learning. Associations with anxiety–comfort (axis 2) and depression–enthusiasm (axis 3) in the left-hand segment of the curve were thus predicted to be of similar magnitude.

A significant association between employees' happiness and increased clarity in the low-to-moderate range was documented earlier. That is consistently found with respect to job-related well-being, but research has mainly examined the first measurement axis, in terms of job satisfaction. Although some evidence is available about job-related anxiety and job-related depression (linking greater well-being to increased clarity), additional research is still needed before the magnitude of effects for the two axes of well-being can be adequately compared. Information is also required about context-free outcomes.

What about the right-hand segment of the curve proposed in Figures 4.1 and 4.2, such that extremely high environmental clarity is viewed as harmful? As with other "additional decrement" features, because threats are generated in this high range through excessive amounts of a feature, stronger (negative) correlations have been suggested with axis 2 (anxiety to comfort) than with axis 3 (depression to enthusiasm). However, it appears that research has not yet addressed that differentiated possibility.

JOB FEATURE 6: CONTACT WITH OTHERS

In addition to the 11 environmental characteristics examined so far, it is clear that happiness depends in several ways on relationships with other people, number 6 in the set introduced in chapter 4. That chapter drew attention to the personal benefits attached to friendship, emotional and instrumental support, social comparisons, norm formation, and the better achievement of goals through interdependent efforts. Social contact is important in those ways in jobs as well as elsewhere. In addition, some people work in interaction with customers or clients, and the nature of those external relationships may also give rise to unhappiness or happiness.

Contact with others was identified earlier as an "additional decrement" feature. As schematized in Figures 4.1 (p. 96) and 4.2 (p. 102), an asymmetric inverted U shape is proposed, with greatest happiness occurring at moderate levels of social contact. That curvilinear pattern is expected for the two aspects of contact identified earlier—its quantity and its quality.

Other People and Happiness

Both those aspects are examined here in terms of the chapter's three questions. First, what information is available about associations with happiness and their possible mechanisms? Second, is there evidence for nonlinearity? And third, what is known about possible differential links with different forms of happiness?

Quantity of Contact. Empirical research in organizations has mainly examined social contact in terms of its quality, for example, as social support or abuse. However, other studies have shown that a moderate amount of interaction with others at work is beneficial. Research into quantity has primarily focused on interaction with colleagues rather than customers. For example, Gardell (1971) found that amount of contact with coworkers was significantly positively associated with employees' overall job satisfaction and life satisfaction, and negatively correlated with job-related tension and context-free anxiety. Research by Hackman and Oldham (1975) showed that employees' reports of the extent to which their job required close working with other people were significantly associated with overall and intrinsic job satisfaction. That pattern was also found by Sims and Szilagyi (1976), in relation to intrinsic job satisfaction ($r = +0.36$) and (facet) satisfactions with colleagues ($r = +0.26$) and supervision ($r = +0.27$). Oldham and Brass (1979) reported that ease of interaction with colleagues was correlated at $+0.32$ with overall job satisfaction and $+0.51$ with satisfaction with those colleagues; in Moch's (1980) study of assembly-plant workers, "isolates" (reporting no close links with others) exhibited significantly lower intrinsic job satisfaction than did "nonisolates."

Links between happiness and quantity of social contact have also been studied with respect to building design. For example, Szilagyi and Holland (1980) monitored a move between buildings made by professional staff. As a result of this transfer, the "social density" of working environments (measured as the number of colleagues within a distance of 50 feet) decreased for some individuals and increased for others. Reductions in social density were found to give rise to declines in overall job satisfaction, and increased density led to greater satisfaction.

These investigations into the quantity of contact with others indicate that low opportunities to interact with others are linked to greater unhappiness at work. However, other research, described later in terms of possible nonlinearity, has shown that social density can also be associated negatively with subjective well-being. Some contact with other people in a job is desirable, but only up to a point. In addition, influences from other aspects of the environment (the present "vitamins") still need to be explored in conjunction with this variable; high-contact and low-contact jobs may also differ from each other in other important respects. Note also that studies have so far concentrated on the first measurement axis of Figure 2.2, failing to examine well-being axes 2 and 3 (from anxiety to comfort and from depression to enthusiasm), and associations between quantity of social contact and context-free indicators of happiness still require investigation.

Quality of Contact.   Much more research has concerned the quality (rather than amount) of social contact that is available in a job. Reported friendship opportunities were correlated at +0.45 with overall job satisfaction in a study by Oldham and Brass (1979) and +0.28 with intrinsic job satisfaction in research by Sims and Szilagyi (1976). A broad measure of good relationships with coworkers was shown by Hendrix, Ovalle, and Troxler (1985) to be associated with low job-related tension, controlling for a range of other features. Birdi et al. (1995) found that quality of working relations was correlated at +0.47 with overall job satisfaction; that association remained significant after statistical controls for several job and personal features.

Many studies of "social support" have revealed similar patterns. Although this is variously defined in the literature, social support is usually viewed in terms of helpful inputs from other people. For example, widely used questionnaire items by Caplan et al. (1975) ask whether colleagues "make your work life easier" and "can be relied on when things get tough." Associations with happiness are likely to arise from variations in both emotional and instrumental assistance, so that well-supported individuals receive help that is both sympathetic and comforting and also of practical problem-solving value. Supportive conversations in work settings may discuss negative or positive job features or be addressed to nonwork issues (e.g., Beehr, King, & King, 1990).

Measures of support from coworkers have repeatedly been shown to be associated with overall and intrinsic job satisfaction. Earlier research has been reviewed by Warr (1987) and others, and later studies include those by Chay (1993) and Moyle (1995), who observed correlations of +0.26 and +0.59 with overall job satisfaction, associations that remained significant despite statistical control for other variables. Across a variety of social support indicators, Viswesvaran, Sanchez, and Fisher (1999) reported an average correlation with job satisfaction of –0.24 (46 samples). Support from coworkers was correlated at +0.50 (average of two values), +0.27, and +0.43, respectively, with overall job satisfaction in studies by de Jonge et al. (2001), Bowling et al. (2004), and Wilson et al. (2004). Podsakoff et al. (1996) found an average correlation of +0.33 between reported group cohesiveness and overall job satisfaction across 16 samples.

Well-being axes 2 and 3 have less often been examined in relation to this environmental feature. Totterdell et al. (2006) observed that emotional support was correlated strongly with job-related axis 3 (depression–enthusiasm; +0.55) but not with job-related anxiety–comfort ($r = +0.02$). That difference was retained despite statistical controls for other variables. With respect to job-related emotional exhaustion, the meta-analysis by Lee and Ashforth (1996) recorded an average correlation with social support of –0.26 across six samples. In later studies, that value was –0.32, –0.30, –0.36 (average of two measurement occasions), and –0.26 (average of two values; Bakker et al., 2005, de Jonge et al., 2001, Houkes et al., 2003, and Zellars & Perrewé, 2001, respectively). Those associations remained significant despite controls for other job and personal variables.

Some research into this job feature has examined subjective well-being that is context-free. For example, Parkes (1990), Chay (1993), and Moyle (1995) observed correlations between wide-ranging distress (the General Health Questionnaire; see chap. 2) and in-job social support of –0.30, –0.36, and –0.34, respectively. Using a different measure of distress, Roxburgh (1996) found that lower levels of coworker support were significantly associated with more distress despite statistical controls for other job features and demographic characteristics. For context-free depression, Beehr et al. (2000) recorded a correlation with coworker support of –0.34.

Low levels of social support extend beyond merely an absence of helpful interactions to include the possibility of interpersonal conflict and explicit hostility or abuse. Some conflict between colleagues, in the form of constructive disagreement and expression of divergent opinions, is central to productive teamwork, but major emotional clashes may of course impair subjective well-being. Examining facet-specific satisfaction targeted on interpersonal relationships, de Dreu and Weingart (2003) reported an average correlation from previous studies of –0.56 (corrected for measurement unreliability) with relationship conflict.

For overall job satisfaction, Grebner et al. (2003) obtained a correlation with relationship conflict of –0.36, and that average value from two samples was –0.48 in research by Guerra, Martinez, Munduate, and Medina (2005). Both sets of investigators reported that this association remained significant despite statistical control for other variables. That was also the case in research by Lubbers, Loughlin, and Zweig (2005), where the bivariate correlation between conflict at work and a broad measure of job-related affect averaged –0.39. Penney and Spector (2005) obtained self-reports of interpersonal conflict at work and also ratings from colleagues of that conflict. Both indicators of low-quality relationships were significantly negatively associated with employees' overall job satisfaction ($r = -0.27$ and -0.36, respectively). For job-related emotional exhaustion, the correlation with relationship conflict in the study by Giebels and Janssen (2005) was $+0.27$.

A significant association with conflict-linked aspects of environmental feature 6 has also been reported for context-free well-being. Applying a broad measure of context-free happiness, Dijkstra, van Diederonck, Evers, and de Dreu (2005) found from two studies an average correlation of –0.23 with reported conflict at work. Related research has examined the impact of offensive remarks, insults, ridicule, criticism, intimidation, malicious rumors, or social isolation enforced by a refusal to communicate with a person (Rospenda & Richman, 2005; Schat & Kelloway, 2005). For example, Schat and Kelloway (2000) and LeBlanc and Barling (2002) reported correlations of $+0.30$ and $+0.32$ between aggression from colleagues (being shouted at, hit, insulted, etc.) and broad psychological distress. This significant pattern was retained despite controls for other possible influences; that was also the case in research by Eriksen and Einarsen (2004).

Although most studies in this area have concerned possibly malicious behaviors by coworkers, "petty tyranny" and "abusive supervision" by managers have been considered by Ashforth (1994) and Tepper (2000) respectively (see chap. 5). The job feature of concern in the present section (6, contact with others) and supportive supervision (10) clearly have many features in common.

Aggressive behaviors that are persistent and repeated are sometimes identified as "bullying." Einarsen, Hoel, Zapf, and Cooper (2003) suggested that "bullying at work is about repeated actions and practices that are directed against one or more workers, that are unwanted by the victim, that may be carried out deliberately or unconsciously, but clearly cause humiliation, offence and distress" (p. 6). Bullying primarily involves pressure on a person that is psychological, but in a minority of cases abuse can bring about physical harm. Workplace violence can itself extend from behaviors that rarely create physical injury (e.g., pushing and shoving) to severe assaults or even murder (Barling, 1996). (Schat and Kelloway [2000] pointed out that homicide was the second most common cause of job-related death in the United States.)

It would not be surprising to find that continuing exposure to aggressive behaviors creates unhappiness. Einarsen and Mikkelsen (2003) have reviewed evidence that bullying is significantly associated with reduced job satisfaction, raised anxiety, and raised depression of both job-related and context-free kinds, and with a wide range of negative psychosomatic conditions. Lapierre et al. (2005) reported findings from a meta-analysis of relationships between overall job satisfaction and several forms of work-place aggression. The uncorrected average correlation was −0.31. In additional analyses that excluded possible gender variation by examining only female samples, they drew attention to the fact that nonsexual aggression had a significantly greater association with women's job satisfaction than did sexual aggression, although both forms of behavior were harmful in that respect (mean $r = -0.41$ and −0.32, respectively).

Although aggression, bullying, or violence usually comes from an individual's coworkers, employees whose role brings them into contact with customers, clients, or the general public may also be exposed to negative behaviors from those sources. For example, the absence of face-to-face contact in telephone interactions may perhaps encourage verbal aggression from unseen customers. This possibility was examined by Grandey et al. (2004), who recorded "communications of anger that violate social norms" (p. 398). They found that verbal aggression so defined occurred in around 15% of interactions in call centers. Its frequency was correlated at +0.30 with job-related emotional exhaustion, and that association remained significant despite controls for dispositional affectivity and other variables.

These negative forms of contact with others are themselves associated with undesirable low levels of other job features. For example, a person who is bullied is likely to perceive a decline in his or her ability to control the environment to reduce harm ("vitamin" 1). Bullied employees may also experience a reduction in predictability (an aspect of feature 5), if aggressive behavior occurs inconsistently or at irregular intervals. With respect to high levels of externally generated goals (feature 3), emotional conflicts with coworkers can create distractions and new behavioral objectives that divert people away from primary work activities.

Note that poor-quality social relations may merely involve interpersonal dislikes rather than actively negative inputs from others. "Not getting on with colleagues" can arise from differences in personal styles and preferences, such that employees can be unhappy at work because of a "personality clash," a mutual dislike between colleagues, or a distaste for one's customers. Those negative themes within feature 6 deserve targeted investigation in their own right.

Barley and Knight (1992) have drawn attention to the fact that processes of interpersonal contact can generate unhappiness, despite being desirable in the terms considered so far. That negative impact can occur within a network of social influence, such that job dissatisfaction experienced by other workers can be transmitted to an employee through between-person "interpretive contagion." In studies of affective similarity within work-groups, Totterdell et al. (2004) found that similarity of job-related feelings was greater when more interaction ties between employees were present, that is, when quantity of social contact was raised. "Groups of employees who are most interconnected in the network of ties show most consistency in this effect" (p. 864). Processes of social contagion are further considered in chapter 9.

Nonlinearity and Social Contact

For both quantity and quality of social contact, evidence about the chapter's second and third questions is limited. Question 2 asks about nonlinear relationships. De Jonge et al. (2000) observed significant nonlinear associations between social support and both job-related emotional exhaustion and context-free depression, with least happiness at low levels of support and an "additional decrement" occurring at very high levels of support in both cases. A nonlinear pattern was also found by Rice et al. (1991) with respect to satisfaction with coworker conversations; this was along the lines proposed here, but details were not presented.

Low to moderate levels of social density were considered earlier. Attention has also been directed at the high (right-hand) segment of the curve in Figures 4.1 and 4.2, with some evidence of "too much of a good thing." For example, Oldham and Rotchford (1983) examined the density of clerical employees' occupation of office space. They found that higher density (more employees in a standard area) was significantly associated with low overall job satisfaction, low satisfaction with colleagues, and low satisfaction with physical surroundings. Greater density was also linked to reduced job feedback from colleagues or supervisors. Sundstrom et al. (1980) reported that lack of privacy was correlated at -0.54 with (facet-specific) satisfaction with one's work place. In the study by Fried, Slowik, Ben-David, and Tiegs (2001), the number of colleagues working close to an office worker was correlated at -0.17 with overall job satisfaction, and results suggested that the negative association between density and well-being was greatest in more complex jobs.

Themes of that kind are illustrated in research into open-plan offices, where a number of employees are located in a single workspace, perhaps with screens, shelving, cabinets, or other furniture serving to group together members of a team. Research comparisons between that setting and traditional, smaller offices have sometimes suggested open-plan benefits in terms of more pleasant working conditions and interactions with colleagues, but negative effects on subjective well-being have often been found. Those arise from increased noise, more interruptions and distractions from others, a sense of overcrowding, a lack of privacy, and fewer friendly conversations because of a lack of confidentiality (Brennan, Chugh, & Kline, 2002; McCoy & Evans, 2005).

For example, in research by Oldham and Brass (1979), a move from separate offices to a single large open-plan site significantly decreased overall job satisfaction, satisfaction with colleagues, and friendship opportunities, as employees reported that they could not hold discussions without being overheard by the larger group. Brennan et al. (2002) pointed out that people might come to adjust to a less private environment after a period of time, so that investigations need to extend beyond merely the point of transition. They tracked office workers for 6 months after their move from traditional offices into an open setting. An early reduction in facet-specific satisfactions (with the environment, physical conditions, and team member relations) was maintained over that period. "The primary complaints listed by employees were lack of privacy and confidentiality and increased noise" (p. 294).

These negative aspects of high social density are consistent with the model of Altman and Chemers (1980), addressed to interpersonal interaction in general. They were concerned with people's attempts to regulate the degree to which they are open to interaction with others, arguing that societies control accessibility by normative behavioral processes and through the creation of environmental structures. Privacy (a reduction in social contact) was seen as important for separate personal development and for the effective management of tasks on either an individual or group basis. In regulating their privacy, people seek both to avoid isolation and to escape crowding; those two conditions (at the two ends of the horizontal axis in Figs. 4.1 and 4.2) were viewed as psychologically harmful. In a general review of problems caused by crowding, Baum and Paulus (1987) showed clear negative impacts of high density on happiness and performance.

One form of privacy regulation is the establishment of personal territory, for oneself and for one's group. Boundaries are created in social networks of all kinds, being valued for the potential they provide for separate activities by individuals and groups and for the effective management of tasks without external interference. Environments that give rise to an extremely high level of interpersonal contact can prevent personal privacy and individual and subgroup development, and bring about levels of crowding that can be disturbing and disruptive.

What about the linearity or nonlinearity of relations between happiness and qualitative aspects of social contact, rather than its quantity? The vitamin model suggests that very high levels of social support can themselves be linked to reduced happiness in comparison with the middle segment of the curve. That is expected from the fact that for environmental features in general what is an opportunity at moderate levels becomes an unavoidable and coercive requirement at very high levels. Being forced to receive help (an instance of very high social support) can in that respect be harmful. Empirical support in organizations was cited in the previous section.

A negative impact was also illustrated in a laboratory study by Deelstra et al. (2003). Research participants worked for 4 hours in a simulated office with a colleague who was in fact a confederate of the researchers. The confederate contributed task assistance in the "imposed support" experimental condition but not in the "no support" condition. (Note that social support here was of the instrumental rather than emotional kind.) The imposition of assistance generated significantly more negative affect than in the comparison condition, except when task problems were unsolvable; in the latter case, the effect of imposed support was not positive but neutral. That negative consequence of very high social support is consistent with the proposed downturn of happiness at the right-hand side of Figures 4.1 and 4.2.

Social Contact and Different Aspects of Happiness

The chapter's third question concerns the pattern of different associations proposed in Tables 4.2 and 5.1. As with other suggested "additional decrement" features, correlations at very high levels of social contact or support are expected to be stronger (negatively) with axis 2 (from anxiety to comfort), and at low levels of the feature to be stronger (positively) with well-being axis 3 (from depression to enthusiasm). That differential expectation is based on the argument presented in chapter 2 that the absence of a desirable feature (here, contact with other people) more gives rise to depression, whereas an excess of a feature (in this case, social overload) represents a potentially harmful threat that brings about anxiety and tension (e.g., Carver, 2003).

The limited amount of research that compares well-being axes 3 and 2 has rarely examined associations with the quantity or quality of social contact. However, initial evidence from Totterdell et al. (2006) has supported the proposed differential pattern: Availability of social support (presumably from low to moderate amounts) was found to be correlated at +0.55 with job-related depression–enthusiasm (axis 3) but at only +0.02 with job-related anxiety–comfort (axis 2; see the earlier section). However, a negative social setting in terms of abuse and bullying appears to be also associated with increased anxiety (a low score on axis 2). That may be due to associated impacts from other features such as reduced opportunity for control and environmental clarity, as suggested earlier. Additional comparative investigations are now desirable. As with the other primary job features considered in this and preceding chapters, a differentiated perspective is required, specifying possibly different associations with different forms of happiness or unhappiness rather than viewing that construct in merely unidimensional terms.

8

Combinations, Measurement, Causes, and Work Profiles

The preceding three chapters examined each primary environmental feature on its own. We now consider some issues that are more general. For example, given that job characteristics do not operate in isolation, what is known about their combined influence on happiness? Measurement themes will also be examined and causal patterns explored through studies that follow employees across time. The chapter will then draw on the vitamin framework to suggest profiles of psychologically bad work and psychologically good work, which may be applied in practical as well as research situations. The main focus is on work as paid employment, but the profiles are also applicable to nonemployment activities of many kinds.

THE COMBINATION OF JOB FEATURES

Although the primary job characteristics have so far been examined singly, they do of course occur in combination with each other. In addition to the importance of a feature on its own, we need also to think about its impact when occurring together with other features.

For example, recognizing that opportunity for personal control (feature 1) has a positive association with job satisfaction in the low to moderate range, are job demands (feature 3) also important over and above variations in control in that range? Warr (1990b) showed that features 1 and 3 were each independently significant in relation to overall job satisfaction despite controlling for the other feature. That was also found, for instance, by Rafferty et al. (2001) after controlling for five demographic variables, and by Bakker et al. (2005) for job-related emotional exhaustion. Many other investigations have shown that primary job features are independently linked to subjective well-being over and above other features. For instance, Schaufeli and Bakker (2004) described independent associations of job demands (feature 3) and forms of supportive social relationships (6) with job-related burnout. It is clear from the many multivariate analyses summarized in chapters 5 to 7 that several job features can be individually important within a compound input.

Interactions Between Features

Combined effects might occur in an additive fashion, with each aspect of a job making an extra contribution without modifying the impact of the others. However, we need also to consider the possibility that environmental features combine together in an interactive rather than additive fashion. In that case, the effect of one variable becomes stronger or weaker when combined with another one. In relation to physical health, interactions of that kind have been demonstrated in some combinations of vitamins and drugs, such that the impact of a particular vitamin can depend on the nature of other inputs. That might also be the case in the area of this book.

Two related possibilities have been of principal interest. First, when two job features are studied in combination, their individual associations with an aspect of well-being can both remain significant, but one or both become(s) modified by the other. Second, as a special case of that interaction, the association between one variable and well-being might become nonsignificant, being removed by a second feature, which itself remains significant. Researchers have not always distinguished between those expectations, and they have also differed among themselves in meaning and use of the terms *interaction, moderation,* and *buffering* in this area (van Vegchel et al., 2005).

Findings about combination have varied considerably between investigations, and the factors determining different research outcomes remain unclear. Most research has concerned the existence or otherwise of an interactive pattern for job features 1 and 3—opportunity for personal control and job demands. Karasek (1979) raised the possibility that those two features combine in an interactive manner. He suggested that one particular combination was disproportionately harmful, when high job demands occur in conjunction with a low level of personal control. On the other hand, when control opportunity is high, raised demands were considered to be less troublesome, or even attractive challenges, because individuals can then decide when and how to deal with them.

In practice, Karasek's (1979) analysis did not test in formal statistical terms for the existence of that pattern. Subsequent research using more rigorous procedures has sometimes obtained significant interactions. For example, van Vegchel et al. (2005) examined job-related emotional exhaustion as a function jointly of demands and control opportunity, and reported a statistical interaction of the kind proposed by Karasek. However, most investigations have failed to find a significant interaction between those two variables. High demands in conjunction with low control do indeed particularly impair well-being, but only in an additive manner to the extent expected by the aggregation of their own individual effects. Terry and Jimmieson (1999) concluded from their review of the field that research "has generally been unsuccessful in establishing empirical support" (p. 107) for interactive combinations between those two job features.

Van der Doef and Maes (1999) drew attention to some evidence that a statistical interaction is more likely when the characteristics have been specified very precisely. That finding was obtained by Wall et al. (1996), who observed a significant interaction with narrow-focus measures of personal control and job demands (asking about particular activities). However, several subsequent studies with focused measures have failed to confirm that interaction (e.g., de Jonge et al., 2001; Totterdell et al., 2006), and in general an additive combination appears more likely for those two variables than is an interactive one.

Possible interactions have also been examined between job demands and social support, an aspect of contact with others (feature 6 in the present framework). Social support might alleviate the harmful effects of high job demands, for example, by providing instrumental or emotional assistance in coping with those demands. Demands that are high would thus be particularly troubling in the absence of social support, and the relationship between demands and subjective well-being would be clearly negative when demands are combined with low support. However, when social support is high, it might lessen the impact of demands, so that the relationship of job demands with happiness or unhappiness would then be significantly less negative or around zero. Although, as summarized in chapter 7, social support up to moderate levels is itself associated with greater well-being, most studies have failed to find evidence for a significant inter-action with job demands of that kind (e.g., Beehr et al., 2000; Bowling et al., 2004; Roxburgh, 1996; van der Doef & Maes, 1999; Viswesvaran et al., 1999).

Research into possible interactions has mainly concerned those three features—opportunity for personal control, job demands, and (to a smaller extent) social support ("vitamins" 1, 3, and 6). Bakker et al. (2005) looked at possible interactive patterns across a wider range of job characteristics. Recording employees' job-related emo-tional exhaustion, they studied feedback (an aspect of feature 5) and supportive supervision (feature 10), as well as features 1, 3, and 6 as already mentioned. In separate analyses for each combination, the level of job demands was studied in conjunction with one of the other four features. Job-related emotional exhaustion was found to be greater when job demands were high and any of the other features was low (and hence negative); however, when the level of another of the features was high (i.e., more positive), demands had a weaker or no relationship with that form of well-being. Significant interactions were present in combinations of job demands and those four job char-acteristics. Bakker et al. (2005) also examined this possibility with respect to a subcomponent of feature 3, work–family conflict, instead of job demands themselves. Significant interactions were found between work–family conflict and control opportunity, feedback, and supportive supervision, but not in combination with social support.

Elovainio et al. (2001) examined feature 1 (opportunity for per-sonal control) in combination with either supportive supervision (labeled in their report as "relational justice") or procedural justice (features 10 and 12). In relation to employees' job-related strain, no evidence for an interactive pattern was found. However, Probst's (2005b) examination of opportunity for control in conjunction with job insecurity (an aspect of 11) revealed significant interactions with respect to job satisfaction; insecurity was related to lower well-being only when the opportunity for control in a job was low.

In the light of these inconsistent reports about the presence or absence of an interaction between job features, a straightforward con-clusion about modes of combination is not possible. It is clear that the environmental features examined in earlier chapters are singly impor-tant for happiness and that they combine together at least additively to affect subjective well-being; for example, several harmful features in combination are likely to create more unhappiness than one alone. However, interactive combinations are found only sometimes and the differentiating conditions have yet to be precisely specified.

We need to build future research on the recognition that different mechanisms account for different combinations of job characteristics. Interpreting their own findings, Bakker et al. (2005) pointed out that "different processes may have been responsible for comparable inter-action effects" (p. 177). For example, the harmful impact of high demands might be reduced by more personal control because that helps in deciding how to deal with (for instance, postpone) those demands. On the other hand, social support in combination with high demands might yield the same statistical pattern in a quite different way, through the provision of assistance from other people, and feed-back could moderate the impact of high demands by providing infor-mation that improves coping activities. For the combination of job insecurity and personal control (described earlier), it is possible that opportunity for personal control as recorded extends in practice beyond the job itself, including greater perceived control over getting a new position if current insecurity leads to job loss.

It is now essential to develop for each principal combination of job features a conceptually appropriate hypothesis about the particular processes that might give rise to either an additive or interactive pattern. The psychological and social mechanisms will often differ between different combinations of characteristics. As noted at several points throughout the book, it is inappropriate to seek a standard explanation for the impact of job features in general or in broad categories; they have their own distinct modes of operation. Furthermore, measures of job features applied with respect to a particular interaction should be linked closely to whatever explanatory themes are hypothesized to be relevant to that interaction, rather than (as has been common) having a more general or conceptually unrelated nature.

It is also important to draw on the fact (emphasized by the vitamin model) that job features' associations with subjective well-being depend on the level of those features. It is usually assumed in this area that studied levels of opportunity for personal control are in the low ("deficiency") range of Figures 4.1 and 4.2 (see chap. 4). However, job demands ("vitamin" 3 in the present framework) may vary more widely between studies. In some cases, demands are primarily of a high ("toxic") kind, but elsewhere they are in the range of acceptable values, and thus likely to generate an association with well-being that is around zero. (See the examples in chap. 6.) Different theoretical explanations are needed for different levels of each environmental characteristic. A universal expectation of a single form of interactive combination is clearly inappropriate.

Compound Inputs

Several aspects of a job have sometimes been combined into a single index of content. This approach is based on the fact that some of the primary job characteristics tend to be associated with each other. For example, high levels of opportunity for personal control or for skill use (features 1 and 2) are linked to raised uncertainty in the environment (5); greater variety in a job (4) can involve more contact with other people (an aspect of 6); a supportive supervisor (10) is likely to provide job feedback (an aspect of 5); a poor career outlook (feature 11) in terms of job insecurity is often accompanied by low environmental clarity (5).

Overlaps of that kind are reflected in empirical intercorrelations. For instance, Xie and Johns (1995) reported that perceived opportunity for personal control (1) was correlated at +0.55, +0.41, and +0.28 with variety (4), task identity (an aspect of 3), and valued social position (9), respectively. A meta-analysis by Jackson and Schuler (1985) found that role conflict (an aspect of feature 3) was on average correlated at −0.28 with considerate supervision (10). Research by Spector (1987) showed that role clarity (an aspect of 5) was correlated at −0.35 with poor-quality relations with others (a negative form of 6). Task significance (9) was correlated on average at +0.40 with feedback (an aspect of 5) in studies by Gerhart (1988), and the correlation between job demands (feature 3) and social support (an aspect of 6) was −0.35 in a study by Janssen et al. (2004).

Recognizing these overlaps, some investigators have created a single index that combines several job features. For example, the Job Diagnostic Survey (Hackman & Oldham, 1975, 1976) included a "motivating potential score" in terms of a weighted (see later discussion) combination of autonomy, feedback, skill variety, task identity, and task significance. Scores of that broad kind have often been found to be positively associated with overall and intrinsic job satisfaction (e.g., Griffin, 1991; Wall et al., 1978). Champoux (1980) combined (without weighting) the five job features into an index of "job scope," reporting across three studies an average correlation of +0.51 with overall job satisfaction and +0.67 with (facet) satisfaction with personal growth in one's job. Correlations between perceived job scope and overall job satisfaction were +0.41 and +0.62 in research by Ganzach (1998) and Judge et al. (2000), respectively.

It was pointed out in chapter 5 that the "additional decrement" components of the vitamin model (features 1 to 6) tend to concern intrinsic aspects of a job, whereas the "constant-effect" characteristics have a more extrinsic emphasis. Measures of "scope" (sometimes referred to as "complexity") mainly cover intrinsic aspects of a job, and that compound variable is therefore expected to be more strongly associated with employees' satisfaction with intrinsic job features (autonomy, variety, etc.) than with their extrinsic satisfaction (with pay, working conditions, etc.). That is indeed the case (e.g., Cordery, Mueller, & Smith, 1991). The same differential pattern was found with respect to facet satisfactions by Judge and Locke (1993). They reported a correlation between perceived intrinsic job characteristics (very similar to "job scope") and satisfaction with the work itself of +0.64, whereas associations of that job index with extrinsic facet satisfactions were lower, averaging only +0.21.

With respect to the second axis of job-related well-being (see Fig. 2.2 in chap. 2), Houkes et al. (2003) reported significant negative associations of job scope with job-related exhaustion, $r = -0.31$ averaged across two measurement occasions. In research by Xie and Johns (1995), that value was −0.28. A compound of intrinsic job characteristics was found by Lee and Allen (2002) to be correlated at +0.43 with activated forms of job-related positive affect (in the top-right section of Figs. 2.1 and 2.2).

Examining "motivational" and other aspects of job content, Campion (1988) combined together responses to 18 questions covering all except 2 of the 12 features in the present framework. (The exceptions were 8 and 12, physical security and equity.) Employees' perceptions of these "motivational" characteristics in aggregation were found to be correlated at +0.62 with their overall job satisfaction. Carlson and Mellor (2004) assessed "self-actualization opportunity" (a compound of personal control and skill use, "vitamins" 1 and 2), finding a correlation with overall job satisfaction of +0.60. Complexity of content rated by independent observers on the basis of job title has also been found to be associated with job holders' overall job satisfaction. For example, Judge et al. (2000) reported a correlation of +0.41, and Gerhart (1987) found that the association remained significant despite controls for other variables. Note that research of that kind treats as identical all jobs with the same title, which is unlikely to be the case, so it may underestimate the true relationship.

In parallel with studies of scope or complexity, some research has placed within an overall compound several job features that are extrinsic (pay, working conditions, etc.) rather than intrinsic. Consistent with the fact that single intrinsic features are in general more closely associated with subjective well-being than are single extrinsic features, extrinsic compounds tend to be less strongly correlated with overall job satisfaction than are compounds of intrinsic characteristics (e.g., Taris, Feij, & van Vianen, 2005).

Combinations of intrinsic job features are also associated with happiness or unhappiness that is context-free. For example, the correlation of unweighted job scope items (see earlier discussion) with life satisfaction averaged +0.32 across three samples in research by Judge, Locke, Durham, and Kluger (1998), and for several measures of context-free happiness it averaged +0.31 in the study by Judge and Locke (1993). In research by Wiener, Vardi, and Muczyk (1981), job complexity was significantly associated with greater life satisfaction and lower depression, as well as with overall job satisfaction and satisfaction with one's career.

Perceived intrinsic job characteristics were measured by Warr et al. (1979) by combining the opportunities for personal control and skill use, variety, feedback, task identity, and valued social position. Manual workers' intrinsic job characteristics were found to be correlated at +0.28 with their life satisfaction and +0.36 with their overall happiness. The correlation of this intrinsic job measure with context-free distress was –0.26 in research by Kemp, Wall, Clegg, and Cordery (1983). House, McMichael, Wells, Kaplan, and Landerman (1979) assessed the degree to which factory workers' jobs permitted personal control and skill use and contained variety and interest; these features (brought together in a scale of "intrinsic rewards") were significantly associated with low levels of context-free distress. In research by Payne et al. (1999), a compound of negative work characteristics (high workload, low control, high role conflict, and low role clarity) was correlated at +0.50 with context-free distress.

With very few exceptions (linked to the Job Diagnostic Survey, already mentioned), these studies of combined inputs from a job have treated as equally important the several elements of a compound. However, variations could arise through the differential weighting of those elements. For example, some features might in general be more important for subjective well-being than others (e.g., opportunity for control rather than physical security). That was assumed in deriving the "motivating potential score" (mentioned earlier), when autonomy and feedback were allocated more weight than task identity, skill variety and task significance: MPS = [(SV + TI + TS)/3] × AU × FB (Hackman & Oldham, 1976).

An alternative weighting possibility is in terms of the current intensity of each input. It could be the case that combined effects on happiness are more influenced by whichever features happen to be more extreme in a particular situation. Such differential weighting has been found widely in studies of social judgment and impression formation. Warr and Jackson (1975) reviewed earlier reports that disproportionate weighting is allocated to more extreme elements. Those (and their own evidence) showed clearly that compound judgments about other people (for instance, deriving from two cues) were principally influenced by the more extreme stimulus.

That form of differential weighting might also operate in the area of this book. Rather than a standard weighting contrast in terms of the continuing nature of a feature (as in, for instance, the job characteristics model, described earlier), the relative importance of environmental features for a person's happiness or unhappiness might depend on the level of those characteristics in a current setting. Research into these weighting possibilities is now required.

Finally in this section about compound inputs from the environment, note that particular combinations of environmental features are likely to underlie several broad variables. Consider, for example, organization size. Job satisfaction is regularly found to be greater in smaller organizations, particularly those that are very small. In a British national sample, Clark et al. (1996) showed that employees in organizations with less than 25 people exhibited significantly greater overall job satisfaction and satisfaction with the work itself than did those in larger organizations. (However, no difference was present for satisfaction with pay or for context-free happiness.) With respect to overall job satisfaction, Clark (1996) examined that data set separately for men and for women, finding the same pattern in both cases, and Clark (2005a) extended the analysis over nine successive years with the same result. Bender et al. (2005) illustrated the generalizability of this negative association with organization size in a national U.S. sample.

Which job features might differ between small organizations and larger ones to account for that difference in some forms of job-related well-being? Average differences might benefit employees in small organizations in terms of features 1, 2, and 4: opportunities for personal control and for skill use and level of variety. For example, specialist staff are rare in small companies, so that individuals there have to deal with a wide variety of tasks and problems themselves, rather than calling in expert colleagues (Poutsma & Zwaard, 1988). However, staff in small organizations might on average have less environmental clarity (5) and lower income (7). Linked to that, different patterns of association might be expected for the three axes of subjective well-being. For example, although employees in small organizations exhibit greater overall job satisfaction (i.e., on measurement axis 1), they may experience greater job-related anxiety (i.e., lower well-being) on axis 2. Empirical research is needed to specify typical levels of job features that underlie organization size and other "container" variables of that kind (those that "contain" other variables of importance).

More generally, environment-centered approaches to employee happiness should more often investigate compounds of features, complementing the traditional emphasis on single or a small number of variables. Findings reviewed above make it clear that sets of job characteristics can be more closely associated with employees' subjective well-being than are the single job features examined in previous chapters. Compound variables are also likely to be important with respect to differences between groups. In seeking environment-based explanations for happiness differences between, say, men and women or between employees in different business sectors, we need to identify the combinations of environmental features that may be responsible for those differences. Procedures to record configurations of primary environmental characteristics are suggested later in the chapter, through the creation of profiles for individual jobs and for groups of jobs.

Nonlinear Relationships

The vitamin model proposes that job characteristics are positively associated with happiness in their lower ("deficiency") range and that this association is reduced (and in some cases reversed) at higher levels of a feature. (See, Fig. 4.2 on p. 102.) Chapters 5 to 7 examined that nonlinear expectation for each job feature separately. Although the possibility of a departure from linearity in relation to employee happiness has rarely been investigated, supportive evidence was described for several of the features on their own. Thus, predicted relationships have been observed in laboratory studies (e.g., for opportunity for personal control and for social contact; chaps. 6 and 7, respectively), and the suggested "additional decrement" pattern is apparent in job settings for "vitamin" 3, externally generated goals (chap. 6). Nevertheless, tests for nonlinearity have been rare, and several investigations have found only a linear association. As noted previously, those have often lacked a wide-enough range of the job feature in question for an adequate examination of the issue.

Based on the earlier theoretical arguments and some empirical evidence about individual job features, it might be expected that, in addition to patterns for single job variables, happiness will also be associated in a nonlinear fashion with combinations of features. Two studies of job scope/complexity (see earlier discussion) have examined this possibility, and both found nonlinearity. Champoux (1980) observed a significant nonlinear pattern in job scope's association with overall job satisfaction and growth satisfaction in two of three samples. (The third sample contained only 66 employees, too few to properly test the hypothesis.) Xie and Johns (1995) also reported significant nonlinearity for job scope, with respect to job-related emotional exhaustion.

Were those nonlinear patterns of the "additional decrement" or "constant effect" kind? The job scope measure used in both studies, based on characteristics assessed by the Job Diagnostic Survey, contained four proposed "additional decrement" components (autonomy, task identity, variety, and feedback; "vitamin" 1, part of 3, 4, and part of 5, respectively), and one assumed "constant effect" characteristic (task significance, 9). An inverted U shape might thus overall be expected, with reduced happiness at very high (as well as low) levels of scope measured in this way. However, the strength of that downturn at the right of Figure 4.2 might be limited by exclusion from the overall compound of job demands (3), which are on their own associated with happiness in an "additional decrement" manner (see chap. 6), and by the inclusion of a "constant effect" characteristic in the form of task significance.

With respect to emotional exhaustion, Xie and Johns (1995) did indeed find an asymmetric U pattern of the additional decrement kind. They suggested that job content "can be stressful when it provokes either understimulation or overstimulation," such that "chronic exposure to too little or too much of a good thing may provoke stress" (p. 1303). Furthermore, the observed pattern was "slightly asymmetric, suggesting insufficiency of job scope was more stressful than excess" (p. 1303). However, that decrement in well-being at very high levels as well as at low values of job scope was not present in the analyses of job satisfaction by Champoux (1980). Although, within an overall nonlinear pattern, a significant leveling off in (raised) satisfaction occurred across moderate levels of scope, the association between job scope and well-being did not turn negative at high levels of these combined job characteristics. The author proposed that a ceiling effect from imperfect measures may have contributed to the absence of a down-turn. (And inadequate coverage of jobs with very high values may also be responsible.)

Strazdins et al. (2004) also obtained results "suggestive of a possible threshold effect" (p. 303), such that high job demands (feature 3), low opportunity for control (1), and low job security (11) combined to substantially impair well-being, whereas at more positive levels of those features a much smaller association was present. Examining context-free anxiety and context-free depression, they found that "very high" pressure from that combination of job features yielded sharp increases in anxiety and depression, whereas variations in the three-variable job score were associated with only small differences in happiness in the range from "low" to "high" pressure. (In effect, because the job features were measured negatively, that latter range was primarily across the right-hand section of Fig. 4.2.) Additional research is clearly needed in this area, but it is very unlikely that job scope and other combinations of features are linearly associated with employee happiness.

ENVIRONMENTAL MEASURES: OBJECTIVE OR SUBJECTIVE?

Environmental features have often been assessed through the perceptions of people taking part in an investigation. When people's happiness is examined in relation to their own view of an environment, problems of interpretation arise that are associated with "common-method variance." This occurs when variance in the two sets of responses (in the present case, about the environment and about one's happiness) may be "attributable to the measurement method rather than to the constructs the measures represent" (Podsakoff, MacKenzie, Lee, & Podsakoff, 2003, p. 879). Common-method influences can increase the correlation between two self-reports, so that a true relationship between variables may be less strong than is indicated by a single person's reports about them. In reviewing these issues, three forms of environmental measurement require consideration: reports by a target person, reports by observers, and indicators that are more objective.

Target Persons' Reports of Environmental Features

Almost all investigations described in previous chapters have assessed the environment through ratings made by research participants themselves. These yield a score for each member of a sample, so that there are multiple indicators of a job (or other) feature, rather than a single statement about "the" environment that is applicable to all job holders in that environment. Target persons' reports are "subjective" assessments, in that measurement is potentially open to influence from the person making a judgment. They record the environment as experienced by a person, rather than an environment existing independently of personal perspectives. As a result, assessments of nominally the same environment can vary between individuals. For example, judgments about the level of externally generated goals (feature 3 in the present framework) derive in part from a person's reference standard; some people view a given environment as more demanding than others. Given that happiness often depends on environmental stimuli as interpreted, rather than on those stimuli without interpretation, subjective assessments of this kind have obvious theoretical advantages in the area of this book.

However, as noted earlier, the presence of a personal viewpoint in measures of the environment may increase correlations with reports of happiness. When the same rater generates both the judgmental scores in a bivariate correlation, seven contaminating influences may be envisaged (Podsakoff et al., 2003). Research participants are likely to seek to maintain some consistency across their responses; they can be influenced by their implicit theories about covariation, giving rise to "illusory correlations" (Berman & Kenny, 1976); a bias toward socially desirable responding to both sets of questions can inflate correlations. Three other possible response biases involve acquiescence (generally agreeing with questions posed), leniency (overrating the desirability of features), and a general tendency toward positive or negative perceptions of the world and oneself (sometimes termed "positive affectivity" or "negative affectivity"). Finally, responses to the two sets of ratings may both be shaped by a transient level of context-free or domain-specific affect.

Although those seven influences are in principle separately possible, they are unlikely to all operate in any one situation. Furthermore, several of them are of concern primarily when assessments are ambiguous. Their collective importance in job settings of different kinds has not yet been specified. Nevertheless, measuring the environment through target persons' reports is expected to inflate correlations with the same people's happiness.

Observers' Ratings of Environmental Features

To avoid possible problems of those kinds, some investigators have obtained descriptions of a person's environment from other people.

Those accounts have sometimes been labeled as "objective," although they are just as subjective as target persons' ratings (just discussed), being potentially open to personal influence from a judge; they are better described as "independent" rather than "objective." The noninvolvement of a target person clearly reduces common-method variance, although some between-source contamination might occur if an observer obtains information about a job through discussion with the job holder himself or herself (e.g., Grebner et al., 2005).

Observers in this form of environmental measurement may be a supervisor or coworker, but sometimes are job analysts whose knowledge of the job in question derives merely from a brief examination. Ratings of job content may be made separately for each person, or they may be at the level of a job title. In the latter case, everyone with the same job title is in effect assumed to be exposed to an identical environment; that is often an unreasonable assumption, especially for employees in different organizations. Ratings at the level of job titles have sometimes been based on summary written accounts (rather than on direct observation of the job), such as in a nationwide Dictionary of Occupational Titles (e.g., Gerhart, 1987, 1988; Spector & Jex, 1991). Those accounts are necessarily much less detailed than the information available to job holders or to observers of the job itself.

Both forms of rating (by a target person and by observers) are thus subjective, but the latter's independence from a target person is helpful in reducing common-method variance. On the other hand, observers' ratings are necessarily based on limited information about the environment in question and they cannot incorporate an individual person's appraisal of factors that impact on him or her. The two forms of rating are thus most likely to diverge when environmental information is less explicit (for instance, when some aspects are unobservable to an outside observer), more variable (so that a brief observation may fail to represent a true average), or when the personal meaning of stimuli differs considerably between individuals.

Subjective rating (by a job holder or an observer) is open to influence from characteristics of the rater and from pressures from other people. Potentially important rater characteristics include biases of the kinds already identified, and also a person's typical frame of reference. In the latter respect, judgments depend in part on an individual's comparison of a job feature with several personal standards, such as previous exposure to that feature, comparisons with other jobs, and estimates of future possibilities (Gerhart, 1988). The second influence, pressure from other people, was emphasized by Salancik and

Pfeffer (1978), who argued that the social context both guides beliefs and knowledge and also focuses individuals' attention on themes to be treated as more salient or less salient. Both judgmental and social influences are reviewed in the next chapter.

Objective Indicators of Environmental Features

A third approach to the specification of a person's environment is through the objective measurement of particular elements. In these cases, subjective influences can be minimal. For example, we might record the temperature in a workplace, the level of pay received, the number of different activities required, or the speed of a production line.

Although objective indicators can be almost free from personal ("subjective") influence, they are inherently very limited. Few of the primary job features examined in earlier chapters can be scored in those terms, and any objective indicator of a feature is likely to be only partial. For example, the speed of a production line indexes one aspect of externally generated goals (feature 3), but jobs that vary in that respect can also differ in other elements of that feature, such as task identity, role conflict, or work–home conflict. Similarly, the fact that broad indicators of multifaceted job "scope" or "complexity" (see earlier discussion) contain many different elements prevents objective quantification of that kind of variable. Researchers have therefore usually preferred the more detailed and comprehensive information that can be obtained from observers or job holders themselves.

Convergent Validity

Job incumbents' ratings of environmental content closely track the objective nature of that content. Spector (1992) reviewed experimental studies that altered the level of job characteristics of the kinds examined in chapters 5 to 8. He reported "considerable consistency" in findings, "demonstrating that manipulations of actual characteristics produced expected changes in self-reports of those characteristics both in the laboratory and in the field" (p. 126).

Correlational research has asked about the magnitude of association between ratings of the same job features made by job holders and by observers. Frese and Zapf (1988) reported an average correlation between analysts' assessments and employees' ratings across two studies of +0.44, with higher values for job features that were more observable. Analysts' and incumbents' ratings of job features were intercorrelated at between +0.66 and +0.89 in the study by Campion (1988). A meta-analysis by Spector (1992) yielded average correlations between job holders and observers (of several different kinds) of +0.30, +0.46, and +0.42 for opportunity for control, skill variety, and workload, respectively. However, for job characteristics that are less observable by nonincumbents, between-rater correlations were reduced. For example, average values for role ambiguity and task significance were +0.11 and +0.14, respectively. Waldenström et al. (2005) examined associations between self-reports and observers' assessments separately for job holders who were either more distressed or less distressed in context-free terms. They found that the pattern was very similar for the two sets of individuals, with an average self–other intercorrelation of +0.69 for personal control opportunity and +0.45 for job demands.

Applying four different measures of objectively defined low variety, Melamed et al. (1995) reported an average correlation of +0.27 between those measures and an incumbent-completed scale of low variety. Xie and Johns (1995) coded the complexity of jobs (see the previous section) on the basis of their titles, and found that this independent description was correlated at +0.40 with job holders' perceptions of job scope as defined earlier. In studies by Ganzach (1998) and Judge et al. (2000), that value was +0.27 and +0.23, respectively. In research by Demerouti et al. (2001), observers' assessments at the level of job titles were correlated with ratings by job holders at +0.39 for opportunity for personal control (feature 1), +0.24 for feedback (an aspect of 5), +0.09 for physical security (8), +0.23 for supervisory support (10), and +0.32 for job security (an aspect of 11).

What about correlations with subjective well-being? Do those vary between the different forms of environmental assessment? Several studies have compared correlations between well-being and job characteristics rated by job holders and by other people. For example, Kiggundu (1980) found that (with one exception) correlations between job satisfaction and features measured through the Job Diagnostic Survey were statistically significant irrespective of rating source: job incumbent, supervisor, or coworker. However, target persons' own job ratings were more strongly associated with their job satisfaction than were other people's assessment of job content. For example, correlations with job complexity were +0.54, +0.20, and +0.34 for ratings by job holders, supervisors, and other workers respectively. Consistent with reduced between-rater convergence for less observable characteristics (described earlier), observer ratings of difficult-to-observe features were less predictive than were ratings of more visible features. For example, although task significance (an aspect of feature 9) was correlated at +0.21 with job satisfaction when rated by a job holder, that value was only +0.02 when the job characteristic was judged by a supervisor.

Algera (1983) compared ratings by job holders with those made by other observers (supervisors or personnel staff), and also reported stronger associations with job-related well-being when job features were assessed by incumbents themselves. For example, multiple correlations with overall job satisfaction were +0.80 and +0.69, respectively, from job holders' and other observers' ratings of job content. In the study by Spector, Dwyer, and Jex (1988), job holders' ratings of the opportunity for personal control were correlated with overall job satisfaction and job-related anxiety at +0.51 and –0.34, respectively; from supervisors' job ratings those correlations were +0.24 and –0.16. For four negative job characteristics, self-reports were in that study on average correlated –0.40 and +0.36 with job satisfaction and job-related anxiety, but those values were reduced to –0.05 and +0.20 for supervisors' job ratings. Xie and Johns (1995) obtained correlations of –0.28 and –0.21 between job-related emotional exhaustion and job holder and independent ratings of job scope respectively.

Campion (1988) avoided problems of common-method variance by analyzing results from two different sets of holders of the same job. He found that average job content ratings (of several "motivational" features; see the earlier description) from one subsample were correlated at +0.32 at the level of job titles with the average job satisfaction of other employees in the same job. Several investigations cited in previous chapters revealed significant associations between job holders' happiness and ratings of job features made by observers. For example, Penney and Spector (2005) reported a correlation of –0.36 between a worker's overall job satisfaction and colleagues' ratings of his or her receipt of low social support (a negative form of "vitamin" 6). Hetland and Sandal (2003) found that employees' satisfaction with their supervisor was correlated at +0.69 with that supervisor's transformational leadership behavior (an aspect of feature 10) as rated by his or her own supervisor.

In overview, target persons' ratings of environmental features tend to be more strongly associated with their own happiness than are the same ratings made by other people. Nevertheless, observers' ratings of primary job features have often been found to be significantly correlated with employees' well-being, and patterns of association are similar. It is notable, however, that research into observer ratings of job content has focused on happiness that is job-related. Observer-derived information about job features is needed in relation to context-free and other indicators to complement the traditional emphasis on job satisfaction.

The fact that job holders' ratings of job content are more correlated with their happiness than are observers' ratings is likely to arise both from the formers' greater understanding of the features that impinge upon them and from their personal interpretations of those features. Linked to that, target persons' reports give rise to common-method variance and thus to inflated correlations with other self-reports, as summarized earlier. On the other hand, the use of ratings by observers can generate inappropriately low job–happiness correlations, because observation has been cursory or job knowledge is limited. In some investigations with independent raters, analyses have been impaired by the creation of a single score for all jobs with the same title, despite the fact that those jobs undoubtedly vary in many ways. Nevertheless, although such homogenization might be expected to reduce observed associations with job holder well-being, ratings of job complexity based on job titles have been found to be significantly associated with job satisfaction, over and above statistical control of other variables (e.g., Gerhart, 1987).

Objective indicators of environmental features (the third measurement approach summarized earlier) have also been found to be associated with employee well-being, for example, evidenced through changes in well-being that follow objective job changes. Objective values are particularly appropriate with respect to employees' income (feature 7), where accurate and precise information may be available to researchers (e.g., Clark, 2005b). With respect to other primary job features, the narrow focus and frequent inapplicability of objective measures mean that those are less likely to be used in the area of this book than are ratings by job holders or other people.

ENVIRONMENTAL CHANGES ACROSS TIME

Although an association between two variables is essential for a causal relationship to be inferred between them, it is clear that a correlation does not necessarily indicate a direct causal influence. If a significant correlation is observed between variables A and B, possible interpretations are:

1. A causes B, for instance, when a job feature causes happiness or unhappiness.
2. B causes A ("reverse causation"), for example, when a person's happiness or unhappiness affects features of his or her job.
3. A causes B and also B causes A ("mutual causation"), when both the preceding processes occur.
4. The association is caused by some other factor(s). Such factors, correlated with both A and B, are often described as "third variables" or (less frequently in psychology) as "omitted variables." They may be background characteristics extended across time, or more localized factors specific to a single point of measurement (sometimes referred to as "occasion factors"; e.g., Zapf, Dormann, & Frese, 1996). Note that this causal process does not exclude the possible simultaneous operation of processes 1, 2, or 3.

"Occasion factors" can include current mood, a social setting, or even the weather, transiently affecting one or both variables under investigation (A or B in the examples just given). Long-term third variables include demographic features such as research participants' age, education, or gender, as well as their ability or personality characteristics. Often considered in the latter respect is a consistent judgmental bias, such that a person may view both an environmental feature and his or her own happiness in a consistently negative or positive manner. (This possibility is examined further in chap. 11.) In addition, differential selection into jobs could sometimes operate as a third factor that is partly responsible for an observed correlation with happiness. For example, dispositionally less happy people may have moved into (or not moved out of) jobs with certain characteristics (sometimes called the "drift" hypothesis), so that a recorded association between those characteristics and unhappiness is at least partly due to continuing differences between subsamples, rather than entirely to job characteristics themselves.

Other third variables that might influence an observed correlation in this area include unmeasured characteristics of a person's job. In addition to the studied variables, other job features not included in the research may also be important. For example, although opportunity for personal control is associated with employees' subjective well-being, perhaps that association (or part of it) arises from between-employee differences in job level, with associated contrasts in some other influential job features.

Researchers can seek to reduce the possible impact of third variables by statistically controlling for features that might perhaps underlie an observed correlation. Previous chapters have described many multivariate analyses of that kind. Nevertheless, one cannot be certain that all important influences have been excluded in any one case, because coverage of variables is necessarily incomplete. Causal interpretation thus usually has to be in terms of probability rather than certainty. In complex environments, statements about causality have to be based in part on the exclusion of plausible alternative influences, rather than only on evidence about a likely cause itself. Confidence in interpretation becomes increased through the accumulation of similar studies in different settings, each one controlling for a number of possible third variables.

Causal inference usually requires examination of patterns across time, with the expectation that a supposed cause precedes a possible effect. For example, it is to be expected that a person who moves from a job with negative features to one with more positive features will in consequence experience an increase in some forms of happiness, and that a move in the opposite direction will contribute to unhappiness. Longitudinal studies of possible causes and effects have been of two kinds.

First are experimental manipulations. These measure an outcome variable (happiness in our case) before and after changing one environmental variable and controlling other possible confounding factors. (However, in practice more than a single environmental feature may be changed.) In addition, it is desirable that a separate control or comparison group is studied, which receives either no or a different treatment. In some cases, "after-only" designs are used, relying, instead of on a prior data collection, on the assumption of random allocation to experimental and control groups, and thus presumably equivalent subsamples in research analyses. It is usual to carry out a "manipulation check," to ensure that changes of the intended kind (e.g., an increase in skill use) have occurred in the treatment group but not in the control or comparison group. Data analyses then compare mean change or outcome scores between the treatment ("experimental") and other groups.

Experimental research has the advantage over other longitudinal analyses (described later) that observed changes in an outcome variable may be attributed to specific environmental manipulations (although third-variable problems still deserve attention). On the other hand, such studies may be influenced by occasion factors in terms of special attention from management or employee (e.g., trade union) groups. A program of experimental intervention in an organization can arouse unusual interest or expectations; participants and observers are likely to be aware of the political importance of certain findings or to expect beneficial or other outcomes. Associated with these "demand characteristics," some intentional or unintentional distortion of questionnaire or interview responses might sometimes occur. In addition to potential enhancement of an experimental group's responses in order to meet expectations or hopes, Cook, Campbell, and Peracchio (1990) drew attention to possible "resentful demoralization" in no-treatment control groups (deprived of new conditions which are considered to be desirable), perhaps leading to unusually negative responses in those cases.

A second longitudinal approach is through the investigation of naturally occurring patterns across time, to record the changes that occur in environmental conditions and also in people's mental state. Some research of this kind has been at the level of individual employees' own localized environments. For example, a researcher may record each employee's job conditions and his or her subjective well-being on two or more occasions. Deriving from management decisions and operational procedures, job conditions are likely to have changed in different directions or by different amounts for different individuals, and changes in individuals' well-being can be examined as a function of those person-specific increases or decreases. Investigations of natural change are more easily carried out and are often less artificial than organizational experiments (described earlier). However, they can leave unspecified the causative changes in job content, because other, unrecorded, features may also have been altered in the period of a study.

Both kinds of longitudinal research have the advantage that some continuing third variables, such as employees' personality characteristics, are held constant across measurement points (although there can be slight variability across time). Longitudinal investigations also make possible statistical examination of potential reverse causal influence (B causes A in the summary above) or mutual causation (A causes B and also B causes A). For example, by measuring job content and employee well-being on two occasions, a two-wave panel design permits cross-lagged correlation analyses, examining across time correlations from variable A at time 1 to B at time 2 and from variable B at time 1 to A at time 2. Other possible longitudinal analyses include hierarchical regressions with lagged effects and the assessment of structural equation models across time. However, Zapf et al. (1996) examined 50 longitudinal studies in the area of this book, and found that less than 20% of them addressed any of those possibilities. Information about reverse causal priority (B affecting A) is thus so far limited.

Attention is here directed at possible longitudinal influences from the 12 primary job features to aspects of happiness (from A to B, as schematized earlier). Some causal influence from B to A is also possible in some cases and is not excluded by the presence of unidirectional effects on their own. Most studies have controlled statistically for a number of potential third variables.

1. Opportunity for Personal Control. Several publications have reported changes in happiness that are linked to changes in this first job feature. Hackman et al. (1978) studied clerical employees before and five months after a technical innovation that on average reduced the amount of personal control they had over their jobs. However, for some employees control was increased, and for those people increases also occurred in overall job satisfaction and satisfaction with opportunities for personal growth in the job. Conversely, reductions in employees' job control were followed by declines in these aspects of subjective well-being. In Griffin's (1981) study over 3 months, changes in employees' autonomy suggested a causal impact on overall job satisfaction and satisfaction with supervisor, although the pattern was not entirely clear.

Bond and Bunce (2003) studied perceived control and overall job satisfaction in call center staff on two occasions a year apart. Examination of nested path analysis models, controlling for several personal variables, showed that prior level of job control was linked to higher subsequent levels of satisfaction and that this pattern was one of unidirectional (rather than reciprocal) causality. Context-free distress was also examined, with a similar finding: Lower distress appeared to be a result of increased job control. Tausig and Fenwick (1999) examined data from a national probability sample of American full-time workers, with questionnaire responses separated by 4 years. Increases or decreases in life satisfaction across that period were predicted by changes in the amount of discretion available in their jobs, over and above the contributions made by more than 30 other variables.

Totterdell et al. (2006) carried out an intra- (rather than inter-) individual study across time, measuring individual workers' job-related anxiety and depression repeatedly over an average of 18 weeks. Multilevel regression analyses included prior measures of well-being. Variations in perceived job control in the previous week were found to be significantly linked as expected to changes in job-related anxiety, but not to changes in job-related depression.

Organizational changes that intentionally modify employees' influence over job activities have also been examined. Wall and Clegg (1981) traced the outcomes of a job redesign process that increased the amount of autonomy available to manufacturing teams. Across a period of 2 years, team members' overall job satisfaction rose significantly after the change, and their level of context-free distress was also seen to decline. Wall et al. (1986) similarly examined an increase in work-team autonomy associated with job redesign, finding that intrinsic job satisfaction rose significantly in the treatment group but not in a comparison setting. However, no change occurred in the level of employees' context-free distress.

Parkes (1982) studied student nurses as they moved between task settings (3 months in each) that differed in the amount of personal discretion available to them. During work in the lower-discretion settings, overall job satisfaction declined significantly and context-free depression was significantly increased. Parkes also examined correlations between each individual's discretion-change score and changes in job satisfaction and other outcomes. Between-setting increases in individuals' job discretion were significantly correlated with increases in their job satisfaction and reductions in context-free depression and anxiety; the greater a person's change in discretion opportunity, the greater was the corresponding change in his or her subjective well-being.

2. Opportunity for Skill Use.   This second job characteristic appears not to have been examined in research across time. However, a study by Feldman et al. (2002) asked laid-off managers who had become reemployed about experienced changes over time. Reported declines in skill utilization between jobs were correlated at -0.33 with overall job satisfaction in their new jobs. Although this negative association with reported change in job content suggests the causal importance of the application of skills, stronger evidence would draw on measures taken at different times, rather than being based merely on a retrospective assessment. And, as in other cases, third variables (such as a decline in income) may have affected the observed pattern.

3. Externally Generated Goals.   Three sets of investigation can be identified for this third environmental feature, concerning changes in level of task demands, in task identity, and in role conflict. In the first respect, de Jonge et al. (2001) examined overall job satisfaction on two occasions a year apart. They showed through structural equation modeling, with controls for other variables, that changes across that period in employees' job demands had a significant causal impact on their satisfaction. Barnett and Brennan (1997) also followed people across a year, recording job characteristics and context-free distress (a mixture of anxiety and depression) at the beginning and end of that period. Controlling for other job, household, and demographic features, the direction and magnitude of change in job demands were significantly predictive of corresponding change in distress. In a study across 4 years, Tausig and Fenwick (1999) found that change in job demands accounted for around 14% of observed change in employees' life dissatisfaction, again controlling for many possible extraneous influences. In all these cases, increases in external demands reduced happiness and reductions in demands led to greater happiness.

Eden (1982) examined qualitative and quantitative overload in the jobs of student nurses as they moved between very demanding and less demanding tasks. Changes in overload were accompanied by parallel increases or decreases in job-related anxiety, again suggesting a causal impact from that job feature. The longitudinal study by Totterdell et al. (2006; see feature 1, already described) found that week-by-week changes in job demands were accompanied by expected changes in job-related anxiety and (to a lesser extent) in job-related depression.

Leitner and Resch (2005) examined context-free depression and life satisfaction on several occasions. In relation to the amount of time that office staff needed to cope with work hindrances (an interrupting form of demand; see chap. 6), cross-lagged correlational analyses over a 1-year period implied a causal influence from time 1 hindrances to (low) time 2 well-being, with no support for a process of reverse causation for either aspect of well-being.

Other aspects of this third job feature reviewed in chapter 6 included task identity and role conflict. Task identity was studied by Wall and Clegg (1981) at the level of teams rather than individuals. Across 2 years, changes in this job characteristic (perceptions that the team undertakes a single, identifiable task with a visible outcome) were significantly linked to corresponding changes in overall job satisfaction and context-free distress.

In a study of managers' role conflict across two measurement points separated by four months, Miles (1975) described longitudinal and cross-sectional correlations with overall job satisfaction and job-related tension that were consistent with a negative causal influence from that conflict. A similar investigation of lower level hospital staff across a 6-month period by Szilagyi (1977) found that increased role conflict reduced satisfaction with work; however, that causal pattern was not observed among staff at higher organizational levels.

4. Variety. The longitudinal study by Hackman et al. (1978; see feature 1, already described) also examined the variety of skills required in employees' jobs. For individual workers, the magnitude of change in skill variety was significantly associated with change of the expected kind in overall job satisfaction and satisfaction with the opportunities for personal growth. In Griffin's (1981) research, a longitudinal impact over three months was suggested for satisfaction with one's supervisor but not for overall job satisfaction.

5. Environmental Clarity. Several investigators have examined changes in role ambiguity, finding that reduced ambiguity in a person's job is followed by an increase in subjective well-being. Both Miles (1975) and Szilagyi (1978) analyzed data from two measurement occasions, finding that increases or decreases in role clarity were linked to enhanced or reduced employee well-being, respectively. Miles reported this effect for overall job satisfaction and job-related tension, and Szilagyi's similar finding (for intrinsic job satisfaction) was significant for higher level and medium-level jobs but not at lower levels.

Eden (1982) investigated changes in job-related anxiety as a function of role ambiguity. Significant increases or decreases in anxiety occurred as student nurses became exposed to different conditions, with greater ambiguity giving rise to more anxiety. Schaubroeck, Ganster, Sime, and Ditman (1993) described an intervention program to clarify employees' role responsibilities and relationships. The program led to a reduction in ambiguity for employees in the treatment group, whereas role ambiguity in a control group remained unchanged. Analyses of variance revealed that an increase in satisfaction with supervision could be attributed to the intervention, but that no effect was present for context-free distress.

Job feedback, another aspect of this environmental feature, was studied by Bechtold, Sims, and Szilagyi (1981). They found that increases or decreases in feedback were accompanied by significant expected changes in overall and intrinsic job satisfaction. Griffin (1981) also examined task feedback over time, with results suggesting a causal impact on satisfaction with supervision but not on overall job satisfaction.

6. *Contact With Others.*   The study by Parkes (1982; see feature 1, already described) recorded changes in social support available to student nurses as they moved between task settings. Increased support from others led to increased overall job satisfaction, and reduced support had the opposite effect. Overall job satisfaction was also found by de Jonge et al. (2001) to be affected by workplace social support across a 12-month period, controlling for other relevant variables. Weekly recordings by Totterdell et al. (2006) indicated that changes in emotional support were accompanied by changes in job-related depression but not in job-related anxiety.

7. *Availability of Money.*   It is obvious from everyday experience that increases or decreases in money availability can affect happiness levels, especially when one is in financial difficulties (to the left of Fig. 4.1). This was illustrated formally by Gerhart (1987) in an examination of data gathered across three years. Controlling for several other variables, increases or decreases in pay were significantly linked to changes as expected in overall job satisfaction. Tausig and Fenwick (1999) studied on two occasions 4 years apart people who had lost their job and had become reemployed by the second measurement point. Despite many statistical controls, changes in income level were strongly related to parallel changes in life dissatisfaction; that predictor variable had the greatest impact of all those examined.

8. *Physical Security.*   A similar longitudinal study of job-changers by Kirjonen and Hänninen (1986) included assessments of the work environment in terms of physical, chemical, and ergonomic hazards. Across a 5-year period, positive or negative changes in that index of physical security were associated with increases or decreases respectively of both job-related and context-free well-being.

9. *Valued Social Position.*   The change study by Hackman et al. (1978; see features 1 and 4, already described) examined employees' perceptions of their job's significance to other people. They found that changes in that respect were associated in the expected direction with increases or decreases in overall job satisfaction and in satisfaction with personal growth opportunities.

10. Supportive Supervision. This job feature appears not to have received much attention in longitudinal research. However, the study by Kirjonen and Hänninen (1986; see feature 8, already described) examined changes in the supportiveness of a person's supervisor. Increases or decreases of that kind were significantly predictive of parallel changes in job-related well-being, but no impact was observed on context-free happiness.

11. Career Prospects. This job characteristic was described earlier in terms either of security of tenure and job conditions or as the potential provided for career advancement or desired change. The former aspect has been examined in terms of perceived job insecurity.

Heaney, Israel, and House (1994) recorded perceptions of job insecurity twice across a 14-month period. Increases or decreases in insecurity predicted corresponding changes in overall job satisfaction, controlling for a range of demographic factors. Hellgren, Sverke, and Isaksson (1999) obtained data on two occasions separated by 12 months. Greater insecurity at time 1 led to a more substantial reduction in overall job satisfaction and a greater increase in context-free distress at time 2, despite statistical controls for positive or negative response bias. The sample's distress scores were examined through latent variable path analyses by Hellgren and Sverke (2003), controlling for gender, age, organizational tenure, family status, and education. Job insecurity emerged clearly as a causal influence on context-free distress.

12. Equity. The final job characteristic in the vitamin model has been examined as fairness within one's organization and also in relations with one's community or society. Although cross-sectional associations with aspects of happiness have been illustrated in chapter 5, longitudinal investigations appear not to have been published.

Sets of Job Characteristics

In addition to these single-feature analyses, longitudinal research has also demonstrated the causal influence of job content when that is defined through multiple characteristics. For example, Karasek (1979) combined together measures of high demands and low opportunity for control, to examine changes in that joint indicator of stressful job content across a period of 6 years. Increases and reductions were accompanied by parallel changes in context-free depression. Barnett and Brennan (1997) derived a summary score that included skill discretion and job demands, finding through hierarchical linear modeling that changes in that score gave rise to corresponding changes in context-free distress. Significant changes across time were also found by Kirjonen and Hänninen (1986), with respect to both job-related and context-free distress as a function of combined job features 1, 2, and 4.

It was pointed out in chapter 4 that the present framework's "additional decrement" features (features 1 to 6) cover aspects of a job that are intrinsic, within its task activities, rather than extrinsic to the role. Studies described in the preceding paragraph all drew on those intrinsic characteristics. Similarly, combinations of job features to represent overall "complexity" or "scope" primarily concern intrinsic content. As described earlier in this chapter, using the Job Diagnostic Survey researchers have brought together scores of perceived autonomy, feedback, skill variety, task identity, and task significance into a single index of job scope. Longitudinal changes in those features collectively have been shown to be followed by expected changes in overall job satisfaction, satisfaction with opportunities for personal growth, and intrinsic (but not extrinsic) satisfaction (Bhagat & Chassie, 1980; Hackman et al., 1978; Wong, Hui, & Law, 1998). Structural equation modeling in the last of those studies suggested that job–happiness effects were reciprocal rather than merely unidirectional.

Griffeth's (1985) experimental study to increase job scope also raised employees' job satisfaction significantly in comparison with a no-redesign control group. Griffin (1981), noting that most research of this kind was of short duration, extended his observations of job scope and overall job satisfaction across four years. Job redesign led to significant short-term increases in both job scope and satisfaction, although satisfaction level subsequently declined. Processes of adaptation across time are considered in the next chapter.

An index of job complexity based on the Job Diagnostic Survey, but describing work-group rather than individual activities, was developed by Wall and Clegg (1981). After manufacturing jobs had been redesigned to increase work complexity at the group level, a significant increase occurred in job holders' overall job satisfaction and a significant decrease in their context-free distress.

Using a slightly different indicator of job scope, Bechtold et al. (1981) showed that increases or decreases in scope over 18 months were related to increases or decreases respectively in intrinsic (but not extrinsic) job satisfaction. Gerhart (1987) reported the same pattern across 3 years with respect to overall job satisfaction, for both a perceptual measure of job scope (as applied in most research) and an objective indicator based on published job descriptions in the Dictionary of Occupational Titles. That significant impact of changes in job scope was obtained despite statistical control for previous and current pay.

Morgeson and Campion (2002) described an investigation in which jobs were redesigned to increase job complexity in terms of 18 "motivational" characteristics (see earlier in this chapter). The intervention was found to enhance "motivational" content from pretest to posttest as intended, and also to bring about significant increases in employees' overall job satisfaction. Changes in work procedures described by Åborg and Billing (2003) reduced employees' job variety and opportunity for personal control and increased their workload. These several reductions in desirable job content were accompanied by a decline in facet-specific satisfaction with ergonomic conditions. (Other forms of subjective well-being were not measured.)

It is clear from the investigations summarized in this section that characteristics of jobs identified in the vitamin framework can have a causal impact on aspects of happiness, as well as being merely correlated cross-sectionally with those variables as shown in chapters 5 to 7. This causal influence is apparent for individual characteristics and especially so for groups of features. The impact of changed job content is expected to be particularly great with respect to consistent changes within a compound of characteristics. When several of the job features change in the same direction within the same period of time, employee happiness is likely to be affected more than if only a single feature is modified.

Further studies should document more systematically possible differential impacts on the several kinds of happiness reviewed in this book. What differences or similarities occur in causal patterns for the three axes of well-being introduced in chapter 2? It is also essential to consider possible nonlinear causal impacts. For example, less pronounced effects on employee happiness are expected from changes in job features which remain in the horizontal section across the middle of Figures 4.1 and 4.2 than in the left-hand section, where the cross-sectional job–happiness association is strong.

Attention needs also to be directed at possible reverse or mutual processes of causation (alternatives 2 and 3 at the beginning of this section). Structural equation analyses of cross-sectional data by Mathieu et al. (1993) pointed to the possibility of reciprocal influences, from job content to job-related well-being as illustrated earlier, but also in the reverse direction. Longitudinal research by Wong et al. (1998) also suggested a reciprocal causal pattern, but effects appeared to be only unidirectional, from job content to happiness, in longitudinal studies by Bond and Bunce (2003; see feature 1, described earlier) and Leitner and Resch (2005; see feature 3, described earlier).

A differentiated view of causal possibilities is required. It is likely that bidirectional influences will occur for only certain aspects of a job, rather than a standard pattern occurring in all cases. Detailed hypotheses are now required about feature-specific processes of influence, in one or both directions, for different job features and for different aspects of happiness.

OTHER MODELS OF THE JOB ENVIRONMENT

Chapters 5 to 8 have taken an environment-centered perspective, examining features external to a person that can influence happiness or unhappiness. Twelve job characteristics (and several components of those) have been explored, and it has been argued that 6 of the 12 illustrate the possibility of "having too much of a good thing." Those "additional decrement" features (numbers 1 to 6 in Table 5.1, emphasizing intrinsic job content) have been viewed as analogous to vitamins that are not only harmful at low levels (in the "deficiency" range) but also at very high ("toxic") levels. They are desirable at levels that are moderately high but not in low or very high ranges; at very high levels, they are thought likely to generate an "additional decrement" in happiness. However, characteristics 7 to 12 (predominantly extrinsic in nature) are more likely to follow the pattern of those vitamins that are harmful at low levels and beneficial at moderate and high levels, without a negative impact in very large doses. Variation in those "constant-effect" features is thought to have little consequence for happiness once they have reached a moderately high level.

Happiness has been considered at three levels of scope: context-free, domain-specific, and facet-specific. Nonlinear patterns are particularly likely in the case of context-free happiness, for which the environmental sources are not restricted to a specific area of a life space (such as a job). Context-free happiness is affected also by many other factors, and those together are likely to outweigh variation in a single domain-specific input within the benign range. At the other (narrow) extreme of scope, facet-specific happiness is by definition focused on an environmental feature itself, for instance as satisfaction with the facet of working conditions. A correlation between that narrow form of well-being and the target environmental feature itself is expected to be almost entirely linear, as features unconnected with the targeted variable have little impact on an association which is strongly determined by conceptual overlap. Nonlinearity is predicted to be of intermediate significance for domain-specific forms of happiness, whose scope lies between context-free and facet-specific happiness. These and associated themes were developed in more detail in chapter 4 and summarized in Figures 4.2a to 4.2c (p. 102).

How does this framework compare to other environment-centered models? Three main areas of difference or similarity need to be considered. First is the number and content of environmental features addressed. Explanatory perspectives differ in their breadth—how far they extend to a wide range of phenomena or restrict the range of issues under investigation. Neither emphasis is universally preferable to the other, and the development of both kinds of framework is desirable. It is in the nature of broad frameworks that they must lack specific detail in some respects. This limitation was viewed by Weick (1979) in terms of the three theoretical ideals of generalizability, accuracy, and simplicity. He pointed out that at best two of these ideals can be realized at any one time; in gaining those two, one must sacrifice the third, so that no theory can at the same time be generalizable, accurate, and simple. It would thus be inappropriate to accuse broadbrush models of being inaccurate in detail, because that is inherent in their nature. However, such frameworks have a special value in providing an overarching structure within which can exist more focused accounts.

The vitamin approach is intentionally broad, seeking to embrace environmental features of many kinds (Warr, 1987). It is applicable to different environments, for example, during unemployment or retirement, and it brings together characteristics that are otherwise rarely viewed within the same account. For example, in job settings, Karasek's model of job strain considers only the presence or absence of discretion, demands and social support (features 1, 3, and 6 in the present framework; e.g., Karasek et al. 1982; Karasek & Theorell, 1990; van der Doef & Maes, 1999), and the job characteristics model of Hackman and Oldham (1975, 1976, 1980) covers only five features— autonomy, task identity, skill variety, feedback and task significance (aspects of "vitamins" 1, 3, 4, 5, and 9).

In this first respect, environmental models in effect differ between themselves in their selection of particular features from a standard set. All the features included in chapters 4 to 8 are likely to be accepted as influential by the supporters of all models; researchers differ in the ones they choose to emphasize. As another example, consider the effort–reward imbalance model of Siegrist (1996, 1998). This is based on the expectation that negative outcomes follow from an imbalance between effort exerted and reward achieved. Effort is generated in part through external demands (feature 3 in the present framework; e.g., Siegrist et al., 2004; but see some person-centered themes described later), and reward has been viewed as raised control ("vitamin" 1), money (7), esteem (9), and career outlook (11). The "imbalance" of concern may thus be described as an environment that yields high levels of feature 3 (effort) and low levels of 1, 7, 9, and 11 (reward). From a wider perspective, other imbalances with effort might of course also be envisaged, against high levels of more "additional decrement" features and low levels of other characteristics.

Another model of environmental influence is the job demands–resources account by Demerouti et al. (2001) and Bakker et al. (2003, 2005). That defines job resources as "those physical, psychological, social, or organizational aspects of the job that may do any of the following: (a) be functional in achieving work goals; (b) reduce job demands and the associated physiological and psychological costs; (c) stimulate personal growth and development" (Demerouti et al., 2001, p. 3). In effect, resources are thus viewed as desirable aspects of a position. Measured resources have included positive forms of autonomy, feedback, social support, and supportive supervision (features 1, 5, 6, and 10). Job demands are taken to refer to "those physical, social, or organizational aspects of the job that require sustained physical or mental effort" (Demerouti et al., 2001, p. 3). Examples of these undesirable features include work overload, work–family conflict, and time pressure (e.g., Bakker et al., 2005)—all within the third feature of the present account. As with the effort–reward imbalance account (just described), the model thus expects harmful effects to arise from jobs that are undesirably low on certain of the "vitamins" and undesirably high on feature 3. That contingency is subsumed in the wider range of combinations envisaged as possible within the vitamin model.

The theoretical benefits of placing together environmental features within groups on the basis of their evaluative direction (as in the last two models) are not entirely clear. Job features within each of the two suggested categories (positive or negative) differ widely in their substance and operation, and their individual impacts are based at least in part on quite different psychological processes. See, for example, the breadth of variation indicated by "any of the following" in the quotation cited in the previous paragraph. Focusing merely on their common evaluative tone distracts attention from the fact that they have different contents and distinct modes of operation. Furthermore, in considering processes of combination between environmental characteristics, different sets of features are expected to join together in different ways, according to each one's specific nature. Combined examination of groups of environmental features defined merely in terms of their overall positive or negative implications does not appear conceptually or pragmatically helpful. (This point was raised more generally in chap. 2, arguing that it is logically inappropriate to treat as equivalent all kinds of "work stressors.")

Another objection to environmental models based on two categories containing features that are either positive or negative derives from nonlinearity within the vitamin framework. Accounts in terms of (for instance) "demands" and "resources" assume that a particular member of one of those categories is unchanging in its personal value as either a "demand" (negative) or a "resource" (positive). Instead, the vitamin model points out that the six "additional decrement" variables and their components may be either positive or negative, depending on their location on the horizontal axis of Figures 4.1 and 4.2. Asserting that job features are always either of positive value or of negative value conceals that change in their evaluative direction at different magnitudes of input.

The vitamin model may also be viewed in relation to the two-factor framework proposed by Herzberg (e.g., 1966). That claimed that "satisfiers" in the job environment should be sharply distinguished from "dissatisfiers." "Dissatisfiers" (supervision, working conditions, company administration, and similar features extrinsic to job content itself) were considered to affect job dissatisfaction but to have no impact on satisfaction, whereas "satisfiers" (possibilities for achievement, recognition, and responsibility) were thought to influence satisfaction but not dissatisfaction.

It has long been clear that a separation between dissatisfaction and satisfaction and between their supposed sources cannot be justified in either conceptual or empirical terms (e.g., Warr & Wall, 1975), and Herzberg's two-category approach, although extremely influential around 1970, now has few adherents. However, an overlap between "dissatisfiers" and the present model's "constant-effect" features may be noted. Although Herzberg wrote in terms of employees' reaction (dissatisfaction or satisfaction) rather than measuring job features themselves, his view of "dissatisfiers" (sometimes called "hygiene factors") may be extended to statements about the levels of environmental characteristics. In effect, his claim with respect to "dissatisfiers" was that for these (extrinsic or, here, "constant effect") features, variations in level influence people's unhappiness or happiness in the low to moderate range, but that at higher levels their variation is of no hedonic consequence. That is also the "constant-effect" perspective of the vitamin model. For "dissatisfiers," the two-factor model and the vitamin framework are thus extremely similar. On the other hand, Herzberg's notion that "satisfiers" are of no importance across lower levels has no empirical support or apparent links to other models.

A second dimension of difference between models in this area concerns their view of pathways between environmental features and outcomes. For example, some frameworks emphasize particular modes of input combination, such as an interactive process in Karasek's model and a weighted compound ("scope") in the job characteristics model. The job demands–resources model assumes an additive combination of its two categories of variables. That is also so the case for the vitamin framework, which contains a larger number of categories for separate investigation. In addition, the vitamin model includes assumptions about nonlinear patterns of input–outcome relationship, and a possibly disproportionate influence from more extreme elements in a compound.

Linked to this variation, some environmental models have placed greater emphasis on within-person mechanisms than others. (Note that there is no reason in principle why any environment-centered model should not be extended in a person-based direction; limitations have so far arisen from increased complexity, which becomes unmanageable.) For example, within-person variables are central to the effort–reward imbalance model of Siegrist. As well as required effort from external demands (discussed earlier), pressures from within the person are viewed as an important source of effort, in terms of individuals' need to control a situation. Within the model, need for control is treated as a broad disposition, covering competitiveness, impatience, desire for approval, and a personal inability to withdraw from work obligations (Siegrist, 1996, 1998; Siegrist et al., 2004).

Considerable emphasis on within-person processes also occurs in Hobfoll's (1989, 2001) conservation-of-resources model. This defines resources as "objects, personal characteristics, conditions, or energies that are valued by the individual or that serve as a means for the attainment of these" (1989, p. 516). This evaluatively positive category of variables is clearly wider than the environmental "vitamins" considered in the present framework, containing both external and within-person features that might be helpful to an individual. With respect to environmental characteristics, Wright and Cropanzano (1998) suggested that in occupational settings the category of "resources" includes positive job features such as autonomy, social support, and good career outlook. The model assumes that "people strive to retain, protect, and build resources and that what is threatening to them is the potential or actual loss of these valued resources" (Hobfoll, 1989, p. 516). With an environmental focus, this appears to be equivalent to the assertion that raised values of features like those viewed here as "vitamins" are important for happiness.

Within-person processes in the effort–recovery model of Meijman and Mulder (1998) are of a psychobiological kind. Taking an environmental perspective that is limited to forms of demand ("vitamin" 3), this argues that employees' expenditure of effort in meeting work demands has both physiological and psychological costs. In normal circumstances, these negative reactions are reversible through a respite from the demands, during which a person's psychobiological systems stabilize again at his or her baseline level. However, recovery is likely to be hampered by continuing expenditure of effort to meet new demands or if an individual is unable to relax adequately. Recovery processes are envisaged within a period of job activity itself if demands are not too great, and also subsequently in periods of rest outside the work setting.

In addition to between-model differences in scope and in person orientation, a third variation occurs in the kinds of outcomes that are of principal concern. For example, different forms of happiness or unhappiness have been emphasized by different authors, such as job satisfaction in the job characteristics model and in Herzberg's theorizing, broadly defined or loosely defined subjective well-being in many cases, and various forms of stress or strain in some recent research. Certain frameworks take a primarily or exclusively physiological or medical perspective. For example, Siegrist's model was developed within medical sociology, and was created to account for variations in cardiovascular ill health. The effort–recovery model originated in exercise physiology, and the job demands–resources model is addressed specifically to forms of job burnout. Given a wide variation in prioritizing of subject matter, it is to be expected that specific predictions and findings will differ somewhat between models.

The vitamin framework may thus be compared with other frameworks in those three respects. It is more comprehensive than others, it sets out to characterize environmental features, with personal processes to be introduced in later chapters, and it has an explicit focus on psychological outcomes that range from the negative (unhappiness) to the positive (happiness). Person-centered themes are explored in chapters 9 to 13, in terms of processes of judgment and comparison with one's own mental standards, and through the impact of demographic features, personality dispositions, wants, and values.

PROFILING PSYCHOLOGICALLY BAD AND GOOD JOBS

The vitamin model emphasizes comprehensive coverage of a wide range of influences from the environment rather than a narrow focus on only a few features. Twelve primary features have been identified in earlier chapters, and those, together with subcategories, are now placed together in Table 8.1.

This table provides, more informally than the previous research-based account, the basis for a profile of 26 psychologically important job characteristics that recognizes the distinction between "additional decrement" and "constant-effect" features. In the former case (numbers 1 to 6 in the table), it is desirable that a job provides moderate or high levels of a feature and that the highest levels of a job characteristic are avoided. That limitation does not arise for the other features (7 to 12 in the table), because those are considered beyond a moderate level to have a beneficial "constant effect" on happiness. The job content labels in Table 8.1 draw on the presentations in earlier chapters, but they have sometimes been reworded for everyday use.

A current or possible job, or a set of jobs, may be assessed in these terms to identify environmental features with potential impact on employee unhappiness or happiness. In many cases, it will be appropriate to ask about a job without specifying a time period, assuming that responses will be stable over the recent past and future. However, in some circumstances instructions might focus on, for instance, the past month or some future period after job redesign.

A possible rating scale is suggested in the top row of Table 8.1. For "additional decrement" characteristics (numbers 1 to 6), desirable job scores are between 4 and 6, with 1, 2, 3, and 7 implying a negative psychological impact. For the "constant-effect" job characteristics (numbers 7 to 12), low scores (1, 2, and 3) are again undesirable, and scores of 4 and above are beneficial. Two exceptions to that general scoring template arise when low values of a feature are themselves

TABLE 8.1

Twenty-Six Features of a Good or Bad Job, to Be Rated by
Job-Holders or Observers

Job Feature	Response Options: 1, Extremely Low; 2, Very Low; 3, Quite Low; 4, Moderate; 5, Quite High; 6, Very High; 7, Extremely High[b].						
1. Control							
1a. Task discretion	1	2	3	4	5	6	7
1b. Influence over the wider organization	1	2	3	4	5	6	7
2. Skill							
2a. Skill use	1	2	3	4	5	6	7
2b. New learning	1	2	3	4	5	6	7
3. Goals							
3a. Number of job demands	1	2	3	4	5	6	7
3b. Difficulty of job demands	1	2	3	4	5	6	7
3c. Task coherence	1	2	3	4	5	6	7
3d. Conflict between job demands	[1]	[2]	[3]	[4]	[5]	[6]	[7]
3e. Conflict between work and home	[1]	[2]	[3]	[4]	[5]	[6]	[7]
4. Variety							
4a. Range of different tasks	1	2	3	4	5	6	7
5. Clarity							
5a. Future predictability[a]	1	2	3	4	5	6	7
5b. Clear role requirements	1	2	3	4	5	6	7
5c. Availability cf feedback	1	2	3	4	5	6	7
6. People							
6a. Amount of social contact	1	2	3	4	5	6	7
6b. Quality of social contact	1	2	3	4	5	6	7
7. Money							
7a. Pay level	1	2	3	4	5	6	7
8. Physical security							
8a. Pleasant environment	1	2	3	4	5	6	7
8b. Safe work practices	1	2	3	4	5	6	7
8c. Adequate equipment	1	2	3	4	5	6	7
9. Significance							
9a. Value to society	1	2	3	4	5	6	7
9b. Significance to self	1	2	3	4	5	6	7
10. Supervision							
10a. Concern for staff	1	2	3	4	5	6	7
11. Career							
11a. Job security	1	2	3	4	5	6	7
11b. Good future prospects	1	2	3	4	5	6	7

(Continued)

TABLE 8.1 (*continued*)

Job Feature	Response Options: 1, Extremely Low; 2, Very Low; 3, Quite Low; 4, Moderate; 5, Quite High; 6, Very High; 7, Extremely High[b].						
12. Fairness							
12a. Fair treatment of employees	1	2	3	4	5	6	7
12b. The organization's morality in society	1	2	3	4	5	6	7

[a]Feature 5a (future predictability) here excludes predictability of job tenure, which is identified as 11a (job security).

[b]A simple alternative rating scale for features 1 to 6 is "too low," "acceptable," or "too high." For features 7 to 12, "too high" might be replaced by "very acceptable." See the discussion in the text.

desirable. Those exceptions are elements 3d and 3e, two forms of role conflict. In those cases, a reverse association with happiness is expected: A score of 1 is most beneficial and 7 is most harmful, so that the zone of threat here extends across scores 5, 6, and 7. To indicate this specific interpretation of responses for job features 3d and 3e, numerical options in Table 8.1 have been placed in brackets.

The profile might in some cases be developed in particularly simple terms by directly evaluating each job feature as its level is assessed. In many practical settings, it would be appropriate to rate each "additional decrement" element in Table 8.1 (numbers 1 to 6) as "too low," "acceptable," or "too high." For "constant-effect" features (7 to 12), which are not expected to be harmful at high levels, "too high" might be replaced by "very acceptable." That simple set of evaluations permits the straightforward identification of potentially troublesome aspects of a work environment.

What about the differential prevalence of high or low scores on the 26 elements in Table 8.1? Information is not available for a representative sample of a nation's jobs, but estimates of frequency might be derived from content analyses of written accounts of people's jobs or working lives. Such analyses have not yet been undertaken in a systematic manner, but a negatively biased sample of personal descriptions has been presented by Kieran (2004). Described as "100 tales of workplace hell," contributions ranged widely over the features in Table 8.1. Most often reported (in almost 25% of the accounts) was poor-quality social contact (6b in the table), as workers were either treated badly by or found distasteful their colleagues or customers. Also common were very high levels of demands (3a and 3b, almost 20%) and low variety in one's activities (feature 4, 11%).

Interpretation of a multiattribute profile is primarily in terms of the score attached to each attribute. Different jobs may be compared with respect to some or all of the elements in Table 8.1. However, it is important also to examine several features in combination. For example, a single undesirable score may be balanced by positive scores elsewhere, so that its impact is less marked than when it is in the context of other undesirable elements. Or a set of negative scores may be attributable to a single aspect of job or organizational design, rather than each one originating from different sources.

Profiles of the happiness potential of different jobs may be constructed from ratings by employees themselves or by knowledgeable observers. Those single-item ratings are appropriate in practical settings, when, for example, an organization wishes to learn about the psychological implications of its work roles or an individual wants to review jobs for which he or she might apply. However, multi-item indicators, assessing a particular job feature through several descriptors, are likely to be more reliable and more acceptable in scientific investigations. Many multi-item scales of that kind have been presented in the academic publications illustrated in earlier chapters, although no single published measure of job content covers all the elements in Table 8.1.

That table hints at both some advantages and a limitation of environment-centered frameworks. On the positive side, a focus on job characteristics can identify the key environmental sources of happiness; important features may be studied individually or collectively, either in overall terms or through detailed examinations casting light on specific causal processes within each; and action implications can be derived about possible changes to job content and organizational processes in order to reduce unhappiness.

On the other hand, it is clear that a particular environmental score may have somewhat different meanings for different individuals. Element scores that are extreme are likely to be similarly distressing or beneficial for everyone, because intense environmental inputs tend to have a substantial impact irrespective of personal interpretation. However, away from extremes the effect of a given feature is likely to vary between people. For example, different individuals' score of 5 ("quite high") on element 3b (difficulty of task demands) may derive from different personal thresholds for what is "high" in this respect, and the same score may be accompanied by considerable job-related anxiety in some cases but not in others. Similarly, a particular amount of social contact (feature 6a) can have different meanings and impacts between people.

It is thus important to complement environment-centered thinking with perspectives about influences on happiness or unhappiness that derive from within a person. Several approaches of that kind are considered in the next five chapters.

9

Social and Judgmental Influences

The preceding chapters have examined particular features in a person's life space that can create happiness or unhappiness. Those environmental characteristics have been placed in 12 principal categories, with subcategories as illustrated in Table 8.1 (p. 239), and their links with subjective well-being (and to a lesser extent self-validation) have been explored. Although causal influences have been demonstrated, observed associations are usually of only moderate size, and environmental accounts leave unexplained a great deal of between-person variation. In seeking to understand why some people are happier than others, we clearly need to go beyond a framework that is based only on inputs from the environment.

The limits of an explanation of happiness oriented only to external stimuli have been emphasized by several investigators. Diener et al. (1999) noted that "researchers are often disappointed by the relatively small effect sizes for ... external, objective variables" (p. 278). Schwarz and Strack (1999) observed that "the relationship between individuals' experiences and objective conditions of life and their subjective sense of well-being is often weak and sometimes counterintuitive" (pp. 61–62). Lyubomirsky (2001) recommended person-centered research because of "the failure of objective variables to predict happiness" (p. 240). Considering "relatively stable" life circumstances, Lyubomirsky, Sheldon, and Schkade (2005) suggested that "all circumstances combined account for only 8% to 15% of variance in happiness levels" (p. 117).

Kim-Prieto et al. (2005) concluded that "while life circumstances can influence reports of well-being, reactions to most life circumstances vary so substantially that there is on average only a modest relation between these circumstances and subjective well-being" (p. 271). From a very different (Buddhist) starting point, the Dalai Lama and Cutler (2003) proposed that "happiness is determined more by the state of one's mind than by one's external conditions, circumstances, or events—at least once one's basic survival needs are met" (p. 1). The poet William Cowper (1731–1800) expressed this well in lines 246–247 of "Table Talk," published in 1782:

> Happiness depends, as Nature shows,
> Less on exterior things than most suppose.

Chapters 9 to 13 thus take a more person-centered approach, exploring influences over and above the aspects of the environment examined so far. In addition to specific environmental features (chaps. 4 to 8), we need to consider the judgments that individuals make in a particular situation, their baseline happiness, their demographic characteristics such as gender or age, and dispositions such as relevant personality traits. Demographic characteristics are reviewed in chapter 10 and dispositional features in chapter 11. Chapter 12 examines the possible moderation of environmental impacts by personal characteristics; issues of person–environment fit and work values are explored in chapter 13. The present chapter looks primarily at judgment processes and variations in baseline happiness. In all cases, the emphasis of research publications has been on the first aspect of happiness, introduced in chapter 1 as subjective well-being. The second aspect, self-validation, has yet to be considered in these respects.

SOCIAL INFLUENCES ON HAPPINESS

Before addressing these individual-based issues, a broad influence from social cues needs to be examined. Those can affect happiness or unhappiness beyond other people's impact within the 12 specific characteristics reviewed so far. For example, although social support (an aspect of feature 6) and supervisor support (10) reflect behaviors and decisions by other people which can affect one's happiness, other individuals might also have a more general influence, not linked to specific inputs of that kind. Subjective well-being may be affected by exposure to other people's views of a situation or their demonstrated well-being, in addition to others' creation of "vitamins" themselves.

That impact was of central interest in early research by Roethlisberger and Dickson (1939). Examining attitudes broadly, they observed that "the meanings which any person in an industrial organization assigns to the events and objects in his environment are often determined by the social situation in which the events or objects occur" (p. 557). Themes of that kind were frequently explored in laboratory and other studies by psychologists in the 1950s and 1960s, emphasizing that a person's mental life is substantially influenced by information and pressures to conformity arising from other people and groups.

Those influences were central to the social information processing model of Salancik and Pfeffer (1978). They argued that attitudes to work are based on the social context, rather than on the impact of a job, such that people construct their attitudes on the basis of information from others—colleagues, supervisors, or customers. That information was said to be of two kinds: direct cues about which attitudes are socially preferred and not preferred, and the creation of differential salience by an emphasis on particular themes and evaluations. Two kinds of social influence were described. Some processes were viewed as implicit, providing hints through particular patterns of behavior and interpersonal relationships, and others involved explicit statements of fact or evaluation. Influences of those kinds may of course be linked to group or community norms, rather than deriving merely from a single person.

Griffin (1983) investigated individual supervisors' influence on perceptual processes, comparing two sets of employees across a period of four months. In one group, supervisors frequently (about five times a day) drew attention to aspects of the complexity (autonomy, variety, etc.) of a person's job. In a control group, no such interventions took place. Employees receiving cues about job features from their supervisor subsequently viewed their jobs as significantly more complex than did the control group, and a substantial difference occurred in overall job satisfaction, which was greater in the socially influenced group.

More recent research has focused on emotional contagion in work groups, examining features that can contribute to the development and maintenance of between-person similarity of feelings at the group level. The presence of a consistent level of well-being in a group of people might arise from three kinds of source. First, all group members might be exposed to the same inputs from the environment ("vitamins" in the present framework). Second, individuals might discuss together local issues and their feelings about them, influencing each other along the lines illustrated above. Some of those influences might derive from processes of social comparison; these are examined later in the chapter. Third, direct emotional contagion might take place among them.

In the last respect, research has pointed to the operation of non-conscious synchronization and convergence processes and possible vicarious affective experiences. Barsade's (2002) model envisaged group members perceiving others' emotions mainly through their nonverbal signals (facial expression, bodily posture, etc.), and trans-lating those inputs through a rapid process of automatic, noncon-scious mimicry. The replication of someone else's bodily activity was proposed to give rise to linked emotional experiences. She reviewed research indicating that "once people engage in the mimicking behav-ior, they then experience the emotion itself" (p. 648).

Barsade (2002) examined themes of that kind in a laboratory experi-ment. In leaderless group discussions, students talked about supposed candidates for a merit bonus. In each group a research confederate, whose role was not known to participants, initiated the presentations. The confederate had been trained to act in either a pleasant or unpleas-ant manner, for example, being either warm, happy, and optimistic, or hostile, pessimistic, and impatient. In addition to self-reports of affect from group members, observer ratings were also obtained from video-recordings of each discussion. Barsade (2002) found that the mood of participants exposed to the pleasant confederate became more positive over time, whereas other participants' mood became less positive in inter-action with a confederate who behaved unpleasantly. (The group discus-sion lasted for 30 minutes.) An impact of the experimental manipulation was also confirmed through the video coders' assessments. Barsade concluded that "group members experience moods at work, those moods ripple out and, in the process, influence ... other group members' emo-tions" (p. 670).

We would thus expect that people who work closely together may acquire similar levels of well-being, for the three kinds of reasons just introduced. Totterdell, Kellett, Teuchmann, and Briner (1998) obtained employees' ratings of their moods on three occasions each day across 3 or 4 weeks (the duration varied between studies). They found that the trend in employees' moods across time was signifi-cantly linked to the collective mood of the rest of their work team, independent of shared negative work events. Totterdell et al. (2004) examined organizational networks more widely, finding that affect converged within interacting work groups and that it was more similar between individuals if there was a work tie between them.

Work colleagues' influence on well-being is likely to be strong in settings of employee-management dispute. When a group's grievances about job content or conditions are a focus of attention and discussion, unhappiness might become more pronounced and widespread. In those settings, the collective experience and negative tone of between-person discussions might elevate strain above that of individual employees alone. Indeed, repeated inputs from other people and the mass media across recent years may have contributed to changed perceptions of the nature and threshold of "work stress," such that this is now reported more frequently than at earlier times (Wainwright & Calnan, 2002; see also chap. 2).

A related influence on employees' happiness comes from their managers. Leaders, especially those of a charismatic kind, can influence followers' emotions, including their experience of subjective well-being. Indeed, leadership trainers often emphasize the importance of communicating optimism and positive activation. The impact of behaviors by a supervisor that are instrumentally or emotionally supportive (job feature 10) has been considered in chapter 5; the focus here is on the possible dissemination of affect itself from a supervisor to his or her subordinates.

That process was examined in a laboratory experiment with students by Sy et al. (2005). Individuals assigned as leaders to task groups were, before their leadership task, exposed to a short videotape presentation that generated either a positive or a negative mood. Following group discussions and activities lasting about 20 minutes, the mood of individual members was found to be significantly more positive in groups whose leaders had a more positive mood.

Extended social pressures can be applied through formal and informal norms within a department or organization as a whole. Kelly and Barsade (2001) have reviewed research into emotion norms in organizational culture, drawing attention to both "feeling rules" and "display rules." The first of those concern expectations about which emotions ought to be experienced, and display rules suggest what should be expressed or concealed in particular situations (creating a form of "vitamin" 3, further discussed in chap. 6). It seems likely that emotion norms of those kinds operate in most roles involving interaction with other people. However, organizationally prescribed rules can be particularly important in customer-facing jobs, when employees are expected to control their emotions and display empathy, agreeableness, or other specific forms of affect (e.g., Wilk & Moynihan, 2005).

Aspects of subjective well-being can thus be influenced in several ways by social pressures and other interpersonal processes. However, factors encouraging or inhibiting the importance of those influences still require more detailed specification. For example, it may be envisaged that, as with social conformity more generally, well-being influences from other people are stronger in settings of ambiguity, when employees are uncertain or ambivalent in their feelings. Effects are also likely to differ between individuals. For instance, Côté (2005) has drawn attention to possible variations arising from neuroticism, self-monitoring and unequal status. Differences may also be expected as a function of individuals' identification with a work-group. Employees who feel committed to a group's aims and processes are likely to respond more strongly than others to cues from other group members. Subjective well-being is likely to be one outcome affected by those cues.

Some empirical findings in this area are ambiguous with respect to possible third variables of the kind that can make difficult causal interpretation in studies of job characteristics (see chap. 8). Outcomes apparently deriving from social contagion might be caused at least in part by unmeasured features that are correlated with those inputs. For example, Griffin (1983) pointed out that cues provided about job content in his investigation (see earlier description) were sometimes accompanied by wider employee–supervisor interactions, as conversations developed around a supervisor's initial remarks. Those conversations could have modified some environmental features such as feedback to an employee or supervisor support. Similarly, the confederate in Barsade's (2002) study may have transmitted information about additional personal characteristics or opinions beyond merely pleasantness or unpleasantness. (However, no evidence of such contamination was found in postexperimental checks.) The two sets of leaders in the research by Sy et al. (2005) could have discussed different issues with their colleagues, not only reflecting a negative or positive mood.

As noted in earlier chapters, causally important unmeasured variables can be present in many areas of psychological research. Although one can never be certain that no other causes exist, it is through the accumulation of research exploring additional possibilities that we can move closer to confident statements of causality. It seems certain that happiness or unhappiness is in part determined by inputs from other people that extend beyond the primary environmental characteristics examined in earlier chapters, but more detailed evidence about potentially relevant features and processes is still required.

JUDGMENTS IN A PARTICULAR SITUATION

In addition to environmental influences (chaps. 4 to 8) and social effects (in the previous section), happiness also derives in part from the ways in which a person processes the information that is available in a particular setting. Psychologists' models of information processing in this area have mainly addressed negative stimuli and ways that people might cope with those. For example, the appraisal–coping model (e.g., Lazarus, 1999; Smith, Haynes, Lazarus, & Pope, 1993) emphasized the mental processes through which people initiate different kinds of coping behavior. "Primary" appraisal was viewed as the assessment of an event's threat or value, and the creation of behaviors to change environmental conditions perceived as undesirable was described as "secondary" appraisal. The framework presented by Daniels, Harris, and Briner (2004) also focuses on unpleasant affect and possible coping procedures, specifying patterns of controlled or automatic processing linked to the development of relevant mental models.

Those approaches take an extended perspective, being concerned with processes all the way from an environmental input to a set of coping behaviors. There is also a complementary need for more detailed examination of particular stages of that process. Of special interest in this book are the activities of primary appraisal, as a person assesses a current situation and makes judgments that might influence his or her happiness or unhappiness.

Those judgments can have two effects on subjective well-being. First is a direct impact, through which a particular interpretation of an environmental feature influences the happiness that is associated with that feature. For example, the judgment that a feature is one with a positive tone can make a person more happy. Second, a moderating influence can occur. It might be the case that the association between the level of a job feature and employee happiness differs when different appraisal judgments have been made. For example, job–happiness correlations may be stronger for individuals who judge the feature in question to be more personally important, and weaker for those who see it as less salient. These possibilities are explored later in this and other chapters.

A framework of 10 judgments is presented in this section, drawing primarily on research in social and cognitive psychology. The framework specifies some ways in which people tend to be cognitively active in determining their own well-being. Individuals are thought to apply some or all of a set of judgments, either by specific intention or through routine habit, thus shaping their affective responses to a particular stimulus from the environment. Each judgment in this framework concerns a reference standard, involving the comparative assessment of an environmental input relative to that standard. Happiness does not depend entirely on what happens to you through inputs from the environment; it is also a function of your perceptions of where you have been, where you might be instead, and where you are likely to go. In addition, your experience is modified by assessments of personal salience, novelty, and self-efficacy.

The 10 judgments are summarized in Table 9.1, together with (in italics) questions that people might ask themselves with respect to each one. Five of them (J1 to J3B in the table) are structurally similar to each other, invoking comparisons with referents outside a person, and the other five have in common the application of personal reference points. First in Table 9.1 are comparisons with other people (J1), asking whether one's own situation, or a particular aspect of that, is better or worse than that of others. Second, comparisons with alternative situations (J2) may be made relative to expectations (J2A) or to counterfactual possibilities (J2B; those that do not exist, being contrary to the facts). Other comparative judgments are time-based (J3), in terms of the direction and speed of change relative to past situations (J3A) or in relation to future possibilities (J3B). In addition, personal reference points are invoked with respect to the salience of an environmental input (J4), the level of one's relevant self-efficacy (J5), and whether an input from the environment is novel or familiar (J6).

Judgments of these 10 kinds are considered to influence a person's well-being in ways illustrated next. The processes can vary in how far they are explicit or implicit, and they may occur in either an automatic or controlled fashion (e.g., Daniels et al., 2004; Schneider & Chein, 2003). Controlled processing is under conscious cognitive management and can be applied flexibly as considered appropriate; it is limited by current attentional resources. Automatic processes, deriving from extended practice, need fewer attentional resources, demand less effort, may be faster than controlled processes, and are resilient in the face of stressors. Automatic processing cannot easily be measured during its occurrence, and research (mainly in cognitive psychology)

TABLE 9.1
Multiple Judgments in the Experience of Well-Being

Type of Judgment	Focus of Judgment
J1: Comparisons with other people: *"How does my situation compare with that of (an)other individual(s) or of the average person?"*	J1. Perceived pleasantness–unpleasantness of one's own situation relative to that of other people
J2: Comparisons with other situations	
J2A. Expected situation: *"How does my situation compare with the situation I expected?"*	J2A. Perceived pleasantness–unpleasantness of one's own situation relative to the situation that was expected
J2B. Counterfactual situation(s): *"How might the situation have developed in other ways?"*	J2B. Perceived pleasantness–unpleasantness of one's own situation relative to that of plausible other possible situations
J3: Comparisons with other times	
J3A. Previous trend: *"Up to now, has the situation deteriorated, improved, or remained unchanged?"*	J3A. Perceived recent changes in the situation
J3B. Likely future trend: *"From now on, is the situation likely to deteriorate, improve, or stay the same?"*	J3B. Expected future changes in the situation
J4: Assessments of personal salience	
J4A. Rated importance of role membership: *"Do I want to be in this role?"*	J4A. The role's personal significance
J4B. Rated importance of a role characteristic: *"Do I value this feature?"*	J4B. The job (or other) feature's personal significance
J4C. Rated attractiveness of core tasks in the role: *"Do I like the things I have to do?"*	J4C. The core tasks' personal attractiveness
J5: Assessments of situation-related self-efficacy: *"Was/is my performance effective in this situation?"*	J5. Perceived adequacy of one's past or future response to the situation
J6: Assessments of novelty or familiarity: *"Is the situation unusual or is it routine?"*	J6. The situation's perceived novelty or routineness

has instead typically examined judgments that are controlled by the individual himself or herself, for example, in response to an investigator's request (Anderson, 1995).

These 10 judgments have been explored by researchers with different interests and theoretical concerns, and they are not usually brought together within a single framework. Empirical research has often been undertaken in the laboratory with student participants, and has so far rarely addressed the well-being of people in employment.

Assessments Against External Standards

The first three judgmental comparisons in Table 9.1 (abbreviated inside the back cover) involve assessments against standards of judgment that are outside the person. These concern other people, other situations, and other times.

J1: Comparisons With Other People.   The experience of well-being is sometimes partly determined by perceptions of relevant similarity with, or difference from, the situation or characteristics of other people (judgment J1). Such comparative perceptions can create a reference point against which one's own well-being can be evaluated. Processes of that kind were illustrated by Wheeler and Miyake (1992), who asked students to record details of social comparisons made over a 2-week period. Reported downward comparisons (against people considered to be worse off than oneself) were found to be associated with subsequent more positive feelings (see also Wheeler, 2000).

Strack, Schwarz, Chassein, Kern, and Wagner (1990) observed that the mere presence of a physically handicapped confederate in a setting of questionnaire completion increased reported well-being, presumably because that person served as a standard of downward comparison. The well-being of cancer patients is greater after comparison with others who are even more ill than oneself (van der Zee, Buunk, de Ruiter, Tempelaar, van Sonderen, & Sanderman, 1996), and satisfaction with one's marriage is greater after experimental exposure to information about another person's unhappy marriage than after information about a happy one (Buunk & Ybema, 2003). Buunk, Oldersma, and de Dreu (2001) asked students to generate reasons why their relationship with a partner was better or worse than most others'. Induced downward comparison led to a more positive evaluation of that relationship, in contrast with other experimental conditions. In general, downward mental comparisons (relative to a referent person who is worse off) are thus expected to enhance the well-being of employees, and upward comparisons are expected to reduce it.

However, although downward social comparisons have been shown to have that positive effect, thinking about oneself in relation to better off reference persons (making comparisons that are upward) can also have personal benefits, although of a different kind. Taylor and Lobel (1989) made that distinction in terms of self-evaluation versus information seeking and affiliation. In cases of self-evaluation (illustrated earlier), assessments of one's own attributes and feelings can become more positive as a result of downward social comparisons, against people who are worse off than oneself. On the other hand, upward comparisons are valuable when an individual wants to gather information, to solve a problem, or to confirm his or her similarity with or make contact with others.

The main concern of this section is with self-evaluation: How does my situation compare with that of other people in its implications for my happiness? Downward social comparisons are thus of special significance (Stapel & Suls, 2004). In other circumstances, for example, when a person is looking for ways to increase his or her knowledge, upward references may be helpful: What can I learn from this person that might enhance my own well-being?

Some studies in employment settings have examined social comparisons related to well-being within the framework of equity theory. As described in chapter 5, this includes the assumption that a situation perceived to be unfair in comparison with other people gives rise to negative affect (Adams, 1963; Walster & Bersheid, 1978). With respect to pay level, satisfaction has been shown to be lower as a function of relevant upward comparison, that is, when the income of others is seen to be inequitably high in relation to their inputs of skill, effort, exposure to working conditions, and so on (Adams, 1965). Similar comparative processes are likely with respect to other environmental contributors to happiness or unhappiness, here treated as "vitamins."

The targets of social comparison range in their specificity from individuals to groups or society in general. Mussweiler and Rüter (2003) showed that undergraduate students' self-knowledge is often based on routine comparisons, proceduralized against an established reference standard and automated through frequent use, rather than through a changing selection of individual referents deemed appropriate to each particular situation. It seems probable that the well-being of employees is also partly determined in that routinized comparative fashion; individuals have standard social comparators that they invoke regularly in appraising stimuli that can affect their well-being.

J2: Comparisons With Other Situations.   Happiness can also be influenced by judgmental comparisons made in relation to two kinds of situation: those that were expected, and those that might otherwise have occurred. In the first case (J2A in Table 9.1), it has been argued that "unexpected success gives pleasure and happiness; unexpected failure gives dissatisfaction and leads to unhappiness" (Freedman, 1978, p. 224). Systematic research into contrasts of that kind has mainly been carried out in laboratory settings. For example, Feather (1969) found that unexpected success or failure in an anagram-solving task was rated as more satisfying or less satisfying, respectively, than expected outcomes. Similarly, bad news felt worse, and good news felt better, when it was unexpected rather than expected in laboratory research by Shepperd and McNulty (2002).

A related possibility has been examined in studies of entry into an organization. Are employees happier if their new job has met their expectations? A met expectation was viewed in employment situations by Porter and Steers (1973) as "the discrepancy between what a person encounters on the job in the way of positive and negative experiences and what he expected to encounter" (p. 152). Confirmation of personally important expectations has been shown to be significantly associated with job satisfaction; the mean uncorrected correlation was +0.33 in a meta-analysis by Wanous, Poland, Premack, and Davis (1992).

Research studies in this area have typically asked job holders at a single point in time to evaluate their current situation in relation to their recalled previous expectations, rather than longitudinally recording expectations in advance of later reality. For example, Taris et al. (2005) obtained from employees direct assessments of 15 job characteristics in comparison with the level they had expected (from "much worse than expected" to "much better than expected"). Met expectations based on recall were on average correlated at +0.31 with overall job satisfaction, and the association remained significant despite controls for levels of the job features themselves and for individuals' ratings of the importance of those features.

However, this recall-based cross-sectional measurement is clearly less than ideal, because distorted memories about what was expected might modify the observed patterns. An investigation across time was reported by Sutton and Griffin (2004), in which preentry expectations were compared with experiences recorded 12 months after commencing a job. That project found no impact on overall job satisfaction from unmet expectations, computed in terms of interactions between expected and actual levels.

It may be that the effect of judgment J2A (against an expected situation) occurs in a briefer period than the 1-year gap in that study. Across an extended period of time, individuals are likely repeatedly to modify their expectations in the light of new knowledge, so that information recorded 12 months earlier may no longer be of personal relevance. Note also that findings are likely to depend on the particular content of an expectation. An employee moving into a job may have expectations about any of the "vitamins" considered earlier, and the disconfirmation of expectations about some of those may be more personally salient than disconfirmation with respect to others. Relevant too is the level of a feature at which a discrepancy occurs. Contrasts within the zones of deficiency or threat (toward low or high extremes of a "vitamin"; see chap. 4) are more significant than discrepancies within the benign middle range of a job characteristic. Although comparative judgments of this kind can be important for well-being, stronger job-related evidence would derive from separate recordings, of expectations before entry into a position and of current levels of each primary feature.

A second judgmental comparison with alternative situations (J2B) is with those that might have occurred but did not occur. Subjective well-being can sometimes be influenced by consideration of either poorer or better counterfactual alternatives, those which are contrary to the facts. People may think about ways in which their current situation might instead have developed, with consequences for their present well-being. For example, "things could be a lot worse than they are."

Upward counterfactual judgments (relative to a more attractive possibility) tend to evoke unpleasant feelings in one's current situation, whereas downward comparisons (which consider an alternative that is worse than reality) can increase a person's happiness (Olson, Buhrman, & Roese, 2000; Roese, 1997; Roese & Olson, 1995). The process was illustrated by Medvec, Madey, and Gilovich (1995) in a study of Olympic medalists. Those receiving silver medals for achieving second place tended to be less happy with their position than were bronze medallists in third place. Many second-place winners appeared to base their feelings in part on upward counterfactual comparisons ("I failed to be the best"), whereas athletes in third place were more likely to make downward comparisons, being pleased to have reached the medal positions ("I did better than all the rest").

These two kinds of comparison with alternative situations (expected or counterfactual) have mainly been examined in the social psychological laboratory, with a focus on study-specific cognitions or satisfaction with a feature that is not job-related. We have almost no research information about the judgments' activation, content, or consequences for well-being inside organizations. Nevertheless, it seems likely that expectancy effects occur in work settings as well as elsewhere, and that counterfactual comparisons are often made: How does my job compare to others that I might have had? Job-related well-being sometimes derives in part from judgments based on prior expectations and about the content of other jobs, known or imagined.

J3: Comparisons With Other Times. Another set of studies has focused on the assessment of temporal trends (judgment J3 in Table 9.1). For example, is this stressful situation getting better or worse? Or have I moved adequately toward a goal? Given that goals may be defined as "internal representations of desired states" (Austin & Vancouver, 1996, p. 338), reduced distance from a goal (from a "desired state") is expected to be associated with better well-being (e.g., Michalos, 1985). Research with university students by Brunstein (1993) and Koestner et al. (2002), in which progress in achieving personal goals predicted change in well-being, was summarized in chapter 6. In overview of that research, "high levels of goal progress or attainment consistently predict increased well-being ... whereas low levels of progress predict reduced well-being" (Lyubomirsky et al., 2005, p. 119). Similarly, employees' attainment of work goals can contribute to their overall job satisfaction (Maier & Brunstein, 2001; Roberson, 1990; Wiese & Freund, 2005), to their end-of-shift job-related affect (Harris et al., 2003), and to their context-free subjective well-being (Wiese & Freund, 2005). A sense that progress is being made is central to the concept of thriving in the model by Spreitzer et al. (2005).

Discrepancy from a desired goal was examined through laboratory manipulations by Solberg, Diener, Wirtz, Lucas, and Oishi (2002). They varied students' hypothetical income or goal attainment in scenarios of imaginary situations, reporting "compelling evidence that the discrepancy between people's desires and actual state [has] a causal influence on their satisfaction" (p. 732). Several kinds of investigation have thus indicated that perceived distance from a goal, usually reflecting judgments about previous movement or nonmovement, can be important for happiness.

An alternative perspective on well-being as a function of progress toward a goal has been explored by Carver and Scheier (e.g., 1990, 1998). Their model was derived from cybernetic theories of feedback in system functioning, emphasizing that responses depend not on goal discrepancy itself (i.e., distance from the goal) but on the speed with which that discrepancy is being reduced. It was assumed that people compare the velocity of discrepancy reduction against a personally acceptable standard of speed of progress, and that their affect arises from a perceived deviation (slower or faster) from that reference rate of movement. "If the rate of movement is too low, negative affect arises. If the rate is high enough (exceeding the criterion), positive affect arises. If the rate is just acceptable but no more, no valence arises" (Carver, 2001, p. 347).

The model is primarily concerned with the regulation of behavior, but implications about well-being include the proposal that the magnitude of a goal discrepancy is itself of no consequence with respect to subjective well-being. The influential factor "is solely whether the perceived *rate of progress* in the action system is adequate" (Carver & Scheier, 1990, p. 23; italics in the original). There is evidence from laboratory studies that speed of progress toward a goal can sometimes contribute in that way (e.g., Carver & Scheier, 1998), and in everyday life this can be seen at times of abrupt change in velocity, when sudden improvement or deterioration in rate of progress toward a goal can be followed by exhilaration or dismay, respectively. In very negative cases, when goal progress is perceived as negligible (the rate is effectively zero), a person may experience unhappiness because "I'm just not getting anywhere." In some more positive settings, it may be "better to travel hopefully than to arrive," and a desirable rate of progress can itself contribute to raised happiness.

However, a model in terms only of rate of progress implies that a current rate that is acceptable in relation to a standard speed generates no feelings, however large is a person's distance from a goal. (See the quotations in the previous paragraphs.) That is improbable, and in fact both distance from a goal and speed of discrepancy reduction have been shown to be influential (e.g., Bandura & Locke, 2003). The two comparisons should therefore be included in J3A. Perceptions of progress velocity relative to a speed standard (as in Carver and Scheier's model) can be important for employee well-being in some conditions, but also important is the perceived magnitude of a goal discrepancy.

The two perspectives (in terms of goal distance and of rate of progress) may in fact be brought together through a consideration of short-term as well as long-term objectives. Research has typically considered only progress toward a single goal at some time in the future. However, people are likely to judge movement trends in relation to a network of goals and subgoals at several levels of specificity. In addition to a substantial overall goal, progress may also be viewed relative to subsidiary and more immediate objectives. A high rate of progress toward a more distant goal may be accompanied by high or low goal discrepancy in relation to particular short-term, subsidiary objectives. For instance, "I'm still a long way from where I wanted to be in this work session." Awareness of both indicators is usual, rather than only one of them, and perceptions of progress rate or goal discrepancy at one level (e.g., overall) can co-occur with assessments of rate or discrepancy at other levels.

Table 9.1 also draws attention to the possible impact on well-being of an expected trend in the future (J3B). This has sometimes been examined as perceived probability of success, and positive expectations of that kind are significantly associated with subjective well-being (e.g., Emmons, 1986); well-being is enhanced when a future trend is envisaged to be positive. In everyday situations, happiness is often felt to depend on "having something to look forward to." One implication of this is that in negative situations, for instance of job stress, it can be predicted that employees' unhappiness will be in part a function of expected future levels of that stress. Examining the extent to which employees mentally "switch off" after a working day, Sonnentag and Bayer (2005) suggested that "it is not primarily the amount of time pressure that one has faced during the working day that makes psychological detachment difficult, but rather the anticipation that time pressure will continue during the working days to come" (p. 409).

More generally, when previous (A) and future (B) trends are similar, a single J3 appraisal may be made. However, when those two diverge, it seems likely that estimates of future progress may be of greater importance for well-being than is a retrospective perception. In evaluating possibilities and making plans, the future is necessarily of major concern.

Assessments Against Internal Standards

The judgments reviewed so far (J1 to J3) have their impact on happiness or unhappiness through the information they provide in relation to reference standards external to the person. J4 to J6 operate instead in relation to a person's own benchmarks, in terms of salience, self-efficacy, and novelty.

J4: Personal Salience.   First is the extent to which an input from the environment is viewed as being of high or low personal salience.

Research in this area has used two sets of descriptive labels, which are in fact conceptually and empirically interdependent. On the one hand, the salience of a situation or environmental feature has been examined in terms of the degree to which it is rated as personally important, significant, of concern, preeminent, or pressing (how much it "matters to" a person). In other studies, descriptions have been in terms of a person's wants, preferences, values, needs, or desires—the extent to which he or she "would like" to retain, attain, or change the feature, sometimes viewed in terms of motivation to approach or avoid.

Those two sets of terms are in practice linked, because an index of perceived importance tells us about the strength of a person's wants: Something that is important to you is something you want to gain, reduce, or maintain. Research findings from the two indicators (importance or want) are in general expected to be similar, but differences are likely to arise from study-specific variations in emphasis. For example, the rated salience of an environmental feature in terms of "importance in your current job" (especially in a study that overall emphasizes negative features) is not necessarily the same as "importance in your ideal job" or "importance in general."

Judgments of salience may concern either negative or positive implications. In negative terms, a situation or feature that is more salient to an individual is one that he or she more strongly needs or wants to escape from or avoid. Salience for negative reasons can derive from a range of emphases—danger, boredom, lack of competence in the current activity, greater desirability of an alternative, and so on. It is obvious that a stimulus appraised as, say, dangerous is likely to have a stronger negative impact on subjective well-being than is the same stimulus when viewed as having no significance for the self. Although in general perceived level of danger tends to reflect the actual negativity of a stimulus, some differences between people in the personal salience of that stimulus can be expected.

Positive forms of salience involve a stronger need or want to gain or retain something that is viewed as personally important in some respect. Students' progress in personal projects (Emmons, 1986) or toward goals (Brunstein, 1993; Sheldon & Elliot, 1999; Sheldon & Houser-Marko, 2001) is more associated with their subjective well-being when those projects or goals are judged to be personally more salient. That differential pattern has also been found for employees in the early months of a job (Maier & Brunstein, 2001) and for pleasant feelings at the end of a work shift (Harris et al., 2003). In addition,

Brunstein, Schultheiss, and Grässmann (1998) observed that the association between students' goal progress and well-being was stronger when personal goals are judged to reflect an individual's dominant motive disposition.

Judgments of personal salience are likely to have a moderating influence on happiness in many domains of life. The construct has been investigated in different ways and with different labels in a variety of research areas. Relevant themes may be brought together here at three levels of generality—concerned with the salience of role membership, role characteristics, or core tasks.

J4A: Rated Importance of Role Membership.   Some research has examined the extent to which different people want to be in (or out of) a particular role. For example, chapter 3 showed that being unemployed involves greater unhappiness for individuals who have a strong commitment to paid work, and conversely that employed people report greater job satisfaction if they have stronger employment commitment of that kind (e.g., Agho et al., 1993; Stafford et al., 1980). Klumb and Lampert's (2004) review of research into women's role preference indicated that well-being is greater for those who are in a role (either employed or home-making) which they value. (See also studies of women and employment examined in chap. 10.) Similar findings, sometimes described in terms of "work-role centrality," have been reported in research with retired individuals; as summarized in chapter 3, wanting less to be a current retired (versus employed) role is linked to greater unhappiness in that role.

More specific roles may also be considered in these terms. For instance, some people undertake their job regularly during the night, and the association between that particular (night shift) role and employee happiness might be thought to depend in part on whether or not an individual prefers such a schedule. Barton (1994) showed that the negative impact of night work was indeed mitigated if it was actively chosen, for instance for reasons of domestic convenience or to earn higher pay.

J4B: Rated Importance of a Role Characteristic.   Other investigations have focused on particular attributes of a role. It has often been found that subjective well-being is more strongly correlated with the absence or presence of a particular attribute if that attribute is viewed as more personally salient. With respect to job satisfaction, this moderating role was demonstrated many years ago, although it has rarely been considered in recent research. Linked to Locke's (1969) perspective, Mobley and Locke (1970) asked about satisfaction with particular features of a job and the personal importance of those features. Correlations between the perceived level of a job feature and satisfaction with that job feature (and with overall work satisfaction) were found to be significantly greater in the case of features that were viewed as more personally salient.

Facet satisfaction was also examined by Rice et al. (1991). They asked about 12 job aspects, such as opportunities for decision-making and for skill learning, effort required, conversations with coworkers, and promotion prospects (features 1, 2, 3, 6, and 11 in the present framework). In relation to satisfaction with each job feature, a significant moderating effect was present in nine out of 12 analyses. The relationship between facet amount and facet satisfaction was stronger for employees rating that facet as more important to them than it was for those viewing it as of lower salience. Consistent with that pattern, the variance of related satisfaction scores was greater for high-salience facets than for low-salience facets. "Workers cannot feel highly satisfied or highly dissatisfied with a facet that is not important to them" (Rice et al., 1991, p. 32).

Chapter 12 illustrates this moderating influence with respect to "growth need strength," the importance or desirability to an employee of intrinsic job features such as autonomy or variety. Research using a summary measure of job content in terms of "scope" (described in chap. 8) has shown that correlations between job scope and job satisfaction differ significantly as a function of growth need strength (e.g., Loher et al., 1985): The association is stronger for employees who more value the job attributes in question than for those who less value those features.

This effect of personal salience will also be demonstrated in chapters 10 and 11, with respect to differences in job-attribute preferences between men and women and in relation to variations of that kind linked to personality. A substantial between-group or between-personality difference in the average salience of a key job characteristic is likely to be accompanied by a between-group difference in the association between that job feature and well-being. In simple terms, the more strongly that a person or group wants something (the more that it is viewed as salient), the more will the happiness of that person or group be affected by its absence or presence.

This moderator pattern is logically necessary. The more that a feature in the environment has implications for a person's happiness or unhappiness, the more it will by definition tend to affect those outcomes. In the present section, the emphasis is on processes of judgment, focusing on whether or not a person attends to a current level of salience. In that respect, the same job feature is expected to influence subjective well-being in different ways as a function of between-person or within-person variations in its perceived importance. This theme is extended into the study of occupational values in chapter 13; dispositional forms of values involve the consistent application of J4B salience judgments across situations and times.

J4C: Rated Attractiveness of Core Tasks. Evaluative judgments may also be focused on activities that are central to a role. An occupational or other environment can be described at several levels of specificity. Attention in earlier chapters was directed at primary characteristics, describing a role in terms of its broad features rather than its specific activities. In that way, jobs vary, for instance, in the opportunity they provide for personal control or the income they produce. But they also vary in the activities that are required, those that are the essence or core of the role.

For example, some jobs require a person to apply physical effort, work with animals, take large risks, cut into human flesh, deal with very ill people, carry out numerical calculations, handle abstract ideas, or make decisions about the life or death of others. Irrespective of the nature of those jobs in terms of the "vitamins" reviewed in chapters 4 to 8, between-job variations are present with respect to core tasks of this kind. And for each core task, people differ in their preferences. The same core task makes some people unhappy and makes other people happy; in a minority of cases, an individual's apparently strange personal preference might suggest that "there's no accounting for taste." (This contrast between preferences is particularly obvious with respect to hobby activities, where between-person differences can be very substantial.) Variations in personal salience of this focused kind (judgment J4C) undoubtedly influence subjective well-being, over and above any impacts from the primary environmental features and the rated salience of those (J4B).

This targeted form of between-person difference in salience has rarely been explored by researchers into job content, although it has been central in other areas such as vocational choice, where different perceptions of the attractiveness of tasks form the basis for classifying people. Its importance in the present framework is that ratings of core-task attractiveness (J4C) influence subjective well-being in ways that are typically ignored by research in this area. An environmental input yields less or more happiness not only as a function of the personal salience of its primary features (J4B as already described), but also in response to a salience judgment of the J4C kind, focusing on the personal attractiveness of core activities in the role.

These two levels of personal salience (J4B and J4C; see, e.g., Table 9.1) both concern attributes of a role. However, they are distinguishable in two respects: their specificity of attribution, and the presence or absence of an objective definition. First, J4C (core-task attractiveness) concerns only a single attribute of (say) a job—its essential activities, those which are central to the role. On the other hand, J4B (role-characteristic importance) may be examined in relation to any feature of interest (e.g., any of the 12 primary features giving rise to 26 subcategories in the present framework; see Table 8.1 in chap. 8). We can in principle envisage jobs that have equivalent levels of all the features, but that differ in the nature of their core task. J4B thus has broad applicability, whereas J4C is pinpointedly specific.

A second difference between these two forms of personal salience is that the features addressed by judgment J4B (about a role characteristic) can be defined independently of a perceiver, whereas (except at the extremes) J4C always involves the reactions of a person. Job characteristics such as variety, externally generated goals, or income can in principle be defined objectively, even though they may also be assessed subjectively through perceptions. On the other hand, the rated attractiveness of core job tasks (J4C) is a subjective concept, with no single objective referent. Different individuals can find the same activity attractive or unattractive; it is often said that attractiveness exists, at least in part, "in the eye of the beholder."

However, this objective–subjective separation is more blurred for tasks that are at the extremes of attractiveness. For example, some tasks are nasty on a universal basis, at least within a particular society. Occupational examples include wringing the necks of animals, handling human debris and body parts, or cleaning particularly soiled toilet areas. Differences between people in rated salience at this third level (about the attractiveness of tasks, J4C) are less likely to be present in those extreme cases (described as "dirty jobs" in chap. 5); between-person variation around the average (clearly unattractive) level is small. On the other hand, for jobs which are moderately attractive for people in general, evaluative reactions can vary considerably between individuals. In those frequent cases, wide interperson variation is likely around a task's average attractiveness value.

Note that all three levels of personal salience draw on the notion of "voluntary" choice. That construct is difficult to operationalize precisely, because many decisions and behaviors involve both voluntary and involuntary activation, being in part personally selected and also externally imposed. However, salience of type J4A (the rated importance of role membership) usually concerns in part the degree to which a person has chosen or would choose a particular role; J4B judgments (about the personal importance of a role characteristic) in part involve a potential choice between aspects of the environment; and attractiveness ratings of core activities (J4C) partly indicate which tasks within a role a person would choose to undertake if he or she were free to do so.

J5: Situation-Related Self-Efficacy.   The second kind of judgment in relation to internal reference points (J5 in Table 9.1; also inside the back cover) concerns a person's perception that he or she is competent in relation to present demands. Two kinds of judgment about situation-related self-efficacy are likely to be important. First are localized judgments, comparing behavior in a current situation against one's benchmark level of competence, in response to questions like "Have I coped well?" or "Have I made a mess of this?" In this way, an employee's perception that he or she has failed to prevent a controllable negative event might give rise to even more unhappiness; these judgments about self-efficacy are expected to contribute to well-being in addition to an impact from the environment itself.

Second, beliefs about one's personal efficacy in a situation are known to enhance current affect, even when a perceived ability to exercise control over that situation is in fact illusory (Bandura, 1997; Bandura & Locke, 2003). Employees' assessments of their self-efficacy during organizational change were found by Scheck and Kinicki (2000) to be linked to perceptions of less threat and potential harm. This second kind of self-efficacy judgment seems likely to operate in part through J3B, considered earlier; self-judgments of current competence (J5) may influence estimates of a likely future trend (J3B) in terms of perceived probability of success or failure.

J6: Novelty or Familiarity.   A third type of judgment against personal reference points involves assessments of the novelty or familiarity of a current situation (J6 in Table 9.1). Continued exposure to a situation tends to reduce its affective potential, either negative or positive, so that more familiar inputs generate feelings that are less extreme. "Over time, events and circumstances that are stable come to have a diminishing impact" (Kim-Prieto et al., 2005, p. 272). In a few cases, it may be said that "familiarity breeds contempt," as an unchanging situation becomes disliked. The review by Frederick and Loewenstein (1999) concluded that the "subjective experience of, and response to, a stimulus depends on more than its current physical intensity; it also depends on the strength, duration, and recency of previously experienced stimuli" (p. 320). In effect, you assess your happiness partly in terms of what you are used to.

Biological and psychological processes of habituation have been widely observed, when the response to a stimulus becomes diminished after repeated presentation of that stimulus. Such a change may be viewed in terms of a raised adaptation level, when exposure to earlier stimuli creates a frame of reference containing standards in relation to which later stimuli are judged. In the area of this book, such judgmental standards have been indexed as the average pleasantness of recent experiences. An increase across time in the average pleasantness of inputs implies that a later event or situation has to exceed a higher threshold (a raised judgmental standard) before it has the same impact on well-being. For example, Parducci's (1995) range-frequency theory sets the evaluation of a new input against the arithmetic mean of previous judgments. Earlier experiences are viewed as providing a reference standard against which new inputs are assessed. Furthermore, that judgmental standard can change with repeated experience, as new stimuli generate a different average level.

Early research examined adaptation in psychophysical judgments (e.g., Helson, 1964), but studies have also focused on hedonic reactions. Feelings of pleasure or satisfaction in response to a constant or repeated environmental stimulus can become reduced or even give way to indifference (e.g., Diener et al., 1999; Frederick & Loewenstein, 1999). Brickman, Coates, and Janoff-Bulman (1978) studied individuals who had won large sums of money in a state lottery. In relation to a comparison group, context-free happiness was somewhat, but not significantly, higher among winners (the group with notionally more positive environments), but rated pleasantness of specific daily activities was significantly lower among that group. In a related study, victims of serious accidents "did not appear nearly as unhappy as might have been expected" (Brickman et al., 1978, p. 921). The authors drew attention to a common perceptual error, when observers see victims of misfortune as more distressed than do those people themselves. "Through overlooking habituation effects, we overestimate the general duration of feeling generated by an event" (p. 926).

Personal adaptation levels were central to Kahneman and Miller's (1986) "norm theory," which proposed that reality is experienced against a background of what is usual (and also what might have been, J2B, described earlier). A stimulus that differs from its current norm is perceived as novel or even surprising, and affective responses to abnormal events were thought to be greater than for the same events when they are normal to a person. This expected emotional amplification relative to a judgmental standard implies that novel events will elicit stronger feelings than familiar ones. More generally, a new, different stimulus takes on special importance, contrasting with an established standard of comparison. However, the special pleasure or pain from a novel input was predicted by norm theory to decline (within the limits created by the nature of the stimulus) as the judgment norm adjusts to stimuli that become routine over time, in a process of "hedonic adaptation."

Landy (1978) and Bowling, Beehr, Wagner, and Libkuman (2005) have examined response changes of this kind in terms of "opponent process" theory (Solomon & Corbit, 1974). This envisages that the primary response to a stimulus is accompanied by an opposite process, which encourages a return to a person's equilibrium state. The opponent process is assumed to operate more slowly than the primary process, and it can "overshoot" beyond an original level. Mental processes of that kind are difficult to examine empirically, especially when experimental manipulation of single variables is not possible, as in organizations. Although several findings about adaptation are consistent with opponent process theory, direct support or refutation is not yet available with respect to its specific mechanisms.

However, processes of hedonic adaptation in organizations have been illustrated in several empirical projects. Boswell, Boudreau, and Tichy (2005) studied well-being changes longitudinally among employees voluntarily moving into a new job. Overall job satisfaction was found to increase immediately after entry into a new position, but in subsequent years it declined significantly as individuals became adapted to the realities of their role. The authors described this longitudinal pattern as "the honeymoon-hangover effect."

Daniels and Guppy (1997) examined employees' strain as a function of particular environmental stressors, finding that experienced strain was less from those stressors that had previously been encountered. Processes of adaptation may thus contribute to an increased ability to handle environmental demands after a period of exposure to those demands. In that respect, everyday experience suggests that many people's capacity to manage a substantial workload becomes "ratcheted up" after a period of coping with increased pressure; workload that would otherwise cause difficulties can more easily be handled after a person has become adapted to its raised level.

Standards of comparison about novelty or familiarity also underlie some between-day differences in the impact of environmental features. Williams et al. (1991) reviewed previous research into variations in daily mood scores. They found that mood has been observed to be more positive on hassle-free days, but primarily when those days are of a particular kind, having yesterday involved many hassles. That contrast-related difference may be interpreted in terms of change in adaptation level. When a high level of stressors has become usual, a new contrasting and low stressor level is judged to be even more positive than it would otherwise be. In their own empirical research, Williams et al. (1991) focused on the reverse process. They examined employed mothers' juggling of their family and work roles, also recording job, home and social satisfaction at the end of each day. It emerged that having to work on both family and job problems did adversely affect end-of-day satisfaction, but only when it followed days in which no juggling had occurred; an absence of role juggling on the previous day had lowered the comparison standard against which a new threat was judged.

Adaptational themes were explored by Suh, Diener, and Fujita (1996) in nonoccupational research. They measured life satisfaction and current affect in relation to previous events classified as either positive (e.g., getting married) or negative (e.g., being a victim of violent crime). Exposure to negative events was found to be significantly associated with lower subjective well-being of all measured kinds, but only if those negative events had occurred within approximately the last three months. The researchers concluded that subjective well-being "does react to external changes in life, but returns to a stable individual baseline rather quickly" (p. 1098). Suh et al. (1996) pointed out that adaptation can involve a downgrading of previous negative experiences, as people come to reorient their attention to more positive themes or try to find a personal meaning in adverse experiences.

More generally, adaptation affects a person's happiness across time in part through the application of other judgments in the framework. For example, changes in J1 and J2B (comparisons with other people and with other possible situations) can contribute to adaptation, as people come to reinterpret previous happenings through new social comparisons or counterfactual possibilities relevant to their later situation. Changes in J2A (comparing against an expectation) are also important contributors to adaptation. An initial environmental input to happiness may be unexpected (e.g., an accident or a big lottery win), and hence be particularly influential. However, across time one comes to expect the resultant continuing state (e.g., physical disability or a life of luxury), so that later J2A judgments tend more to a neutral norm. Processes of forgetting also aid adaptation, as a person gradually forgets previously influential aspects of other situations, modifying counterfactual assessments (J2B) about how things might have been if they had remained unchanged.

Similarly, people may come to want either less or more as they adjust to a situation's constraints and opportunities. Their experiences of discrepancy from future goal attainment (judgment J3B) can thus become modified, with different goals becoming important in these comparisons. Linked to that, new motivational emphases can develop, with associated changes in personal salience (J4) as different aspects of life come to take on different importance. Judgments of one's self-efficacy (J5) are also likely to increase across time in a stable situation, as one learns to cope with what were originally novel demands.

Adaptation to an environmental feature or set of features can thus involve the other judgment processes considered here. In addition, adaptation can give rise to changes in the environmental features considered in previous chapters. For example, environmental clarity (feature 5) can increase across time, and contact with others (6) may be varied as mutual learning occurs between an individual and people in his or her setting. Adjustment to a situation may also involve changes in externally generated goals (3), as different activities are undertaken or a person's ability to attain particular goals becomes enhanced or reduced.

It may thus be that the happiness or unhappiness of employees whose job features have improved or deteriorated subsequently returns toward an equilibrium level, perhaps being held under personal homeostatic control (Cummins, 2000a). The "dynamic equilibrium model" of Headey and Wearing (1989, 1992) proposed that each person has a "normal" level of well-being and of experienced life events. "Human beings construct their world to arrive at a psychologically consistent set of perceptions—an equilibrium state—which supports or bolsters a feeling of well-being" (1992, p. 7). Subjective well-being was predicted to remain stable except in response to novel events outside the "normal" range. However, well-being changes were expected to be temporary, as adaptation occurred. Headey and

Wearing observed that pattern in a community sample across a 6-year period. The longitudinal "honeymoon-hangover" pattern reported for job changers by Boswell et al. (2005; described earlier) also illustrated a return to people's setpoint after a temporary shift.

In another longitudinal study, Lucas, Clark, Georgellis, and Diener (2003) showed that life satisfaction shifted positively after marriage and negatively after widowhood, but that on average people returned toward their baseline level in subsequent years (more rapidly after marriage than after widowhood). Within banking organizations, Griffin (1991) found that although the content of employees' jobs remained enhanced for several years after job redesign, their overall job satisfaction increased only temporarily before falling back to its original level. There is thus a theoretical rationale and accumulating empirical evidence to suggest that happiness is in part a function of people's assessment of an environmental feature's novelty or familiarity. However, this theme has not often been investigated in employment settings.

Differential Activation of Judgments

Given the manifest importance of these judgment processes, the environmental model of happiness in chapters 4 to 8 needs to be extended to include a person's mental processes as well as inputs from his or her situation. The relative impact of those two sets of influences is likely to depend on the strength of stimulation from the environment (e.g., Frese & Zapf, 1999). Job characteristics are expected to take priority over personal judgments when they command attention by their intensity, whereas cognitive processes can more readily influence happiness when an event or situation does not demand all of a person's attention. Thus, as illustrated earlier with respect to J4C (the rated attractiveness of core tasks), judgment processes are likely to be particularly important in the determination of well-being when an environmental input is of moderate rather than extreme intensity.

Similarly, the ambiguity of a situation can affect the activation of these judgments. Subjective processes are likely to assume greatest importance when objective conditions are unclear. In considering specific attitudes, Salancik and Pfeffer (1978) argued that "the more ambiguous the job aspects, the more the worker will rely on social comparisons to assess them" (p. 228). In a study of marital satisfaction, Buunk, Collins, Taylor, van Yperen, and Dakof (1990) found that situations which are ambiguous in well-being terms did indeed encourage comparisons with other people (judgment J1). More generally, environmental ambiguity creates a need for additional information, for example, also through counterfactual comparisons (J2B). In addition, when implications for well-being are unclear, a person might particularly emphasize the referent of personal novelty or familiarity (J6), for example, seeking information about previous instances. However, no research investigations into these possible contingencies in job situations have been located.

Differences in judgment activation are also expected in relation to discrepancies from an expected trend. Disconfirmation of an expectation about one's progress may create a need to review a prior prediction (J2A) or to reflect about alternative possible outcomes (J2B). Conversely, when an expectation is being met, attention is likely to be directed elsewhere. Similarly, variations in the clarity of a temporal trend are likely to be important for the two comparisons with other times (judgments J3A and J3B); the more that a trend is explicit, the more can those temporal comparisons be applied in assessing one's well-being.

Parallel themes concern differences in the activation of salience and novelty judgments. When salience or novelty is high, conceptually linked judgment processes (J4 or J6 respectively) are more likely to be initiated. Thus greater assessed salience of a stimulus will necessarily point to issues of possible impacts on the self, and rated stimulus novelty directs attention to new elements in the situation. Consistent with patterns reviewed at the beginning of the chapter, salience judgments may be initiated or modified by pressures from other people. For example, Wilk and Moynihan (2005) explored the emphasis placed by different supervisors on particular rules of emotional display in call centers.

Additional factors that may encourage or discourage the application of judgments against reference standards are specific additional cognitions. Social comparisons (J1) and counterfactual judgments (J2B) are more likely to be activated, with potential impact on well-being, when relevant comparators can readily be envisaged. In addition, it has been shown (but not in job settings) that counterfactual thinking (J2B) is more common when the counterfactual possibility might in practice be realized (Roese, 1997). Employee well-being is thus likely to be more influenced by judgments about other possibilities when such possibilities are known to exist rather than merely imagined.

More generally, well-being is expected to be more open to the influence of comparative judgment when a person reflects on his or her situation, rather than responding immediately to a new stimulus. That differential possibility is similar to the distinction made by Forgas (1995) between substantive and other forms of information processing. He found in laboratory research that moods had a stronger impact on social judgments when processing of information about the environment was required to be complex rather than routine.

Judgments and Well-Being: Research Needs

Most studies reviewed in the previous section were conducted outside organizations, with a focus on self-description, social judgment, or well-being that is not job-related. In seeking to learn more about the happiness of people in work situations, it is important that occupational research focuses more on the ten judgments presented above. For example, we require information about patterns of their occurrence and their impact in work settings: How prevalent is each judgment, and how strong are associations with employee happiness or unhappiness? In that respect, conventional investigations of well-being as a function of job characteristics can easily be expanded, so that they also record judgments of the kind outlined here in addition to their customary measurement of environmental features.

One approach of this kind would investigate reports of some or all of the judgments in Table 9.1 in conjunction with perceptions of job characteristics, analyzing employee well-being as a function of reported judgments as well as of the environmental inputs. An initial analysis could examine findings about the environment and well-being without consideration of intervening judgments (as in the traditional manner); more detailed analyses could then identify (for instance, through multiple regression) which of the judgments have a significant incremental impact on well-being, over and above job features themselves. Other investigations of the judgments could helpfully obtain information about employees' ratings of the personal relevance of each one; which of the judgments are considered by job holders to be most influential in determining their own experienced well-being? Some kinds of judgment appear likely to operate as moderators rather than providing direct effects, but alternative modes of impact have yet to be explored.

The influence on employee well-being of different forms of judgment might also be examined through content analyses of open-ended self-descriptions. In research into undergraduate students' accounts of their own characteristics (friendliness, intelligence, etc.),

Wilson and Ross (2000) coded the presence of social comparisons and temporal comparisons in their written statements. Such analyses can be applied in the area of this book, asking employees to describe the sources of feelings about their job. The presence in self-accounts of the judgments described here might then be related to measured well-being and other variables of concern in a particular setting.

Parallel studies should investigate mental processes that occur outside settings created by an investigator. It will usually be necessary to examine retrospective accounts of judgments made previously, learning about earlier processes as recalled by research participants. In general terms, the desirable research strategy is one that combines both idiographic and nomothetic approaches, encouraging people to identify the judgments and comparisons that are idiosyncratically important to them in a particular situation but indexing those in standard terms for all participants (Emmons, 1986).

The mental processes considered here are likely often to extend or be repeated across time. Although most research in the area of this book has involved a single occasion of measurement, the study of happiness-relevant judgments and their activation could particularly benefit from exploration across an extended period. Longitudinal studies in this area could valuably focus on causal direction and seek to exclude possible third-variable interpretations. Experience-sampling procedures have considerable potential in that respect, taking a within-person (rather than the usual between-person) perspective across time (e.g., Fisher & Noble, 2004). In addition, longitudinal research of a qualitative kind is needed, using observation and/or repeated interviews to explore patterns of thinking, types of comparators in each judgment category, and possible links between those categories.

Research should also build on the fact that a person can apply several types of judgment in a single setting or period. Subjective well-being derives from many stimuli and mental activities within a particular episode (e.g., when dealing with a specific task demand). That episode is rarely restricted to a brief instant of time (as usually is research measurement), but extends across a period of minutes, hours or days. In the course of such an episode, many judgments may be made, against different reference standards or repeatedly against the same standard. However, research procedures to explore multiple cognitive processes within the same episode are poorly developed, and now deserve attention.

SELF-HELP EXERCISES

Processes examined in this chapter are present in different guises in many published programs for self-help or self-improvement. Although such programs may contain valuable insights and recommendations, evidence about their impact is extremely limited. "More than 95% of self-help books are published without any research documenting their effectiveness" (Norcross et al., 2000, p. 3). However, some researchers have recently focused on particular judgments and activities, comparing those in experimental settings against each other or against control conditions.

For example, Emmons and McCullough (2003) experimentally compared the impact on students of writing down each day for a fortnight "up to five things in your life that you are grateful or thankful for" (p. 379; Study 2). They found that grateful thinking on that regular basis led to significantly more positive affect during the fortnight than for students who focused on their daily hassles. That difference was also observed (Study 3) in neuromuscular patients against a no-activity control group across 3 weeks; in addition, the experimental (gratitude) group exhibited within the period significantly greater life satisfaction than the controls.

Gratitude involves a recognition that a positive feature in one's life has been caused by another person. Reflecting on that desirable development draws attention to the fact that one's position might otherwise have been more negative (a downward counterfactual judgment, J2B) and possibly worse than that of other people (J1), and may imply that matters are improving (J3B). "Counting your blessings" through grateful reflection can also counteract adaptation processes (J6), as an otherwise stable awareness is modified. It thus brings into play a compound of the judgments introduced earlier, and also emphasizes connectedness with other people, perhaps encouraging reciprocated behaviors that in turn further contribute to well-being.

Also examining the hedonic value of grateful thinking, Sheldon and Lyubomirsky (2006) asked students to write on a single occasion about the things in life for which they were grateful, giving reasons for the gratitude. Students were also encouraged to reflect thankfully in that way during the following 4 weeks, but no specific instructions were given. Although subjective well-being increased relative to changes in other experimental conditions, the impact was not statistically significant, perhaps because of limited adherence to the routine and its insubstantial nature. A more effortful gratitude activity was examined in an Internet study by Seligman et al. (2005). Participants were asked to "write and then deliver a letter of gratitude in person to someone who had been especially kind to them but who had never been properly thanked" (p. 416). Gratitude visits of that kind increased happiness significantly more than in a placebo control group for some days after the event, but the effect did not extend into a longer period.

Seligman et al. (2005) also examined other self-guided exercises. For example, individuals were asked to write down three things that went well each day for a week and describe their causes. This activity led to well-being improvements that continued for 6 months (the longest period examined). It can involve a mixture of judgments J1, J2, and J3, again directing a person's thoughts to positive aspects of his or her situation. That optimistic perspective is also required in exercises that ask people to reflect on their future "best possible selves," making the assumption that life has gone as well as it could. King (2001) asked undergraduate students to write narrative descriptions of their best possible futures for 20 minutes each day for 4 consecutive days, and Sheldon and Lyubomirsky (2006) obtained that written reflection once and asked students to repeat the exercise at least twice over the next 4 weeks. A significant increase in positive affect was found in both studies, and King (2001) also reported an increase in composite well-being after 3 weeks. However, follow-up checks after 4 weeks by Sheldon and Lyubomirsky (2006) indicated that in their study the benefit was only short-lived. They pointed out that the magnitude of impact was likely to depend on the extent to which a person continues with the activity over a period; repeated positive thinking may be more beneficial than merely a single episode. In their study and in the research by Seligman et al. (2005), continued exercising rather than merely a short-term activity was associated with greater happiness.

Other self-guided exercises investigated by Seligman and colleagues (2005) asked people to focus on their own personal strengths. In one case, participants were asked both to identify their particular strengths and to use them more often during the next week. In another experimental condition, the instruction was to use one of your principal strengths in a new and different way every day for a week. Both interventions led to increased happiness relative to a placebo control group, with the impact of the second one extending further into the study's 6-month follow-up period.

Experimental studies of this kind are important for both theoretical and practical reasons. In theoretical terms, experimental comparisons between exercise conditions can increase understanding of causality, advancing beyond the correlational research into judgment processes summarized earlier in the chapter. It also permits examination of possible contingency factors. The hedonic value of an intervention depends not only on its content, but also on its intensity, duration, and frequency, as well as on the characteristics of the individuals involved and on the indicators of happiness that are examined. For example, thinking in a grateful manner is a less substantial activity than making a visit to express gratitude in a face-to-face encounter; further, in terms of particular outcomes, gratitude might have more impact on well-being that involves low arousal (the bottom-right section of Figs. 2.1 and 2.2), whereas reflecting on your personal strengths may more bear on the top-right section—activated pleasure. Additional experimental research into main and interactive effects is clearly much needed.

Possible moderators of those kinds are also important in practical terms, in the development of self-guidance activities to increase happiness. For example, variations in duration and frequency point to possible issues of boredom and adaptation across time. Although extended application of an exercise is likely to be needed for continued effectiveness, repeating a procedure day after day is liable to become boring and to reduce motivation to continue. It may be possible to identify an optimal time interval between repeated applications of an exercise, or to specify particular compounds of exercises which have greatest impact. Perhaps a program that applies several different activities in successive blocks is necessary, especially if that is constructed to fit within a person's daily activities, becoming a habitual routine.

Fordyce (1977, 1983) observed that different activities were considered valuable by different individuals, so that some personal selection of exercises may prove desirable. Fordyce himself offered 14 "fundamentals" to increase personal happiness, and noted that student participants particularly favored "stop worrying," "spend more time socializing," "lower your expectations," and "develop positive, optimistic thinking" (Fordyce, 1983). However, there are of course many obstacles to the successful initiation and maintenance of those behaviors, and research knowledge and practical certainty are very limited in this field. Studies in organizations have yet to be reported.

BASELINE HAPPINESS AND ASSOCIATED
MENTAL PROCESSES

In addition to differences between individuals in their judgment processes in a particular episode, and despite the occurrence of some changes across time, people are likely to carry with them different continuing baselines of happiness. Consistency across time and between different locations has often been shown. For example, Diener and Larsen (1984) reported that people's average levels of affect in work and leisure situations were intercorrelated at +0.70 and +0.74 for positive and negative indicators respectively. Combining findings about employees' overall and facet-specific job satisfaction, Dormann and Zapf (2001) reported from previous studies an average uncorrected test–retest correlation of +0.42 across a range of intervals.

Consistency of well-being is in part a function of stability of the environment. For example, test-retest correlations of job-related well-being are higher when previous and subsequent job content remain similar. That pattern was demonstrated by Staw and Ross (1985) in several analyses. For example, across 3 years the test–retest correlation for overall job satisfaction was +0.47 for employees remaining in the same occupation and +0.36 for those who changed occupation. Parallel values over 10 years in research by Steel and Rentsch (1997) were +0.46 and +0.23, and across a variety of durations in the review by Dormann and Zapf (2001) average stability coefficients were +0.42 for job stayers and +0.18 for job changers. Dormann, Fay, Zapf, and Frese (2006) presented findings from job stayers only. Across two data sets, average test–retest correlations for overall job satisfaction were +0.52, +0.49, +0.47, and +0.32 for gaps of 1, 2, 3, and 4 years, respectively.

Other evidence of consistent between-person rank-ordering of subjective well-being across time comes from the study by Grandey et al. (2005). Across a 12-month period the test–retest correlation for overall job satisfaction was +0.66 for men and +0.52 for women. In research by de Jonge et al. (2001) and Grebner et al. (2005), the 12-month values were +0.55 and +0.44, respectively, for men and women combined. Boswell et al. (2005) presented consistency data across 1-year, 2-year and 3-year gaps. Average test–retest correlations of job satisfaction from overlapping groups of respondents across those gaps were +0.40, +0.29, and +0.25, respectively. High levels of stability across 12 months have also been found for job-related emotional exhaustion (e.g., +0.66, +0.68, and +0.70 in studies by de Jonge et al., 2001, Houkes et al., 2003, and Demerouti et al., 2004, respectively), context-free distress (e.g., +0.60 across a year; Hellgren & Sverke, 2003), and context-free depression (e.g., +0.57 across four years; Frone et al., 1997). Most individuals in those studies remained in the same job throughout, but separate analyses for stayers and changers were not provided.

The notion of a continuing baseline of happiness was central to Headey and Wearing's (1989, 1992) dynamic equilibrium model (see earlier discussion), which argued that people tend to return into their personal narrow range of happiness despite temporary changes in response to environmental stimuli. They reported a test–retest correlation for life satisfaction of +0.52 across 6 years. Similarly, Cummins (2000a) proposed that well-being is held under personal homeostatic control around each person's regular level. Well-being stability appears to be greatest for individuals who are generally more satisfied. In research by Fujita and Diener (2005), members of that group were more consistent in their well-being across 17 years than were less satisfied people. Aspects of stability have also been considered earlier in the chapter among processes of hedonic adaptation; links with continuing dispositions of personality are examined in chapter 11.

Those consistent differences between people in their baseline of subjective well-being are important for hedonic processing in two ways. First is a simple incremental impact on observed levels, added to whatever is the impact of a stimulus. Measured happiness can be viewed as resulting from a combination of the impact of a stimulus and a person's continuing baseline. For example, a stimulus that has a standard effect on everyone will give rise in individual cases to happiness that is a person's baseline plus a constant environmental impact. Second, baselines are important for a more proactive reason. People who are consistently either happy or unhappy "are not just passively acted on by life events—instead they actively interpret and respond to situations" in different ways (Abbe, Tkach, & Lyubomirsky, 2003, p. 386). This means that variations in baseline happiness can be associated with characteristically different approaches to the processing of hedonically relevant information. As a result of different processing by the two kinds of people, a high or low baseline can itself become more strongly established (Lyubomirsky, 2001).

For example, happy individuals are more likely to positively rationalize the outcomes of personally significant decisions (Lyubomirsky & Ross, 1999). After rejection of their applications to certain colleges, chronically happy students were found to value those colleges less and to value even more the college that accepted them. They thus created an evaluative contrast between positive and negative outcomes of their choice. That form of postdecision rationalization was less usual for unhappy individuals, with both the accepting and rejecting colleges being similarly evaluated. As a result, unhappy students were more likely to remain disappointed about being rejected by certain of the colleges.

Other research has contrasted more broadly the way that happy and unhappy people evaluate and think about events in their life. Longitudinal comparisons indicate that happy individuals tend to have more positive memories and more pleasant thoughts about previous events than do people who are unhappy (Lyubomirsky & Tucker, 1998). In a similar vein, happy individuals are less likely to engage in reflection and rumination about previous failures and possible short-comings. Such rumination can lead to a wider concern about one's negative experiences and perhaps to still greater unhappiness. A downward spiral of that kind has been implicated in the self-sustaining nature of clinical depression, as extended rumination deepens a person's negative feelings (Ingram, 1990).

Happy and unhappy individuals also differ in their use of social comparison processes. Those judgments (identified as J1 in the earlier section) can improve or depress well-being when made in relation to a reference standard that is either less or more favorable than one's own position. Unhappy individuals have been found to be particularly sensitive to comparison information of a negative kind, whereas happy people's well-being is largely unaffected by knowledge about other people's position in relation to their own (Abbe et al., 2003; Lyubormirsky, 2001). Happy people's relative insensitivity to social comparisons allows them to maintain high levels of well-being despite fluctuations in their own position relative to others.

As illustrated in the previous section, practical routines and mental exercises to increase one's happiness often emphasize the establishment of new baseline patterns of this kind. For example, many self-help guides urge people to "count your blessings" or "look on the bright side" every day. Development of "the power of positive thinking" (e.g., Peale, 1952) is largely based on personal disciplines to reduce negative comparisons between oneself and others. Although baselines of the kind considered here differ between people in a consistent way, there is also scope for some modification of an individual's level.

Most research reviewed in this section has been undertaken outside employment settings. However, Miner et al. (2005) examined across several weeks employees' average (baseline) hedonic tone at the beginning of a working day. On four occasions each day, information was gathered about recent events and current affect. As expected, positive events at work were associated with raised positive affect, but that was especially the case for high-baseline employees. Individuals who generally arrived at work in a more positive mood reported greater improvement in mood following positive events than did low-baseline employees.

The baseline-related differences considered so far have mainly concerned differences in cognitive processes: Happier people tend to think in ways that sustain or increase their happiness. Other cognitive processes of this kind are examined in chapter 14. In addition, differences in behavior as well as cognition are important; more happy individuals tend to behave in ways that increase the probability of later happiness. Lyubomirsky et al. (2005) reviewed the correlates of several forms of positive affect, showing that affect is significantly associated with more activity, involvement with other people, energy, and a greater investment in one's surroundings. "Happy moods appear to lead people to seek out others and to engage with the environment at large, to be more venturesome, more open, and more sensitive to other individuals" (p. 836). Those perspectives and activities increase the probability of further pleasant episodes and also encourage success in many domains of life.

In overview, the fact that some people are consistently ("as a person") more happy than others provides for each individual a baseline against which responses to environmental inputs are set. Two kinds of baseline-relevant mechanism can be envisaged. First is a straightforward incremental effect in responding to the environment. For the same input, people are differentially happy beforehand, and a constant stimulus impact will make them similarly differentially happy (perhaps at an altered level) afterward. Second is a more variable process. Research has made a start in detailing characteristic ways of thinking about and acting on the environment that are associated with different personal baselines. Happiness-related differences in behavior mean that happier individuals are more likely to engage in new activities and be exposed to new challenges. And, because people with different baselines of happiness process new information in divergent ways, baseline-related differences in mental processes are expected to reduce the observed correlation between environmental features and well- being.

Finally in this section, note that even a high baseline of well-being can be associated with negative as well as positive affective experiences.

Diener and Seligman (2002) identified subsets of students who were either very happy or very unhappy, assessed through a range of indicators across several weeks. In addition to specifying behavioral differences (e.g., very happy individuals spent more time in social encounters), they reported that some periods of unhappiness were experienced in all cases—on as many as half the days for the most happy subgroup. A high level of baseline happiness does not exclude periods of low subjective well-being.

10

Differences Between Sets of People

C hapter 9 examined two forms of influence that operate in addition to the impact of specific environmental stimuli. First were social processes, through which happiness can be in part determined by opinions and pressures from other people. Second, 10 kinds of judgment were shown to be important, when an input from the environment is appraised against reference standards. As well as their involvement in specific episodes, judgment processes were seen also to be repeated consistently within persons between situations, such that people who are in general happy or in general unhappy tend to construe their world regularly through repeated application of thought processes that support a continuing level.

Chapter 9 also drew attention to the part played by demographic and personality variables. Those are considered in the present and the following chapters. Research into demographic features and happiness may be viewed at three levels of specificity, each examining one kind of possible difference between people or groups. The levels concern cultural, demographic, and occupational themes, as follows.

Cultural Differences. Most publications cited in this book have been written within a Western tradition, emphasizing issues of Euro-American concern. However, happiness and its sources might be different in other cultures, for example, in parts of Asia. Research attention has recently turned to possible differences between

Euro-American and East Asian conceptions of happiness, and those are first examined.

Demographic Differences. A second kind of variation (e.g., within a particular culture) is between sets of people identified in terms of characteristics such as sex, age or race. For example, we might ask whether female employees are on average more happy or less happy than male employees. There are difficulties in obtaining samples that represent an entire population, for example, covering all men or all women, and small-sample studies can be misleading because of the particular job content or conditions that happen to be investigated. However, consistent differences are emerging, and some of those are examined in this chapter.

Occupational Differences. Other investigations have focused on possible differences between occupational groups. For example, are part-time employees on average more satisfied or less satisfied than full-time ones, or do temporary staff differ from more permanent staff in that respect? As in the previous case, it is difficult to obtain representative samples of a population (e.g., all part-time employees), and observed differences between studied groups might arise from discrepancies between job content, rather than from an occupational status itself.

For each of those kinds of difference, four issues are addressed. First, we need to ask about different conceptions of happiness itself. The account presented in chapters 1 and 2 and applied in subsequent chapters has emphasized specified forms of subjective well-being and self-validation. Those are likely to be primary in any group, such that happiness can generally be construed through the dimensions summarized in Figures 2.2 and 2.3. However, the relative importance and principal contents of particular aspects of happiness may vary between sets of people. For example, self-validating aspects might be more significant for some groups than others.

Second, we should ask about average levels of happiness associated with the between-person difference under investigation. For example, are older workers in general more happy than younger ones? Such comparisons are descriptively important, but, as indicated earlier, interpretation can sometimes be uncertain because of possible inequalities between studied groups in the environments to which they are exposed. Third, it is important to learn whether individual or group characteristics are linked to differential exposure to environmental features that influence happiness. As shown in previous chapters, happiness is influenced by external features, but exposure to those features might itself be affected by characteristics of a person. That may come about because an individual's attributes caused him or her to move into or out of certain kinds of environments, or because of decisions made by other people, such as managers responsible for personnel selection.

Fourth is the question of possible moderators. Chapters 4 to 8 have shown that all the primary job features are important. But it may be that the magnitude of job–happiness associations differs between sets of people. For instance, some research has asked about statistical interactions with gender in the correlations between job features and job satisfaction. It may be some of those job–happiness correlations are, for example, greater for men than for women. If so, how might that difference in correlation magnitude be explained? One possibility is that an environmental feature (such as opportunity for skill use or contact with other people) is in general more strongly associated with happiness when it is more personally salient to the individuals in question. In that case, an observed between-group difference in correlations could arise from a difference in the average salience of that feature between the two sets of people under investigation. This moderating possibility is explored throughout the chapter.

CULTURAL DIFFERENCES

Most research reviewed in this book has been undertaken from a Euro-American perspective, with underlying expectations about the nature of self and society. It may be that different expectations in other parts of the world are linked to alternative notions of happiness. That construct is likely to be in part socially determined, being embedded in the network of meanings and values of a particular cultural tradition.

For example, Eid and Diener (2001) reviewed previous research indicating that Americans particularly value enthusiasm (the top-right section of well-being in Fig. 2.2 in chap. 2), and that Chinese people appear to see more value in negative emotions. From their own analysis of data from college students, Eid and Diener (2001) concluded that Americans and Australians view positive emotions in general as very much more desirable and appropriate than do Chinese people. Examining subcultures within the United States, Oishi (2002) asked about memory processes that may feed into overall assessments of life satisfaction or other forms of subjective well-being. When asked to recall a previous week, European Americans remembered it as very good but Asian Americans remembered it as only mildly good, despite the fact that both groups had at the time described the period as mildly good. In research with undergraduate students, Tsai, Knutson, and Fung (2006) focused on "ideal affect," that which "people value and would ideally like to feel" (p. 289). They reported that Americans valued activated positive feelings such as excitement more than did Chinese, and that Asian students more valued low-arousal positive feelings such as calmness. People are likely to construct their experience of happiness in ways that in part reflect cultural norms of thinking and feeling.

That general theme has been developed with respect to cultures that are either "individualist" or "collectivist." In the former case (represented by the United States and some European countries), social norms emphasize personal accountability, self-sufficiency, independence, the pursuit of self-oriented goals, and a focus on enhancing one's well-being. Although social relationships are important in such a culture, they operate within the assumption that each person is independent, being free to choose whether or not to enter such relations (e.g., Lu & Gilmour, 2004; Suh, Diener, Oishi, & Triandis, 1998; Triandis, 1995; Uchida, Norasakkunkit, & Kitiyama, 2004).

On the other hand, more collectivist cultures, such as in China, Japan and other East Asian countries, place greater emphasis on social harmony and role obligations. Priority is given to collective welfare, self-control, and the diligent performance of roles within social networks. Lu and Gilmour (2004) identified the core issues for happiness in collectivist cultures as "the fulfilment of role obligations in interdependent social relationships, the creation and maintenance of interpersonal harmony, [and] striving to promote the welfare and prosperity of the collective (e.g., family)" (p. 276). Self-referenced evaluations appear to be less central in those cultures (e.g., Suh et al., 1998), although positive feelings about the self are also valued (e.g., Piccolo, Judge, Takahashi, Watanabe, & Locke, 2005). The difference appears to be one of emphasis; a focus on the self is important in both kinds of culture but it is stronger in cultures that are individualistic.

Linked to that relative difference in the salience of the self, it is expected that a more independent notion of selfhood (as in the Euro-American tradition) will be accompanied by stronger associations between self-esteem and indicators of happiness than in the case of more interdependent conceptions; subjective well-being is likely to be more linked to positive evaluation of an autonomous self within a more individualistic framework. Consistent with that differential expectation, correlations between subjective well-being and self-esteem have been found to be less strong in collectivist countries (Diener & Diener, 1995). Similarly, life satisfaction is more strongly predicted by positive and (in reverse) negative feelings in individualist countries than in collectivist ones (Suh et al., 1998). (See also Lu, Gilmour, & Kao, 2001.)

Differences between individualist and collectivist notions of happiness are thus to be expected. In the former case (e.g., for North Americans), happiness is largely a function of successful development of an independent self through actively striving to master the environment. The collectivist form of happiness (e.g., for East Asians) is achieved more through nurturance of a self that is dependent on others, which strives to merge with the social environment and to meet culturally mandated obligations. In that case, the perceived boundary between the self and others is more blurred and is repeatedly negotiated through social interaction. "In short, happiness is constructed as *realization of social harmony*" (Uchida et al., 2004, p. 226, italics in the original). In both kinds of culture, happiness arises in part from goal-achievement, but the goals that are primarily valued differ between them.

Another characteristic of East Asian conceptions of happiness is a stronger awareness of dialectical balance, perhaps linked to the yin-yang philosophy that everything is part of a cyclical process of change between good and bad, between well-being and ill-being, and between several other states that contrast with each other. "Happiness is dependent on unhappiness, while unhappiness is hidden in happiness" (Lu & Gilmour, 2004, p. 277). In Euro-American cultures positivity and negativity are typically considered to be in clear opposition to each other, but in East Asian cultures they are more viewed as complementary (Uchida et al., 2004). That dialectical perspective can lead in East Asian settings to a lesser concern for the maximization of current well-being and a more willing acceptance of negative situations, because those are more explicitly recognized as essential to the later emergence of positive outcomes. For example, research with students has indicated that the experience of happiness is viewed as less important in China than in the United States or Australia, with a reduced attention to one's own state of well-being (Diener, Suh, Smith, & Shao, 1995). The here-and-now occurrence of negative feelings can from that perspective be viewed as of limited concern, whereas to many Euro-American investigators negative experiences are seen as harmful, stressful, and in need of support or remediation.

In relation to the chapter's first theme (the conception of happiness), it may thus be the case that the construct has a partly different meaning in more individualist and collectivist countries. Other research has suggested that the measurement axes identified in chapter 2 are generally important across cultures. For example, Russell (1983) found similar conceptual structures in Japanese, Gujarati, Croatian, and Chinese speakers. The three-dimensional structure of experiences in Figure 2.3 thus appears to be broadly applicable, based on pleasure, mental arousal, and self-validation. However, between-culture differences can occur in terms of content: The individualist emphasis in the construct of happiness is more on personal achievement of self-relevant goals, whereas the collectivist concern is more for the fulfillment of role obligations to maintain harmony in interdependent social relationships. This difference points to a possible divergence in the relative importance of self-validation, as described in chapters 1 and 2. Self-validating aspects of happiness, in particular with a focus on standards of social worth, appear likely to be particularly salient in collectivist cultures.

The chapter's second theme concerns the average level of happiness in different people or sets of people. For example, is there a difference in the level of subjective well-being between individualist and collectivist cultures? Diener et al. (1995) showed that significantly higher average scores for life satisfaction and context-free happiness were obtained in more individualist nations. Veenhoven (1999) reported a correlation of +0.55 across 38 nations. He pointed out that the direction of causality remains ambiguous, but speculated that "individualistic society fits human nature better than a collectivist society does" (p. 176). Given that any society sets restrictions on members' freedom, Veenhoven argued that the less strong restrictions in more individualistic settings provide more opportunities for people, giving them "a better chance of living a life that fits their nature" (p. 177). (On the other hand, he recognized that increased freedom has costs, e.g., in terms of difficulty in choosing and the consequences of poor choice; see the "additional decrement" discussed earlier for "vitamin" 1.) Uchida et al. (2004) pointed out that the between-nation correlation of subjective well-being with individualism is linked to a general tendency of, for instance, Americans to emphasize positive feelings and positive self-views more than, say, Japanese people (see the earlier discussion).

In addition to an impact of cultural features of the individualist or collectivist kind illustrated earlier, this difference between countries in average context-free well-being may arise in part from other ("third-variable") differences. For example, individualist countries tend also to have greater national wealth (e.g., Huang & van de Vliert, 2004; Veenhoven, 1999), a factor shown in chapter 4 to be linked to average context-free well-being. Diener et al. (1995) controlled for countries' economic prosperity in partial correlation analyses, finding that the positive association with individualism remained significant despite that control. Veenhoven (1999) also examined the individualism–happiness association after controlling for national wealth. He reported that in his data the positive association between those variables was present only across richer nations. One explanation offered was that only in those countries do people have environmental choices and rewards that are enhanced by individualism; in undeveloped countries, favorable opportunities tend to be absent.

What about between-culture differences in average well-being that is job-related? Studying overall job satisfaction in a single company across 39 countries, Huang and van de Vliert (2004) observed a correlation of +0.10 between a country's individualism and that form of well-being. The job satisfaction of employees in two American companies was correlated at +0.02 with their self-rated individualism in research by Probst and Lawler (2006). Additional research is needed, but a significant association seems unlikely.

The chapter's third theme (differential exposure to environmental influences) has been touched on already. Collectivist cultures embody norms of social interdependence and harmony that value goal achievement in those respects more than is the case in individualist settings. Living in a particular culture necessarily involves exposure to normatively valued behaviors and role relationships that can differ from other cultures. However, research is still required into those normative sources of happiness in employment settings in different cultures.

Fourth, do differences in culture moderate the associations between specific (here job-related) inputs and happiness? The 39-country investigation by Huang and van de Vliert (2004; already mentioned) indicated that job level and associated features were more strongly associated with overall job satisfaction in individualist rather than collectivist countries. They suggested that more individualist cultures may more encourage goals of self-actualization that can be better attained at higher job levels in those cultures (hence the positive correlation between job level and satisfaction in those countries); alternatively, lower level jobs may have a more attractive content in collectivist countries (so that in those cases the level–satisfaction correlation is smaller).

The same project also found that some intrinsic job characteristics (opportunity for skill use and feedback from one's supervisor) were more strongly associated with job satisfaction in individualist countries than in collectivist ones (Huang & van de Vliert, 2003).

Probst and Lawler (2006) examined associations between employees' perceived job security (an aspect of feature 11) and their job satisfaction. They predicted that a greater emphasis on communal welfare and between-person links in more collectivistic countries would be accompanied by stronger correlations between security and job satisfaction than in more individualistic countries. That was found to be the case in comparisons between China and the United States, and also in the form of a significant interaction between perceived security and employees' own individualism in a separate study in the United States.

Despite the fact that relevant empirical research has been limited, it is clear that cultural differences can be important for the four themes examined here: the conception of happiness, average levels, differential exposure, and moderating influences in combination with environmental effects. Nevertheless, it is possible that individualist–collectivist differences may become less significant in future years, as Eastern and Western perspectives draw from each other in continuing processes of globalization and homogenization.

DEMOGRAPHIC DIFFERENCES

A second set of between-group investigations has concerned happiness as a function of personal attributes determined by one's birth. Two such features are examined here, gender and age, with particular reference to people in employment.

Men and Women

Before asking the chapter's four principal questions (about conceptions of happiness, average levels, possible differential exposure, and moderation by gender), a related issue should be considered. Several investigations have asked whether having a paid job in addition to meeting family and domestic commitments is psychologically beneficial or harmful for women in general. This research originated in the 1950s, when married women's employment was relatively unusual and there was considerable debate about the personal and family impacts of its additional and sometimes conflicting demands.

Studies in this area have differed widely in their sample composition—for example, examining only women who are married, those with children of certain ages, particular subgroups (like the highly educated), or women in particular geographical locations. A range of different outcome indicators has been studied, and findings have varied somewhat between investigations. Nevertheless, it is now clear from a large amount of research that on average context-free happiness is similar between women in jobs and women who are not employed (Klumb & Lampert, 2004).

Happiness in either role depends on the two sets of variables introduced in chapter 3 for unemployed and retired people—a person's preference for a role and the characteristics of that role. In the first respect, the psychological benefits of paid employment depend on a woman's wish either to be in a job or to be a homemaker. Preferences are often ambivalent, but in general a greater commitment to paid work is associated with greater subjective well-being in women who are employed (Barnett & Hyde, 2001; Repetti, Matthews, & Waldron, 1989; Ross et al., 1983; Warr & Parry, 1982). This pattern was described in chapter 3 for employed people in general, with the converse association being found in unemployment or retirement, when greater employment commitment is associated with lower well-being (e.g., McKee-Ryan et al., 2005; Paul & Moser, 2006).

Second, as was illustrated throughout chapters 4 to 8, happiness is influenced by the characteristics of a woman's environment, both at work and at home. Within the vitamin framework of this book, particularly relevant characteristics include externally generated goals (feature 3), which are likely to increase if a woman has both family and job responsibilities. For example, chapter 6 examined work–family conflict, the magnitude of which derives from the demands of a parental role as well as of a job (e.g., Grzywacz & Marks, 2000). The more negative is a woman's employment and/or family profile on the dimensions of Table 8.1 in chapter 8 (including 3e, work–home conflict), the lower is her subjective well-being expected to be.

Turning to the present section's more specific focus, on variations between employees themselves, the chapter's first question asks about possible between-group differences in the conception of happiness. Do men and women on average differ in the way they think about that notion? The framework presented in chapter 2, in terms of the dimensions of pleasure, mental arousal and self-validation, seems likely to be generally appropriate for both men and women, although that generality has apparently not been empirically tested.

However, between-gender differences might occur in terms of the relative salience of different measurement axes or with respect to average baselines or reference standards. In the first case, men and women might differ in the emphasis given either to anxiety–comfort or to depression–enthusiasm when reflecting on their happiness. Second, if women tend on average to experience, for instance, more anxiety than men, their conception of that form of happiness in a particular situation could be in relation to a baseline expectation that is more anxious than that of men. In thinking about the meaning of low or high well-being, they would thus apply a more negative reference point for comparisons. More generally, it is possible that women differ from men in their application of certain of the judgment processes outlined in chapter 9. For example, women more than men might emphasize social comparisons (J1), leading to a partly different conception of well-being.

These themes appear not to have been explored empirically. However, some research has asked whether women tend toward more intense experiences of well-being, both positive and negative (Fujita, Diener, & Sandvik, 1991). It appears that this might be so, although the possibility has yet to be explored in employment settings.

In thinking about the chapter's first question, it is easy to slip from the "meaning" of happiness into a consideration of its "sources." It may be the case that, when thinking about their happiness, men and women identify partly different contributing events and features. Those are outside the conception of happiness itself, being factors that promote or restrict it. Evidence about those sources of happiness includes correlations of specific environmental features with well-being for the two sexes separately; some of those are reviewed later in a discussion of statistical moderators. In terms of possibly different meanings of this concept to men and women, attention needs instead to be directed to the nature and structure of the experience itself.

Men and Women: Average Happiness.   Second, do men and women on average report the same amount of happiness? Meta-analyses of context-free patterns for the first axis of subjective well-being have suggested either equivalent levels or very small differences in one direction or the other. Observed happiness differences in published reviews have been either slightly in favor of men (Haring, Stock, & Okun, 1984) or of women (Wood, Rhodes, & Whelan, 1989). It seems appropriate to conclude with respect to measurement axis 1 in Figure 2.2 (from feeling bad to feeling good, irrespective of mental arousal) that context-free happiness levels are in general similar between the sexes.

However, a gender difference is consistently observed on context-free axes 2 and 3 (from anxiety to comfort and from depression to enthusiasm). On average, in research with community samples women report significantly more anxiety (e.g., Feingold, 1994) and depression (e.g., Nolen-Hoeksema & Rusting, 1999). Substantial gender differences of that kind are also present in clinical disorders with those labels (e.g., Kessler et al., 1994; Keyes, 2002). Jick and Mitz (1985) reviewed previous published studies (mainly of community samples), reporting that those consistently indicated greater context-free distress, anxiety, and depression among women. That difference also occurs in samples of employees only, with greater context-free distress (low scores across axes 2 and 3) found in women workers compared to male workers by Loscocco and Spitze (1990), Piltch, Walsh, Mangione, and Jennings (1994), Pugliesi (1995), Clark et al. (1996), Roxburgh (1996), and Mullarkey et al. (1999). In a comparison of workers all in similar jobs, Lowe and Northcott (1988) observed greater context-free depression (on axis 3) in women than in men, before and after statistical controls for other variables.

Are those gender patterns present for well-being that is job-related? As indicated earlier, results are partly dependent on the nature of influential job characteristics in a particular study, and large-sample investigations are desirable to statistically control for those or to balance differences in male and female job environments. Analyzing data from seven representative samples of the American working population, Weaver (1980) found that average overall job satisfaction scores (axis 1) were almost identical for men and women. That was also found by D'Arcy, Syrotuik, and Siddique (1984) with Canadian respondents, by Neil and Snizek (1988) in an Australian government organization, by Aryee et al. (2005) in an Indian sample, and by Mottaz (1986), Brush, Moch, and Pooyan (1987), Pugliesi (1995), Carlson and Mellor (2004), and Rode (2004) in different U.S. samples.

However, in recent studies American female samples have tended to report greater overall job satisfaction than men (e.g., Erickson et al., 2000; Grandey et al., 2005). Data from a U.S. national sample indicated that women on average have significantly higher job satisfaction despite control for many other variables (Bender et al., 2005). In the United Kingdom, nationally representative studies have also found that women on average report significantly higher job satisfaction (overall, with their pay, and with the work itself) than men, before and after statistical controls for other variables (Clark, 1996, 1997; Clark et al., 1996). Aggregating across 10 Western nations (including the United States), Birdi et al. (1995) found a small but significant average gender difference in overall job satisfaction, with women scoring more highly, both before and after statistical controls for many other variables. This significant difference was also demonstrated through regression analysis by Clark (2005b) in survey data gathered from 19 countries. That study further revealed that women on average reported significantly greater satisfaction at the facet level—with the work itself, pay, job security, and hours of work.

Gender patterns in overall job satisfaction separately in 21 different countries were examined by Sousa-Poza and Sousa-Poza (2000). In one case (Spain) women employees were substantially less satisfied than men, and in 15 countries the difference was negligible. However, in United Kingdom, United States, Hungary, and New Zealand, women on average reported greater job satisfaction than did men.

Those between-country differences are considered shortly. In general, however, it appears that men and women score similarly on job-related measures on the first axis of well-being or that women on average have higher scores. As described earlier, similar findings occur for context-free happiness on that axis. For job-related indicators on the other two axes in Figure 2.2, the pattern is again like that found for context-free measures. For example, in separate analyses of blue-collar and white-collar employees in a Finnish representative sample, Kauppinen-Toropainen, Kandolin, and Mutanen (1983) reported that job-related emotional exhaustion was significantly greater among women than among men. In separate analyses of full-time and part-time employees, British women were found to report higher levels of stress at work than men by Smith, Johal, Wadsworth, Smith, and Peters (2000). In a nationally representative sample of British workers, Warr (1992) observed that women had significantly lower well-being on the job-related depression–enthusiasm axis, after controls for job characteristics, family life cycle and other demographic characteristics; however, that difference was not significant for job-related anxiety–comfort after including the statistical controls.

In at least the countries just identified, women thus tend to report lower subjective well-being than men on axes 2 and 3. How might that difference be explained? In addition to potential differences in job characteristics (see the following), there may exist some more person-based sources of variation. Nolen-Hoeksema and Rusting (1999) evaluated three broad possibilities: biological, dispositional, and responses to the social context. They concluded that suggested biological explanations for greater anxiety and depression among women (e.g., with respect to hormones or genetic variation) are poorly supported. Dispositional differences were thought to be more important, for example, women's greater intensity of emotional experiences, stronger empathy with other people, more self-focused rumination about negative emotional states, and greater investment in interpersonal relationships. Nolen-Hoeksema and Rusting's (1999) review also pointed to possible social-context effects, in terms of women's overload from home as well as employment, more limited power in social relationships, possible physical or sexual abuse, and stereotypical expectations about emotionality in men and women. For example, with respect to the first of those, significantly more women than men in the study by Zappert and Weinstein (1985) reported worrying about household responsibilities while at work.

However, as noted already, findings about job satisfaction (on the first measurement axis in Fig. 2.2) often take a different form: either no difference or women report higher well-being. Given that women often receive lower pay and may have less positive job features than men (e.g., Bielby & Baron, 1986; Jacobs, 1995; see also later discussion), it might be predicted that women's average job satisfaction would be lower than that of men. For example, Blau and Kahn (1996) described gender earnings gaps in different countries that ranged from 18% to 37% in favor of men. Why is that expected well-being deficit not consistently found? Two sets of possible explanations may be suggested, in terms either of different processes of judgment or of differences in job content.

First, it could be that the mental processes of women and men differ on average when thinking about their job in relation to other jobs (Clark, 1997; Mottaz, 1986). As illustrated in the within-person processes examined in chapter 9, the impact of an environmental feature on happiness can depend on a person's thoughts relative to his or her judgmental standards.

Particularly important in the present section are five of those judgments—related to other people (social comparisons, J1), with respect to relevant expectancies (J2A), against alternative possibilities (counterfactual assessments, J2B), and in terms of several forms of personal salience (J4). In general, it is possible that women more think of their own jobs in comparison with others that are of lower quality (e.g., held by other women, or typically through downward counterfactual comparisons). As shown in chapter 9, downward comparisons (in judgments J1 or J2B) provide evidence for a more positive evaluation of one's own position. Similarly, women may on average expect their job to contain only modest levels of certain desirable features (J2A), viewing the actual levels positively against those modest expectations. Another possibility is that certain job characteristics may on average be judged as less personally salient by women than by men (J4B), so that lower levels of those features have a smaller negative impact on women's well-being. With respect to judgment J4C, certain core tasks might on average be more attractive (e.g., caring activities?) or less attractive (e.g., physical labor?) to women, so that between-gender happiness patterns in certain studies partly reflect divergent evaluations of the tasks they are required to undertake.

With specific reference to job satisfaction, Clark (1997) showed that British women on average expected to earn less than men. Those low expectations about income partly accounted for their high level of job satisfaction; their own position was perceived as reasonable against lower income expectations, a form of judgment J2A in chapter 9. Clark recognized that more comprehensive measurement of expectations was needed, and suggested that the gender pattern in British data (with greater job satisfaction on average among women than among men) may be changing. For example, given that men and women are coming more to undertake similar jobs, women's social and counter-factual comparisons might gradually change to invoke higher standards of job features, yielding a reduction in women's job satisfaction relative to those raised comparison levels.

The possibility of a reduced female–male discrepancy over time was supported cross-sectionally by Clark's (1997) finding that younger women's job satisfaction was similar to that of younger men, rather than being significantly higher than men's as in the overall sample. Younger women may have more positive expectations about jobs than older ones, so that their comparative judgments of experienced job features tend to be reduced, coming more to parallel the judgments made by men. Sousa-Poza and Sousa-Poza (2003) examined the job satisfaction trend between 1991 (the year of Clark's data) and 2000, using the same (repeated) UK national survey as Clark (1997). They found that women's overall job satisfaction (but not men's) declined substantially over that decade, but that a (smaller) female–male discrepancy was still present in 2000.

This trend across time might perhaps reflect a more general increase in the involvement of paid work in women's life satisfaction (linked to judgment J4A in chapter 9—the rated importance of role membership). Tait et al. (1989) examined the association between job satisfaction (domain-specific) and life satisfaction (context-free) reported in published studies in two time periods. Before 1974, the average correlation for women between those two forms of subjective well-being was low (+0.16), but thereafter it increased to around the level found for men (+0.31).

With respect to judgment J4B in chapter 9, judgments of personal salience in terms of the rated importance of a role characteristic are often described in employment settings as "job attribute preferences" or "work values." In an early study, Centers and Bugental (1966) found that employed American women tended more than men to value social support in their jobs (an aspect of "vitamin" 6), and that male employees assessed as more important the opportunity for skill use (feature 2). An Australian investigation by Neil and Snizek (1988) also found that female employees rated good personal relations at work as more important to them than did men. Conversely, men viewed opportunities for personal control and for skill use (features 1 and 2) as more important than did women.

Mottaz (1986) studied the perceived importance of job features separately at upper and lower job levels in American organizations. In upper level jobs, the rated importance of each feature did not differ between men and women. However, at lower levels men attached greater importance to autonomy (feature 1) and task significance (9), and women more valued supportive supervision (10). Examining job attribute preferences in American national samples, Lacy, Bokemeier, and Shepard (1983) found that job security (an aspect of 11) was considered to be more important by men than by women, and that this difference was particularly strong at lower occupational levels and older ages.

American studies of men's and women's job attribute preferences were reviewed by Konrad, Ritchie, Lieb, and Corrigall (2000). Their meta-analysis confirmed that women more than men tend to view as important supportive coworkers and supervisors and the opportunity to work with and help others (job features 6, 10, and 9); women also on average more valued the opportunity for self-development (2) and the presence of variety in a job (4). Conversely, on average men have been found to rate as more important the opportunities for autonomy and personal influence (feature 1). However, previous patterns differed somewhat between analyses, and specific details remain in need of further investigation.

Clark's (1997) examination of responses from a British national sample also found gender differences in average salience. Men ranked pay (feature 7) and both promotion prospects and job security (aspects of 11) as significantly more important than did women. Conversely, women more valued supportive supervision (10) and convenient hours of work (an aspect of 3). Examining survey data from 19 different countries, Clark (2005a) again found that male employees were more likely than women to rate a high income (7) as very important. On the other hand, women more valued flexible working hours, helpfulness to society, and helpfulness to other people (aspects of 3, 9, and 6). In that study, promotion prospects (11) were equally valued by the two sexes (see also Clark, 2005b). In another British sample, Sloane and Williams (2003) analyzed the importance of particular job features in terms of correlations between satisfaction with those features and overall job satisfaction. In those terms, job security and opportunity for promotion (11) were more important to male employees, and convenient working hours (an aspect of 3) and good interpersonal relations (6) were more important to women. Results from a U.S. national sample also emphasized the importance to female employees of personally suitable working hours (Bender et al., 2005; see the next section).

Overall, those studies of personal salience suggest (at least for the countries examined) that women, in comparison with men, on average more value mutually supportive relations with colleagues and convenient working schedules. However, men tend on average to see autonomy, skill use, income, and job security as more important than do female employees. In considering women's greater job satisfaction in several studies (described earlier), it is possible that those job features that are more negative for women are on average of relatively low salience to them, and thus have a smaller impact on their well-being. On the other hand, the features in women's work that tend to be positive might be rated as of higher personal salience to them, and thus more enhance their well-being. This possibility has yet to be explored across the full set of features examined in earlier chapters.

A second possible explanation for gender patterns in job satisfaction concerns the level of those job characteristics. In their examination of male and female job satisfaction across countries (above), Sousa-Poza and Sousa-Poza (2000) asked whether the different national patterns might be accounted for by average differences in men's and women's job characteristics. Their data permitted examination of average job holders' perceptions of six of the features described earlier: opportunity for personal control (1), contact with others (6), availability of money (7), valued social position (9), supportive supervision (10), and career outlook (11).

In general, the average male–female pattern of perceived job content of those kinds was similar across countries. However, gender divergence was present for those countries in which male and female job satisfaction most differed. For example, in the United Kingdom and United States (which exhibited the greatest discrepancy in overall job satisfaction in favor of women), female employees reported higher levels of features 6, 9, 10, and 11 than did men. On the other hand, in Spain (where women's job satisfaction was particularly low relative to men's) female employees reported particularly low levels of those job characteristics.

Analyzing overall job satisfaction in each country through ordered probit regressions, Sousa-Poza and Sousa-Poza (2000) found that gender differences in job satisfaction were statistically accounted for by differences in job content of these kinds in nearly all cases. However, in the United Kingdom and United States women remained significantly more satisfied with their jobs despite statistical controls for job content. The authors concluded that women's greater job satisfaction is primarily "an Anglo-Saxon paradox" (p. 137). They speculated that other job characteristics in addition to those examined might be important in explaining the pattern, and also that different male and female expectations may be involved, in ways described earlier in this section.

More generally, in addition to comparing male and female employees in terms of subjective well-being, it is important to expand research to examine the second form of happiness—self-validation. For example, are women in general more likely than men to appraise their work activities against standards of interpersonal service? Carlson and Mellor (2004) considered the possibility that women more than men seek self-realization through mutual support in relationships with other people, weighing the needs of others against their own. Their scale of "relational self-definition" contained items like "I feel I have a responsibility to look out for the well-being of others," and scores were significantly higher for female employees than for male employees. Possible gender differences in happiness as self-validation now deserve targeted investigation.

Men and Women: Average Job Features.   The chapter's third question asks about differential exposure to environmental features that may affect happiness. Do men and women on average undertake jobs that differ in ways that might give rise to different average levels of happiness or unhappiness? As noted in the previous section, some variability occurs between countries, but it is clear that in general female employees tend to receive lower incomes and are less likely to be in senior managerial positions than men (e.g., Blau & Kahn, 1996; Wright & Ermisch, 1991). However, male–female comparisons have not yet considered levels of exposure to all the environmental features examined in this book. Is there a difference between the average male and female job profile as set out in Table 8.1 of chapter 8, and (if so) what are the consequences for happiness?

Results reported to date often derive from samples that are small or imperfectly comparable between studies, and findings about male and female exposure to different job characteristics have varied between studies. However, it has frequently been found that male employees tend to report greater opportunity for personal control than do women (feature 1; Grandey et al., 2005; Loscocco & Spitze, 1990; Lowe & Northcott, 1988; Mottaz, 1986; Neil & Snizek, 1988; Pugliesi, 1995; Roxburgh, 1996; Rode, 2004). That pattern was also observed for opportunity for skill use (2) by Lowe and Northcott (1988) and Rode (2004).

On the other hand, women's jobs have sometimes been found to provide significantly more supportive supervision (10; Mottaz, 1986; Sousa-Poza & Sousa-Poza, 2000), coworker support (an aspect of 6; Roxburgh, 1996), and job security (an aspect of 11; Neil & Snizek, 1988; Rode, 2004; Sousa-Poza & Sousa-Poza, 2000), and to involve less physical danger (an aspect of 8; Sousa-Poza & Sousa-Poza, 2000). No gender differences in job demands (feature 3) or variety (4) were present in Roxburgh's (1996) comparison, but hard physical demands (an aspect of 3) were less prevalent for women in Clark's (2005a, 2005b) analysis of multination data. The female subsample examined by Grandey et al. (2005) reported lower job variety (4) than did men. In a U.S. national sample, Grzywacz and Dooley (2003) found that 7% of men and 23% of women were in jobs identified as "economically inadequate" (low levels of feature 7), and a high income was significantly more common for men than for women in Clark's (2005a, 2005b) analyses across several countries.

Gallie et al. (1998) asked about main job activities (taking up more than half of an employee's time). In a British national sample, they found that although 60% of women had some type of "people work" as their main activity, this was the case for only 33% of men. Good relations at work (an aspect of feature 6) were reported significantly more often by women than by men in Clark's (2005a, 2005b) multicountry analyses. One form of low social support was examined by Eriksen and Einarsen (2004). They studied bullying in those work settings in which a person is in a numerical minority. Pointing out that women tend more to report being bullied at work than do men (Zapf, Einarsen, Hoel, & Vartia, 2003), they drew attention to the "outsider" position often held by women in predominantly male environments. It may be that bullying of females is more likely because women are in a "socially exposed" or numerically "deviant" minority. If so, we would expect men to be more bullied than women when they work in such a minority position. That was found to be the case in a study of male nurses in mainly female work groups; 10% and 4% of male and female respondents, respectively, had been subject to bullying in the past 6 months.

Carlson and Mellor (2004) examined two compounds of job attributes, finding a gender difference in exposure to one of those only. One compound was an extension of the present feature 6, interpersonal contact, recording the opportunity to be part of a caring group that values team contributions and mutual assistance; female employees reported greater exposure than men to that work characteristic. The second compound brought together the present job features 1 and 2 (opportunities for personal control and for skill use), and was described as the opportunity for self-actualization; men and women reported the same amount of this feature in their jobs. Characteristics of that second kind have sometimes been studied in terms of "complexity" (see chap. 8). For example, Erickson et al. (2000) reported that male workers' job complexity was significantly greater than that of women. However, inconsistency of findings between samples was illustrated by differing correlations with gender in three studies by Shaw and Gupta (2004): -0.05, -0.16, and $+0.35$.

An issue of particular research interest in recent years is the extent to which work and family responsibilities conflict with each other, an aspect of feature 3 in the present framework. Findings about links with happiness have been reviewed in chapter 6; we should here ask about possible male–female differences in the amount of that conflict. As with exposure to other job features, above, results have varied between samples. Although some studies have found that women report more overall interference between work and home than do men, no gender difference was observed in several other investigations (Butler et al., 2005; Eby et al., 2005; Grzywacz & Marks, 2000; Parasuraman et al., 1996).

This inconsistency also occurs in research that looks separately at the two directions of influence. For example, in samples studied by

Frone et al. (1996, 1997) and Grandey et al. (2005), conflict from family to work was more common in women than men, whereas no gender difference occurred in work-to-family conflict. On the other hand, Cinamon and Rich (2002) found more work-to-family conflict in women but no gender difference in the family-to-work direction; no gender difference in either respect was present in research by Aryee et al. (2005). The meta-analysis by Byron (2005; of studies up to 2002) indicated that men and women reported very similar levels of conflict in either direction. However, studying only interference from work to family, Demerouti et al. (2004) reported that this direction of conflict was significantly greater in men than in women.

Research needs now to focus on the personal and environmental variables that may influence these patterns. For example, a high level of demands in a job could increase conflict between job and home, particularly for child-caring women more than for men. In that case, greater male–female differences in exposure to work–family conflict would be observed in studies where women's home and job demands are high. A study by Kinnunen et al. (2004) found no gender difference in (overall) work–home conflict for the complete sample, but among employees in high-level jobs women reported significantly more conflict with home life than did men. Byron's (2005) review suggested that although no gender differences are present overall, a difference does occur when study participants are parents; women exposed to child-care demands tended to report more conflict in both directions than did men.

As noted earlier in the chapter, accurate average information about large segments of the population (here, men and women in general) is difficult to obtain. Research samples have tended to be small and to vary between studies in unspecified ways. Given that in many countries men tend to be in jobs with greater influence and income, gender differences in those respects (features 1 and 7) are widely expected. However, average male and female exposure to other characteristics seems likely to vary between settings, and more substantial investigations are still required.

Men and Women: Moderators of Job–Happiness Links. The chapter's fourth question asks whether an individual or group characteristic serves as a moderator of the associations between job features and aspects of happiness. In this section, we need to learn whether particular job features are differently correlated with happiness for men and for women. In fact, many job–happiness correlations have been found to be similar between the sexes. However, a consistent pattern of difference is emerging for a number of features.

Mottaz (1986) examined correlations with overall job satisfaction separately for the two sexes. Holding constant other variables, such as age, education, income, and other job characteristics, he found that opportunity for control (feature 1) made a greater contribution to job satisfaction for men, and that supportive supervision (10) was more strongly correlated with job satisfaction for women. This differential pattern was present in both upper level and lower level jobs. However, for seven other features (pay, working conditions, promotion prospects, etc.) job–happiness correlations were similar for men and women. In a study by Piltch et al. (1994), of managers in a single company, context-free distress was also differentially linked to those two job features—opportunity for control more strongly for men, and social support more strongly for women.

Pugliesi (1995) found a similar moderating impact of gender on the association between opportunity for control and overall job satisfaction, with a stronger correlation for men than for women. Comparing employees in similar jobs, Bryce and Haworth (2003) reported those values for men and women to be +0.58 and +0.39, respectively; that difference was retained despite statistical controls for other variables. In Weaver's (1978) comparison between full-time male and female employees in national U.S. samples, the correlation between job autonomy and overall job satisfaction was larger for men than for women in bivariate analyses; however, the difference became nonsignificant after controls for other variables. Opportunity for personal control and skill use combined (features 1 and 2 together) was more strongly related to overall job satisfaction in men than women in research by Carlson and Mellor (2004). They also found that the presence of a caring and supportive work group (an aspect of feature 6) was more strongly associated with women's job satisfaction than with men's, although that difference was not statistically significant. Similarly, the presence of good relations at work was more strongly associated in multiple regressions with overall job satisfaction for women than for men in Clark's (2005b) multination sample.

Negative forms of the sixth environmental feature (contact with others) were examined in a meta-analysis by Lapierre et al. (2005), in terms of aggression from others. Between-gender comparison was possible for nonsexual aggression, but not for sexual aggression, which had mainly been studied in female samples. Reported nonsexual aggression was more closely negatively associated with overall job satisfaction for women than for men, with average uncorrected r values of -0.41 and -0.29, respectively.

With respect to feature 7 (availability of money), Bender et al. (2005) found that men's earnings were significantly associated with overall job satisfaction, but that the association was nonsignificant for women, controlling for the same demographic and occupational variables in both cases. Job security (an aspect of "vitamin" 11) was more strongly associated with overall job satisfaction for men than for women in Clark's (2005b) data from several countries. Gender also appeared to moderate the association between equity in a job (an aspect of 12) and job-related well-being in a study by Sweeney and McFarlin (1997). They examined perceptions of distributive justice (the fairness of reward allocation in an organization) and of procedural justice (the fairness of decision-making procedures; see chap. 5). It was suggested that women tend to have lower expectations of pay, and might thus be less concerned than men about their organization's distribution of rewards, including pay. That pattern was indeed found: The correlations between perceived distributive equity and overall job satisfaction were significantly greater for men than for women after statistical controls.

There is thus some evidence that gender moderates the association between several job features and subjective well-being. Specifically, associations seem to be stronger for women with respect to contact with others (feature 6), supportive supervision (10), and perhaps aspects of equity (12). On the other hand, job–happiness correlations tend to be greater for men with respect to opportunity for control (1) and possibly opportunity for skill use (2). Other patterns are less clear, and more extensive data are still needed.

Why should those particular patterns of moderation occur? As indicated in several ways throughout the book, it is logically necessary that the well-being of individuals or groups is more associated with environmental characteristics that are judged to be more personally salient to them (J4 in chap. 9), whereas features of lesser perceived importance are necessarily less strongly linked to happiness. As described previously with respect to judgment J4B, that general pattern can be illustrated specifically for the salience of job characteristics.

Empirical support at the individual level has been presented in chapter 9, where correlations between job features and employee well-being were reported to be greater for those features viewed by an individual to be more personally salient. Similar patterns are expected at the aggregate level, between sets of workers who differ on average in the importance accorded to a job feature. Correlations are thus predicted to differ for men and women between a job feature and well-being when those two groups view that feature on average as differently salient. Conversely, when job features are on average equally important to the two groups (as they often are), they are expected to be similarly linked to well-being for men and for women.

As outlined earlier, empirical results support that prediction, but they are not entirely consistent. In seeking reasons for varied findings in this area, four methodological considerations deserve attention: the magnitude of the between-group salience difference in a particular study, the nature of samples, the manner in which statistical interactions are examined, and the appropriateness of the importance ratings included in an analysis.

In the first case, when the average rated importance of a job feature is considerably different between men and women, a moderating effect of gender is more likely than when importance ratings are only slightly different between the two groups. Average personal salience needs to be adequately contrasted between men and women for a proper test of its moderating role, and that may not always be the case. (However, because salience has not been measured in most studies, we cannot be sure.) Second, attention needs to be directed at the composition of male and female samples. For example, there may be some confounding influence from a mixing of part-time and full-time respondents; more part-timers are likely in female than male subsamples (see later in this chapter), and part-timers' preferences for certain job features may differ from those of full-timers. Similarly, preferences might vary between upper level and lower level job holders, with more men at upper levels. Sample composition is not always clear in published reports, and its impact has not been explored in this area.

Third, procedures to assess statistical interaction have varied between studies, in some cases including simultaneously several interaction terms in a single analysis. For instance, interactions between gender and several job features have sometimes all been examined in the same step of an analysis. However, in seeking to learn about a single job feature, it is inappropriate to remove variance associated with other interactions before examining an interaction with the feature under examination. As considered in chapter 6 with respect to quadratic terms, we cannot adequately learn whether, for instance, gender and job autonomy on their own have an interactive relationship with happiness if we also include in the same analysis several interactions between gender and other job features. Such an analysis instead tells us about the interaction of interest only after variance explained by other interactions has been taken out. Allowing the focal interaction to be conditioned by other interactions in the same analysis distorts findings about the interaction of concern. Furthermore, the effect recorded in those cases can vary according to which other interactions happen to be included in an equation. Different research reports have been inconsistent in the nature of a cited interaction and its statistical constraints, despite that interaction being described with the same name in each case.

A fourth methodological concern arises from possible between-sample variations in the rated salience of job features. For example, it may be the case that differences occur between the job attribute preferences of women in more "masculine" and more "feminine" occupations, perhaps through differential self-selection into the roles, or because the two subgroups have different comparison standards arising from their exposure to different job content (Konrad, Ritchie, Lieb, & Corrigall, 2000). However, between-sample generalizability has been widely assumed, and possible salience moderators are often proposed on the basis of ratings made by a separate sample in a different location and time period. Those ratings may be inappropriate for the newly studied employees. A preferable approach is to analyze data gathered only from a single set of respondents, obtaining from them ratings of both the amount and perceived importance of each job feature.

Bender et al. (2005) considered gender differences in job satisfaction as a function of occupational segregation as well as of personal salience. In an American national sample, women overall reported significantly greater job satisfaction than men, and their job-related well-being was particularly high in gender-segregated occupations; women's job satisfaction was greater as the proportion of women in a workplace was greater. (For men, exclusively male workplaces were also linked to greater job satisfaction, but across other proportions of men no association with well-being was present.)

In seeking to explain that pattern for female employees, Bender and colleagues found that it was linked to the availability of family friendly policies about work scheduling. Employees indicated the extent to which they were able to take time off work when needed for family or personal reasons. It emerged that this job characteristic (a form of personal control, the present feature 1, in conjunction with reduced work–family conflict, an aspect of 3) was of particular importance to women's job-related happiness. After statistically controlling for scheduling flexibility of that kind, the gender composition of a workplace was no longer significant with respect to women's job satisfaction; the influential factor was scheduling flexibility, which itself varied positively with the proportion of women in a workplace. Bender et al. (2005) concluded that "flexibility is a crucial element in the bundle of job characteristics that appeal to women and that it plays an important role explaining the relationship between job satisfaction and gender segregation" (p. 481).

Some investigators have examined particular compounds of job features, reporting correlations of those with well-being that are similar for men and women (Barnett & Brennan, 1995; Lowe & Northcott, 1988; Strazdins et al., 2004). However, those studies have not assessed the perceived importance of the examined compounds for the studied employees themselves, and the compounds' salience may be similar for men and women. There is a general need to examine systematically the moderating impact job features' personal importance assessed in the sample of employees whose well-being is examined. As illustrated earlier, it is likely that average between-gender differences in salience are accompanied by differences in the strength of association with the same employees' happiness. However, more evidence is needed, and possible differences in that pattern between different forms of well-being have yet to be investigated.

Finally, it may be that gender differences in the perceived importance of job features are becoming less marked. Recent decades have seen structural changes that have increased women's employment opportunities relative to men's and strengthened their role as an income-provider for themselves and their family. These shifts may on average have modified women's views about desirable job features, bringing those more into line with the job attribute preferences of male workers. Additional longitudinal evidence about gender-linked changes in perceptions and values is clearly desirable.

Younger and Older People

The chapter's four questions are next asked about employee age and happiness. First, do different people (here, older and younger ones) have different conceptions of happiness? The three-dimensional framework of Figure 2.3, representing happiness in terms of dimensions of pleasure, mental arousal, and self-validation, seems likely to be equally appropriate at all adult ages. However, there may be some variation in the relative importance of the three dimensions. In that way, older people on average might have a reduced concern for hedonic aspects of happiness, and more strongly emphasize self-validating activities. However, empirical evidence appears to be lacking for or against this possibility.

Another difference between happiness as construed at different ages concerns temporal perspective. Older people's experiences are necessarily set within a future time perspective that is more limited than that of younger ones. Birren and Renner (1981) pointed out that in their later years people often review their past, mentally integrating their characteristics and activities so that they come to accept as valuable their life's experiences. That "life review and reconciliation" consists of "adding up where one has been rather than a preoccupation with what will be achieved" (pp. 248–249). Such a process may also be envisaged within a specific domain such as paid employment. Job-related happiness may thus have a partly different meaning for younger and older workers.

A third possible age difference in the conception of happiness might occur with respect to the intensity of experience. Diener, Sandvik, and Larsen (1985) concluded that the intensity of both positive and negative affect is lower at older ages. In thinking about their own and other people's happiness, older people may thus have a somewhat truncated conceptual space, excluding feelings that are more extreme in their intensity.

Younger and Older People: Average Happiness.   The chapter's second question asks about average levels of happiness as a function of the individual or group variable under consideration, in this case age. Many studies have focused on age-patterns with respect to subjective well-being, but happiness as self-validation appears not to have been examined.

Looking first at well-being that is context-free, age patterns on the first axis in Figure 2.2 (from feeling bad to feeling good, irrespective of arousal level) have often been studied in terms of life satisfaction. Although findings are not entirely consistent, older people are often found to be happier in this respect to a significant but modest degree (e.g., Campbell, 1981; Cheng, 2004; Diener et al., 1999; Judge & Watanabe, 1993). Diener and Suh (1998) reported that this age difference occurred widely across countries, in a study of approximately 60,000 people in 43 nations. However, as described in relation to retirement (chap. 3), a slight average decline in well-being occurs above the late sixties. For example, Mroczek and Spiro (2005) analyzed longitudinal data across 22 years, finding that average life satisfaction increased to about age 65 and then declined.

The trend is different for aroused forms of well-being, in the top-right quadrant of Figure 2.2 (the positive pole of axis 3). Older individuals have been found to be on average about as happy as, or slightly less happy than, younger ones in those activated positive respects (e.g., Andrews & Withey, 1976; Campbell, 1981; Charles, Reynolds, & Gatz, 2001; Diener & Suh, 1998). One way of interpreting this difference between axes 1 and 3 is that older people may be more satisfied (up to about 65 years) in a less aroused way; their experience of well-being may tend to become overall more positive, but they might move from 3b in the diagram (away from happiness of an active kind) toward 1b (more satisfaction of a relatively passive kind).

With respect to the negative pole of axis 3, concerned with feelings of depression, there is evidence for a J-shaped age pattern. Among the population as a whole, feelings of depression first decline cross-sectionally up to the mid-forties and then increase up to higher average levels among people in their eighties, associated with impaired physical health, death of family members and friends, and reduced personal control and interpersonal bonds (Mirowsky & Ross, 1992; Neumann, 1989; see also Ryff, 1989). For example, in a national U.S. sample studied by Mirowsky and Ross (1992), depression scores declined by about 25% between the ages of 20 and 45 and increased by around 70% between 45 and 80. In research by Charles et al. (2001), a decline in depression to about 60 years was accompanied by stability thereafter. Within the employed population, which is mainly around middle age and below, Frone et al. (1996) reported a correlation of age with context-free depression of –0.16 (average of two studies), and Lowe and Northcott (1988) showed that this negative association remained significant despite controls for many other variables.

For context-free indicators on the second axis of affective well-being in Figure 2.2 (from anxiety to comfort), there is also evidence of curvilinearity, but in the opposite direction. The General Health Questionnaire (GHQ; Goldberg & Williams, 1988; see chap. 2) might be thought to emphasize the top-left quadrant of Figure 2.2, particularly reflecting activated forms of distress. Results from a national UK sample presented by Warr (1997) showed that GHQ scores were low among teenagers but were at a peak around the age of 40. Distress was then successively lower up to the early sixties, after when it tended again to be higher. This pattern was confirmed for general negative affect in a U.S. community sample by Teachman (2006).

In a study of employed respondents, Clark et al. (1996) observed that GHQ distress was low among 16- to 19-year-olds and greater up to age 38, with a decline to particularly low levels among employed people in their sixties. This curvilinear relationship is consistent with findings of greater family, financial and occupational pressures in the middle years (Folkman, Lazarus, Pimley, & Novacek, 1987); below and above those middle years, distress is less pronounced. Using another measure with employed people, Warr (1990b) also observed lower context-free anxiety after the middle years; Campbell (1981) reported the same pattern in a sample of nonemployed as well as employed respondents, as did Warr et al. (1988) in samples of unemployed individuals.

The different age relationships for anxiety and depression may be interpreted in terms of greater psychological arousal in the middle years of life. Around the age of 40, people tend to experience more anxiety (involving higher arousal in terms of Fig. 2.2 in chap. 2) and less depression (which also involves more arousal, at higher levels on axis 3). After about 40 years, environmental demands and daily hassles are likely to decline somewhat for most people, resulting in reduced psychological arousal potentially linked both to less anxiety (2a in Fig. 2.2) and to more depression (3a).

We should also ask about between-person variation at different ages. It is possible that there is a greater inter-individual spread of happiness at older ages than in younger groups. That occurs in several cognitive and physiological processes, for which between-person variance is greater in older samples (e.g., Fozard, Vercruyssen, Reynolds, Hancock, & Quilter, 1994). This possible age increase in between-person differences has not usually been examined with respect to happiness, and now deserves more attention. An age-related increase in variance was found for positive affect by Charles et al. (2001), but for negative affect between-person variance was greatest around the age of 35. In parallel research, Warr, Miles, and Platts (2001) examined interindividual variance at different ages with respect to personality attributes such as neuroticism and extraversion (see the next chapter), but found no differences in the spread of scores between low and high ages. However, the moderate association between subjective well-being and perceived health (see chap. 2) suggests that greater between-person variation in health at older ages will be accompanied by a similar pattern for some aspects of happiness.

Turning to subjective well-being that is job-related, it is regularly found that overall job satisfaction (axis 1) is significantly higher among older workers (e.g., Abraham & Hansson, 1995; Brush et al., 1987; Clark, 2005a, 2005b; Clark et al., 1996; Rhodes, 1983; Rode, 2004; Warr, 1994b; Weaver, 1980). The positive correlation is not high, usually falling between +0.10 and +0.20, but it remains significant despite statistical controls for other demographic and environmental variables (Birdi et al., 1995; Clark et al., 1996; Pugliesi, 1995; Sloane & Williams, 2000). It is often assumed that this association is purely linear, with no significant curvilinear component of the kinds illustrated earlier.

That view is inconsistent with early research. On the basis of evidence up to the mid-1950s, Herzberg, Mausner, Peterson, and Capwell (1957) suggested that "in general, morale is high among young workers. It tends to go down during the first few years of employment. The low point is reached when workers are in their middle and late twenties, or early thirties. After this period, job morale climbs steadily with age" (pp. 5–6). That decline in job well-being from a raised level immediately after entry into the labor market is plausible in terms of young people's initial enthusiasm for the adult role being followed by a gradual discouragement in the face of routine activities with few opportunities for change. The pattern may be described as J-shaped, rather than U-shaped, because it is asymmetrical with higher job satisfaction values at older ages than at younger ones. Such a pattern of scores was found in an early British study (Handyside, 1961), and has more recently been observed in a large sample of British employees (Clark, 1996; Clark et al., 1996) and in a multinational study (Birdi et al., 1995). Overall job satisfaction was found to be at its minimum at 31 and 26 years of age, respectively, in the latter two studies.

The J-shaped and the linear patterns differ only with respect to the youngest employees. Job satisfaction is relatively high for them in cases where a J-shaped association is observed; however, in a purely linear pattern the youngest respondents are the least satisfied. Discrepancies between findings for the youngest individuals in different studies seem likely to arise for reasons of the following kinds: differences in sample composition (e.g., the number and age of young respondents; whether or not students working part-time are included in a study); variations in labor market characteristics, perhaps between studies conducted at different times (e.g., young job holders may feel particularly positive when jobs are extremely scarce, but less so when jobs are plentiful); differences in job content (e.g., young job holders in dead-end jobs may experience a greater decline in job satisfaction than those receiving training and advancement).

At the third level of scope, facet-specific job satisfactions have been found to be associated in different ways with employee age. Satisfaction with the work itself tends to be greater at older ages, but a significant age gradient is often absent in relation to more extrinsic satisfactions, with promotion opportunities, coworkers, and supervisors (Rhodes, 1983; Warr, 1994b). This does not preclude the possibility that significant relationships are present in particular settings, and findings about facet satisfaction vary depending on the nature of the sample, the organization, and the measures applied (e.g., Clark et al., 1996; Lee & Wilbur, 1985; Morrow & McElroy, 1987; Oliver, 1977). In terms of compounds of facets, intrinsic job satisfaction is more positively correlated with age than is extrinsic satisfaction (Schwab & Heneman, 1977), linked to the stronger correlation with overall job satisfaction of intrinsic rather than extrinsic indicators (see chap. 2).

What about the second axis of job-related well-being shown in Figure 2.2, from feelings of anxiety to comfort? Job-related anxiety and feelings of strain were found to be significantly curvilinearly associated with employee age by Warr (1992) and Birdi et al. (1995), with greatest job anxiety in the middle years. A similar but less pronounced pattern was found for axis 3 (depression to enthusiasm) in the study by Warr (1992), with employees in the middle age groups reporting most job-related depression. In both cases, the positive relationship between employee age and greater job-related well-being was statistically significant before and after controls for other variables.

In a study of employees aged between 40 and 69, Abraham and Hansson (1995) found that older individuals in that range reported less job-related anxiety and depression than did younger ones. Smith (2001) examined British employees' reports that they were stressed at work, finding that job strain increased cross-sectionally from age 18 to the forties, declining again thereafter. Overall, there is thus consistent evidence that job-related well-being is greater in older employees, and several investigations have suggested that the pattern is curvilinear, with raised well-being also found at the youngest ages.

These age patterns all summarize cross-sectional evidence, and do not themselves demonstrate within-person change across time. Cross-sectional information describes what is the case at the time of an investigation, and is essential for descriptive understanding, in this case about the well-being of people of different ages. However, cross-sectional differences between older and younger people could derive from cohort (sometimes called "generation") effects. In the case of a positive age gradient (as here after the twenties), the members of older generations might always have been more happy, so that the cross-sectional pattern may reflect stable characteristics that differ between cohorts rather than changes as people age. In order to examine this possibility directly, it is desirable to compare the same individuals over a period of years. Such comparisons are rare for the variables discussed here, and evidence about cohort differences in job satisfaction is limited (Glenn & Weaver, 1985; Janson & Martin, 1982). In addition, the presence of curvilinear relationships, as in several studies summarized earlier, would require an interpretation in terms of age-linked reversals of previous cohort differences. It seems likely that the reported age gradients primarily reflect changes across time, but the evidence remains incomplete.

Cross-sectional increases with age in both job-related and context-free well-being were documented earlier. Chapter 2 described how happiness scores at those two levels of scope are moderately correlated with each other (e.g., Rice et al, 1992; Tait et al., 1989), and it might be that the job-related pattern is caused by an overarching effect of context-free happiness. This issue was addressed by Clark et al. (1996), by inserting context-free distress scores (GHQ; see the earlier description) into analyses of relationships between age and overall job satisfaction. GHQ score was itself a significant predictor of job satisfaction, even after inclusion of a range of other variables, but the J-shaped relationship of job satisfaction with age remained almost unchanged despite control for this context-free indicator. Even though the same curvilinear relationship may be present between age and both job-specific and context-free well-being, age-related variations in job well-being cannot be explained in terms of happiness that is context-free.

So, how might that age difference (with older employees exhibiting greater job-related happiness) be accounted for? Some cohort effects cannot be entirely ruled out (see earlier discussion), and differential participation in the labor market at different ages also deserves consideration. In that respect, it might be that at older ages the more unhappy individuals have excluded themselves from jobs (for instance, retiring early), whereas subsamples at younger ages extend more widely across the happiness range. Variations between average subjective well-being at different ages would then be at least in part a result of different sample composition, rather than demonstrating a true difference between people of different ages. However, this latter possibility is unlikely between the ages of about 30 to 50, when labor-market participation is consistently high and the age trend is also found; possible differences in sample composition are relevant only above about 50, when increasing proportions of people are absent from the labor force.

Over and above possible cohort and sample-composition effects, two sets of reasons for greater job-related happiness at older ages are plausible. These parallel the themes introduced earlier for gender patterns: different ways of thinking about job characteristics, and possible differential exposure to those characteristics.

First, we need to consider possible differences in judgment processes that underlie employees' experience of well-being. Of those introduced in chapter 9, four are particularly relevant to age-patterns. First, it may be the case that older and younger employees have different expectations about the quality of jobs available to them (judgment J2A in the earlier presentation). Older workers' accumulated employment experiences might have created expectations that jobs tend to be relatively unattractive. If younger people have more positive expectations about jobs in general, their assessments of their own current job characteristics relative to those higher expectations could be more negative than the assessments made by older employees.

Linked to that, older employees may make more downward social or counterfactual comparisons than do younger ones, comparing their job with others that are inferior to their own (J1 and J2B). That might occur because older workers have become aware over time of a wider range of job characteristic levels; similarly, they may less use as reference standards high-quality jobs to which they no longer aspire. If older workers tend to compare their jobs against reference standards that are lower than those of younger workers, their job-related well-being might be correspondingly raised.

Another judgment process that may bear on the job-related well-being of older and younger individuals is in terms of personal salience (judgment J4). For example, it could be the case that older employees have specific work preferences (J4B), which make more attractive to them job characteristics that are available but are less desirable to younger people. A given level of a current job feature can affect well-being more in people who view its presence as personally more important. In a similar way, older employees might be less concerned about job characteristics that are troublesome at younger ages.

Wright and Hamilton (1978) and Kalleberg and Loscocco (1983; in secondary analyses of the same data) found that the rated importance of many job features was similar across ages, but that income and promotion opportunities were of less importance to older employees. Lacy et al. (1983) showed that this pattern was the same for both men and women. Possible age variations in the perceived importance of the 12 primary job features require more comprehensive investigation. Warr (1997) has reviewed the limited evidence for several of them, speculating that older workers relative to younger ones may less value variety (4), money (7) and future prospects (11b in Table 8.1), but view as more important physical security (8) and job security (11a). In addition, an age difference has often been observed in terms of opportunity for the acquisition of new skills (part of the second job feature); older employees tend to regard that opportunity as less important than do younger ones (Maurer, Weiss, & Barbeite, 2003; Warr & Birdi, 1998). Empirical investigations into personal salience at different ages across the full range of primary job characteristics are now needed.

Younger and Older People: Average Job Features.   The second possible explanation introduced above for older employees' greater job-related well-being coincides with the chapter's third general question: Are there subgroup differences in the exposure to job characteristics? If older workers tend to occupy better quality jobs (with more positive levels of the key characteristics), a positive age trend in job-related well-being can be expected.

Some differences of that kind are evident. For example, opportunity for personal control (feature 1) is likely to be greater at older ages. This may arise from promotion to more senior jobs or from extended tenure in a single job, or it may be associated with norms about more relaxed supervision of older workers. As noted in chapter 6, increased control can include greater potential to adjust task activities to meet one's preferences. Availability of money (7) tends also to be greater at older ages, as income is linked to job level or tenure (Birdi et al., 1995; Warr, 1992). For example, the correlation between income and age was +0.20 in the study of employed individuals by Judge and Watanabe (1993).

Little information is available about age patterns in other job features. However, national statistics in many countries, as well as within-organization findings (e.g., Aronsson, Gustafsson, & Dallner, 2002; Warr & Birdi, 1998), make it clear that older workers are exposed less to one aspect of feature 2, the opportunity to enhance their skills; training and development provision is substantially reduced at older ages. It is likely that work–family conflict (an aspect of 3) also changes with age. Frone et al. (1996) reported that older employees experienced less conflict of that kind than younger ones, perhaps in part because of reduced parental commitments. The same pattern was found in a U.S. national sample by Grzywacz and Marks (2000), for both work-to-family and family-to-work influences in the case of men. However, women's age was related negatively only to conflict that was from family to work.

Across the job features examined here, differences in exposure at different ages are expected to be reflected in parallel differences in subjective well-being. A related issue concerns the possibility of a wider between-person range of exposure at older ages. Some individuals proceed successfully through a career, being exposed to job features that are desirable, perhaps increasingly so across the years. Others have consistently poor-quality jobs, and may become more and more marginalized in employment terms. If such between-individual content divergence does increase with age, statements merely about average levels of exposure can become increasingly inappropriate in older samples. This possibility has yet to be investigated.

Younger and Older People: Moderators of Job–Happiness Links. The chapter's fourth question asks about possible moderators. A general expectation in the present framework is that environmental features of greater personal salience will be more strongly correlated with happiness than will features of lower salience. (See, e.g., judgment J4B in chap. 9.) In terms of contrasted groups (older and younger workers in this case), we need to ask about the average salience of each primary job feature for each group, expecting job–happiness correlations to be greater for a particular group when its average importance rating of a job feature is higher.

Evidence about this possible moderating pattern is not yet available with respect to employee age. As noted earlier, few studies have considered differences in the rated importance of job characteristics at different ages. Issues of statistical moderation, contrasting the correlations between job features and well-being observed for younger and older workers, have apparently not been examined at all.

OCCUPATIONAL DIFFERENCES

The third difference between employees to be examined concerns the nature of their contracts, for example, full-time versus part-time or in relatively permanent versus temporary roles. Work that is "part-time" is usually defined as less than 30 or 35 hours a week, and part-time workers make up around 15% to 25% of many countries' workforce (e.g., Aronsson et al., 2002; Barling & Gallagher, 1996; European Commission, 2005; Gallagher, 2005; McOrmond, 2004). However, there are clear differences between men and women. For example, in the United Kingdom almost 45% of female workers are part-timers, compared to only about 10% of men; stated differently, around 80% of part-time workers in Britain are women (Office for National Statistics, 2005, Table B1). In the United States, around 26% of employed women are part-timers, but only 11% of men (Bureau of Labor Statistics; see www.bls.gov).

Part-time work is also distributed unevenly in relation to age. Male part-timers are primarily to be found at the extremes of the age-range, as young students or men retired from full-time employment, whereas most female part-timers are either students or mothers of younger children. Linked to that pattern, many part-time workers do not want a job that is full-time. Among British part-timers excluding students, that overall percentage (satisfied with a part-time role) is 88, and 70% of men and 92% of women are in that satisfied subgroup (Office for National Statistics, 2005, Table B1). In the United States, only about a third of part-time employees would prefer a full-time role (Probst, 2005a).

Part-time work is most common in retail, service, and health-care organizations (e.g., Barling & Gallagher, 1996; Feldman, 1990; Feldman & Doerpinghaus, 1992; McOrmond, 2004). At the risk of some oversimplification, we can distinguish between two main categories. On the one hand are "peripheral," "secondary," or "poor-quality" part-time jobs, but in addition "core," "primary," or "standard" work might be undertaken on a part-time instead of a full-time basis. In jobs that are "peripheral," content is impoverished in terms of some or all of the primary characteristics examined here, whereas that is not necessarily the case in "core" positions. This distinction is sometimes made as "old-concept" versus "new-concept" part-time jobs (van Rijswijk et al., 2004). "New-concept" part-time work has characteristics similar to full-time employment, with contractual rights protected, but differs in the number of hours worked. Some countries have encouraged the new-concept practice of "job-sharing," when a single core job is undertaken in different sections of the week by two employees.

The second distinction examined in this section is between permanent and temporary employees. Recent years have seen a shift in many countries from an expectation of long-term attachment to a single organization to more frequent transitions between employers. Those transitions arise both from individuals' wishes to obtain wider experience and also from some employers' preferences for more flexible arrangements. There are between-country differences in definition, but temporary employees make up between about 5% and 15% of many developed countries' work force (Aronsson et al., 2002; Booth, Francesconi, & Frank, 2002; European Commission, 2005; Gallagher, 2005; Mauno, Kinnunen, Mäkikangas, & Nätti, 2005). That proportion has increased in many countries in the last decade (McOrmond, 2004)

Although research has often examined temporary employees as a whole, it is desirable to differentiate between them in the "peripheral" and "core" terms introduced earlier. All nonpermanent employees might in one sense be viewed as outside an organization's "core," but some temporary staff are more "peripheral" than others. It is helpful to separate short-term "casual" appointments from those that are also short but with a previously agreed duration, perhaps for a particular project. Casual work is the most "peripheral," often requiring little expertise, being potentially subject to abrupt termination, and more likely to be followed by unemployment or insecure work elsewhere in the secondary labor market. On the other hand, temporary work on a specific project may be subject to a contract similar (except for duration) to that of permanent staff. It can be organized either through an intermediate hiring agency or by direct contact. In many countries, project work is primarily undertaken by skilled or professional staff, and it can be perceived as relatively secure because subsequent positions are available through a hiring agency that has links to many employers.

As with other forms of group membership, temporary employees differ between themselves in additional respects. For example, as well as gender or age variations, they can be either full-time or part-time (Booth et al., 2002; Feldman & Doerpinghaus, 1992); in the study of temporary staff by Aronsson et al. (2002), 46% were part-timers. Emphasizing the wide variations between different temporary roles, McLean-Parks, Kidder, and Gallagher (1998) presented a framework in terms of employees' psychological contract. As introduced in chapter 5 in relation to job feature 12 (equity), that embodies the expectations of each other held by an employee and employer. McLean-Parks et al. (1998) explored differences between temporary employees in those expectations, for example, whether a person's psychological contract was oriented to a particular individual versus being applicable to employees more generally and whether it was open-ended versus time-limited.

Recognizing these variations, the four issues raised earlier are considered for full-time versus part-time and permanent versus temporary workers: conceptions of happiness, average levels, exposure to job features, and role occupancy versus nonoccupancy as a possible moderator of associations between job features and happiness. In the first respect, there is no apparent reason for differences in the applicability of the happiness framework set out in chapter 2, for example, because members of one category have at other times been in a different category. In all the roles, an account in terms of the dimensions of pleasure, mental arousal, and self-validation (as in Fig. 2.3) seems to be appropriate.

Full-Time and Part-Time Employees

Average Happiness.   The chapter's second issue concerns average levels of happiness. Studies comparing overall job satisfaction between full-timers and part-timers in general have produced a variety of different findings (Barling & Gallagher, 1996; Conway & Briner, 2002; Bernhard-Oettel, Sverke, & de Witte, 2005). Thorsteinson's (2003) meta-analysis indicated that on average the two groups have similar levels of satisfaction (axis 1 in Fig. 2.2). Consistent with that general pattern, no difference was found between the overall job satisfaction of full-time and part-time employees in later studies by Krausz et al. (2000), Sloane and Williams (2000), van Rijswijk et al. (2004), and Näswall et al. (2005). However, Sinclair, Martin, and Michel (1999) reported higher job satisfaction among part-timers, particularly those (mainly mothers of young children) whose pay supplemented a primary family income from someone else.

Clark's (1996) analysis of a British national sample revealed significantly greater satisfaction with pay, the work itself and the job overall among part-timers than full-timers. That pattern was retained for overall satisfaction and satisfaction with pay after statistical controls for gender and many other variables (Clark et al., 1996). Two smaller British samples were investigated by Conway and Briner (2002), with overall job satisfaction significantly higher among part-timers in one sample and no difference in the other. Part-time employees in both cases reported slightly but significantly greater well-being in terms of job-related anxiety–comfort (axis 2 in Fig. 2.2), but in neither sample was there a difference in depression–enthusiasm (axis 3). Reports of strain from one's job were examined by Smith (2001), with substantially more full-timers (22%) scoring above the threshold than part-timers (9%). (See also Smith et al., 2000.) However, job-induced tension was at the same level for full-time and part-time employees in the study by Bernhard-Oettel et al. (2005). Warr and Payne (1983) found that strain on the previous day was attributed to their job by more full-time (10%) than part-time (4%) women workers. Full-time female employees were also more likely to attribute pleasure yesterday to their job than were part-timers (16% vs. 11%), consistent with full-timers' more extended activity in an employed role.

In terms of facet-specific well-being, Thorsteinson's (2003) meta-analysis indicated that, after omission of a single anomalous study, average differences between full-timers and part-timers are negligible with respect to satisfaction with pay, coworkers, promotion prospects, one's supervisor, and the work itself. However, significant differences in specific facet satisfactions have been found in some studies (e.g., McGinnis & Morrow, 1990). Barling and Gallagher (1996) concluded that well-being divergence between part-timers and full-timers in particular organizations is more likely at the facet level than in overall terms, linked to the varying nature of local conditions.

In addition to domain-specific and facet-specific well-being (discussed earlier), we need to ask about context-free indicators. Few such comparisons between full-time and part-time employees appear to have been published, but Clark et al. (1996) and Bernhard-Oettel et al. (2005) reported no difference in general distress, and van Rijswijk et al. (2004) found that context-free emotional exhaustion was similar in the two groups. As emphasized in chapter 4, context-free forms of well-being are more dependent on other aspects of individuals and their life space, rather than primarily on the focused issue of, for instance, whether a job is part-time or full-time.

Average Job Features.   The chapter's third question asks about differential group exposure to features that may influence happiness or unhappiness. What comparative evidence is available for full-time versus part-time staff? The pattern might be envisaged to depend on whether the studied part-time jobs are more peripheral or less peripheral in the terms introduced above. For part-time employees in jobs that might otherwise be held by full-timers (those which are "less peripheral," "core," or "new concept" in the terms used earlier), a part-time versus full-time role seems unlikely to affect most of the job characteristics to which one is exposed. However, average differences in job content are more expected between core full-time staff and those part-timers who are in peripheral or secondary jobs.

Job characteristics have rarely been studied from that differentiated perspective, and little information is available about average differences in job content between those subgroups. For workers as a whole (without differentiation according to core versus periphery or role preference), Barling and Gallagher (1996) thought it likely that part-timers are on average likely to have less opportunity for personal control (feature 1), lower task identity (an aspect of 3), less job variety (4), greater role ambiguity (an aspect of 5), and lower overall job scope (see chap. 8). However, Gallagher (2005) suggested that average levels of role ambiguity were likely to be the same.

In a comparison of female workers' job content, Gallie et al. (1998) found that part-timers as a group reported less task discretion (1), opportunity for skill use and development (2), variety (4), pay and benefits (7), safe working conditions (8), and future prospects (11). (Other characteristics in the present framework were not examined.) Opportunity for learning and development (an aspect of feature 2) was also reported to be lower in part-time jobs by Aronsson et al. (2002). In one of two samples studied by Conway and Briner (2002), equity in one's job (12) was perceived to be greater in part-time than full-time work; however, no difference was present in the second sample. In comparisons between full-time and part-time employees with permanent contracts in the same occupational domain (health care), Bernhard-Oettel et al. (2005) found no differences in the level of control opportunity (1), demands (3), or insecurity (11). In general, evidence about patterns of exposure is limited in this area, and additional research that more carefully characterizes subgroups of part-timers in relation to their job content and role preferences is clearly needed.

Of particular relevance to part-time workers is a possible reduction in conflict between work and home, included here in job feature 3. Recognizing that most part-time employees are women, often with parental responsibilities, freedom from full-time attendance in a place of employment can be attractive to help manage conflicting demands between different domains. As summarized earlier, female employees tend particularly to value flexibility in their working schedules. Higgins, Duxbury, and Johnson (2000) and van Rijswijk et al. (2004) reported that part-timers experienced less work–home interference than full-timers. As well as reducing this form of between-domain conflict (feature 3), working part-time can also increase more generally the opportunity to control time allocations (an aspect of 1). Less time spent at work may make possible more control over other, apparently unconnected, aspects of one's life space.

Moderators of Job–Happiness Links.   The chapter's fourth question asks about possible moderator effects. Do we expect the magnitude of associations between particular environmental features and employee happiness to differ between full-time and part-time employees? Differences in the strength of association have been shown earlier for other groups to be linked to variations in the salience of a role characteristic (judgment J4B in chap. 9). In general, correlations between job features and happiness are greater when individuals or groups (e.g., men or women) view an environmental characteristic as more desirable or important to them. Differences might thus be expected in job–happiness correlations between full-time and part-time employees with respect to those job features that are viewed by the two groups as substantially different in their personal salience.

Evidence about this possibility is limited. A few studies have examined correlations between specific job features and happiness for the two groups separately, without assessing the rated importance of those features. For example, those correlations were found to be similar between full- and part-time workers in research by Conway and Briner (2002; examining equity) and by Strazdins et al. (2004; for job pressure). Bernhard-Oettel et al. (2005) reported that no statistical moderation was present for control opportunity or job demands, but that a significant interaction was present for job insecurity; insecurity was significantly more strongly associated with job-induced tension for full-timers than for part-timers. However, that difference was not present with respect to context-free distress. Information is not yet available about correlations of that kind as a function of job attribute salience as rated by the two subgroups.

Related research has examined employees' choice of their role. Part-time workers who actively choose a part-time position have been found to report greater job-related well-being than those who take up part-time work reluctantly (Barling & Gallagher, 1996; Feldman, 1990; Gallagher, 2005; Thorsteinson, 2003). For example, Krausz, Sagie, and Biderman (2000) studied nurses' overall job satisfaction as a function of preferred and actual working hours; a greater mismatch was associated with reduced well-being.

Before leaving part-time employment, we should note that some people have more than a single job. When an individual undertakes both a full-time job and a part-time one, he or she is sometimes said in the latter role to be "moonlighting"; in other cases, a person holds two, or possibly more, part-time positions. Estimates of two-job holding in the United States vary between 6% and 18% of the work force

(Zickar, Gibby, & Jenny, 2004), and in the United Kingdom around 4% of those in employment have two positions (Simic & Sethi, 2002).

For such people, overall job satisfaction has been found to be similar in both roles, although reported strain is greater in a primary job (Zickar et al., 2004). Part-time employees in their second job (the one requiring fewer hours) were found by Sinclair et al. (1999) to have lower satisfaction in that job than part-timers who had only a single job. Zickar et al. (2004) observed that satisfaction with a primary job is more closely related to life satisfaction ($r = +0.50$) than is satisfaction with one's secondary (in practice, part-time) job ($r = +0.18$). That difference was repeated for job-related strain ($r = -0.41$ and -0.25, respectively).

Permanent and Temporary Employees

Next, let us consider issues 2, 3, and 4 for workers in relatively permanent versus temporary positions: average levels of happiness in each group, patterns of exposure to job characteristics, and possible moderation of job–happiness associations.

Average Happiness. Comparisons between permanent and temporary employees' average happiness have typically examined subjective well-being that is job-related. Findings about the two groups as a whole have been inconsistent, suggesting that in overall terms no well-being differences are present (e.g., Allen & van der Velden, 2001; Aronsson et al., 2002; Bernhard-Oettel et al., 2005; Clark, 1996; Clark, 2005a; Feldman & Doerpinghaus, 1992; Mauno et al., 2005; McLean-Parks et al., 1998; Näswall et al., 2005). Bender et al. (2005) found that temporary male employees had lower job satisfaction than permanent ones, but that this difference was not significant for women.

As implied by that last finding, results depend in part on characteristics of particular samples. For example, Krausz, Brandwein, and Fox (1995) recorded no difference between the overall job satisfaction of permanent and temporary workers as a whole, but differences were present for subsets of temporary employees. Satisfaction was greatest among temporary staff who had chosen to be in that role, lowest among involuntary temporary workers, and in between among permanent staff. Booth et al. (2002) found that temporary staff employed on a casual basis had significantly lower job satisfaction than permanent employees, but that no difference was present between permanent staff and those temporary employees on fixed-term contracts.

That pattern was also found for several facet satisfactions (e.g., with the work itself), but not for satisfaction with job security or with promotion prospects; in those respects, permanent employees were significantly more satisfied than either group of temporary workers.

Job-related strain was examined by Parker, Griffin, Sprigg, and Wall (2002) in temporary manufacturing employees. They found that this form of strain was less marked among temporary workers than among permanent ones, and attributed temporary workers' relatively better well-being of that kind to a reduced load from their job. They drew attention to Pearce's (1993) finding that managers tend to allocate less difficult tasks to temporary workers, with permanent staff being more often asked to cope with complex problems, the ones that are particularly likely to generate job-related strain. Similar levels of job strain in temporary and permanent work were reported by Gallie et al. (1998), who attributed that absence of a difference to temporary employees' lower work pressure counterbalancing the problems of higher insecurity. Note that some temporary employees' well-being may be enhanced by a judgment that they are likely to be offered a permanent position in the future (judgment J3B, about a likely future trend, introduced in chap. 9).

Average Job Features.   Possible differences in work pressure link into the chapter's third question: Are the two subgroups exposed to different job features? For the first primary characteristic, opportunity for personal control, Aronsson et al. (2002) found that temporary employees as a whole had less discretion in their work than permanent ones, although available discretion was greater for temporary staff hired for specific projects than for casual workers. In the study by Gallie et al. (1998), casual temporary workers had substantially less autonomy than permanent ones, but that difference from permanent employees was absent for less peripheral temporary staff. Parker et al. (2002) also found that temporary employees had lower opportunity for personal control than did permanent ones, although the difference emerged less strongly in longitudinal analyses.

A similar pattern has been found for opportunity for skill use (feature 2), especially with respect to development opportunities. Temporary employees tend to receive less training than permanent ones, although the difference is again less marked for project employees than for casual temporary staff (Aronsson et al., 2002; Booth et al., 2002). With respect to feature 3, work demands were lower for casual temporary workers than for permanent ones in the study by Gallie et al. (1998). Parker et al. (2002) reported that temporary workers' less complex jobs involved a lower workload than did permanent positions. Their results suggested a parallel difference for role conflict (an aspect of 3), but that pattern (with less role conflict in temporary work) was not found in all analyses. In the study by Krausz et al. (1995), role conflict did not differ between permanent and temporary jobs. Social support (an aspect of 6) and supportive supervision (10) were similar for permanent and temporary staff in the investigation by Aronsson et al. (2002).

Expected differences between the groups have been found for job features 7 and 11. Income level (7) is generally lower for those without a permanent contract, partly because temporary workers on average undertake less responsible jobs. That is particularly the case for temporary staff who are casual, whose pay tends also to be significantly lower than that of temporary workers employed on a contract (Booth et al., 2002). In a similar manner, perceived job security (11) is lower for temporary than permanent workers (Mauno et al., 2005; Parker et al., 2002), although that difference is much more marked for casual employees than for project workers (Gallie et al., 1998).

Levels of well-being are expected to depend in particular studies on the nature of the job characteristics to which permanent and temporary employees are exposed. For example, Parker et al. (2002) interpreted the lower job strain of temporary workers in their study in terms of their reduced role overload and role conflict, despite the fact that they received less pay and were in less secure jobs. Additional research is needed to provide more substantial evidence for the completion of a Table 8.1 profile (see chap. 8) for the average permanent versus temporary employee; in the latter case, supplementary consideration of more peripheral and less peripheral roles is clearly also needed.

Moderators of Job–Happiness Links.   The chapter's fourth question asks about possible between-group differences in the magnitude of associations between job features and happiness. For other categories (e.g., unemployed or retired people, men vs. women), the perceived importance of a role or environmental feature has been shown to be critical in this respect: Job–happiness correlations tend to be greater when a subgroup views the role or feature in question as more personally important. We should thus focus on possible differences in the salience of particular job features to temporary and permanent employees. However, studies of their subjective well-being have not yet explored that issue.

Some research has examined whether or not individuals occupy roles with a tenure they find desirable. This preference has been considered in chapter 9 in terms of the personal salience of role membership, judgment 4A. Although permanent employment is in general preferred to a temporary role (Booth et al., 2002; Parker et al., 2002), employees who are temporary by choice have been found to report greater job satisfaction than involuntary temporary workers (Connelly & Gallagher, 2004; Krausz, Brandwein, & Fox, 1995). As in other cases, individuals' role preference is related to their happiness.

Self-Employment, Telework, and Portfolio Careers

This section on occupational differences has so far identified for consideration employment that is full-time or part-time and that which is permanent or temporary. We might also ask about groups such as the self-employed, "teleworkers," and "portfolio workers." However, the subjective well-being of those sets of workers has infrequently been examined, and evidence is not yet available for detailed consideration of the chapter's four principal questions.

Self-employed people make up around 16% of Europe's work force (European Commission, 2005), and the rate is around 8% in the United States (Hipple, 2004). (However, inclusion of self-employed individuals with their own incorporated business increases the U.S. rate to around 11%.) Self-employment is more common for men than for women, and above 65 years most people still working are self-employed. Self-employed people may work as single-person units or they might employ other people, owning a (usually small) business. In the latter case (less than 20% of self-employed people), their role includes many features common to managerial activities as employee members of an organization.

"Telework" has expanded in recent years, as more people carry out their job activities for some part of their time in a location away from an employer's site. That location is usually their own home, but might be space rented elsewhere for the purpose. All definitions of telework emphasize separation from an organizational site, but they vary in their concern for the regularity and frequency of that arrangement, the minimum weekly duration required for inclusion in the category, and whether or not computers and computer networks are central to a job.

A British national survey indicated that almost 8% of the work force were teleworkers, defined in terms of at least 1 day per week (Hotopp, 2002). Ruiz and Walling (2005) reported from their later UK data that most teleworkers (around 62% of them) were self-employed and that most (about 65%) were men. (Linked to that, self-employment is more common in men than in women; see earlier discussion.) Around an overall prevalence of 8%, the rates of teleworking were 11% and 6% for men and women respectively. Teleworkers were predominantly managerial, professional and technical workers. That is also the case in the United States. A national survey of working at home at least once a week as part of a primary job found that overall 15% of American workers fell in that category, but that for management, professional, and related occupations the figure was 28%; 34% of those reporting some work at home were self-employed (Bureau of Labor Statistics; see www.bls.gov, accessed September 22, 2005). (Note that the teleworking definition in that survey is both broader than in the United Kingdom, including shorter periods, and more narrow, concerning only home locations.)

Some teleworkers are in part-time roles, and they also vary in other ways considered in this chapter, for example, in their age and the temporary or permanent nature of their job. Lamond, Daniels, and Standen (2005) drew attention to additional variations, for example, between-job differences in the level of expertise required (feature 2), the amount of intraorganizational contact involved (an aspect of 6), and the extent of use of computer-based technology.

Golden and Veiga (2005) also emphasized differences between teleworkers, with particular focus on the number of hours each week spent away from an employing organization. Reviewing previous research, they noted that findings about job satisfaction in contrast with non-teleworkers' satisfaction have varied between investigations. Studying the temporal extent of each employee's teleworking, they found that overall job satisfaction was progressively greater up to a threshold of about 15 hours a week away from an employer and then slightly lower at longer durations. Examining possible moderator variables, they reported that job satisfaction was higher for teleworkers whose work less required interdependence with colleagues (an aspect of feature 6) and for those who had a greater opportunity for personal control in their job (1; see also Golden, 2006).

The notion of a "portfolio" career was introduced by Handy (1985) to describe the possibility of a combination of paid work, voluntary work, periods of study, and working from home. The term is now used more widely to refer to self-employed people who work for a number of different organizations or clients. In each of several employment relationships a person works part-time and/or on a temporary basis. Arrangements of that kind have long been common for self-employed electricians, plumbers, and so on, who move from customer to customer, but portfolio working appears to be increasing in frequency for knowledge workers of several kinds. However, comprehensive information about its prevalence is not yet available.

There have been few studies that compare the happiness of these groups with more traditional workers, and published results are inconsistent (e.g., Eden, 1975; Hotopp, 2002; Lewis, 2003). Influential variables are likely to be the same as in other groups—the unemployed, retired, part-time, temporary, and so on. As illustrated throughout the book, people are more happy or less happy as a function of key environmental characteristics and of their preference for a current role or role features relative to alternatives (judgment J4 in chap. 9). In terms of role preference, some individuals actively choose self-employment, telework, or a portfolio combination because they value the perceived advantages, whereas others are pressed into that position because of the lack of alternatives or for family or medical reasons. Subjective well-being is expected to differ accordingly, but research evidence has yet to be obtained.

What about exposure to key job characteristics in these employment roles? Self-employed people are likely to have raised opportunities for personal control (feature 1) and for skill use (2), as well as potentially high work–family conflict (an aspect of 3; Parasuraman et al., 1996). A similar pattern is expected for teleworkers, and that group may receive less training (an aspect of feature 2) and have more limited social contact (6). Aspects of working conditions (space and facilities at home; feature 8) may also be impaired for some teleworkers (Lamond et al., 2005). Portfolio workers are likely to experience substantial personal control and job variety (features 1 and 4), but also greater uncertainty (5) and insecurity (11). Members of that group may have difficulty regulating role demands, with either too little or too much work (feature 3; Totterdell et al., 2006).

Given that the number of people in self-employment, telework, and portfolio careers is increasing in many countries, it is clear that research attention should shift to investigate their jobs and happiness in addition to those of traditional employees. That is also the case for other subgroups considered in this section—part-time and temporary workers. In all cases, happiness is likely to be a function of key job characteristics and of individuals' wish to be in their current role. The latter preference (a form of personal salience, introduced as judgment J4 in chap. 9) depends in part on those job characteristics themselves, but also on a range of personal attributes and values; the latter are explored in the next three chapters.

11

Personality, Genes,
and Happiness

Chapters 11 to 13 continue the general theme of the previous two: A person's happiness or unhappiness is a function of himself or herself as well as of inputs from the environment. As in chapter 10, four questions are addressed. Is the personal feature under consideration linked to differences in people's conception of the nature of happiness? Is that personal feature associated with differences in levels of happiness? Are different kinds of individuals exposed to different inputs from the environment, with possible varying impacts on happiness? Is the strength of the association between job characteristics and happiness influenced by the personal attribute under investigation? The first three issues are examined in the present chapter, and chapter 12 considers the fourth possibility. Some of these themes are carried forward into chapter 13, which reviews a range of perspectives on person–environment fit, and further explores personal salience and occupational values.

PERSONALITY, VALUES, AND MOTIVES

It is clear that stable attributes of several kinds have the potential to affect a person's behavior and experiences. For example, physical differences in strength, bodily characteristics, and appearance are all of continuing importance in interactions with the environment. People

TABLE 11.1
Some Overlapping Dispositions at Three Levels of Generality

Principal Emphasis or Breadth of Scope	Dispositional Construct		
	Value	Personality	Motive
Principal emphasis	On thoughts	On both thoughts and actions	On actions
Breadth of scope			
Broad scope: across themes and/or times	Ideology	Temperament	Life goal
Medium scope	Value	Trait	Motive
Narrow scope: restricted to a specific theme and/or time	Interest	Habit	Want

with different physical attributes enter different (as well as similar) situations, and they handle some situations in a different manner. However, psychologists' interest in stable characteristics has primarily concerned consistency in cognitive-affective dispositions, with particular reference to personality and associated features, and that is the focus here.

Personality dispositions are members of a wider family of concepts, each of which has some elements in common with others despite differences between them. Several members of that family are presented in Table 11.1, with particular reference to their breadth of scope and their relative emphasis on thought processes or action possibilities, although both of those are involved to some degree in all cases. Thus, in considering personality (the middle column) we are likely to incorporate themes that are both cognitive (labeled as "thoughts" in the table) and also concerned with a tendency to actions of certain kinds. That dual perspective is illustrated in the content of many personality inventories, whose items ask either what an individual enjoys, prefers or likes (i.e., about thought processes of several kinds) or about what he or she routinely or typically does (forms of action).

Also in Table 11.1 are the constructs of value (to the left) and motivation (to the right). Many authors have offered definitions of a value in terms of a person's idea about what is desirable or good (e.g., Roe & Ester, 1999). For example, Locke (1976) considered that a "value is that which one acts to gain and/or keep" (p. 1304), and Hofstede's (1984) definition was in terms of "a broad preference for one state of affairs over others" (p. 389). Ros, Schwartz, and Surkiss (1999) defined values as "desirable trans-situational goals that vary in importance as guiding principles in people's lives" (p. 51); they were summarized as "conceptions of the desirable" by Schwartz (1999, p. 24). In the same way, Cable and Edwards (2004) viewed individuals' values as "what they believe is important" (p. 823). More formally, "values are (a) beliefs that transcend specific situations, (b) pertain to desirable end states or behaviors, (c) guide selection of behavior and events, and (d) vary in terms of relative importance" (p. 823).

After reviewing literature in this field, Dawis (1991) concluded that there is agreement "that values function as the standards, or criteria, by which persons evaluate things and that such evaluation is on the basis of the relative importance of things to the person" (p. 838). In general, statements about values thus concern people's relative evaluations of alternative possibilities; they provide one indication of the perceived differential salience of situations, activities or ideas (judgment J4 in chap. 9).

As summarized in column 2 of Table 11.1, values range in scope from broad perspectives on, say, the organization of society ("ideologies" in the table) to more specific outlooks that have been investigated under the label of "interest" or "preference" (e.g., Dawis, 1991). Edwards (1996) concluded that "values represent conscious desires held by the person, and thus encompass preferences, interests, motives, and goals" (p. 294). Focusing on employment situations, Shaw and Gupta (2004) viewed some values narrowly as "the desired level of a task characteristic," and noted that as a whole values "are typically defined operationally as preferences or interests, although they can also include motives and goals" (p. 848).

Although the three dispositions toward the left of Table 11.1 (ideologies, values, and interests) vary in their scope, they have in common some within-person continuity of affect between settings. That continuity is reflected also in attributes of personality, considered in the middle column of the table. Indeed, a personality feature might be viewed largely as a syndrome of values. Empirical overlaps between the two constructs have been demonstrated with respect to values identified as vocational interests. Those were described by Mount, Barrick, Scullen, and Rounds (2005) as "long-term dispositional traits inherent in the person that influence behavior primarily through one's preferences for certain environments, activities, and types of people" (p. 449). Particular vocational preferences of that kind have often been found to be moderately associated with certain aspects of personality (e.g., Hogan & Blake, 1999; Mount et al., 2005; Tokar & Fischer, 1998; Tokar, Fischer, & Subich, 1998). For example, measures of extraversion are correlated at around +0.25 or +0.30 with vocational interests labeled as "social" and "enterprising," as are personality scores of openness to experience in relation to "investigative" and "artistic" vocational interests. Indeed, for Holland (1973, 1999), "what we have called 'vocational interests' are simply another aspect of personality" (1973, p. 7).

Those correlations arise from the fact that the constructs of interest and personality are in some ways overlapping. Nevertheless, despite the associations summarized in the previous paragraph, the majority of personality–interest correlations are nonsignificant. That absence of association is sometimes taken to indicate the nonequivalence of the two kinds of variable. In practice, however, observed low correlations between them are attributable to a lack of conceptual overlap in those particular cases, rather than to an overall separateness. When particular personality traits and interests are conceptually linked, as they are in a minority of combinations, they tend to be empirically related. However, even the statistically significant correlations are of only moderate strength, indicating that the two sets of variables may be treated as partly distinct from each other.

A related concept is that of motivation, in the right-hand column of Table 11.1. Motives in the form of broad-scope life goals (toward the top of the table) are retained over periods of years. Extension across time can also occur at other levels of generality; even specific wants (at the bottom of the table) reflect in part a continuing directedness of mental and behavioral processes. Wants do not arise independently of previous motives or values. In part, they derive repetitively from mental schemata that recur as a person continues to want the same kinds of outcome. Although personality traits are less dependent on current stimuli than are motives, those two concepts both involve continuing action tendencies, behavioral routines, and associated thought processes (Winter, John, Stewart, Klohnen, & Duncan, 1998). For example, individuals whose personality is more extraverted than others' have associated dispositional motives that differ from those who are less extraverted.

Manifestations of personality (in the middle of Table 11.1) may also be viewed at several levels of generality. Very broad perspectives are sometimes described in terms of temperament. That notion has been characterized in several ways, but aspects of temperament are often considered to differ from personality traits in terms of their more fundamental and global nature, possibly emphasizing an inherited biological origin (Strelau & Angleitner, 1991). With narrower scope, specific habits (at the bottom of the table) can also reflect a consistency in personality, as people's targeted routines are often linked with their more general dispositions (Aarts & Dijksterhuis, 2000; Ouellette & Wood, 1998).

This chapter mainly examines the involvement in happiness of consistent orientations that have been studied under the label of personality. However, being located in the center of Table 11.1, personality traits are surrounded by overlapping constructs of the kind shown there. Although differing in some respects between themselves, the concepts in Table 11.1 are similar in embracing gradations of personal salience. Many findings and possibilities examined below in terms of personality may thus also be viewed in terms of other constructs in Table 11.1; dividing lines between cells in the table are fuzzy and imprecise.

The constructs in that table are often described in terms of dimensions through which people might differ from each other. Many dimensions of difference within personality have been suggested, and it has become conventional to group those into five principal categories (e.g., Goldberg, 1990; McRae & Costa, 1997). Although investigators have sometimes used alternative labels, the so-called "Big Five" personality factors may be described as follows:

> *Neuroticism* (**N**), usually taken to include anxiety, depression, hostility and moodiness, with low levels of neuroticism sometimes labeled positively as "emotional stability."
>
> *Extraversion* (**E**), sometimes examined through two overlapping components: sociability, friendliness, gregariousness, and talkativeness (an "affiliative" tendency); and assertiveness, social potency, energy, optimism, and influence on others (perhaps described as "surgency").
>
> *Openness to experience* (**O**), which can be separated into either an artistic orientation (a sensitivity to aesthetic and cultural issues) or a more general intellectual emphasis on conceptual and abstract topics.
>
> *Agreeableness* (**A**), covering features such as cooperativeness, modesty, trustworthiness, sympathy for others, and consideration of people's wishes.
>
> *Conscientiousness* (**C**), a tendency to initiate actions of two kinds: first in terms of achievement orientation, proactivity, striving, and a determination to attain goals; and second as dependability, planfulness, self-discipline, a concern for order, and an acceptance of routines and authority.

There has been argument about whether all aspects of personality can be fitted into this structure, and about how to cope with the possibility that certain dispositions may extend across more than a single factor (e.g., Block, 1995). In addition, the item composition of some factors differs between inventories claiming to measure the same construct, so that the same labels can in fact refer to somewhat different aspects of a person. A more differentiated perspective (in terms of, say, 20 different attributes) can sometimes have conceptual and explanatory advantages (e.g., Bartram, 2005; Hough, 1992; Paunonen, 1998), for example, in examining combinations of multiple traits or seeking to predict narrowly specified behaviors. However, the Big Five structure has undoubted descriptive value, and findings about personality and happiness are here presented mainly in those terms.

PERSONALITY AND HAPPINESS: MEANINGS AND ASSOCIATIONS

The chapter's first question asks about possible differences in the meaning of happiness. Do people with different personality attributes think about happiness in systematically different ways? As pointed out in chapter 10, examination of the construct's meaning should not include possible sources of raised or lowered happiness (which may well vary for different kinds of people), but be concerned only with its intrinsic nature. In psychological (rather than, say, philosophical) terms, we need to ask whether happiness is construed differently by individuals with different characteristics.

This issue has rarely been raised, and evidence is lacking about possible variations between people in, for instance, applicability of the dimensional structure of happiness suggested in chapter 2. It seems appropriate to assume that this structure is similarly applied by people with different personalities, but research evidence is still required.

However, personality-linked differences might be expected in terms of variations in people's baselines and associated perceptions of happiness. For instance, if higher scorers on neuroticism (N) tend on average to report more unhappiness than do low-N individuals, they may generally think about hedonic experiences within a different comparative framework. That may involve different levels and kinds of judgmental standards of the kind examined in chapter 9. The construct of happiness as understood by more neurotic people might thus have a more somber tone, because all instances of happiness are evaluated against less positive judgmental norms. At present, we know little about differences in the meaning of happiness to people with different personality and related characteristics.

Levels of Context-Free Happiness

The chapter's second question has more often been investigated: Are there average differences in happiness between high and low scorers on key dimensions of personality? Patterns are first considered for context-free, rather than domain-specific or facet-specific, happiness.

Reviewing previous findings within the Big Five framework (discussed earlier), DeNeve and Cooper (1998) grouped well-being indicators into those assessing more affective forms of happiness (type 1 in Table 2.1 in chap. 2) and those recording life satisfaction (type 2). For type 1 context-free measures of happiness, average correlations were −0.25 with neuroticism, +0.27 with extraversion, +0.06 with openness to experience, +0.19 with agreeableness, and +0.16 with conscientiousness. For life satisfaction, corresponding values were −0.24, +0.17, +0.14, +0.16, and +0.22, respectively.

In fact, average associations of happiness with Big Five factors are likely to be larger than was reported in that review. Different procedures for accumulating evidence about associations with a composite score (here, a Big Five factor) can yield different estimates of correlations. For calculating correlations with a Big Five factor, it is desirable to examine a composite factor score for each individual. However, research reviews have often only had access to findings about elements within a factor (more focused scales that retrospectively can be viewed as components of a factor), so that they have averaged the correlations found for each of those elements. The average of the correlations with elements of a composite is necessarily smaller than the correlation with that composite itself (e.g., Warr, Bartram, & Brown, 2005). DeNeve and Cooper (1998) computed the average value of correlations with separate elements of that kind, that is, with individual scales considered to fall within a Big Five compound. Their average correlations between a personality factor and subjective well-being, based on elements rather than an overall composite, are thus likely to underestimate the correlations for composite factors themselves.

Underestimation of that kind can be avoided if Big Five factors are measured directly as compound scores for each respondent, rather than in terms of separate elements whose correlations are later aggregated. Some personality inventories are of that kind, and research into those composite Big Five values has suggested even stronger correlations with happiness. For example, the meta-analysis by Lucas and Fujita (2000) examined only scales that measured extraversion as a single factor, finding an average correlation with positive affect of +0.37. Law, Wong, and Song (2004) found average correlations of compound personality scales with life satisfaction across two samples of –0.42 (N), +0.35 (E), +0.10 (O), +0.23 (A), and +0.23 (C). Steel and Ones (2002) described a nation-level study, in which average values for each country (rather than scores for individual persons) were examined with respect to composite factor scores from a single inventory. Across 16 countries, they reported correlations with life satisfaction of –0.59 (N), +0.48 (E), +0.23 (O), +0.08 (A), and –0.21 (C) [sic]. Both neuroticism and extraversion accounted (in separate analyses) for substantial variance in happiness over and above the effect of national income.

Some research has examined context-free distress. In Chay's (1993) study, the correlations between employees' distress and their neuroticism and extraversion were +0.54 and –0.36, respectively. Parkes (1990), Moyle (1995), Dijkstra et al. (2005), and Jones et al. (2005) reported correlations between neuroticism and distress of +0.31, +0.55, +0.67, and +0.60, respectively, and showed that the neuroticism–distress association remained significant despite contributions from several job and other personal characteristics.

Employees' neuroticism and extraversion significantly predicted context-free affective well-being and life satisfaction 2 years later in an investigation by Suh et al. (1996). In research by Judge et al. (1998), a significant association between neuroticism and life satisfaction (r = –0.30 averaged across three samples) was paralleled by an average value of –0.29 when participants' life satisfaction was estimated by a "significant other" (spouse, partner, etc.). Self-reported life satisfaction was correlated at –0.38 with neuroticism measured 2 months earlier in the study by Judge et al. (2005). Rode (2004) asked about the link between neuroticism scores and an aggregate of nonwork satisfactions (with one's marriage, home, etc.), finding a correlation of –0.32. The association was similar (r = –0. 28) when this aggregate nonwork satisfaction was recorded 3 years later than the personality indicator. In research by Dijkstra et al. (2005), a broad index of context-free well-being was correlated at +0.27 and +0.14 with extraversion and agreeableness, respectively. However, the association of extraversion with context-free depression was nonsignificant (r = –0.08) in research by Schaubroeck, Ganster, and Fox (1992); between that measure of unhappiness and trait neuroticism the correlation was +0.69.

A related set of studies has examined two personality dispositions that have usually been viewed as more comprehensive than Big Five characteristics—tendencies to experience negative affect or positive affect (e.g., Watson & Tellegen, 1985). Negative affectivity (NA) has been treated as a general proneness to experience distress, dissatisfaction, fear, anger, sadness and other negative feelings; it has been viewed as "a broad and pervasive personality trait" (Watson & Clark, 1984, p. 465). The disposition of positive affectivity (PA) reflects a tendency to joy, interest, excitement, alertness, cheerfulness, and exhilaration. Agho et al. (1993) took as a definition "the degree to which an individual is predisposed to be happy" (p. 1012).

Scales constructed by Watson et al. (1988; in the Positive and Negative Affect Schedule, PANAS) record those orientations, although, as pointed out in chapter 2, they mainly cover high-activation feelings to the exclusion of lower levels of psychological arousal (see Figs. 2.1 and 2.2). Positive affectivity (PA) and negative affectivity (NA) are strongly correlated with extraversion (E) and neuroticism (N), respectively (e.g., Watson & Clark, 1992), and E and N scales have sometimes been used to assess PA and NA themselves. Across 76 previous studies, Thoresen et al. (2003) recorded an average correlation between PA and NA of −0.29.

In view of significant associations between E and N and aspects of happiness (discussed earlier), and based on the nature of PA and NA themselves, significant correlations of happiness with those affectivity variables are also expected. Substantial associations have often been reported. For example, in the American study by Judge and Locke (1993), PA and NA were correlated with context-free happiness at +0.50 and −0.64, respectively, and with life satisfaction at +0.36 and −0.48. In Japan, correlations of PA and NA with measured happiness were +0.40 and −0.49, and with life satisfaction those values were +0.47 and −0.27 (Piccolo et al., 2005). The research review by Watson and Slack (1984) found negative affectivity to be highly related to state anxiety and negative affect, even when the state measures were completed 10 years after the trait measurement. Significant associations of that kind across more than 6 years (especially for NA) were also reported by Watson and Walker (1996). Those two aspects of continuing personality are thus highly correlated with current well-being, and they predict states of happiness or unhappiness even after several years.

Such correlations are partly a reflection of conceptual overlap between particular traits and states. Positive affect and negative affect can be measured with varying time-frames, for example, "as you generally are" (a dispositional trait) or "as you feel at the moment" (a state). Dispositionally worded indicators tap long-term characteristics, whereas subjective well-being assessed with a more immediate focus usually concerns an episodic state. States are by definition of short duration, and it is in the nature of a (longer term) disposition that it is exhibited repeatedly in particular examples of linked behavior or experience (short-term states). That is sometimes described in terms of "trait-state overlap," viewing a continuing trait, such as the propensity to negative affect, as a dispositional tendency that is evidenced through multiple episodes of states with similar content. Fleeson, Malanos, and Achille (2002) concluded that "the frequencies with which individuals enact various levels of states are a large part (but not all) of the nature of individual differences in traits" (p. 1411).

The significant between-person association between trait neuroticism and low (state) subjective well-being is thus in part logically necessary. That is also the case for the observed positive correlation with extraversion. Scale items to tap that personality dimension (especially those that focus on the surgency component; see earlier) tend to emphasize energy and positive emotions of the kind that can be reflected in raised subjective well-being in particular settings. For trait measures of neuroticism and extraversion, Williams et al. (1991) reported significant associations in different episodes with employees' situation-specific positive mood and task enjoyment (negative for N, and positive for E); in many different tasks (studied across eight days), less neurotic and more extraverted employees were typically in a more happy state.

Fleeson et al. (2002) also asked about patterns across time, but they focused on consistency within persons rather than between persons (discussed earlier). Examining on each measurement occasion state extraversion (in particular the surgency component) and activated forms of positive affect, they showed that students' self-reports of more extraverted behavior in particular episodes were strongly correlated with more positive affect of that activated kind. This within-person association was found to occur for each individual studied, and to be present in separate analyses of particular kinds of situation (studying, at a party, during paid work, at a meal, etc.).

Associations of some personality traits with episodic happiness or unhappiness are thus in part logically necessary. Other relevant causal processes are likely to include personality-linked variations in the perception of situations and also in behavior that might create differences in environmental conditions. For example, it could be the case that high-N individuals generally (but not necessarily accurately) perceive their environment as more threatening than do other people, or they may behave in ways that bring about more troublesome inputs. Those possibilities are examined later.

As illustrated earlier, associations of context-free well-being with the other Big Five dispositions (openness to experience, agreeableness, and conscientiousness) are less marked than for neuroticism and extraversion. However, modestly significant associations were reported in previous paragraphs. Those links with happiness might sometimes arise from high scorers' movement into relevant happiness-promoting situations. In addition, indirect associations are expected from links between dispositions themselves. A personality trait can be associated with a particular outcome, not primarily because of its own content, but because it happens to be correlated with another disposition which is itself conceptually linked to the outcome in question (Warr, 2000). In that way, a particular trait may be correlated with happiness because it is (even modestly) associated with, say, neuroticism, a characteristic that itself logically overlaps with low levels of that outcome.

Other research into context-free subjective well-being has examined associations with personality features that may cut across several of the Big Five constructs. For example, "hardiness" has been defined in terms of "a constellation of personality characteristics that function as a resistance resource in the encounter with stressful life events" (Kobasa, Maddi, & Kahn, 1982, p. 169). The main components have been viewed as a high level of commitment to one's activities, a sense of control over features in one's life space, and a perception that changes provide challenge rather than threat. Several hardiness scales have been developed, and examinations of internal consistency have confirmed that the first two of those features (commitment and perceived control) are both important components of the disposition, but that challenge is best treated as a separate construct (e.g., Florian, Mikulincer, & Taubman, 1995; Funk, 1992; Hull, van Treuren, & Virnelli, 1987).

Overall hardiness or the first two components have often been found to be related to context-free happiness (positively) or unhappiness (negatively). For example, Hull et al. (1987) reviewed correlations of the overall hardiness score with general distress that were around −0.38 and with depression around −0.32. In the study by Florian et al. (1995), the commitment component of hardiness was correlated at +0.44 with current positive affect and −0.55 with current negative feelings; for the control component, those values were +0.38 and −0.44, respectively. Florian and colleagues followed military trainees across 4 months of stressful activity, finding that dispositional commitment and control had subsequent benefits on subjective well-being that appeared to arise from more effective processes of situational appraisal and coping in difficult situations.

Hardiness is significantly correlated with other traits, negatively with neuroticism (e.g., Funk, 1992) and positively with extraversion (Parkes & Rendall, 1988), and it is presumably part of a broader positive orientation toward oneself and one's life space. A related concept is the "sense of coherence"—the extent to which a person sees the world as comprehensible, meaningful, and manageable (Antonovsky, 1987). Roskies, Louis-Guerin, and Fournier (1993) reported a correlation of −0.53 between that variable and employees' context-free distress, and Höge and Büssing (2004) found that this association remained significant beyond the impact of negative affectivity and other variables. As is the case for hardiness, sense of coherence as conventionally measured is strongly negatively associated with neuroticism; for example, $r = -0.61$ in the study by Höge and Büssing (2004).

A characteristic studied as "resilience" is also linked to subjective well-being. That variable has been characterized as the ability to bounce back from negative experiences, flexibly adapting to changing demands (Block & Block, 1980). Scores on a scale of resilience have been shown to predict subjective well-being after working on stressful tasks (Tugade & Fredrickson, 2004). The construct has some similarities with other concepts reviewed here, but Tugade and Fredrickson (2004) have emphasized differences in cognitive processing: Resilient individuals may experience high anxiety (as e.g., do high-NA people), but they respond to that anxiety and the anxiety-provoking situation in ways that allow them better to recover. Variations in this disposition appear not to have been investigated in employment settings.

A broad perspective on personality orientations of the kinds illustrated earlier was adopted by Judge et al. (1998). They suggested that the construct of "core self-evaluations" embodies key personality features relevant to people's view of themselves in relation to others. Principal elements were considered to be low neuroticism and high locus of control, self-efficacy and self-esteem. Together those form a composite that may be viewed as similar to self-confidence.

High and low scorers on core self-evaluations have often been found to differ significantly in context-free well-being. The average correlation with life satisfaction in three American samples studied by

Judge, Erez, Bono, and Thoresen (2003) was +0.51, and in a Japanese sample that value was +0.52 (Piccolo et al., 2005). Measuring personality 2 months before life satisfaction, the correlation was +0.33 in the study by Judge et al. (2005). Using a different measure of core self-evaluations, Rode (2004) found that the relationship with life satisfaction was significant across 3 years, also after controls for job and demographic features. A meta-analysis of studies of unemployed individuals revealed an average cross-sectional correlation with life satisfaction of +0.38 (McKee-Ryan et al., 2005). For a broad measure of happiness, the correlation with core self-evaluations was +0.67 in the study by Piccolo et al. (2005).

As pointed out by Judge and colleagues, core self-evaluations clearly overlap with certain more specific personality traits (for instance, by including neuroticism in the composite). However, significant incremental validity over Big Five factors in the prediction of life satisfaction has been demonstrated (Judge et al., 2003). The broader variable thus can account for additional variance in the relationship between particular personality traits and happiness.

Different processes are associated with "perfectionism," the tendency to work unremittingly toward particularly high standards. Three forms of this construct have received attention—perfectionism that is self-oriented, other-oriented, or socially prescribed (e.g., Blatt, 1995; Flett & Hewitt, 2002). Self-oriented perfectionism is an extended striving to be flawless; it involves continuous high levels of motivation, unrealistic self-expectations, stringent self-evaluation and self-criticism, and a recurrent concern about one's failings and shortcomings. Other-oriented perfectionism places similar demands on other people; socially prescribed perfectionism is centered on an insistent personal conviction that other people's extremely high expectations of oneself must be met if their approval is to be gained.

As with other dispositions, this personality trait embodies particular assessments of personal salience, with a continuing emphasis on one's own excellence. It has consistently been found to be associated with greater context-free anxiety and depression (e.g., Blatt, 1995; Flett & Hewitt, 2002). In a study of performing artists, Mor, Day, Flett, and Hewitt (1995) examined some of those links. They found that self-oriented perfectionism and socially prescribed perfectionism were significantly predictive of more anxiety and less happiness during a stage performance. Other research has suggested that influential processes include perfectionists' maladaptive coping procedures (e.g., avoidance and denial, rather than active attempts at problem solution) and a perception of lower social support (e.g., Dunkley, Zuroff, & Blankstein, 2003). Some perfectionist thinking is of course important for resourcefulness and the achievement of difficult goals, but persistently raised levels of self-criticism can clearly cause personal difficulties.

Finally, in this consideration of context-free happiness, some evidence about the second component—self-validation—may be reviewed. As described in chapters 1 and 2, this form of happiness is difficult to operationalize, and it has less frequently been the target of empirical research than has subjective well-being. The focus of self-validation is on people's attainment of standards that somehow reflect what they feel they should be. For example, Ryff's (1989) scale of personal growth asked about respondents' sense of continued development, and her purpose in life scale recorded the presence of valued life goals and a sense of directedness toward those.

Schmutte and Ryff (1997) examined the associations between self-reports about those aspects of self-validating happiness and the Big Five dimensions of personality. Across two samples, average correlations with personal growth were: N –0.36, E +0.48, O +0.40, A +0.30, and C +0.38. For purpose in life, average correlations were: N –0.57, E +0.43, O +0.16, A +0.28, and C +0.58. The researchers recognized that correlations between personality and self-validation (they did not use that term) might derive in part from linked differences in subjective well-being, the first kind of happiness. Statistical controls for positive affect and negative affect did indeed reduce the observed correlations between Big Five factors and self-validation. However, extraversion and openness to experience remained important for personal growth, and conscientiousness remained significantly linked to purpose in life, despite the controls for affective state.

King et al. (2006) also examined the sense of purpose in life, for example, focusing on students' experiences in the last 2 days (e.g., "In the last two days my life had very clear goals and aims"). This form of recent self-validation was found to be correlated at +0.41 with trait extraversion.

In overview, it is clear that context-free happiness is in part a function of people's continuing personality dispositions. That pattern is linked to the stable differences in mental processes examined at the end of chapter 9. It was there pointed out that variations between people in a continuing baseline of happiness are associated with systematically different ways of processing hedonically relevant information. Individuals differ from each other in many dispositional ways, some of which can be described as values, personality traits or motives. (See Table 11.1 at the beginning of this chapter.) All of those dispositions involve consistent application of happiness-related judgments of the kind explored in chapter 9 (and further in chap. 12). These work together in behaviors and linked mental processes to sustain a person's typical level of happiness.

Levels of Domain-Specific and Facet-Specific Happiness

The context-free processes that have been considered so far are expected also to occur for happiness that is domain-specific. Research attention in the domain of employment has primarily been directed at overall job satisfaction (on measurement axis 1 in Fig. 2.2), and average correlations with Big Five personality attributes parallel those summarized earlier for the first axis of well-being that is context-free.

The meta-analysis by Judge, Heller, and Mount (2002) found the following uncorrected average correlations with overall job satisfaction in previous research: neuroticism −0.24, extraversion +0.19, openness to experience +0.01, agreeableness +0.13, and conscientiousness +0.20. Very similar values were obtained in studies that were either cross-sectional or longitudinal. A separate meta-analysis by Bruk-Lee et al. (2005) yielded uncorrected average correlations with overall job satisfaction of −0.25 (N), +0.12 (E), −0.02 (O), +0.13 (A), and +0.16 (C). Composite factor scores were examined in the meta-analysis by Thoresen et al. (2003), yielding average uncorrected correlations with job satisfaction of −0.23 and +0.18 with neuroticism and extraversion, respectively. In other research into job satisfaction, Wayne et al. (2004), Aryee et al. (2005), and Jones et al. (2005) reported correlations with neuroticism of −0.23, −0.33, and −0.30, respectively, and a study by Judge et al. (2005) found a correlation with N measured 2 months earlier of −0.37. In Tokar and Subich's (1997) investigation, "nearly identical" cross-sectional correlation values were obtained for men and women. For the trait of conscientiousness, Lubbers et al. (2005) reported a correlation of +0.25 with a broad index of job-related affect.

Bruk-Lee et al. (2005) also included in their meta-analysis specific traits that might be classified as components of Big Five factors. For example, anger (sometimes viewed as an aspect of neuroticism) was found to be on average correlated −0.23 with overall job satisfaction. For achievement striving (one component of conscientiousness), the average correlation was +0.28.

Examining facet satisfactions rather than a domain-level indicator of well-being, Schaubroeck, Ganster, and Kemmerer (1996) reported correlations with neuroticism and extraversion on two separate occasions. Average cross-sectional correlations with neuroticism were: satisfaction with the work content –0.27, pay satisfaction –0.05, security satisfaction –0.24, supervisor satisfaction –0.18, coworker satisfaction –0.27, and workload satisfaction –0.18. For extraversion, those values were +0.04, –0.03, +0.08, +0.02, +0.20, and +0.08, respectively. As emphasized in chapters 2 and 4, well-being that is specific to a single facet of a person's environment is particularly affected by that environmental facet itself. Correlations of facet satisfaction with predictors such as personality traits are thus expected generally to be low, because that narrow form of well-being is particularly driven by the targeted aspect of the environment in question. Thus, for instance, the correlation between neuroticism and pay satisfaction in the already described study averaged only –0.05, as pay level itself (rather than personality) strongly determines that pay-linked form of satisfaction. Similarly, extraversion was unrelated in the study to most facet satisfactions, but it was significantly linked to the conceptually related satisfaction with coworkers.

Research has also asked about job-related well-being as a function of continuing dispositions in the form of positive affectivity (PA) and negative affectivity (NA). As indicated earlier, those are often tapped through scales of extraversion and neuroticism, respectively, although the constructs were originally conceptualized more broadly (e.g., Watson & Clark, 1984). In a meta-analysis of findings with several different personality scales, Connolly and Viswesvaran (2000) found average uncorrected correlations of overall job satisfaction with PA and NA of +0.41 and –0.27, respectively; the meta-analysis by Thoresen et al. (2003) yielded average uncorrected values of +0.28 and –0.28; in the review by Bruk-Lee et al. (2005), average correlations with PA and NA were +0.41 and –0.25; and in a Japanese sample those values were +0.64 and –0.33 (Piccolo et al., 2005). Averaged across four analyses, the correlation between NA and overall job satisfaction was –0.31 in research by Dormann et al. (2006). For satisfaction with personal growth opportunities, Munz, Huelsman, Konold, and McKinney (1996) reported correlations with PA and NA, respectively of +0.62 and –0.33. It is clear that job satisfaction is significantly linked to those aspects of personality.

Watson and Slack (1993) examined associations of this kind longitudinally, with personality scales administered 2 years before the measurement of well-being. Correlations with subsequent overall job satisfaction were +0.29 (PA) and –0.09 (NA) across that period. For (facet) satisfaction with the work itself (a variable that is significantly correlated with overall job satisfaction), the 2-year longitudinal values were +0.42 and –0.32, respectively. Staw, Bell, and Clausen (1986) reported longitudinal analyses across some 30 years. Independent observers' ratings of positive affective disposition from data provided during adolescence were found to be correlated at +0.26 with self-reported overall job satisfaction when employees were in their forties; the concurrent correlation (when positive disposition and job satisfaction were both measured in adulthood) was +0.40. Employees' dispositional positive affectivity and negative affectivity were rated by "significant others" in the study by Judge and Ilies (2004). Those independent ratings of the personality traits were found to be correlated with employees' own reports of overall job satisfaction +0.35 and –0.16. There is thus a variety of evidence for the trait-state association of PA and NA with job-related well-being. The pattern is consistent across time, and with separate persons' recording of trait and state.

Strongest correlations between personality and subjective well-being are expected when trait and state are measured in similar terms that differ only in time-span. In that way, Brief et al. (1988) found a high correlation of +0.57 between trait negative affectivity and state negative affect at work during the previous week, tapping the same kind of construct but with different time perspectives. Substantial associations with NA are also expected for the second well-being axis of Figure 2.2, from anxiety to comfort. For that axis, content overlap between the trait and (low values of) the state is greater than for the state variable of satisfaction (axis 1, considered earlier). Jex and Spector (1996) reported a correlation of trait negative affectivity with job-related (state) anxiety of +0.43, against only –0.21 for job satisfaction. The same correlations were +0.32 and –0.18 longitudinally across 15 months in a separate sample (Spector & O'Connell, 1994). In research by van Rijswijk et al. (2004), trait neuroticism was correlated at +0.59 and –0.24 with job-related emotional exhaustion (mainly tapping low levels of well-being on axis 2; see chap. 2) and overall job satisfaction (axis 1), respectively. For trait anxiety, those two correlations were +0.45 and –0.34 in a study by de Jonge et al. (2001). Dispositional negative affectivity is thus more linked to well-being axis 2 than to axis 1, at least as axis 2 has typically been measured with an emphasis on its low values.

Both negative and positive affects were studied in combined measures along well-being axes 2 and 3 by Totterdell et al. (2006). Trait neuroticism was found to be equally correlated with job-related anxiety–comfort (–0.44) and job-related depression–enthusiasm (–0.45), both scored so that higher values represent raised well-being. Job-related emotional exhaustion (primarily reflecting well-being axis 2) was studied by Zellars and Perrewé (2001). They found correlations with neuroticism, extraversion, and agreeableness of +0.48, −0.24, and −0.24, respectively. The meta-analysis of previous findings by Thoresen et al. (2003) yielded average uncorrected correlations with job-related emotional exhaustion of +0.48 from employee neuroticism and −0.20 from extraversion. That form of low well-being was correlated at +0.56 with dispositional negative affectivity in research by Grandey et al. (2004). Cherry (1984) recorded a significant correlation between neuroticism scores and job-related strain measured as long as 16 years later, but an r value was not cited.

Job-related emotional exhaustion was measured on two occasions by Houkes et al. (2003). The synchronous correlation with negative affectivity was +0.58 on each occasion; between measurement occasions, the correlation was +0.47 with NA recorded a year earlier. Both the synchronous and longitudinal associations remained significant despite statistical controls for other job and personal variables. Job-related forms of well-being axis 3 (from depression to enthusiasm) have rarely been studied in relation to personality. However, for job-related depression in the past 30 days (low scores on the third axis), Heinisch and Jex (1997) reported a correlation with trait negative affectivity of +0.52.

Among other stable dispositions (in addition to the Big Five and positive and negative affectivity) that have been studied in relation to job-related happiness or unhappiness is employees' sense of coherence (see the earlier description). Höge and Büssing (2004) found a correlation of −0.61 between sense of coherence and a broad measure of job-related strain; this remained significant despite statistical control for negative affectivity. Dispositional optimism is another personality attribute that is linked to job-related well-being. This general tendency to expect favorable experiences and outcomes was found by Aryee et al. (2005) to be correlated at +0.37 with overall job satisfaction. Jex and Spector (1996) reported average optimism correlations across two samples of +0.18 and −0.31 with job satisfaction and job-related anxiety, respectively. The correlation between trait anxiety and optimism was −0.57 in that research, and −0.54 in the study by Totterdell et al. (2006). Totterdell and colleagues also measured job-related anxiety–comfort and depression–enthusiasm (axes 2 and 3 in Fig. 2.2), finding correlations with dispositional optimism of +0.37 and +0.63, respectively (where higher scores on those axes indicate higher well-being).

Overall job satisfaction is also linked to employees' core self-evaluations. That broad personality construct (embracing neuroticism, locus of control, self-efficacy and self-esteem; see earlier) was correlated with job satisfaction +0.45 on average across two American samples in research by Judge et al. (2003), +0.46 in another American sample by Best, Stapleton, and Downey (2005), and +0.49 in a Japanese sample studied by Piccolo et al. (2005). Measuring job satisfaction 2 months later than core self-evaluations, Judge et al. (2005) found a correlation of +0.38. In Rode's (2004) study, a longitudinal correlation across 3 years was also significant despite controls for several job and personal variables. In a secondary analysis of previously collected data (Judge, Bono, & Locke, 2000), a measure of core self-evaluations (but not originally using that term) taken when employees were in their teens was correlated at +0.27 with their job satisfaction 30 years later. When the personality measure was again administered 10 years before the job satisfaction measure, the correlation was +0.43. The latter association remained significant despite statistical control for variations in job complexity.

Dispositional proactivity (looking for and acting on opportunities, showing initiative, and being persistent) was correlated at +0.37 with overall job satisfaction in research by Aryee et al. (2005). However, a scale of self-reported personal initiative emphasizing short-term action was associated at only +0.10 with overall job satisfaction in research by Frese, Fay, Hilburger, Leng, and Tag (1997). Another personality variable of potential interest in this section is individualism–collectivism (see the cultural themes explored in chap. 10). Employees with a more collectivist orientation have a greater concern for harmony and interdependence with others. In two Chinese samples, employees' collectivism was on average found to be correlated at +0.22 with overall job satisfaction (Hui, Yee, & Eastman, 1995), but this association appears not to have been examined in Western societies.

In considering domain-specific well-being, the focus in this chapter has been on the domain of paid employment, for example, reviewing research into job satisfaction or job-related anxiety. Another important domain identified in chapter 2 is the person himself or herself. Domain-specific happiness of that kind has been examined in terms of self-esteem, which is also significantly associated with certain aspects of personality. For instance, across three samples of students, Watson et al. (2002) reported average correlations of self-esteem with neuroticism, extraversion, openness to experience, agreeableness, and conscientiousness of –0.61, +0.44, +0.22, +0.20, and +0.36, respectively.

In overview, it is clear that happiness is in part a function of stable characteristics of a person himself or herself. Psychologists' research has usually focused on dispositions of personality, and some patterns of overlap are now established. Other continuing attributes are likely also to be important. For example, abilities of cognitive and other kinds might affect the ways in which people approach and respond to certain situations. Ganzach (1998) asked about overall job satisfaction in relation to a broad index of intelligence. Across a range of jobs of varying complexity, the bivariate correlation was only –0.02. Possible statistical moderation (such that intelligence and subjective well-being are differently interrelated in different kinds of jobs) are considered in the next chapter.

Other possible correlates of happiness include particular abilities in the form of practical problem solving or social competence, as individuals who are more able in those respects are likely to deal more effectively with complex situations. For example, more socially competent people may more readily move through interpersonally threatening episodes into social encounters that enhance rather than continue to impair subjective well-being. These issues deserve more research attention than they have so far received.

Within the vitamin analogy set out in chapters 4 to 8, we might also ask about between-person variations in the shape of the expected curve linking environmental features with happiness. As illustrated in Figures 4.1 and 4.2, environment–happiness associations are expected to be nonlinear, with (for instance) a downturn in happiness at very high levels of "additional decrement" features. It may be that these curves differ in systematic ways for individuals with different personality traits. For example, the high-level downturn for externally generated goals ("vitamin" 3) might occur sooner for more neurotic individuals, as they experience a raised level of demands as more threatening than do low-neurotic individuals. Conversely, that downturn might occur later in relation to environmental clarity (feature 5) for people who are more open to experience and who thus more highly value situations that are ambiguous.

Finally in this section, we should consider the involvement of personality in overlaps between different kinds of happiness. Given that dispositions can be linked to several forms of subjective well-being, it is likely that those dispositions are also involved in within-person associations between well-being of different kinds. For example, chapter 2 reviewed evidence that employees' life satisfaction and job satisfaction were significantly intercorrelated. Possible explanations include the spillover of affect from one domain to another, but also may involve overarching dispositional consistency.

Heller et al. (2002) examined this possibility, by comparing the association between life satisfaction and job satisfaction before and after statistical controls for several attributes of personality. The uncontrolled intercorrelation of +0.46 (average across two occasions) was reduced to +0.30 after controlling for neuroticism, extraversion, and conscientiousness together, +0.28 after controlling for core self-evaluations, +0.31 after controlling for positive affectivity and negative affectivity, and +0.27 after controlling for all of those dispositions. It thus seems that personality attributes contribute to between-level consistency in happiness, but that other causal processes are also involved, because the association between life and job satisfaction remained statistically significant despite the controls. As described in chapter 2, findings by Judge and Watanabe (1993) suggested mutual influence across levels: Life satisfaction and job satisfaction have an impact on each other.

THE INHERITANCE OF HAPPINESS

The importance to happiness of continuing aspects of a person has also been explored in terms of possible genetic influences. Perhaps subjective well-being is in part inherited? Arvey, Bouchard, Segal, and Abraham (1989) studied the job satisfaction of monozygotic (identical) twins who had been reared apart. Pairs of such twins brought up together share the same genetic structure and principal environmental influences. However, when reared apart their environment is varied but their genetic makeup remains identical. Partitioning between-individual variance into environmental and genetic components, Arvey et al. (1989) inferred from between-twin comparisons that approximately 30% of the variance in overall job satisfaction and in intrinsic job satisfaction was associated with genetic factors, but that extrinsic satisfaction (directed at contextual aspects of a job) was unaffected by inheritance. Two replications of this study were reported by Arvey, McCall, Bouchard, Taubman, and Cavanaugh (1994). Parallel investigations into subjective well-being that is context-free have been reviewed by Diener et al. (1999), with heritability found in general to be at about the level cited earlier for overall job satisfaction; an even higher value (44%) was computed for context-free well-being by Røysamb et al. (2003).

Such statistically based inferences depend on several assumptions, which may not always be completely met. For instance, a pair of twins defined as "reared apart" may in fact have lived in the same environment for several initial months or years, or their separate environments may be similar to each other. There is thus room to question some details of these studies (Cropanzano & James, 1990; Diener et al., 1999; see also Bouchard, Arvey, Keller, & Segal, 1992), but the general conclusion is not in doubt: Happiness is subject to a significant genetic influence. Parallel research has revealed genetic effects also for many other personal features—cognitive abilities, personality, vocational interests, and broad orientations such as religious or political conservatism and racial prejudice (e.g., Arvey & Bouchard, 1994; Loehlin, 1992).

How should the genetic contribution to subjective well-being be explained? In part, the effect might be a direct one: Some people are born with a greater propensity to be happy than are others. However, indirect effects are also likely through inheritance-linked cognitive and personality attributes and through preferred behaviors that encourage or discourage happiness. For example, individuals with similar inherited attributes may tend to move into similar jobs, with similar potentials for happiness or unhappiness. Some similarity of job content between separated twins was recorded by Arvey et al. (1989). In that way, a genetic influence on job satisfaction may arise in part from inherited abilities and behavioral tendencies, which in turn lead people into jobs with certain implications for their happiness. With respect to relevant job characteristics, Behrman, Hrubec, Taubman, and Wales (1980) concluded that genetic influences account for about 35% of the variance in people's occupational status and about 45% of the variance in their earnings at maturity.

Personality mediation of inherited variation in well-being was examined by Ilies and Judge (2003). In secondary analyses of previous summary data, they investigated the extent to which Big Five personality traits and (in a separate analysis) positive and negative affectivity accounted for genetic differences in overall job satisfaction. They concluded that personality features explained significant proportions of the genetic variance in that form of satisfaction—around 24% and 45% in separate analyses of the Big Five traits and PA and NA, respectively.

Although percentage allocations to environmental and genetic influences should be viewed as approximations rather than exact values, it seems appropriate to conclude from twin studies that genetic effects (although significant) are generally smaller than is the influence of environmental features (e.g., Arvey & Bouchard, 1994; Bouchard et al., 1992). However, research into potential genetic effects has typically left unmeasured features of the environment. The participants in published studies were in many different jobs and settings, but those were not specified in research accounts and we do not know how similar or different they were within a twin pair. Although twin research has contrasted genetic sources, analyses have so far not examined differences or similarities in possible environmental influences. It is of course difficult to record and summarize inputs from a person's environment across the years prior to his or her participation in a research investigation.

A similar uncertainty is present in research more generally into well-being as a function of personality traits. It appears that all published investigations have combined within their sample individuals holding a variety of jobs, rather than seeking to statistically control that form of environmental influence or to hold it constant by studying a single job (Staw & Cohen-Charash, 2005). Published bivariate correlations between a personality attribute and, for example, job satisfaction are therefore also determined by unmeasured between-person variations in job characteristics. To record an uncontaminated association between personality and subjective well-being, we ideally require that environmental inputs are the same for everyone.

COMBINED EFFECTS: ENVIRONMENT AND PERSONALITY

Nevertheless, correlations with happiness from both job content and personality traits have been shown throughout the book to be widely significant. That is found in investigations that examine separately only the job (chaps. 4 to 8) or the person (this chapter), and also in bivariate analyses of job features and personality within the same study (e.g., Agho et al., 1993; Chen & Spector, 1991; Grandey et al., 2004; Höge & Büssing, 2004; Judge et al., 1998, 2000; Levin & Stokes, 1989; Munz et al., 1996). In addition to examining those bivariate correlations on their own, it is desirable to learn about personality–happiness associations and environment–happiness associations together in combined analyses of traits and job features together.

Such analyses have often indicated that the two categories of variable, in the person and in the environment, contribute to subjective well-being in addition to the other. For example, both employee extraversion and poor social relationships (low values of job feature 6) made independent contributions to job-related affect in research by Dijkstra et al. (2005). Agho et al. (1993) found in multiple regression analysis that trait positive affectivity was significantly associated with overall job satisfaction in addition to significant inputs from several job and demographic features. In research by Chen and Spector (1991), negative affectivity remained significant in relation to overall job satisfaction and job-related strain over and above significant associations with job features. Similar results, with both job features and negative affectivity making significant independent contributions in multiple regressions, were (for instance) reported for overall job satisfaction and intrinsic job satisfaction by Levin and Stokes (1989), and for job-related emotional exhaustion by Houkes et al. (2003), Grandey et al. (2004), and Höge and Büssing (2004).

Näswall et al. (2005) included affectivity traits in analyses with demographic and job-related variables. Their main focus was on perceived job insecurity (an aspect of feature 11), which was itself associated with overall job satisfaction (on well-being axis 1) and job-related strain (a negative index on axis 2). In combined analyses, separately for each aspect of well-being, both the personality and job variables were important. Positive affectivity and job insecurity were both significant in relation to job satisfaction (but negative affectivity was not), and for job-related strain significant predictors included NA and insecurity (but not PA).

That difference (in which PA is associated more with satisfaction, and NA is linked more to negative forms of well-being) may be a general one, possibly arising from divergence in the customary direction of item-wording in the two sets of measures (Burke, Brief, & George, 1993; Munz et al., 1996; Thoresen et al., 2003). It appears generally desirable in research to examine the full spread of a well-being axis (e.g., from anxiety to comfort), rather than restricting attention to only one pole (e.g., anxiety alone).

The compound personality construct of core self-evaluations was shown by Judge et al. (1998, 2000) to be significantly associated with overall job satisfaction in combination with an impact of intrinsic job characteristics; that joint pattern was also present despite the use of independent raters' assessments of either job characteristics or well-being. A significant combined pattern was also found by Best et al. (2005), with job satisfaction linked both to core self-evaluations and to over-restrictive organizational regulations. In Rode's (2004) investigation, core self-evaluations measured 3 years earlier and current job content were both related to overall job satisfaction in combined analyses. Ferguson, Daniels, and Jones (2006) presented a meta-analysis of previous studies, creating two categories of variable, either "negatively oriented" personality traits (neuroticism, negative affectivity, etc.)

or negative job characteristics. In relation to context-free distress measured at a subsequent time, both sets of variables (negative personality features and negative job characteristics) were found independently (i.e., over and above the other one) to be significantly predictive.

Happiness is undoubtedly a function of both environmental and personal variables at the same time, but we are some way from understanding the nature and varying strength of incremental effects in this area. It is now important in the same study to gather both kinds of information, about job and other environmental features as well as about aspects of the person, to complement the traditional emphasis on only one of those sets of variables.

PERSONALITY AND EXPOSURE TO ENVIRONMENTAL FEATURES

The third question of this and the previous chapter concerns individuals' exposure to different environmental conditions. Are certain kinds of people more exposed than others to particular features in the environment? If so, differences in their happiness might derive partly or wholly from the impact of those different features, rather than directly from associated personal attributes. One possible explanation of the personality–happiness link is thus of the third-variable kind considered in chapter 8: Environmental features (which may covary with personality) might be causally important, rather than (or in addition to, as described earlier) the studied dispositions themselves.

Relations between personality and job content have been reported by Bowling, Beehr, and Schwader (2005), Chay (1993), Heinisch and Jex (1997), Jones et al. (2005), Moyle (1995), Parkes (1990), Schaubroeck et al. (1992), Totterdell et al. (2006), van Rijswijk et al. (2004), Wayne et al. (2004), and Zellars and Perrewé (2001). Each of those covered a different set of perceived job features; their studies are referenced alphabetically in the summary that follows as studies 1 to 11, respectively.

Research has concentrated mainly on the dispositions of neuroticism and extraversion. Neuroticism (N) was found to be correlated with perceived opportunity for personal control in one's job (feature 1) on average –0.23 (in studies 2, 4, 5, and 8) and with job demands (feature 3) on average +0.16 (studies 2 to 6, 8, 9, and 11). For particular aspects of that third environmental characteristic, average correlations of N with role conflict at work were +0.21 (studies 3, 7, and 11) and with work–family conflict +0.36 (studies 9 and 10). Grzywacz and Marks

(2000), Wayne et al. (2004), and Aryee et al. (2005) found that neu-roticism was significantly associated in separate analyses with both directions of conflict: from work to family and from family to work. Correlation values were cited only by the latter two sets of authors, averaging +0.36 in both directions. For facilitation (rather than con-flict) between the two roles, Grzywacz and Marks observed no associ-ation with neuroticism, and correlations were also low in studies by Wayne et al. (2004) and Aryee et al. (2005), averaging –0.07 and –0.12 with work-to-family and family-to-work facilitation, respectively. Van Rijswijk et al. (2004) found that employees' neuroticism was corre-lated at +0.26 with perceived home demands.

For job variety (the fourth primary feature), Schaubroeck et al. (1992) reported a correlation with neuroticism of –0.04. Low environmental clarity (feature 5) includes role ambiguity, perceptions of which were found to be correlated with N on average at +0.23 in studies 3, 4, 7, and 11. For social support (an aspect of contact with others, feature 6), the average correlation with neuroticism was –0.20 (from all studies except 9 and 10). In additional investigations, Judge et al. (1998, 2000) studied employees' perceptions of a compound of intrinsic job characteristics. The average correlation of intrinsic job content with neuroticism across four samples was –0.29. More neurotic and less neurotic employees thus tend to be in jobs with partly different characteristics, at least as those are perceived by job holders themselves.

Some differences have also been found for extraversion (E), although less research has so far been published. Correlations in the studies listed earlier between perceived job features and extraversion were singly or on average as follows: opportunity for personal control +0.26 (study 2), externally generated goals –0.02 (studies 2 and 11), role conflict –0.05 (studies 7 and 11), work–family conflict –0.06 (study 10), variety +0.03 (study 7), role ambiguity –0.12 (studies 7 and 11), and social support +0.25 (studies 1, 2, 7, and 11). The analysis by Grzywacz and Marks (2000) indicated that both male and female extraverts reported more facilitation from work to family and from family to work than did intro-verts; in the study by Wayne et al. (2004) those correlations (for men and women combined) were +0.22 and +0.24.

Wayne et al. (2004) also examined other Big Five traits in relation to experienced work–family conflict. Reported conflict between work and family (averaged here across both directions of conflict) was cor-related at –0.13, –0.05, and –0.18 with agreeableness, openness to experience, and conscientiousness, respectively. For facilitation between the two roles, those average r values were +0.18, +0.18, and

+0.12, respectively. Zellars and Perrewé (2001) found that agreeableness was correlated at –0.04 with reported demands, –0.25 with role conflict, –0.22 with role ambiguity, and on average +0.10 with forms of social support. In the study by Bowling et al. (2005), agreeableness correlated at +0.29 on average with the receipt of positive work and nonwork support.

Further research is clearly desirable in this field. However, it appears that high scorers on neuroticism scales see their job's characteristics as more negative than do low scorers: less personal discretion, more demands, greater conflict and ambiguity, less support from others, and lower complexity in general. Extraversion seems at present to be linked only to perceptions of two primary features (more control opportunity and greater social support) and also to more facilitation between work and family. Note that (consistent with the point made earlier) significant associations with E tend to concern the perception of positive features, whereas for N the features are usually negative. However, no research has examined a full set of job characteristics in relation to a wide range of personality attributes.

Parallel findings have been reported for negative affectivity (NA) and positive affectivity (PA). As indicated earlier, those dispositions are closely linked with neuroticism and extraversion, respectively, and some researchers have in fact assessed NA and PA through scales of N and E. Relevant data have been located in studies by Chen and Spector (1991), de Jonge et al. (2001), Grandey et al. (2004), Houkes et al. (2003), Judge and Locke (1993), Munz et al. (1996), and Spector, Jex, and Chen (1995); these are referenced next in alphabetical sequence as studies 1 to 7, respectively.

Almost all research has concerned negative affectivity alone. Average or individual NA correlations with key job features are: opportunity for personal control –0.24 (studies 2, 3, 4, 6, and 7), externally generated goals +0.15 (studies 1 and 2), role conflict +0.23 (study 1), task identity –0.20 (studies 6 and 7), skill variety –0.13 (studies 6 and 7), role ambiguity +0.26 (study 1), feedback –0.24 (studies 6 and 7), social support –0.30 (studies 1, 2, and 4), and task significance –0.20 (studies 6 and 7). Examining perceived job insecurity (an aspect of feature 11), Näswall et al. (2005) found correlations with NA of +0.26 and with PA of –0.19. Those negative correlations with NA are reflected in findings about more comprehensive measures of job content. For perceived job scope (see chap. 8), the correlation with NA averaged –0.34 in studies 4 and 7; for a summary measure of perceived intrinsic job characteristics, that correlation was –0.24 (study 5). Study

5 also found that employees' positive affectivity was correlated at +0.40 with perceived intrinsic job characteristics.

The NA pattern parallels that for the overlapping construct of neuroticism, discussed earlier: High-NA employees tend to see the characteristics of their jobs as less positive than do low-NA employees. A similar trend has been found for core self-evaluations, dispositional optimism, and sense of coherence. A compound measure of core self-evaluations (covering neuroticism, locus of control, self-efficacy, and self-esteem; see earlier) was found by Judge et al. (2000) to be correlated at +0.39 with employees' ratings of the complexity of their job. For dispositional optimism, Spector et al. (1995) reported correlations with perceived opportunity for control of +0.15, task identity of +0.14, task variety of +0.17, feedback of +0.18, and task significance of +0.19; with overall job complexity that correlation was +0.22. In the study by Totterdell et al. (2006), trait optimism was correlated at +0.35 with employee-perceived opportunity for control, −0.05 with job demands, and +0.41 with social support. For sense of coherence (discussed earlier), a correlation of −0.34 with a summary self-rating of job stressors was found by Höge and Büssing (2004).

Are personality traits linked to the objective nature of jobs in those ways, so that people with different personality traits are exposed to partly different stimuli from the environment? Or are the personality-linked differences described earlier due to a perceptual bias, such that individuals with higher negative affectivity or similar traits view their world more negatively, even though such a difference may not exist in reality? Or are both possibilities important? It is desirable to examine whether personality-linked differences in job content are also found when that content is measured independently of the job holder himself or herself. Spector et al. (1995) used the limited information in written job descriptions to derive independent ratings of several job features. Associations between job holders' negative affectivity (NA) and job content independently assessed in this manner were lower than for self-ratings of content, but they usually remained significant. Correlations with NA were −0.14 for opportunity for personal control, −0.10 for task identity, −0.19 for skill variety, and −0.14 for overall complexity. For feedback and task significance (job features that depend heavily on individual perceptions, and are thus difficult to rate from a job description alone), associations of employee NA with independent job ratings were nonsignificant ($r = -0.03$ and -0.09, respectively).

Spector et al. (1995) also examined independently rated job content in relation to employees' dispositional optimism. Correlations of optimism were +0.22 with independently assessed opportunity for control, +0.14 with task identity, +0.26 with task variety, and +0.22 with overall complexity. For feedback and task significance, correlations between independent job ratings and employees' optimism were again low: −0.02 and +0.16.

Attributes of the environment were also identified independently in (nonemployment) research by Suh et al. (1996). Respondents summarized clearly defined events in their life in the previous four years by checking items identified by independent judges as either positive or negative (e.g., getting married or losing a job). Neuroticism was found to be linked to reports of prior negative events (average r across two measurement points = +0.24), and extraversion was associated with reports of prior positive events (average r = +0.19). However, the causal sequence between life events and personality remains unclear in this investigation, with simultaneous cross-sectional measurement of both personality and recalled exposure to events. Some longitudinal evidence is considered in the next chapter.

Judge and colleagues sought to avoid problems of common-method variance by measuring employees' personality through judgments made by people who know them well. Across three samples, neuroticism assessed by "significant others" was on average correlated −0.15 with employees' perceptions of intrinsic characteristics in their job (Judge et al., 1998). For independent ratings of employees' core self-evaluations, the correlation with employee-perceived intrinsic characteristics was +0.23 (Judge et al., 2000).

However, causal interpretation of those findings remains unclear. It is possible that the association between independent ratings of personality and employee-reported job content is influenced by the same personality-linked bias in the perception of job features that might be present in studies based entirely on self-reports (discussed earlier). That perceptual bias could still affect findings if the independent ratings accurately represent employees' personality, which itself remains operative in perception. It is desirable to avoid that possible distortion by measuring job content in a manner that cannot be influenced by the personality of the job holder. Estimating job complexity from current job titles, Judge et al. (2000) reported a correlation with employees' core self-evaluations assessed independently during childhood of +0.22.

There is thus some evidence that employees of certain kinds (differing primarily in neuroticism, extraversion, and similar traits) tend to be in jobs that diverge in some ways from the jobs of other employees.

That is shown in a few (but not yet enough) investigations that avoid possible perceptual bias by obtaining independent assessments of job content. Nevertheless, most studies in this section have depended on self-reports of job features, and observed correlations between personality traits and job content may in those cases derive in part from a perceptual influence. More investigations that reduce common-method variance are clearly required.

Some links between personality and exposure to particular job features may be due in part to processes of self-selection into particular settings or to individuals' own shaping of environmental conditions. For example, exposure to environmental feature 6 in terms of social support is significantly linked with employees' own supportive behavior to others; the average correlation between (self-reported) support received and support given was +0.53 in the study by Bowling et al. (2005). Furthermore, it was the more extraverted employees who gave greater amounts of support to others. It may thus be that those individuals (primarily extraverts) who more offer support to colleagues increase the amount of support they receive, with associated gains in happiness. In that case, extraverts would tend to be more exposed to this positive form of job feature 6 because of their own behavior. Additional person–environment possibilities of that kind are considered in the next chapter.

12

Moderator Effects and Differential Salience

Chapter 11 has shown that some continuing personality dispositions are reflected in states of happiness or unhappiness. Furthermore, people with certain personality attributes may be exposed to
environments that differ in some respects from the environments of
other people.

EXPLAINING DISPOSITIONAL EFFECTS

How might we explain those two kinds of association—between personality traits and happiness, and between traits and the environment
to which one is exposed? Examining negative affectivity, Spector et al.
(2000) drew attention to six possible causal mechanisms. Based on their
framework, personality links with happiness and with environmental
exposure might be explained in the following ways. The suggested alternatives are expected to operate in combination, and the mode of that
combination is likely to vary between settings and studies. Separate
examination is needed of the two kinds of link: from traits to subjective
well-being, and from traits to environmental exposure.

1. The Perception Mechanism. A first possibility is in terms of perceptual differences. Perhaps high scorers on certain personality scales
see the world differently from low scorers, provoking different levels

of well-being which are at least in part independent of environmental reality. As one example, Staw et al. (1986) suggested that "people may bring a positive or negative disposition to the work setting, process information about the job in a way that is consistent with this disposition, and then experience job satisfaction or dissatisfaction as a result" (p. 61). As described in chapter 11, the negative and positive emphases of neuroticism and extraversion respectively are such that some perceptual influences on experienced well-being are very likely.

What about the second kind of link, between personality and exposure to specific environmental features? The fact that correlations between employees' job features and certain of their personality dispositions are higher when both variables are rated by employees themselves, rather than when the environment is independently measured (see chap. 11), suggests that perceptual processes are important contributors to observed associations between personality and environmental exposure. On the other hand, measured associations between personality dispositions and independently rated job content may themselves be artificially reduced, because estimates of job features by nonincumbents can have restricted validity (see chap. 8), and evidence about personality and independently assessed job content remains limited. It thus not yet clear whether associations between, say, neuroticism and exposure to particular job features derive from different perceptions of the environment by high and low scorers. More systematic comparisons are needed between the associations of personality with actual environments and with those environments as perceived.

2. The Responsivity Mechanism.   Second, high scorers on a personality dimension may differ from low scorers in their happiness reactions to the same environmental input. This possibility (a difference in affective response, not merely in perception as above) is sometimes described in terms of between-person variations in "susceptibility." It seems particularly relevant for personality-linked outcomes in terms of high or low well-being, rather than with respect to personality-based differences in exposure to environments. For example, happiness might differ between individuals in part because extraverts are particularly responsive in happiness terms to the presence of rewards (e.g., Rusting & Larsen, 1997) or because neurotic individuals are especially reactive to stressful stimuli (e.g., Bolger & Zuckerman, 1995; Parkes, 1990).

In that case, we would expect to observe significant statistical moderation, such that the strength of some associations between job features and job holders' happiness varies between people; for individuals who are more susceptible to the job feature, correlations should be greater. Research into that possibility is reviewed shortly, when it is shown that environment–happiness associations do tend to be stronger when the personal salience of a studied environmental feature is greater.

Between-person differences in responsivity might also be viewed in a more comprehensive manner, examining behavioral as well as perceptual themes. For example, some people respond routinely to a particular kind of situation with behaviors that are different from those of other people. Consistent differences in responsivity of a behavioral kind can shape subsequent developments and thus subjective well-being. For example, certain kinds of coping behavior may solve a problem, whereas others increase the threat. Links between variations in happiness-related behavioral responsivity and personality dispositions deserve more empirical investigation.

3. The Selection Mechanism.   High scorers and low scorers on a personality scale may select themselves into (or out of) different settings, in consequence creating different environmental inputs, which themselves yield different levels of happiness for the two subgroups. In parallel with that process, choices about people are made by organizations. Employers might differentially select or retain individuals according to particular personality characteristics, giving rise to different environments and thus to different happiness levels for different kinds of people. In both cases (self-selection and selection by others) significant associations would be expected between personality and happiness and between personality and environmental exposure, because different personality types have become located in jobs with different happiness-inducing characteristics. In those terms, a significant correlation between job content and subjective well-being would derive at least in part from selection processes that occurred before the measurement of environmental features. This possibility is considered shortly.

4. The Context-Creation Mechanism.   A fourth, linked possibility is that high scorers may behave in certain ways that create or enhance certain environmental conditions. "For example, high NAs might get into conflicts with others more often, do a worse job of managing their workflow, and perform worse on the job than low NAs. These behaviors would result in a higher level of job stressors for high-NA people" (Spector et al., 2000, p. 88). More generally, "the effects of personality appear ... to include behaviors that increase or decrease the probability of rewarding events" (Diener et al., 1999, p. 282). A possible sequence of that kind was illustrated at the end of the last chapter, such that the behavior of extraverts may encourage others to provide them with more social support. Another relevant behavior is job performance. Certain dispositional characteristics might give rise to good or bad performance, with associated differences in rewards or punishments that can affect happiness (Staw & Cohen-Charash, 2005). If disposition-linked behaviors influence happiness-inducing or happiness-reducing environmental conditions in those ways, differences in happiness will tend to follow. Other illustrations are cited shortly.

Although the present emphasis is on dispositions in terms of personality characteristics, Table 11.1 drew attention to conceptual overlaps between personality and other continuing psychological attributes, particularly people's values and motives. It was pointed out that constructs of personality, values, and motives all embody between-person differences in the perceived attractiveness of certain environmental features. Given that people tend to behave in ways that are intended to increase attractive outcomes, their current environment will often have been determined in part by behaviors arising from value-laden dispositions of many kinds, not merely from personality alone.

The third and fourth possible mechanisms (selection and context-creation) overlap with each other, in that creating particular environmental conditions (mechanism 4) in part requires that a person chooses to enter the environment or behavior setting in question (mechanism 3). Both possibilities would receive support from significant longitudinal patterns in which job content was predicted by earlier assessments of personality.

A few studies have examined that longitudinal possibility. For example, both de Jonge et al. (2001) and Houkes et al. (2003) showed that measures of negative affectivity significantly predicted perceived job demands and social support in a job one year later. In research with students, Bolger and Zuckerman (1995) examined diary reports of interpersonal conflicts across a two-week period after the measurement of neuroticism. Subsequent conflict was reported significantly more often by high-N individuals than by those with lower scores. In that respect, Einarsen and Mikkelsen (2003) considered the possibility that behaviors associated with certain personality traits might predispose some people to be bullied at work; however, direct evidence was not presented.

Headey and Wearing (1989) examined neuroticism and extraversion as predictors of future experienced events. In a community sample across 6 years, they found that more neurotic individuals were more likely to report negative events in future years, and that extraversion predicted subsequent reports of favorable events. (Links between N and positive events and between E and negative events were non-significant.) Magnus, Diener, Fujita, and Pavot (1993) also measured inputs from the environment through reports of experienced events. They found that neuroticism significantly predicted the occurrence of negative (but not positive) events in the next 4 years ($r = +0.23$). The longitudinal correlation between extraversion and positive events was +0.24, with that value nonsignificant for negative events. In addition, although the correlation between the Big Five trait of conscientious-ness and future positive events was +0.25, links with future events (either positive or negative) for agreeableness and openness to expe-rience were nonsignificant (see also Suh et al., 1996).

Longitudinal research by van Os, Park, and Jones (2001) studied only negative life events, examining the occurrence of those at ages 36 and 43 as a function of neuroticism and extraversion measured at age 16. Controlling for symptoms of anxiety and depression at the later occasion, neuroticism, but not extraversion, was significantly associ-ated with reports of negative events that occurred after more than 20 years. Together, these studies indicate that the importance in this respect of neuroticism and extraversion is restricted to either negative or positive events respectively. Furthermore, personality's influence on event exposure apparently does not extend to all kinds of trait.

Processes whereby different kinds of employees select themselves or become selected into systematically different environments have been illustrated within Schneider's (e.g., 1987) attraction–selection–attrition model. Schneider suggested three processes by which organizations become increasingly homogeneous across time. First, individuals are differentially attracted to certain kinds of organizational culture on the basis of their personal characteristics; second, during the organization's recruitment process applicants may be selected to match and sustain that culture on the basis of possessing similar characteristics; and third, individuals might leave the organization if they do not adequately fit within its culture. A key proposal of this model is that people prefer organizations that have characteristics similar to their own, particularly in terms of their personality (Schneider, Goldstein, & Smith, 1995).

The involvement of personality in organizational preference was demonstrated by Warr and Pearce (2004). They examined people's importance ratings of features of organizational culture (e.g., "there are clear rules and procedures to follow" or "things change very quickly") as a function of personality attributes. Significant associations were found between certain traits and conceptually similar culture preferences. For instance, a preference for working in organizations with a high-performance culture was stronger among people scoring more highly on scales representing the Big Five factor of conscientiousness. A similarly differentiated pattern was found in relation to Schein's (e.g., 1993) "career anchors," preferences for principal attributes of careers such as security and stability, entrepreneurial activity, or dedication to service, with significant associations observed with conceptually linked personality traits.

Those patterns support one part of the attraction–selection–attrition model, illustrating the process through which people are attracted to organizations that are similar to themselves. However, longitudinal research is still needed to examine more substantially the model's predictions. It is not yet known how strongly personality-related preferences give rise to actual self-selection, or to what extent individuals considered to be suited to an organization's culture are more likely to be selected and in turn choose to remain in that organization.

Longitudinal studies are also needed with respect to personality and differential self-selection into careers. A person's career provides an extended set of environments that influence his or her happiness over a period. However, research into career interests has mainly concerned cross-sectional associations between personality traits and vocational interests of particular kinds. The review by Tokar et al. (1998; see also chap. 11) drew attention to personality links with some of Holland's (e.g., 1997) interest types. For example, significant positive associations have been found between the trait of extraversion and vocational interests defined as enterprising and social, and between the trait of conscientiousness and interests that are conventional. It is likely that those personality-linked vocational preferences will lead to self-selection into different kinds of career, with corresponding variations in job content and consequences for individuals' happiness. However, many other variables (such as the availability of personality-related kinds of jobs) also affect the unfolding of careers, and possible impacts of personality still need investigation across time.

In general terms, this fourth (context-creation) mechanism envisages that people act in ways that modify their environments, which in turn have consequences for their happiness. Those actions are not always intentional, but purposeful examples occur in processes of "job crafting" (Wrzesniewski & Dutton, 2001). Within the constraints of their organizational role, individuals are likely to adjust their task activities and relationships with others, with linked changes in the way that they think about their job. It seems likely that particular forms of job crafting are associated with certain personality traits. For example, openness to experience may be accompanied by a shaping of one's work role to permit greater novelty-seeking, or high-neuroticism employees may modify their situation to restrict activities to comfortable routines. However, these possibilities remain in need of empirical exploration.

In overview, there are several reasons to expect that personality-based differences in processes of selection into, or creation of, current situations will result in environments that differ somewhat according to people's personality. Those environmental differences are likely in turn to yield variations in happiness. However, details have yet to be specified in empirical research.

Selection and context-creation mechanisms are expected also to operate for attributes other than personality and conceptually related variables (values and motives, as described above). For example, between-person variation in cognitive abilities is clearly linked to differential movement into jobs and careers of different kinds, and physical attributes such as strength or attractiveness also partly determine entry into certain kinds of work. As a result of these differences in entry, subsequent inputs from the environment (with potential impact on happiness) indirectly derive in part from the personal attributes in question. That person–situation–person process is a cyclical one across time; it now requires more intensive research investigation.

5. The Reverse-Causation Mechanism.   A fifth possible process in this section involves a reversal of causal priority. First, with respect to a possible connection between personality and level of happiness, personality traits may be malleable across time through the repeated occurrence of parallel short-term states. In that way, a repetition of happiness states, perhaps across several years, could come to influence certain attributes of personality. For instance, a sequence of anxiety states might contribute to longer term raised levels of neuroticism, or a long period of positive affect might increase extraversion or dispositional optimism.

A reverse sequence might also occur with respect to the second link considered in this section, between personality and the environment to which one is exposed. In that way, a personality trait might be modified by the environments that one has experienced. Rather than (or as well as) a personality trait leading to entry into a certain kind of environment, exposure to that environment over an extended time might bring about a changed level of personality disposition. In that case, an observed association between a personality trait and environmental exposure (here, to a certain job feature) would be due at least in part to the job feature having influenced the trait, rather than because personality moved the person into that environment.

These two possible influences (from happiness to personality, and from the environment to personality) are clearly difficult to examine empirically. They may have some significance as causal mechanisms extended across time, but research evidence is not yet available.

6. The Trait–State Mechanism. Finally, continuing traits of any kind are necessarily linked to conceptually related temporary states in particular episodes of activity. The nature of those states matches the disposition in question. As outlined in chapter 11, trait–state overlap ensures that periods of temporary unhappiness are present within dispositions such as neuroticism and negative affectivity. For example, "it is a defining feature of NA that people with high NA are more often in a negative mood" (Höge & Büssing, 2004, p. 397). Similarly, some aspects of extraversion, particularly its emphasis on surgency, entail that a continuing trait of that kind will be reflected in specific, localized instances of more positive well-being. As a result, a state of well-being in a given setting is in part a specific instance of a person's continuing disposition toward happiness or unhappiness.

Trait–state overlap is also necessarily present for other personality dimensions, in that particular behaviors and experiences in single episodes reflect the nature of more extended dispositions. However, the linked short-term states corresponding to a trait in those cases (e.g., within openness to experience) appear less directly to embody forms of well-being. Thus it is not clear how straightforward conceptual overlap of trait and state might bear on happiness states with respect to dispositions other than neuroticism and extraversion.

Nevertheless, a wider range of traits may be reflected indirectly in specific states of happiness because of personality's involvement in consistent patterns of cognitive processing. As described in chapter 9, mental comparisons with other people or situations, or against personal reference standards such as novelty or personal salience, can shape people's reactions to environmental inputs. Judgments with that impact on happiness derive in part from personality styles, so that some trait–state overlap may occur through the mediation of personality-linked judgment processes. Aspects of this possibility are explored later in the chapter.

In overview, it appears that all six personality-linked mechanisms are potentially important in this area: perception (mechanism 1), responsivity (2), selection (3), context-creation (4), reverse causation (5), and trait–state overlap (6). They operate in varying combinations to create the two outcomes considered in this and the previous chapter: happiness itself, and the environments to which people are exposed (here, aspects of job content).

For the second outcome, characteristics of a person's job, personality is likely to be important primarily through mechanisms 3 and 4: People may select themselves, or be selected, into certain environments, or they may create particular kinds of environmental characteristics. In addition, perceptual differences (mechanism 1) are likely to play a part in studies of job content which obtain employees' ratings of their job. However, very little research evidence is available to account for the associations observed between personality dispositions and individuals' exposure to particular kinds of environments.

For personality-linked causes of happiness, the first outcome considered in this section, all those mechanisms (perception, selection, and context-creation) appear to be important. Mechanisms 2 and 6 also deserve consideration, in that differential responsivity and trait–state mechanisms are also likely to contribute to the influence of personality on happiness. Mechanism 5 (reverse causation) may also operate as outlined above, but empirical investigation has not been reported. More generally, research in this field has been mainly cross-sectional, examining synchronous correlations rather than possible causal processes across time. Evidence about mechanisms is thus sparse, and more complex research designs are now required.

DIPOSITIONAL MODERATORS OF JOB–HAPPINESS ASSOCIATIONS

The previous two chapters asked through their fourth question whether employees' characteristics affect the strength of associations between job content and happiness. That moderator possibility is considered here with respect to personality dispositions. For example, is the correlation between opportunity for personal control in a job and an aspect of job-related well-being systematically larger for employees with certain types of personality than for others? Such a finding would suggest differential responsivity (mechanism 2 just described), but other processes may also be important. Two sets of studies are relevant. First are investigations into the possible moderating impact of personality traits of the kinds examined in the previous chapter, and second is research into the differing priority that people attach to particular job characteristics. Findings have been inconsistent in the first case, but personal salience is consistently found to be important.

Personality Attributes

In the first respect, job-based research in this area has mainly focused on neuroticism and other indicators of negative affectivity. The subjective well-being of employees with higher dispositional negative affectivity might be more affected by threatening job features than is the case for lower NA employees. Parkes (1990) viewed this possibility in terms of differential vulnerability or reactivity to environmental stressors, such that higher NA individuals might be more affected by environmental threat than are lower NA people. A significant moderated pattern of that kind was observed: Job demands were positively associated with context-free distress for more neurotic employees, but not for less neurotic people. However, that differential pattern was not present for the environmental feature of social support.

Moyle (1995) also observed a significant moderating influence of neuroticism in relation to context-free distress. However, in that study a significant interaction was not present for job demands, being found instead for opportunity for control and for social support. Parallel analyses for domain-specific well-being (overall job satisfaction) failed to reveal any moderating impact of neuroticism with respect to those job features. The moderating impact of negative affectivity was also nonsignificant in the study by Munz et al. (1996) of overall satisfaction and growth satisfaction as a function of intrinsic job features. However, a broad measure of job-related distress was found by Dijkstra et al. (2005) to be more strongly associated with reported conflict at work for high-N than for low-N employees.

With respect to well-being axis 2 (from anxiety to comfort), Houkes et al. (2003) hypothesized that the correlation between high workload and job-related emotional exhaustion would be significantly greater for employees with higher NA scores. They found that to be the case in concurrent correlations, and also in longitudinal analyses in which negative affectivity was measured a year before the other variables. On the other hand, examining emotional dissonance generated by job requirements (see chap. 6), Zapf and Holz (2006) found in two different samples that a significant association between dissonance and job-related emotional exhaustion was not affected by the level of employees' neuroticism. With broader measures of negative job characteristics and job-related strain, Höge and Büssing (2004) also failed to find an interactive pattern; the association between job features and strain was similar for higher NA and lower NA employees. That was also the case for the associated disposition of sense of coherence (see chap. 11).

Heinisch and Jex (1997) examined associations with job-related depression (low scores on well-being axis 3). Their results were internally inconsistent, with the interaction between job features and neuroticism found to be significant in two cases (for role ambiguity and role conflict) but not in two others (for workload and low social support). They suggested that the pattern might differ between men and women, but again found mixed results. The association between job content and depression was moderated by neuroticism for women but not for men, and that difference was present only in two out of four analyses (for workload and role ambiguity, but not for role conflict or low social support). As Heinisch and Jex pointed out, it is not clear how such a three-way interaction (job feature by personality trait by gender) might be explained. At present, it appears unlikely to be general occurrence.

In overview, there is some evidence that negative affectivity can moderate the association between job features and employee subjective well-being, but results have been inconsistent and the pattern of findings is far from clear. As for positive affectivity, Moyle (1995) reported (without details) that no interactions were present, measuring PA through a scale of extraversion. Using the PANAS scale (see chap. 2), Munz et al. (1996) reported that "PA played a small role" (p. 804) in associations between job content and job satisfaction, but additional information was not presented. A significant moderating impact of extraversion was observed by Dijkstra et al. (2005) with respect to conflict at work and job-related distress: Reported conflict was more closely associated with that form of distress for low-E than for high-E employees.

As described in chapter 11, dispositional hardiness is known to correlate positively with context-free well-being. Does that continuing disposition moderate the relationship between environmental features and happiness? Despite some initial supporting evidence (when less hardy samples exhibited stronger relations between negative environmental features and subjective well-being), several later investigations have indicated that environment–happiness associations do not in general differ as a function of the level of respondent hardiness (Funk, 1992; Hull et al., 1987).

Other personality features and environmental features appear not to have been examined from this moderator perspective. For example, it might be the case that the association between amount of social contact and subjective well-being is stronger for people who are more extraverted than others, although Moyle's (1995) finding described earlier, about support rather than contact, did not support this possibility. A moderating influence might also be expected in relation to perfectionism: High job demands could be more negatively associated with unhappiness for more perfectionist employees than for others. Additional research in this area would be valuable; at present, it is difficult to reach a general conclusion because studies are few and findings are contradictory.

Values, Wants, and Personal Salience

The pattern has been more clearly established in relation to a second form of moderation. Instead of assessing personality directly, between-person variations have sometimes been examined in terms of occupational values or preferences. This research tradition explores forms of what have been referred to in earlier chapters as judgments of "personal salience." Chapter 9 drew attention to three levels of scope: the rated importance of role membership (J4A), the rated importance of particular role characteristics (J4B), and the rated attractiveness of core tasks in the role (J4C; see, e.g., Table 9.1, also inside the back cover). In the first case (J4A), well-being is likely to be affected by whether or not a person wishes to be in the role in question. Chapter 3 showed that this form of personal salience (for instance, assessed as employment commitment, work-role centrality, or role preference) was linked to a person's happiness or unhappiness in several different roles—during unemployment, in a job, or when retired. Similarly, chapter 10 indicated that, among women all of whom are employed, those with a stronger desire to be in a job tend to be more happy.

At the second level of scope of salience, subjective well-being is likely also to be affected by the importance which a person attaches to primary features of a role (judgment J4B). A moderator pattern is expected in analyses of data at both the individual and the group level.

For example, in group-level comparisons chapter 10 reviewed differences between men and women in the correlations between job features and well-being as a function of those features' importance to male and female employees. Gender appears to moderate those correlations when men and women on average differ substantially in their preference for the job characteristic in question. In those cases of large average salience differences between subgroups, the subsample (either men or women here, but the point is a general one) who more value the environmental feature yields stronger correlations between subjective well-being and the presence or absence of that feature than do members of the subgroup for whom the feature is on average less personally salient.

The absence of a feature is thus particularly bad for well-being, and its presence is particularly desirable, if that feature is seen as personally important. However, if the feature is of lower concern to a person, variations in its level are less likely to affect happiness. Preferences for a role, a role feature, or a core task can vary from situation to situation. However, they are particularly relevant to this chapter because they can also exist in dispositional form, extending for each individual across time and space. In that form, they may be viewed as examples of personal values (see chaps. 11 and 13), embodying assessments of relative importance at the heart of personal salience. In the same way, personality traits also involve preferences, giving rise to consistently different ratings of salience across situations. For instance, high scorers on an extraversion scale might generally view social contact as more personally important than do low scorers.

Instead of examining possible personality moderators of job–happiness associations (as in the previous section), some research into job content has approached salience more directly, examining for a particular environmental feature its "perceived importance," "salience," "priority," or how strong is a person's "preference" for it compared to other features. A traditional focus has been on job satisfaction as a function of the salience as well as the level of job features, and studies have often been from the perspective of the job characteristics model (Hackman & Oldham, 1975, 1976, 1980). As summarized in earlier chapters, this emphasized five features (autonomy, skill variety, task identity, feedback, and task significance) and their relations with job satisfaction and other variables. The model suggested that correlations with those outcomes depend on the level of a continuing individual difference variable, which was described as "higher order need strength," "growth need strength," or (less often) "need for self-actualization." This personal variable was described as "strength of the desire for satisfaction of 'higher order' needs (e.g., obtaining feelings of accomplishment, personal growth)" (Hackman & Lawler, 1971, p. 259). It is a consistent disposition with high stability across time. For instance, the test–retest correlation across a year was +0.63 in research by Houkes et al. (2003).

It was assumed in the job characteristics model that the five principal job features (sometimes labeled as "intrinsic" characteristics) would be more strongly associated with job satisfaction for employees scoring more highly on measures of this individual-difference construct. "Growth need" has been measured in terms of a person's preference for those job features. Some studies have asked how much of each intrinsic characteristic an employee would like to have in his or her job (e.g., Hackman & Lawler, 1971; Hackman et al., 1978; Houkes et al., 2003), and others measured the rated importance of those characteristics (e.g., Jackson, Paul, & Wall, 1981; Sims & Szilagyi, 1976).

Growth need strength (GNS) can thus be placed within the concept of personal salience examined in different ways throughout the book. It involves a form of judgment J4B described in chapter 9—the rated importance of a role characteristic. The focus in this case is on intrinsic job features such as autonomy and skill utilization, and (as with other instances of salience variation) it is expected to moderate the association between those characteristics and subjective well-being. Research has often examined intrinsic job characteristics as a whole through a summary measure of job "scope" (see chap. 8), and correlations between perceived job scope and job satisfaction have frequently been found to differ significantly as a function of employees' growth need strength. Loher et al. (1985) reported from previous studies average uncorrected scope–satisfaction correlations of +0.57 and +0.32 for higher and lower GNS employees respectively. In Spector's (1985) review of overlapping research, those values were +0.51 and +0.29. Although job scope is in general associated with job-related well-being, that association is stronger for employees who more strongly value scope of that kind.

Jackson et al. (1981) examined this pattern longitudinally, in order to reduce the possibility that previous (cross-sectional) results had been influenced by research participants' striving for consistency in their responses. For instance, if a job feature has been described as both present and personally important, an employee may experience pressure to say that he or she is satisfied with that feature. Jackson and colleagues observed the usual pattern, despite measuring job content and satisfaction a year after growth need strength. Scope–satisfaction correlations were +0.68 and +0.35 for higher and lower GNS employees.

Hackman et al. (1978) asked about changes in well-being after job content had been modified by management action. Reduction or enhancement of job scope gave rise to expected negative or positive changes in overall job satisfaction and satisfaction with growth opportunities. Those satisfaction changes were found to be greater for higher GNS employees. However, the differences failed to reach statistical significance, perhaps because between-employee variations in GNS were not large and/or because of small sample sizes (27 and 28 in the two subgroups).

Sims and Szilagyi (1976) examined moderation with respect to associations with specific job characteristics, rather than with job scope more broadly. Higher GNS employees exhibited stronger correlations between satisfaction with work content and perceived autonomy, variety, dealing with others, and friendship opportunities. Wanous (1974) looked at this pattern for individual job facets and employees' satisfaction with those facets. Average correlations were +0.53 and +0.09 for higher and lower scorers on a measure of growth need strength in terms of composite preference for intrinsic features. A difference in correlations as a function of the perceived importance of individual facets was reported by Rice et al. (1991), although their research (see chap. 9) was not presented in terms of growth need strength. In addition to reviewing correlations with domain-specific well-being (satisfaction with one's job) as a function of job scope (above), Spector (1985) summarized previous findings about facet-specific satisfactions. A significant moderating impact of growth need strength was found for correlations between perceived job scope and several satisfactions—with work content, growth opportunities, promotion prospects, pay, and coworkers.

O'Brien and Dowling (1980) obtained measures of desired levels of single job features. Examining the relationship between the presence of these features and overall job satisfaction, they found that the interaction between desired and reported levels of a feature was significant for skill use, high job demands and variety (features 2, 3, and 4). Kahn et al. (1964) examined role ambiguity in one's job (an aspect of feature 5), as well as the matching personal characteristic of need for certainty or inability to tolerate ambiguity. That characteristic may be viewed as indicating the personal salience of the particular job feature; for individuals who desire clarity in their environment, the presence of ambiguity is by definition of particular concern. Kahn and colleagues found that employees' need for clarity moderated in the expected manner the relationship of role clarity in a job with their context-free tension.

Lyons (1971) reported a similar finding with respect to overall job satisfaction, with significantly different correlations between role clarity and satisfaction among higher and lower scorers on a measure of need for clarity (+0.54 and +0.20, respectively); however, a parallel difference in relation to job-related tension (−0.69 and −0.40) was not statistically significant. Focusing on role ambiguity (i.e., low clarity), Keenan and McBain (1979) found significantly different correlations between perceived role ambiguity in a job and overall job satisfaction for high scorers and low scorers on a measure of ambiguity intolerance ($r = -0.62$ and -0.28, respectively). For the negative pole of well-being axis 2, in terms of job-related tension, correlations with role ambiguity were +0.48 for employees highly intolerant of ambiguity and +0.14 for those less concerned about that feature.

Personality dispositions such as authoritarianism or need for independence are also expected to embody different levels of personal salience. Vroom (1959) found that perceived opportunity for personal control (feature 1) was more strongly correlated with job satisfaction for employees with matching levels of these dispositions, that is, low authoritarianism and high independence. Average correlations were +0.54 and +0.08 for preference-matched and preference-unmatched groups, respectively. Workman and Bommer (2004) measured individuals' orientation toward working in groups, in a study that redesigned call center jobs to involve more team-based activities (an aspect of feature 6). The change in job content increased intrinsic job satisfaction to a greater extent for those employees who had a stronger preference for group work.

Research by Rogelberg, Leach, Warr, and Burnfield (2006) considered possible interruptions to the achievement of work goals (feature 3). They noted that attending meetings at work can interrupt personal goal achievement by taking employees away from current goal-directed activities, and might thus be less attractive to employees who score more highly on a dispositional measure of achievement striving. Two studies were reported, examining meetings either in a typical week or in a single day. Consistent with the expected moderation by personality, correlations of demands (number and duration of meetings) with overall job satisfaction (axis 1) and job-related depression–enthusiasm (axis 3) were significantly different between higher and lower striving individuals. For those with lower achievement striving, the correlation between time spent in meetings and job well-being was positive, whereas for higher striving employees that meeting–happiness association was negative. However, that interaction in relation to job-related anxiety–comfort (axis 2) was not statistically significant.

Moderation by personal salience presumably occurs throughout the framework of Table 11.1, covering what are conventionally described as values and motives as well as personality. Stated simply, the more that something is important to you, the more strongly will you be affected by its absence or presence. However, refinements are needed in the definition and measurement of this moderating construct, in part linked to differences in traditional approaches to positive and negative features. Researchers into job content and job redesign have emphasized salience judgments about positive features (e.g., in terms of growth need strength), whereas those concerned about the impact of stressors from the environment have tended to focus on between-person differences in perceptions of danger and threat. It would be helpful to expand models in either area to cover also processes that are oppositely evaluated.

It is not yet clear in detail how the rated importance of particular environmental features can be mapped onto conventionally studied dimensions of personality. By definition, personality dispositions subsume specific preferences and emphases, such that certain aspects of an environment are of greater salience for, say, more neurotic versus less neurotic individuals. However, targeted forms of trait-related personal salience require more investigation. For example, extraverts might regard certain forms of contact with colleagues as more personally salient than do introverts, so that variations in those forms of the environmental feature (an aspect of number 6) will be more strongly associated with aspects of their well-being than is the case for introverts. Similarly, statistical moderation might occur because high scorers on openness to experience more value the opportunity to develop new skills at work (feature 2) than do low scorers; or high-conscientiousness employees may rate as more personally important a high level of job goals (3) than do low-conscientious individuals.

It would also be useful to look at more specific facets within the Big Five personality compounds. In examples in the previous paragraph, of particular relevance are affiliative (rather than surgency) components of extraversion, intellectual (rather than artistic) aspects of openness to experience, and achievement orientation (rather than dependability) within conscientiousness. (These within-factor distinctions were summarized at the beginning of chap. 11.) Note also that, although growth need strength is stable across time (e.g., Houkes et al., 2003), links between that dispositional form of salience and constructs of personality have yet to be explored.

Empirical investigations of this central construct now need systematically to cover different levels of judgment scope (the rated importance of role membership, of particular role characteristics, and of core tasks—J4A to J4C in chap. 9) and also salience-linked networks of personality traits, broader values, and demographic categorizations (by gender, age, etc.). It is also important to determine the pattern of moderator influences of this kind across different aspects of happiness—context-free, domain-specific, and facet-specific. Personal salience clearly warrants much greater research attention than it has recently received.

Ability and Education

In addition to the moderating influence of personal salience, some job–happiness associations might be expected to differ as a function of individuals' abilities. Abdel-Halim (1981) measured ability in one's job through self-report rather than through an objective test, finding a significant moderating impact with respect to role conflict and subjective well-being. Role conflict in one's job was less strongly correlated with low intrinsic job satisfaction for higher ability employees than for those reporting lower job ability, presumably because more able individuals could better cope with threats from the environment. Investigations of this kind that apply more objective measures of individuals' job ability are now needed.

What about broad indices of employees' intelligence? Context-free well-being appears to be unrelated to measured intelligence (e.g., Hartog & Oosterbeek, 1998). For job satisfaction, Ganzach's (1998) literature review and analysis of empirical data indicated that intelligence scores are in general also unrelated to that form of domain-specific well-being. However, multivariate analyses suggested that intelligence was negatively associated with satisfaction in less complex jobs. Ganzach pointed out that this finding may overlap with an impact of growth need strength, "in that it suggests that people with higher intelligence desire more interesting and challenging work" (p. 536).

That theme was developed by Ganzach (2003). He argued that intelligence is linked to a desire for more complex jobs, so that the correlation between employees' intelligence and their overall job satisfaction is likely to be negative after statistical control for job complexity. In two national U.S. samples of employees aged between 24 and 38, the average bivariate correlation between intelligence and overall job satisfaction was +0.04. However, that association became significantly negative in both samples after control for the complexity level of a person's job (defined through analysts' ratings of job titles), pay level, and several demographic characteristics. Although more intelligent people tended to be in more complex jobs (mean $r = +0.35$), high-intelligence employees who were exposed to relatively low complexity tended to be less satisfied.

Cognitive ability may also contribute to job–happiness associations through linked differences in job performance. It could be the case that cognitively able employees in more complex jobs perform better than others, with associated differences in goal attainment, rewards, and consequential well-being. On the other hand, in less complex jobs cognitive ability might be unrelated to performance and associated well-being. (Associations between job performance and happiness are examined in chap. 14.)

Some research has looked indirectly at this issue, in terms of employees' level of education. Intelligence and education received are strongly associated with each other; for example, the correlation was +0.55 in research by Ganzach (2003). Given that more educated individuals tend to obtain jobs that provide greater income (e.g., Grzywacz & Dooley, 2003), it might be expected that the association between education and subjective well-being would be positive. For context-free indicators, a small but significant average correlation (around +0.13) was reported from community samples by Diener et al. (1999). However, that association between education and context-free well-being tended to become zero or negative after controls for income or occupational status.

With respect to job-related well-being in samples of employees, correlations with level of education have been found to be significantly negative in several British samples—by Warr (1992; for job-related anxiety–comfort), by Clark (1996; for overall job satisfaction and satisfaction with the work itself), and by Clark (2005a; for overall job satisfaction). In all cases, that negative association was retained after control for income and other job and personal characteristics; see Clark and Oswald (1996) for multivariate analyses of data in Clark (1996). (Control variables included employees' age, which is important with respect to education, because later cohorts have usually received more education than earlier ones.) Sousa-Poza and Sousa-Poza (2003) combined the data of Clark (1996) with nine later nationally representative

UK data sets, observing again that more educated employees reported lower job satisfaction than did employees with less education after controls had been added for other variables.

Birdi et al. (1995) analyzed the responses from national surveys in 10 different countries, finding a correlation of 0.00 between education and overall job satisfaction. That correlation was +0.08 for men and +0.02 for women in Weaver's (1978) analyses of national U.S. samples. Ganzach (2003) examined facet satisfaction with pay as well as overall job satisfaction in two national U.S. samples aged between 24 and 38. In those cases, level of education was again unrelated to overall job satisfaction, without and with controls for other variables, but higher levels of education were linked with significantly lower pay satisfaction after controls. Studying overall job satisfaction in a U.S. national sample, Bender et al. (2005) reported that more educated employees had significantly lower well-being in the full-sample and male-only analyses after many demographic controls; however, for women that negative difference was nonsignificant.

Clark and Oswald (1996) suggested that more educated individuals tend to view their current situation against an expectation of obtaining jobs that are above average in attractiveness (a form of comparative judgment identified as J2A in chap. 9), and that those expectations often remain unmet in reality. Greater education, especially when income level is controlled, may thus be accompanied by a greater perceived failure to meet personal expectations, and unmet expectations tend to be accompanied by lower subjective well-being.

Another form of this mismatch was examined by Quinn and Mandilovitch (1980). They asked employees about both their actual education level and the level required in their job, finding that overall job satisfaction was significantly linked to the match between those. Particularly low job satisfaction was observed among workers who had been educated substantially beyond the level required for their job. That possibility was studied by Allen and van der Velden (2001) in a sample of university and college graduates. In that case, self-reported over-education (working in a job that requires a lower level of education than one's own) was unrelated to overall job satisfaction after control for a range of job characteristics. (Those additional variables accounted for a substantial proportion of variance; the importance of education level on its own was not reported.) Links between education level and employee well-being thus vary somewhat between investigations, and additional multivariate research in this area remains needed.

PERSONALITY AND JUDGMENT PROCESSES

Developing the theme that judgments of personal salience may some-times reflect preferences that are part of a personality disposition, this section asks about judgment–personality links more broadly. Chapter 9 introduced 10 judgment processes that may operate as people appraise their environment, with expected effects on subjective well-being over and above an impact from environmental stimuli themselves. That chap-ter was mainly concerned with average patterns of judgment, those occurring for people in general. Let us now look at possible between-person variations in the activation of those judgments.

Table 12.1 suggests possible influences from a range of personality attributes. Twelve dispositions are listed to the left of the table, and the judgments are set out along the top row. To simplify the presenta-tion, J4A, J4B, and J4C have there been combined into an overall account of the fourth judgment; separate research findings are not yet available. In a few cases it is possible to indicate that empirical evi-dence for differential activation is available. Those instances are shown as "Supported" in particular cells of the table, described as either "job" (in occupational settings) or "nonjob" (in the laboratory or elsewhere outside paid employment). Some other personality–judgment associations are described as "Hypothesized," with expecta-tions based on related evidence and the nature of the constructs involved. All other cells in Table 12.1 have been left blank, because no rationale for an expected influence from one of the activating vari-ables is yet apparent. (An earlier version of these ideas appeared in Warr, 2006b.)

As pointed out in chapter 9, comparative judgments made in rela-tion to other people, other situations or other times (identified as J1, J2, and J3 respectively) can provide frames of reference within which a current input from the environment is appraised. Those three kinds of judgment can involve comparisons that are either upward or down-ward. Upward comparisons are made against a reference person or event with more positive characteristics than one's own, and down-ward comparisons are against a worse-off referent than oneself. As described in chapter 9, upward and downward comparative judg-ments tend to be associated with lower or higher subjective well-being, respectively.

Neuroticism (disposition 1 in Table 12.1) is expected to be linked to the activation of judgmental comparisons J1, J2A, and J2B in an upward direction, because that disposition includes scanning the

TABLE 12.1

Possible Personality Influences on the Activation of Principal Judgments in the Experience of Well-Being

Disposition	J1. Comparisons With Other People	J2A. Comparisons With Other Situations: Expected	J2B. Comparisons With Other Situations: Counterfactual	J3A. Comparisons With Other Times: Previous Trend	J3B. Comparisons With Other Times: Likely Future Trend	J4. Judgments of Personal Salience (See the Text for Three Three Subtypes)	J5. Judgments of Situation-Related Self-Efficacy	J6. Judgments of Novelty of Familiarity
1. Neuroticism	Hypothesized (upward)	Hypothesized (upward)	Hypothesized (upward)			Hypothesized (positive)		
2. Self-esteem	Supported (downward) (nonjob)		Supported (downward) (nonjob)			Hypothesized (negative)		
3. Trait depression	Hypothesized (upward)		Hypothesized (upward)	Hypothesized				
4. Extraversion	Supported (downward) (nonjob)	Hypothesized (downward)	Hypothesized (downward)					
5. Optimism	Supported (downward) (nonjob)		Supported (downward) (nonjob)		Hypothesized			
6. Future orientation					Hypothesized			
7. Novelty-seeking style								Hypothesized
8. Maximizing style	Supported (nonjob)		Hypothesized					
9. Perfectionism	Hypothesized (upward)		Hypothesized (upward)					

TABLE 12.1 (*continued*)

Disposition	J1. Comparisons With Other People	J2A. Comparisons With Other Situations: Expected	J2B. Comparisons With Other Situations: Counterfactual	J3A. Comparisons With Other Times: Previous Trend	J3B. Comparisons With Other Times: Likely Future Trend	J4. Judgments of Personal Salience (See the Text for Three Three Subtypes)	J5. Judgments of Situation-Related Self-Efficacy	J6. Judgments of Novelty of Familiarity
10. Collectivist orientation	Supported (job)						Hypothesized (negative)	
11. Social comparison orientation	Supported (nonjob and job)							
12. Field dependence	Supported (nonjob)							

379

environment for negative possibilities. Such a neuroticism-linked pattern was found by van der Zee, Buunk, and Sanderman (1996), but was not consistently present in Wheeler's (2000) review. Associations between neuroticism and upward judgmental comparisons are therefore indicated in Table 12.1 as Hypothesized rather than Supported. In addition, more neurotic individuals (with an enhanced anxiety about themselves) are thought more likely to emphasize the perceived significance of a stimulus for oneself (judgment J4); more neurotic individuals are hypothesized to be particularly sensitive to the personal salience of an environmental input.

Other continuing aspects of a person that are linked conceptually and empirically with scores on neuroticism scales include self-esteem and trait depression. As indicated in Table 12.1, nonorganizational research has found that high self-esteem (disposition 2 in the table) is associated with both downward social comparisons (J1; Crocker, Thompson, McGraw, & Ingerman, 1987; Wheeler, 2000) and downward counterfactual comparisons (J2B; Kasimatis & Wells, 1995). Table 12.1 also proposes that employees with greater self-esteem are less likely to focus on the presence or absence of potential personal threat (judgment J4; because high self-esteem includes a relatively lower concern about potential dangers to the self), and that with respect to J1 and J2B, trait depression (disposition 3) operates similarly to neuroticism and to self-esteem that is low. In addition, depression tends to be associated with retrospective rumination about oneself (Ingram, 1990), so that a Hypothesized link with trait depression is also indicated in the table for judgment J3A (comparison with a previous trend).

The Big Five factor of extraversion (disposition 4 in Table 12.1) is also likely to be associated with differential activation of certain judgments underlying well-being. For example, extraverts have been shown to be more likely than introverts to make downward social comparisons (J1; Wheeler, 2000). This tendency is also expected for parallel self-enhancing comparisons with alternative situations (judgments J2A and J2B), and those are shown as Hypothesized in the table.

Three other continuing dispositions that are likely to be linked to trait extraversion concern optimism (5), future orientation (6), and novelty-seeking style (7). With respect to optimism, Lyubomirsky (2001) reported that pessimists (i.e., low scorers on optimism) were highly sensitive in laboratory situations to upward social comparisons (J1; see also Abbe et al., 2003). In addition, Kasimatis and Wells (1995) found that optimistic students were more likely than pessimists to make downward (self-enhancing) counterfactual comparisons (judgment J2B). Mental comparisons with a likely future trend (J3B) may also be made more often by optimistic than by pessimistic individuals, linked to the formers' positive outlook on the future. Similarly, a forward-looking dispositional emphasis (6) in the appraisal of a situation or event is by definition likely to encourage reference to a perceived future trend (J3B); and a continuing emphasis on novelty (disposition 7 in Table 12.1) is expected to promote J6 comparison processes, relative to the personal reference point of novelty or familiarity.

Schwartz et al. (2002) explored students' tendency to seek to maximize their gains by thoughts and behaviors that were aimed at a perfect choice (disposition 8); such "maximizers" were found to be more likely than satisficers to engage in social comparison judgments (J1). It seems likely that maximizers will also more often engage in counterfactual thinking (J2B), but no evidence about that has been found. Maximizing processes may be viewed as an aspect of the more general construct of perfectionism (disposition 9 in the table), a tendency to seek unrealistically high achievements and unreasonably to see one's performance as falling below an acceptable level. As summarized in chapter 11, perfectionism is associated with reduced well-being, and it is hypothesized in Table 12.1 that higher levels of that disposition encourage the activation of two kinds of upward judgment, J1 and J2B.

Differences in collectivist-individualist orientation (disposition 10) have been shown by Bordia and Blau (2003) to be linked to processes underlying pay satisfaction, such that collectivist concerns (for group norms, interdependence, sacrifice to help others, etc.) are more associated with the use of other people as judgmental referents (J1) than is an individualist orientation. Such a collectivism-linked emphasis on social comparisons is likely to occur with respect to other forms of well-being. Conversely, judgments about one's own effectiveness in the current situation (J5) seem more likely to be activated by people with an individualist rather than collectivist orientation, because their focus is particularly on success of a self-referring kind. This possibility is identified as Hypothesized in Table 12.1.

Table 12.1 also indicates that a person's stable tendency to make social comparisons (disposition 11) has been shown to be related to the occurrence of comparative social judgments (J1) in nonorganizational settings (Gibbons & Buunk, 1999). Individuals with high social comparison orientation were found to be more likely to compare themselves with others and to be satisfied after downward social comparisons. Those people appeared to be uncertain about themselves in relation to other people, being more strongly dependent on social cues for self-evaluation. Similar findings were obtained in work settings by Buunk, Zurriaga, Peiro, Nauta, and Gosalvez (2005), with employees who scored highly on social comparison orientation reporting more negative affect after upward comparisons. Finally in Table 12.1, disposition 12 is the general tendency to field dependence rather than independence. That characteristic has been measured through perceptual tasks (in an embedded figures test), recording the degree to which a person sees a focal object as separate from its surrounding field. The tendency to see a stimulus figure as dependent on its background rather than as independent from other information, has been found in laboratory research to be related to greater receptivity to social information (judgment J1; O'Connor & Barrett, 1980; Weiss & Shaw, 1979; Witkin & Goodenough, 1977).

It will be clear from the lack of cited empirical evidence in this section that research has rarely explored the personality correlates of judgment activation. More studies are needed in job settings of the two issues underlying Table 12.1: the typical occurrence of judgments that influence subjective well-being (J1 to J6, in the top row, reviewed in chap. 9), and personality-linked differences in the activation of those judgments (in the cells in Table 12.1, linking dispositions to judgments). In seeking to understand the bases of happiness in a particular situation, we need to know more about relevant mental processes and about differences between people in the initiation and operation of those processes.

13

Person–Environment Fit and Work Values

P rincipal job features were examined in chapters 4 to 8 within a perspective that can be described as "environment-centered." Employees' happiness or unhappiness were there seen to be affected by key aspects of the work environment, grouped within 12 principal categories or in 26 categories and subcategories (see Table 8.1 in chap. 8). On the other hand, the influences on happiness considered in chapters 9 to 12 have primarily concerned individuals themselves, such as their judgment processes, cultural settings, demographic characteristics, personality attributes, and the salience that they accord to particular elements of their environment. Approaches of those kinds can be referred to as "person-centered."

Despite their primary emphasis on either the environment or the person, both approaches in fact embody themes from the other. Features of the environment are important for subjective well-being because they are desirable or undesirable in relation to individuals' needs or wants. (Consistent with much of the literature, those two terms are here treated as largely interchangeable. However, the term *need* sometimes implies a stronger biological infrastructure than *want*.) And individuals' attributes are relevant to well-being when they influence the level or personal salience of environmental features or involve cognitive processes in reaction to those features. It is clear that happiness arises not from the environment or the person alone, but from some combination of the two.

FRAMEWORKS OF PERSON–ENVIRONMENT FIT

Conceptual frameworks that embody both environmental and personal features have sometimes been directed at the "fit," "congruence," "compatibility," "correspondence," "matching," or "similarity" between a person (P) and his or her environment (E). Several approaches of that kind, often referred to as addressing "person–environment (P-E) fit," explicitly require the simultaneous consideration of environmental and personal characteristics. In the area of this book, the primary focus is on congruence or incongruence between a person and his or her occupational setting.

The idea that people tend to be happier in settings into which they better fit is immediately plausible, and many research investigations into person–environment fit (or with similar labels) have been published. (See reviews by, Kristof, 1996; Spokane, Meir, & Catalano, 2000; Verquer, Beehr, & Wagner, 2003; and Kristof-Brown, Zimmerman, & Johnson, 2005.) Researchers have differed in their methods, but the fit/misfit paradigm requires that both P and E be scored in parallel terms. The broadest perspective is on the match between a person and his or her environment as a whole, but employment-related studies have also examined congruence between a person and his or her career (actual or potential), employing organization, work group, or current job.

"Fit" can be viewed either cross-sectionally or dynamically. In cross-sectional examination, parallel information from both the person (P) and the environment (E) is compared on a single measurement occasion to specify how closely the studied variables match each other. For example, the level of a job feature (an aspect of E) may be compared against a job holder's preference for that feature (P). On the other hand, a dynamic approach to P-E fit emphasizes processes of interaction that are extended across time, as both an individual and, for instance, his or her organization make mutual adjustments in the light of each other's characteristics and behavior. Empirical research in this area has mainly examined fit of the first, cross-sectional kind, rather than exploring the mutual influences of person and environment on each other across time.

P-E fit studies have also differed in their source of data. Measures of fit have been derived from three types of indicator—"self-rated" assessments, "single-source" comparisons, or "multiple-source" comparisons. In the first ("self-rated") case, individuals assess directly through a single judgment the degree of compatibility between themselves and their environment on presented dimensions, providing a direct rating of P-E congruence itself, rather than separate ratings of the two components for later matching with each other. "Single-source" comparisons are also made by the same person (e.g., a job holder), but in this case involve separate ratings about oneself (P) and about one's environment (E). Those two sets of ratings are later placed in relation to each other to generate fit or misfit scores. In "multiple-source" assessments, self-descriptive information from the person is compared with information about the environment obtained from a different source, such as a supervisor or job analyst. Alternative terminologies include that by Kristof-Brown et al. (2005), referring to the three kinds of measure as "perceived," "subjective" and "objective" respectively. As those authors pointed out, reviews of this field are made difficult by "the proliferation of conceptualizations, measures, and analytic approaches" (p. 282).

Additional measurement decisions must be taken about the content of fit (which features of the environment should be covered) and the quantification of fit itself (how P-E compatibility should be calculated on whatever features are studied). Two kinds of content have been studied, either more affective or more ability-related. First, aspects of the environment may or may not match a person's needs, wants, or preferences; second, demands posed by the environment might or might not be congruent with a person's abilities. For example, the theory of work adjustment (Dawis & Lofquist, 1984) sets out propositions of those two kinds. In the first case, the correspondence is examined between a job's provision of "reinforcers" (E) and a job holder's needs (sometimes grouped together in the theory as "values"; P). The second set of comparisons is between a job's skill requirements (E) and a job holder's response capabilities (P). Those two approaches to P-E fit have sometimes been described as "supplies–needs" and "demands–abilities" perspectives, respectively (e.g., Edwards, 1996; French et al., 1982; Kristof, 1996; Tinsley, 2000).

Although it is generally agreed that a comprehensive assessment of person–environment fit requires attention to both sets of content, most research has taken merely a "supplies–needs" approach, examining environmental features that are relevant to well-being. Within that perspective, studied characteristics of an organization (E) have included culture, climate, norms, or job content; person variables examined relative to those environmental features have included goals, values, preferences, and aspects of personality (P).

For example, the model of Dawis and Lofquist (1984) covered P-variables in terms of six basic values derived through factor analysis from 20 "work-related needs." Those values concerned needs for achievement, altruism, autonomy, comfort, safety, and status. Job environments were construed in parallel terms, yielding profiles of "occupational reinforcers" in different roles. The degree to which those "reinforcers" in the environment matched employees' "needs" was predicted to determine the level of their job satisfaction, summarizing the level of that fit through a single P-E score across the 20 dimensions.

Different investigations have studied different kinds of P and E variables, such that results are not always readily comparable between publications. A common procedure is to ask simply about actual and desired levels of an environmental feature. For example, French et al. (1982) paired an environmental item "How much [e.g., workload] do you have?" with a P-item "How much [e.g., workload] would you like to have?" Shaw and Gupta (2004) compared perceptions of actual levels with ratings of "ideal" levels.

Irrespective of its particular content, how should the magnitude of person–environment fit of the cross-sectional kind be quantified? Many studies have derived algebraic difference (or discrepancy, or D) scores between the P and E indicators, for example subtracting a measure of the environment from a measure of the person. D-scores of that algebraic kind can take either a positive or a negative value, representing an environmental deficit or an excess in relation to a person's score. D-scores have either been examined for single dimensions of P and E (e.g., workload or social contact) or summed across all studied dimensions to create an index of overall fit. Between-feature summation of that kind conceals possible differences between the impact of separate environmental features, and more targeted information is required in investigations into the content of particular jobs. In those cases, we need to learn about specific job features (rather than merely an overall compatibility), if actions are planned to improve specific aspects of a situation identified as problematic.

Some investigations have examined the amount of misfit irrespective of whether that discrepancy is an environmental deficit ($P > E$) or an excess ($P < E$). It is then usual to record absolute scores (ignoring the sign) or to square algebraic difference values to remove information about direction of discrepancy. Such analyses assume that a given misfit value is equivalent irrespective of its direction, that is, whether a person has too little or too much of the feature(s). Given the very different personal implications of deficit and excess, that assumption is likely to be widely inappropriate.

Other researchers have instead examined the direction of an observed misfit. Caplan et al. (1975) and French et al. (1982) computed two directional scores ("deficit" or "excess") for a range of individual job features, and also took a measure of "poor fit" (in either direction, ignoring the sign of a discrepancy). In comparisons between those three P-E fit measures and the environmental scores on their own (perceptions of a job feature by a job holder), predictions of subjective well-being were only sometimes improved by one or other of the indices of misfit rather than an environmental score on its own. In addition, effects were inconsistent between the several misfit measures, and no overarching principles were identified to account for the varying patterns of correlations of well-being with E-scores on their own and with the different kinds of P-E indicator. Rounds, Dawis, and Lofquist (1987) compared as many as 19 alternative P-E fit scores, showing that they differed considerably in their association with job satisfaction. However, the pattern of those correlations with fit scores varied between different occupational groups, and clear recommendations about preferred procedures were not apparently possible.

Despite their widespread use, difference scores on their own are unsatisfactory as indicators of congruence (e.g., Edwards, 1993, 1994; Kalliath, Bluedorn, & Strube, 1999; Kristof, 1996; Tinsley, 2000). For instance, D-scores are ambiguous in that they conceal the contribution of each component itself (P and E in this case). Associations with, say, job satisfaction may in practice derive from the level of one of the components rather from the difference between them. For example, Wall and Payne (1973) showed that relationships between job facet satisfaction and the difference between perceived and wanted facet amounts were no longer significant after controlling for perceived facet scores; the latter (measures of E) were the important ones. Edwards and Cooper (1990) demonstrated that "because a difference score is a simple linear combination of its components, it can *never* contain more predictive power than the combined effect of its components and, in most cases, will contain *less* predictive power" (p. 301, italics in original). In general, environmental (E) scores on their own explain substantially more variance in subjective well-being than do indicators of P or combinations of E and P (Edwards, 1996; Kalliath et al., 1999; Kristof-Brown et al., 2005; Taris et al., 2005).

It is clear that reported findings about P-E fit depend on a range of measurement decisions. Differences in the variance of responses can also be important. If the between-person variance in E- or P-scores differs considerably from variance in the other, P-E fit values can be determined primarily by the set with the larger variances. Other problems concern unreliability: Low reliability of component scores (P or E) is reduced further by their joint incorporation into a D-score compound. In addition, there can be problems of multicollinearity, because P, E, and P-E scores tend to be strongly correlated with each other.

Rather than analyzing associations with the computed difference between two features (P and E), which conceals the impact of the actual level of those variables, it is preferable to examine in the same analysis relationships with each of those components themselves. In that way, one might explore associations between, say, job satisfaction and separate indicators of P and E, rather than merely the associations with some kind of P-E discrepancy. Regression procedures for E and P scores have been advocated by Edwards (e.g., 1993, 1994), also including quadratic or multivariate interaction terms and nonlinear relationships between P, E, and outcome variables. That more comprehensive procedure allows separate assessment of personal and environmental influences on their own and in various forms of combination with each other. For example, Edwards (1996) considered nonlinear relationships of well-being with both person–job (P-E) misfit and also with aspects of job content (E) itself.

Nevertheless, examination of several possible interactions between a range of indicators can generate problems of multicollinearity between the many linked scores. There is also a danger that several compound inferences in regression equations will magnify sample-specific error variance, and conclusions can depend on which particular sequence of analytic decisions is followed (Edwards, 1993). In addition, it is often difficult for readers to assimilate complex and inconsistent patterns of multiple relationships described in regression analyses. These "are likely to contain coefficients on curvilinear and interactive terms that are difficult to interpret" (Edwards, 1993, p. 660). Linked to that, statistical analyses have sometimes involved a level of abstractness that is somewhat divorced from day-to-day variables. Tinsley (2000) wondered "how the results for the quadratic and interaction terms increased our understanding of P-E fit," and concluded from previous regression presentations that "a conceptual interpretation is not apparent" (p. 171).

Despite these methodological uncertainties, subjective well-being has often been reported to be greater when a person's needs or wants are more closely matched by features in his or her environment. (That finding reflects the impact on happiness of reduced goal distance, as considered in earlier chapters.) Research in the P-E fit tradition has typically examined overall fit (aggregated across all dimensions studied) and irrespective of the direction of any misfit. In a meta-analysis of previous studies of the congruence between the attributes of an employee (P) and his or her organization (O; a form of E), Verquer et al. (2003) recorded an average uncorrected correlation between overall fit and job satisfaction of +0.25. That value was found to depend on the type of measurement used, being +0.57 for respondents' direct ratings of similarity between self and organization (referred to as "self-rated" earlier), +0.30 for single-source perceptions (by the job holder alone, separately of P and O and later matched with each other), and +0.20 for multiple-source comparisons (the job holder for P and another person for O).

The meta-analysis by Kristof-Brown et al. (2005) of a similar but larger data set revealed an average uncorrected correlation between overall person–organization fit and job satisfaction of +0.35. Differences between the three kinds of measure identified earlier were again observed, with average values of +0.45, +0.37, and +0.23, respectively. The raised values for self-rated congruence (+0.57 and +0.45 in the two analyses) presumably arise from studies' reliance on personal reports of both P-E fit (in a joint assessment) and also of subjective well-being. Some research has confirmed the robustness of this fit-satisfaction correlation over and above other possible influences on well-being. For example, Bretz and Judge (1994) showed that a significant association with overall job satisfaction was retained despite controls for demographic, job, and industry-sector variables.

In addition to a focus on congruence with one's organization (just discussed), other studies have examined fit or misfit combined across the characteristics of jobs. In the review by Kristof-Brown et al. (2005), the average uncorrected correlation between overall person-job fit and overall job satisfaction was found to be +0.44. As in other cases, the closeness of association depended on the method of assessing fit; the average correlation was +0.45, +0.46, and +0.22 for self-rated, single-source, and multiple-source measurements, respectively.

Similar findings have been obtained in research examining vocational interests (P) and the nature of a person's career (a form of E; rather than organizational, job, or other attributes of the environment). A review by Tranberg, Slane, and Ekeberg (1993) covered studies of individuals' career fit in terms of Holland's (e.g., 1997) six personal styles—vocational interests that are Realistic, Investigative, Artistic, Social, Enterprising, or Conventional. The closeness of person–career match in one of those terms was correlated on average at +0.20 with job satisfaction; career interests that are fulfilled tend to be accompanied by greater well-being. In a later review, Spokane et al.

(2000) concluded that this average value for career interests was around +0.25. Tranberg et al. (1993) showed that links with satisfaction varied between different kinds of content. For example, P-E fit with respect to the match between Social vocational interest and a person's career type in that respect were correlated with job satisfaction on average at +0.33, whereas for other career interests (e.g., Realistic, mean r = +0.05) congruence appeared to be of little importance. Conceptual and methodological problems in the study of vocational interests as a function of P-E congruence have been explored by Spokane et al. (2000) and Tinsley (2000).

The second form of fit introduced earlier, between demands and abilities, has less been often investigated. Edwards (1996) asked about three kinds of task—planning and organizing, decision-making, and motivating and rewarding others. Respondents indicated the level of skill required in each task in their job (the environmental demands score) and also their own skill level in that task (the indicator of personal ability). P-E fit of this demands–abilities kind was examined in relation to experienced well-being in performing each one. Although findings varied somewhat between the three tasks, P-E fit in terms of demands and self-reported abilities was generally unrelated to job holder well-being measured in that way.

Allen and van der Velder (2001) examined one direction of skill mismatch in terms of employees' own judgments of whether "I would perform better in my current job if I possessed additional knowledge and skills" (p. 438). After controls for job and demographic characteristics, greater self-rated skill deficit was found to be significantly associated with lower overall job satisfaction. The opposite possibility (that an excess of skill may sometimes yield reduced well-being) was illustrated in chapter 12; some research has suggested that higher levels of intelligence or education are associated with reduced job satisfaction in less complex jobs. However, evidence remains limited in this area, and the effects of incongruence between demands and abilities are not yet clearly defined.

Note that some questionnaires that purportedly ask only about the environment (E) are in fact worded in ways that instead address P-E fit or misfit. Thus, although the opportunity for skill use ("vitamin" 2; see chap. 5) is itself an aspect of E, some researchers have instead asked about skill "underutilization," directly assessing desired increases in this environmental feature (a P-variable). Similarly, externally generated goals (feature 3) are sometimes examined in terms of work or role "underload" or "overload," explicitly as a deficit or an excess in relation to the level that a person considers to be acceptable. It is clearly important that studies of P-E fit distinguish conceptually and operationally between their P and E variables.

Research into person–environment fit in general has heavily emphasized satisfaction indicators rather than other forms of subjective well-being. It is desirable now also to consider the additional measurement axes presented in Figure 2.2 and throughout the book. For example, we might expect that different patterns will be observed relative to axes 2 and 3 of subjective well-being (from anxiety to comfort and from depression to enthusiasm). Between-feature differences in the associations with those two axes have been suggested in Tables 4.2 and 5.1, and divergence might also be observed in associations with P-E fit. For example, consistent with the generally expected different impacts of low or high levels of environmental features (see chap. 2), P-E incongruence might more affect depression-enthusiasm at low levels of E and more affect anxiety-comfort in the high range. With respect to well-being axes 1 and 2, Edwards's (1996) results suggested that job satisfaction (axis 1) was more affected by fit or misfit in terms of supplies (E) and values (P), whereas job-related tension (axis 2) might be more linked to mismatches between demands (E) and abilities (P). It is desirable in future P-E studies to examine a wider range of indicators of happiness, both job-related and context-free.

More generally, there has long been controversy about the merit of calculating P-E congruence at all (Tinsley, 2000). As noted earlier, main effects from environmental features on their own are substantially larger than those from fit or misfit, detailed findings about correlates of fit are inconsistent, and it remains unclear whether conventional computations of congruence are conceptually and statistically acceptable. Kalliath et al. (1999) argued that "with only a single exception, *all* empirical tests of value congruence effects have used flawed statistical procedures, which renders their results inconclusive at best" (p. 1176, italics in original). They applied multiple regression procedures recommended by Edwards (1994), and found "a general lack of support for congruence effects" (p. 1192).

Examining overall congruence measures, Tranberg et al. (1993) pointed out that fit investigations "take an overly simple view" (p. 261) of the many different influences on subjective well-being. They concluded that overall P-E information adds little to our understanding of the variables and processes that might be important in the development and maintenance of happiness. In effect, an observed significant association between closeness of P-E fit and subjective well-being restates the fact that people are more happy if they have what they want than if they lack what they want. There is now a need to ask more specific and varied questions than have been conventional in this area. For instance, P-E fit or misfit may be more influential in certain kinds of situation. In that way, Shaw and Gupta (2004) suggested that person-job congruence may be more associated with subjective well-being when an employee's job performance is low rather than high. There are also hints in the literature that P-E misfit is most associated with reduced satisfaction when measured dimensions are judged to be of greater personal salience (Kristof-Brown et al., 2005, p. 322; Rounds et al., 1987, p. 303); this possibility is developed in a later section.

Particularly desirable is a move away from merely assessing overall fit irrespective of its direction (e.g., Edwards, 1993). The review by Kristof-Brown et al. (2005) drew attention to the prevalence of non-symmetrical patterns, such that environmental deficiencies (P > E), when people want more than they have, are often more strongly associated with unhappiness than is an environmental excess (P < E), when people want less than a current level. Within the present framework, that difference is consistent with the asymmetric nature of the inverted-U curves in Figures 4.1 and 4.2. Considering relationships envisaged in the present framework, different patterns of association are expected between specific types of job feature ("constant effect" vs. "additional decrement"), between environmental levels (e.g., in the "deficiency" or "toxic" range), and between measurement content (the three well-being axes at each of three levels of scope). (Themes of this kind are expanded in the next section.) The traditional overall assessment of P-E congruence is widely unsatisfactory, in that it ignores distinctions and processes of those several kinds.

That general failing does not mean that combined P and E influences on happiness are unimportant. Person–environment relationships have been studied in many other, more informative ways. As illustrated in chapters 9 to 12, alternative approaches to the study of joint P and E contributions to subjective well-being have avoided problems of the kind illustrated in this section. For example, as described in previous chapters, between-group comparisons (e.g., by gender or personality) of environment–happiness associations, statistical analyses of E-by-P interactions, and studies of individuals' cognitive processes have all proved informative. The greater flexibility and conceptual richness of other approaches to between-person variation in responding to environmental features make them more attractive and potentially productive than traditional research of the kind that has been labeled as "P-E fit."

P-E FIT, WANTS, AND THE VITAMIN FRAMEWORK

Concepts of value, need, want, preference, and so on, overlap substantially with notions of well-being and satisfaction, because both sets of construct concern desired states and their achievement. It seems clear from this conceptual interdependence that the relative absence of a desired feature (i.e., a P-E deficit) will usually be accompanied by lower well-being with respect to that feature: people are unhappy if they lack what they want. At low environmental levels (in the zone of deficiency, to the left of Figs. 4.1 and 4.2), it is usual for individuals to want more of a desirable feature. For example, most employees have been shown to want greater personal influence over activities in their workplace than they currently have (Greenberger et al., 1989; Wall & Lischeron, 1977). Within that lower range, P-E misfit will thus generally reflect an environmental deficit: People want more than they have, or P > E. And in general the lower the level of the environmental feature, the greater the increase that is wanted. For the lower range of happiness-relevant environmental features, correlations between job well-being and the magnitude of P-E misfit will thus necessarily be at least moderate.

But what about a P-E excess, when an E-score exceeds a P-score? In those cases, an environment contains more of a feature than a person wants. It is important here to distinguish between "additional decrement" (AD) and "constant effect" (CE) characteristics, as described in chapters 4 to 8. Within the higher environmental range, correlations with well-being are expected to be negative for AD job features (see, e.g., Fig. 4.1), but around zero for CE characteristics.

That difference is linked to dissimilar personal preferences across the higher range of environmental values for the two kinds of feature. As spelled out in chapter 4, the two different categories of environmental feature are assumed to be maximally desirable across different levels. The AD variables (control, demands, variety, etc.) are considered to become coercively negative beyond moderate levels, so that a negative association between environmental level and well-being is expected in the higher range; moderate levels are for those features the most desirable ones. Because people want progressively greater reductions in an AD feature across its higher range (i.e., P < E to an increasing extent across higher values), a significant association between greater P-E misfit and lower feature-related well-being is assured across high levels of that category of job feature. On the other hand, constant-effect (CE) environmental characteristics are thought to be on average consistently desirable beyond moderate levels (i.e., P = E in general in that range), so that P-E fit scores are expected across high levels of those features to be unrelated to subjective well-being.

Stating that with respect to both low and high levels of an environmental feature, for AD characteristics a P-E discrepancy is predicted to be associated with reduced well-being both at low levels of E (when usually P > E) and at high levels (when usually P < E). However, for CE features, a discrepancy is expected to matter only below a threshold level of the feature (when usually P > E), whereas above that threshold level P = E on average. Scores that are low on environmental variables of either kind imply P-E deficits (where P > E), and high E-scores imply either P-E excess (where P < E; for AD features) or P-E fit (where P = E; for CE features).

The standard expectation of P-E fit models, that a close fit is always more desirable than a difference in either direction, is clearly inappropriate in such a differentiated framework; the pattern depends on the nature and level of an environmental feature. It is thus important to examine separate predictions for different aspects of the environment. Furthermore, measurements of an environmental feature alone can themselves provide information about likely fit without giving rise to conceptual and measurement problems of the kind outlined in this chapter.

SALIENCE AND PERSON–ENVIRONMENT FIT

As illustrated in several chapters, the magnitude of associations between job features and subjective well-being can be influenced by an individual's characteristics and judgments. One such judgment has been described in many sections of the book in terms of personal salience. In general terms, the judged personal salience of an environmental feature is the strength with which a person wants to avoid, attain or retain that feature; it thus denotes the extremity of a personal evaluation in terms of undesirability or desirability. Employment commitment, role preferences, job-attribute preferences, occupational values, priorities within personality traits, growth need strength, and judged personal significance in primary appraisal of the environment are all instances of that broader construct.

As noted earlier, judgments of personal salience can often reflect dispositional characteristics. For example, externally generated goals ("vitamin" 3) are by definition more desirable to individuals with stronger achievement orientation than to those who less value goal achievement; the absence or presence of those goals will thus be particularly salient to such individuals. Similarly, a negative feature of the environment, sometimes termed a "stressor," can be particularly unwanted by certain kinds of people but less so by others. For instance, as shown in chapter 12, role ambiguity (an aspect of feature 5) is more threatening to job holders who have a strong need for clarity.

In addition to this dispositional consistency in priority allocations, salience judgments are also affected by more temporary wants or needs in particular situations. Those short-term influences arise from the requirements of a current setting. For example, current wants or active motives may emphasize features and activities that are personally desirable at the present time in order to meet specific objectives. In that way, a project may have reached a point at which a person desires a certain feature in order to advance further to a goal; or substantial deprivation may temporarily provoke an increase in need. In both those cases, a feature's current personal salience becomes temporarily greater.

Judgments of personal salience are brought together with the vitamin model's nonlinear expectations in Table 13.1. In that table, the salience of an environmental characteristic is described in terms of the strength of a current want in relation to that characteristic. If something is viewed as personally salient, it is by definition more strongly wanted, or, if it is negative, avoidance is more strongly wanted. As described earlier, any salience level can derive from dispositional preferences, situational emphases, or both of those.

In the first section of the table is summarized the general pattern of wants for AD and CE features, irrespective of variations in personal salience. As summarized earlier, the expected pattern of wants is the same for both AD and CE features at low to medium levels of those features (column 2). For both kinds of characteristic in this range, people in general want higher levels, indicated in the table as "+ +." In the language of person–environment (P-E) fit (see the previous sections), P > E. At high levels of an environmental characteristic (in the right-hand column), Table 13.1 sets out the previously described differences between AD and CE features; people generally want less ("– –") of an AD feature (P < E), and on average want the same amount (P = E) of a CE feature ("00" in the table).

In the two lower sections of column 2, the strength of wants for an increased level of a currently low environmental feature (either AD or

TABLE 13.1

Wants and Personal Salience in Lower and Higher Ranges of "Additional Decrement" (AD) and "Constant-Effect" (CE) Environmental Features

Type of Environmental Feature and Level of Salience	Range of Environmental Variable	
	Low to Medium	High
The general pattern, irrespective of personal salience:		
AD features	All/most want more (+ +)	Most want less (– –)
CE features	All/most want more (+ +)	Most want same (00)
Additional decrement features, separately at high or low salience:		
AD features, high personal salience	All/most strongly want more (+ + +)	Most would like less (–)
AD features, low personal salience	All/most would like more (+)	Most strongly want less (– – –)
Constant effect features, separately at high or low salience:		
CE features, high personal salience	All/most strongly want more (+ + +)	Most would like more (+)
CE features, low personal salience	All/most would like more (+)	Most want same (00)

CE) is described as either "+" (when it is low salience) or "+ + +" (when the feature is high salience). Those symbols represent strength of wants on either side of the average level ("+ +") at the top of the table. The "+" for low salience is described as "would like" (a more tentative form of want) and the "+ + +" for high salience as "strongly want" (a more intense desire). In both cases (AD and CE), the expected pattern at low to medium environmental levels (in the second column) is straightforward and logically necessary. Up to medium quantities of an environmental characteristic, those that are highly salient are more strongly wanted ("+ + +") than are low-salience features ("+").

However, the pattern is more surprising in the higher range of AD features, in the middle of column 3. In that case, a reverse salience pattern is expected. When an environmental feature is more salient to a person, he or she will be relatively less averse to that feature's negative qualities in a particular episode. Although the nature of AD features (control, demands, variety, etc.) makes them generally undesirable at very high levels, their overall more positive evaluation by high-salience perceivers makes high levels relatively less troublesome to those individuals (shown as "–" in Table 13.1). Conversely, the negative AD association at high levels is likely to be particularly marked for individuals who view the environmental feature as not very attractive (i.e., of low personal salience). Those people will more strongly wish to avoid high levels of a threatening feature that they do not in general greatly value ("– – –" in the table).

As outlined in chapter 4 and elsewhere, constant-effect (CE) features (availability of money, career outlook, equity, etc.) are assumed not to become generally aversive at high levels, and in those cases a desired reduction is not on average expected at high environmental levels. However, for individuals who generally view a CE feature (i.e., availability of money) as personally very important (i.e., they strongly desire large amounts of money), a continuing positive association with subjective well-being across higher levels of that CE feature might be envisaged ("+" in the bottom right-hand cell of Table 13.1). On the other hand, for those who see high income as less personally important, the general CE pattern is expected. On that basis, a leveling off after moderate CE amounts ("00") is shown at the bottom of column 3.

Those salience-related trends are logically entailed by the definition of personal salience as the perceived desirability of an environmental feature. At lower levels of an environmental feature, well-being is impaired by the absence of something wanted, and that impairment is particularly strong if the absent feature is very much wanted. However, the absence of a desirable environmental feature is of relatively less concern to people who view that feature as less salient ("+" in column 2 of Table 13.1). Conversely, for those who view the feature as highly salient, its deficiency is more significant and a remedy is more strongly wanted ("+ + +" in the table). The general expectation displayed to the left of Figure 4.2 in chapter 4 can thus be moderated by dispositional salience.

Across higher environmental levels (in the right-hand column), the pattern in Table 13.1 is again logically necessary, but it is less intuitively obvious than in the summary in column 2. When an AD characteristic is raised to a level that becomes negative in a particular situation, individuals who view that feature as personally desirable are expected to respond less negatively than others ("–" in the right-hand column of Table 13.1), because they are favorably disposed to that feature. However, AD attributes which have become threatening in the higher range will be more troubling to those who perceive the feature as of low salience, because for them the feature's desirability is not great enough to outweigh its negative impact at high levels; they will more strongly ("– – –") want to remedy the excess. The same relative pattern is expected to occur for CE features ("+" and "00"), around an overall stability of association at higher levels (at the top of the table).

Dispositional salience effects of these kinds have been demonstrated in several earlier chapters for low-to-medium environmental levels, but research into possible nonlinear patterns (to the right of Fig. 4.2 and Table 13.1) is generally lacking. Given that personal salience operates in conjunction with environmental influences on people's happiness in employment settings and elsewhere, the correlates, causes and consequences of the wants that underlie salience deserve greater research attention. Some differential predictions are illustrated in Table 13.1. Furthermore, as illustrated in chapter 11, wants belong to the family of constructs that includes ideologies, values, attitudes, personality traits, habits, motives, and preferences. Much of the earlier discussion might thus be presented alternatively in some of those terms, generating a wide range of hypotheses about those other constructs.

OCCUPATIONAL VALUES

Developing one example of that theme, between-person differences in personal salience are central to the study of values. Chapter 11 described how conventional definitions of that construct have been based on a person's view about what is desirable or goals to be sought. Three levels of scope may be considered. In broad terms, people differ in the extent to which they see particular roles as desirable. For example, between-person variations occur in the personal centrality of having a paid job. At more specific levels, values have been examined in terms of preferences for particular aspects of role content or for key tasks. In all cases, they embody salience processes identified in chapter 9 as judgment J4. Broader values involve judgment J4A, the rated importance of role membership; and J4B (the rated importance of a role characteristic) and J4C (the rated attractiveness of core tasks) operate at the more specific levels. Values are considered here mainly in terms of J4B, with a particular emphasis on occupational themes.

The relevant literature is substantial, also covering job attribute preferences, particular career interests, and job-related needs, and there have been many attempts to specify and classify principal work values. Categorization is made difficult by the large number of possible targets that can be desirable to a person and by the several levels of abstractness at which they might be described. For example, authors have varied in their emphasis either on preferences that are restricted to occupations or also extend to a life space as a whole. There is at present no agreement about a single system of value categorization.

For example, the theory of work adjustment (Dawis & Lofquist, 1984) was built around six principal work values (achievement, altruism, autonomy, comfort, safety, and status; see earlier in the chapter), and an international group proposed a structure with a different six components (comfort, income, interpersonal contact, learning and improvement opportunity, religious and social service, and self-expression; MOW International Research Team, 1987). Super (e.g., 1970) focused on a set of 15, including security, achievement, surroundings, and prestige. Hofstede's (1990) framework was in terms of four value dimensions (power distance, uncertainty avoidance, individualism, and masculinity–femininity), and Ros et al. (1999) emphasized extrinsic, intrinsic, prestige, and social categories.

Based on the characteristics of organizations, Quinn and Rohrbaugh (1983) created a model of "competing values" around two axes, extending from flexibility to control (concerning different degrees of routinization and regulation) and from an internal to an external focus (concerned with a person or organization versus a more outgoing perspective). Cable and Edwards (2004) also suggested two principal axes, in their case from conservatism to openness to change and from self-enhancement to self-transcendance, with eight core values such as relationships, pay, and autonomy.

Several models have sought to place both individuals and organizations within the same value structure (e.g., Cable & Edwards, 2004; Kalliath et al., 1999; Dawis & Lofquist, 1984; O'Reilly, Chatman, & Caldwell, 1991). That procedure is applied here. Principal work values (indicators of personal salience; see earlier discussion) can be viewed in the same 12 categories as have been proposed for key environmental characteristics (described here as "vitamins"). Although no single number can be generally "correct," a presentation in terms of 12 categories (with subcategories in some cases) is attractive to balance the conflicting needs for differentiated precision and manageable simplicity.

Given the primary importance of the book's 12 environmental features, we might thus envisage occupational values in the terms suggested in Table 13.2. In each case, labels used by other authors are illustrated in the right-hand column. (But constructs described elsewhere are sometimes overlapping rather than completely identical with the values defined here.) As indicated in the note to the table, the

TABLE 13.2

Twelve Principal Categories of Occupational Value, Parallel
to the "Vitamins" Examined in Chapters 4 to 8

"Vitamin"-Related Label	*Some Related Targets of Value in Other Models*
1. Desire for autonomy and influence	Autonomy, control, empowerment, independence, individualism, independence, self-direction, self-expression, self-determination
2. Desire for skill use	Creative problem-solving, creativity, growth, learning and development, self-development
3. Desire for goals and challenge	Achievement, goal attainment, output orientation, pressure to achieve, task focus
4. Desire for variety	Low continuity, novelty, different experiences
5. Need for clarity	Predictability, uncertainty avoidance, certainty
6. Concern for social relationships	Affiliation, associates, friendliness, human relations, relationships, interpersonal contact, social interaction, warm group relations
7. Desire for money	Economic gain, financial return, wealth, pay
8. Concern for physical comfort and security	Comfort, good surroundings, safety, security
9. Desire for a significant role	Altruism, desired task significance, religious and social service, contribution to community, status, prestige
10. Desire for supervisory support	Supervisory relations, supportive leadership
11. Concern about career outlook	Good career, promotion emphasis, continuity of employment, future progression
12. Concern for fairness	Equity, morality, trust, avoidance of discrimination

Note. Values 1 to 6 may be viewed as more "intrinsic," whereas 7 to 12 are more "extrinsic" to job activities.

12 values can be viewed in terms that are primarily "extrinsic" or "intrinsic" to the activities in a job, as can the characteristics reviewed in chapters 4 to 8. They all reflect differences between individuals in assessments of personal salience, illustrated as judgment J4 in previous chapters. (See, e.g., Table 9.1, also inside the back cover.) Like other forms of personal salience, values operate simultaneously at several levels of temporal specificity; dispositional themes are of primary importance in this section.

Additional research into dispositional forms of personal salience is now needed in many of the areas examined in previous chapters. For instance, at the level of between-group comparisons we lack a comprehensive understanding of differences and similarities between younger and older employees in their ratings of the personal importance of job features. Psychologists' research into age and employment has mainly concentrated on processes that are cognitive, emphasizing declines in speed of information processing and in forms of abstract perception and reasoning (e.g., Warr, 1994b). Complementary research into the causes and consequences of between-age differences in personal salience (here described as values) would help to remedy the current imbalance in our knowledge about older versus younger workers.

It is important to take a comprehensive approach, extending across the full range of work values in Table 13.2. Many studies of differences between individuals and groups have examined the salience of only a few environmental aspects, so that current explanations are necessarily partial. It will sometimes be desirable to go beyond a broad value category to examine subcategories relevant to the groups in question, parallel to the components of job features in Table 8.1 in chapter 8. For example, comparisons between the work values of employed women and men should include the personal salience of work–home conflict, an aspect of feature and value number 3. Similarly, studies of managers need to look within value 1, at several aspects of the desire for autonomy and influence. That broad construct can include a preference for supervisory responsibility for other people and policy, as well as a desire for influence over one's immediate tasks.

Chapter 10 concluded that men and women tend on average to differ in their concern for social relationships (here, value 6) and in their desire for autonomy (1). Consistent with those average value differences, associations between subjective well-being and those two job characteristics appear to differ between male and female employees; correlations are larger for a group's more valued characteristic. This salience-linked difference in the correlates of happiness is also seen through measures of growth need strength, covering the personal salience of several intrinsic job features. That form of work value was shown in chapter 12 to moderate the association between the perceived presence of those features and forms of job satisfaction; correlations are significantly stronger among individuals reporting greater growth need strength.

Patterns of that kind are likely in relation to values within certain personality traits. For instance, as described earlier, dispositional need for clarity and trait authoritarianism in personal relationships moderate associations of job-related happiness with role ambiguity and with opportunity for personal control respectively. The value-related elements of personality constructs now need to be specified more precisely in their own right, focusing on the J4-type assessments of salience (see chaps. 9 and 12) that are made within each trait. How do specific assessments of salience contribute to and draw from particular personality traits, and what is their moderating impact on associations between environmental characteristics and aspects of happiness?

The focus in this section has been mainly on judgment J4B, assessing the importance to oneself of particular characteristics of a role. However, parallel arguments apply to judgments J4A (rating the importance of membership of a particular role) and J4C (judgments about the attractiveness of core tasks in a role). Although research into personal salience may initially appear somewhat peripheral to the book's overarching question, "Why are some people at work happier than others?" it is in fact of central importance at the present stage of research. We now know in broad terms which aspects of the environment promote or impair happiness, but we remain relatively ignorant about when and how those features are of more or of less importance. Judgments of salience are at the heart of a network of variables that give rise to between-person variations in happiness. By focusing on salience processes in terms of values, preferences, needs, and wants, we will increase knowledge that is directly linked to the impact of environmental characteristics; the environment and the person are interdependent.

14

Some Consequences of Happiness

This chapter considers how happiness or unhappiness can affect behavior, in contrast to the emphasis in previous chapters on possible causes. The state of happiness is clearly desirable at a personal level, but it might also be important because of implications that are themselves valued. For example, it could be that happy people are more likely than unhappy ones to behave effectively in organizations. Research has suggested that such a causal process can occur, but that other directions of influence (from behavior to happiness, for instance) may also be important in some cases. As in earlier chapters, the presentation emphasizes findings from employment settings, but nonoccupational investigations are also considered.

GENERAL CONSIDERATIONS

In studying possible consequences of different levels of happiness, researchers have strongly emphasized subjective well-being rather than self-validation. (See the two components examined in chaps. 1 and 2.) Most studies have been correlational, examining the strength of association between a form of well-being and a particular behavior at one point in time. As in other areas of correlational study (and illustrated particularly in chap. 8), the presence of a significant association does not necessarily indicate that one variable (e.g., high job satisfaction) has caused the other (e.g., good work performance). The opposite might be true: Good performers might be more satisfied as a result of their better performance. Alternatively, both those processes might occur in a bidirectional pattern, and/or a third factor (or several of them) might bring about both high performance and high satisfaction.

Correlations between subjective well-being and behavior are thus on their own causally ambiguous. Furthermore, given that behavior is determined by many different factors (organizational policies, group pressures, individual abilities, available options, etc.), the maximum observed correlation with well-being alone is expected to be much less than +1.00.

As in other areas of research, investigators have sought methodological procedures to assist in the identification of causal processes. For example, some correlational studies, examining associations between happiness and possible outcomes, have applied statistical controls to rule out other variables that might be influential, holding constant demographic features, job characteristics, or other factors. Other investigations have obtained information longitudinally, with happiness measured before its potential effects. A longitudinal association is usually required as evidence of potential causality, but cannot itself exclude an impact from continuing influences (see chap. 8). In addition, it is usually unclear within a longitudinal design what is theoretically the most appropriate duration between two measurement occasions; longitudinal studies have varied widely in the time lag applied.

Causal processes might in principle be identified through experimental research, in the present case manipulating people's happiness to examine differences in behavioral outcomes. However, research of that kind is difficult to undertake in everyday settings. Procedures explicitly to alter employees' well-being in order to learn about behavioral consequences are open to ethical and pragmatic objections. For example, individuals may object to interference in their personal life for research purposes, and research designs in organizations are likely to be compromised by unbalanced samples (e.g., comprising only volunteers, who may be atypical), by the influence of participants' expectations on measured outcomes, or by synchronous effects from other operational changes (because decisions about working procedures continue to be taken throughout an investigation). In general, it may not be possible in an occupational setting to modify happiness (here the "independent" variable) without at the same time changing other variables such as the content of a job, thus increasing the difficulty of causal interpretation. For these varied reasons, few experimental findings are available from organizations about the impact on behavior of changes in well-being.

Instead, some investigators have employed experimental manipulation in short-term, often laboratory-based, research. In those studies, mild happiness has been induced by a free gift, returned money from a slot machine, victory in a computer game, unexpected food or drink, thinking about a happy occasion, or praise from another person (e.g., Isen, 1999; Isen & Baron, 1991). These experimental investigations have usually covered only feelings that are positive, avoiding the generation of negative affect for research purposes. Findings (illustrated later) may be qualitatively different from those in organizations. For example, research into job satisfaction as a potential causal variable concerns a form of subjective well-being that is sustained, based on continuing environmental influences, and repeatedly experienced across days or weeks. On the other hand, laboratory inductions of happiness give rise only to brief affective states, with an impact that is localized and that may be overridden by more extended forms of well-being or unavoidable inputs from the environment.

It is clear that caution is required in the integration of findings from organizational studies and short-term experimental inductions. It could be that more established well-being is linked to different kinds and levels of behavior than are brief states. Or, short-term states could typically influence behavior in combination with more extended forms of well-being. Research in this field is still limited, and detailed understanding of these and similar issues is lacking.

Some relevant themes were considered by Beal, Weiss, Barros, and MacDermid (2005) in terms of more distal and more proximal influences on performance. They pointed out that most research in organizations has taken a between-person approach, studying behavioral differences between people in their relatively long-term affect (e.g., their job satisfaction). Instead, a focus on short-term emotional variability within a person might better contribute to understanding links with performance in particular episodes. Their emphasis was mainly on affective experiences that originate outside a particular task. Those create distractions that can draw away resources, increase the need for effortful emotional regulation, and possibly impair performance. However, when positive affect is integral to the task, "the attentional pull of the task is likely to increase, allowing the worker to stay focused on the task while expending a minimum of regulatory resources" (p. 1063).

Context-free rather than domain-specific happiness was considered by Kim-Prieto et al. (2005). They examined patterns of more proximal and more distal influences in terms of sequences of affect across time. Distinguishing between different time frames, they illustrated how happiness measured with a long-term emphasis (such as life satisfaction) derives in complex ways from more short-term experiences. They pointed out that shorter term forms of happiness might be more closely associated with other variables than is, for instance, life satisfaction. It may thus be the case that behavior in some settings is strongly associated with short-term affective states (e.g., current mood), but is less related to the longer term indicators that are conventionally studied.

Those possibilities link with other general issues. As described in chapter 2 and illustrated throughout the book, happiness takes a variety of forms, for instance differing in degree of scope, the involvement of pleasure or self-validation, relative affective or cognitive emphasis, the presence of psychological arousal as well as pleasure, and also duration of the experience. In thinking about the behavioral consequences of happiness, it is important to ask about particular forms, rather than assuming that findings about one type of happiness will be replicated with others.

For example, differences in the scope of happiness have been illustrated throughout the book at context-free, domain-specific, and facet-specific levels. In examining the causes of happiness, chapter 4 drew attention to the fact that for subjective well-being that is context-free many different kinds of influence may be operative, involving varied features in the environment and in the person. For context-free well-being, any single cause is thus expected usually to be of limited importance on its own among many other causes. On the other hand, facet-specific well-being is influenced in a targeted manner by a narrow set of variables concerned with the facet in question, which can have a substantial impact on (the conceptually linked) satisfaction with that facet. (See, e.g., Fig. 4.2c.) A similar gradation may be suggested for the consequences of well-being. A facet-specific form of happiness, such as satisfaction with pay, is likely to give rise to behavior associated narrowly with its own particular issue (here, pay), whereas context-free well-being (e.g., global satisfaction with one's life) may have implications that are more diffuse but each fairly weak.

This scope-related contrast in outcomes can be augmented by differing affective or cognitive emphases in the happiness measure that is applied. In general, affective indicators are more likely than cognitive ones to be associated with behavior, because affect is central to the motives and wants that generate activity; cognition itself has no motivational properties. Thus, for example, facet-specific happiness that is primarily affective may directly influence behaviors relevant to that facet, whereas facet-specific well-being indicators that are more cognitively based may have fewer links with behavior. Indeed, facet-specific well-being, here viewed primarily as a targeted form of happiness, comes close to what some other commentators have viewed as an attitude, with clear expectations of conceptually related attitude–behavior links. On the other hand, context-free well-being is conceptually distinct from an attitude, with fewer implications for specific actions. (See Table 2.2 and the associated discussion in chap. 2.)

Differences in behavioral consequences are also expected between subjective well-being assessed on measurement axis 1 and on axes 2 and 3. Axis 1 (see Fig. 2.2) ranges from feeling bad to feeling good without concern for degree of psychological arousal. The other two axes reflect also the experience of raised or lowered activation. For instance, active pleasure (3b, in the top-right section of Figs. 2.1 and 2.2) can involve interest, energy, or enthusiasm, feelings that are clearly oriented to action. Indeed, the terms *activation* and *action* have the same origin and conceptual base, both having *act* as their stem. It may thus be that activated forms of well-being are more strongly associated with behavior than is more tranquil well-being which involves less psychological arousal. The general point is that we need to ask separately about the consequences of different forms of happiness, rather than treating all indicators as interchangeable.

JOB PERFORMANCE

First, what about behavior in a job? It is widely believed that high subjective well-being and effective job performance are linked. Across three samples, Fisher (2003) found that 92% of nonpsychologists agreed with the statement that "a happy worker is likely to be a productive worker." She showed in a within-person study that this belief about people in general is supported by personal experience of oneself. Research participants described on up to five occasions a day their current well-being, in terms of mood (from negative to positive) and of satisfaction with a current task. In addition, they rated their performance in whatever task they were undertaking at the time, for example, from poor to excellent. Individuals' well-being covaried systematically with their self-ratings of task performance, yielding within-person across-time correlations of +0.41 between performance and current mood and +0.57 between performance and satisfaction with the current task (see also Fisher & Noble, 2004).

People are thus less happy when their task performance is felt to be poor, and more happy when they are working well. However, information in Fisher's (2003) study was (by design) all provided by the same person, and it might be argued that assessments of task performance were biased by an individual's feelings at the time. So we also need information about indicators of behavioral effectiveness that are independent of the target person.

Research of that kind has examined patterns across a sample of people, rather than within-person associations as in the example above, asking whether people who are happy behave differently (in independent assessments) from those who are less happy. Most occupational studies have measured behavior in terms of overall job performance as rated by a person's supervisor. Overall performance scores have been of two kinds, either a combined value from separate ratings of several job activities, or a global assessment of work performance as a whole. Well-being in this area has traditionally been examined in terms of overall job satisfaction. As described in chapter 2, that job-related construct is located on measurement axis 1, from feeling bad to feeling good without concern for psychological arousal, and scales often have a cognitive emphasis rather than being strongly affective (see Table 2.1).

Before reviewing findings from research in this field, let us consider again possible forms of causal influence and potential underlying processes. As outlined earlier in this chapter and in chapter 8, four causal patterns can be envisaged:

- Well-being causes performance.
- Performance causes well-being.
- Well-being and performance cause each other.
- One or more additional variables cause both well-being and performance.

The first two possibilities illustrate sequences that are unidirectional, with the second sometimes described as "reverse causation." The third possibility suggests bidirectional or reciprocal influences, and the last one is sometimes said to reflect the impact of one or more "third variables" or "third factors."

These possibilities are not mutually exclusive, in that more than one may be important in any situation, and their relative importance is expected to vary between studies. For instance, different kinds of well-being may be related to behavior in different ways, and the nature of desired performance (and thus possible links with happiness) clearly varies between different jobs. The general sketch offered next requires more detailed specification of contingencies with respect to particular jobs and particular kinds of subjective well-being and performance.

Possibility 1: Well-Being Causes Performance.   This unidirectional pattern might come about because raised well-being generates behaviors that promote good performance, whereas low well-being inhibits those behaviors. For example, happy individuals might be more active, energetic, interested in their environment, sympathetic to other people, and persistent in the face of difficulties than are unhappy individuals. Locke's (1970) view was that "satisfaction and dissatisfaction are important incentives to action in that they entail action tendencies (i.e., approach and avoidance)" (p. 484), with performance determined by a person's goals, the attainment of which brings satisfaction.

Other possible causal processes are indirect through interpersonal consequences. An employee's happiness might generate responses from other people that enhance his or her performance. For example, a worker's positive affect and associated behaviors might encourage colleagues to provide instrumental assistance and emotional support, or supervisors to allocate more challenging or personally suitable tasks. Individual and social processes of these kinds are further examined later in the chapter.

Possibility 2: Performance Causes Well-Being.   Reverse causation might occur because effective job performance changes environmental inputs in ways that can enhance happiness. "Briefly stated, good performance may lead to rewards, which in turn lead to satisfaction" (Lawler & Porter, 1967, p. 23). For example, several of the environmental features examined in chapters 4 to 8 can become more available to a person as a result of his or her organizationally desired behavior. An obvious example is increased pay (feature 7) deriving from successful job performance, but the attainment of job targets (feature 3) is often also a major source of happiness, leading to rewards that can be either self-generated or provided by the organization. Or supervisors might be more supportive (feature 10) to workers whose performance is viewed as good. More generally, effective job performance can bring about greater personal control over the environment and more extensive skill utilization (features 1 and 2), with widespread positive implications for happiness as illustrated in chapter 6.

Certain behaviors are more likely than others to contribute to happiness or unhappiness in these ways. For example, Spreitzer et al.

(2005) have emphasized the desirable consequences of three particular sets of activity in employment settings. Those involve focusing on the task in hand, exploring new ideas and possibilities, and relating to others in an attentive manner. "Each of those behaviors can help people to experience thriving at work" (p. 540).

Possibility 3: Well-Being and Performance Cause Each Other. In this case, the two previous processes are viewed as operating in conjunction with each other. Well-being may be a response to previous goal-achievement, job effectiveness, and associated personal rewards (as suggested by possibility 2). In turn, raised well-being might generate activities and goal-seeking that influence performance and thus subsequent well-being (possibility 1). Reciprocal cycles of influence across time (performance-reward-performance) were emphasized in a review of motivational processes by Latham and Pinder (2005). They pointed out that effective performance can yield reward-linked happiness, and that this encourages the continuation of the rewarding behavior.

Possibility 4: Additional Variables Cause Both Well-Being and Performance. As in other areas of research, it may be the case that observed correlations between happiness and behavior have been influenced by additional, perhaps unmeasured, features. For example, continuing influences might be envisaged from personality traits such as extraversion or neuroticism (see chap. 11). In that way, more extraverted individuals might both feel more happy and also exhibit behaviors that are important in the particular job under investigation. Similarly, continuing levels of the 12 primary environmental features might yield both raised or impaired well-being and matching levels of performance. For instance, supportive supervision (feature 10) might increase job satisfaction and also create the conditions for effective job performance. Observed associations between employee happiness and performance would in these cases be due, at least in part, to the influence of other factors.

It is difficult to assess empirically the relative impact of these four causal possibilities. Some conceptual and methodological problems are illustrated below. In practice, most studies to date have merely asked about the existence or otherwise of a significant association between well-being and behavior. A research review by Lyubomirsky et al. (2005) combined many types of happiness (both context-free and job-related) and grouped together many forms of success in employment (performance, income, job content, and low labor turnover). Aggregating across those very diverse indicators of both kinds, the average correlation in previous studies between happiness and success in work was found to be +0.27.

Job-Specific Well-Being

With a more specific focus, examining the correlates of job satisfaction, Iaffaldano and Muchinsky (1985) recorded an average uncorrected correlation in previous investigations of +0.25 with overall job performance. Petty, McGee, and Cavender (1984) reported very similar findings (the average uncorrected correlation was +0.23), and noted that the association with rated performance was stronger for managerial and professional employees than for others (average uncorrected correlations of +0.31 and +0.15, respectively). In the review by Podsakoff et al. (1996), the mean satisfaction–performance correlation was +0.24. Examining several hundred studies, Judge, Thorensen, Bono, and Patton (2001) observed an average uncorrected correlation between job satisfaction and performance of +0.18, with a stronger association (mean $r = +0.26$) when a person's work was of higher complexity and thus permitted greater freedom of action. Their review also indicated that the average correlation was slightly higher for overall measures of job satisfaction (+0.22) than for a composite of facet satisfactions (+0.18). Later research by Schleicher, Watt, and Greguras (2004) yielded correlations in two nonmanagerial samples between overall job satisfaction and supervisor-rated overall performance of +0.38 and +0.23.

Several investigators have examined activities at work described as "organizational citizenship behavior" or "contextual performance" (i.e., outside a prescribed main task; Smith, Organ, & Near, 1983). Such "extrarole" behaviors include providing assistance to colleagues, being friendly, volunteering to undertake needed tasks, adhering closely to the organization's rules, and making suggestions to improve effectiveness. Organizational citizenship behavior can more readily be distinguished from core-task performance in lower level jobs. Required task activities in those tend to be more closely specified than in managerial or professional roles, when conceptual or empirical separation between citizenship and task behaviors is less straightforward.

Ratings of citizenship behavior by a boss or colleagues have frequently been found to be significantly associated with an employee's overall job satisfaction (e.g., McNeely & Meglino, 1994; Motowidlo, 1984; Podsakoff et al., 2000; Smith et al., 1983). In a meta-analytic

review, Organ and Ryan (1995) summarized correlations of job satisfaction with specific forms of citizenship behavior rated by other
people. For altruism, the mean uncorrected r was +0.23, and for generalized compliance that value was +0.20. Considering overall citizenship behavior, the average correlation of single citizenship scales with
job satisfaction was found to be +0.38. (As pointed out in chap. 11, the
average of correlations with constituent scales tends to underestimate
the correlation with an overall composite, here citizenship behavior as
a whole.)

George (1991, 1996) has suggested that associations with citizenship
behavior are due to more satisfied employees experiencing more positive short-term mood (in the top-right section of Figs. 2.1 and 2.2),
which she showed to be linked to altruistic behaviors rated by supervisors ($r = +0.24$). Lee and Allen (2002) found that job-related positive
affect of that activated kind was correlated at +0.18 with colleagues' ratings of help provided to other individuals and +0.24 with their ratings
of a person's citizenship behavior directed at the organization more
broadly. Active forms of positive mood were correlated at +0.17 with a
broad index of citizenship behavior rated by supervisors in research by
Eisenberger, Jones, Stinglhamber, Shanock, and Randall (2005).

Employees' behavior has also been studied in terms of voluntary
overtime. Many jobs offer the possibility of undertaking some unpaid
work outside the required hours, and employees' job-specific well-
being might be associated with such behavior. This was found to be
the case by Gechman and Wiener (1975) in a study of schoolteachers.
Controlling for age (itself strongly associated with the well-being indicator), overall job satisfaction was correlated at +0.25 with the amount
of additional unpaid time devoted to work-related activities.

Participation in learning activities was studied by Birdi, Gardner,
and Warr (1998). Overall job satisfaction was found to be greater
among those who were more active in self-determined development
activities (undertaking personal projects, serving on working groups,
etc.). This positive association remained significant after statistical
control for demographic variables which were themselves predictive
of participation in these forms of activity. (For instance, younger and
more educated employees are more likely to undertake development
projects; e.g., Maurer et al., 2003.)

Deviant activities at work have been investigated under the heading
of "counterproductive work behavior," covering theft, sabotage, lying,
physical assault, and other forms of delinquency. This kind of activity
is difficult to record accurately (e.g., because people tend to conceal

it), but it has been found to be more common among employees with lower job-related well-being. For example, Penney and Spector (2005) reported correlations between overall job satisfaction and an employee's self-reported and peer-reported counterproductive behavior of –0.33 and –0.25, respectively.

However, from these cross-sectional investigations alone we cannot determine whether greater well-being promoted the behaviors in question, whether the behaviors enhanced well-being, whether both effects occurred, or (in many cases) whether third variables were causally important (possibilities 1 to 4, listed earlier). Note also that almost all studies cited in this section have looked at employee well-being in relation to behavior in the recent past. It is usual to obtain happiness reports and information about behavior at about the same time. Ratings of job performance thus typically concern an earlier period, so that a reported correlation represents a postdiction rather than a prediction of behavior. A shift to multiple assessments that permit analyses across time is clearly needed.

With that in mind, Lyubomirsky et al. (2005) asked from previous research findings whether happiness precedes job success, rather than being linked only cross-sectionally. As in their cross-sectional review (already described), they combined very diverse indicators of the two constructs. Across several time intervals and mixed measures of happiness or job success, the average longitudinal correlation was found to be +0.24.

Note that happiness might have an impact on performance through a sequence of social influences as well as in entirely individual terms. One influence of that kind could be in terms of reciprocal social support, an aspect of "vitamin" 6. As summarized in chapter 11, an employee's contribution of social support to others tends to be associated with the receipt of social support in return (Bowling et al., 2005). Given that more happy individuals tend more to offer that support (summarized earlier), it could sometimes be the case that their job performance is also better because of supportive inputs from other employees.

Between-person influences and the development of performance-relevant cultural norms are also assumed in research at the organizational level. Several investigators have predicted that organizations whose employees are on average more satisfied will be more productive than other organizations. In a study of 298 schools, Ostroff (1992) found that standardized measures of academic performance, administrative efficiency and student behavior were significantly associated with their teachers' mean overall job satisfaction (an average coefficient of +0.28). This pattern was retained after statistical controls were introduced for differences between the schools in student characteristics and the resources available. Robertson et al. (1995) applied standardized observational procedures in a study of nurses' delivery of health care. Analyses of variance for six caring activities at the unit level revealed substantial differences in the quality of care between wards with nurses whose average overall job satisfaction was either high or low.

Other studies have measured organizational performance in financial terms. Across 28 retail stores, Koys (2001) found that employees' mean job satisfaction was correlated at +0.35 with store profitability in the subsequent year. (For subsequent customer satisfaction ratings, that value was +0.61.) A significant company-level association was also observed in relation to productivity by Harter, Schmidt, and Hayes (2002), although the temporal sequence of measurement was not clear from that report. In a study of manufacturing companies, Patterson et al. (2004) obtained a correlation of +0.44 between average overall job satisfaction and company productivity in the subsequent year. That longitudinal association remained significant after several statistical controls, and was present in separate analyses of the average satisfaction of managers and nonmanagers in each company ($r = +0.41$ and $+0.39$, respectively).

Cross-sectional analyses of unit-level data by Ryan, Schmit, and Johnson (1996) revealed correlations (controlling for unit size, and here averaged across two measurement points) between employees' average overall job satisfaction and market share of +0.25 and between average job satisfaction and customer satisfaction of +0.20. Longitudinal analyses suggested that a reverse causal pattern (possibility 2, identified earlier) may be involved for customer satisfaction, with customer reactions influencing employees' feelings about their job. However, attempts to specify the direction of causality for the financial indicator were inconclusive. Schneider, Hanges, Smith, and Salvaggio (2003) found that, although companies' average overall job satisfaction significantly predicted earnings per share in each of the following two years (mean $r = +0.23$), correlations were somewhat higher (averaging +0.33) in the reverse direction, from that financial indicator to average job satisfaction in the following two years. These organization-level studies make it clear that well-being and performance can influence each other in several ways.

Nevertheless, longitudinal evidence about organizations' average happiness and financial performance remains limited, and very few studies have examined both kinds of variable on two or more occasions. More substantial data sets are still required for confident interpretation. For example, sample sizes in the analyses by Schneider and colleagues ranged from only 12 to 35 companies. It is also desirable to restrict attention to single business sectors, rather than (as is common) bringing together information about organizations with different products or services, which can be operating in very different conditions. Average organizational scores are also more meaningful if they are from single locations, rather than combining multiple subsamples of employees from different sites.

Furthermore, as with all longitudinal research, it is sometimes difficult to disentangle specific directional effects from the influence of continuing levels of a studied variable. For example, if the rank order of satisfaction scores remains stable across years, as it often does, it may be unclear which year's level is the causally important one. Measured performance will be similarly associated with both earlier and later well-being, because the two values are similar, so that causal priority will be ambiguous. A similar stability is found in performance scores. For example, at the level of individual employees the correlation across 12 months was +0.75 in research by Takeuchi, Wang, and Marinova (2005). This point is illustrated further in relation to absence behavior later in the chapter.

The performance studies reviewed so far have focused on well-being axis 1, particularly on job satisfaction. However, it could be that variations in the second dimension introduced in chapter 2 (psychological arousal) are also important. What about job-related forms of axis 2, from feelings of anxiety to comfort? For low well-being of that kind, it seems likely that employees who report more job anxiety might be experiencing difficulty in coping with job demands and thus be liable to perform relatively less effectively; an inverse association between job-related anxiety and job performance is thus probable.

Few investigations have addressed this possibility, but Jamal (1984) found that unhappiness in terms of job-related tension was associated with lower supervisory ratings (a median correlation of –0.35), and Spector et al. (1988) reported a correlation of –0.16. Takeuchi et al. (2005) examined negative job-related affect in a measure that appears to be primarily loaded on axis 2. They found a correlation of –0.36 with contemporary ratings by supervisors of overall job performance and one of –0.19 with that performance measure 1 year later.

A particular form of job behavior was considered by Karasek and Theorell (1990). They hypothesized that, if sustained over a long period, job-related anxiety (a low score on well-being axis 2) would inhibit learning. More anxious employees might thus be less likely to acquire procedures and skills to protect themselves from future stressors or to undertake work effectively, perhaps becoming still more anxious. Evidence for this longitudinal possibility has yet to be published.

Another hypothesis is in terms of an optimal amount of demand, with lower performance occurring on either side of that optimum. It may be the case that the relationship between job anxiety and performance is one of an inverted U, such that moderate demands are linked to raised job-related anxiety and also to more effective performance, but that lower and higher levels of demand and anxiety are accompanied by lower performance. Anderson (1976) suggested that this was the case in data from a sample of small-business owners, but the possibility remains in need of more substantial examination. In a study of hair stylists, van Dyne, Jehn, and Cummings (2002) found a tendency for more sales to be achieved by those with more negative job feelings (mainly tension, 2a in Fig. 2.2), but reported that the association with supervisor-rated performance was negligible. The study by Takeuchi et al. (2005) revealed a significant inverted-U pattern in addition to a linear relationship (see the earlier description): Job performance was best when employees reported moderate levels of strain. It seems likely that some anxiety is a common accompaniment of effectiveness in many job tasks.

The emotional exhaustion component of job-related burnout primarily represents negative forms of well-being axis 2 (see chap. 2). In studies by Wright and Bonett (1997) and Wright and Cropanzano (1998), cross-sectional correlations with supervisor-rated overall performance were found to be -0.16 and -0.27, respectively. In the first of those studies, employees' performance was measured again after 3 years; the longitudinal correlation with prior job-related emotional exhaustion was -0.31. Cropanzano, Rupp, and Byrne (2003) reported significant cross-sectional associations of emotional exhaustion with supervisor ratings both of overall job performance and of organizational citizenship behavior. The average correlations from two studies were -0.22 and -0.20, respectively, and those remained significant despite statistical controls for age, gender and ethnicity. Leiter, Harvie, and Frizzell (1998) studied this form of well-being in terms of work-unit averages. Examining assessments by patients of the quality of hospital care they had received, they found that patients treated in units whose nursing staff on average exhibited greater job-related emotional exhaustion were much less satisfied with their nurses, doctors and overall quality of care (average unit-level $r = -0.68$).

The third axis of job-specific well-being in Figure 2.2 ranges from depression to enthusiasm. It appears likely that employees with positive feelings of this kind (in the top-right, activated section of Fig. 2.2) will be among the more productive, but few relevant studies have been reported. George (1991) found a correlation of +0.26 between activated forms of positive mood and supervisors' ratings of salespeople's helpful customer behavior; however, the correlation with actual sales performance was only +0.10. With respect to low well-being on axis 3, Motowidlo, Packard, and Manning (1986) examined the association between nurses' job-related depression and ratings by supervisors and coworkers of their interpersonal effectiveness (sensitivity to patients, cooperation, warmth, etc.) and of their cognitive/motivational effectiveness (concentration, perseverance, etc.). In both bivariate and multivariate analyses, job-related depression was significantly associated with lower effectiveness of both kinds.

Context-Free Well-Being

All studies cited so far in this section have examined job performance as a function of well-being that is job-specific. We might also ask about happiness-behavior links at the other two levels of scope—context-free and facet-specific well-being. Research into job performance has less often used those indicators, of greater or less abstractness than the domain-specific constructs considered so far.

With respect to context-free well-being, Wright, Bonett, and Sweeney (1993) used items that mainly fell on measurement axis 3, from depression to enthusiasm. Across a 1-year period, well-being scores were correlated at +0.48 with later ratings of job performance. In two other studies, this context-free measure was correlated at +0.40 (average of two assessments) and +0.46 with supervisor-rated composite performance 1 year later. Those significant patterns were retained after controls for demographic characteristics and prior level of well-being.

Cropanzano and Wright (1999) illustrated the expected reduction in that association across longer periods of prediction. Although the correlation between rated performance and their measure of context-free well-being was +0.34 and +0.36 in cross-sectional and 1-year analyses, respectively, that value was only +0.18 when performance was measured 5 years after happiness. In two cross-sectional multiple regression analyses by Wright and Cropanzano (2000), context-free well-being was found to explain significant variance in rated performance beyond that accounted for by job satisfaction.

A study by Beehr et al. (2000) bears on the second causal possibility introduced earlier, in terms of reverse influence. They examined the association between context-free depression and sales achieved by door-to-door booksellers, recording sales in the previous few months. The observed correlation was –0.38. Given that responses to questions about depressive symptoms were made in the knowledge of prior success or failure (and in the context of other questions drawing attention to earlier job difficulties), some influence from that awareness of performance onto current well-being can be envisaged. Note, however, that this reverse causal process is a general occurrence in many job settings; awareness of previous poor or good performance is likely often to bear upon a person's feelings about his or her job.

Staw, Sutton, and Pelled (1994) used a measure of subjective well-being that combined self-reports of both context-free and job-specific affects with some ratings by observers of job-related affect. That mixed indicator was found to be correlated with supervisors' ratings of overall job performance at +0.30 in simultaneous assessment (i.e., of recently observed behavior) and +0.16 when performance was measured around 19 months later. The latter association became highly significant after controls were introduced for demographic variables and individuals' performance recorded on the previous measurement occasion.

Facet-Specific Well-Being

There is thus some evidence that happiness that is context-free is predictive of later job performance. Significant associations at the medium (domain-specific) level of scope, with job-related well-being, were documented earlier. What about the third level of abstractness, with respect to facet-specific indicators? As pointed out previously, these come close to measures of specific attitudes, and attitudes are by definition expected to influence conceptually linked behavior. Kraus (1995) examined 88 previous studies in nonemployment settings, finding that attitudes were on average correlated at +0.38 with subsequent behavior (for instance, voting for political parties, adhering to a diet, discriminating racially, or driving rapidly). Attitude investigations have recorded behavior either through observations by other people or through self-reports by research participants themselves. Correlations were found to be smaller, but still significant, when behavioral indicators were from observers (mean r = +0.32) rather than being self-reported (mean r = +0.51), and they were particularly high when both variables (attitude and behavior) were of similar scope (mean r = +0.54, including both observed and self-reported behaviors).

Despite this nonoccupational evidence of attitude–behavior links, few investigations have been published of associations between facet-specific well-being and job performance. Iaffaldano and Muchinsky (1985) and Petty et al. (1984) reviewed early research with the scales of the Job Descriptive Index (JDI; see chap. 2). Examining overlapping but not identical data sets, the two reviews yielded slightly different average correlations between the five studied facets and overall job performance. Mean values (with Iaffaldano and Muchinsky's results first) were: +0.18 and +0.27 for satisfaction with work content, +0.16 and +0.27 for satisfaction with supervision, +0.12 and +0.22 for satisfaction with promotion opportunities, +0.10 and +0.18 for satisfaction with coworkers, and +0.05 and +0.15 for satisfaction with pay.

For "hard criteria" of job performance (which were not detailed), Kinicki et al. (2002) reported from previous JDI studies an average uncorrected correlation of +0.22 with satisfaction with work content. For performance that was supervisor-rated, the average correlation with work-content satisfaction in that review was +0.16. In addition, supervisor-rated performance was correlated on average at +0.21, +0.16, +0.17, and +0.13 with facet-specific satisfactions with supervision, promotion opportunities, coworkers, and pay, respectively.

Pay satisfaction was examined by Currall, Towler, Judge, and Kohn (2005) at the organizational level. Average performance of school districts was assessed through standardized academic tests administered to all students in certain age-groups, and districts' average pass rate for those students was examined as a function of their teachers' average pay satisfaction. The bivariate correlation between those variables at the district level was +0.23, and that association remained significant despite controls for teacher's salary and experience, students' socioeconomic status, and school facilities. The authors speculated that greater pay satisfaction might give rise to a greater willingness to engage in more positive teaching practices.

Organization-level links between facet satisfaction and performance were studied longitudinally by Schneider et al. (2003; see earlier in the section). They found that average company-level satisfaction with job security was unrelated to subsequent company financial performance, but that average satisfaction with security was itself predicted by previous company performance. It seems likely that a company's success caused employees to hold positive beliefs and feelings about future security, and that relative company failure increased their feelings of insecurity—a form of reverse causality, the second possibility suggested earlier. However, for other facet satisfactions, that reverse process on its own was not apparent. For satisfaction with pay, reciprocal causal influences on company performance appeared to be present (both from and to well-being), but longitudinal links were nonsignificant for satisfaction with empowerment, with job fulfilment, or with the work group.

Future investigations of employee well-being at the facet level could usefully draw on models of attitude-behavior links (e.g., Eagly & Chaiken, 1993; Kraus, 1995). Those emphasize the importance of matched scope; behaviors are more likely to be predicted by attitudes if both variables are similarly narrow. In that respect, facet-specific well-being is likely to be more closely associated with facet-specific behavior than with the overall performance indicators that have traditionally been studied.

An Expanded Perspective

Generally, studies in this field should adopt a more comprehensive perspective beyond the customary concern for job satisfaction, examining different forms of subjective well-being at other levels of scope as well as across the three axes of measurement. It is likely that particular unidirectional or bidirectional influences are restricted to only certain aspects of well-being in relation to certain kinds of job performance.

Within an expanded perspective of that kind, it is desirable to examine together people's happiness or unhappiness and also the environmental sources of that experience. Significant happiness–performance associations are likely sometimes to arise from "third variables" in the job environment, such that certain job features give rise to both employee well-being and particular job activities, as in possibility 4 introduced earlier.

Linked to that, unhappiness in the form of job-related strain may be associated either negatively or positively with job performance depending on the environmental source of that strain, either from challenging demands that draw out activity and creativity or from oppressive conditions or disliked colleagues. Lepine et al. (2005) examined previous findings about very broad categories described as "challenge" stressors and "hindrance" stressors. Although both kinds of negative environmental feature were significantly linked to broadly defined strain, "hindrance" stressors in the environment were negatively correlated with job performance (mean $r = -0.14$) and "challenge" stressors yielded a small positive association (average $r = +0.09$). That secondary analysis of summary data did not permit more complex interpretation, and empirical research that brings together both measured job characteristics and employee happiness in the prediction of job performance is now needed.

ASSOCIATED THOUGHTS AND BEHAVIORS

What mechanisms might underlie causal relationships between employees' well-being and their job performance? Several possibilities were mentioned earlier in the chapter, and some combination of those is likely to be important in particular settings. Findings are here grouped in terms of cognitive processes, energy-related effects, and social activities. Most investigations cited below have involved the experimental induction of short-term positive affect, and the generalizability of results to more extended forms of happiness has not yet been established.

Mental Processes

Cognitive outcomes have sometimes been examined in terms of effects on perception and memory, with a general finding that affective state provides a guideline for people's information processing. Research reviews supporting statements in this section have been provided by Isen and Baron (1991), Staw et al. (1994), Isen (1999), Forgas (2001), Forgas and George (2001), Lucas and Diener (2003), Russell (2003), and Lyubomirsky et al. (2005). Additional references are cited in the text.

For example, the induction of mild positive affect has been shown to encourage more positive perceptions, to facilitate the recall of positive material, and to give rise to more positive judgments about neutral material. Positive themes are thus more often cognitively accessed by people who are feeling good. Findings from laboratory research are less clear about the converse effects of unhappiness (Isen, 1985). However, it is a characteristic of clinically depressed people to emphasize memories and thoughts that are negative (Beck, Rush, Shaw, & Emery, 1979; Teasdale, Taylor, & Fogarty, 1980), and such an effect might also occur for unhappiness that is less extreme.

Happiness-related positive priming has also been shown for judgments of expectancy and valence. Models of motivation and related processes deriving from expectancy theory (e.g., Vroom, 1964) envisage that people assess the probability that certain actions or events will lead to certain outcomes (expectancy judgments) and also appraise the attractiveness of those outcomes (utility or valence judgments). Both forms of judgment appear to be more positive when research participants are more happy (Seo et al., 2004; Wright & Staw, 1999). After positive mood induction, people thus tend to be more optimistic and to see more opportunities for pleasure around them.

Laboratory research has also suggested that happy people process complex information more speedily, and that they adopt a wider perspective across the range of issues requiring consideration. For example, positive affect appears to make additional cognitive material available for processing, and encourages a wider span of attention. Associated with that, other laboratory studies have indicated that positive mood can impair detailed reasoning processes. For example, Phillips, Bull, Adams, and Fraser (2002) recorded limitations in happier people's controlled switching of attention between focal ideas.

Stressful conditions have long been known to lead to a narrowing of attention. This was first observed in simulated flying tasks in World War II, when pilot error in difficult activities often arose from a failure to respond to signals from the periphery of a display (Russell Davis, 1948). Subsequent research by cognitive psychologists has consistently demonstrated this strain-related narrowing of perceptual focus. By restricting their attention to tasks considered to be central, people under strain maintain or enhance performance in those central activities, but their effectiveness on peripheral tasks can become impaired (e.g., Hockey, 1986).

Linked to that, negative affect has been found to give rise to more attentiveness to detail, with less happy people thinking in a more analytical manner. Happy individuals appear to base judgments more readily on prior assumptions, perhaps relying on established stereotypes, rather than checking and working through new information. Induced happiness also increases risk-taking in hypothetical situations or when the chances of winning are high. The practical benefits or costs of those different cognitive implications of happiness do of course depend on the nature of the task in hand; for example, does that require risk-taking or considerable attention to detail?

Experimental research has also suggested that happiness inductions can promote creativity, in terms of the elicitation of more unusual and more diverse associations to neutral stimulus words. The applicability of those laboratory findings to job-related innovation might however be questioned, because innovation in organizational settings involves the successful exploitation of ideas that are useful as well as merely being novel. Practical creativity thus requires extended activities to overcome obstacles across time in addition to intellectual creativity (e.g., DeGraff & Lawrence, 2002). Measures of mental associations to stimulus words (as in laboratory research) clearly fail to tap much of that wider process.

Nevertheless, an organizational diary study by Amabile, Barsade, Mueller, and Staw (2005) found evidence of a causal link between positive mood and creativity among employees. Significant cross-sectional associations between those variables were accompanied by lagged effects into the following day, but not across a longer period. Amabile and colleagues drew attention to the possible operation of an affect-induced incubation process. Such a process would involve unconscious recombination of ideas in the period subsequent to conscious problem solving, such that creativity would be apparent at a later time. It may be that incubation of this kind is more likely during periods of positive affect.

However, it is also important to explore the ways in which creativity might be linked to affect that is negative. Creativity is often provoked by external pressure: "Necessity is the mother of invention" and "threat is the engine of innovation." Threatening events can disrupt familiar procedures and create unhappiness, at the same time generating novel solutions to the imposed problem that might otherwise have remained unconsidered (e.g., James, Broderson, & Eisenberg, 2004). In some circumstances, a negative association is thus expected between happiness and creativity.

Cognitive outcomes of these several kinds have been viewed by Russell (2003) in terms of the two-dimensional framework of Figures 2.1 and 2.2 (see chap. 2). Findings reviewed in this section have mainly concerned differences in terms of feeling bad to feeling good (the horizontal axis in the figures), but differences in activation (the vertical dimension) may also be important. Russell drew attention to possible curvilinear associations in that respect, such that optimal cognitive performance may be associated with intermediate levels of mental activation, rather than with levels that are low or high. This possibility with respect to job performance was considered earlier in the chapter.

In addition, the influence of positive affect on cognitive processing may be particularly great when that affect takes on an activated form.

For example, a feeling of enthusiasm (raised well-being in the top-right section of Figs. 2.1 and 2.2) might particularly increase optimism and involvement in problem-solution, whereas greater well-being in terms of tranquility and peacefulness (the bottom-right section) seems likely instead to promote comfortable inaction. As emphasized throughout the book, deeper understanding in this area requires a differentiated view of its central construct.

Energy-Related Themes

A second set of potential outcomes from happiness may be described in terms of people's energy, persistence and level of activity. The fact that happiness is associated with more positive assessments of future possibilities (above) suggests it will also facilitate task activity and encourage continued efforts toward a goal (Staw et al., 1994). For example, a happy person's anticipation of success and thoughts about ways to achieve that success may encourage task activity and persistence. Some evidence for this possibility is available, but causal evidence is still limited.

Csikszentmihalyi and Wong (1991) reported from a within-person investigation that students' level of positive affect was greater when they were more active. In a between-employee study, Parker and Sprigg (1999) showed that proactive behavior (measured through self-reports of personal initiative and perseverance) was greater for individuals whose job-related anxiety was low. Baron (1990) found that experimentally induced positive mood increased feelings of task-related self-efficacy. Self-confidence may thus be greater when a person is more happy, with a greater willingness to engage in difficult or novel activities. Lyubomirsky et al. (2005) reviewed nonoccupational evidence in this field, showing that a significant happiness–activity association has been found in longitudinal as well as cross-sectional investigations.

Several general perspectives are based on the notion that feelings and action are interdependent. For example, action theory (Frese & Sabini, 1985; Hacker, 1986) focuses on the ways in which behavior is oriented to the achievement of goals, which both reflect previous satisfaction and suggest new objectives. Locke's (1970) analysis of job satisfaction and job performance illustrated how positive feelings arising from previous behavior are likely to lead to future actions that might sustain feelings of that kind. Job satisfaction from the attainment of previous goals is inherently overlapping with motivation to achieve similar goals and associated satisfaction in the future. Happiness is thus often linked to affect-laden constructs of a purposive kind, implying activity in the pursuit of objectives. That seems to be especially probable in the case of well-being axis 3, when positive feelings also embody raised activation (the top-right section of Figs. 2.1 and 2.2).

Fredrickson's (e.g., 2001) "broaden-and-build" theory has brought together several of the themes illustrated here. That theory focuses specifically on individual emotions such as pride, love, and interest, as well as happiness in the forms of joy or contentment. As outlined in chapter 2, all emotions involve affect, and the two emotions of joy and contentment illustrate the different forms of subjective well-being in the two right-hand sections of Figures 2.1 and 2.2. Fredrickson pointed out that positive affect functions as an internal signal to approach or continue, and argued that positive emotions broaden people's repertoire of thoughts and actions, widening the array of possibilities that come to mind. For example, Fredrickson and Joiner (2002) observed upward spirals in a longitudinal study across five weeks. Initial positive feelings were followed by increases in students' reports of broad-minded coping (e.g., thinking of a variety of different ways to deal with a problem), which in turn appeared to enhance subsequent affect.

Fredrickson also proposed that broaden-and-build processes increase people's resilience in the face of adversity and serve to maintain positive feelings across time. "The personal resources accrued during states of positive emotions are conceptualized as durable. They outlast the transient emotional states that led to their acquisition" (Fredrickson, 2001, p. 220). Evidence for this consequential resilience so far remains indirect, and the possibility clearly deserves further systematic investigation.

Interpersonal Effects

A third set of outcomes from raised happiness is in terms of behavior toward other people and their reactions to that behavior. Several studies of induced positive mood have revealed increases in sociability, helpfulness, generosity, and cooperativeness. (For reviews see Isen and Baron, 1991, George and Brief, 1992, Staw et al., 1994, and Lucas and Diener, 2003.) Those interpersonal effects parallel the associations between employees' job satisfaction and organizational citizenship behavior summarized in the earlier section. Carlson, Charlin, and Miller (1988) examined previous studies of mood and helping behavior in order to identify possible causal mechanisms. Their analysis suggested that positive mood inductions increase people's sensitivity to positive reinforcement and to ways of achieving that reinforcement. Some processes giving rise to that impact involve cognitive priming (described earlier), but Carlson and colleagues concluded that in addition happy people tend more to emphasize to themselves the attractiveness of helping others and the value of social interaction more broadly.

Individuals in a positive mood thus seem to be more sensitive than others to the reward value of actual and potential events, and appear to be more motivated to seek further pleasant experiences. As outlined earlier in this chapter and in chapter 9, the maintenance of positive mood is achieved in part through one's own thoughts and behaviors, but it is also influenced by the responses of other people. Given that happy individuals are more likely to attract positive reactions from others, those positive inputs from others will often enhance or maintain an initial state of happiness. As one aspect of that, helping behavior (increased by happiness) may lead to equity-based reciprocity from others, with more cooperative behavior in return (e.g., Bowling et al., 2005). It may also be the case that happy people are more likely to be successful in attempts to influence others because of their more pleasing manner, so that they come to experience outcomes that are more personally desirable than those of low-affect individuals. From their review of nonoccupational research, Lyubomirsky et al. (2005) concluded that happy people's better social relationships were "one of the most robust findings in the literature" (p. 823).

However, Staw et al. (1994) pointed out that there "may be hidden costs to conveying positive emotions" in interactions with others (p. 65). A consistently high level of helpfulness, for instance, in responding positively to unscheduled interruptions, may encourage further interruptions, more than are perceived as desirable. That possibility is linked with the present specification of the environmental "vitamin" of social contact as an "additional decrement" feature (see chaps. 4 and 7). It is possible to "have too much of a good thing," and in some circumstances positive mood and associated behaviors may cause a person to exceed the threshold level of social interaction beyond which negative inputs become more likely.

In overview, several different processes (here grouped as cognitive, energy-related, and interpersonal) may contribute to the associations between happiness and job performance. Details of their operation have rarely been examined in organizational settings, and patterns of reciprocal (rather than unidirectional) causality are expected in many cases. The impact of any one process is likely to vary between situations, for instance depending on the extent to which a job involves detailed, analytic thinking. Similarly, patterns are likely to differ between settings with considerable social interaction and those of more independent working. In addition, the joint operation of states and traits may often be important. Much research summarized in this section has involved only the induction of short-term positive mood. However, individual differences are also expected in dispositional terms (linked for instance to personality traits; see chap. 11), and dispositional forms of happiness may have a greater impact on behavior in organizations than does transitory feeling. Similarly, temporally extended motives toward a particular goal are likely to be more influential than brief changes in mood (Forgas & George, 2001). In addition to positive states, low levels of well-being (e.g., as a result of job stressors) are likely to have negative impacts on the specific processes considered here. Those negative possibilities have rarely been explored, and research in this area clearly deserves to be expanded.

ABSENCE FROM WORK

Another form of employee behavior that might be affected by happiness or unhappiness is absenteeism, or its converse, attendance at work. Those behaviors are important in both theoretical and practical terms. Theoretical accounts of absenteeism are of particular interest because they incorporate a wide range of environmental and individual variables, pointing to complex networks of intervening processes (e.g., Johns, 1997). Possible overlaps with themes in earlier sections are suggested by the fact that an employee's absence level is significantly associated with less effective job performance, assessed both from company records and by supervisory ratings (Viswesvaran, 2002). In practical terms, the cost of absenteeism to organizations can be considerable—in lost output, in the identification and training of temporary replacements, and in the management of uncertainty. So too can be the additional load on colleagues, for whom targets are made less attainable by a reduction in resources.

Absence from work is determined by a range of factors, in addition to medical constraints imposed by being ill. Social and family pressures can affect decisions to attend (e.g., Brook & Price, 1989; Erickson, Nichols, & Ritter, 2000; Nicholson, 1977), and organizational influences on attendance or absence include some job characteristics (e.g., Rhodes & Steers, 1990), specific policies to encourage attendance (Farrell & Stamm, 1988), support from a supervisor (Tharenou, 1993), and more broadly the "absence culture" in which a person works—norms and sanctions (informal as well as formal) about reasonable levels of absence (Johns, 1997; Martocchio, 1994). Although absenteeism might be expected to vary as a function of job-related well-being, other factors are clearly also important.

Absenteeism is conventionally measured in two different ways, through the time-lost index and the frequency index (e.g., Bakker et al., 2003; Farrell & Stamm, 1988; Hackett, 1989; Kohler & Mathieu, 1993). The time-lost index is computed as the total duration of absence during a specified period, perhaps expressed as a proportion of the total time examined; the frequency index is the number of separate incidents of absence in a specified period, regardless of their duration. The time-lost index, in terms of absence duration, gives greater emphasis to long periods away from work, and is often considered primarily to represent involuntary responses to incapacitating sickness. On the other hand, the frequency index, in which a single day's absence is given the same weight as, say, a 3-month absence, is widely thought to describe more voluntary choices to take time off work for brief periods of time. Correlations between the time-lost and frequency indicators have varied between studies, but are on average moderately positive (Farrell & Stamm, 1988; Kohler & Mathieu, 1993).

How do the three axes of job-specific well-being correlate with these two indices of absenteeism? We might expect that the frequency index (with its possibly greater emphasis on voluntary nonattendance) will be more linked to unhappiness than the duration measure, but that the underlying causal relationships will be multidirectional. However, the extent to which each index represents either voluntary or involuntary behavior is far from clear, so that a sharp distinction might not occur. Note also that a studied distribution of absence scores is usually highly skewed, with most people having zero or very low values, and this nonnormality might reduce the magnitude of correlations obtained in some investigations.

A meta-analysis of previous findings by Farrell and Stamm (1988) found that overall job satisfaction (a job-related form of the first axis in Fig. 2.2) was on average correlated at only -0.10 with the frequency index and -0.13 with the time-lost index. Examining an overlapping but not identical sample of studies, Hackett (1989) obtained similar findings (mean $r = -0.09$ and -0.15, respectively), but found that job satisfaction was more associated with absence frequency for women than for men. He suggested that this difference might arise from many women's greater family responsibilities. As a result, "their 'threshold' at which dissatisfaction is manifested in absenteeism may be lower than it is for males" (p. 245). A later study by Melamed et al. (1995) also found that difference. Correlations of intrinsic job satisfaction with the frequency of sickness absence were -0.11 for men and -0.20 for women. With respect to job-related facet satisfactions, the meta-analysis by Hackett (1989) indicated that satisfaction with work content (for men and women combined) was somewhat more associated with absence frequency (mean $r = -0.13$) and duration (mean $r = -0.09$) than were satisfactions with coworkers, pay, supervision, and promotion opportunities; for those, the average correlations with absence frequency and duration were -0.06 and -0.05, respectively.

Several investigators have reported that job satisfaction remains significantly associated with absenteeism despite controls for other variables. For example, Brooke and Price (1989) showed that overall job satisfaction was significantly related to absence frequency over and above significant job content and other correlates, such as lack of variety, role ambiguity, low pay, kinship responsibility, and work involvement. In Clegg's (1983) study, that association remained unchanged after control for demographic variables—age, sex, marital status, tenure, job level, and job category.

Clegg (1983) also pointed out that most research in this area has examined information about absenteeism that is in the past (immediately before completion of well-being measures) rather than in the future. Reported findings thus usually concern retrospective associations rather than predictions about future behavior. Clegg analyzed absence frequency twice—in the 6 months before and the 6 months after employees reported their overall job satisfaction. The correlations were similar, -0.16 from prior absence to later job satisfaction, and -0.14 from prior satisfaction to later absence. Given that both variables tend to be stable across time, methodological concerns about the timing of data collection may in fact have little impact on the conclusions that are drawn, because similar scores for well-being or absence might be entered into analyses at both times. Despite that, many studies (with absence data covering a previous rather than a subsequent period) clearly fail to demonstrate directly a causal impact of well-being on later behavior.

With that in mind, Hardy, Woods, and Wall (2003) examined absenteeism in the following 12 months, finding that overall job satisfaction was correlated at -0.25 with subsequent absence frequency and -0.27 with subsequent absence duration. Investigation of satisfaction and absence levels at two measurement points showed that this pattern also occurred in terms of changes across time: Increases or decreases in job satisfaction over 2 years were accompanied by decreases or increases, respectively, in absenteeism.

Turning to well-being axis 2, the average correlations of job-related anxiety with the frequency index and the time-lost (duration) index were +0.11 and +0.18, respectively in Farrell and Stamm's (1988) analysis. Job-related emotional exhaustion (mainly tapping the negative pole of axis 2; see chap. 2) was found by Bakker et al. (2003) to be correlated at +0.06 and +0.16 with absence frequency and duration, respectively; in research by van Vegchel et al. (2005), those values averaged +0.24 and +0.26 across two samples. Erickson et al. (2000) reported a correlation of +0.23 between job-related emotional exhaustion and absence frequency. The frequency index was also examined by Jamal (1984) and Spector et al. (1988), who reported correlations with job-related anxiety of +0.25 (median value) and +0.15, respectively. In the longitudinal study by Hardy et al. (2003; described earlier), correlations of job anxiety with absence frequency and duration in the subsequent 12 months were +0.11 and +0.15.

The third axis of well-being ranges from feelings of depression to enthusiasm. It might be expected that higher job-related well-being on this axis (indicating more active pleasure in one's job) will be accompanied by less time off work. George (1989) examined positive feelings of this kind, and observed a correlation of −0.28 with the number of single-day absences (thought to emphasize voluntary time off work). In the review by Farrell and Stamm (1988), measures of job involvement (reflecting an active interest in one's role, as in positive forms of axis 3) were on average correlated at −0.28 with the frequency index of absenteeism, but only −0.10 with absence duration.

Hardy et al. (2003) contrasted predictions from job-related depression (the negative pole of axis 3) with those from job-related anxiety (axis 2, just described). For employees' depression scores, correlations were +0.24 and +0.28 with subsequent absence frequency and duration, respectively. Placing both forms of well-being in a single regression analysis, they showed that job-related depression was a stronger predictor of absenteeism than was job-related anxiety.

Mason and Griffin (2003) examined active forms of job-related well-being (high scores on axis 3) in terms of positive affective tone at the level of a work group; employees indicated how far their group exhibited enthusiasm, energy, pride, and high morale. They found across 97 groups that average group tone and the frequency of absence in the following 3 months were intercorrelated at −0.20 and −0.33 in separate analyses of data collected at two different times. Those longitudinal associations remained significant after the inclusion of information about age, gender, and group size.

It thus appears that the third axis of well-being is more linked to absenteeism than are the other two measurement axes. Evidence is so far limited, but this possibility receives support from clinical research suggesting that absenteeism from a job is more common in depressed patients than among those diagnosed with anxiety alone (Kessler & Frank, 1997).

In addition, it is clear that explanations of absence require consideration of multiple variables. In some cases, statistical interactions may be significant, with one variable moderating the effect of another. For example, Erickson et al. (2000) found that although employees' job-related emotional exhaustion was overall significantly correlated with the frequency of absence (see earlier), this correlation was particularly strong for subsamples who had young children at home or had problems obtaining child care assistance. Some effects of happiness on behavior thus depend on additional features.

That influence from other variables was illustrated by Smith (1977) in a study of between-group patterns in average job satisfaction and attendance at work on a single day. Groups were contrasted in terms of environmental conditions: In Chicago there had been an unexpected and severe snowstorm that greatly hampered travel to work, whereas in New York the weather was unexceptional. Samples in each city were closely matched and drawn from the same company. Personal choice and special effort were required for individuals to attend work in Chicago, but less so in the more routine conditions of New York. That difference was reflected in different associations with job satisfaction. Average correlations between attendance and job-facet satisfactions (measured 4 months previously) were +0.44 in Chicago but only +0.08 in New York.

Context-free well-being as a predictor of absenteeism has rarely been studied. A general measure of psychological distress was shown by Ulleberg and Rudmo (1997) to be related to self-reported absence frequency, and the longitudinal investigation by Hardy et al. (2003; see the earlier description) also included measurement of distress levels. They found that prior context-free distress predicted both absence frequency ($r = +0.23$) and absence duration ($r = +0.26$). Those associations remained significant despite controls for age, gender, and job, as well as for earlier levels of absence and satisfaction: Changes in distress over a 2-year period were accompanied by parallel changes in absenteeism.

Hardy and colleagues also cited the actual amount of absenteeism recorded for high scorers versus the rest of the sample. Members of the most distressed quarter of the sample were subsequently absent almost twice as often as the less distressed three-quarters. That substantial difference between the behavior of subgroups, linked to a correlation with unhappiness around +0.25 (mentioned earlier), is likely to be present in other settings where a similar degree of association is found between well-being and the studied variable.

STAFF TURNOVER

Another behavioral measure that might be expected to be related to job-specific well-being is whether or not people remain with their current employer. It is widely assumed that unhappiness in a job leads people to leave that job, although such transitions clearly depend also on other factors such as the availability of relevant alternatives. Research attention has focused on overall job satisfaction, within measurement axis 1 of the present framework. It is consistently found that people who subsequently leave a job tend to have been somewhat less satisfied. In the meta-analysis by Griffeth, Hom, and Gaertner (2000), the average correlation across 67 samples was –0.17. For intrinsic job satisfaction (with the work itself) and satisfaction with colleagues, average correlations were –0.14 and –0.10, respectively. In an earlier meta-analysis, Tett and Meyer (1993) showed that turnover associations were stronger with multi-item than with single-item reports of job satisfaction (–0.16 and –0.09, respectively).

Clark (2001) examined voluntary job quitting across seven waves of an annual British national panel survey. Low overall job satisfaction was a highly significant predictor of voluntary turnover in the next year. That significant prediction was retained after controls for a wide range of demographic and occupational variables, and was also present in separate analyses of data from men and women. Clark (2001) also studied job quitting as a function of previous facet satisfactions. Dissatisfaction with job security was particularly influential, and dissatisfactions with pay, personal discretion, hours of work, and the work itself were all about equally predictive.

Voluntary turnover was in that research differently associated with forms of facet-specific well-being for men and for women. Male employees' quitting was predicted most by earlier dissatisfaction with job security (an aspect of feature 11), whereas the most predictive dissatisfaction for women was with the opportunity for personal discretion (feature 1). Examining subsamples below and above age 30, Clark (2001) found that voluntary quitting among younger employees was most linked to dissatisfaction with opportunity for personal discretion, and that above 30 years dissatisfactions with pay (feature 7) and promotion opportunities (an aspect of 11) were most predictive of turnover.

Kinicki et al. (2002) reviewed previous research into facet satisfactions measured with the Job Descriptive Index (see chap. 2). In relation to staff turnover (not necessarily defined as voluntary, as in Clark's study), the average uncorrected correlation with prior satisfaction with work content was –0.24. Correlations between turnover and other measured facet satisfactions were lower, ranging between –0.17 (coworkers) and –0.12 (supervision).

Studies of staff turnover as a function of subjective well-being on the other two axes have been infrequent. In one small sample, Wright and Cropanzano (1998) reported a correlation of job-related exhaustion (mainly reflecting low scores on axis 2) with voluntary turnover in the following year of +0.34. Additional research in this area would be valuable.

This form of behavior is potentially linked with the previous one, in that both movement out of a job and absenteeism are likely to be influenced by prior negative feelings, perhaps each being part of a progression of withdrawal responses. Reviewing previous research, Griffeth et al. (2000) found that the average correlation between absence and subsequent job quitting was +0.20 (see also Mitra, Jenkins, & Gupta, 1992).

Boswell et al. (2005) tracked across several years individuals who voluntarily moved between organizations into similar (managerial) jobs. In comparison with nonchangers, those employees' overall job satisfaction was found to be significantly lower prior to their move, and it increased substantially in their new position.

Low job-related well-being thus predicts movement from a job, but, as in other cases, additional variables also influence that form of behavior. For example, staff turnover has been found to be greater when role conflict is high or role clarity is low, when job tenure is short, and when relations with a supervisor are poor (e.g., Griffeth et al., 2000). In addition, job satisfaction better predicts staff turnover when the local unemployment rate is low (Carsten & Spector, 1987; Hom, Caranikas-Walker, Prussia, & Griffeth, 1992). In that respect, Hom and Kinicki (2001) showed that local unemployment rates are important for determining the perceived utility of searching for another job; job seeking is less worth the effort if few jobs are available.

Almost all research has examined staff turnover in general, but low job-related well-being may predict some categories of movement more than others. Fields, Dingman, Roman, and Blum (2005) studied movements of three kinds: into a different job in the same organization, into the same job in a different organization, and into a different job in a different organization. It is difficult accurately to specify from summary information which jobs are "the same" or "different," but results suggested that low job satisfaction predicted transitions of only the first two kinds. For radical turnover of the third kind (into a different job and different organization), additional factors may have been more important. For example, low job security in the earlier job was particularly linked to this kind of move, suggesting that radical shifts were more enforced by personal layoff or company closure than by job-holder unhappiness.

Some investigators have asked about people's future plans, finding that low job satisfaction is more strongly associated with employees' intention to leave than with actual turnover (e.g., George & Jones, 1996; Hom et al., 1992; Zaccaro & Stone, 1988). In the meta-analysis by Tett and Meyer (1993), the uncorrected mean correlation with intention to leave was –0.48. Lee and Ashforth (1996) reported from previous studies an average correlation between job-related emotional exhaustion (mainly covering low values on axis 2; see chap. 2) and turnover intention of +0.37. For job-related anxiety, Spector et al. (1988) found a single-sample value of +0.41. Intentions to leave are themselves significantly correlated with actual turnover, +0.38, +0.33, and +0.35 on average in reviews by Carsten and Spector (1987), Hom et al. (1992), and Griffeth et al. (2000).

Research into employee unhappiness and turnover would benefit from more targeted examination of specific forms of well-being and of other investigated constructs. For example, the traditional emphasis on overall job satisfaction, which tends to ignore differences in mental activation, may have reduced predictive power relative to that of axes 2 and 3. Labor market conditions are also clearly important, as is a study's base rate of turnover. In many investigations the number of employees leaving their job is very small. In order to increase the subsample of leavers, researchers have often combined data across many months, creating a long and sometimes theoretically inappropriate gap between the measurement of well-being and subsequent behavior. There has also been a widespread failure to distinguish between staff turnover that is voluntary and that which is imposed by an employer or by economic conditions.

Unhappiness is expected to be a strong influence on self-generated transition out of an unhappiness-creating situation, but only when some threshold of unhappiness has been reached, when personal benefits are expected to arise from the alternative, and when such an alternative is available. As in other areas of this book, more differentiated specification of variables and additional tests of multivariate hypotheses are required.

References

Aarts, H., & Dijksterhuis, A. (2000). Habits as knowledge structures: Automaticity in goal-directed behavior. *Journal of Personality and Social Psychology, 78*, 53–63.

Abbe, A., Tkach, C., & Lyubomirsky, S. (2003). The art of living by dispositionally happy people. *Journal of Happiness Studies, 4*, 385–404.

Abdel-Halim, A. A. (1981). A re-examination of ability as a moderator of role perceptions-satisfaction relationship. *Personnel Psychology, 34*, 549–561.

Åborg, C., & Billing, A. (2003). Health effects of "the paperless office": Evaluations of the introduction of electronic document handling systems. *Behaviour and Information Technology, 22*, 389–396.

Abraham, J. D., & Hansson, R. O. (1995). Successful aging at work: An applied study of selection, optimization, and compensation through impression management. *Journal of Gerontology: Psychological Sciences, 50B*, P94–P103.

Abraham, K. (1950). Observations on Ferenczi's paper on Sunday neuroses. In R. Fliess (Ed.), *The psycho-analytic reader*. London: Hogarth Press. (Original work published 1918)

Adams, G. A., King, L. A., & King, D. W. (1996). Relationships of job and family involvement, family social support, and work-family conflict with job and life satisfaction. *Journal of Applied Psychology, 81*, 411–420.

Adams, J. S. (1963). Toward an understanding of inequity. *Journal of Abnormal and Social Psychology, 67*, 422–436.

Adams, J. S. (1965). Inequity in social exchange. In L. Berkowitz (Ed.), *Advances in experimental social psychology* (pp. 267–299). San Diego, CA: Academic Press.

Adelmann, P. K. (1987). Occupational complexity, control, and personal income: Their relation to psychological well-being in men and women. *Journal of Applied Psychology, 72*, 529–537.

Agho, A. O., Mueller, C. W., & Price, J. L. (1993). Determinants of employee job satisfaction: An empirical test of a causal model. *Human Relations, 46*, 1007–1027.

Algera, J. A. (1983). Objective and perceived task characteristics as a determinant of reactions by task performers. *Journal of Occupational Psychology, 56,* 95–107.

Allen, J., & van der Velden, R. (2001). Educational mismatches versus skill mismatches: Effects on wages, job satisfaction, and on-the-job search. *Oxford Economics Papers, 3,* 434–452.

Allen, T. D., Herst, D. E. L., Bruck, C. S., & Sutton, M. (2000). Consequences associated with work-to-family conflict: A review and agenda for future research. *Journal of Occupational Health Psychology, 5,* 278–308.

Allport, G. W. (1937). *Personality: A psychological interpretation.* New York: Henry Holt.

Altman, I., & Chemers, M. (1980). *Culture and environment.* Monterey, CA: Brooks Cole.

Amabile, T. M., Barsade, S. G., Mueller, J. S., & Staw, B. M. (2005). Affect and creativity at work. *Administrative Science Quarterly, 50,* 367–403.

Anderson, C. R. (1976). Coping behaviors as intervening mechanisms in the inverted-U stress-performance relationship. *Journal of Applied Psychology, 61,* 30–34.

Anderson, J. R. (1995). *Learning and memory: An integrated approach* (2nd ed.). New York: Wiley.

Andrews, F. M., & Withey, S. B. (1974). Developing measures of perceived life quality: Results from several national surveys. *Social Indicators Research, 1,* 1–26.

Andrews, F. M., & Withey, S. B. (1976). *Social indicators of well-being: Americans' perceptions of life quality.* New York: Plenum.

Angyal, A. (1965). *Neurosis and treatment: A holistic theory.* New York: Wiley.

Antonovsky, A. (1987). *Unraveling the mystery of health.* San Francisco: Jossey-Bass.

Applebaum, H. (1992). *The concept of work: Ancient, medieval, and modern.* Albany: State University of New York Press.

Aquino, J. A., Russell, D. W., Cutrona, C. E., & Altmeier, E. M. (1996). Employment status, social support, and life satisfaction among the elderly. *Journal of Counseling Psychology, 43,* 480–489.

Arneson, R. J. (1999). Human flourishing versus desire satisfaction. *Social Philosophy and Policy, 16,* 113–142.

Arnold, J. (1997). *Managing careers into the 21st century.* London: Chapman.

Aronsson, G., Gustafsson, K., & Dallner, M. (2002). Work environment and health in different types of temporary jobs. *European Journal of Work and Organizational Psychology, 11,* 151–175.

Arvey, R. D., & Bouchard, T. J. (1994). Genetics, twins, and organizational behavior. *Research in Organizational Behavior, 16,* 47–82.

Arvey, R. D., Bouchard, T. J., Segal, N. L., & Abraham, L. M. (1989). Job satisfaction: Environmental and genetic components. *Journal of Applied Psychology, 74,* 187–192.

Arvey, R. D., McCall, B. P., Bouchard, T. J., Taubman, P., & Cavanaugh, M. A. (1994). Genetic influences on job satisfaction and work values. *Personality and Individual Differences, 17,* 21–33.

Aryee, S., Srinivas, E. S., & Tan, H. H. (2005). Rhythms of life: Antecedents and outcomes of work-family balance in employed parents. *Journal of Applied Psychology, 90,* 132–146.

Ashford, S., Lee, C., & Bobko, P. (1989). Content, causes, and consequences of job insecurity: A theory-based measure and substantive test. *Academy of Management Journal, 32*, 803–829.

Ashforth, B. (1994). Petty tyranny in organizations. *Human Relations, 47*, 755–778.

Ashforth, B. E., & Kreiner, G. E. (1999). "How can you do it?" Dirty work and the challenge of constructing a positive identity. *Academy of Management Review, 24*, 413–434.

Austin, J. T., & Vancouver, J. B. (1996). Goal constructs in psychology: Structure, process, and content. *Psychological Bulletin, 120*, 338–375.

Avolio, B. J., Bass, B. M., & Jung, D. J. (1999). Re-examining the components of transformational and transactional leadership using the Multifactor Leadership Questionnaire. *Journal of Occupational and Organizational Psychology, 72*, 441–462.

Bakker, A. B., Demerouti, E., de Boer, E., & Schaufeli, W. (2003). Job demands and job resources as predictors of absence duration and frequency. *Journal of Vocational Behavior, 62*, 341–356.

Bakker, A. B., Demerouti, E., & Euwema, M. C. (2005). Job resources buffer the impact of job demands on burnout. *Journal of Occupational Health Psychology, 10*, 170–180.

Baldamus, W. (1961). *Efficiency and effort: An analysis of industrial administration.* London: Tavistock.

Bandura, A. (1997). *Self-efficacy: The exercise of control.* New York: Freeman.

Bandura, A. (2001). Social cognitive theory: An agentic perspective. *Annual Review of Psychology, 52*, 1–26.

Bandura, A., & Locke, E. A. (2003). Negative self-efficacy and goal effects revisited. *Journal of Applied Psychology, 88*, 87–99.

Barker, B. M., & Bender, D. A. (Eds.). (1980). *Vitamins in medicine* (4th ed., Vol. 1). London: Heinemann.

Barker, B. M., & Bender, D. A. (Eds.). (1982). *Vitamins in medicine* (4th ed., Vol. 2). London: Heinemann.

Barley, S. R., & Knight, D. B. (1992). Toward a cultural theory of stress complaints. *Research in Organizational Behavior, 14*, 1–48.

Barling, J. (1996). The prediction, experience, and consequences of workplace violence. In G. R. VandenBos & E. Q. Bulatao (Eds.), *Violence on the job* (pp. 29–49). Washington, DC: American Psychological Association.

Barling, J., & Gallagher, D. G. (1996). Part-time employment. In C. L. Cooper & I. T. Robertson (Eds.), *International review of industrial and organizational psychology* (pp. 243–277). Chichester, UK: Wiley.

Barling, J., Kelloway, E. K., & Iverson, R. D. (2003). Accidental outcomes: Attitudinal consequences of workplace injuries. *Journal of Occupational Health Psychology, 8*, 74–85.

Barnett, R. C., & Brennan, R. T. (1995). The relationship between job experiences and psychological distress: A structural equation approach. *Journal of Organizational Behavior, 16*, 259–276.

Barnett, R. C., & Brennan, R. T. (1997). Change in job conditions, change in psychological distress, and gender: A longitudinal study of dual-earner couples. *Journal of Organizational Behavior, 18*, 253–274.

Barnett, R. C., & Hyde, J. S. (2001). Women, men, work, and family: An expansionist theory. *American Psychologist, 56*, 781–796.

Baron, R. A. (1990). Environmentally induced positive affect: Its impact on self-efficacy, task performance, negotiation, and conflict. *Journal of Applied Social Psychology, 20*, 368–384.

Barringer, T. (2005). *Men at work: Art and labour in Victorian Britain.* New Haven, CT: Yale University Press.

Barsade, S. G. (2002). The ripple effect: Emotional contagion and its effect on group behavior. *Administrative Science Quarterly, 47*, 644–675.

Barton, J. (1994). Choosing to work at night: A moderating influence on individual tolerance to shift work. *Journal of Applied Psychology, 79*, 449–454.

Bartram, D. (2005). The Great Eight competencies: A criterion-centric approach to validation. *Journal of Applied Psychology, 90*, 1185–1203.

Bass, B. M. (1985). *Leadership and performance beyond expectations.* New York: Free Press.

Baum, A., & Paulus, P. (1987). Crowding. In D. Stokols & I. Altman (Eds.), *Handbook of environmental psychology* (pp. 534–570). New York: Wiley.

Beal, D. J., Weiss, H. M., Barros, E., & MacDermid, S. M. (2005). An episodic process model of affective influences on performance. *Journal of Applied Psychology, 90*, 1054–1068.

Bechtold, S. E., Sims, H. P., & Szilagyi, A. D. (1981). Job scope relationships: A three-wave longitudinal analysis. *Journal of Occupational Behaviour, 2*, 189–202.

Beck, A. T., Rush, A. J., Shaw, B. F., & Emery, G. (1979). *Cognitive therapy of depression.* New York: Guilford Press.

Beehr, T. A., Glaser, K. A., Canali., K. G., & Wallwey, D. A. (2001). Back to basics: Re-examination of demand-control theory of occupational stress. *Work and Stress, 15*, 115–130.

Beehr, T. A., Glazer, S., Nielson, N. L., & Farmer, S. J. (2000). Work and non-work predictors of employees' retirement ages. *Journal of Vocational Behavior, 57*, 206–225.

Beehr, T. A., Jex, S. M., Stacy, B. A., & Murray, M. A. (2000). Work stressors and co-worker support as predictors of individual strain and job performance. *Journal of Organizational Behavior, 21*, 391–405.

Beehr, T. A., King, L. A., & King, D. W. (1990). Social support and occupational stress: Talking to supervisors. *Journal of Vocational Behavior, 36*, 61–81.

Behrman, J. R., Hrubec, Z., Taubman, P., & Wales, T. J. (1980). *Socioeconomic success: A study of the effects of genetic endowments, family environments, and schooling.* New York: North-Holland.

Bellavia, G. M., & Frone, M. R. (2005). Work-family conflict. In J. Barling, E. K. Kelloway, & M. R. Frone (Eds.), *Handbook of work stress* (pp. 113–147). Thousand Oaks, CA: Sage.

Bender, K. A., Donohue, S. M., & Heywood, J. S. (2005). Job satisfaction and gender segregation. *Oxford Economic Papers, 57*, 475–496.

Berman, J. S., & Kenny, D. A. (1976). Correlational bias in observer ratings. *Journal of Personality and Social Psychology, 34*, 263–273.

Bernhard-Oettel, C., Sverke, M., & de Witte, H. (2005). Comparing three alternative types of employment with permanent full-time work: How do employment contract and perceived job conditions relate to health complaints? *Work and Stress, 19*, 301–318.

Best, R. G., Stapleton, L. M., & Downey, R. G. (2005). Core self-evaluations and job burnout: The test of alternative models. *Journal of Occupational Health Psychology, 10*, 441–451.

Bhagat, R. S., & Chassie, M. B. (1980). Effects of changes in job characteristics on some theory-specific attitudinal outcomes: Results from a naturally-occurring quasi-experiment. *Human Relations, 33*, 297–313.

Bielby, W. T., & Baron, J. N. (1986). Men and women at work: Sex segregation and statistical discrimination. *American Journal of Sociology, 91*, 759–799.

Birdi, K. S., Gardner, C. R., & Warr, P. B. (1998). Correlates and perceived outcomes of four types of employee development activity. *Journal of Applied Psychology, 82*, 845–857.

Birdi, K. S., Warr, P. B., & Oswald, A. (1995). Age differences in three components of employee well-being. *Applied Psychology: An International Review, 44*, 345–373.

Birren, J. E., & Renner, V. J. (1981). Concepts and criteria of mental health and aging. *American Journal of Orthopsychiatry, 51*, 242–254.

Blatt, S. J. (1995). The destructiveness of perfectionism. *American Psychologist, 50*, 1003–1020.

Blau, F., & Kahn, L. (1996). Wage structure and gender earnings differentials: An international study. *Economica, 63*, S39-S62.

Block, J. (1995). A contrarian view of the five-factor approach to personality description. *Psychological Bulletin, 117*, 187–215.

Block, J. H., & Block, J. (1980). The role of ego-control and ego-resiliency in the origination of behavior. In W. A. Collins (Ed.), *The Minnesota symposia on child psychology* (Vol. 13, pp. 39–101). Hillsdale, NJ: Lawrence Erlbaum Associates.

Bolger, N., & Zuckerman, A. (1995). A framework for studying personality in the stress process. *Journal of Personality and Social Psychology, 69*, 890–902.

Bonanno, G. A. (2004). Loss, trauma, and human resilience. *American Psychologist, 59*, 20–28.

Bond, F. W., & Bunce, D. (2003). The role of acceptance and job control in mental health: Job satisfaction and work performance. *Journal of Applied Psychology, 88*, 1057–1067.

Booth, A. L., Francesconi, M., & Frank, J. (2002). Temporary jobs: Stepping stones or dead ends? *Economic Journal, 112*, F189-F213.

Bordia, P., & Blau, G. (2003). Moderating effect of allocentrism on pay referent comparison-pay level satisfaction relationship. *Applied Psychology: An International Review, 52*, 499–514.

Bordia, P., Hunt, E., Paulsen, N., Tourish, D., & Difonzo, N. (2004). Uncertainty during organizational change: Is it all about control? *European Journal of Work and Organizational Psychology, 13*, 345–365.

Bossé, R., Aldwin, C. M., Levenson, M. R., & Ekerdt, D. J. (1987). Mental health differences among retirees and workers: Findings from the Normative Aging Study. *Psychology and Aging, 2*, 383–389.

Boswell, W. R., Boudreau, J. W., & Tichy, J. (2005). The relationship between employee job change and job satisfaction: The honeymoon-hangover effect. *Journal of Applied Psychology, 90*, 882–892.

Bouchard, T. J., Arvey, R. D., Keller, L. M., & Segal, N. L. (1992). Genetic influences on job satisfaction: A reply to Cropanzano and James. *Journal of Applied Psychology, 77*, 89–93.

Bowling, N. A., Beehr, T. A., Johnson, A. L., Semmer, N. K., Hendricks, E. A., & Webster, H. A. (2004). Explaining potential antecedents of workplace social support: Reciprocity or attractiveness? *Journal of Occupational Health Psychology, 9*, 339–350.

Bowling, N. A., Beehr, T. A., & Schwader, W. M. (2005). Giving and receiving social support at work: The roles of personality and reciprocity. *Journal of Vocational Behavior, 67*, 476–489.

Bowling, N. A., Beehr, T. A., Wagner, S. H., & Libkuman, T. M. (2005). Adaptation-level theory, opponent process theory, and dispositions: An integrated approach to the stability of job satisfaction. *Journal of Applied Psychology, 90*, 1044–1053.

Bradburn, N. M. (1969). *The structure of psychological well-being*. Chicago: Aldine.

Bradburn, N. M., & Caplovitz, D. (1965). *Reports on happiness*. Chicago: Aldine.

Brandstädter, J., & Rothermund, K. (1994). Self-percepts of control in middle and later adulthood: Buffering losses by rescaling goals. *Psychology and Aging, 9*, 265–273.

Brayfield, A. H., & Rothe, H. F. (1951). An index of job satisfaction. *Journal of Applied Psychology, 35*, 307–311.

Breaugh, J. A., & Colihan, J. P. (1994). Measuring facets of job ambiguity: Construct validity evidence. *Journal of Applied Psychology, 79*, 191–202.

Brennan A., Chugh, J. S., & Kline, T. (2002). Traditional versus open office design: A longitudinal field study. *Environment and Behavior, 34*, 279–299.

Bretz, R. D., & Judge, T. A. (1994). Person-organization fit and the theory of work adjustment: Implications for satisfaction, tenure, and career success. *Journal of Vocational Behavior, 44*, 32–54.

Brickman, P., Coates, D., & Janoff-Bulman, R. (1978). Lottery winners and accident victims: Is happiness relative? *Journal of Personality and Social Psychology, 36*, 917–927.

Brief, A. P. (1998). *Attitudes in and around organizations*. Thousand Oaks, CA: Sage.

Brief, A. P., Burke, M. J., George, J. M., Robinson, B. S., & Webster, J. (1988). Should negative affectivity remain an unmeasured variable in the study of job stress? *Journal of Applied Psychology, 73*, 193–198.

Briner, R. B., & Reynolds, S. (1999). The costs, benefits, and limitations of organizational level stress interventions. *Journal of Organizational Behavior, 20*, 647–664.

Broadbent, D. E. (1981). Chronic effects from the physical nature of work. In B. Gardell and G. Johansson (Eds.), *Working life* (pp. 39–51). Chichester, UK: Wiley.

Brooke, P. P., & Price, J. L. (1989). The determinants of absenteeism: An empirical test of a causal model. *Journal of Occupational Psychology, 62*, 1–19.

Brotheridge, C. M., & Lee, R. T. (2002). Testing a conservation of resources model of the dynamics of emotional labor. *Journal of Occupational Health Psychology, 7*, 57–67.

Bruck, C. S., Allen, T. D., & Spector, P. E. (2002). The relation between work-family conflict and job satisfaction: A finer-grained analysis. *Journal of Vocational Behavior*, 60, 336–353.

Bruk-Lee, V., Goh, A., Khoury, H., & Spector, P. E. (2005, April). *Beyond the Big Five: A meta-analysis of job satisfaction and personality factors.* Paper presented to SIOP Conference, Los Angeles.

Brunstein, J. C. (1993). Personal goals and subjective well-being: A longitudinal study. *Journal of Personality and Social Psychology*, 65, 1061–1070.

Brunstein, J. C., Schultheiss, O. C., & Grässmann, R. (1998). Personal goals and emotional well-being: The moderating role of motive dispositions. *Journal of Personality and Social Psychology*, 75, 494–508.

Brush, D. H., Moch, M. K., & Pooyan, A. (1987). Individual demographic differences and job satisfaction. *Journal of Occupational Behaviour*, 8, 139–156.

Bryce, J., & Haworth, J. (2003). Psychological well-being in a sample of male and female office workers. *Journal of Applied Social Psychology*, 33, 565–585.

Bullinger, H.-J., Kern, P., & Braun, M. (1997). Controls. In G. Salvendy (Ed.), *Handbook of human factors and ergonomics* (2nd ed., pp. 697–728). New York: Wiley.

Burger, J. M. (1989). Negative reactions to increases in perceived personal control. *Journal of Personality and Social Psychology*, 56, 246–256.

Burke, M. J., Brief, A. P., & George, J. M. (1993). On the role of negative affectivity in understanding relations between self-reports of stressors and strains: A comment on the applied psychology literature. *Journal of Applied Psychology*, 78, 402–412.

Burke, M. J., Brief, A. P., George, J. M., Roberson, L., & Webster, J. (1989). Measuring affect at work: Confirmatory analyses of competing mood structures with conceptual linkage to cortical regulatory systems. *Journal of Personality and Social Psychology*, 57, 1091–1102.

Burns, D. D., & Eidelson, R. J. (1998). Why are depression and anxiety correlated? A test of the tripartite model. *Journal of Consulting and Clinical Psychology*, 66, 461–473.

Büssing, A. (1992). A dynamic view of job satisfaction in psychiatric nurses in Germany. *Work and Stress*, 6, 239–259.

Butler, A. B., Grzywacz, J. G., Bass, B. L., & Linney, K. D. (2005). Extending the demands-control model: A daily diary study of job characteristics, work-family conflict and work-family facilitation. *Journal of Occupational and Organizational Psychology*, 78, 155–169.

Buunk, B. P., Collins, R. L., Taylor, S. E., van Yperen, N. W., & Dakof, G. A. (1990). The affective consequences of social comparison: Either direction has its ups and downs. *Journal of Personality and Social Psychology*, 59, 1238–1249.

Buunk, B. P., Oldersma, F. L., & de Dreu, C. K. W. (2001). Enhancing satisfaction through downward comparison: The role of relational discontent and individual differences in social comparison orientation. *European Journal of Social Psychology*, 37, 452–467.

Buunk, B. P., & Ybema, J. F. (2003). Feeling bad, but satisfied: The effects of upward and downward comparison upon mood and marital satisfaction. *British Journal of Social Psychology*, 42, 613–628.

Buunk, B. P., Zurriaga, R., Peiró, J. M., Nauta, A., & Gosalvez, I. (2005). Social comparisons at work as related to a co-operative social climate and to individual differences in social comparison orientation. *Applied Psychology: An International Review, 54,* 61–80.

Bycio, P., Hackett, R. D., & Allen, J. S. (1995). Further assessments of Bass's (1985) conceptualization of transactional and transformational leadership. *Journal of Applied Psychology, 80,* 468–478.

Byron, K. (2005). A meta-analytic review of work-family conflict and its antecedents. *Journal of Vocational Behavior, 67,* 169–198.

Cable, D. M., & Edwards, J. R. (2004). Complementary and supplementary fit: A theoretical and empirical integration. *Journal of Applied Psychology, 89,* 822–834.

Campbell, A. (1981). *The sense of well-being in America.* New York: McGraw-Hill.

Campion, M. A. (1988). Interdisciplinary approaches to job design: A constructive replication with extensions. *Journal of Applied Psychology, 73,* 467–481.

Campion, M. A., & Thayer, P. W. (1985). Development and field evaluation of an interdisciplinary measure of job design. *Journal of Applied Psychology, 70,* 29–43.

Caplan, R. D., Cobb, S., French, J. R. P., Van Harrison, R., & Pinneau, S. R. (1975). *Job demands and worker health.* Washington, DC: US Department of Health, Education, and Welfare.

Carlopio, J. R. (1996). Construct validity of a physical work environment satisfaction questionnaire. *Journal of Occupational Health Psychology, 1,* 330–344,

Carlson, J. H., & Mellor, S. (2004). Gender-related effects in the job-design-job-satisfaction relationship: An interactional approach. *Sex Roles, 51,* 237–247.

Carlson, M., Charlin, V., & Miller, N. (1988). Positive mood and helping behavior: A test of six hypotheses. *Journal of Personality and Social Psychology, 55,* 211–229.

Carsten, J. M., & Spector, P. E. (1987). Unemployment, job satisfaction, and employee turnover: A meta-analytic test of the Muchinsky model. *Journal of Applied Psychology, 72,* 374–381.

Carstensen, L. L. (1995). Evidence for a life-span theory of socio-emotional selectivity. *Current Directions in Psychological Science, 4,* 151–156.

Carver, C. S. (2001). Affect and the functional bases of behaviour: On the dimensional structure of affective experience. *Personality and Social Psychology Review, 5,* 345–356.

Carver, C. S. (2003). Pleasure as a sign you can attend to something else: Placing positive feelings within a general model of affect. *Cognition and Emotion, 17,* 241–261.

Carver, C. S., & Scheier, M. F. (1990). Origins and functions of positive and negative affect: A control-process view. *Psychological Review, 97,* 19–35.

Carver, C. S., & Scheier, M. F. (1998). *On the self-regulation of behavior.* Cambridge, UK: Cambridge University Press.

Centers, R., & Bugental, D. E. (1966). Intrinsic and extrinsic job motivations among different segments of the working population. *Journal of Applied Psychology, 50,* 193–197.

Champoux, J. E. (1980). A three-sample test of some extensions to the job characteristics model. *Academy of Management Journal, 23,* 466–478.

Charles, C. T., Reynolds, C. A., & Gatz, M. (2001). Age-related differences and change in positive and negative affect over 23 years. *Journal of Personality and Social Psychology, 80,* 136–151.

Chay, Y. W. (1993). Social support, individual differences and well-being: A study of small business entrepreneurs and employees. *Journal of Occupational and Organizational Psychology, 66,* 285–302.

Chen, G., Gully, S. M., & Eden, D. (2004). General self-efficacy and self-esteem: Toward theoretical and empirical distinction between correlated self-evaluations. *Journal of Organizational Behavior, 25,* 375–395.

Chen, P. Y., & Spector, P. E. (1991). Negative affectivity as the underlying cause of correlations between stressors and strains. *Journal of Applied Psychology, 76,* 398–407.

Cheng, S.-T. (2004). Age and subjective well-being revisited: A discrepancy perspective. *Psychology and Aging, 19,* 409–415.

Cherry, N. (1984). Nervous strain, anxiety and symptoms among 32-year old men at work in Britain. *Journal of Occupational Psychology, 57,* 95–105.

Cinamon, R. G., & Rich, Y. (2002). Gender differences in the importance of work and family roles: Implications for work-family conflict. *Sex Roles, 47,* 531–541.

City and Guilds Institute. (2005). *Hairdressers are cutting it in the league table of happiest jobs.* Retrieved February 25, 2005, from http://www.city-and-guilds.co.uk

Clark, A. E. (1996). Job satisfaction in Britain. *British Journal of Industrial Relations, 34,* 189–217.

Clark, A. E. (1997). Job satisfaction and gender: Why are women so happy at work? *Labour Economics, 4,* 341–372.

Clark, A. E. (2001). What really matters in a job? Hedonic measurement using quit data. *Labour Economics, 8,* 223–242.

Clark, A. E. (2003). Unemployment as a social norm: Psychological evidence from panel data. *Journal of Labor Economics, 21,* 323–351.

Clark, A. E. (2005a). Your money or your life: Changing job quality in OECD countries. *British Journal of Industrial Relations, 43,* 377–400.

Clark, A. E. (2005b). What makes a good job? Evidence from OECD countries. In S. Bazen & C. Luciflora (Eds.), *Job quality and employer behaviour* (pp. 11–30). Basingstoke, UK: Palgrave Macmillan.

Clark, A. E., & Oswald, A. J. (1996). Satisfaction and comparison income. *Journal of Public Economics, 61,* 359–381.

Clark, A. E., Oswald, A., & Warr, P. B. (1996). Is job satisfaction U-shaped in age? *Journal of Occupational and Organizational Psychology, 69,* 57–81.

Clark, D. A., Beck, A. T., & Brown, G. (1989). Cognitive mediation in general psychiatric outpatients: A test of the content-specificity hypothesis. *Journal of Personality and Social Psychology, 56,* 958–964.

Clark, L. A., & Watson, D. (1991). Tripartite model of anxiety and depression: Psychometric evidence and taxonomic implications. *Journal of Abnormal Psychology, 100,* 316–336.

Clegg, C. W. (1983). Psychology of employee lateness, absence, and turnover: A methodological critique and an empirical study. *Journal of Applied Psychology, 68,* 88–101.

Clegg, C. W., Carey, N., Dean, G., Hornby, P., & Bolden, R. (1997). Users' reactions to information technology: Some multivariate models and their implications. *Journal of Information Technology, 12*, 15–32.

Cobb, S., & Kasl, S. V. (1977). *Termination: The consequences of job loss*. Cincinatti: US Department of Health Education and Welfare.

Cohen, J., Cohen, P., West, S. G., & Aiken, L. S. (2003). *Applied multiple regression/correlation analysis for the behavioral sciences* (3rd ed.) Mahwah, NJ: Lawrence Erlbaum Associates.

Colquitt, J. A. (2001). On the dimensionality of organizational justice: A construct validation of a measure. *Journal of Applied Psychology, 86*, 386–400.

Colquitt, J. A., Conlon, D. E., Wesson, M. J., Porter, C. O. L. H., & Ng, K. Y. (2001). Justice at the millennium: A meta-analytic review of 25 years of organizational justice research. *Journal of Applied Psychology, 86*, 425–445.

Compton, W. C., Smith, M. L., Cornish, K. A., & Qualls, D. L. (1996). Factor structure of mental health measures. *Journal of Personality and Social Psychology, 71*, 406–413.

Connelly, C. E., & Gallagher, D. C. (2004). Emerging trends in contingent work research. *Journal of Management, 30*, 956–983.

Connolly, J. J., & Viswesvaran, C. (2000). The role of affectivity in job satisfaction: A meta-analysis. *Personality and Individual Differences, 29*, 265–281.

Conway, N., & Briner, R. B. (2002). Full-time versus part-time employees: Understanding the links between work status, the psychological contract, and attitudes. *Journal of Vocational Behavior, 61*, 279–301.

Cook, J. D., Hepworth, S. J., Wall, T. D., and Warr, P. B. (1981). *The experience of work*. London: Academic Press.

Cook, T. D., Campbell, D. T., & Peracchio, L. (1990). Quasi experimentation. In M. D. Dunnette & L. M. Hough (Eds.), *Handbook of industrial and organizational psychology* (Vol. 1, pp. 491–576). Palo Alto, CA: Consulting Psychologists Press.

Cooper, J. M. (1975). *Reason and the human good in Aristotle*. Cambridge, MA: Harvard University Press.

Coopersmith, S. (1967). *The antecedents of self-esteem*. Palo Alto, CA: Consulting Psychologists Press.

Cordery, J. L., Mueller, W. S., & Smith, J. M. (1991). Attitudinal and behavioral effects of autonomous group working: A longitudinal field study. *Academy of Management Journal, 34*, 464–476.

Côté, S. (2005). A social interaction model of the effects of emotion regulation on work strain. *Academy of Management Review, 30*, 509–530.

Cranny, C. J., Smith, P. C., & Stone, E. F. (1992). *Job satisfaction: How people feel about their jobs and how it affects their performance*. New York: Lexington Press.

Creed, P. A., & Macintyre, S. R. (2001). The relative effects of deprivation of the latent and manifest benefits of employment on the well-being of unemployed people. *Journal of Occupational Health Psychology, 6*, 324–331.

Crocker, J., Thompson, L. L., McGraw, K. M., & Ingerman, C. (1987). Downward comparison prejudice and evaluations of others: Effects of self-esteem and threat. *Journal of Personality and Social Psychology, 52*, 907–916.

Crocker, M. J. (1997). Noise. In G. Salvendy (Ed.), *Handbook of human factors and ergonomics* (2nd ed., pp. 790–827). New York: Wiley.

Cropanzano, R., Byrne, Z. S., Bobocel, D. R., & Rupp, D. E. (2001). Moral virtues, fairness heuristics, social entities, and other denizens of organizational justice. *Journal of Vocational Behavior, 58,* 164–209.

Cropanzano, R., Goldman, B. M., & Benson, L. (2005). Organizational justice. In J. Barling, E. K. Kelloway, & M. R. Frone (Eds.), *Handbook of work stress* (pp. 63–87). Thousand Oaks, CA: Sage.

Cropanzano, R., & James, K. (1990). Some methodological considerations for the behavioral genetic analysis of work attitudes. *Journal of Applied Psychology, 75,* 433–439.

Cropanzano, R., Rupp, D. E., & Byrne, Z. S. (2003). The relationship of emotional exhaustion to work attitudes, job performance, and organizational citizenship behaviors. *Journal of Applied Psychology, 88,* 160–169.

Cropanzano, R., Weiss, H. M., Hale, J. M. S., & Reb, J. (2003). The structure of affect: Reconsidering the relationship between negative and positive affectivity. *Journal of Management, 29,* 831–857.

Cropanzano, R., & Wright, T. A. (1999). A 5-year study of change in the relationship between well-being and job performance. *Consulting Psychology Journal, 51,* 252–265.

Csikszentmihalyi, M. (1997). *Finding flow.* New York: Basic Books.

Csikszentmihalyi, M. (1999). If we are so rich, why aren't we happy? *American Psychologist, 54,* 821–827.

Csikszentmihalyi, M., & Wong, M. M. (1991). The situational and personal correlates of happiness: A cross-national comparison. In F. Strack & M. Argyle (Eds.), *Subjective well-being: An interdisciplinary perspective* (pp. 193–212). Elmsford, NY: Pergamon Press.

Cummins, R. A. (2000a). Objective and subjective quality of life: An interactive model. *Social Indicators Research, 52,* 55–72.

Cummins, R. A. (2000b). Personal income and subjective well-being: A review. *Journal of Happiness Studies, 1,* 133–158.

Cummins, R. A., McCabe, M., Romeo, Y., & Gullone, E. (1994). The Comprehensive Quality of Life Scale (ComQol): Instrument development and psychometric evaluation on college staff and students. *Educational and Psychological Measurement, 54,* 372–382.

Currall, S. C., Towler, A. J., Judge, T. A., & Kohn, L. (2005). Pay satisfaction and organizational outcomes. *Personnel Psychology, 58,* 613–640.

Dalai Lama, H. H., & Cutler, H. C. (2003). *The art of happiness at work.* London: Hodder & Stoughton.

Daniels, K., & Guppy, A. (1997). Stressors, locus of control, and social support as consequences of affective psychological well-being. *Journal of Occupational Health Psychology, 2,* 156–174.

Daniels, K., Harris, C., & Briner, R. B. (2004). Linking work conditions to unpleasant affect: Cognition, categorization and goals. *Journal of Occupational and Organizational Psychology, 77,* 343–363.

D'Arcy, C., Syrotuik, J., & Siddique, C. M. (1984). Perceived job attributes, job satisfaction, and psychological distress: A comparison of working men and women. *Human Relations, 37,* 603–611.

Davis, M. A. (2003). Factors related to bridge employment participation among private sector early retirees. *Journal of Vocational Behavior, 63,* 55–71.

Dawis, R. V. (1991). Vocational interests, values, and preferences. In M. D. Dunnette & L. M. Hough (Eds.), *Handbook of industrial and organizational psychology* (2nd ed., pp. 833–871). Palo Alto, CA: Consulting Psychologists Press.

Dawis, R. V., & Lofquist, L. H. (1984). *A psychological theory of work adjustment*. Minneapolis: University of Minnesota Press.

De Dreu, C. K. W., & Weingart, L. R. (2003). Task versus relationship conflict, team performance, and team member satisfaction: A meta-analysis. *Journal of Applied Psychology, 88*, 741–749.

Deelstra, J. T., Peeters, M. C. W., Schaufeli, W. B., Stroebe, W., Zijlstra, F. R. H., & van Doornen, L. P. (2003). Receiving instrumental support at work: When help is not welcome. *Journal of Applied Psychology, 88*, 324–331.

DeGraff, J., & Lawrence, K. A. (2002). *Creativity at work*. San Francisco: Jossey-Bass.

De Jonge, J., & Schaufeli. W. B. (1998). Job characteristics and employee well-being: A test of Warr's Vitamin Model in health-care workers using structural equation modeling. *Journal of Organizational Behavior, 19*, 387–407.

De Jonge, J., Dormann, C., Janssen, P. P. M., Dollard, M. F., Landeweerd, J. A., & Nijhuis, F. J. N. (2001). Testing reciprocal relationships between job characteristics and psychological well-being: A cross-lagged structural equation model. *Journal of Occupational and Organizational Psychology, 74*, 29–46.

De Jonge, J., Reuvers, M. M. E. N., Houtman, I. L. D., Bongers, P. M., & Kompier, M. A. J. (2000). Linear and non-linear relations between psychosocial job characteristics, subjective outcomes, and sickness absence: Baseline results from SMASH. *Journal of Occupational Health Psychology, 5*, 256–268.

Demerouti, E., Bakker, A. B., & Bulters, A. J. (2004). The loss spiral of work pressure, work-home interference, and exhaustion: Reciprocal relations in a three-wave study. *Journal of Vocational Behavior, 64*, 131–149.

Demerouti, E., Bakker, A. B., Nachreiner, F., & Schaufeli. W. B. (2001). The job demands-resources model of burnout. *Journal of Applied Psychology, 86*, 499–512.

DeNeve, K. M., & Cooper, H. (1998). The happy personality: A meta-analysis of 137 personality traits and subjective well-being. *Psychological Bulletin, 124*, 197–229.

Den Uyl, D., & Machan, T. R. (1983). Recent work on the concept of happiness. *American Philosophical Quarterly, 20*, 115–134.

Dew, M. A., Bromet, E. J., & Penkower, L. (1992). Mental health effects of job loss in women. *Psychological Medicine, 22*, 751–764.

De Witte, H. (1999). Job insecurity and psychological well-being: Review of the literature and exploration of some unresolved issues. *European Journal of Work and Organizational Psychology, 8*, 155–177.

Diener, E. (1994). Assessing subjective well-being: Progress and opportunities. *Social Indicators Research, 31*, 103–157.

Diener, E., & Biswas-Diener, R. (2002). Will money increase subjective well-being? *Social Indicators Research, 57*, 119–169.

Diener, E., & Diener, M. (1995). Cross-cultural correlates of life satisfaction and self-esteem. *Journal of Personality and Social Psychology, 68*, 653–663.

Diener, E., Diener, M., & Diener, C. (1995). Factors predicting the subjective well-being of nations. *Journal of Personality and Social Psychology, 69*, 851–864.

Diener, E., Emmons, R. A., Larsen, R. J., & Griffin, S. (1985). The Satisfaction with Life Scale. *Journal of Personality Assessment, 49*, 71–75.

Diener, E., & Larsen, R. J. (1984). Temporal stability and cross-situational consistency of affective, behavioral, and cognitive responses. *Journal of Personality and Social Psychology, 47,* 580–592.

Diener, E., & Lucas, R. E. (1999). Personality and subjective well-being. In D. Kahneman, E. Diener, & N. Schwartz (Eds.), *Well-being: The foundations of hedonic psychology* (pp. 213–229). New York: Russell Sage Foundation.

Diener, E., Sandvik, E., & Larsen, R. J. (1985). Age and sex effects for emotional intensity. *Developmental Psychology, 21,* 542–546.

Diener, E., Sandvik, E., Seidlitz, L, & Diener, M. (1993). The relationship between income and subjective well-being: Relative or absolute? *Social Indicators Research, 28,* 195–223.

Diener, E., & Seligman, M. E. P. (2002). Very happy people. *Psychological Science, 13,* 81–84.

Diener, E., & Suh, E. M. (1998). Subjective well-being and age: An international analysis. *Annual Review of Gerontology and Geriatrics, 17,* 304–324.

Diener, E., & Suh, E. M. (1999). National differences in subjective well-being. In D. Kahneman, E. Diener, & N. Schwartz (Eds.), *Well-being: The foundations of hedonic psychology* (pp. 434–450). New York: Russell Sage Foundation.

Diener, E., Suh, E. M., Lucas, R. E., & Smith, H. L. (1999). Subjective well-being: Three decades of progress. *Psychological Bulletin, 125,* 276–302.

Diener, E., Suh, E. M., Smith, H. L., & Shao, L. (1995). National and cultural differences in reported subjective well-being: Why do they occur? *Social Indicators Research, 31,* 103–157.

Dijkstra, M. T. M., van Dierondonck, D., Evers, A., & de Dreu, C. K. W. (2005). Conflict and well-being at work: The moderating role of personality. *Journal of Managerial Psychology, 20,* 87–104.

Dooley, D., Catalano, R., & Wilson, G. (1994). Depression and unemployment: Panel findings from the Epidemiological Catchment Area Study. *American Journal of Community Psychology, 22,* 745–765.

Dooley, D., Prause, J., & Ham-Rowbottom, K. A. (2000). Underemployment and depression: Longitudinal relationships. *Journal of Health and Social Behavior, 41,* 421–436.

Dooley, D., Rook, K., & Catalano, R. (1987). Job and non-job stressors and their moderators. *Journal of Occupational Psychology, 60,* 115–132.

Dormann, C., Fay, D., Zapf, D., and Frese, M. (2006). A state-trait analysis of job satisfaction: On the effect of core self-evaluations. *Applied Psychology: An International Review, 55,* 27–51.

Dormann, C., & Zapf, D. (2001). Job satisfaction: A meta-analysis of stabilities. *Journal of Organizational Behavior, 22,* 483–504.

Dunham, R. B., & Herman, J. B. (1975). Development of a female faces scale for measuring job satisfaction. *Journal of Applied Psychology, 60,* 629–631.

Dunkley, D., Zuroff, D. C., & Blankstein, K. R. (2003). Self-critical perfectionism and daily affect: Dispositional and situational influences on stress and coping. *Journal of Personality and Social Psychology, 84,* 234–252.

Dyer, L., & Theriault, R. (1976). The determinants of pay satisfaction. *Journal of Applied Psychology, 61,* 596–604.

Eagly, A. H., & Chaiken, S. (1993). *The psychology of attitudes.* Orlando, FL: Harcourt Brace.

Easterlin, R. A., (2001). Income and happiness: Towards a unified theory. *The Economic Journal, 111,* 465–484.

Eby, L. T., Casper, W. J., Lockwood, A., Bordeaux, C., & Brinley, A. (2005). Work and family research in IO/OB: Content analysis and review of the literature (1980–2002). *Journal of Vocational Behavior, 66,* 124–197.

Eden, D. (1975). Organizational membership versus self-employment: Another blow to the American dream. *Organizational Behavior and Human Performance, 13,* 79–94.

Eden, D. (1982). Critical job events, acute stress, and strain: A multiple interrupted time series. *Organizational Behavior and Human Performance, 30,* 312–329.

Edwards, J. R. (1993). Problems with the use of the profile similarity indices in the study of congruence in organizational research. *Personnel Psychology, 46,* 641–665.

Edwards, J. R. (1994). The study of congruence in organizational behaviour research: Critique and a proposed alternative. *Organizational Behavior and Human Decision Processes, 58,* 51–100.

Edwards, J. R. (1996). An examination of competing versions of the person-environment fit approach to stress. *Academy of Management Journal, 39,* 292–339.

Edwards, J. R., & Cooper, C. L. (1990). The person-environment fit approach to stress: Recurring problems and some suggested solutions. *Journal of Organizational Behavior, 11,* 293–307.

Eid, M., & Diener, E. (2001). Norms for experiencing emotions in different cultures: Inter- and intranational differences. *Journal of Personality and Social Psychology, 81,* 869–885.

Einarsen, S., Hoel, H., Zapf, D., & Cooper, C. L. (2003). The concept of bullying at work: The European tradition. In S. Einarsen, H. Hoel, D. Zapf, & C. L. Cooper (Eds.), *Bullying and emotional abuse in the workplace* (pp. 3–30). London: Taylor & Francis.

Einarsen, S., & Mikkelsen, E. G. (2003). Individual effects of exposure to bullying at work. In S. Einarsen, H. Hoel, D. Zapf, & C. L. Cooper (Eds.), *Bullying and emotional abuse in the workplace* (pp. 127–144). London: Taylor & Francis.

Eisenberg, P., & Lazarsfeld, P. F. (1938). The psychological effects of unemployment. *Psychological Bulletin, 35,* 358–390.

Eisenberger, R., Jones, J. R., Stinglhambler, F., Shanock, L., & Randall, A. T. (2005). Flow experiences at work: For high achievers alone? *Journal of Organizational Behavior, 26,* 755–775.

Elovainio, M., Kivimäki, M., & Helkama, K. (2001). Organizational justice evaluations, job control, and occupational strain. *Journal of Applied Psychology, 86,* 418–424.

Emmons, R. A. (1986). Personal strivings: An approach to personality and subjective well-being. *Journal of Personality and Social Psychology, 51,* 1058–1068.

Emmons, R. A., & McCullough, M. E. (2003). Counting blessings versus burdens: An experimental investigation of gratitude and subjective well-being in daily life. *Journal of Personality and Social Psychology, 84,* 377–389.

Erickson, R. J., Nichols, J., & Ritter, C. (2000). Family influences on absenteeism: Testing an expanded process model. *Journal of Vocational Behavior, 57,* 246–272.

Eriksen, W., & Einarsen, S. (2004). Gender minority as a risk factor of exposure to bullying at work: The case of male assistant nurses. *European Journal of Work and Organizational Psychology, 13,* 473–492.

European Commission. (2005). *Employment in Europe 2005: Recent trends and prospects*. Brussels: Directorate-General for Employment, Social Affairs and Equal Opportunities.

Faragher, E. B., Cass, M., & Cooper, C. L. (2005). The relationship between job satisfaction and health: A meta-analysis. *Occupational and Environmental Medicine, 62*, 105–112.

Farrell, D., & Stamm, C.L. (1988). Meta-analysis of the correlates of employee absence. *Human Relations, 41*, 211–227.

Feather, N. T. (1969). Attribution of responsibility and valence of success and failure in relation to initial confidence and task performance. *Journal of Personality and Social Psychology, 13*, 129–144.

Feingold, A. (1994). Gender differences in personality: A meta-analysis. *Psychological Bulletin, 116*, 429–456.

Feldman, D. C. (1990). Reconceptualizing the nature and consequences of part-time work. *Academy of Management Review, 15*, 103–112.

Feldman, D. C. (1994). The decision to retire early: A review and conceptualization. *Academy of Management Review, 19*, 285–311.

Feldman, D. C., & Doerpinghaus, H. I. (1992). Patterns of part-time employment. *Journal of Vocational Behavior, 41*, 282–294.

Feldman, D. C., Leana, C. R., & Bolino, M. C. (2002). Underemployment and relative deprivation among re-employed executives. *Journal of Occupational and Organizational Psychology, 75*, 453–471.

Feldman, L. A. (1993). Distinguishing depression and anxiety in self-report: Evidence from confirmatory factor analysis in non-clinical and clinical samples. *Journal of Consulting and Clinical Psychology, 61*, 631–638.

Feldman, L. A. (1995). Variations in the circumplex structure of mood. *Personality and Social Psychology Bulletin, 69*, 153–166.

Feldman Barrett, L., & Russell, J. A. (1998). Independence and bipolarity in the structure of current affect. *Journal of Personality and Social Psychology, 74*, 967–984.

Ferenczi, S. (1926). Sunday neuroses. In *Further contributions to the theory and technique of psycho-analysis* (pp. 174–177). London: Hogarth Press. (Original work published 1918)

Ferguson, A. (1767/1966). *An essay on the history of civil society*. Edinburgh: Edinburgh University Press.

Ferguson, E., Daniels, K., & Jones, D. (2006). Negatively oriented personality and perceived negative job characteristics as predictors of future psychological and physical symptoms: A meta-analytic structural modelling approach. *Journal of Psychosomatic Research, 60*, 45–52.

Festinger, L. (1954). A theory of social comparison processes. *Human Relations, 7*, 117–140.

Fields, D., Dingman, M. E., Roman, P. M., & Blum, T. C. (2005). Exploring predictors of alternative job changes. *Journal of Occupational and Organizational Psychology, 78*, 63–82.

Finlay-Jones, R. T., & Brown, G. W. (1981). Types of stressful life event and the onset of anxiety and depressive disorders. *Psychological Medicine, 11*, 803–815.

Fisher, C. D. (1993). Boredom at work: A neglected concept. *Human Relations, 46*, 395–417.

Fisher, C. D. (2000). Mood and emotions while working: Missing pieces of job satisfaction? *Journal of Organizational Behavior, 21,* 185–202.

Fisher, C. D. (2003). Why do lay people believe that satisfaction and performance are correlated? Possible sources of a commonsense theory. *Journal of Organizational Behavior, 24,* 753–777.

Fisher, C. D., & Gitelson, R. (1983). A meta-analysis of the correlates of role conflict and ambiguity. *Journal of Applied Psychology, 68,* 320–333.

Fisher, C. D., & Noble, C. S. (2004). A within-person examination of correlates of performance and emotions while working. *Human Performance, 17,* 145–168.

Fleeson, W., Malanos, A. B., & Achille, N. M. (2002). An intra-individual process approach to the relationship between extraversion and positive affect: Is acting extraverted as "good" as being extraverted? *Journal of Personality and Social Psychology, 83,* 1409–1422.

Fleishman, E. A., & Harris, E. F. (1962). Patterns of leadership behavior related to employee grievances and turnover. *Personnel Psychology, 15,* 43–56.

Fletcher, B. C., & Jones, F. (1993). A reputation of Korasek's demand-discretion model of occupational stress with a range of dependent measures. *Journal of Organizational Behavior, 14,* 319–330.

Flett, G. L., & Hewitt, P. L. (Eds.) (2002). *Perfectionism: Theory, research, and treatment.* Washington, DC: American Psychological Association.

Florian, V., Mikulincer, M., & Taubman, O. (1995). Does hardiness contribute to mental health during a stressful real-life situation? The roles of appraisal and coping. *Journal of Personality and Social Psychology, 68,* 687–695.

Flügel, J. C. (1948). "L'appetit vient en mangeant." Some reflexions on the self-sustaining tendencies. *British Journal of Psychology, 38,* 171–190.

Folkman, S., Lazarus, R. S., Pimley, S., & Novacek, J. (1987). Age differences in stress and coping. *Psychology and Aging, 2,* 171–184.

Fordyce, M. W. (1977). Development of a program to increase personal happiness. *Journal of Counseling Psychology, 24,* 511–521.

Fordyce, M. W. (1983). A program to increase happiness: Further studies. *Journal of Counseling Psychology, 30,* 483–498.

Forgas, J. P. (1995). Mood and judgment: The Affect Infusion Model. *Psychological Bulletin, 117,* 39–66.

Forgas, J. P. (Ed.) (2001). *Handbook of affect and social cognition.* Mahwah, NJ: Lawrence Erlbaum Associates.

Forgas, J. P., & George, J. M. (2001). Affective influences on judgments and behavior in organizations: An information processing perspective. *Organizational Behavior and Human Decision Processes, 86,* 3–34.

Fozard, J. L., Vercruyssen, M., Reynolds, S. L., Hancock, P. A., & Quilter, R. E. (1994). Age differences and changes in reaction time: The Baltimore longitudinal study of aging. *Journal of Gerontology, 49,* P179-P189.

Frederick, S., & Loewenstein, G. (1999). Hedonic adaptation. In D. Kahneman, E. Diener, & N. Schwarz (Eds.), *Well-being: The foundations of hedonic psychology* (pp. 302–329). New York: Russell Sage Foundation.

Fredrickson, B. L. (2001). The role of positive emotions in positive psychology. *American Psychologist, 56,* 218–226.

Fredrickson, B. L., & Joiner, T. (2002). Positive emotions trigger upward spirals toward emotional well-being. *Psychological Science, 13*, 172–175.

Freedman, J. L. (1978). *Happy people: What happiness is, who has it, and why.* New York: Harcourt Brace Jovanovich.

French, J. R. P., Caplan, R. D., & van Harrison R. (1982). *The mechanisms of job stress and strain.* Ann Arbor, MI: Institute for Social Research.

Frese, M., Fay, D., Hilburger, T., Leng, K, & Tag, A. (1997). The concept of personal initiative: Operationalization, reliability and validity in two German samples. *Journal of Occupational and Organizational Psychology, 70*, 139–161.

Frese, M., & Sabini, J. (1985). *Goal-directed behaviour: The concept of action in psychology.* Hillsdale NJ: Lawrence Erlbaum Associates.

Frese, M., & Zapf, D. (1988). Methodological issues in the study of work stress: Objective vs. subjective measurement of work stress and the question of longitudinal studies. In C. L. Cooper & R. L. Payne (Eds.), *Causes, coping and consequences of stress at work* (pp. 375–411). Chichester, UK: Wiley.

Frese, M., & Zapf, D. (1999). On the importance of the objective environment in stress and attribution theory. Counterpoint to Perrewé and Zellars. *Journal of Organizational Behavior, 20*, 761–765.

Freud, S. (1930). *Civilization and its discontents.* London: Hogarth Press.

Frey, B., & Stutzer, A. (2001). *Happiness and economics: How the economy and institutions affect well-being.* Princeton, NJ: Princeton University Press.

Fried, Y. (1991). Meta-analytic comparison of the Job Diagnostic Survey and Job Characteristics Inventory as correlates of work satisfaction and performance. *Journal of Applied Psychology, 76*, 690–697.

Fried, Y., Slowik, L. H., Ben-David, H. A., & Tiegs, R. B. (2001). Exploring the relationship between workplace density and employee attitudinal reactions: An integrative model. *Journal of Occupational and Organizational Psychology, 74*, 359–372.

Frone, M. R. (2000). Work-family conflict and employee psychiatric disorders: The National Comorbidity Study. *Journal of Applied Psychology, 85*, 888–895.

Frone, M. R., Russell, M., & Barnes, G. M. (1996). Work-family conflict, gender, and health-related outcomes: A study of employed parents in two community samples. *Journal of Occupational Health Psychology, 1*, 57–69.

Frone, M. R., Russell, M., & Cooper, M. L. (1992). Antecedents and outcomes of work-family conflict: Testing a model of the work-family interface. *Journal of Applied Psychology, 77*, 65–78.

Frone, M. R., Russell, M., & Cooper, M. L. (1997). Relation of work-family conflict to health outcomes: A four-year longitudinal study of employed parents. *Journal of Occupational and Organizational Psychology, 70*, 325–335.

Fujita, F., & Diener, E. (2005). Life satisfaction set point: Stability and change. *Journal of Personality and Social Psychology, 88*, 158–164.

Fujita, F., Diener, E., & Sandvik, E. (1991). Gender differences in negative affect and well-being: The case for emotional intensity. *Journal of Personality and Social Psychology, 61*, 427–434.

Funk, S. C. (1992). Hardiness: A review of theory and research. *Health Psychology, 11*, 335–345.

Gagné, M., & Deci, E. L. (2005). Self-determination theory and work motivation. *Journal of Organizational Behavior, 26*, 331–362.

Gall, T. L., Evans, D. R., & Howard, J. (1997). The retirement adjustment process: Changes in the well-being of male retirees across time. *Journal of Gerontology: Psychological Sciences, 52B*, P110-P117.

Gallagher, D. G. (2005). Part-time and contingent employment. In J. Barling, E. K. Kelloway, and M. R. Frone (Eds.), *Handbook of work stress* (pp. 517–541). Thousand Oaks, CA: Sage.

Gallie, D., White, M., Cheng, Y., & Tomlinson, M. (1998). *Restructuring the employment relationship*. Oxford: Clarendon Press.

Ganster, D. C. (1989). Worker control and well-being: A review of research in the workplace. In S. L. Sauter, J. J. Hurrell, and C. L. Cooper (Eds.), *Job control and worker health* (pp. 3–23). Chichester, UK: Wiley.

Ganzach, Y. (1998). Intelligence and job satisfaction. *Academy of Management Journal, 41*, 526–539.

Ganzach, Y. (2003). Intelligence, education, and facets of job satisfaction. *Work and Occupations, 30*, 97–122.

Gardell, B. (1971). Alienation and mental health in the modern industrial environment. In L. Levi (Ed.), *Society, stress and disease* (Vol. 1, pp. 148–180). Oxford: Oxford University Press.

Gardell, B. (1982). Worker participation and autonomy: A multi-level approach to democracy in the workplace. *International Journal of Health Services, 12*, 527–558.

Gaskins, R. W. (1999). "Adding legs to a snake": A re-analysis of motivation and the pursuit of happiness from a Zen Buddhist perspective. *Journal of Educational Psychology, 91*, 204–215.

Gechman, A. S., & Wiener, Y. (1975). Job involvement and satisfaction as related to mental health and personal time devoted to work. *Journal of Applied Psychology, 60*, 521–523.

George, J. M. (1989). Mood and absence. *Journal of Applied Psychology, 74*, 317–324.

George, J. M. (1991). State or trait: Effects of positive mood on prosocial behaviors at work. *Journal of Applied Psychology, 76*, 299–307.

George, J. M. (1996). Trait and state effect. In K. R. Murphy (Ed.), *Individual differences and behavior in organizations* (pp. 145–171). San Francisco: Jossey-Bass.

George, J. M., & Brief, A. P. (1992). Feeling good–doing good: A conceptual analysis of the mood at work–organizational spontaneity relationship. *Psychological Bulletin, 112*, 310–329.

George, J. M., & Jones, G. R. (1996). The experience of work and turnover intentions: Interactive effects of value attainment, job satisfaction, and positive mood. *Journal of Applied Psychology, 81*, 318–325.

George, L. K., Okun, M. A., & Landerman, R. (1985). Age as a moderator of the determinants of life satisfaction. *Research on Aging, 7*, 209–233.

Gerhart, B. (1987). How important are dispositional factors as determinants of job satisfaction? Implications for job design and other personnel programs. *Journal of Applied Psychology, 72*, 366–373.

Gerhart, B. (1988). Sources of invariance in incumbent perceptions of job complexity. *Journal of Applied Psychology, 73*, 154–162.

Geurts, S. A. E., Kompier, M. A. J., Roxburgh, S., & Houtman, I. L. D. (2003). Does work-home interference mediate the relationship between workload and well-being? *Journal of Vocational Behavior, 63*, 532–559.

Geurts, S. A. E., Taris, T. W., Kompier, M. A. J., Dikkers, J. S. E., van Hooff, M. L. M., & Kinnunen, U. M. (2005). Work-home interaction from a work psychological pespective: Development and validation of a new questionnaire, the SWING. *Work and Stress, 19*, 319–339.

Gibbons, F. X., & Buunk, B. P. (1999). Individual differences in social comparison: Development of a scale of social comparison orientation. *Journal of Personality and Social Psychology, 76*, 129–142.

Gibson, J. J. (1979). *The ecological approach to visual perception.* Boston: Houghton Mifflin.

Giebels, E., & Janssen, O. (2005). Conflict stress and reduced well-being at work: The buffering effect of third party help. *European Journal of Work and Organizational Psychology, 14*, 137–155.

Gilbreath, B., & Benson, P. G. (2004). The contribution of supervisor behaviour to employee psychological well-being. *Work and Stress, 18*, 255–266.

Glazer, S., & Beehr, T. A. (2005). Consistency of implications of three role stressors across four countries. *Journal of Organizational Behavior, 26*, 467–487.

Glenn, N. D., & Weaver, C. N. (1985). Age, cohort, and reported job satisfaction in the United States. In Z. S. Blau (Ed.), *Current perspectives on aging and the life-cycle* (pp. 89–109). Greenwich, CT: JAI Press.

Glomb, T. M., Kammeyer-Mueller, J. D., & Rotundo, M. (2004). Emotional labor demands and compensating wage differentials. *Journal of Applied Psychology, 89*, 700–714.

Goldberg, D. P., & Williams, P. (1988). *A user's guide to the General Health Questionnaire.* Windsor: NFER-Nelson.

Goldberg, L. R. (1990). An alternate "description of personality": The big-five factor structure. *Journal of Personality and Social Psychology, 59*, 1216–1229.

Golden, T. D. (2006). The role of relationships in understanding telecommuter satisfaction. *Journal of Organizational Behavior, 27*, 319–340.

Golden, T. D., & Veiga, J. F. (2005). The impact of extent of commuting on job satisfaction: Resolving inconsistent findings. *Journal of Management, 31*, 301–318.

González-Romá, V., Schaufeli, W. B., Bakker, A. B., & Lloret, S. (2006). Burnout or work engagement: Independent factors or opposite poles? *Journal of Vocational Behavior, 68*, 165–174.

Goodman, P. S. (1974). An examination of referents used in the evaluation of pay. *Organizational Behavior and Human Performance, 12*, 170–195.

Gosserand, R. H., & Diefendorff, J. M. (2005). Emotional display rules and emotional labor: The moderating role of commitment. *Journal of Applied Psychology, 90*, 1256–1264.

Grandey, A. A. (2000). Emotion regulation in the workplace: A new way to conceptualize emotional labor. *Journal of Occupational Health Psychology, 5*, 95–110.

Grandey, A. A., Cordeiro, B. L., & Crouter, A. C. (2005). A longitudinal and multisource test of the work-family conflict and job satisfaction relationship. *Journal of Occupational and Organizational Psychology, 78*, 305–323.

Grandey, A. A., Dickter, D. N., & Sin, H.-P. (2004). The customer is *not* always right: Customer aggression and emotion regulation of service employees. *Journal of Organizational Behavior, 25*, 397–418.

Grebner, S., Semmer, N. K., & Elfering, A. (2005). Working conditions and three types of well-being: A longitudinal study with self-report and rating data. *Journal of Occupational Health Psychology, 10*, 31–43.

Grebner, S., Semmer, N. K., Lo Faso, L., Gut, S., Kälin, W., & Elfering, A. (2003). Working conditions, well-being, and job-related attitudes among call centre agents. *European Journal of Work and Organizational Psychology, 12*, 341–365.

Green, D. P., Goldman, S. L., & Salovey, P. (1993). Measurement error masks bipolarity in affect ratings. *Journal of Personality and Social Psychology, 64*, 1029–1041.

Greenberger, D. B., Strasser, S., Cummings, L. L., & Dunham, R. B. (1989). The impact of personal control on performance and satisfaction. *Organizational Behavior and Human Decision Processes, 43*, 29–51.

Greenhaus, J. H., & Beutell, N. J. (1985). Sources of conflict between work and family roles. *Academy of Management Review, 10*, 76–88.

Greenhaus, J. H., & Powell, G. N. (2006). When work and family are allies: A theory of work-family enrichment. *Academy of Management Review, 31*, 72–92.

Griffeth, R. W. (1985). Moderation of the effects of job enrichment by participation: A longitudinal field experiment. *Organizational Behavior and Human Decision Processes, 35*, 73–93.

Griffeth, R. W., Hom, P. W., & Gaertner, S. (2000). A meta-analysis of antecedents and correlates of employee turnover: Update, moderator tests, and research implications for the next millennium. *Journal of Management, 26*, 463–488.

Griffin, M. A. (1997). Multilevel influences on work attitudes: Organisational and individual predictors of pay satisfaction. *Australian Psychologist, 32*, 190–195.

Griffin, R. W. (1981). A longitudinal investigation of task characteristics relationships. *Academy of Management Journal, 24*, 99–113.

Griffin, R. W. (1983). Objective and social sources of information in task redesign: A field experiment. *Administrative Science Quarterly, 28*, 184–200.

Griffin, R. W. (1991). Effects of work redesign on employee perceptions, attitudes, and behaviors: A long-term investigation. *Academy of Management Journal, 34*, 425–435.

Grzywacz, J. D., & Dooley, D. (2003). "Good jobs" to "bad jobs": Replicated evidence of an employment continuum from two large surveys. *Social Science and Medicine, 56*, 1749–1760.

Grzywacz, J. D., & Marks, N. F. (2000). Reconceptualizing the work-family interface: An ecological perspective on the correlates of positive and negative spillover between work and family. *Journal of Occupational Health Psychology, 5*, 111–126.

Guerra, J. M., Martinez, I., Munduate, L., & Medina, F. J. (2005). A contingency perspective on the study of the consequences of conflict types: The role of organizational culture. *European Journal of Work and Organizational Psychology, 14*, 157–176.

Hacker, W. (1986). *Arbeitspsychologie*. Bern, Switzerland: Huber.

Hackett, R. D. (1989). Work attitudes and employee absenteeism: A synthesis of the literature. *Journal of Occupational Psychology, 62*, 235–248.

Hackman, J. R., & Lawler, E. E. (1971). Employee reactions to job characteristics. *Journal of Applied Psychology, 55*, 259–286.

Hackman, J. R., & Oldham, G. R. (1975). Development of the Job Diagnostic Survey. *Journal of Applied Psychology, 60*, 159–170.

Hackman, J. R., & Oldham, G. R. (1976). Motivation through the design of work: Test of a theory. *Organizational Behavior and Human Performance, 16*, 250–279.

Hackman, J. R., & Oldham, G. R. (1980). *Work redesign*. Reading, MA: Addison-Wesley.

Hackman, J. R, Pearce, J. L., & Wolfe, J. C. (1978). Effects of changes in job characteristics on work attitudes and behaviors: A naturally occurring quasi-experiment. *Organizational Behavior and Human Performance, 21*, 289–304.

Hagerty, M. R., & Veenhoven, R. (2003). Wealth and happiness revisited—Growing national income *does* go with greater happiness. *Social Indicators Research, 64*, 1–27.

Haider, S., & Loughran, D. (2001). *Elderly labor supply: Work or play?* Retrieved May 16, 2006, from www. bc.edu/centers/crr/papers/wp-2001-04.pdf

Hall, D. T., & Chandler, D. E., (2005). Psychological success: When the career is a calling. *Journal of Organizational Behavior, 26*, 155–176.

Hammer, L. B., Cullen, J. C., Neal, M. B., Sinclair, R. R., & Shafiro, M. V. (2005). The longitudinal effects of work-family conflict and positive spillover on depressive symptoms among dual-earner couples. *Journal of Occupational Health Psychology, 10*, 138–154.

Handy, C. (1984). *The future of work: A guide to a changing society*. Oxford: Blackwell.

Handyside, J. D. (1961). Satisfaction and aspirations. *Occupational Psychology, 35*, 213–243.

Hanisch, K. A. (1994). Reasons people retire and their relations to attitudinal and behavioral correlates in retirement. *Journal of Vocational Behavior, 45*, 1–16.

Hanisch, K. A. (1999). Job loss and unemployment research from 1994 to 1998: A review and recommendations for research and intervention. *Journal of Vocational Behavior, 55*, 188–220.

Hannan, D. F., Oriain, S., & Whelan, C. T. (1997). Youth unemployment and psychological distress in the Republic of Ireland. *Journal of Adolescence, 20*, 307–320.

Hardy, G. E., Woods, D., & Wall, T. D. (2003). The impact of psychological distress on absence from work. *Journal of Applied Psychology, 88*, 306–314.

Hardy, M. A., & Quadagno, J. (1995). Satisfaction with early retirement: Making choices in the auto industry. *Journal of Gerontology: Social Sciences, 50B*, S217-S228.

Haring, M. J., Stock, W. A., & Okun, M. A. (1984). A research synthesis of gender and social class as correlates of subjective well-being. *Human Relations, 37*, 645–657.

Harkness, A. M. B., Long, B. C., Bermbach, N., Patterson, K., Jordan, S., & Kahn, H. (2005). Talking about work stress: Discourse analysis and implications for stress interventions. *Work and Stress, 19*, 121–136.

Harlow, R. E., & Cantor, N. (1996). Still participating after all those years: A study of life task participation in later life. *Journal of Personality and Social Psychology, 71*, 1235–1249.

Harris, C., Daniels, K., & Briner, R. B. (2003). A daily diary study of goals and affective well-being at work. *Journal of Occupational and Organizational Psychology, 76*, 401–410.

Harter, J. K., Schmidt, F. L., & Hayes, T. L. (2002). Business-unit relationship between employee satisfaction, employee engagement, and business outcomes: A meta-analysis. *Journal of Applied Psychology, 87,* 268–279.

Hartog, J., & Oosterbeek, H. (1998). Health, wealth and happiness: Why pursue a higher education? *Economics of Education Review, 17,* 245–256.

Hartman, G. W. (1934). Personality traits associated with variations in happiness. *Journal of Abnormal and Social Psychology, 29,* 202–212.

Harvey, S., Kelloway, E. K., & Duncan-Leiper, L. (2003). Trust in management as a buffer of the relationships between overload and strain. *Journal of Occupational Health Psychology, 8,* 306–315,

Hathcock, J. N., Azzi, A., Blumberg, J., Bray, T., Dickinson, A., Frei, B., Jialal, I., Johnston, C. S., Kelly, F. J., Kraemer, K., Packer, L., Parthasarathy, S., Sies, H., & Traber, M. G. (2005). Vitamins E and C are safe across a broad range of intakes. *American Journal of Clinical Nutrition, 81,* 736–745.

Haworth, J. T. (1997). *Work, leisure and well-being.* London: Routledge.

Headey, B., Holmström, E., & Wearing, A. (1984). The impact of life events and changes in domain satisfactions on well-being. *Social Indicators Research, 15,* 203–227.

Headey, B., & Wearing, A. (1989). Personality, life events, and subjective well-being: Toward a dynamic equilibrium model. *Journal of Personality and Social Psychology, 57,* 731–739.

Headey, B., & Wearing, A. (1992). *Understanding happiness: A theory of subjective well-being.* Melbourne, Australia: Longman Cheshire.

Heaney, C. A., Israel, B. A., & House, J. S. (1994). Chronic job insecurity among automobile workers: Effects on job satisfaction and health. *Social Science and Medicine, 38,* 1431–1437.

Heinisch, D. A., & Jex, S. M. (1997). Negative affectivity and gender as moderators of the relationship between work-related stressors and depressed mood at work. *Work and Stress, 11,* 46–57.

Helander, M. G., Landauer, T. K., & Prabhu, P. V. (Eds.). (1997). *Handbook of human-computer interaction* (2nd. ed). Amsterdam: Elsevier.

Heller, D., Judge, T. A., & Watson, D. (2002). The confounding role of personality and trait affectivity in the relationship between job and life satisfaction. *Journal of Organizational Behavior, 23,* 815–835.

Hellgren, J., & Sverke, M. (2003). Does job insecurity lead to impaired well-being or vice versa? Estimation of cross-lagged effects using latent variable modeling. *Journal of Organizational Behavior, 24,* 215–236.

Hellgren, J., Sverke, M., & Isaksson, K. (1999). A two-dimensional approach to job insecurity: Consequences for employee attitudes and well-being. *European Journal of Work and Organizational Psychology, 8,* 179–195.

Helson, H. (1964). *Adaptation-level theory.* New York: Harper and Row.

Hendrix, W. H., Ovalle, N. K., & Troxler, R. G. (1985). Behavioral and physiological consequences of stress and its antecedent factors. *Journal of Applied Psychology, 70,* 188–201.

Herz, D. E. (1995). Work after early retirement: An increasing trend among men. *Monthly Labor Review, 118*(4), 13–20.

Herzberg, F. (1966). *Work and the nature of man.* Chicago: World Publishing.

Herzberg, F. I., Mausner, B., Peterson, R. O., & Capwell, D. R. (1957). *Job attitudes: Review of research and opinion.* Pittsburgh, PA: Psychological Service of Pittsburgh.

Herzog, A. R., House, J. S., & Morgan, J. N. (1991). Relation of work and retirement to health and well-being in older age. *Psychology and Aging, 6,* 202–211.

Hetland, H., & Sandal, G. M. (2003). Transformational leadership in Norway: Outcomes and personality correlates. *European Journal of Work and Organizational Psychology, 12,* 147–170.

Higgins, C., Duxbury, L., & Johnson, K. L. (2000). Part-time work for women: Does it really help balance work and family? *Human Resource Management, 39,* 17–32.

Hipple, S. (2004). Self-employment in the United States: An update. *Monthly Labor Review, 127*(7), 13–23.

Hobfoll, S. E. (1989). Conservation of resources: A new attempt at conceptualizing stress. *American Psychologist, 44,* 513–524.

Hobfoll, S. E. (2001). The influence of culture, community, and the nested self in the stress process: Advancing conservation of resources theory. *Applied Psychology: An International Review, 50,* 337–370.

Hockey, G. R. J. (1986). Changes in operator efficiency as a function of environmental stress, fatigue, and circadian rhythms. In K. Boff, L. Kaufman, & J. P. Thomas (Eds.), *Handbook of perception and performance* (Vol. 2, pp. 44/1–44). New York: Wiley.

Hofstede, G. (1984). The cultural relativity of the quality of life concept. *Academy of Management Review, 9,* 389–398.

Hofstede, G. (1990). *Cultures and organizations: Software of the mind.* London: McGraw-Hill.

Hogan, R., & Blake, R. (1999). John Holland's vocational typology and personality theory. *Journal of Vocational Behavior, 55,* 41–56.

Höge, T., & Büssing, A. (2004). The impact of sense of coherence and negative affectivity on the work stressor-strain relationship. *Journal of Occupational Health Psychology, 9,* 195–205.

Holland, J. L. (1973). *Making vocational choices: A theory of careers.* Englewood Cliffs, NJ: Prentice Hall.

Holland, J. L. (1997). *Making vocational choices: A theory of vocational personalities and work environments.* Odessa, FL: Psychological Assessment Resources.

Holland, J. L. (1999). Why interest inventories are also personality inventories. In M. Savickas & A. Spokane (Eds.), *Vocational interests: Their meaning, measurement, and use in counseling* (pp. 87–101). Palo Alto, CA: Davies-Black.

Holman, D. (2002). Employee well-being in call centres. *Human Resource Management Journal, 12,* 35–50.

Holman, D., & Wall, T. D. (2002). Work characteristics, learning-related outcomes, and strain: A test of competing direct effects, mediated, and moderated effects. *Journal of Occupational Health Psychology, 7,* 283–301.

Hom, P. W., Caranikas-Walker, F., Prussia, G. E., & Griffeth, R, W. (1992). A meta-analytical structural equations analysis of a model of employee turnover. *Journal of Applied Psychology, 77,* 890–909.

Hom, P. W., & Kinicki, A. J. (2001). Toward a greater understanding of how dissatisfaction drives employee turnover. *Academy of Management Journal, 44,* 975–987.

Homans, G. C. (1961). *Social behavior: Its elementary forms*. New York: Harcourt Brace.

Horley, J., & Lavery, J. J. (1995). Subjective well-being and age. *Social Indicators Research, 34*, 275–282.

Hotopp, U. (2002). Teleworking in the UK. *Labour Market Trends, 110*, 311–318.

Hough, L. M. (1992). The "big five" personality variables—construct confusion: Description versus prediction. *Human Performance, 5*, 139–155.

Houkes, I., Janssen, P. P. M., de Jonge, J., & Bakker, A. B. (2003). Personality, work characteristics, and employee well-being: A longitudinal analysis of additive and moderating effects. *Journal of Occupational Health Psychology, 8*, 20–38.

House, J. S., McMichael, A. J., Wells, A. J., Kaplan, B. H., & Landerman, L. R. (1979). Occupational stress and health among factory workers. *Journal of Health and Social Behavior, 20*, 139–160.

Huang, X., & van de Vliert, E. (2003). Where intrinsic job satisfaction fails to work: National moderators of intrinsic motivation. *Journal of Organizational Behavior, 24*, 159–179.

Huang, X., & van de Vliert, E. (2004). Job level and national culture as joint roots of job satisfaction. *Applied Psychology: An International Review, 53*, 329–348.

Hughes, E. C. (1951). Work and the self. In J. H. Rohrer & M. Sherif (Eds.), *Social psychology at the crossroads* (pp. 313–323). New York: Harper and Brothers.

Hughes, G. J. (2001). *Aristotle on ethics*. London: Routledge.

Hui, C. H., Yee, C., & Eastman, K. L. (1995). The relationship between individualism-collectivism and job satisfaction. *Applied Psychology: An International Review, 44*, 276–282.

Hull, J. G., van Treuren, R. R., & Virnelli, S. (1987). Hardiness and health: A critique and alternative approach. *Journal of Personality and Social Psychology, 53*, 518–530.

Iaffaldano, M. T., & Muchinsky, P. M. (1985). Job satisfaction and job performance: A meta-analysis. *Psychological Bulletin, 97*, 251–273.

Ilgen, D. R., Fisher, C. D., & Taylor, M. S. (1979). Consequences of individual feedback on behavior in organizations. *Journal of Applied Psychology, 64*, 349–371.

Ilies, R., & Judge, T. A. (2003). On the heritability of job satisfaction: The mediating role of personality. *Journal of Applied Psychology, 88*, 750–759.

Ingram, R. (1990). Self-focused attention in clinical disorders: Review and conceptual model. *Psychological Bulletin, 107*, 156–176.

Ironson, G. H., Smith, P. C., Brannick, M. T., Gibson, W. M., & Paul, K. B. (1989). Construction of a job in general scale: A comparison of global, composite, and specific measures. *Journal of Applied Psychology, 74*, 193–200.

Isen, A. M. (1985). The asymmetry of happiness and sadness in effects on memory in normal college students. *Journal of Experimental Psychology: General, 114*, 388–391.

Isen, A. M. (1999). Positive affect. In T. Dagleish & M. Power (Eds.), *Handbook of cognition and emotion* (pp. 521–539). New York: Wiley.

Isen, A. M., & Baron, R. A. (1991). Positive affect as a factor in organizational behavior. *Research in Organizational Behavior, 13*, 1–53.

Iyengar, S. S., & Lepper, M. R. (2000). When choice is demotivating: Can one desire too much of a good thing? *Journal of Personality and Social Psychology, 79*, 995–1006.

Jackson, P. R., Paul, L. J., & Wall, T. D. (1981). Individual differences as moderators of reactions to job characteristics. *Journal of Occupational Psychology*, *54*, 1–8.

Jackson, P. R., Stafford, E. M., Banks, M. H., & Warr, P. B. (1983). Unemployment and psychological distress in young people: The moderating role of employment commitment. *Journal of Applied Psychology*, *68*, 525–535.

Jackson, P. R., & Walsh, S. (1987). Unemployment and the family. In D. Fryer & P. Ullah (Eds.), *Unemployed people* (pp. 194–216). Milton Keynes, UK: Open University Press.

Jackson, P. R., & Warr, P. B. (1984). Unemployment and psychological ill-health: The moderating role of duration and age. *Psychological Medicine*, *14*, 605–614.

Jackson, P. R., & Warr, P. B. (1987). Mental health of unemployed men in different parts of England and Wales. *British Medical Journal*, *295*, 525.

Jackson, P. R., Wall, T. D., Martin, R., & Davids, K. (1993). New measures of job control, cognitive demand, and production responsibility. *Journal of Applied Psychology*, *78*, 753–762.

Jackson, S. A., & Marsh, H. W. (1996). Development and validation of a scale to measure optimal experience: The Flow State Scale. *Journal of Sport and Exercise Psychology*, *18*, 17–35.

Jackson, S. E. (1983). Participation in decision-making as a strategy for reducing job-related strain. *Journal of Applied Psychology*, *68*, 3–19.

Jackson, S. E., & Schuler, R. S. (1985). A meta-analysis and conceptual critique of research on role ambiguity and role conflict in work settings. *Organizational Behavior and Human Decision Processes*, *36*, 16–78.

Jacobs, J. A. (Ed.) (1995). *Gender inequality at work*. Thousand Oaks, CA: Sage.

Jahoda, M. (1958). *Current concepts of positive mental health*. New York: Basic Books.

Jahoda, M. (1981). Work, employment, and unemployment: Values, theories, and approaches in social research. *American Psychologist*, *36*, 184–191.

Jahoda, M. (1982). *Employment and unemployment: A social-psychological analysis*. Cambridge, UK: Cambridge University Press.

Jahoda, M., Lazarsfeld, P. F., & Zeisel, H. (1971). *Marienthal: The sociography of an unemployed community*. New York: Aldine-Atherton. (Original work published 1933)

Jamal, M. (1984). Job stress and job performance controversy: An empirical assessment. *Organizational Behavior and Human Performance*, *33*, 1–21.

James, K., Brodersen, M., & Eisenberg, J. (2004). Workplace affect and workplace creativity: A review and preliminary model. *Human Performance*, *17*, 169–194.

Janson, P., & Martin, J. K. (1982). Job satisfaction and age: A test of two views. *Social Forces*, *60*, 1089–1102.

Janssen, O. (2001). Fairness perceptions as a moderator in the curvilinear relationships between job demands and job performance and job satisfaction. *Academy of Management Journal*, *44*, 1039–1050.

Janssen, P. P. M., Peeters, M. C. W., de Jonge, J., Houkes, I., & Tummers, G. E. R. (2004). Specific relationships between job demands, job resources and psychological outcomes and the mediating role of negative work-home interference. *Journal of Vocational Behavior*, *65*, 411–429.

Jeurissen, T, & Nyklíciek, I. (2001). Testing the vitamin model of job stress in Dutch health care workers. Work and Stress, 15, 254–264.

Jex, S., & Spector, P. E. (1996). The impact of negative affectivity on stressor-strain relations: A replication and extension. *Work and Stress, 10*, 36–45.

Jick, T. D., & Mitz, L. F. (1985). Sex differences in work stress. *Academy of Management Review, 10*, 408–420.

Johansson, G. (1989). Job demands and stress reactions in repetitive and uneventful monotony at work. *International Journal of Health Services, 19*, 365–377.

Johns, G. (1997). Contemporary research on absence from work: Correlates, causes and consequences. In C. L. Cooper & I. T. Robertson (Eds.), *International review of industrial and organizational psychology* (pp. 115–173). Chichester, UK: Wiley.

Jones, M. C., Smith, K., & Johnston, D. W. (2005). Exploring the Michigan model: The relationship of personality, managerial support and organizational structure with health outcomes in entrants to the healthcare environment. *Work and Stress, 19*, 1–23.

Judge, T. A., Bono, J. E., & Locke, E. A. (2000). Personality and job satisfaction: The mediating role of job characteristics. *Journal of Applied Psychology, 85*, 237–249.

Judge, T. A., Bono, J. E., Erez, A., & Locke, E. A. (2005). Core self-evaluations and job and life satisfaction: The role of self-concordance and goal attainment. *Journal of Applied Psychology, 90*, 257–268.

Judge, T. A., & Colquitt, J. A. (2004). Organizational justice and stress: The mediating role of work-family conflict. *Journal of Applied Psychology, 89*, 395–404.

Judge, T. A., Erez, A., Bono, J. E., & Thoresen, C. J. (2003). The core self-evaluations scale: Development of a measure. *Personnel Psychology, 56*, 303–331.

Judge, T. A., Heller, D., & Mount, M. K. (2002). Five-factor model of personality and job satisfaction: A meta-analysis. *Journal of Applied Psychology, 87*, 530–541.

Judge, T. A., & Ilies, R. (2004). Affect and job satisfaction: A study of their relationship at work and at home. *Journal of Applied Psychology, 89*, 661–673.

Judge, T. A., & Locke, E. A. (1993). Effect of dysfunctional thought processes on subjective well-being and job satisfaction. *Journal of Applied Psychology, 78*, 475–490.

Judge, T. A., Locke, E. A., Durham, C. A., & Kluger, A. N. (1998). Dispositional effects on job and life satisfaction: The role of core evaluations. *Journal of Applied Psychology, 83*, 17–34.

Judge, T. A., & Piccolo, R. F. (2004). Transformational and transactional leadership: A meta-analytic test of their relative validity. *Journal of Applied Psychology, 89*, 755–768.

Judge, T. A., Piccolo, R. F., & Ilies, R. (2004). The forgotten ones? The validity of consideration and initiating structure in leadership research. *Journal of Applied Psychology, 89*, 36–51.

Judge, T. A., Thoresen, C. J., Bono, J. E., & Patton, G. K. (2001). The job satisfaction-job performance relationship: A qualitative and quantitative review. *Psychological Bulletin, 127*, 376–407.

Judge, T. A., & Watanabe, S. (1993). Another look at the job satisfaction–life satisfaction relationship. *Journal of Applied Psychology, 78*, 939–948.

Kafka, G. J., & Kozma, A. (2001). The construct validity of Ryff's scales of psychological well-being (SPWB) and their relationship to measures of subjective well-being. *Social Indicators Research, 57*, 171–190.

Kahn, R. L., Wolfe, D. M., Quinn, R. P., & Snoek, J. D. (1964). *Organizational stress: Studies in role conflict and ambiguity*. New York: Wiley.

Kahneman, D., & Miller, D. (1986). Norm theory: Comparing reality to its alternatives. *Psychological Review, 93*, 136–153.

Kalleberg, A. L., & Loscocco, K. A. (1983). Aging, values, and rewards: Explaining age differences in job satisfaction. *American Sociological Review, 48*, 78–90.

Kalliath, T. J., Bluedorn, A. C., & Strube, M. J. (1999). A test of value congruence effects. *Journal of Organizational Behavior, 20*, 1175–1198.

Kantowitz, B. H., & Sorkin, R. D. (1983). *Human factors: Understanding people–system relationships*. New York: Wiley.

Karasek, R. A. (1979). Job demands, job decision latitude, and mental strain: Implications for job design. *Administrative Science Quarterly, 24*, 285–308.

Karasek, R. A., & Theorell, T. (1990). *Healthy work*. New York: Basic Books.

Karasek, R. A., Triantis, K. P., and Chaudhry, S. S. (1982). Coworker and supervisor support as moderators of associations between task characteristics and mental strain. *Journal of Occupational Behavior, 3*, 181–200.

Kasimatis, M., & Wells, G. L (1995). Individual differences in counterfactual thinking. In N. J. Roese & J. M. Olson (Eds.), *What might have been: The social psychology of counterfactual thinking* (pp. 81–101). Mahwah, NJ: Lawrence Erlbaum Associates.

Kauppinen-Toropainen, K., Kandolin, I., & Mutanen, P. (1983). Job dissatisfaction and work-related exhaustion in male and female work. *Journal of Occupational Behaviour, 4*, 193–207.

Keenan, A., & McBain, G. D. M. (1979). Effects of type A behaviour, intolerance of ambiguity, and locus of control on the relationship between role stress and work-related outcomes. *Journal of Occupational Psychology, 52*, 277–285.

Kehr, H. M. (2003). Goal conflicts, attainment of new goals, and well-being among managers. *Journal of Occupational Health Psychology, 8*, 195–208.

Kelloway, E. K., & Barling, J. (1991). Job characteristics, role stress and mental health. *Journal of Occupational Psychology, 64*, 291–304.

Kelly, J. R., & Barsade, S. G. (2001). Mood and emotions in small groups and work teams. *Organizational Behavior and Human Decision Processes, 86*, 99–130.

Kemp, N. J., Wall, T. D., Clegg, C. W., & Cordery, J. L. (1983). Autonomous work groups in a green-field site: A comparative study. *Journal of Occupational Psychology, 56*, 271–288.

Kendler, K. S., Hettema, J. M., Butera, F., Gardner, C. O., & Prescott, C. A. (2003). Life event dimensions of loss, humiliation, entrapment, and danger in the prediction of onsets of major depression and generalized anxiety. *Archives of General Psychiatry, 60*, 789–796.

Kessler, R. C., & Frank, R. G. (1997). The impact of psychiatric disorders on work loss days. *Psychological Medicine, 27*, 861–873.

Kessler, R. C., McGonagle, K. A., Zhao, S., Nelson, C. B., Hughes, M., Eshleman, S., Wittchen, H., & Kendler, K. S. (1994). Lifetime and twelve-month prevalence of DSM-III-R psychiatric disorders in the United States. *Archives of General Psychiatry, 51*, 8–19.

Keyes, C. L. M. (2002). The mental health continuum: From languishing to flourishing in life. *Journal of Health and Social Behavior, 43*, 207–222.

Keyes, C. L. M., Schmotkin, D., & Ryff, C. D. (2002). Optimizing well-being: The empirical encounter of two traditions. *Journal of Personality and Social Psychology, 82*, 1007–1022.

Kieran, D. (2004). *The Idler book of crap jobs.* London: Bantam Books.

Kiggundu, M. N. (1980). An empirical test of job design using multiple job ratings. *Human Relations, 33*, 339–351.

Kilpatrick, R., & Trew, K. (1985). Life-styles and psychological well-being among unemployed men in Northern Ireland. *Journal of Occupational Psychology, 58*, 207–216.

Kim, S., & Feldman, D. C. (2000). Working in retirement: The antecedents of bridge employment and its consequences for quality of life in retirement. *Academy of Management Journal, 43*, 1195–1210.

Kim-Prieto, C., Diener, E., Tamir, M., Scollon, C., & Diener, M. (2005). Integrating the diverse definitions of happiness: A time-sequential framework of subjective well-being. *Journal of Happiness Studies, 6*, 261–300.

King, L. A. (2001). The health benefits of writing about life goals. *Personality and Social Psychology Bulletin, 27*, 798–807.

King, L. A., Hicks, J. A., Krull, J. L., & Del Gairo, A. K. (2006). Positive affect and the experience of meaning in life. *Journal of Personality and Social Psychology, 90*, 179–196.

Kinicki, A. J., McKee-Ryan, F. M., Schriesheim, C. A., & Carson, K. P. (2002). Assessing the construct validity of the Job Descriptive Index: A review and meta-analysis. *Journal of Applied Psychology, 87*, 14–32.

Kinnunen, U., Geurts, S., & Mauno, S. (2004). Work-to-family conflict and its relationship with satisfaction and well-being: A one-year longitudinal study on gender differences. *Work and Stress, 18*, 1–22.

Kirjonen, J., & Hänninen, V. (1986). Getting a better job: Antecedents and effects. *Human Relations, 39*, 503–516.

Kirmeyer, S. L. (1988). Coping with competing demands: Interruption and the Type A pattern. *Journal of Applied Psychology, 73*, 621–629.

Kivimäki, M., Elovainio, M., Vahtera, J., Virtanen, M., & Stansfeld, S. A. (2003). Association between organizational inequity and incidence of psychiatric disorders in female employees. *Psychological Medicine, 33*, 319–326.

Klumb, P. L., & Lampert, T. (2004). Women, work, and well-being 1950–2000: A review and methodological critique. *Social Science and Medicine, 58*, 1007–1024.

Kobasa, S. C., Maddi, S. R., & Kahn, S. (1982). Hardiness and health: A prospective study. *Journal of Personality and Social Psychology, 42*, 168–177.

Koestner, R., Lekes, N., Powers, T. A., & Chicoine, E. (2002). Attaining personal goals: Self-concordance plus implementation intentions equals success. *Journal of Personality and Social Psychology, 83*, 231–244.

Kohler, S. S., & Mathieu, J. E. (1993). Individual characteristics, work perceptions, and affective reactions influences on differentiated absence criteria. *Journal of Organizational Behavior, 14*, 515–530.

Konrad, A. M., Ritchie, J. E., Lieb, P., & Corrigall, E. (2000). Sex differences and similarities in job attribute preferences: A meta-analysis. *Psychological Bulletin, 126*, 593–641.

Kornhauser, A. W. (1965). *Mental health of the industrial worker: A Detroit study*. New York: Wiley.

Kossek, E. E., & Ozeki, C. (1998). Work-family conflict, policies, and the job-life satisfaction relationship: A review and directions for organizational behavior— human resources research. *Journal of Applied Psychology, 83*, 139–149.

Koys, D. J. (2001). The effects of employee satisfaction, organizational citizenship behavior, and turnover on organizational effectiveness: A unit-level, longitudinal study. *Personnel Psychology, 54*, 101–114.

Kraus, S. J. (1995). Attitudes and the prediction of behavior: A meta-analysis of the empirical literature. *Personality and Social Psychology Bulletin, 21*, 58–75.

Krausz, M., Brandwein, T., & Fox, S. (1995). Work attitudes and emotional responses of permanent, voluntary, and involuntary temporary-help employees: An exploratory study. *Applied Psychology: An International Review, 44*, 217–232.

Krausz, M., Sagie, A., & Biderman, Y. (2000). Actual and preferred work schedules and scheduling control as determinants of job-related attitudes. *Journal of Vocational Behavior, 56*, 1–11.

Kristof, A. L. (1996). Person-organization fit: An integrative review of its conceptualizations, measurement, and implications. *Personnel Psychology, 49*, 1–49.

Kristof-Brown, A. L., Zimmerman, R. D., & Johnson, E. C. (2005). Consequences of individuals' fit at work: A meta-analysis of person-job, person-organization, person-group, and person-supervisor fit. *Personnel Psychology, 58*, 281–342.

Kunin, T. (1955). The construction of a new type of attitude measure. *Personnel Psychology, 9*, 65–78.

Lacy, W. B., Bokemeier, J. L., & Shepard, J. M. (1983). Job attribute preferences and work commitment of men and women in the United States. *Personnel Psychology, 36*, 315–329.

Lamond, D., Daniels, K., & Standen, P. (2005). Managing virtual workers and virtual organizations. In D. Holman, T. D. Wall, C. W. Clegg, P. Sparrow, & A. Howard (Eds.), *The essentials of the new workplace* (pp. 173–195). Chichester, UK: Wiley.

Landeweerd, J. A., & Boumans, N. P. G. (1994). The effect of work dimensions and need for autonomy on nurses' work satisfaction and health. *Journal of Occupational and Organizational Psychology, 67*, 207–217.

Landy, F. J. (1978). An opponent process theory of job satisfaction. *Journal of Applied Psychology, 63*, 533–547.

Lapierre, L. M., Spector, P. E., & Leck, J. D. (2005). Sexual versus nonsexual workplace aggression and victims' overall job satisfaction: A meta-analysis. *Journal of Occupational Health Psychology, 10*, 155–169.

Latham, G. P., & Pinder, C. C. (2005). Work motivation theory and research at the dawn of the twenty-first century. *Annual Review of Psychology, 56*, 485–516.

Law, K. S., Wong, C.-S., & Song, L. J. (2004). The construct and criterion validity of emotional intelligence and its potential utility for management studies. *Journal of Applied Psychology, 89*, 483–496.

Lawler, E. E., & Porter, L. W. (1967). The effect of performance on job satisfaction. *Industrial Relations, 7*, 20–28.

Lazarus, R. (1999). *Stress and emotion: A new synthesis*. New York: Springer.

LeBlanc, M. M., & Kelloway, E. K. (2002). Predictors and outcomes of workplace violence and aggression. *Journal of Applied Psychology, 87*, 444–453.

Lee, K., & Allen, N. J. (2002). Organizational citizenship behavior and workplace deviance: The role of affect and cognition. *Journal of Applied Psychology, 87*, 131–142.

Lee, R., & Wilbur, E. R. (1985). Age, education, job tenure, salary, job characteristics, and job satisfaction: A multivariate analysis. *Human Relations, 38*, 781–791.

Lee, R. T., & Ashforth, B. E. (1996). A meta-analytic examination of the correlates of the three dimensions of job burnout. *Journal of Applied Psychology, 81*, 123–133.

Leiter, M. P., Harvie, P., & Frizzell, C. (1998). The correspondence of patient satisfaction and nurse burnout. *Social Science and Medicine, 47*, 1611–1617.

Leitner, K., & Resch, M. G. (2005). Do the effects of job stressors on health persist over time? A longitudinal study with observational stressor measures. *Journal of Occupational Health Psychology, 10*, 18–30.

Lepine, J. A., Podsakoff, N. P., & Lepine, M. A. (2005). A meta-analytic test of the challenge stressor-hindrance stressor framework: An explanation for inconsistent relationships among stressors and performance. *Academy of Management Journal, 48*, 764–775.

Leventhal, G. S. (1980). What should be done with equity theory? New approaches to the study of fairness in social relationships. In K. Gergen, M. Greenberg, & R. Willis (Eds.), *Social exchange: Advances in theory and research* (pp. 27–55). New York: Plenum.

Levin, I., & Stokes, J. P. (1989). Dispositional approach to job satisfaction: Role of negative affectivity. *Journal of Applied Psychology, 74*, 752–758.

Lewig, K. A., & Dollard, M. F. (2003). Emotional dissonance, emotional exhaustion and job satisfaction in call centre workers. *European Journal of Work and Organizational Psychology, 12*, 366–392.

Lewin, K., Dembo, T., Festinger, L., & Sears, P. S. (1944). Level of aspiration. In J. McV. Hunt (Ed.), *Personality and behavior disorders* (pp. 333–378). New York: Ronald Press.

Lewis, S. (2003). Flexible working arrangements: Implementation, outcomes, and management. In C. L. Cooper & I. T. Robertson (Eds.), *International Review of Industrial and Organizational Psychology* (pp. 1–28). Chichester, UK: Wiley.

Lim, V. (1996). Job insecurity and its outcomes: Moderating effects of work-based and non-work-based social support. *Human Relations, 49*, 171–194.

Locke, E. A. (1969). What is job satisfaction? *Organizational Behavior and Human Performance, 4*, 309–336.

Locke, E. A. (1970). Job satisfaction and job performance: A theoretical analysis. *Organizational Behavior and Human Performance, 5*, 484–500.

Locke, E. A. (1976). The nature and causes of job satisfaction. In M. D. Dunnette (Ed.), *Handbook of industrial and organizational psychology* (pp. 1297–1343). Chicago: Rand McNally.

Loehlin, J. C. (1992). *Genes and environment in personality development.* Newbury Park, CA: Sage.

Loevinger, J. (1980). *Ego development: Conceptions and theories.* San Francisco: Jossey-Bass.

Loher, B. T., Noe, R. A., Moeller, N. L., & Fitzgerald, M. P. (1985). A meta-analysis of the relation of job characteristics to job satisfaction. *Journal of Applied Psychology, 70*, 280–289.

Loscocco, K. A., & Spitze, G. (1990). Working conditions, social support, and the well-being of female and male factory workers. *Journal of Health and Social Behavior, 31*, 313–327.

Lowe, G. S., & Northcott, H. C. (1988). The impact of working conditions, social roles, and personal characteristics on gender differences in distress. *Work and Occupations, 15*, 55–77.

Lu, L., & Gilmour, R. (2004). Culture and conceptions of happiness: Individual oriented and social oriented SWB. *Journal of Happiness Studies, 5*, 269–291.

Lu, L., Gilmour, R., & Kao, S. F. (2001). Culture, values, and happiness: An East-West dialogue. *Journal of Social Psychology, 141*, 477–493.

Lubbers, R., Loughlin, C., & Zweig, D. (2005). Young workers' job self-efficacy and affect: Pathways to health and performance. *Journal of Vocational Behavior, 67*, 199–214.

Lucas, R. E., Clark, A. E., Georgellis, Y., & Diener, E. (2003). Reexamining adaptation and the set point model of happiness: Reactions to changes in marital status. *Journal of Personality and Social Psychology, 84*, 527–539.

Lucas, R. E., Clark, A. E., Georgellis, Y., & Diener, E. (2004). Unemployment alters the set point for life satisfaction. *Psychological Science, 15*, 8–15.

Lucas, R. E., & Diener, E. (2003). The happy worker: Hypotheses about the role of positive affect in worker productivity. In M. R. Barrick & A. M. Ryan (Eds.), *Personality and work* (pp. 30–59). San Francisco: Jossey-Bass.

Lucas, R. E., Diener, E., & Suh, E. (1996). Discriminant validity of well-being measures. *Journal of Personality and Social Psychology, 71*, 616–628.

Lucas, R. E., & Fujita, F. (2000). Factors influencing the relation between extraversion and pleasant affect. *Journal of Personality and Social Psychology, 79*, 1039–1056.

Lyons, T. F. (1971). Role clarity, need for clarity, satisfaction, tension, and withdrawal. *Organizational Behavior and Human Performance, 6*, 99–110.

Lyubomirsky, S. (2001). Why are some people happier than others? The role of cognitive and motivational processes in well-being. *American Psychologist, 56*, 239–249.

Lyubomirsky, S., King, L., & Diener, E. (2005). The benefits of frequent positive affect: Does happiness lead to success? *Psychological Bulletin, 131*, 803–855.

Lyubomirsky, S., & Ross, L. (1999). Changes in attractiveness of elected, rejected, and precluded alternatives: A comparison of happy and unhappy individuals. *Journal of Personality and Social Psychology, 76*, 988–1007.

Lyubomirsky, S., Sheldon, K. M., & Schkade, D. (2005). Pursuing happiness: The architecture of sustainable change. *Review of General Psychology, 9*, 111–131.

Lyubomirsky, S., & Tucker, K. L. (1998). Implications of individual differences in subjective happiness for perceiving, interpreting, and thinking about life events. *Motivation and Emotion, 22*, 155–186.

MacDonald, L. A., Karasek, R. A., Punnett, L., & Scharf, T. (2001). Covariation between workplace physical and psychosocial stressors: Evidence and implications for occupational health research and prevention. *Ergonomics, 44*, 696–718.

Magnus, K., Diener, E., Fujita, F., & Pavot, W. (1993). Extraversion and neuroticism as predictors of objective life events: A longitudinal analysis. *Journal of Personality and Social Psychology, 65*, 1046–1053.

Maier, G. W., & Brunstein, J. C. (2001). The role of personal work goals in new-comers' job satisfaction and organizational commitment. *Journal of Applied Psychology, 86,* 1034–1042.

Major, V. S., Klein, K. J., & Erhart, M. G. (2002). Work time, work interference with family, and psychological distress. *Journal of Applied Psychology, 87,* 427–436.

Markides, K. S., & Martin, H. W. (1979). A causal model of life satisfaction among the elderly. *Journal of Gerontology, 34,* 86–93.

Marmot, M. (2004). *Status syndrome.* London: Bloomsbury.

Martin, R., & Wall, T. D. (1989). Attentional demand and cost responsibility as stressors in shopfloor jobs. *Academy of Management Journal, 32,* 69–86.

Martocchio, J. J. (1994). The effects of absence culture on individual absence. *Human Relations, 47,* 243–262.

Maslach, C. (1982). *Burnout: The cost of caring.* New York: Prentice Hall.

Maslach, C. (1998). A multidimensional theory of burnout. In C. L. Cooper (Ed.), *Theories of work stress* (pp. 68–85). Oxford, UK: Oxford University Press.

Maslach, C., Schaufeli, W. B., & Leiter, M. P. (2001). Job burnout. *Annual Review of Psychology, 52,* 397–422.

Maslow, A. H. (1943). A theory of human motivation. *Psychological Review, 50,* 370–396.

Maslow, A. H. (1968). *Toward a psychology of being,* second edition. New York: Van Nostrand.

Mason, C. M., & Griffin, M. A. (2003). Group absenteeism and positive affective tone: A longitudinal study. *Journal of Organizational Behavior, 24,* 667–687.

Mathieu, J. E., Hofman, D. A., & Farr, J. L. (1993). Job perception-job satisfaction relations: An empirical comparison of three competing theories. *Organizational Behavior and Human Decision Processes, 56,* 370–387.

Mauno, S., Kinnunen, U., Mäkikangas, A., & Nätti, J. (2005). Psychological conse-quences of fixed-term employment and perceived job insecurity among health care staff. *European Journal of Work and Organizational Psychology, 14,* 209–237.

Maurer, T. J., Weiss, E. M., & Barbeite, F. G. (2003). A model of involvement in work-related learning and development activity: The effects of individual, situational, motivational, and age variables. *Journal of Applied Psychology, 88,* 707–724.

McCoy, J. M., & Evans, G. W. (2005). Physical work environment. In J. Barling, E. K. Kelloway, & M. R. Frone (Eds.), *Handbook of work stress* (pp. 219–245). Thousand Oaks, CA: Sage.

McDougall, W. (1932). *The energies of man.* London: Methuen.

McFall, L. (1982). *Happiness.* New York: Lang.

McGinnis, S. K., & Morrow, P. C. (1990). Job attitudes among full- and part-time employees. *Journal of Vocational Behavior, 36,* 82–96.

McGregor, I., & Little, B. R. (1998). Personal projects, happiness, and meaning: On doing well and being yourself. *Journal of Personality and Social Psychology, 74,* 494–512.

McKee-Ryan, F. M., & Kinicki, A. J. (2002). Coping with job loss: A life-facet per-spective. In C. L. Cooper & I. T. Robertson (Eds.), *International review of indus-trial and organizational psychology* (Vol. 17, pp. 1–29). Chichester, UK: Wiley.

McKee-Ryan, F. M., Song, Z., Wanberg, C. R., & Kinicki, A. J. (2005). Psychological and physical well-being during unemployment: A meta-analytic study. *Journal of Applied Psychology, 90*, 53–76.

McLean-Parks, J., Kidder, D. L., & Gallagher, D. G. (1998). Fitting square pegs into round holes: Mapping the domain of contingent work arrangements onto the psychological contract. *Journal of Organizational Behavior, 19*, 697–730.

McNeely, B. L., & Meglino, B. M. (1994). The role of dispositional and situational antecedents in prosocial organizational behavior: An examination of the intended beneficiaries of prosocial behavior. *Journal of Applied Psychology, 79*, 836–844.

McOrmond, T. (2004). Changes in working trends over the past decade. *Labour Market Trends, 112*, 25–35.

McRae, R. R., & Costa, P. T. (1997). Personality trait structure as a human universal. *American Psychologist, 52*, 509–516.

Medvec, V. H., Madey, S. F., & Gilovich, T. (1995). When less is more: Counterfactual thinking and satisfaction among Olympic athletes. *Journal of Personality and Social Psychology, 69*, 603–610.

Meijman, T. F., & Mulder, G. (1998). Psychological aspects of workload. In P. J. D. Drenth, H. Thierry, & C. J. de Wolff (Eds.), *Handbook of work and organizational psychology*, second edition (pp. 5–33). Hove, UK: Psychology Press.

Meijman, T. F., Mulder, G., van Dormolen, M., & Cremer, R. (1992). Workload of driving examiners: A psycho-physiological field study. In H. Kragt (Ed.), *Enhancing industrial performance* (pp. 245–260). Frankfurt, Germany: Lang.

Melamed, S., Ben-Avi, I., Luz, J., & Green, M. S. (1995). Objective and subjective work monotony: Effects on job satisfaction, psychological distress, and absenteeism in blue-collar workers. *Journal of Applied Psychology, 80*, 29–42.

Mesmer-Magnus, J. R., & Viswesvaran, C. (2005). Convergence between measures of work-to-family and family-to-work conflict: A meta-analytic investigation. *Journal of Vocational Behavior, 67*, 215–232.

Michalos, A. C. (1985). Multiple discrepancies theory (MDT). *Social Indicators Research, 16*, 347–413.

Midanik, L. T., Soghikian, K., Ransom, L. J., & Tekawa, I. S. (1995). The effect of retirement on mental health and health behaviors: The Kaiser Permanente Retirement Study. *Journal of Gerontology: Social Sciences, 50B*, S59–S61.

Miles, R. H. (1975). An empirical test of causal inference between role perceptions of conflict and ambiguity and various personal outcomes. *Journal of Applied Psychology, 60*, 334–339.

Miller, S. M. (1981). Predictability and human stress. In L. Berkowitz (Ed.), *Advances in experimental social psychology* (Vol. 14, pp. 203–256). New York: Academic Press.

Miner, A. G., Glomb, T. M., & Hulin, C. (2005). Experience sampling mood and its correlates at work. *Journal of Occupational and Organizational Psychology, 78*, 171–193.

Miner, J. B. (1992). *Industrial-organizational psychology*. New York: McGraw-Hill.

Mirowsky, J., & Ross, C. E. (1992). Age and depression. *Journal of Health and Social Behavior, 33*, 187–205.

Mitra, A., Jenkins, G. D., & Gupta, N. (1992). A meta-analytic review of the relationship between absence and turnover. *Journal of Applied Psychology, 77*, 879–889.

Mobley, W. H., & Locke, E. A. (1970). The relationship of value importance to satisfaction. *Organizational Behavior and Human Performance, 5*, 463–483.

Moch, M. (1980). Job involvement, internal motivation, and employees' integration into networks of work relationships. *Organizational Behavior and Human Performance, 25*, 15–31.

Mor, S., Day, H. I., Flett, G. L., & Hewitt, P. L. (1995). Perfectionism, control, and components of performance anxiety in professional performers. *Cognitive Therapy and Research, 19*, 207–225.

Morgeson, F. P., & Campion, M. A. (2002). Minimizing trade-offs when redesigning work: Evidence from a longitudinal quasi-experiment. *Personnel Psychology, 55*, 589–612.

Morris, J. A., & Feldman, D. C. (1996). The dimensions, antecedents, and consequences of emotional labor. *Academy of Management Review, 21*, 986–1010.

Morrison, D., Cordery, J., Girardi, A., & Payne, R. L. (2005). Job design, opportunities for skill utilization, and intrinsic job satisfaction. *European Journal of Work and Organizational Psychology, 14*, 59–79.

Morrow, P. C., & McElroy, J. C. (1987). Work commitment and job satisfaction over three career stages. *Journal of Vocational Behavior, 30*, 330–346.

Motowidlo, S. J. (1984). Does job satisfaction lead to consideration and personal sensitivity? *Academy of Management Journal, 27*, 910–915.

Motowidlo, S. J., Packard, J. S., & Manning, J. S. (1986). Occupational stress: Its causes and consequences for job performance. *Journal of Applied Psychology, 71*, 618–629.

Mottaz, C. J. (1986). Gender differences in work satisfaction, work-related rewards and values, and the determinants of work satisfaction. *Human Relations, 39*, 59–378.

Mount, M. K., Barrick, M. R., Scullen, S. M., & Rounds, J. (2005). Higher-order dimensions of the Big Five personality traits and the Big Six vocational interest types. *Personnel Psychology, 58*, 447–478.

MOW International Research Team (1987). *The meaning of working*. London: Academic Press.

Moyle, P. (1995). The role of negative affectivity in the stress process: Tests of alternative models. *Journal of Organizational Behavior, 16*, 647–668.

Mroczek, D. K., & Kolarz, C. M. (1998). The effect of age on positive and negative affect: A developmental perspective on happiness. *Journal of Personality and Social Psychology, 75*, 1333–1349.

Mroczek, D. K., & Spiro, A. (2005). Change in life satisfaction during adulthood: Findings from the Veterans Affairs Normative Aging Study. *Journal of Personality and Social Psychology, 88*, 189–202.

Mullarkey, S., Wall, T. D., Warr, P. B., Clegg, C. W., & Stride, C. (1999). *Measures of job satisfaction, mental health and job-related well-being*. Sheffield, UK: Sheffield Academic Press.

Munz, D. C., Huelsman, T. J., Konold, T. R., & McKinney, J. J. (1996). Are there methodological and substantive roles for affectivity in Job Diagnostic Survey relationships? *Journal of Applied Psychology, 81*, 795–805.

Murphy, G. C., & Athanasou, J. A. (1999). The effect of unemployment on mental health. *Journal of Occupational and Organizational Psychology, 72,* 83–99.

Murray, H. A. (1938). *Explorations in personality.* New York: Oxford University Press.

Muse, L. A., Harris, S. G., & Feild, H. S. (2003). Has the inverted-U theory of stress and job performance had a fair test? *Human Performance, 16,* 349–364.

Mussweiler, T., & Rüter, K. (2003). What friends are for! The use of routine standards in social comparison. *Journal of Personality and Social Psychology, 85,* 467–481.

Mutchler, J. E., Burr, J. A., Pienta, A. M., & Massagli, M. P. (1997). Pathways to labor force exit: Work transitions and work instability. *Journal of Gerontology: Social Sciences, 52B,* S4-S12.

Myers, D. A. (1991). Work after cessation of career job. *Journal of Gerontology: Social Sciences, 46,* S93-S102.

Myers, D. G., & Diener, E. (1995). Who is happy? *Psychological Science, 6,* 10–19.

Nakamura, J., & Csikszentmihalyi, M. (2002). The concept of flow. In C. R. Snyder & S. J. Lopez (Eds.), *Handbook of positive psychology* (pp. 89–105). Oxford, UK: Oxford University Press.

Näswall, K., Sverke, M., & Hellgren, J. (2005). The moderating role of personality characteristics on the relationship between job insecurity and strain. *Work and Stress, 19,* 37–49.

Neil, C. C., & Snizek, W. E. (1988). Gender as a moderator of job satisfaction: A multivariate assessment. *Work and Occupations, 15,* 201–219.

Netemeyer, R. G., Johnston, M. W., & Burton, S. (1990). Analysis of role conflict and role ambiguity in a structural equations framework. *Journal of Applied Psychology, 75,* 148–157.

Neumann, J. P. (1989). Aging and depression. *Psychology and Aging, 4,* 150–165.

Nezu, A. M. (1985). Differences in psychological distress between effective and ineffective problem solvers. *Journal of Counseling Psychology, 32,* 135–138.

Nicholson, N. (1977). Absence behaviour and attendance motivation: A conceptual synthesis. *Journal of Management Studies, 14,* 231–252.

Niklas, C. D., & Dormann, C. (2005). The impact of state affect on job satisfaction. *European Journal of Work and Organizational Psychology, 14,* 367–388.

Nix, G. A., Ryan, R. M., Manly, J. B., & Deci, E. L. (1999). Revitalization through self-regulation: The effects of autonomous and controlled motivation on happiness and vitality. *Journal of Experimental Social Psychology, 35,* 266–284.

Nolen-Hoeksema, S., & Rusting, C. (1999). Gender differences in well-being. In D. Kahneman, E. Diener, & N. Schwarz (Eds.), *Well-being: The foundations of hedonic psychology* (pp. 330–350). New York: Russell Sage Foundation.

Norcross, J. C., Santrock, J. W., Campbell, L. F., Smith, T. P., Sommer, R., & Zuckerman, E. L. (2000). *Authoritative guide to self-help resources in mental health.* New York: Guilford Press.

Nordenmark, M. (1999). Non-financial employment motivation and well-being in different labour market situations: A longitudinal study. *Work, Employment and Society, 13,* 601–620.

O'Brien, G. E. (1980). The centrality of skill utilization for job design. In K. D. Duncan, M. M. Gruneberg, & D. Wallis (Eds.), *Changes in working life* (pp. 167–187). Chichester, UK: Wiley.

O'Brien, G. E. (1982). The relative contribution of perceived skill utilization and other perceived job attributes to the prediction of job satisfaction: A cross-validation study. *Human Relations, 35*, 219–237.

O'Brien, G. E. (1983). Skill utilization, skill variety and the job characteristics model. *Australian Journal of Psychology, 35*, 461–468.

O'Brien, G. E., & Dowling, P. (1980). The effects of congruency between perceived and desired attributes upon job satisfaction. *Journal of Occupational Psychology, 53*, 121–130.

O'Connor, G. J., & Barrett, G. V. (1980). Informational cues and individual differences as determinants of subjective perceptions of task enrichment. *Academy of Management Journal, 23*, 697–716.

Office for National Statistics. (2005). *Labour market trends* (Vol. 113). London: Her Majesty's Stationery Office.

Oishi, S. (2002). The experiencing and remembering of well-being: A cross-cultural analysis. *Personality and Social Psychology Bulletin, 28*, 1398–1406.

Okun, M. A., Stock, W. A., Haring, M. J., & Witter, R. A. (1984). Health and subjective well-being: A meta-analysis. *International Journal of Aging and Human Development, 19*, 111–132.

Oldham, G. R., & Brass, D. J. (1979). Employee reactions to an open-plan office: A naturally occurring quasi-experiment. *Administrative Science Quarterly, 24*, 267–284.

Oldham, G. R., & Rotchford, N. L. (1983). Relationships between office characteristics and employee reactions: A study of the physical environment. *Administrative Science Quarterly, 28*, 542–556.

Oliver, R. L. (1977). Antecedents of salemen's compensation perceptions: A path analysis interpretation. *Journal of Applied Psychology, 62*, 20–28.

Olson, J. M., Buhrman, O., & Roese, N. J. (2000). Comparing comparisons: An integrative perspective on social comparison and counterfactual thinking. In J. Suls & L. Wheeler (Eds.), *Handbook of social comparison: Theory and research* (pp. 379–398). New York: Kluwer/Plenum.

O'Reilly, C. A., Chatman, J., & Caldwell, D. F. (1991). People and organizational culture: A profile comparison approach to assessing person-organization fit. *Academy of Management Journal, 34*, 487–516.

Organ, D. W., & Ryan, K. (1995). A meta-analytic review of attitudinal and dispositional predictors of organizational citizenship behavior. *Personnel Psychology, 48*, 775–802.

Ostroff, C. (1992). The relationship between satisfaction, attitudes, and performance: An organizational level analysis. *Journal of Applied Psychology, 77*, 963–974.

Ouellette, J. A., & Wood, W. (1998). Habit and intention in everyday life: The multiple processes by which past behavior predicts future behavior. *Psychological Bulletin, 124*, 54–74.

Palmore, E. B., Burchett, B. M., Fillenbaum, G. G., George, L. K., & Wallman, L. M. (1985). *Retirement: Causes and consequences*. New York: Springer.

Parasuraman, S., Purohit, Y. S., Godshalk, V. M., & Beutell, N. J. (1996). Work and family variables, entrepreneurial career success, and psychological well-being. *Journal of Vocational Behavior, 48*, 275–300.

Parducci, A. (1995). *Happiness, pleasure, and judgment*. Mahwah, NJ: Lawrence Erlbaum Associates.

Parfit, D. (1984). *Reasons and persons*. Oxford, UK: Oxford University Press.

Parker, S. K. (2003). Longitudinal effects of lean production on employee outcomes and the mediating role of work characteristics. *Journal of Applied Psychology, 88,* 620–634.

Parker, S. K., & Sprigg, C. (1999). Minimizing strain and maximizing learning: The role of job demands, job control, and proactive personality. *Journal of Applied Psychology, 84,* 925–939.

Parker, S. K., Griffin, M. A., Sprigg, C. A., & Wall, T. D. (2002). Effect of temporary contracts on perceived work characteristics and job strain: A longitudinal study. *Personnel Psychology, 55,* 689–719.

Parkes, K. R. (1982). Occupational stress among student nurses: A natural experiment. *Journal of Applied Psychology, 67,* 784–796.

Parkes, K. R. (1990). Coping, negative affectivity, and the work environment: Additive and interactive predictions of mental health. *Journal of Applied Psychology, 75,* 399–409.

Parkes, K. R., & Rendall, D. (1988). The hardy personality and its relationship to extraversion and neuroticism. *Personality and Individual Differences, 9,* 785–790.

Patterson, M. J., Warr, P. B., & West, M. A. (2004). Organizational climate and company productivity: The role of employee affect and employee level. *Journal of Occupational and Organizational Psychology, 77,* 193–216.

Paul, K. I., & Moser, K. (2006). Incongruence as an explanation for the negative mental health effects of unemployment: Meta-analytic evidence. *Journal of Occupational and Organizational Psychology, 79,* 595–621.

Paunonen, S. V. (1998). Hierarchical organization of personality and prediction of behavior. *Journal of Personality and Social Psychology, 74,* 538–556.

Pavot, W., & Diener, E. (1993). Review of the Satisfaction with Life Scale. *Psychological Assessment, 5,* 164–172.

Payne, E. C., Robbins, S. B., & Dougherty, L. (1991). Goal directedness and older-adult adjustment. *Journal of Counseling Psychology, 38,* 302–308.

Payne, R. L., Wall, T. D., Borrill, C., & Carter, A. (1999). Strain as a moderator of the relationship between work characteristics and work attitudes. *Journal of Occupational Health Psychology, 4,* 3–14.

Peale, N. V. (1952). *The power of positive thinking*. New York: Prentice Hall.

Pearce, J. L. (1993). Toward an organizational behavior of contract laborers: Their psychological involvement and effects on employee co-workers. *Academy of Management Journal, 36,* 1082–1096.

Peeters, M. A. G., & Rutte, C. G. (2005). Time management behavior as a moderator for the demand-control interaction. *Journal of Occupational Health Psychology, 10,* 64–75.

Penney, L. M., & Spector, P. E. (2005). Job stress, incivility, and counterproductive work behavior (CWB): The moderating role of negative affectivity. *Journal of Organizational Behavior, 26,* 777–796.

Peterson, C., Park, N., & Seligman, M. E. P. (2005). Orientations to happiness and life satisfaction: The full life versus the empty life. *Journal of Happiness Studies, 6,* 25–41.

Petty, M. M., McGee, G. W., & Cavender, J. W. (1984). A meta-analysis of the relationship between individual job satisfaction and individual performance. *Academy of Management Review, 9*, 712–721.

Petty, R. E., Wegener, D. T., & Fabrigar, L. R. (1997). Attitudes and attitude change. *Annual Review of Psychology, 48*, 609–647.

Phillips, L. H., Bull, R., Adams, E., & Fraser, L. (2002). Positive mood and executive function: Evidence from Stroop and fluency tasks. *Emotion, 2*, 12–22.

Piccolo, R. F., Judge, T. A., Takahashi, K., Watanabe, N., & Locke, E. A. (2005). Core self-evaluations in Japan: Relative effects on job satisfaction, life satisfaction, and happiness. *Journal of Organizational Behavior, 26*, 965–984.

Pierce, J. L., & Gardner, D. J. (2004). Self-esteem within the work and organizational context: A review of the organization-based self-esteem literature. *Journal of Management, 30*, 591–622.

Piltch, C. A., Walsh, D. C., Mangione, T. W., & Jennings, S. E. (1994). Gender, work, and mental distress in an industrial labor force. In G. P. Keita & J. J. Hurrell (Eds.), *Job stress in a changing workforce* (pp. 39–54). Washington, DC: American Psychological Association.

Pinquart, M. (2001). Age differences in perceived positive affect, negative affect, and affect balance in middle and old age. *Journal of Happiness Studies, 2*, 375–405.

Pinquart, M., & Sörensen, S. (2000). Influences of socio-economic status, social network, and competence on subjective well-being in later life: A meta-analysis. *Psychology and Aging, 15*, 187–224.

Piotrkowski, C. S. (1978). *Work and the family system*. New York: The Free Press.

Podsakoff, P. M., MacKenzie, S. B., & Bommer, W. H. (1996). Meta-analysis of the relationships between Kerr and Jermier's substitutes for leadership and employee job attitudes, role perceptions, and performance. *Journal of Applied Psychology, 81*, 380–399.

Podsakoff, P. M., MacKenzie, S. B., Lee, J.-Y., and Podsakoff, N. (2003). Common method biases in behavioral research: A critical review of the literature and recommended remedies. *Journal of Applied Psychology, 88*, 879–903.

Podsakoff, P. M., MacKenzie, S. B., Paine, J. B., & Bachrach, D. G. (2000). Organizational citizenship behaviors: A critical review of the theoretical and empirical literature and suggestions for future research. *Journal of Management, 26*, 513–563.

Pollock, K. (1988). On the nature of social stress: Production of a modern mythology. *Social Science and Medicine, 26*, 381–392.

Porter, L. W., & Steers, R. M. (1973). Organizational, work, and personal factors in employee turnover and absenteeism. *Psychological Bulletin, 80*, 151–176.

Poulton, E. C. (1978). Blue collar stressors. In C. L. Cooper & R. L. Payne (Eds.), *Stress at work* (pp. 51–79). Chichester, UK: Wiley.

Poutsma, E., & Zwaard, A. (1988). Programming CNC equipment: The effects of automation in small industrial enterprises. *International Small Business Journal, 72*(2), 35–43.

Price, R. D., Choi, J. N., & Vinokur, A. D. (2002). Links in the chain of adversity following job loss: How financial strain and loss of personal control lead to depression, impaired functioning and poor health. *Journal of Occupational Health Psychology, 7*, 302–312.

Probst, T. M. (2005a). Economic stressors. In J. Barling, E. K. Kelloway, & M. R. Frone (Eds.), *Handbook of work stress* (pp. 267–297). Thousand Oaks, CA: Sage.

Probst, T. M. (2005b). Countering the negative effects of job insecurity through participative decision making: Lessons from the demand-control model. *Journal of Occupational Health Psychology, 10,* 320–329.

Probst, T. M., & Lawler, J. (2006). Cultural values as moderators of employee reactions to job insecurity: The role of individualism and collectivism. *Applied Psychology: An International Review, 55,* 234–254.

Pugliesi, K. (1995). Work and well-being: Gender influences on the psychological consequences of employment. *Journal of Health and Social Behavior, 36,* 57–71.

Quick, H. E., & Moen, P. (1998). Gender, employment, and retirement quality: A life course approach to the differential experiences of men and women. *Journal of Occupational Health Psychology, 3,* 44–64.

Quinn, R. E., & Rohrbaugh, J. (1983). A spatial model of effectiveness criteria: Toward a competing values approach to organizational analysis. *Management Science, 29,* 363–377.

Quinn, R. P., & Mandilovitch, M. S. B. (1980). Education and job satisfaction, 1962–1977. *Vocational Guidance Quarterly, 29,* 100–111.

Quinn, R. W. (2005). Flow in knowledge work: High performance experience in the design of national security technology. *Administrative Science Quarterly, 50,* 610–641.

Rafferty, Y., Friend, R., & Landsbergis, P. A. (2001). The association between job skill discretion, decision authority and burnout. *Work and Stress, 15,* 73–85.

Rainwater, L. (1974). *What money buys: Inequality and the social meanings of income.* New York: Basic Books.

Reisenzein, R. (1994). Pleasure-arousal theory and the intensity of emotions. *Journal of Personality and Social Psychology, 67,* 525–539.

Reitzes, D. C., Mutran, E. J., & Fernandez, M. E. (1996). Does retirement hurt well-being? Factors influencing self-esteem and depression among retirees and workers. *The Gerontologist, 36,* 649–656.

Remington, N. A., Fabrigar, L. R., & Visser, P. S. (2000). Re-examining the circumplex model of affect. *Journal of Personality and Social Psychology, 79,* 286–300.

Repetti, R. L., Matthews, K. A., & Waldron, I. (1989). Employment and women's health. *American Psychologist, 44,* 1394–1401.

Rhodes, S. R. (1983). Age-related differences in work attitudes and behavior: A review and conceptual analysis. *Psychological Bulletin, 93,* 328–367.

Rhodes, S. R., & Steers, R. M. (1990). *Managing employee absenteeism.* Reading, MA: Addison-Wesley.

Rice, R. W., Frone, M. R., & McFarlin, D. B. (1992). Work-nonwork conflict and the perceived quality of life. *Journal of Organizational Behavior, 13,* 155–168.

Rice, R. W., Gentile, D. A., & McFarlin, D. B. (1991). Facet importance and job satisfaction. *Journal of Applied Psychology, 76,* 31–39.

Rice, R. W., Phillips, S. M., & McFarlin, D. B. (1990). Multiple discrepancies and pay satisfaction. *Journal of Applied Psychology, 75,* 386–393.

Rizzo, J. R., House, R. J., & Lirtzman, S. I. (1970). Role conflict and ambiguity in complex organizations. *Administrative Science Quarterly, 15*, 150–163.

Robbins, S. B., Lee, R. M., & Wan, T. T. H. (1994). Goal continuity as a mediator of early retirement adjustment: Testing a multidimensional model. *Journal of Counseling Psychology, 41*,18–26.

Roberson, L. (1990). Prediction of job satisfaction from characteristics of personal work goals. *Journal of Organizational Behavior, 11*, 29–41.

Robertson, A., Gilloran, A., McGlew, T., McKee, K., McInley, A., & Wight, D. (1995). Nurses' job satisfaction and the quality of care received by patients in psychogeriatric wards. *International Journal of Geriatric Psychiatry, 10*, 575–584.

Rode, G. C. (2004). Job satisfaction and life satisfaction revisited: A longitudinal test of an integrated model. *Human Relations, 57*, 1205–1230.

Roe, R. A., & Ester, P. (1999). Values and work: Empirical findings and theoretical perspective. *Applied Psychology: An International Review, 48*, 1–21.

Roese, N. J. (1997). Counterfactual thinking. *Psychological Bulletin, 121*, 133–148.

Roese, N. J., & Olson, J. M. (1995). Counterfactual thinking: A critical overview. In N. J. Roese & J. M. Olson (Eds.), *What might have been: The social psychology of counterfactual thinking* (pp. 1–55). Mahwah, NJ: Lawrence Erlbaum Associates.

Roethlisberger, F., & Dickson, W. J. (1939). *Management and the worker.* Cambridge, MA: Harvard University Press.

Rogelberg, S. G., Leach, D. J., Warr, P. B., & Burnfield, J. (2006). "Not another meeting!" Are meeting time demands related to employee well-being? *Journal of Applied Psychology, 91*, 83–96.

Ronan, W. W. (1970). Relative importance of job characteristics. *Journal of Applied Psychology, 54*, 192–200.

Ros, M., Schwartz, S. H., & Surkiss, S. (1999). Basic individual values, work values, and the meaning of work. *Applied Psychology: An International Review, 48*, 49–71.

Rose, M. (2003). Good deal, bad deal? Job satisfaction in occupations. *Work, Employment and Society, 17*, 503–530.

Rosenberg, M. (1965). *Society and the adolescent self-image.* Princeton, NJ: Princeton University Press.

Roskies, E., Louis-Guerin, C., & Fournier, C. (1993). Coping with job insecurity: How does personality make a difference? *Journal of Organizational Behavior, 14*, 617–630.

Rospenda, K. M., & Richman, J. A. (2005). Harrassment and discrimination. In J. Barling, E. K. Kelloway, & M. R. Frone (Eds.), *Handbook of work stress* (pp. 149–188). Thousand Oaks, CA: Sage.

Ross, C. E., & Drentea, P. (1998). Consequences of retirement activities for distress and sense of personal control. *Journal of Health and Social Behavior, 39*, 317–344.

Ross, C. E., Mirowsky, J., & Huber, J. (1983). Dividing work, sharing work, and in-between: Marriage patterns and depression. *American Sociological Review, 48*, 809–823.

Rothbard, N. P. (2001). Enriching or depleting? The dynamics of engagement in work and family roles. *Administrative Science Quarterly, 46*, 655–684.

Rounds, J. B., Dawis, R. V., & Lofquist, L. H. (1987). Measurement of person-environment fit and prediction of satisfaction in the theory of work adjustment. *Journal of Vocational Behavior, 31*, 297–318.

Rousseau, D. M. (1995). *Psychological contracts in organizations: Understanding written and unwritten agreements.* Thousand Oaks, CA: Sage.

Roxburgh, S. (1996). Gender differences in work and well-being: Effects of exposure and vulnerability. *Journal of Health and Social Behavior, 37*, 265–277.

Roy, D. F. (1960). "Banana time," job satisfaction, and informal interaction. *Human Organization, 18*, 158–168.

Røysamb, E., Tambs, K., Reichborn-Kjennerud, T., Neale, M. C., & Harris, J. R. (2003). Happiness and health: Environmental and genetic contributions to the relationship between subjective well-being, perceived health, and somatic illness. *Journal of Personality and Social Psychology, 85*, 1136–1146.

Ruhm, C. J. (1990). Bridge jobs and partial retirement. *Journal of Labor Economics, 8*, 482–501.

Ruiz, Y., & Walling, A. (2005). Home-based working using communication technologies. *Labour Market Trends, 113*, 417–426.

Russell, J. A. (1979). Affective space is bipolar. *Journal of Personality and Social Psychology, 37*, 345–356.

Russell, J. A. (1980). A circumplex model of affect. *Journal of Personality and Social Psychology, 39*, 1161–1178.

Russell, J. A. (1983). Pancultural aspects of the human conceptual organization of emotions. *Journal of Personality and Social Psychology, 45*, 1281–1288.

Russell, J. A. (2003). Core affect and the psychological construction of emotion. *Psychological Review, 110*, 145–172.

Russell Davis, D. (1979). Pilot error: Some laboratory experiments. In E. J. Dearnaley and P. B. Warr (Eds.), *Aircrew stress in wartime operations* (pp. 179–218). London: Academic Press. (Original work published 1948)

Rusting, C. L., & Larsen, R. J. (1997). Extraversion, neuroticism, and susceptibility to positive and negative affect: A test of two theoretical models. *Personality and Individual Differences, 22*, 607–612.

Ryan, A. M., Schmit, M. J., & Johnson, R. (1996). Attitudes and effectiveness: Examining relations at an organizational level. *Personnel Psychology, 49*, 853–882.

Ryan, R. M., & Deci, E. L. (2001). On happiness and human potentials: A review of research on hedonic and eudaimonic well-being. *Annual Review of Psychology, 52*, 141–166.

Ryan, R. M., & Frederick, C. M. (1997). On energy, personality, and health: Subjective vitality as a dynamic reflection of well-being. *Journal of Personality, 65*, 529–565.

Ryff, C. D. (1989). Happiness is everything, or is it? Explorations on the meaning of psychological well-being. *Journal of Personality and Social Psychology, 57*, 1069–1081.

Ryff, C. D., & Keyes, C. L. M. (1995). The structure of psychological well-being revisited. *Journal of Personality and Social Psychology, 69*, 719–727.

Salancik, G. R., & Pfeffer, J. (1978). A social information processing approach to job attitudes and task design. *Administrative Science Quarterly, 23*, 224–253.

Schat, A. C. H., & Kelloway, E. K. (2000). Effects of perceived control on the outcomes of workplace aggression and violence. *Journal of Occupational Health Psychology, 5,* 386–402.

Schat, A. C. H., & Kelloway, E. K. (2005). Workplace aggression. In J. Barling, E. K. Kelloway, & M. R. Frone (Eds.), *Handbook of work stress* (pp. 189–218). Thousand Oaks, CA: Sage.

Schaubroeck, J., Ganster, D. C., & Fox, M. L. (1992). Dispositional affect and work-related stress. *Journal of Applied Psychology, 77,* 322–335.

Schaubroeck, J., Ganster, D. C., & Kemmerer, B. (1996). Does trait affect promote job attitude stability? *Journal of Organizational Behavior, 17,* 191–196.

Schaubroeck, J., Ganster, D. C., Sime, W. E., & Ditman, D. (1993). A field experiment testing supervisory role clarification. *Personnel Psychology, 46,* 1–25.

Schaufeli, W. B., & Bakker, A. B. (2004). Job demands, job resources, and their relationship with burnout and engagement: A multi-sample study. *Journal of Organizational Behavior, 25,* 293–315.

Scheck, C. L., & Kinicki, A. (2000). Identifying the antecedents of coping with an organizational acquisition: A structural assessment. *Journal of Organizational Behavior, 21,* 627–648.

Schein, E. (1993). *Career anchors: Discovering your real values,* revised edition. London: Pfeiffer.

Schleicher, D. J., Watt, J. D., & Greguras, G. J. (2004). Re-examining the job satisfaction-performance relationship: The complexity of attitudes. *Journal of Applied Psychology, 89,* 165–177.

Schmitt, N., & Stults, D. M. (1985). Factors defined by negatively keyed items: The result of careless respondents? *Applied Psychological Measurement, 9,* 367–373.

Schmutte, P. S., & Ryff, C. D. (1997). Personality and well-being: Re-examining methods and meanings. *Journal of Personality and Social Psychology, 73,* 549–559.

Schneider, B. (1987). The people make the place. *Personnel Psychology, 40,* 437–454.

Schneider, B., Goldstein, H. W., & Smith, D. B. (1995). The ASA framework: An update. *Personnel Psychology, 48,* 747–773.

Schneider, B., Hanges, P. J., Smith, D. B., & Salvaggio, A. N. (2003). Which comes first: Employee attitudes or organizational and financial market performance? *Journal of Applied Psychology, 88,* 836–851.

Schneider, W., & Chein, J. M. (2003). Controlled and automatic processing: Behavior, theory, and biological mechanisms. *Cognitive Science, 27,* 525–559.

Schriesheim, C. A., Eisenback, R. J., & Hill, K. D. (1991). The effect of negation and polar opposite item reversals on questionnaire reliability and validity: An experimental investigation. *Educational and Psychological Measurement, 51,* 67–78.

Schultz, D. (1977). *Growth psychology: Models of the healthy personality.* Pacific Grove, CA: Brooks/Cole.

Schwab, D. P., & Heneman, H. G. (1977). Age and satisfaction with dimensions of work. *Journal of Vocational Behavior, 10,* 212–220.

Schwarz, B. (2000). Self determination: The tyranny of freedom. *American Psychologist, 55,* 79–88.

Schwarz, B. (2004). *The paradox of choice.* New York: Harper Collins/Ecco.

Schwarz, B., Ward, A., Monterosso, J., Lyubomirsky, S., White, K., & Lehman, D. R. (2002). Maximizing versus satisficing: Happiness is a matter of choice. *Journal of Personality and Social Psychology, 83*, 1178–1197.

Schwartz, N., & Strack, F. (1999). Reports of subjective well-being: Judgmental processes and their methodological implications. In D. Kahneman, E. Diener, & N. Schwarz (Eds.), *Well-being: The foundations of hedonic psychology* (pp. 61–84). New York: Russell Sage Foundation.

Schwartz, S. H. (1999). A theory of cultural values and some implications for work. *Applied Psychology: An International Review, 48*, 23–47.

Seligman, M. E. P. (2002). *Authentic happiness*. New York: Free Press.

Seligman, M. E. P., Steen, T. A., Park, N., & Peterson, C. (2005). Positive psychology progress: Empirical validation of interventions. *American Psychologist, 60*, 410–421.

Seltzer, J., & Numeroff, R. E. (1988). Supervisory leadership and subordinate burnout. *Academy of Management Journal, 31*, 439–446.

Seo, M.-G., Feldman Barrett, L., & Bartunek, J. M. (2004). The role of affective experience in work motivation. *Academy of Management Review, 29*, 423–439.

Sevastos, P., Smith, L., & Cordery, J. L. (1992). Evidence on the reliability and construct validity of Warr's (1990) well-being and mental health measures. *Journal of Occupational and Organizational Psychology, 65*, 33–49.

Shamir, B. (1986a). Self-esteem and the psychological impact of unemployment. *Social Psychology Quarterly, 49*, 61–72.

Shamir, B. (1986b). Protestant work ethic, work involvement and the psychological impact of unemployment. *Journal of Occupational Behaviour, 7*, 25–38.

Shaw, J. D., & Gupta, N. (2004). Job complexity, performance, and well-being: When does supplies-values fit matter? *Personnel Psychology, 57*, 847–879.

Sheldon, K. M., & Elliot, A. J. (1999). Goal striving, need satisfaction, and longitudinal well-being: The self-concordance model. *Journal of Personality and Social Psychology, 76*, 482–497.

Sheldon, K. M., & Houser-Marko, L. (2001). Self-concordance, goal attainment, and the pursuit of happiness: Can there be an upward spiral? *Journal of Personality and Social Psychology, 80*, 152–165.

Sheldon, K. M., & Kasser, T. (1995). Coherence and congruence: Two aspects of personality integration. *Journal of Personality and Social Psychology, 68*, 31–543.

Sheldon, K. M., & Lyubomirsky, S. (2006). How to increase and sustain positive emotion: The effects of expressing gratitude and visualizing best possible selves. *Journal of Positive Psychology, 1*, 73–82.

Shepperd, J. A., & McNulty, J. K. (2002). The affective consequences of expected and unexpected outcomes. *Psychological Science, 13*, 85–88.

Siegrist, J. (1996). Adverse health effects of high-effort/low-reward conditions. *Journal of Occupational Health Psychology, 1*, 27–41.

Siegrist, J. (1998). Adverse health effects of effort-reward imbalance at work. In C. L. Cooper (Ed.), *Theories of organizational stress* (pp. 190–204). Oxford, UK: Oxford University Press.

Siegrist, J., Starke, D., Chandola, T., Godin, I., Marmot, M., Niedhammer, I, & Peter, R. (2004). The measurement of effort-reward imbalance at work: European comparisons. *Social Science and Medicine, 58*, 1483–1499.

Simic, M., & Sethi, S. (2002). People with second jobs. *Labour Market Trends, 110,* 239–246.

Simoens, S., Scott, A., & Sibbald, B. (2002). Job satisfaction, work-related stress and intentions to quit of Scottish GPs. *Scottish Medical Journal, 47*(4), 80–86.

Sims, H. P., & Szilagyi, A. D. (1976). Job characteristic relationships: Individual and structural moderators. *Organizational Behavior and Human Performance, 17,* 211–230.

Sims, H. P., Szilagyi, A. D., & Keller, R. T. (1976). The measurement of job characteristics: *Academy of Management Journal, 19,* 195–212.

Sinclair, R. R., Martin, J. E., & Michel, R. P. (1999). Full-time and part-time subgroup differences in job attitudes and demographic characteristics. *Journal of Vocational Behavior, 55,* 337–357.

Sloane, P. J., & Williams, H. (2000). Job satisfaction, comparison earnings, and gender. *Labour, 14,* 473–502.

Smith, A. (2001). Perceptions of stress at work. *Human Resource Management Journal, 11,* 74–86.

Smith, A., Johal, S., Wadsworth, E., Smith, G. D., & Peters, T. (2000). *The scale of occupational stress: The Bristol stress and health at work study.* Sudbury, UK: HSE Books.

Smith, C. A., Haynes, K. N., Lazarus, R. S., & Pope, L. (1993). In search of the "hot" cognitions: Attributions, appraisals, and their relation to emotion. *Journal of Personality and Social Psychology, 65,* 916–929.

Smith, C. A., Organ, D. W., & Near, J. P. (1983). Organizational citizenship behavior: Its nature and antecedents. *Journal of Applied Psychology, 68,* 653–663.

Smith, F. J. (1977). Work attitudes as predictors of attendance on a specific day. *Journal of Applied Psychology, 62,* 16–19.

Smith, M. J. (1997). Psychosocial aspects of working with video display terminals (VDTs) and employee physical and mental health. *Ergonomics, 40,* 1002–1015.

Smith, P. C., Kendall, L. M., & Hulin, C. L. (1969). *The measurement of satisfaction in health and retirement.* Chicago: Rand McNally.

Solberg, E. C., Diener, E., Wirtz, D., Lucas, R. E., & Oishi, S. (2002). Wanting, having, and satisfaction: Examining the role of desire discrepancies in satisfaction with income. *Journal of Personality and Social Psychology, 83,* 725–734.

Solomon, R. L., & Corbit, J. D. (1974). An opponent-process theory of motivation: I. Temporal dynamics of affect. *Psychological Review, 81,* 119–145.

Sonnentag, S. (2000). Expertise at work: Experience and excellent performance. In C. L. Cooper & I. T. Robertson (Eds.), *International review of industrial and organizational psychology* (Vol. 15, pp. 223–264). Chichester, UK: Wiley.

Sonnentag, S., & Bayer, U.-V. (2005). Switching off mentally: Predictors and consequences of psychological detachment from work during off-job time. *Journal of Occupational Health Psychology, 10,* 393–414.

Sousa-Poza, A., & Sousa-Poza, A. A. (2000). Taking another look at the gender/job-satisfaction paradox. *Kyklos, 53,* 135–152.

Sousa-Poza, A., & Sousa-Poza, A. A. (2003). Gender differences in job satisfaction in Great Britain, 1991–2000: Permanent or transitory? *Applied Economics Letters, 10,* 691–694.

Spector, P. E. (1985). Higher-order need strength as a moderator of the job scope–employee at come relationship: A meta-analysis. *Journal of Occupational Psychology, 58*, 118–127.

Spector, P. E. (1986). Perceived control by employees: A meta-analysis of studies concerning autonomy and participation at work. *Human Relations, 39*, 1005–1016.

Spector, P. E. (1987). Interactive effects of perceived control and job stressors on affective reactions and health outcomes for health workers. *Work and Stress, 1*, 155–162.

Spector, P. E. (1992). A consideration of the validity and meaning of self-report measures of job conditions. In C. L. Cooper & I. T. Robertson (Eds.), *International review of industrial and organizational psychology* (Vol. 7, pp. 123–151). Chichester, UK: Wiley.

Spector, P. E., Chen, P. Y., & O'Connell, B. J. (2000). A longitudinal study of relations between job stressors and job strains while controlling for prior negative affectivity and strains. *Journal of Applied Psychology, 85*, 211–218.

Spector, P. E., Dwyer, D. J., & Jex, S. M. (1988). Relation of job stressors to affective, health, and performance outcomes: A comparison of multiple data sources. *Journal of Applied Psychology, 73*, 11–19.

Spector, P. E., & Jex, S. M. (1991). Relations of job characteristics from multiple data sources with employee affect, absence, turnover intentions, and health. *Journal of Applied Psychology, 76*, 46–53.

Spector, P. E., Jex, S. M., & Chen, P. Y. (1995). Relations of incumbent affect-related personality traits with objective measures of characteristics of jobs. *Journal of organizational Behavior, 16*, 59–65.

Spector, P. E., & O'Connell, B. J. (1994). The contribution of personality traits, negative affectivity, locus of control and Type A to the subsequent reports of job stressors and job strains. *Journal of Occupational and Organizational Psychology, 67*, 1–11.

Spector, P. E., van Katwyk, P. T., Brannick, M. T., & Chen, P. Y. (1997). When two factors don't reflect two constructs: How item characteristics can produce artifactual factors. *Journal of Management, 23*, 659–677.

Spector, P. E., Zapf, D., Chen, P. Y., & Frese, M. (2000). Why negative affectivity should not be controlled in job stress research: Don't throw out the baby with the bath water. *Journal of Organizational Behavior, 21*, 79–95.

Spokane, A. R., Meir, E. I., & Catalano, M. (2000). Person-environment congruence and Holland's theory: A review and reconsideration. *Journal of Vocational Behavior, 57*, 137–187.

Spreitzer, G., Sutcliffe, K., Dutton, J., Sonenshein, S., & Grant, A. M. (2005). A socially embedded model of thriving at work. *Organization Science, 16*, 537–549.

Srivastava, A., Locke, E. A., & Bartol, K. M. (2001). Money and subjective well-being: It's not the money, it's the motives. *Journal of Personality and Social Psychology, 80*, 959–971.

Stafford, E. M., Jackson, P. R., & Banks, M. H. (1980). Employment, work involvement and mental health in less qualified young people. *Journal of Occupational Psychology, 53*, 291–304.

Stapel, D. A., & Suls, J. (2004). Method matters: Effects of explicit versus implicit social comparisons on activation, behavior, and self-views. *Journal of Personality and Social Psychology, 87*, 860–875.

Staw, B. M., Bell, N. E., & Clausen, J. A. (1986). The dispositional approach to job attitudes: A life-time longitudinal test. *Administrative Science Quarterly, 31*, 56–77.

Staw, B. M., & Cohen-Charash, Y. (2005). The dispositional approach to job satisfaction: More than a mirage, but not yet an oasis. *Journal of Organizational Behavior, 26*, 59–78.

Staw, B. M., & Ross, J. (1985). Stability in the midst of change: A dispositional approach to job attitudes. *Journal of Applied Psychology, 70*, 469–480.

Staw, B. M., Sutton, R. I., & Pelled, L. H. (1994). Employee positive emotion and favorable outcomes in the workplace. *Organization Science, 5*, 51–71.

Steel, P., & Ones, D. S. (2002). Personality and happiness: A national-level analysis. *Journal of Personality and Social Psychology, 83*, 767–781.

Steel, R. P., & Rentsch, J. R. (1997). The dispositional model of job attitudes revisited: Findings of a 10-year study. *Journal of Applied Psychology, 82*, 873–879.

Strack, F., Schwarz, N., Chassein, B., Kern, D., & Wagner D. (1990). The salience of comparison standards and the activation of social norms: Consequences for judgments of happiness and their communication. *British Journal of Social Psychology, 29*, 303–314.

Strazdins, L., D'Souza, R. M., Lim, L. L.-Y., Broom, D. H., & Rodgers, B. (2004). Job strain, job insecurity, and health: Rethinking the relationship. *Journal of Occupational Health Psychology, 9*, 296–305.

Strelau, J., & Angleitner, A. (Eds.). (1991). *Explorations in temperament: International perspectives on theory and measurement.* London: Plenum Press.

Suh, E., Diener, E., & Fujita, F. (1996). Events and subjective well-being: Only recent events matter. *Journal of Personality and Social Psychology, 70*, 1091–1102.

Suh, E., Diener, E., Oishi, S., & Triandis, H. C. (1998). The shifting basis of life satisfaction judgments across cultures: Emotions versus norms. *Journal of Personality and Social Psychology, 74*, 482–493.

Sundstrom, E., Burt, R. E., & Kamp, D. (1980). Privacy at work: Architectural correlates of job satisfaction and job performance. *Academy of Management Journal, 23*, 101–117.

Super, D. E. (1970). *Work values inventory.* Boston: Houghton-Mifflin.

Sutton, G., & Griffin, M. A. (2004). Integrating expectations, experiences, and psychological contract violations: A longitudinal study of new professionals. *Journal of Occupational and Organizational Psychology, 77*, 493–514.

Sverke, M., Hellgren, J., & Näswall, K. (2002). No security: A meta-analysis and review of job insecurity and its consequences. *Journal of Occupational Health Psychology, 7*, 242–264.

Swan, G. E., Dame, A., & Carmelli, D. (1991). Involuntary retirement, type A behavior, and current functioning in elderly men: 27-year follow-up of the Western Collaborative Group Study. *Psychology and Aging, 6*, 384–391.

Sweeney, P. D., & McFarlin, D. B. (1997). Process and outcome: Gender differences in the assessment of justice. *Journal of Organizational Behavior, 18*, 83–98.

Sweeney, P. D., & McFarlin, D. B. (2004). Social comparisons and income satisfaction: A cross-national examination. *Journal of Occupational and Organizational Psychology, 77*, 149–154.

Sweeney, P. D., & McFarlin, D. B. (2005). Wage comparisons with similar and dissimilar others. *Journal of Occupational and Organizational Psychology, 78,* 113–131.

Sweeney, P. D., McFarlin, D. B., & Inderrieden, E. J. (1990). Using relative deprivation theory to explain satisfaction with income and pay level: A multi-study examination. *Academy of Management Journal, 33,* 423–436.

Sy, T., Côté, S., & Saavedra, R. (2005). The contagious leader: Impact of the leader's mood on the mood of group members, group affective tone, and group processes. *Journal of Applied Psychology, 90,* 295–305.

Szilagyi, A. D. (1977). An empirical test of causal inference between role perceptions, satisfaction with work, performance, and organizational level. *Personnel Psychology, 30,* 375–388.

Szilagyi, A. D., & Holland, W. E. (1980). Changes in social density: Relationships with functional interaction and perceptions of job characteristics, role stress and work satisfaction. *Journal of Applied Psychology, 65,* 28–33.

Taber, T. D., & Alliger, G. M. (1995). A task-level assessment of job satisfaction. *Journal of Organizational Behavior, 16,* 101–121.

Taber, T. D., Beehr, T. A., & Walsh, J. T. (1985). Relationships between job evaluation ratings and self-ratings of job characteristics. *Organizational Behavior and Human Decision Processes, 35,* 27–45.

Tait, M., Padgett, M. Y., & Baldwin, T. T. (1989). Job and life satisfaction: A re-evaluation of the strength of the relationship and gender effects as a function of the date of the study. *Journal of Applied Psychology, 74,* 502–507.

Takeuchi, R., Wang, M., & Marinova, S. V. (2005). Antecedents and consequences of psychological workplace strain during expatriation: A cross-sectional and longitudinal investigation. *Personnel Psychology, 58,* 925–948.

Taris, R., Feij, J. A., & van Vianen, A. E. M. (2005). Met expectations and supplies-values fit of Dutch young adults as determinants of work outcomes. *International Journal of Human Resource Management, 16,* 366–382.

Taris, T. W., Kalimo, R., & Schaufeli, W. B. (2002). Inequity at work: Its measurement and association with worker health. *Work and Stress, 16,* 287–301.

Tausig, M., & Fenwick, R. (1999). Recession and well-being. *Journal of Health and Social Behavior, 40,* 1–16.

Taylor, S. E., & Lobel, M. (1989). Social comparison activity under threat: Downward evaluation and upward contacts. *Psychological Review, 96,* 569–575.

Teachman, B. A. (2006). Aging and negative affect: The rise and fall and rise of anxiety and depression symptoms. *Psychology and Aging, 21,* 201–207.

Teasdale, J. D., Taylor, R., & Fogarty, S. J. (1980). Effects of induced elation-depression on the accessibility of memories of happy and unhappy experiences. *Behavior Research and Therapy, 18,* 339–346.

Telfer, E. (1980). *Happiness: An examination of a hedonistic and a eudaemonistic concept of happiness and of the relations between them.* London: Macmillan.

Tellegen, A., Watson, D., & Clark, L. A. (1999). On the dimensional and hierarchical structure of affect. *Psychological Science, 10,* 297–303.

Tepper, B. J. (2000). Consequences of abusive supervision. *Academy of Management Journal, 43,* 178–190.

Terkel, S. (1972). *Working: People talk about what they feel about what they do.* New York: Pantheon Books.

Terry, D. J., & Jimmieson, N. L. (1999). Work control and employee well-being: A decade review. In C. L. Cooper & I. T. Robertson (Eds.), *International review of industrial and organizational psychology* (Vol. 14, pp. 95–148). Chichester, UK: Wiley.

Tett, R. P., & Meyer, J. P. (1993). Job satisfaction, organizational commitment, turnover intention, and turnover: Path analysis based on meta-analytic findings. *Personnel Psychology, 46,* 259–293.

Tharenou, P. (1993). A test of reciprocal causality for absenteeism. *Journal of Organizational Behavior, 14,* 193–210.

Thomas, K. (Ed.). (1999). *The Oxford book of work.* Oxford, UK: Oxford University Press.

Thomas, L. T., & Ganster, D. C. (1995). Impact of family-supportive work variables in work-family conflict and strain: A control perspective. *Journal of Applied Psychology, 80,* 6–15.

Thompson, S. C. (2002). The role of personal control in adaptive functioning. In C. R. Snyder & S. J. Lopez (Eds.), *Handbook of positive psychology* (pp. 202–213). Oxford, UK: Oxford University Press.

Thoresen, C. J., Kaplan, S. A., Barsky, A. P., Warren, C. R., & de Chermont, K. (2003). The affective underpinnings of job perceptions and attitudes: A meta-analytic review and integration. *Psychological Bulletin, 129,* 914–945.

Thorsteinson, T. J. (2003). Job attitudes of full- and part-time employees: A meta-analytic review. *Journal of Occupational and Organizational Psychology, 76,* 151–177.

Tiberius, V. (2004). Cultural differences and philosophical accounts of well-being. *Journal of Happiness Studies, 5,* 293–314.

Tinsley, H. E. A. (2000). The congruence myth: An analysis of the efficacy of the person-environment fit model. *Journal of Vocational Behavior, 56,* 147–179.

Tokar, D. M., & Fischer, A. R. (1998). More on RIASEC and the five-factor model of personality: Direct assessment of Prediger's (1982) and Hogan's (1983) dimensions. *Journal of Vocational Behavior, 52,* 246–259.

Tokar, D. M., Fischer, A. R., & Subich, L. M. (1998). Personality and vocational behavior: A selective review of the literature, 1993–1997. *Journal of Vocational Behavior, 53,* 115–153.

Tokar, D. M., & Subich, L. M. (1997). Relative contributions of congruence and personality dimensions to job satisfaction. *Journal of Vocational Behavior, 50,* 482–491.

Toossi, M. (2004). Labor force projections to 2012: The graying of the U.S. workforce. *Monthly Labor Review, 127,* 37–57.

Totterdell, P., Kellett, S., Teuchmann, K., & Briner, R. B. (1998). Evidence of mood linkage in work groups. *Journal of Personality and Social Psychology, 74,* 1504–1515.

Totterdell, P., Wall, T., Holman, D., Diamond, H., & Epitropaki, O. (2004). Affect networks: A structural analysis of the relationship between work ties and job-related affect. *Journal of Applied Psychology, 89,* 854–867.

Totterdell, P., Wood, S., & Wall, T. (2006). An intra-individual test of the demands-control model: A weekly diary study of psychological strain in portfolio workers. *Journal of Occupational and Organizational Psychology, 79*, 63–84.

Tranberg, M., Slane, S., & Ekeberg, S. E. (1993). The relation between interest congruence and satisfaction: A meta-analysis. *Journal of Vocational Behavior, 42*, 253–264.

Triandis, H. C. (1995). *Individualism and collectivism*. Boulder, CO: Westview Press.

Tsai, J. L., Knutson, B., & Fung, H. H. (2006). Cultural variation in affect valuation. *Journal of Personality and Social Psychology, 90*, 288–307.

Tucker, P., & Rutherford, C. (2005). Moderators of the relationship between long work hours and health. *Journal of Occupational Health Psychology, 10*, 465–476.

Tugade, M. M., & Fredrickson, B. L. (2004). Resilient individuals use positive emotions to bounce back from negative emotional experiences. *Journal of Personality and Social Psychology, 86*, 320–333.

Uchida, Y., Norasakkunkit, V., & Kitayama, S. (2004). Cultural constructions of happiness: Theory and empirical evidence. *Journal of Happiness Studies, 5*, 223–239.

Ullah, P., Banks, M. H., & Warr, P. B. (1985). Social support, social pressures and psychological distress during unemployment. *Psychological Medicine, 15*, 283–295.

Ulleberg, P., & Rudmo, T. (1997). Job stress, social support, job satisfaction and absenteeism among offshore oil personnel. *Work and Stress, 11*, 215–228.

Van der Doef, M., & Maes, S. (1995). The job-demand (support) model and psychological well-being: A review of 20 years of empirical research. *Work and Stress, 13*, 87–114.

Van der Zee, K. I., Buunk, B. P., de Ruiter, J. H., Tempelaar, R., van Sonderen, E., & Sanderman, R. (1996). Social comparison and the subjective well-being of cancer patients. *Basic and Applied Social Psychology, 34*, 53–65.

Van der Zee, K. I., Buunk, B. P., & Sanderman, R. (1996). The relationship between social comparison processes and personality. *Personality and Individual Differences, 20*, 551–565.

Van Dijkhuizen, N. (1980). *From stressors to strains*. Lisse: Swets and Zeitlinger.

Van Dyne, L., Jehn, K. A., & Cummings, A. (2002). Differential effects of strain on two forms of work performance: Individual employee sales and creativity. *Journal of Organizational Behavior, 23*, 57–74.

Van Katwyk, P. T., Fox, S. Spector, P. E., & Kelloway, E. K. (2000). Using the Job-related Affective Well-being Scale (JAWS) to investigate affective responses to work stressors. *Journal of Occupational Health Psychology, 5*, 219–230.

Van Os, J., Park, S. B. G., & Jones, P. B. (2001). Neuroticism, life events and mental health: Evidence for person–environment correlation. *British Journal of Psychiatry, 178* (suppl. 40), s72–s77.

Van Rijswijk, K., Bekker, M. H. J., Rutte, C. G., & Croon, M. A. (2004). The relationships among part-time work, work-family interference, and well-being. *Journal of Occupational Health Psychology, 9*, 286–295.

Van Schuur, W. H., & Kiers, H. A. L. (1994). Why factor analysis is often the wrong model for analyzing bipolar concepts and what model to use instead. *Applied Psychological Measurement, 18*, 97–110.

REFERENCES

Van Vegchel, N., de Jonge, J., & Landsbergis, P. A. (2005). Occupational stress in (inter)action: The interplay between job demands and job resources. *Journal of Organizational Behavior, 26,* 535–560.

Van Yperen, N. W., & Janssen, O. (2002). Fatigued and dissatisfied or fatigued but satisfied? Goal orientations and responses to high job demands. *Academy of Management Journal, 45,* 1161–1171.

Veenhoven, R. (1984). *Conditions of happiness.* Dordrecht: Reidel.

Veenhoven, R. (1991). Is happiness relative? *Social Indicators Research, 24,* 1–34.

Veenhoven, R. (1999). Quality-of-life in individualistic society. *Social Indicators Research, 48,* 157–186.

Veit, C. T., & Ware, J. E. (1983). The structure of psychological distress and well-being in general populations. *Journal of Consulting and Clinical Psychology, 51,* 730–742.

Verquer, M. L., Beehr, T. A., & Wagner, S. H. (2003). A meta-analysis of relations between person-organization fit and work attitudes. *Journal of Vocational Behavior, 63,* 473–489.

Vinokur, A. D., Price, R. H., & Caplan, R. D. (1996). Hard times and hurtful partners: How financial strain affects depression and relationship satisfaction of unemployed persons and their spouses. *Journal of Personality and Social Psychology, 71,* 166–179.

Viswesvaran, C. (2002). Absenteeism and measures of job performance: A meta-analysis. *International Journal of Selection and Assessment, 10,* 12–17.

Viswesvaran, C., Sanchez, J. I., & Fisher, J. (1999). The role of social support in the process of work stress: A meta-analysis. *Journal of Vocational Behavior, 54,* 314–334.

Von Hofsten, C. (1985). Perception and action. In M. Frese & J. Sabini (Eds.), *Goal-directed behavior: The concept of action in psychology* (pp. 80–96). Hillsdale, NJ: Lawrence Erlbaum Associates.

Vroom, V. H. (1959). Some personality determinants of the effects of participation. *Journal of Abnormal and Social Psychology, 59,* 322–327.

Vroom, V. H. (1964). *Work and motivation.* New York: Wiley.

Wainwright, D, & Calnan, M. (2002). *Work stress: The making of a modern epidemic.* Buckingham: Open University Press.

Waldenström, K., Lundberg, I., Waldenström, M., and Härenstam, A. (2005). Does psychological distress influence the reporting of demands and control at work? *Occupational and Environmental Medicine, 60,* 887–891.

Wall, T. D., & Clegg, C. W. (1981). A longitudinal field study of group work design. *Journal of Occupational Behaviour, 2,* 31–49.

Wall, T. D., Clegg, C. W., & Jackson, P. R. (1978). An evaluation of the job characteristics model. *Journal of Occupational Psychology, 51,* 183–196.

Wall, T. D., Jackson, P. R., Mullarkey, S., & Parker, S. K. (1996). The demands-control model of job strain: A more specific test. *Journal of Occupational and Organizational Psychology, 69,* 153–166.

Wall, T. D., Kemp, N. J., Jackson, P. R., & Clegg, C. W. (1986). The outcomes of autonomous workgroups: A long-term field experiment. *Academy of Management Journal, 29,* 280–304.

Wall, T. D., & Lischeron, J. A. (1977). *Worker participation*. London: McGraw-Hill.

Wall, T. D., & Payne, R. L. (1973). Are deficiency scores deficient? *Journal of Applied Psychology*, 58, 322–326.

Walster, G. W., & Berscheid, E. (1978). *Equity: Theory and research*. Boston: Allyn and Bacon.

Wanous, J. P. (1974). Individual differences and reactions to job characteristics. *Journal of Applied Psychology*, 59, 616–622.

Wanous, J. P., Poland, T. D., Premack, S. L., & Davis, K. S. (1992). The effects of met expectations on newcomer attitudes and behaviors: A review and meta-analysis. *Journal of Applied Psychology*, 77, 288–297.

Warr, P. B. (1982). A national study of non-financial employment commitment. *Journal of Occupational Psychology*, 55, 297–312.

Warr, P. B. (1987). *Work, unemployment, and mental health*. Oxford: Oxford University Press.

Warr, P. B. (1990a). The measurement of well-being and other aspects of mental health. *Journal of Occupational Psychology*, 63, 193–210.

Warr, P. B. (1990b). Decision latitude, job demands and employee well-being. *Work and Stress*, 4, 285–294.

Warr, P. B. (1992). Age and occupational well-being. *Psychology and Aging*, 7, 37–45.

Warr, P. B. (1994a). A conceptual framework for the study of work and mental health. *Work and Stress*, 8, 84–97.

Warr, P. B. (1994b). Age and employment. In H. C. Triandis, M. D. Dunnette, & L. M. Hough (Eds.), *Handbook of industrial and organizational psychology* (Vol. 4, pp. 485–550). Palo Alto, CA: Consulting Psychologists Press.

Warr, P. B. (1997). Age, work, and mental health. In K. W. Schaie & C. Schooler (Eds.), *The impact of work on older adults* (pp. 252–296). New York: Springer.

Warr, P. B. (1999). Well-being and the workplace. In D. Kahneman, E. Diener, & N. Schwarz (Eds.), *Well-being: The foundations of hedonic psychology* (pp. 392–412). New York: Russell Sage Foundation.

Warr, P. B. (2000). Indirect processes in criterion-related validity. *Journal of Organizational Behavior*, 21, 731–745.

Warr, P. B. (2005). Work, well-being, and mental health. In J. Barling, K. Kelloway, & M. Frone (Eds.), *Handbook of work stress* (pp. 547–573). Thousand Oaks, CA: Sage.

Warr, P. B. (2006a). Some historical developments in I-O psychology outside USA. In L. L. Koppes (Ed.), *Historical perspectives in industrial and organizational psychology* (pp. 81–107). Mahwah, NJ: Lawrence Erlbaum Associates.

Warr, P. B. (2006b). Differential activation of judgments in employee well-being. *Journal of Occupational and Organizational Psychology*, 79, 225–244.

Warr, P. B., Bartram, D., & Brown, A. (2005). Big Five validity: Aggregation method matters. *Journal of Occupational and Organizational Psychology*, 78, 377–386.

Warr, P. B., & Birdi, K. (1998). Employee age and voluntary development activity. *International Journal of Training and Development*, 2, 190–204.

Warr, P. B., Butcher, V., & Robertson, I. T. (2004a). Activity and psychological well-being in older people. *Aging and Mental Health*, 8, 172–183.

Warr, P. B., Butcher, V., Robertson, I. T., & Callinan, M. (2004b). Older people's well-being as a function of employment, retirement, environmental characteristics and role preference. *British Journal of Psychology, 95,* 297–324.

Warr, P. B., Cook, J. D., & Wall, T. D. (1979). Scales for the measurement of some work attitudes and aspects of psychological well-being. *Journal of Occupational Psychology, 52,* 129–148.

Warr, P. B., & Jackson, P. R. (1975). The importance of extremity. *Journal of Personality and Social Psychology, 32,* 278–282.

Warr, P. B., & Jackson, P. R. (1983). Self-esteem and unemployment among young workers. *Le Travail Humain, 46,* 355–366.

Warr, P. B., & Jackson, P. R. (1984). Men without jobs: Some correlates of age and length of unemployment. *Journal of Occupational Psychology, 57,* 77–85.

Warr, P. B., & Jackson, P. R. (1985). Factors influencing the psychological impact of prolonged unemployment and re-employment. *Psychological Medicine, 15,* 795–807.

Warr, P. B., Jackson, P. R., & Banks, M. H. (1988). Unemployment and mental health: Some British studies. *Journal of Social Issues, 44,* 47–68.

Warr, P. B., Miles, A., & Platts, C. (2001). Age and personality in the British population between 16 and 64 years. *Journal of Occupational and Organizational Psychology, 74,* 165–199.

Warr, P. B., & Parry, G. (1982). Paid employment and women's psychological well-being. *Psychological Bulletin, 91,* 498–516.

Warr, P. B., & Payne, R. L. (1983). Affective outcomes of paid employment in a random sample of British workers. *Journal of Occupational Behaviour, 4,* 91–104.

Warr, P. B., & Pearce, A. (2004). Preferences for careers and organisational cultures as a function of logically related personality traits. *Applied Psychology: An International Review, 53,* 423–435.

Warr, P. B., & Wall, T. D. (1975). *Work and well-being.* Harmondsworth, UK: Penguin.

Waterman, A. S. (1984). *The psychology of individualism.* New York: Praeger.

Waterman, A. S. (1993). Two conceptions of happiness: Contrasts of personal expressiveness (eudaimonia) and hedonic enjoyment. *Journal of Personality and Social Psychology, 64,* 678–691.

Waters, L. E., & Moore, K. A. (2002). Self-esteem, appraisal and coping: A comparison of unemployed and re-employed people. *Journal of Organizational Behavior, 23,* 593–604.

Watson, D., Clark, L. A., & Tellegen, A. (1988). Development and validation of brief measures of positive and negative affect: The PANAS scales. *Journal of Personality and Social Psychology, 54,* 1063–1070.

Watson, D., & Clark, L. A. (1984). Negative affectivity: The disposition to experience aversive states. *Psychological Bulletin, 96,* 465–490.

Watson, D., & Clark, L. A. (1992). On traits and temperament: General and specific factors of emotional experience and their relation to the five-factor model. *Journal of Personality, 60,* 441–476.

Watson, D., & Slack, A. K. (1993). General factors of affective temperament and their relation to job satisfaction over time. *Organizational Behavior and Human Decision Processes, 54,* 181–202.

Watson, D., Suls, J., & Haig, J. (2002). Global self-esteem in relation to structural models of personality and affectivity. *Journal of Personality and Social Psychology*, *83*, 185–197.

Watson, D., & Tellegen, A. (1985). Toward a consensual structure of mood. *Psychological Bulletin*, *98*, 219–235.

Watson, D., & Walker, L. M. (1996). The long-term stability and predictive validity of trait measures of affect. *Journal of Personality and Social Psychology*, *70*, 567–577.

Wayne, J. H., Musisca, N., & Fleeson, W. (2004). Considering the role of personality in the work-family experience: Relationships of the Big Five to work-family conflict and facilitation. *Journal of Vocational Behavior*, *64*, 108–130.

Weaver, C. N. (1978). Sex differences in the determinants of job satisfaction. *Academy of Management Journal*, *21*, 265–274.

Weaver, C. N. (1980). Job satisfaction in the United States in the 1970s. *Journal of Applied Psychology*, *65*, 364–367.

Weick, K. E. (1979). *The social psychology of organizing*. New York: McGraw-Hill.

Weick, K. E. (1995). *Sensemaking in organizations*. Thousand Oaks, CA: Sage.

Weick, K. E., Sutcliffe, K. M., & Obstfeld, D. (2005). Organizing and the process of sensemaking. *Organization Science*, *16*, 409–421.

Weiss, D. J., Dawis, R. V., England, G. W., & Lofquist, L. H. (1967). *Manual for the Minnesota Satisfaction Questionnaire*. Minneapolis, MN: University of Minnesota.

Weiss, H. M., & Shaw, J. B. (1979). Social influences on judgments about tasks. *Organizational Behavior and Human Performance*, *24*, 126–140.

Westman, M., Etzion, D., & Horovitz, S. (2004). The toll of unemployment does not stop with the unemployed. *Human Relations*, *57*, 823–844.

Wheeler, L. (2000). Individual differences in social comparison. In J. Suls & L. Wheeler (Eds.), *Handbook of social comparison: Theory and research* (pp. 141–158). New York: Kluwer/Plenum.

Wheeler, L., & Miyake, K. (1992). Social comparison in everyday life. *Journal of Personality and Social Psychology*, *62*, 760–773.

Whiting, E. (2005). The labour market participation of older people. *Labour Market Trends*, *113*, 285–296.

Wiener, Y., Vardi, Y., & Muczyk, J. (1981). Antecedents of employees' mental health: The role of career and work satisfaction. *Journal of Vocational Behavior*, *19*, 50–60.

Wiese, B. S., & Freund, A. M. (2005). Goal progress makes one happy, or does it? Longitudinal findings from the work domain. *Journal of Occupational and Organizational Psychology*, *78*, 287–304.

Wiesner, M., Windle, M, & Freeman, A. (2005). Work stress, substance use, and depression among young adult workers: An examination of main and moderator effect models. *Journal of Occupational Health Psychology*, *10*, 83–96.

Wilk, S. L., & Moynihan, L. M. (2005). Display rule "regulators": The relationship between supervisors and worker emotional exhaustion. *Journal of Applied Psychology*, *90*, 917–927.

Williams, K. J., Suls, J., Alliger, G. M., Learner, S. M., & Wan, C. K. (1991). Multiple role juggling and daily mood states in working mothers: An experience sampling study. *Journal of Applied Psychology*, *76*, 664–674.

Williams, R. D. (2004). An introduction to the UK time use survey from a labour market perspective. *Labour Market Trends*, *112*(2), 63–70.

Wilson, A. E., & Ross, M. (2000). The frequency of temporal-self and social comparisons in people's personal appraisals. *Journal of Personality and Social Psychology, 78,* 928–942.

Wilson, M. G., DeJoy, D. M., Vandenberg, R. J., Richardson, H. A., & McGrath, A. L. (2004). Work characteristics and employee health and well-being: Test of a model of healthy work organization. *Journal of Occupational and Organizational Psychology, 77,* 565–588.

Winefield, A. H. (1995). Unemployment: Its psychological costs. In C. L. Cooper & I. T. Robertson (Eds.), *International review of industrial and organizational psychology* (Vol. 10, pp. 169–212). Chichester, UK: Wiley.

Winter, D. G., John, O. P., Stewart, A. J., Klohnen, E. C., & Duncan, L. E. (1998). Traits and motives: Toward an integration of two traditions in personality research. *Psychological Review, 105,* 230–250.

Witkin, H. A., & Goodenough, R. R. (1977). Field dependence and interpersonal behavior. *Psychological Bulletin, 84,* 661–689.

Wong, C.-S., Hui, C., & Law, K. S. (1998). A longitudinal study of the job perception–job satisfaction relationship: A test of the three alternative specifications. *Journal of Occupational and Organizational Psychology, 71,* 127–146.

Wood, W., Rhodes, N., & Whelan, M. (1989). Sex differences in positive well-being: A consideration of emotional style and marital status. *Psychological Bulletin, 106,* 249–264.

Workman, M., & Bommer, W. (2004). Redesigning computer call center work: A longitudinal field experiment. *Journal of Organizational Behavior, 25,* 317–337.

Wright, J. D., & Hamilton, R, F. (1978). Work satisfaction and age: Some evidence for the "job change" hypothesis. *Social Forces, 56,* 1140–1158.

Wright, R. E., & Ermisch, J. F. (1991). Gender discrimination in the British labour market: A reassessment. *Economic Journal, 101,* 508–522.

Wright, T. A., & Bonett, D. G. (1997). The contribution of burnout to work performance. *Journal of Organizational Behavior, 18,* 491–499.

Wright, T. A., Bonett, D. G., & Sweeney, D. A. (1993). Mental health and work performance: Results of a longitudinal field study. *Journal of Occupational and Organizational Psychology, 66,* 277–284.

Wright, T. A., & Cropanzano, R. (1998). Emotional exhaustion as a predictor of job performance and voluntary turnover. *Journal of Applied Psychology, 83,* 486–493.

Wright, T. A., & Cropanzano, R. (2000). Psychological well-being and job satisfaction as predictors of job performance. *Journal of Occupational Health Psychology, 5,* 84–94.

Wright, T. A., & Staw, B. M. (1999). Affect and favorable work outcomes: Two longitudinal tests of the happy-productive worker thesis. *Journal of Organizational Behavior, 20,* 1–23.

Wrzesniewski, A., & Dutton, J. E. (2001). Crafting a job: Revisioning employees as active crafters of their work. *Academy of Management Review, 26,* 179–201.

Wrzesniewski, A., Dutton, J. E., & Debebe, G. (2003). Interpersonal sensemaking and the meaning of work. In B. Staw & R. Kramer (Eds.), *Research in organizational behavior* (Vol. 25, pp. 93–135). San Francisco: Interscience.

Wrzesniewski, A., McCauley, C., Rozin, P., & Schwartz, B. (1997). Jobs, careers, and callings: People's reactions to their work. *Journal of Research in Personality, 31,* 21–33.

Wyatt, S., Fraser, J. A., & Stock, F. G. L. (1928). *The comparative effects of variety and uniformity in work.* Report 52. London: Industrial Health Research Board.

Wyatt, S., & Langden, J. N. (1938). *The machine and the worker: A study of machine-feeding processes.* Report 82. London: Industrial Health Research Board.

Wyatt, S., & Ogden, D. A. (1924). *On the extent and effects of variety in repetitive work.* Report 26. London: Industrial Fatigue Research Board.

Xie, J. L., & Johns, G. (1995). Job scope and stress: Can job scope be too high? *Academy of Management Journal, 38,* 1288–1309.

Yik, M. S. M., Russell, J. A., & Feldman Barrett, L. (1999). Structure of self-reported current affect: Integration and beyond. *Journal of Personality and Social Psychology, 77,* 600–619.

Zaccaro, S. J., & Stone, E. F. (1988). Incremental validity of an empirically based measure of job characteristics. *Journal of Applied Psychology, 73,* 245–252.

Zapf, D. (2002). Emotion work and psychological well-being: A review of the literature and some conceptual considerations. *Human Resource Management Review, 12,* 237–268.

Zapf, D., Dormann, C., & Frese, M. (1996). Longitudinal studies in organizational stress research: A review of the literature with reference to methodological issues. *Journal of Occupational Health Psychology, 1,* 145–169.

Zapf, D., Einarsen, S., Hoel, H., & Vartia, M. (2003). Empirical findings on bullying in the workplace. In S. Einarsen, H. Hoel, D. Zapf, & C. L. Cooper (Eds.), *Bullying and emotional abuse in the workplace* (pp. 103–126). London: Taylor and Francis.

Zapf, D., & Holz, M. (2006). On the positive and negative effects of emotion work in organizations. *European Journal of Work and Organizational Psychology, 15,* 1–28.

Zapf, D., Vogt, C., Seifert, C., Mertini, H., & Isic, A. (1999). Emotion work as a source of stress: The concept and development of an instrument. *European Journal of Work and Organizational Psychology, 8,* 371–400.

Zappert, L. T., & Weinstein, H. M. (1985). Sex differences in the impact of work on physical and psychological health. *American Journal of Psychiatry, 142,* 1174–1178.

Zellars, K. L., & Perrewé, P. L. (2001). Affective personality and the content of emotional social support: Coping in organizations. *Journal of Applied Psychology, 86,* 459–467.

Zickar, M. J., Gibby, R. E., & Jenny, T. (2004). Job attitudes of workers with two jobs. *Journal of Vocational Behavior, 64,* 222–235.

Zohar, D. (1999). When things go wrong: The effect of daily work hassles on effort, exertion and negative mood. *Journal of Occupational and Organizational Psychology, 72,* 265–283.

Author Index

Subject Index

O